Adobe®
InDesign™ Bible

Adobe® InDesign™ Bible

Galen Gruman, John Cruise, and Kelly Kordes Anton

IDG Books Worldwide, Inc.
An International Data Group Company

Foster City, CA ✦ Chicago, IL ✦ Indianapolis, IN ✦ New York, NY

Adobe® InDesign™ Bible

Published by
IDG Books Worldwide, Inc.
An International Data Group Company
919 E. Hillsdale Blvd., Suite 400
Foster City, CA 94404
www.idgbooks.com (IDG Books Worldwide Web site)

Library of Congress Catalog Card No.: 99-67137

ISBN: 0-7645-3243-X

Printed in the United States of America

10 9 8 7 6 5 4 3 2 1

1B/SX/RQ/ZZ/FC

Distributed in the United States by IDG Books Worldwide, Inc.

Distributed by CDG Books Canada Inc. for Canada; by Transworld Publishers Limited in the United Kingdom; by IDG Norge Books for Norway; by IDG Sweden Books for Sweden; by IDG Books Australia Publishing Corporation Pty. Ltd. for Australia and New Zealand; by TransQuest Publishers Pte Ltd. for Singapore, Malaysia, Thailand, Indonesia, and Hong Kong; by Gotop Information Inc. for Taiwan; by ICG Muse, Inc. for Japan; by Intersoft for South Africa; by Eyrolles for France; by International Thomson Publishing for Germany, Austria and Switzerland; by Distribuidora Cuspide for Argentina; by LR International for Brazil; by Galileo Libros for Chile; by Ediciones ZETA S.C.R. Ltda. for Peru; by WS Computer Publishing Corporation, Inc., for the Philippines; by Contemporanea de Ediciones for Venezuela; by Express Computer Distributors for the Caribbean and West Indies; by Micronesia Media Distributor, Inc. for Micronesia; by Chips Computadoras S.A. de C.V. for Mexico; by Editorial Norma de Panama S.A. for Panama; by American Bookshops for Finland.

For general information on IDG Books Worldwide's books in the U.S., please call our Consumer Customer Service department at 800-762-2974. For reseller information, including discounts and premium sales, please call our Reseller Customer Service department at 800-434-3422.

For information on where to purchase IDG Books Worldwide's books outside the U.S., please contact our International Sales department at 317-596-5530 or fax 317-596-5692.

For consumer information on foreign language translations, please contact our Customer Service department at 800-434-3422, fax 317-596-5692, or e-mail rights@idgbooks.com.

For information on licensing foreign or domestic rights, please phone +1-650-655-3109.

For sales inquiries and special prices for bulk quantities, please contact our Sales department at 650-655-3200 or write to the address above.

For information on using IDG Books Worldwide's books in the classroom or for ordering examination copies, please contact our Educational Sales department at 800-434-2086 or fax 317-596-5499.

For press review copies, author interviews, or other publicity information, please contact our Public Relations department at 650-655-3000 or fax 650-655-3299.

For authorization to photocopy items for corporate, personal, or educational use, please contact Copyright Clearance Center, 222 Rosewood Drive, Danvers, MA 01923, or fax 978-750-4470.

ABOUT IDG BOOKS WORLDWIDE

Welcome to the world of IDG Books Worldwide.

IDG Books Worldwide, Inc., is a subsidiary of International Data Group, the world's largest publisher of computer-related information and the leading global provider of information services on information technology. IDG was founded more than 30 years ago by Patrick J. McGovern and now employs more than 9,000 people worldwide. IDG publishes more than 290 computer publications in over 75 countries. More than 90 million people read one or more IDG publications each month.

Launched in 1990, IDG Books Worldwide is today the #1 publisher of best-selling computer books in the United States. We are proud to have received eight awards from the Computer Press Association in recognition of editorial excellence and three from Computer Currents' First Annual Readers' Choice Awards. Our best-selling ...For Dummies® series has more than 50 million copies in print with translations in 31 languages. IDG Books Worldwide, through a joint venture with IDG's Hi-Tech Beijing, became the first U.S. publisher to publish a computer book in the People's Republic of China. In record time, IDG Books Worldwide has become the first choice for millions of readers around the world who want to learn how to better manage their businesses.

Our mission is simple: Every one of our books is designed to bring extra value and skill-building instructions to the reader. Our books are written by experts who understand and care about our readers. The knowledge base of our editorial staff comes from years of experience in publishing, education, and journalism — experience we use to produce books to carry us into the new millennium. In short, we care about books, so we attract the best people. We devote special attention to details such as audience, interior design, use of icons, and illustrations. And because we use an efficient process of authoring, editing, and desktop publishing our books electronically, we can spend more time ensuring superior content and less time on the technicalities of making books.

You can count on our commitment to deliver high-quality books at competitive prices on topics you want to read about. At IDG Books Worldwide, we continue in the IDG tradition of delivering quality for more than 30 years. You'll find no better book on a subject than one from IDG Books Worldwide.

IDG BOOKS WORLDWIDE

John Kilcullen
Chairman and CEO
IDG Books Worldwide, Inc.

Steven Berkowitz
President and Publisher
IDG Books Worldwide, Inc.

WINNER

*Eighth Annual
Computer Press
Awards ≥1992*

WINNER

*Ninth Annual
Computer Press
Awards ≥1993*

WINNER

*Tenth Annual
Computer Press
Awards ≥1994*

WINNER

*Eleventh Annual
Computer Press
Awards ≥1995*

IDG is the world's leading IT media, research and exposition company. Founded in 1964, IDG had 1997 revenues of $2.05 billion and has more than 9,000 employees worldwide. IDG offers the widest range of media options that reach IT buyers in 75 countries representing 95% of worldwide IT spending. IDG's diverse product and services portfolio spans six key areas including print publishing, online publishing, expositions and conferences, market research, education and training, and global marketing services. More than 90 million people read one or more of IDG's 290 magazines and newspapers, including IDG's leading global brands — Computerworld, PC World, Network World, Macworld and the Channel World family of publications. IDG Books Worldwide is one of the fastest-growing computer book publishers in the world, with more than 700 titles in 36 languages. The "...For Dummies®" series alone has more than 50 million copies in print. IDG offers online users the largest network of technology-specific Web sites around the world through IDG.net (http://www.idg.net), which comprises more than 225 targeted Web sites in 55 countries worldwide. International Data Corporation (IDC) is the world's largest provider of information technology data, analysis and consulting, with research centers in over 41 countries and more than 400 research analysts worldwide. IDG World Expo is a leading producer of more than 168 globally branded conferences and expositions in 35 countries including E3 (Electronic Entertainment Expo), Macworld Expo, ComNet, Windows World Expo, ICE (Internet Commerce Expo), Agenda, DEMO, and Spotlight. IDG's training subsidiary, ExecuTrain, is the world's largest computer training company, with more than 230 locations worldwide and 785 training courses. IDG Marketing Services helps industry-leading IT companies build international brand recognition by developing global integrated marketing programs via IDG's print, online and exposition products worldwide. Further information about the company can be found at www.idg.com.   1/24/99

Credits

Acquisitions Editor
Michael Roney

Development Editor
Katharine Dvorak

Technical Editor
Dennis Cohen

Copy Editors
Michael D. Welch
Timothy Borek
Marti Paul

Project Coordinators
Ritchie Durdin
Linda Marousek

Graphics and Production Specialists
Mario Amador
Stephanie Hollier
Jude Levinson
Dina F. Quan
Ramses Ramirez

Quality Control Specialist
Chris Weisbart

Cover Art
Joann Vuong

Proofreading and Indexing
York Production Services

About the Authors

Galen Gruman is the executive editor of *Upside* magazine and the coauthor of 11 books on desktop publishing, including *Macworld QuarkXPress 4 Bible* and *PageMaker 6.5 For Dummies Internet Edition*, as well as a contributor to *The PC Bible, 3rd Edition*. Originally a news reporter and editor, Gruman got caught by the production-technology bug in 1979 and hasn't recovered. He led one of the first successful conversions of a national magazine to desktop publishing in 1986 and has covered publishing technology since then for several publications, including the trade weekly *InfoWorld*, for which he began writing in 1986; *Macworld*, whose staff he joined in 1991 and for which was executive editor from 1994 to 1998; and the magazines *Magazine Design & Production* and *Publish*.

John Cruise is a Denver-based technical writer and editor who has written numerous magazine articles and two books — *Macworld QuarkXPress 4 Bible* and *QuarkXPress 4 For Dummies* — about desktop publishing. In the late 1980s and early 1990s, he was a managing editor at Quark, Inc., and later worked as editor of *X-Ray Magazine*, a publication for users of publishing software products. He is currently teaching graphic design and doing technical writing, editing, and consulting for several software companies.

Kelly Kordes Anton develops documentation and marketing materials for high-end Macintosh publishing products, copy-edits and writes for Denver-area magazines, and provides QuarkXPress training. A veteran of Quark, Inc., she started on the QuarkXPress 3.2 team and eventually led the development of the QuarkXPress 4.0 documentation. She has developed training materials for Quark, provided technical review for several QuarkXPress books, and is a coauthor of the book *Using QuarkXPress*. Continual involvement with magazine publishers and students keeps her firmly entrenched in the day-to-day realities of publishing. Her main interest, however, is her three-year-old son Robert, who has known the difference between "good" and "well" for more than a year.

Foreword: Your Guide to InDesign's Challenge

As an editor and author, first at *Macworld* and now at *Publish*, I've followed Adobe and its products for many years. Like others involved in graphic design and publishing, I've seen Adobe stake out its leadership in image-editing and vector illustration software — and I've also watched it struggle to do the same in the page-layout arena. There, Adobe has had a tough hill to climb.

Practically since its inception, QuarkXPress was the program of choice for professional desktop publishers, leaving what was then Aldus PageMaker in the dust as the perennial runner-up. When PageMaker became an Adobe product, many of my colleagues thought it had a chance to regain its former glory, but PageMaker was never able to loosen QuarkXPress's iron grip on the hearts and wallets of desktop publishers.

Now, however, with the release of Adobe InDesign, the publishing landscape is finally poised for a change. Adobe is determined to shake up the status quo and provide XPress with its first real competition — and publishing pros with their first real choice in design and production tools.

Of course, Adobe's challenge is to convince XPress's legions that they'd rather switch than fight (with Quark, that is). Will InDesign succeed? Can publishers be persuaded to accept this new layout program as the future model for electronic publishing? The answers depend on a number of factors, including how compatible InDesign is with XPress, how well Adobe has implemented InDesign's professional publishing features, and how well those features stack up against XPress's. But it also depends on whether publishing pros can find an experienced guide to help them navigate the program, exploit its strengths, and circumvent its weaknesses.

Fortunately, that's exactly what you can expect from this book. Its lead writer is a long-time colleague of mine, the former Macworld executive editor Galen Gruman, a veteran writer, editor, and coauthor of several books on QuarkXPress. In the *Adobe InDesign Bible*, Galen and his coauthors, John Cruise and Kelly Kordes Anton, thoroughly cover all of InDesign's tools, commands, strengths, and quirks to get you quickly up to speed and help you master its many features.

I've known Galen since we began working together at Macworld, where he rose quickly through the ranks by demonstrating exceptional writing skills, an ability to clarify dense technical information, and a knack for assembling a cohesive team of talented people. Although as a computer journalist he's covered a wide range of topics, publishing and its related technologies have always held a special interest for him. You should be glad that Galen has decided to lend his considerable talents to the *Adobe InDesign Bible* because he and his coauthors have the tenacity to dig deep into this program's intricacies to make it work harder — so you won't have to.

Cathy Abes
Senior Editor
Publish magazine

Foreword: Getting the Most from InDesign

I started in the desktop publishing industry by working on a book called *Whale Song* (Beyond Words Publishing, 1986) — the first book desktop-published on a Macintosh. Bob Goodman, the publisher, a friend, and a mentor taught me how to explain new publishing technologies at traditional publishing trade shows. He was very patient and forgiving of the new technologies. At that time you were limited to one-page documents in PageMaker. *Whale Song* was unique because it included a section on how it was digitally produced. I sold over 500 of those books in three days, and this forever changed my career. I was hooked on technology and the process of explaining it to new users.

Over the years, I have educated art directors, artists, designers, photographers, typographers, and publishers on new technology. Books are essential to the learning process. My challenge as an educator has always been finding a book that speaks to the software user regardless of his or her level of expertise.

The authors of this book — Galen Gruman, John Cruise, and Kelly Kordes Anton — make the process of learning InDesign fun and easy. They discuss technical concepts in an effective way so even nontechnical designers can follow and learn the essentials. An entire appendix is dedicated to the transition to InDesign from QuarkXPress or PageMaker. This appendix alone makes the book worth purchasing! The organization also makes it possible for you to find what you need when you need it. I highly recommend this book.

Electronic publishing has come a long way since the early days of desktop publishing. InDesign is the tool I've been waiting for. It is from Adobe, a company that is a pleasure doing business with. I recently spent some time with the InDesign team — they have what it takes and they listen.

Helene DeLillo
President
Dancing Icon, Inc.

Foreword:
The InDesign Mission

InDesign was conceived by a small, dedicated group of engineers in 1993. It began as a research project that sought to create a desktop-publishing product that could be responsive to customers' needs, extensible for external developers, and serve as a foundation for future development. The team grew to full size in early 1997, and InDesign shipped in late summer 1999.

Many software products were built in the 1980s using the programming language C. They have been updated frequently, with many features being added that weren't originally planned for. The end result is like trying to build a truck on a subcompact frame. The foundation is just not strong or flexible enough, and so it takes a long time to get the truck to work. InDesign (formerly code-named Shuksan and then K2) was conceived to address this very problem. We know a lot more now about desktop publishing than we did back in the 1980s when programs such as PageMaker were first created. With InDesign, we've built an architectural foundation for the publishing of the future.

Furthermore, in the software industry, third-party developers usually have to write their plug-ins to a restrictive API (application program interface). With InDesign, external developers can access the same interfaces that Adobe engineers can. InDesign 1.0 is actually a collection of over 100 plug-ins developed by Adobe. Many more are being written by third-party developers. The application itself is very small — just a couple of megabytes. It is written entirely in C++ using object-oriented technology. It is written explicitly to be extensible, not as an afterthought or with a separate API. All the plug-ins are loaded at runtime, so when a new plug-in is available, it's just dropped in the Plug-ins folder, and it's automatically used by InDesign when InDesign launches.

Most important, however, InDesign was created to be responsive to customer needs. The desktop-publishing community has a startling range and number of customers, operating systems are frequently updated, and the Web has created a whole new medium for communicating information. InDesign plug-ins can be updated individually or as a group. New plug-ins can easily be created. Furthermore, features such as multiple undo are very hard to implement in a complex application if the underlying architecture wasn't created with this functionality in mind. The InDesign engineering team wanted to create a product that helps customers be more creative in their jobs and get their work done more efficiently. We have created the basis for this future in the 1.0 version and will be enhancing it in upcoming versions with functionality that customers are asking for.

It is very unusual for products to be rewritten from scratch. Adobe has created a whole new desktop-publishing product with InDesign. The dedication of the engineering team has been incredible. Many, many late nights and weekends have seen engineers typing away. We have created a revolutionary product, of which InDesign 1.0 is just the tip of the iceberg.

Stacy Molitor
InDesign Engineering Manager
Adobe Systems, Inc.

Preface

Welcome to the *Adobe InDesign Bible* — your personal guide to a new, powerful, full-featured publishing program that offers precise but flexible control over all aspects of page design. Our goal is to guide you each step of the way through the publishing process, showing you as we go how to make Adobe Systems' InDesign work for you. You'll also learn tips and tricks about publishing design that you can use in any document, whether it was created in InDesign or not.

Although InDesign is new, it is hardly a novice. Taking the best from the two schools of thought on desktop publishing, InDesign merges the highly structured approach of programs such as QuarkXPress and Corel Ventura Publisher with the more naturalistic approach of Adobe PageMaker. Thus it offers a smart range of desktop publishing capabilities to sophisticated designers who develop magazines, books, ads, and product brochures. And it gives the power of the press to individuals and groups who use the program's impressive set of publishing tools to communicate their thoughts, dreams, and philosophies.

InDesign is also poised to take advantage of electronic publishing. Not only can you produce high-quality, lively flyers, newsletters, magazines, and similar publications in InDesign, you can also create rich, colorful documents that can be viewed on the Web, distributed on CD-ROM, or sent directly to a printing press for faithful print reproduction.

In a nutshell, InDesign is meant to help those who educate, inform, and document the world in which we live. Join us in learning how to use these tools.

What This Book Offers

So, because InDesign comes with good documentation that is full of examples, why do you need this book? In a phrase, to see the bigger picture. Publishing design involves much more than understanding a particular program's tools — it involves knowing when, how, and most important, why to use them. In this book, we help you realize the potential of InDesign by applying its tools to real-world publishing design needs.

Some desktop publishers have years of high-end creative, design-intensive experience. Others are just getting started in publishing, perhaps by producing simple newsletters or flyers to advertise a community event. Not a few are exploring the brave new world of Web publishing.

Desktop publishers fall into several classes:

+ Designers new to InDesign but familiar with other desktop-publishing software

+ Designers familiar with print publishing but new to electronic publishing

+ Experienced designers new to desktop technologies

+ Novice designers new to desktop technologies

No matter which class you're in, you'll find that this book addresses your needs. You don't need a degree in design or ten years of experience producing national ad campaigns — you can use this book if you're responsible for developing and implementing the look of documents, whether a four-page black-and-white company newsletter or a four-color billboard ad. The basic techniques and issues are the same for both ends of the spectrum. And we, of course, cover in detail the specialized needs — such as table creation, image control, color output, and electronic publishing — of specialty designers. (For those just learning such advanced techniques, be sure to read the sidebars that explain the underlying issues.) Regardless of your level of experience with desktop publishing, this book helps you use InDesign.

What distinguishes this book from others is that it does not attempt to substitute for the documentation that accompanies InDesign. Instead, it guides you through the process of publishing a document, regardless of whether that document is your first or one-thousandth.

How to Read This Book

The *Adobe InDesign Bible* is made up of 39 chapters divided into 11 parts. If you are a novice publisher or designer, we suggest you read the book in order because the process of page design is presented in increasing levels of sophistication. You first learn how (and why) to create placeholders, and then how to work with common elements (such as text), and finally how to use special effects and deal with high-end publishing issues (such as output control, image manipulation, and printing).

If you are experienced, read the book in any order you want — pick the sections or chapters that cover the design issues you want to know more about, either as basic design issues or as InDesign implementation issues. You should also find the exhaustive index a real aid in finding what you're looking for.

Following is a brief description of the parts you will find in the *Adobe InDesign Bible*:

Part I, Welcome to InDesign, walks you through the initial steps of using InDesign to create your publications. We give you a basic introduction to InDesign itself, explaining the concepts it uses in its layout approach. We highlight what's special about InDesign and define a whole passel of publishing and InDesign terms to make sure that we're all working from the same page.

Part II, Frame and Line Fundamentals, explains how InDesign's frame and line tools work so you can create and manipulate layout objects. With these building blocks, you construct almost all the components in a layout: from the frame containers that hold text and pictures to original artwork you create in InDesign.

Part III, Text Fundamentals, shows you how to prepare, import, and format your text for use with InDesign. For many designers, text is the gray stuff that flows around picture and headlines, but text is actually a key component of the layout and its design, as we discuss in this part.

Part IV, Typography Fundamentals, shows you how to use typography effectively in any program, and then teaches you how to take advantage of InDesign's typographic power to really jazz up your layout.

Part V, Picture Fundamentals, discusses how to use InDesign to manipulate and work with images — in all popular formats — in your layout. Although text carries the message, it's a picture that gets your attention and that often can say more than any collection of words. This part helps you get the most out of your images in InDesign.

Part VI, Drawing Fundamentals, shows you how you can use the tools in InDesign to create a variety of shapes that you can use as original artwork or as specialty containers for text and images.

Part VII, Color Fundamentals, explains how to use InDesign's color tools to create colors, tints of colors, and even blends of colors, so you'll have plenty of ways to jazz up your document's objects.

Part VIII, Page Fundamentals, discusses the tools InDesign sports to work with pages. InDesign comes with a set of tools that let you automate repetitive work, apply common elements to a range of pages, and customize page settings, among other capabilities. This part walks you though the ins and outs of all of them.

Part IX, Output Fundamentals, walks you though the output steps of publishing. This part shows you what you need to be aware of as well as shows you how to output your documents for printing or for use in the Adobe Portable Document Format often used for network- and CD-ROM-based documents, as well as for Web-based documents.

Part X, Web Fundamentals, discusses how InDesign can help you convert print documents for use online as well as create basic Web pages. You'll still need a dedicated Web tool, but for those times where InDesign should be part of the process, the two chapters in this part will help you do things right.

Part XI, Advanced Issues, expands your horizons a little, once you've become an expert at InDesign. Very few publishers work by themselves, and most have a whole raft of tools to work their miracles. The chapters in this part expose you to key insights into working beyond InDesign.

The appendixes at the back of the book take you through the ins and outs of how to install Adobe InDesign, provide some shortcuts and tricks for using the program, as well as offer tips for switching from PageMaker or QuarkXPress to InDesign.

Whether you're reading the book sequentially or nonsequentially, you'll find the many cross-references helpful. Publication design is ultimately successful because the result is more than the sum of its parts — and the tools used to create and implement your designs cannot be used in isolation. Because this is true, it is impossible to have one "right" order or grouping of content; the cross-references let you know where to get additional information when what you're seeking to understand or learn doesn't fit the way we've organized this book.

Conventions Used in This Book

Before we begin showing you the ins and outs of InDesign, we need to spend a few minutes reviewing the terms and conventions used in this book.

InDesign commands

The InDesign commands that you select by using the program menus appear in this book in normal typeface. When you choose some menu commands, a related pull-down menu or a pop-up menu appears. If we describe a situation in which you need to select one menu and then choose a command from a secondary menu or list box, we use an arrow symbol. For example, *Choose Edit ⇨ Margins and Columns to set up the locations of the pages margins and default text columns* means that you should choose the Margins and Columns command from the Edit menu.

Like most modern programs, InDesign has an interface feature — proving to be quite popular — called *tabbed panes*. This is a method of stuffing several dialog boxes into one dialog box. You see tabs, like those in file folders, and by clicking a tab, the pane of options for that tab comes to the front of the dialog box. You can even move tabs from one dialog box to another to make an arrangement that best suits your work style. This book tells you to select the tab (where the name of the pane is) to display the pane.

Mouse conventions

Because you use a mouse to perform many functions in InDesign, you need to be familiar with the following terms and instructions. And, yes, by "mouse," we include other pointing devices, such as trackballs and pen tablets.

✦ **Pointer:** The small graphic icon that moves on the screen as you move your mouse is a *pointer* (also called a *cursor*). The pointer takes on different shapes depending on the tool you select, the current location of the mouse, and the function you are performing.

✦ **Click:** To *click* means to quickly press and release the mouse button once. Most Mac mice have only one button, but some have two or more, and all PC mice have at least two buttons; if you have a multibutton mouse, click the left-most button when we say to click the mouse.

✦ **Double-click:** To *double-click* means to quickly press and release the mouse button twice. On some multibutton mice, one of the buttons can function as a double-click (you click it once, the mouse clicks twice); if your mouse has this feature, use it because it saves strain on your hand.

✦ **Right-click:** A Windows feature since Windows 95, *right-click* means to click the right-hand mouse button. On a Mac's one-button mouse, hold the Control key when clicking the mouse button. On multibutton Mac mice, assign one of the buttons to the Control+click combination.

✦ **Drag:** *Dragging* is used for moving and sizing items in an InDesign document. To drag an item, first position the mouse pointer on it, then press *and hold down* the mouse button, and then slide the mouse across a flat surface to "drag" the item.

Dealing with Computer Platform Issues

InDesign runs on Mac OS 8.5 and 8.6, Windows 98, and Windows NT 4.0 with Service Pack 3 or later installed. (It should also run on the forthcoming Mac OS X and Windows 2000, although you may need to reinstall it. However, because both operating systems were still in development when this book went to press, and InDesign was available before they were, you should verify compatibility directly with Adobe—which you can reach on the Internet at www.adobe.com—before moving to Windows 2000 or Mac OS X.)

Most desktop publishers use Apple Computer's Macintosh, and thus most readers of this book will likely be Mac-based. That's why this book uses Mac screens for the majority of its examples. But the minority in publishing who use Microsoft's Windows continues to grow, especially for business-oriented and personal publishing, so we also use Windows screens in many chapters to acknowledge that group. In all cases, we provide both Mac and Windows instructions for processes and commands.

Adobe has done a good job to ensure that the interface for InDesign is almost identical, within the natural differences between Mac and Windows, on both platforms. So looking at a Windows screen will show a Mac user a near replica of what that Mac user sees onscreen. In the few cases where the two interfaces differ, we provide both screens.

When there are differences from one platform to another in how InDesign looks, operates, or interacts with other programs or the operating system, we alert you using the Platform Differences icon. (Though the most visible platform differences are between Mac and Windows, you'll likely encounter a few subtle differences in how InDesign runs on Windows 98 versus Windows NT 4.0, and we'll point them out as well.)

Keyboard conventions

This book provides both the Macintosh and Windows shortcuts throughout, with the Mac shortcut first. In most cases, the Mac and Windows shortcuts are the same, except the names of the keys differ, as follows:

✦ ⌘ is the Mac's Command key—the most-used shortcut key. Its Windows equivalent is Ctrl.

✦ Shift is the same on the Mac and Windows.

✦ The Option key on the Mac is usually the same as the Alt key in Windows. In many Mac programs' menus—including in InDesign—you'll see Option used; in Windows, InDesign simply uses "Alt" in the menus.

✦ The Control key on the Mac has no Windows equivalent (Ctrl, remember, is the Windows equivalent of the Mac's ⌘ key).

If you're supposed to press several keys together, we indicate this by placing plus signs (+) between them. Thus Shift+⌘+A means press and hold both the Shift and ⌘ keys, and then press A. After you've pressed the A key, let go of all the keys. (The last letter in the sequence does not need to be held down.)

We also use the plus sign to join keys to mouse movements: For example, Option+ drag means to hold the Option key when dragging the mouse on the Mac, whereas Alt+drag means to hold the Alt key when dragging the mouse in Windows.

Also note that InDesign lets you change the shortcuts associated with menu and other commands. Throughout the book, we assume the shortcuts in use are the default ones.

Icons

You will notice special graphic symbols, or *icons*, throughout this book. We use these icons to call your attention to points that are particularly important or worth noting:

The Caution icon warns you of potential hang-ups or pitfalls you may encounter while using InDesign (and tells how to avoid them).

The Cross-Reference icon points you to different parts of the book that contains related or expanded information on a particular topic.

The Design Advice icon indicates a technique or approach to layout that will enhance your publication's design.

The Note icon indicates information that you should remember for future use — something that may seem minor or inconsequential but will in reality resurface.

The Platform Difference icon alerts you to differences using InDesign on the Macintosh versus in Windows, as well as between Windows 98 and Windows NT 4.0.

The Tip icon indicates a technique or action in InDesign that can save you time or effort.

The Oddity icon indicates something that works contrary to expectations and thus could cause confusion unless known in advance.

Working the Magic

We've all had long association with the publishing and creative services industry, and we've never lost the excitement and magic of turning ideas into pages. InDesign helps you work that magic. We hope this book helps you use that magic effectively.

Acknowledgments

In creating a book of such scope, many people contribute: family, friends, vendors, colleagues, and the staff at IDG Books Worldwide. The authors thank everyone who has provided software, images, layouts, editing, production assistance, and of course, morale, support, and encouragement.

The following people provided permission to reproduce their copyrighted works in this book:

✦ Dan Brogan of 5280 Publishing Co. provided several layouts from *5280* magazine and its Web site, using stories by Amanda M. Faison and photography by Steven Adams, for us to use as examples.

✦ Sheryl Perri and Lisa Zimmerman of Buzz Publishing also provided layouts from *Buzz in the 'Burbs*, using designs by Debra Novara Jones and Tom Visocchi, for use in our examples.

✦ Photos for the color insert were provided by Ingall W. Bull III, Angela Burgess, Darius Gruman, Galen Gruman, John Henning, Jr., and Leah Walthert.

In all cases, the providers retain all rights to their intellectual property.

Also thanks to Tim Cole and the Adobe InDesign beta team for providing quick, accurate technical answers.

A list of software providers is in Appendix E.

Contents at a Glance

Contents

Part III: Text Fundamentals   171

Part VI: Drawing Fundamentals   441

Chapter 24: Drawing Free-Form Shapes and Curved Paths 443

Chapter 25: Modifying Shapes and Paths 457

Chapter 26: Special Effects for Drawings 469

Part VII: Color Fundamentals   479

Chapter 27: Defining Colors and Gradients 481

Welcome to InDesign

You're ready to go — you've bought InDesign, installed it, you've even launched it. But now what? It's a new program, and while the program is familiar because it looks like most other Macintosh or Windows programs, it *is* a new program, so you're not really sure what to do next. The answer is simple: Read on.

The chapters in Part I walk you through the initial steps of using InDesign to create your publications. First, **Chapter 1** gives you a basic introduction to InDesign, explaining the concepts it uses in its layout approach. We highlight what's special about InDesign and define a passel of publishing and InDesign terms to make sure that we're all working from the same page, and so you're not confused when you see new terms in InDesign's menus and help system, or hear them from colleagues.

With the basic context out of the way, **Chapter 2** gives you a tour through InDesign's interface — its array of tools, menus, palettes, panes, dialog boxes — and covers all the components you get with the program. This sets the stage for **Chapter 3**, which shows you how to adjust the InDesign interface by setting global preferences, changing view zooms for your documents, and setting your own keyboard shortcuts.

Finally, with InDesign tuned to your liking, **Chapter 4** shows you how to create a document, save it, convert documents in other formats (such as QuarkXPress, Portable Document Format, and PageMaker) into InDesign formats, and open documents. When you finish this chapter, you'll be ready to start creating.

What InDesign Can Do for You

Adobe InDesign is a new desktop publishing program, but don't let that fool you. Its history stretches more than 12 years, as it succeeds the venerable Adobe PageMaker, the first popular desktop publishing program. InDesign *is* an all-new program — make no mistake about that — but it does draw on the experience and design of PageMaker, which Adobe Systems acquired in 1994 and significantly modified in the intervening years. PageMaker is now being aimed at business publishers, and InDesign is Adobe's entry into the professional publishing space that has been dominated by QuarkXPress.

Why does this matter? Because chances are you already use PageMaker or QuarkXPress and are switching to InDesign, or adding InDesign to your software toolkit. You'll find a lot of familiar features in InDesign, but InDesign is a new product that borrows from PageMaker and other Adobe products, as well as from chief rival QuarkXPress. It also adds new components of its own. So draw upon your experience with PageMaker, QuarkXPress, or other Adobe software, but don't let yourself think you can run InDesign on autopilot. Instead, be sure to really learn InDesign's own approaches.

Cross-Reference If you are switching to InDesign from PageMaker or QuarkXPress, be sure to check out Appendix D in the back of this book. It will help you translate the old expertise into InDesign's frame of reference.

So what can InDesign do for you? A lot. For years, layout designers had to choose between a free-form but manual approach to layout (PageMaker) and a structured but easily revised approach (QuarkXPress). Most chose the latter. With InDesign you can choose both. That's important for both novice and experienced users, because page layout has no one-size-fits-all answer. Sometimes creating a layout from scratch—almost as if you were doing it by hand on paper—is the best approach, such as if your project is a one-time publication or an experiment. And sometimes using a highly-formatted template that you can modify as needed is the best approach, because there's no need to reinvent the wheel for common documents.

InDesign can handle sophisticated tasks such as magazine and newspaper page layout, but its simple approach to publishing also makes it a good choice for smaller projects such as flyers and newsletters. InDesign is also a good choice for corporate publishing tasks such as proposals and annual reports. As plug-in software from Adobe Systems and other companies becomes available to add extra capabilities, InDesign could also be a good tool for books and other lengthy publications.

Cross-Reference   For more on using plug-in software, see Chapter 38.

But that's not all. InDesign is not merely a merger of QuarkXPress and PageMaker— though it may seem that way to experienced users. It is designed from the ground up as an *electronic* publishing tool. That means documents can easily be sent to service bureaus and printing presses for direct output, and save you lots of time and lots of money. It also means you can create documents for electronic distribution, particularly using the Adobe Acrobat Portable Document Format (PDF). You can also create Web pages from InDesign, but you still need a Web page design tool to do anything that a Web reader would expect to see, such as hyperlinks.

Cross-Reference   See Parts IX and X for more in-depth coverage of output and Web topics.

This chapter details InDesign's range of uses and features, points out the ways in which the program can be useful to you, and describes the basic metaphor on which the program is based. You'll also find a comprehensive list of the terms— clearly and concisely defined—that we use throughout the book. So whether you're an expert or novice, please read on and prepare yourself for a great nDesign adventure.

What Makes InDesign Special

The release of PageMaker in 1986 launched the desktop publishing revolution. Since then, PageMaker and its competitors added tons of cool features. It may be hard to imagine that there's any thing new to add to this publishing toolkit.

Well, InDesign's creators have managed to add a few. And expect more in the months to come. InDesign uses a technology called *plug-in software* that lets Adobe and other companies create features (via plug-ins) you drop into a special folder to add additional capability to InDesign (see Chapter 38 for details).

Following are the significant additions to the desktop publishing toolkit, courtesy of InDesign (note that this list doesn't include enhanced versions of features found in competitors such as QuarkXPress and Ventura Publisher, as well as PageMaker):

✦ **Multi-line Composer**, which lets InDesign adjust the spacing and hyphenation over several lines of text at once — rather than the typical one-line-in-isolation of other programs — to achieve the best possible spacing and hyphenation. (See Chapter 13.)

✦ **Optical margin alignment**, which actually moves some characters past the margin of your columns to create the optical illusion that all the characters line up. This works because some characters' shapes fool the eye into thinking they begin before or after where they really do, so while technically aligned, they appear not to be. Optical margin alignment fixes this problem. (See Chapter 13.)

✦ **Optical kerning**, which adjusts the spacing between characters, based on their shapes, for the most natural look possible without resorting to hand-tuning their spacing. (See Chapter 13.)

✦ **A menu for inserting special characters**, so you no longer have to remember codes or use separate programs such as the Mac's KeyCaps or Windows's Character Map to add special symbols such as bullets (•) and section indicators (§). Your word processor has likely had this feature for a few years, but this is a first in desktop publishing. (See Chapter 10.)

✦ **Glyph scaling**, which lets InDesign stretch or compress characters to make them fit better in a line. (A *glyph* is a character.) This works in addition to tracking and kerning, which adjust the spacing between characters to make them fit better in a line. (See Chapter 13.)

✦ **Custom strokes for characters**, which lets you change the look of characters by making their outlines thicker or thinner. You can also give the part of the characters inside the outlines a different color, to create an outline effect. (Normally, the part inside the stroke is the same color as the stroke, so the reader sees a normal, solid character.) (See Chapter 19.)

✦ **EPS display**, so you can now see the detailed contents of an EPS file rather than rely on a poor-quality preview image or, worse, see an X or gray box in place of the image. (See Chapter 20.)

✦ **PDF import and export**, so you can place PDF files in your layout directly. (See Chapters 4 and 20.)

✦ **Illustrator and Photoshop file import**, so you can place these graphics files directly in your layout. (See Chapter 20.)

✦ **Multiple views of the document**, so you can have several windows open for the same document, letting you see different sections at the same time. (See Chapter 3.)

Continued

(continued)

Still, InDesign is a first-generation product, so it's not surprising that it is missing some features found in some of its competitors. These include:

✦ **Vertical justification**, to adjust spacing between lines to fill out a frame of text vertically.

✦ **A table editor**, to create tables through an easier method than defining dozens of tab stops.

✦ **Styles for lines and frames** to automate their formatting.

✦ **Trapping controls for individual objects**; InDesign offers just global trapping controls.

✦ Support for **Pantone Hexachrome**, the high-fidelity color model.

✦ **Intercolumn rules**, which let you automatically have thin lines placed in the spaces (gutters) between columns.

✦ **Indexing** and other book-creation features.

✦ **Ability to add hyperlinks** for pages exported to HTML or PDF for use on the Web or in interactive media such as CD-ROMs.

✦ **Ability to have text run along a path** such as a curved line. You'll have to create such text in CorelDraw, Adobe Illustrator, or a similar program and import it into InDesign as a graphic.

InDesign may have the preceding shortcomings, but it's very likely that other companies will fill in the gaps by offering plug-in software to add such capabilities.

Discovering the InDesign Approach

Publishing programs, although similar in many ways, differ in their approach to the publishing task. One way to describe a program's approach to publishing is to talk about its *metaphor*, or the overall way that it handles publishing tasks. Some programs use a *free-form metaphor*, which means that the method used to assemble a document is based on assembling page elements as you would if they were placed on a pasteboard until ready for use (this is also called the *pasteboard metaphor*, although that's a less precise term because software using other metaphors can still include a pasteboard). Other programs approach page layout using a *frame-based metaphor* in which frames (or boxes) hold both the page elements and the attributes that control the appearance of those elements. InDesign uses both.

The frame-based metaphor

Under a frame-based metaphor, you build pages by assembling a variety of frames that will contain your text and graphics. First, you set up the basic framework of the document—the page size and orientation, margins, number of columns, and so on. You then fill that framework with text, pictures, and lines.

Note   Frames and lines need not be straight or square. With InDesign 1.0, you can create frames that are shaped by Bézier curves. (In the 1970s, French engineer Pierre Bézier, pronounced *BAY-zyay* or *Bez-ee-AY*, created the mathematics that make these adjustable curves work.)

You have several reasons to use frames:

✦ *To create a template for documents such as newsletters and magazines that use the same basic elements for many articles.* You create the frames and then add the text and graphics appropriate for each specific article—modifying, adding, and deleting frames as necessary for each article.

✦ *To get a sense of how you want your elements to be placed and sized before you start working with the actual elements.* This is similar to creating a pencil sketch on paper before doing a formal layout.

✦ *To ensure specific size and placement of elements up front.* In this case, you're often working with a template or guidelines that limit size and placement of elements. In many cases, you can copy an existing frame, because its size is one you're using in several locations of your layout. For structured or partly structured documents such as newsletters and magazines, we find it easier to set up our documents so elements are sized and placed correctly up front than to resize elements one at a time later.

Note   Bear in mind that whether you start by creating frames in which you will later place graphics or text or you simply place the text and graphics directly on your page, you're using frames. In the case of direct placement of elements on the page, InDesign creates a frame automatically for each element. The difference is that the frame InDesign creates is based on the amount of text or the size of the graphic, rather than on your specific specifications. Of course, in either case, you can modify the frames and the elements within them.

The free-form metaphor

Under a free-form (pasteboard) metaphor, you draw the pages' content as if you're working on paper. Depending on how long you've been in this business, you may well remember having paste-up boards with strips of type, camera-ready line drawings, and halftone pictures strewn about, sticking to the pasteboard thanks to the wax on their backs. You would then assemble all these pieces until you got the combination that looked right to you. The free-form metaphor encourages an experimental approach, which is particularly well-suited to one-of-a-kind documents such as ads, brochures, annual reports, and marketing materials.

Note   In a frame-based approach, you can certainly experiment by using the frames as placeholders for actual text and graphics. But visual thinkers like to work with actual objects, and that's why the free-form metaphor works much better for them. With InDesign, you pick the metaphor that works for your style, your current situation, and your mood. After all, both approaches can lead to the same design.

Understanding Global and Local Control

The power of desktop publishing in general, and InDesign in particular, is that it lets you automate time-consuming layout and typesetting tasks while letting you customize each step of the process according to your needs. The dual structure and flexibility of the frame-based and free-form layout metaphors carries over to all operations, from typography to color: You can use *global* controls to establish general settings for layout elements and then use *local* controls to modify those elements to meet specific publishing requirements. The key to using global and local tools effectively is to know when each is appropriate.

Global tools include:

✦ General preferences and application preferences (see Chapter 3)

✦ Master pages (see Chapter 31)

✦ Styles (see Chapter 15)

✦ Sections of page numbers (see Chapter 32)

✦ Color definitions (see Chapter 28)

✦ Hyphenation and justification (see Chapter 13)

✦ Libraries (see Chapter 31)

Note   Styles and master pages are the two main global settings that you can expect to override locally throughout a document. You shouldn't be surprised to make such changes often because while the layout and typographic functions that styles and master pages automate are the fundamental components of any document's look, they do not always work for all of a publication's specific content.

Local tools include:

✦ Frame tools (see Chapters 11 and 21 through 26)

✦ Character and paragraph tools (see Chapters 12 through 14)

✦ Graphics tools (see Chapters 20 through 26)

Knowing which tools to use

In many cases, it's obvious which tool to use. If you maintain certain layout standards throughout a document, for example, then using master pages is the obvious way to keep your work in order. Using styles is the best solution if you want to apply standard character and paragraph formatting throughout a document. When you work with special-case documents, such as a single-page display ad, it doesn't make much sense to spend time designing master pages and styles — it's easier just to format one-of-a-kind elements on-the-fly.

In other cases, it's harder to decide which tool is appropriate. For example, you can create drop caps (large initial letters set into a paragraph of type) as a character option in the Character pane, or you can create a character style (formatting that you can apply to any selected text, ensuring the same formatting is applied each time) that contains the drop-cap settings and apply that style to the drop cap. The method you choose will depend on the complexity of your document and how often you need to perform the action. The more often you find yourself doing something, the more often you should use a global tool (such as character styles).

Fortunately, you don't have to decide between global and local tools right away while designing a document. You can always create styles from existing formatting later or add elements to a master page if you need them to appear on every page.

Specifying measurement values

Another situation in which you can choose between local or global controls is when specifying measurement values. Regardless of the default measurement unit you set (and that appears in all dialog boxes, panes, and palettes), you can use any unit when entering measurements in an InDesign dialog box. If, for example, the default measurement is picas, but you're accustomed to working with inches, go ahead and enter measurements in inches.

InDesign accepts any of the following codes for measurement units, which are defined later in this chapter:

✦ xi *or* x inch *(for inches)*

✦ xp *(for picas)*

✦ $x$pt *or* 0px *(for points)*

✦ xc *(for ciceros)*

✦ $x$cm *(for centimeters)*

✦ $x$mm *(for millimeters)*

Note   The *x* indicates where you specify the value, such as *1i* for 1 inch. It doesn't matter whether you put a space between the value and the code: *1inch* and *1 inch* are the same as far as InDesign is concerned.

Tip   You can enter fractional picas in two ways: in decimal format (as in *8.5p*) and in picas and points (as in *8p6*). Either of these settings results in a measurement of 8¹/₂ picas (there are 12 points in a pica).

Defining Terms and Concepts

As with many specialized functions, desktop publishing tools have their own unique terms. Not too long ago, only a few publishing professionals knew — or cared — what the words *pica*, *kerning*, *crop*, or *color model* meant. Today, these words are becoming commonplace. Almost everyone who wants to produce a nice-looking report, a simple newsletter, or a magazine encounters these terms in the menus and manuals of their layout programs. Occasionally, the terms are used incorrectly or are replaced with general terms to make nonprofessional users feel less threatened, but such a substitution ends up confusing professional printers, people who work in service bureaus, and Internet service providers. The following definitions, grouped by publishing task, cover the basic terms and concepts you need to know as you work with InDesign.

Typography terms

Typography terms include words that describe the appearance of text in a document or on a computer screen. These terms refer to such aspects of typography as the size and style of the typeface used and the amount of space between lines, characters, and paragraphs.

Characters

✦ **Font:** This is a set of characters at a certain size, weight, and style (for example, 10-point Palatino Bold). This term is now used often as a synonym for *typeface*, which is a set of characters at a certain style in *all* sizes, weights, and stylings (for example, Palatino).

✦ **Face:** A face is a combination of a weight and styling at all sizes (for example, Palatino Bold Italic).

✦ **Font family:** This is a group of related typefaces (for example, the Franklin family includes Franklin Gothic, Franklin Heavy, and Franklin Compressed).

✦ **Weight:** This term describes typeface thickness. Typical weights, from thinnest to thickest, are *ultralight*, *light*, *book*, *medium*, *demibold* or *semibold*, *bold*, *heavy*, *ultrabold*, and *ultraheavy*. You may also see some nonstandard terms used such as *thin* and *thick*; these correspond to *light* and *heavy*.

✦ **Style:** Type can have one of three basic stylings: *Roman* type is upright type; *oblique* type is slanted type; and *italic* type is both slanted and curved (to appear more like calligraphy than roman type). Type also may be *expanded* (widened), *condensed* (narrowed), or *compressed* (severely narrowed). See Figure 1-1 for examples of some of these stylings.

Syntax Medium

Syntax Medium Italic

Syntax Bold

Syntax Bold Italic

Syntax Black

Syntax Black Italic

Syntax Ultrablack

Syntax Ultrablack Italic

Figure 1-1: A sample sans-serif typeface with different stylings.

✦ **x height:** This term refers to the height of the average lowercase letter (this is based on the letter *x*). The greater the height, the bigger the letter looks when compared to letters in other typefaces that are the same point size but have a smaller x height.

✦ **Cap height:** Cap height is similar to x height. It refers to the size of the average uppercase letter (based on the letter *C*).

✦ **Descender:** In a letter such as *q*, the part of the letter that goes below the baseline is called a *descender*.

✦ **Ascender:** The part of a letter that extends above the x height (as in the letter *b*) is called an *ascender* (see Figure 1-2).

✦ **Baseline:** The invisible line on which text rests, usually at the bottom of descender-less characters such as *x*, *v*, *b*, and *m*.

✦ **Strokes:** The lines and curves that make up the characters. These are outlines of the character that can be thickened (to produce an outline effect) or distorted (to change the character's shape).

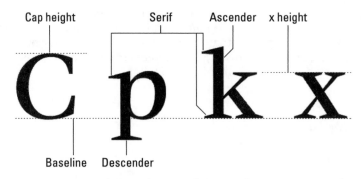

Cap height   Serif   Ascender   x height

Baseline   Descender

Figure 1-2: Sample text showing different elements of a typeface.

✦ **Serif:** This is a horizontal stroke used to give letters visual identity and help lead your eye across a line. The horizontal strokes on the upper-left and bottom of the letter *p* in a typeface such as Times are serifs (refer to Figure 1-2).

✦ **Sans serif:** This means that a typeface does not use serif embellishments. Helvetica is an example of a sans-serif typeface (refer to Figure 1-1).

✦ **Block:** This type of font uses strokes to give the characters a more distinct look than a sans-serif font, but not to the extent of a traditional serif. A block typeface, such as Lubalin Graph, often looks as if it had been carved from wooden blocks.

✦ **Calligraphic script:** This is a font that is meant to emulate a stylized handwritten form, such as Murray Hill or Fraktur.

✦ **Decorative:** This refers to a font that is designed almost as a graphic, such as Critter.

✦ **Pi symbol**: This is a font of special symbols rather than standard alphanumeric characters, such as Wingdings and Mathematical Pi.

Other types of fonts exist that don't fit into the preceding common classes. Chapter 16 covers typography in more detail, and shows examples of these classes.

✦ **Ligature:** A *ligature* is a set of joined characters, such as fi , fl , ffi , or ffl . The characters are joined because the characters' shapes almost blend together by default, so typographers decided to make them blend together naturally.

Automatic ligatures are available only in InDesign for Mac OS, due to the differences between how the Mac OS handles fonts and how Windows handles fonts. Also, very few Windows fonts come with ligatures, so you will likely not be able to manually use ligatures on a PC.

Measurement units

✦ **Pica:** A *pica* is a measurement unit that specifies the width and depth of columns and pages. A traditional publisher's pica is just a little less than $^1/_6$ of an inch, but in desktop publishing, it's an even $^1/_6$ inch.

✦ **Point:** A *point* is a measurement used to specify type size and the space between lines. Each pica has 12 points, so there are about 72.27 traditional points to the inch — and an even 72 in desktop publishing.

✦ **Cicero:** A *cicero* is a unit of measure used in many parts of Europe. One inch equals about 5.62 ciceros, so a cicero is a little bigger than a pica (1.07 picas, actually).

✦ **Em, en, and punctuation spaces:** The terms *em*, *en*, and *punctuation space* (also called a *thin space*) are units of measurement that reflect, respectively, the horizontal space taken up by a capital *M*, capital *N*, and lowercase *t*.

Note

Typically, an em space is the same width as the current point size; an en space is half of the current point size, and a punctuation (thin) space is one quarter of the current point size. In other words, for 12-point type, an em space is 12 points wide, an en space is 6 points wide, and a punctuation or thin space is 3 points wide.

✦ **Figure space:** This refers to the width of a numeral, which usually is the same as an en space. (In most typefaces, all numerals are the same width so that tables align naturally.)

Spacing

✦ **Leading:** This term, also called *line spacing*, refers to the space from the base of one line (the *baseline*) to another. (Leading is named after the pieces of lead once used to space out lines on old letterpresses, and is pronounced as "ledding.") See Figure 1-3 for examples of leading.

✦ **Composition:** This is the adjustment of character spacing across lines of text to produce a visually pleasing result that keeps letters within words together and individual words distinct from others, all with out cramming or awkward gaps. Most programs compose text one line at a time, which can lead to awkward spacing in adjacent lines because what makes sense for one line may cause a bigger problem in the next line. InDesign uses the one-line-at-a-time method but can also use multi-line composition, in which it adjusts spacing across several lines at once, minimizing awkward results.

✦ **Tracking:** *Tracking* determines the overall space between letters within a word (not to be confused with *kerning*).

✦ **Word spacing:** *Word spacing* defines the preferred, minimum, and maximum spacing between words.

This is 14-point type set to 1 point of leading.
As you can see, the lines are simply too close to each other.
See how the text almost overlaps between the first two lines?

This is 14-point type with the leading set to Auto—the normal setting
for leading. Notice how the space in between lines is more than
enough to avoid text overrunning other text, but not so much that
there are large gaps between lines. Note that Auto sets the leading to
be 20 percent more than the point size, which usually results in the
correct 1.5 to 3 points of extra space between lines (for 14-point text,
that means leading of 16.8 points, or 2.8 points extra space). As text gets
larger than about 18 points, you'll want to avoid Auto and use a specific
leading amount (usually 2 points more than the text size). You can specify
your own Auto value.

This is 14-point type with the leading set to 20 points. Notice how the space
in between lines is far more than enough to avoid text overrunning other
text,; in fact, it's an unusually large amount that probably looks a little
strange. You might find such large leading in a kid's book, since young children need help distinguishing characters and the extra space does that. It
also makes sense in very wide columns, so people can keep the long lines
separated visually. You'll also find it in some layouts for parts of an introduction or other special elements that you want to call attention to. But you
rarely find this amount of leading in regular body text.

Figure 1-3: The same type with different leading can have a very different appearance.

✦ **Letter spacing:** *Letter spacing* (sometimes called *character spacing*) defines the preferred, minimum, and maximum spacing between letters.

Note

InDesign uses your preferred spacing specifications unless you justify the text or apply manual spacing adjustments. If you justify text, the program spaces letters and words within the limits you set for maximum and minimum spacing.

✦ **Kerning:** *Kerning* refers to an adjustment of the space between two letters. You kern letters to accommodate their specific shapes. For example, you probably would use tighter kerning in the letter pair *to* than in *oo* because *to* looks better if the *o* fits partly under the crossbar in the *t*. Practically every font already adjusts kerning for you, so any kerning you do will usually be for large type used in ads and headlines, rather than in body copy where the fonts' kerning settings are typically fine.

✦ **Pair kerning:** This is a table, called the *kerning table* in InDesign, that indicates the letter pairs you want the publishing program to kern automatically. Kerning is used most frequently in large headlines where the inconsistent letter spacing is more noticeable. See Figure 1-4 for an example of kerning.

✦ **Justification:** *Justification* adds space between words (and sometimes between letters) so that each line of text aligns at both the left and right margin of a column or page. *Justification* also refers to the type of alignment used: justified, ragged right, centered, or ragged left (see the following definitions).

AV to just

AV to just

Figure 1-4: An example of unkerned (top) and kerned letter pairs.

✦ **Ragged right and flush left:** These terms both refer to text that aligns against a column's left margin but not its right margin.

✦ **Ragged left and flush right:** These terms refer to text that aligns against the right margin but not the left margin.

✦ **Centered:** This refers to text that aligns so there is equal space between the ends of the line of text and both margins.

✦ **Vertical justification:** This adds space between paragraphs (and sometimes between lines) so that the tops and bottoms of each column on a page align. (This term is often confused with *column balancing*, which ensures that each column has the same number of lines.) Unfortunately, InDesign offers no vertical-justification controls.

Paragraphs

✦ **Indent:** You typically indicate a new paragraph with a first-line *indent*, which inserts a space (often an em space in newspapers and magazines) in front of the paragraph's first letter.

✦ **Outdent:** An *outdent* (also called an *exdent*) shifts the first character to the left past the left margin and places the other lines at the left margin. This paragraph alignment is typically used in lists.

✦ **Block indent:** A *block indent*, a style often used for long quotes, moves an entire paragraph in from the left margin, and sometimes from the right margin as well.

✦ **Hanging indent:** A *hanging indent* is like an outdent except that the first line begins at the left margin and all subsequent lines are indented.

✦ **Bullet:** This is a character (often a filled circle) used to indicate that a paragraph is one element in a list of elements. Bullets can be indented, outdented, or kept at the left margin.

✦ **Drop cap:** A *drop cap* is a large capital letter that extends down several lines into the surrounding text (the rest of the text wraps around it). Designers and typesetters use drop caps at the beginning of a section or story to attract the reader's attention. A *raised cap* is the same as a drop cap except that it does not extend down into the text. Instead, it rests on the baseline of the first line and extends several lines above the baseline.

✦ **Keep:** This specifies that a specific number of lines or paragraphs are kept together, rather than being split at the top or bottom of a column.

✦ **Styles:** These contain named sets of such attributes as spacing, typeface, indent, leading, and justification.

✦ **Style or style tag:** A set of attributes is known as a *style* or *style tag*. You can have styles that apply to entire paragraphs — called *paragraph styles* — and styles that apply to a range of characters you highlight — called *character styles*.

Note

Essentially, styles are text-formatting macros. You *tag* each paragraph or a set of characters with the name of the style that you want to apply. Any formatting changes made to one paragraph or character style are automatically reflected in all paragraphs or characters tagged with the same style.

Hyphenation

✦ **Hyphen:** A *hyphen* is used to indicate the division of a word at the end of a line and to join words that combine to modify another word.

✦ **Hyphenation:** This is determining where to place the hyphen in split words.

✦ **Consecutive hyphenation:** This determines how many lines in a row can end with a hyphen (in most situations, three or more hyphens in a row is considered by some to be bad typographic practice).

✦ **Hyphenation zone:** The *hyphenation zone* determines how far from the right margin a hyphen can be inserted to split a word.

✦ **Exception dictionary:** An *exception dictionary* lists words with nonstandard hyphenations. You can add words that the publishing program's default dictionary does not know and override the default hyphenations for a word such as *project*, which is hyphenated differently as a noun (*proj-ect*) than as a verb (*pro-ject*).

✦ **Discretionary hyphen:** Placing a *discretionary hyphen* (also called a *soft hyphen*) in a word tells the program to hyphenate the word at that place if the word must be split. A discretionary hyphen affects only the word in which it is placed.

Layout terms

Document layout—the placement of text, pictures, and other items on a page or, in the case of Web publishing, on a screen—involves many elements. A brief primer on layout terms follows.

Cross-Reference You'll find more detailed explanations of layout terms later in this book, particularly in Parts II and VIII.

Layout tools

✦ **Galleys:** These are single columns of type that are not laid out in any sort of final-page format. Publishers typically use galleys to check for proper hyphenation and proof for errors. Galleys also are sent to authors for proofreading so that corrections can be made before the text is laid out. Galleys are fast becoming a thing of the past, replaced by *proofs*, which are simply laser-printed or otherwise inexpensively produced printouts of laid-out pages used for proofreading. An advantage to using a galley is that there's only one column on the page, leaving more room to mark problems.

✦ **Grid:** A *grid* is the basic layout design of a publication. It includes standard positions of folios, text, graphics, bylines, and headlines. A layout artist modifies the grid when necessary. These are more often called *templates* in desktop publishing.

✦ **Dummy:** A *dummy* is a rough sketch of the layout of a particular publication.

✦ **Pasteboard:** The work area around the document page on which you might place elements you are considering using but haven't yet figured out where they should go.

✦ **Guidelines:** These show the usual placement of columns and margins in the grid. In some programs, guidelines are nonprinting lines that you can use to ensure that elements align.

✦ **Baseline grid:** A *baseline grid* indicates the location of lines of text for normal text—this grid of horizontal lines is essentially a ruler based on the leading of the body text, and is usually used to position other text elements relative to the main body text.

✦ **Overlay:** An *overlay* is a piece of transparent paper or film laid over a layout board. On the overlay, the artist can indicate screens in a different color or overprinted material such as text or graphics. Some programs have electronic equivalents of overlays. InDesign is one of those programs, and it calls its overlays *layers*.

✦ **Knockout:** A *knockout* is when one element cuts out the part of another element that it overlaps.

Note

A designer would say that one element knocks out the other or that one element is knocked out of the other. In either phrasing, it means the first element covers up the part of the other element under it. This differs from overlaying the other element, because in an overlay, both elements are visible (like a superimposed image).

Design elements

✦ **Column:** A *column* is a block of text.

✦ **Gutter:** When you place two or more columns side by side, the space between columns is called the *gutter*. (In newspapers and magazines, gutter space is usually one or two picas.)

✦ **Margin:** The *margin* is the space between the edge of a page and the nearest standard block of text. Some designers let text or graphics intrude into the margin for visual effect.

✦ **Bleed:** This is a graphic element or block of color that extends past the trimmed edge of the page.

✦ **Wrap:** A *wrap* refers to a textual cutout that occurs when a column is intruded by graphics or other text. The column margins are altered so that the column text goes around — wraps around — the intruding graphic or text instead of being overprinted by the intruding element.

Note

Depending on what the text wraps around and the capabilities of the layout program, a wrap can be rectangular, polygonal, or curved. InDesign supports all three shapes.

✦ **Folio:** A *folio* is the page number and identifying material (such as the publication name or month) that appears at the bottom or top of every page.

✦ **White space:** This is the part of the page left empty to create contrast to the text and graphics. White space provides visual relief and emphasizes the text and graphics.

✦ **Frames:** Most desktop publishing programs, including InDesign, use *frames* to hold layout elements (text and graphics) on a page. (Some programs refer to these frames as *boxes*.) Using a mouse, you can delete, copy, resize, reshape, or otherwise manipulate frames in your layout.

✦ **Stroke:** The frames that hold layout elements can have ruling lines around them; InDesign calls these lines *strokes*. (Text can have strokes as well.)

✦ **Template:** You can create a *template* by filling a document with empty frames and defining styles in advance; you then can use the template repeatedly to create documents that use the same frames and styles.

Image manipulation

✦ **Cropping:** *Cropping* an image means to select a part of it for use on the page.

✦ **Sizing:** *Sizing* an image means to determine how much to reduce or enlarge the image (or part of the image). Sizing is also called *scaling*.

Note

With layout programs, you often can *distort* an image by sizing it differently horizontally and vertically, which creates special effects such as compressing or stretching an image.

✦ **Skewing:** Also called *slanting*, this distorts the object or text along one axis but leaves the other alone. For example, in horizontal skewing, an object is slanted in one direction (perhaps to the right), but the top and bottom are unaffected.

✦ **Shearing:** This effect is similar to skewing, except that it adjusts both axes. For example, the frame that is being sheared will have both the x and y axes slanted, but the top and bottom lines of the frame remain parallel to each other, as do the left and right lines. Chapter 22 shows examples.

✦ **Reversing:** Also called *inverting* in some programs, *reversing* exchanges the black and white portions of an image. This effect is similar to creating a photographic negative.

Color terms

Color is an expansive (and sometimes confusing and esoteric) concept in the world of publishing. The following definitions, however, should start you on your way to a clear understanding of the subject.

Cross-Reference

Part VII covers color in detail.

✦ **Spot color:** This is a single color applied at one or more places on a page, such as for a screen or as part of an illustration. You can use more than one spot color per page. Spot colors can also be process colors — such as if you are printing just black and magenta, with magenta being used just for part of a logo.

✦ **Process color:** A *process color* refers to any of the four primary colors in publishing: cyan, magenta, yellow, and black (known as a group as *CMYK*).

✦ **Color model:** A *color model* is an industry standard for specifying a color.

✦ **Swatchbook:** The printer uses a premixed ink based on the color model identifier you specify; you look up the numbers for various colors in a table of colors (which is often put together as a series of color samples, or *swatches*, known as a *swatchbook*).

✦ **Four-color printing:** This is the use of the four process colors in combination to produce most other colors.

✦ **Color separation:** A *color separation* is a set of four photographic negatives — one filtered for each process color — shot from a color photograph or image. When overprinted using the process-color inks, the four negatives reproduce that image.

✦ **Build:** A *build* attempts to simulate a color-model color by overprinting the appropriate percentages of the four process colors.

✦ **Color space:** This is a method of representing color in terms of measurable values such as the amount of red, yellow, and blue in a color image. The color space *RGB* represents the red, green, and blue colors on video screens. CMYK is another color space.

✦ **CIE LAB:** This color-space standard specifies colors by one lightness coordinate and two color coordinates — green-red and blue-yellow.

✦ **CMYK:** This standard specifies colors as combinations of cyan, magenta, yellow, and black.

✦ **Color gamut:** This is the range of colors that a device, such as a monitor or a color printer, can produce.

✦ **High-fidelity color:** This is a form of process color that builds from more than the four CMYK plates.

InDesign does not include the Pantone Hexachrome color model, the standard high-fidelity color ink set that includes orange, green, and black, along with enhanced versions of cyan, magenta, and yellow inks. But it preserves Hexachrome definitions in imported PDF files, and converts Hexachrome colors from QuarkXPress and EPS documents to the less-exact CMYK color model.

Production terms

The following definitions refer to some of the issues you need to know about when you are preparing documents for printing.

✦ **Registration marks:** These tell a printer where to position each negative relative to other negatives (the registration marks must line up when the negatives are superimposed). Registration marks also help printers keep different-colored plates aligned with one another on the press.

✦ **Crop marks:** These show a printer where to trim pages down to their final size. An image or page element may extend past the area defined by the crop marks, but anything beyond that area is cut away by the printer. Crop marks are used both to define page size and to indicate which part of an image is to be used.

✦ **Screen:** A *screen* is an area printed at a particular percentage of a color (including black). For example, the border of a page may have a 20-percent black screen, which appears light gray if printed on white paper.

✦ **Trapping:** This refers to the technique of extending one color so that it slightly overlaps an adjoining color. Trapping is done to prevent gaps between two abutting colors. Such gaps are sometimes created by the misalignment of color plates on a printing press.

✦ **Preflight:** Checking a document to ensure that all linked graphics files are located, that all fonts are available, and that there are no other issues that could prevent accurate output is called *preflighting*. InDesign comes with a built-in utility to do this check.

Web publishing terms

Paperless publishing on the Web is the topic of the hour and the following terms are only a taste of what we'll be covering later in this book.

See Part X for more on Web fundamentals.

✦ **Home page:** A *home page* is an HTML page (a Web page) that usually summarizes what your *Web site*, or entire group of Web pages, offers.

✦ **HTML:** HyperText Markup Language (HTML) is a page description language that is interpreted (turned into page images) by HTML *browsers* such as Netscape Navigator and Microsoft Internet Explorer.

✦ **Hyperlinks:** A *hyperlink* (also called simply a *link*) is an area in a Web or PDF page (often an icon or an underlined word) that, when clicked with the mouse, takes a user to a different location on a Web or PDF page or to an altogether different Web or PDF page.

InDesign terms

InDesign comes with its own terminology, much of it adopted from other Adobe products. The general ones (not covered elsewhere) include the following:

✦ **Link:** A reference to an imported file containing the location, last modification date, and last modification time. This information lets InDesign notify you when source text or a graphics file has changed so you can choose whether to update the version in your layout.

✦ **PDF:** The Adobe Portable Document Format is the standard for electronic documents. No matter what kind of computer it is viewed on (Windows, Macintosh, or Unix), a PDF document retains high fidelity to the original in typography, graphics representation, and layout. InDesign can both place PDF files as if they were graphics and export its own pages to PDF format.

✦ **Place:** To import a picture or text file.

✦ **Plug-ins:** A piece of software that loads into InDesign and becomes part of InDesign, to add more capabilities. One form of plug-ins is called an *XTension*, which is designed to work in the rival QuarkXPress page layout program. InDesign also can run some XTensions as plug-ins in InDesign.

Summary

InDesign offers a strong set of features for professional publishers working on brochures, magazines, advertisements, and similar publications. While it lacks specialized tools for database publishing (such as for catalogs), for book publishing, and for Web publishing, InDesign may at some point gain those capabilities if Adobe or other companies design plug-in software for such purposes.

InDesign's use of both the free-form and structured layout metaphors makes it very flexible, letting you pick the layout style that works best for you and for your document's specific needs.

Now that you understand the capabilities of InDesign and have learned the basic terminology of desktop publishing, you're ready to see how InDesign actually operates. Chapter 2 shows you InDesign's tools and user interface, so you can get started using the program.

✦   ✦   ✦

A Tour of InDesign

◆ ◆ ◆ ◆

In This Chapter

What's inside the
application folder

Exploring the
document window

Using tools, panes,
and palettes

Reviewing menu
commands

◆ ◆ ◆ ◆

The first time you use a program, it can be overwhelming. It's unclear what you can actually do with the program, and each program has its own idiosyncrasies in how to use it effectively. InDesign is no different. If you're familiar with other Adobe applications, such as PageMaker or Photoshop, the InDesign software interface will be familiar to you. Even if you've been using QuarkXPress, you'll be able to translate much of what you've learned about QuarkXPress into InDesign terms.

But because every program is unique, each one has its own style and approaches. So, now that you're ready to start using InDesign, follow through this chapter to find out where InDesign puts its capabilities and how to access them. When you first launch InDesign, you'll see a Toolbox palette on the left, a Transform pane at the bottom of the screen, and several other palettes on the right. It's ready and waiting for you to open a document and start working.

However, taking some time to familiarize yourself with the interface is invaluable when learning new software. After all, without a basic understanding of what you're looking at onscreen, it's difficult to begin working in InDesign.

Note InDesign lets you change the shortcuts associated with menu and other commands (Chapter 3 covers this feature in more detail). Throughout the book, we assume the shortcuts in use are the default ones.

Checking Out the InDesign Application Folder

Often, users simply launch an application from an alias or shortcut and never even look in the application folder. This is fine, until it comes time to install a new plug-in or share important information with other users. Familiarizing yourself with the application folder's basic contents helps prevent you from throwing anything important away and ensures that you're working with the correct files and folders.

If you locate the InDesign application folder on your hard drive and open it, as shown in Figure 2-1, you'll see it's chock full of stuff that you may not even recognize. The three items you need to know about in this folder are the InDesign Defaults file, the Plug-ins folder, and the Required folder.

Figure 2-1: The InDesign application folder contains the application along with other files required to run InDesign.

InDesign Defaults file

The InDesign Defaults file stores all your preference settings for new documents such as the measurement system you prefer to work in and the way your graphics display. To specify these defaults, you modify settings in the Preferences dialog box (File menu) when no documents are open, as shown in Figure 2-2. All new documents you create will be based on these settings.

Because some of the information affects how text flows and how documents look, you may wish to standardize it for a workgroup by setting preferences once and sharing the InDesign Defaults file. (Sharing the file is a simple matter of giving copies of the file to other InDesign users to place in their application folder.)

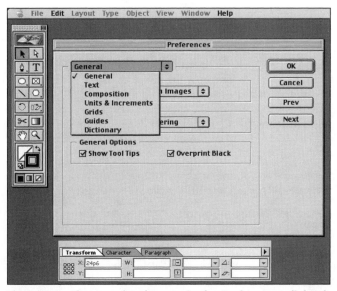

Figure 2-2: If you make changes in the Preferences dialog box when no documents are open, the settings become defaults for all new documents.

Note   If you make changes to preferences while a document is open, the change is saved with that document and not in the InDesign Defaults file. The document remembers its own preference settings so it will look the same when it's opened on other machines running InDesign.

Making InDesign Easy to Access

If you haven't created an alias or shortcut for InDesign yet, now is a good time to do so. You can move the alias to a place in your system that's easier to get to than in the application folder. Here's how:

✦ On the Mac, select the program icon, and use File ⇨ Make Alias or press ⌘+M. You can move the alias to the desktop for easy access, or place it in the Apple menu by moving it to the Apple Menu Items folder in your System Folder. Or you can place it in the Favorites folder (also in the System folder) by using File ⇨ Add to Favorites or Ctrl+clicking the icon and choosing the Add to Favorites option from the contextual menu. The Favorites folder will appear in your Apple menu, in Open and Save dialog boxes, and in the Network Browser program. Another option for creating an alias is to press Option+⌘ while you drag the program icon to the location where you want an alias.

Continued

(continued)

✦ In Windows, right-click the program icon and select Create Shortcut from the contextual menu that appears. You can move the alias to the desktop for easy access, or place it in the Start menu by dragging the shortcut to the Start button. If you want to have the shortcut in a specific folder in your Start menu (we tend to keep our Start menu organized that way), right-click the Start menu and select Open from the contextual menu to open it, and then open or create the folder you want to move it to (use File ➪ New ➪ Folder to create a folder). Then drag the shortcut to the desired location.

If you use the program all day every day, you might as well make InDesign a start-up application so it launches itself automatically when you turn on your computer:

✦ On the Mac, place the InDesign alias in the Startup Items folder inside your System folder.

✦ In Windows, place the InDesign shortcut in the Startup folder in your Start menu's Programs folder. You can open the Start menu by right-clicking it and choosing Open from the contextual menu.

Plug-ins folder

The Plug-ins folder in the InDesign folder contains small software modules, called *plug-ins*, that add both core features and additional, optional features to InDesign. As Figure 2-3 shows, the Plug-ins folder contains a variety of subfolders such as Dictionaries, Filters, and Graphics, which make it easy to locate files.

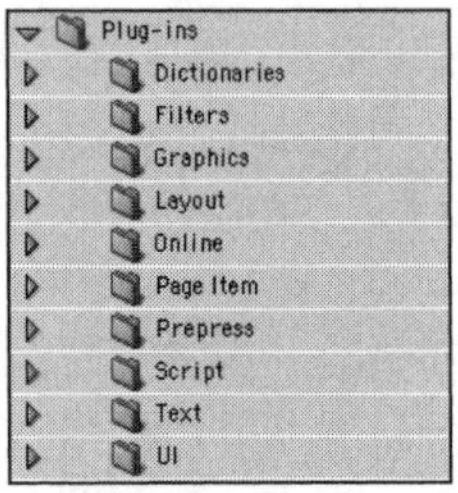

Figure 2-3: The Plug-ins folder contains subfolders for dictionaries used for checking spelling and hyphenation, along with folders for different types of plug-ins.

To install additional plug-ins from Adobe or other companies, add them to the Plug-ins folder. Follow the instructions provided by each vendor — some will have an installation program, while others simply have you copy the plug-in file to this folder.

To remove a plug-in, simply move it out of the subfolder of the Plug-ins folder and store it someplace else, or delete it.

You also use the Plug-ins folder to get access to any customizations you make to the spelling or hyphenation dictionaries in InDesign. These custom settings are saved in the files inside the Dictionaries folder. If you're in a workgroup, the only way to ensure that everyone is working with the same spelling and hyphenation standards — so that text flows the same way on everyone's machine — is to share the dictionary files. (See Chapter 37 for more information on maintaining standards across workgroups.)

Note   If you're a QuarkXPress user, don't compare plug-ins directly to XTensions. XTensions are plug-ins that add features to the core product but are not required to run QuarkXPress. The InDesign plug-ins installed by Adobe, on the other hand, actually provide many core features and must be installed.

Required folder and remaining files

As you might guess from its name, the Required folder contains software components required to run InDesign. The program is structured with many small pieces such as plug-ins and required files so that these small files can be updated or fixed as necessary. You should leave this folder alone. In fact, it's probably best that you leave most of the remaining files in the InDesign application folder as you found them.

Tip   To keep track of required files and plug-ins versus optional ones, you might create an Optional Plug-ins folder and install any optional plug-ins there rather than to the existing folders in the Plug-ins folder. On the Mac, you might use the Label feature (available in the contextual menu by Ctrl+clicking the icon or via File ⇨ Label) to give optional plug-ins a different icon color so you can tell quickly what is optional.

Exploring the Document Window

Once you're running InDesign, the first thing to do is create a new, empty document by choosing File ⇨ New, or ⌘+N or Ctrl+N, and clicking OK immediately. This gives you a document window so you can start exploring the application. (Never mind the settings for now — you're exploring.)

No matter what size document you're working on or how many pages it has, all documents are displayed within a standard window. The window provides controls that help in creating and placing objects, changing the view scale, and navigating among pages. Figure 2-4 shows all the standard elements of a new document window.

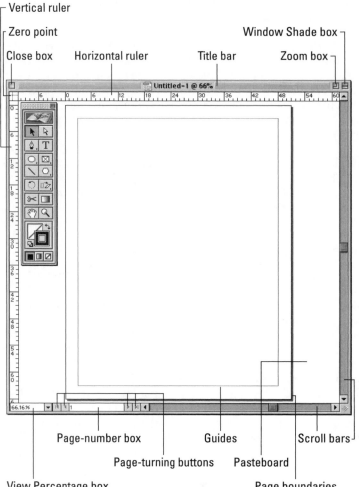

Vertical ruler

Zero point

Window Shade box

Close box   Horizontal ruler   Title bar   Zoom box

Untitled-1 @ 66%

Page-number box   Guides   Scroll bars

Page-turning buttons   Pasteboard

View Percentage box   Page boundaries

Figure 2-4: The standard document window provides controls for managing documents onscreen, changing the view scale, displaying different pages, and placing objects on pages.

Title bar

The bar across the top of the window is called the title bar. InDesign's title bar not only displays the name of the document, but also the magnification at which it's being displayed. For example, the words "Herb Article @ 68%" centered in the title bar mean that you're looking at an InDesign document file called "Herb Article" and you're viewing it at 68 percent of full size — a typical percent value you'll land at when using Fit Page In Window view on a 17-inch monitor. The title bar also includes three boxes for manipulating the document window, as shown in Figure 2-5.

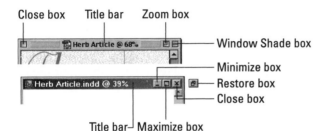

Figure 2-5: The title bar of each document window contains a Close box, Zoom (Mac) or Restore (Windows) box, and WindowShade (Mac) or Minimize (Windows) box. The Mac title bar is shown at top, Windows at bottom.

Macintosh/Windows Interface Differences

The Macintosh and Windows have slight interface differences for title bars, as noted here.

✦ The Close box in the upper-left corner on Mac OS or the X in the upper-right corner in Windows lets you close the document. When you click it, if you've made any changes to the document without saving it, a save alert will appear.

✦ The Zoom box near the upper-right corner lets you expand the document window to fit the screen. On the Mac, clicking it again toggles the window back to its previous size and position. (In Windows, use the Restore box to do this, or the Maximize box to have the document fill the entire window.)

✦ On the Mac, the WindowShade box lets you shrink the document window down to only the title bar, called a WindowShade. Clicking the WindowShade box again restores the document window. (You can double-click the title bar to create a WindowShade if Double-click title bar to collapse windows is selected in the Appearance control panel's Options pane.) In Windows, clicking the Minimize box has the same effect as a WindowShade on the Mac, except that Windows moves the minimized title bar to the bottom of the InDesign windows, while the Mac will *not* move the title bar. And in Windows, you click the Restore box (which replaces the Minimize box) to get the document back to its previous size.

Rulers

New document windows always display a horizontal ruler across the top and a vertical ruler down the left side. The horizontal ruler measures from the top-left corner of the page across the entire spread; the vertical ruler measures from the top to the bottom of the current page.

You can use these rulers to judge the size and help with the placement of frames and lines on your page. Although InDesign provides more precise methods for placing objects — such as the Transform pane in which you can enter exact values — designers often use the rulers for rough placement while experimenting with a design, as shown in Figure 2-6.

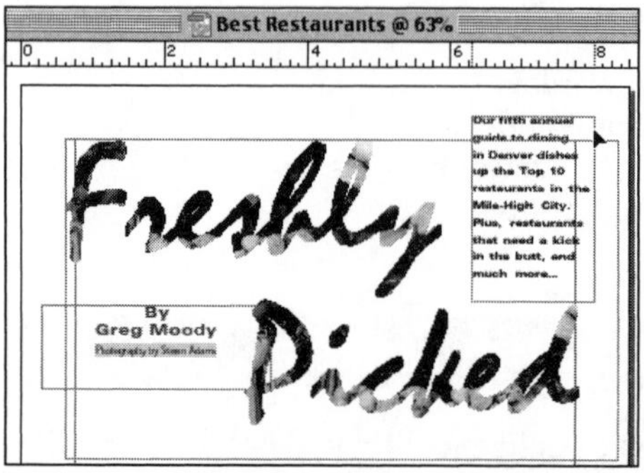

Figure 2-6: This article's kicker (or subhead) is right-aligned with the 8-inch mark on the ruler.

By default, both rulers display increments in picas, but you can change the measurement system for each ruler in the Units & Increments pane of the Preferences dialog box (File ➪ Preferences, or ⌘+K or Ctrl+K). If you do this while no documents are open, the rulers in all new documents will display in your preferred measurement systems.

Cross-Reference   Chapter 29 explains the increments on the ruler in more detail.

If you need more space onscreen or want to preview a design without all the layout tools, you can hide rulers by choosing View ➪ Hide Rulers, or by pressing ⌘+R or Ctrl+R. Most users show the rulers all the time out of habit, but they're really not necessary in template-driven documents such as magazines where all the placement decisions are indicated by guides and master pages. Or, if you're editing text on a smaller monitor, you might appreciate the space gain, minimal though it might be.

The zero point

The intersection of the rulers in the upper-left corner of the page is called the *zero point*. Known as the *ruler origin* in other applications, this is the starting place for all horizontal and vertical measurements. If you need to place items in relation to another spot on the page — for example, from the center of a spread rather than from the left-hand page — you can move the zero point by clicking and dragging it to a new location. The X and Y values in the Transform pane update as you drag the zero point so you can place it precisely. The zero point is document-wide, so it changes for all pages or spreads in the document. To restore the zero point to the upper-left corner of the left-most page, double-click the intersection of the rulers in the upper-left corner.

Once you move the zero point, all the objects on the page display new X and Y values even though they haven't moved. Objects above or to the left of the zero point will have negative X and Y values, and the X and Y values of other objects will not relate to their actual position on the page or spread.

All this can be potentially confusing, especially in a workgroup when other users may change the zero point and forget to restore it to the upper-left corner. To solve this problem, you can lock the ruler origin, making it more difficult for users to change it. Ctrl+click or right-click the ruler origin and choose Lock Zero Point, as shown in Figure 2-7. Granted, the Unlock Zero Point command is right there as well so users can just as easily unlock it. Even though it's easy to undo, it's still worth using. Some users won't know how to unlock it, and others will be reminded that you don't want them messing with the zero point.

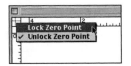

Figure 2-7: A contextual menu, accessed by Ctrl+clicking or right-clicking the intersection of the horizontal and vertical ruler, lets you lock or unlock the zero point.

Scroll bars

Standard scroll bars run down the right side and across the bottom of the document window. As in most applications, you can either drag the scroll boxes or click the scroll arrows to move around on a page or move to other pages in the document.

Pasteboard, pages, and guides

Inside the rulers you'll see a white area surrounding the black, drop-shadowed outlines of your pages, as shown in Figure 2-8. The work area surrounding the page is called the *pasteboard*, and it's designed as a workspace for creating, experimenting with, and temporarily storing objects. You can also use the pasteboard to bleed objects off a page so they'll print to the edge of a trimmed page.

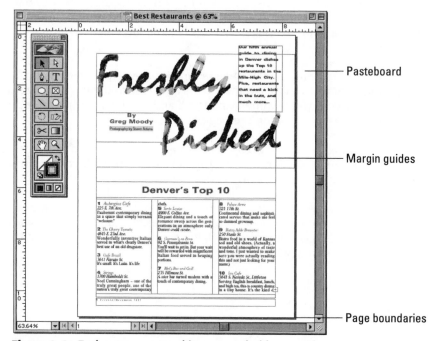

Figure 2-8: Each page or spread is surrounded by a work area called a pasteboard.

Unlike PageMaker (and like QuarkXPress), each page or spread in InDesign has its own pasteboard. There's an inch of pasteboard above and below each page, and a space equal to the page width to the left and right of each page or spread. For example, a spread consisting of two 4-inch pages will have four inches of pasteboard to the left and four inches to the right.

Tip   Although the pasteboard is designed as a work and temporary storage area, don't clutter it up with too many objects. Unnecessary objects on the pasteboard won't print, true, but they do increase file size resulting in slower opening, closing, and saving.

Pages, drawn with black outlines, reflect the page size you set up in the New Document dialog box (File ⇨ New, or ⌘+N or Ctrl+N). If it looks like pages are touching, you're looking at a multipage spread. By default, you'll see magenta lines across the top and bottom of each page showing the top and bottom margins you specified when you created the document. Violet-colored lines indicate the left and right margins (for single-page documents) or inside and outside margins (for facing-page documents). These lines are nonprinting guides that can help you position objects.

You can change the placement of these guides using the Margins and Columns dialog box (in the Layout menu), and you can create additional guides by dragging them from the horizontal or vertical rulers. (Chapter 4 covers guides in detail.)

If you can't see the guide colors well, you can change them for all new documents. When no documents are open, choose new colors in the Guides pane of the Preferences dialog box (File ⇨ Preferences, or ⌘+K or Ctrl+K). The Margins color applies to horizontal guides and the Columns color applies to vertical guides.

View percentage box

The lower-left corner of the document window contains a field/pop-up menu that lets you change the document's view percent. The view scale can be as small as 5 percent and as large as 4,000 percent, and you can modify it in 0.01 percent increments. You have three options for using the view percentage box:

✦ To change the view to a preset value, click the arrow on the field and choose an option from the pop-up menu, as shown in Figure 2-9.

✦ To change the view to a specific value, highlight the value in the field, enter a new value, and press Return or Enter.

✦ To jump into the field quickly and enter a specific value, press Option+⌘+5 or Ctrl+Alt+5, enter a new value, and press Return or Enter. This method lets you change the view without taking your hands off the keyboard.

Figure 2-9: You can choose from a list of preset view percentages using the menu on the View percentage box.

Page-turning buttons

Next to the view percentage box you'll find a page number field encased by two sets of arrows, as shown in Figure 2-10. These arrows are page-turning buttons, which let you turn pages sequentially or jump to the first or last page in the document. From left to right, clicking these arrows takes you to the first page, previous page, next page, and last page.

Figure 2-10: Buttons on the document window enable you to flip from page to page.

Page-number box

The lower-left corner of the document window also provides a control for jumping to a specific page or master page in a document. To jump to a specific page number, highlight the number in the Page Number field, enter a new page number, and press Return or Enter. A shortcut to highlighting the field is ⌘+J or Ctrl+J.

To jump to a master page, enter the first few characters of the master page's name in the field, and then press Return or Enter. Jumping to document pages can be a little more complicated. Because the page number that displays and prints on the document page does not have to match the position of the page in the document — for example, the third page might be labeled "iii" — you have two methods for entering the page number you want to jump to: section page numbers and absolute page numbers.

Section page numbers

A section page number, specified through the Section Options dialog box (in the Pages pane's palette menu) is a customized page number. You would use section numbers if your document needs to start on a page other than 1 — for example, if you're working on a magazine and each article is saved in a different document. You can also split a single document into separate sections of page numbers, and use section page numbers to change the format of numbers to roman numerals, letters, and so on.

To jump to or print a page with a section page number, you need to indicate which section it is and what page number is displayed on the page. InDesign provides a default name for sections, starting at Sec1. When you enter a section page number, you must separate the section name and the page number with a colon. For example, if you start the page numbering on page 51, you will need to enter Sec1:51 in the Page number box to jump to that page. (See Figure 2-11.) Having to include this undisplayed section information makes this option fairly unappealing, so you may prefer to use absolute page numbers.

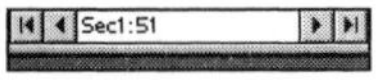

Figure 2-11: To use section page numbers to jump to pages, enter the name of the section, followed by a colon, and then the page number.

Absolute page numbers

An absolute page number indicates a page's position in the document, such as 1 for the first page, 2 for the second page, and so on. To specify an absolute page number, you enter a plus sign before the number that represents the page's position. For example, the first page in the document is always +1, the second page is always +2, and so on.

Using Tools

InDesign always displays a floating palette called the Toolbox, which contains more than 25 tools. By default, it appears in the upper-left corner of your screen, but you can move it to any location you wish. The tools let you create and manipulate the objects that make up your pages. The tools work the same way as they do in other Adobe products — such as Photoshop, Illustrator, and PageMaker — and they work somewhat like the tools in QuarkXPress. But the tools do not work like the toolbars in your word processor, which are more like macros that make something happen. With InDesign's tools, for the most part you select the tool and do something with it — draw a new frame, rotate a line, crop an image, and so on.

With so many tools, all of which perform limited functions, it's imperative that you understand what each tool does. When it comes to tools, InDesign has little intuition — you must select the correct tool for the action you want to complete. The software is unable to predict that you might want to make a box slightly larger while you're editing text, or that you might want to reshape a frame at the same time you're resizing it. You need to learn which tool to use and get used to switching tools — frequently.

Note The limited functionality of each tool may be familiar to PageMaker users, but is likely to drive a QuarkXPress convert crazy. In recent years, Quark has made its tools more flexible, so users don't have to switch as often as they go from, for example, moving a picture box to importing a picture. QuarkXPress users should pay special attention to the tool definitions that follow so you can translate the InDesign tools to tools that you understand.

Using ToolTips and keyboard shortcuts

To start getting familiar with the tools, first make sure Show ToolTips is checked in the General pane of the Preferences dialog box (File ➪ Preferences, or ⌘+K or Ctrl+K). Point at each tool to learn its official name, as shown in Figure 2-12 (the pointer will need to rest on the tool for a second or two for the ToolTip to display). Knowing the actual name is the key to learning about any tool — after all, the documentation's index doesn't list "little black pointer" or "empty square," but rather "Selection tool" and "Rectangle tool."

Figure 2-12: ToolTips display the name of each tool along with the shortcut key (in parenthesis) that you can use to select that tool.

While you're learning the tool names, you'll notice a single letter in parenthesis next to each tool name. This is the shortcut key for selecting that tool. For example, the (Z) next to the Zoom tool indicates that pressing Z selects the Zoom tool.

The Toolbox's shortcuts don't use modifier keys such as ⌘ and Ctrl. (And even though they're displayed as capital letters, you don't have to press Shift either.) If you're editing text or otherwise have the Type tool selected — or if you're in a text-entry field in pane or dialog box — entering these shortcuts will simply insert the text where your cursor is. If you're not careful, you can enter nonsense text in your articles because of this. This shortcut makes no sense in a program that includes significant text-handling functionality. Adobe's graphics programs, such a Photoshop and Illustrator, use such single-letter shortcuts, which made sense because artists rarely used text in them. Adobe has decided to standardize the interface across all its products, which in this case results in an unintuitive and potentially damaging approach.

Once you learn all the keyboard commands, you can create and refine a layout without ever reaching for the Toolbox. In no time you'll be switching from the Scale tool to the Rotate tool with a quick punch on R, and then hitting T to add a text frame. Obviously, you can't use the keyboard commands for selecting tools while typing or editing text, but they are worth remembering for switching tools while designing a layout. In many production environments, copy editors handle text changes, while layout artists handle design issues — in such environments, the layout artists would learn these shortcuts, while the copy editors would avoid them.

Opening and closing the Toolbox

Opening the Toolbox is easy because there's only one obscure method for closing it in the first place. Pressing the Tab key (with any tool but the Type tool selected) closes all open palettes including the Toolbox. This is the only time you'll find the Toolbox closed. To reopen the Toolbox, choose Window ➪ Tools. The Window menu command doesn't toggle between Show Tools and Hide Tools, and the Toolbox doesn't include a close box, so your only option for closing it is to hide all the palettes again.

If the Toolbox is in the way onscreen, you can click its minimize box to shrink it to its title bar. (On Mac OS, you can also double-click the title bar to make the Toolbox into a WindowShade.) You can then tuck the remains of the Toolbox into the document title bar, as shown in Figure 2-13, so it doesn't obstruct your document view at all. While the Toolbox is minimized, you can still use keyboard shortcuts to change tools.

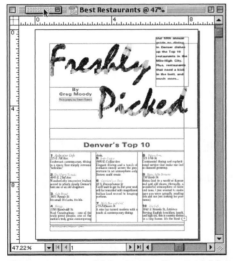

Figure 2-13: To hide the Toolbox quickly, you can minimize it and tuck it up into the document title bar.

Selecting tools

To select a tool and start using it, click it in the Toolbox. As long as you're not using the Type tool, you can also press a keyboard shortcut displayed in parentheses in the ToolTips.

In addition to the tools you can see, the Toolbox contains a few hidden tools that are consolidated into little pop-out menus. Any tool with a small arrow in its lower-right corner is hiding one or more similar tools, as shown in Figure 2-14. To access hidden tools, click and hold on a tool with a pop-out indicator. To choose a hidden tool, drag the pointer over it and release the mouse button. When you select a hidden tool, it replaces the previous tool in the Toolbox.

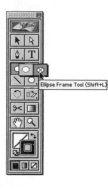

Figure 2-14: If a small triangle appears in the lower-right corner of a tool, you can click and hold on it to display pop-out tools.

> **Tip**
> The pop-out tools also have keyboard shortcuts, most of which include the Shift key. For example, the Scale tool uses the shortcut key S. The Scale tool's pop-out provides access to the Shear tool, which has the keyboard shortcut of Shift+S.

Tool definitions

In real life you can often get by using the wrong tool for a job — using a flat screwdriver instead of a Phillips, or a shoe instead of a flyswatter. This won't work in InDesign. Whether you're typing, reshaping an object, or applying a color, there's one — and only one — tool for the job. Loosely organized with the most commonly used tools appearing at the top, the Toolbox includes tools for creating and manipulating frames and lines — the objects that make up your designs. (See Figure 2-15.)

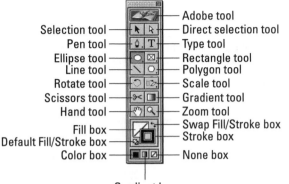

Selection tool — Adobe tool
Selection tool — Direct selection tool
Pen tool — Type tool
Ellipse tool — Rectangle tool
Line tool — Polygon tool
Rotate tool — Scale tool
Scissors tool — Gradient tool
Hand tool — Zoom tool
Fill box — Swap Fill/Stroke box
Default Fill/Stroke box — Stroke box
Color box — None box

Gradient box

Figure 2-15: The Toolbox contains tools for creating and manipulating InDesign objects.

Note

Frames are shapes and containers that you can size, position, and reshape with precision. InDesign has three types of frames: empty (unassigned) for blocks of color, text frames for containing type, and graphics frames for imported images. By default, most frames are empty, but can be easily converted to text or graphics frames. Other frames are created specifically as text or graphics frames. (See Chapter 5 for basic information about creating frames.)

Adobe tool

In the Adobe Toolbox world, the first item is actually a big button that takes you to the Adobe Web site. A fairly large, prominent tool for something you can do just as easily many other ways, the Adobe tool does show the product icon (the butterfly for InDesign) so you always know by looking at the Toolbox that InDesign is active.

Selection tool

The Selection tool, shortcut V, lets you select objects on the page and move or resize them. You might want to rename this tool in your mind to the Mover tool because it's the only tool that lets you drag objects around onscreen.

QuarkXPress users: Think of this as half your Item tool.

Tip

If you're working with text and have the Type tool selected, you can switch to the Selection tool by holding ⌘ or Ctrl, rather than use the Toolbox palette.

Here's how the Selection tool works:

✦ To select any object on a document page, click the object. If you can't seem to click it, it might be an object placed by a *master page* (a preformatted page used to format pages automatically) or it might be behind another object.

✦ To select an object placed by a master page, press Shift+⌘ or Ctrl+Shift while you click.

✦ To select an object that is completely behind another object, ⌘+click it or Ctrl+click it.

✦ To select multiple objects, click and drag a rectangular shape around the objects or Shift+click them individually. Because you need to press the Shift key anyway while selecting objects placed by master pages, you can always multiple-select those objects.

✦ To move selected objects, click somewhere within the objects and drag the mouse.

✦ To resize a selected object, drag any handle, as shown in Figure 2-16. Press Shift+⌘ or Ctrl+Shift while you drag to maintain the proportions of the object.

✦ To resize both a selected frame and its graphic, press ⌘ or Ctrl while you drag. Press Shift+⌘ or Ctrl+Shift to keep things proportional.

Our fifth annual guide to dining in Denver dishes up the Top 10 restau-rants in the Mile-High City. Plus, res-taurants that need a kick in the butt,

Figure 2-16: Dragging a text frame's handle lets you enlarge it to make, for example, all the text fit.

Tip   To resize multiple objects simultaneously, you must first group them (Object ➪ Group, or ⌘+G or Ctrl+G). Otherwise, only the object whose handle is being dragged will resize. Ungroup via Object ➪ Ungroup, or Shift+⌘+G or Ctrl+Shift+G.

Direct Selection tool

The Direct Selection tool, shortcut A, lets you select individual handles on objects to reshape them, and it lets you move graphics independently of their frames.

QuarkXPress users: Think of the Direct Selection tool as the other half of your Item tool and as the Content tool for pictures.

Here's how the Direct Selection tool works:

✦ To select an object to reshape it, click the object. This displays anchor points on the edges (the anchor points are hollow handles that you can select individually, as shown in Figure 2-17), which you can drag to reshape the object.

✦ Like the Selection tool, selecting objects placed by a master page requires you to Shift+⌘+click or Ctrl+Shift+click. However, the Direct Selection tool does let you easily select objects behind other objects and to select items within groups.

✦ To select multiple objects, click and drag around the objects or Shift+click them. Because you need to press the Shift key anyway while selecting objects placed by master pages, you can always multiple-select those objects.

✦ To move a graphic within its frame, click inside the frame and drag the graphic.

✦ To move a frame while leaving the graphic in place, click an edge of the frame and drag it.

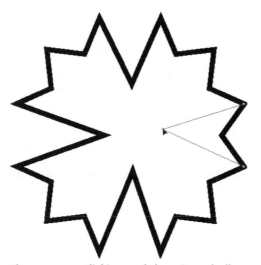

Figure 2-17: Clicking and dragging a hollow anchor point with the Direct Selection tool lets you reshape items.

Note In addition to using the Selection tool for threading (linking) text frames (see Chapter 11), you can use the Direct Selection tool. This is one of the few cases where you have more than one tool to handle a task.

Pen tool

The Pen tool, shortcut P, lets you create paths consisting of straight and curved segments. Modeled after the pen tools in Illustrator and Photoshop, this is the tool for creating simple illustrations within InDesign.

If a path you create with the Pen tool is left open, the object is essentially a line that you can color or adjust stroke settings for. If the path is closed, the object is basically an empty frame. You can import text or graphics into the paths using the Place command (File ➪ Place, or ⌘+D or Ctrl+D) or you can type into the path using the Type tool. If you decide to place text or graphics in an open path, the path closes automatically and becomes a frame.

Oddity You cannot place text on an open path to have it follow the path's shape, as you can in Illustrator and QuarkXPress. To have such text, create it first in a program such as Illustrator, FreeHand, or CorelDraw and then export it as an EPS file for import into InDesign.

To use the Pen tool:

✦ To create straight segments of a path, click and release to establish an anchor point, and then move the mouse to the next location, click again, and so on. To move an anchor point after clicking, press the spacebar and drag the segment.

✦ To create curved segments of a path, click and drag, and then release the mouse button to end the segment, as shown in Figure 2-18.

✦ To close a path and create a frame, click over the first anchor point created (the hollow one).

✦ To create an open path (a line), ⌘+click or Ctrl+click away from the path or select another tool.

Figure 2-18: Clicking and dragging with the Pen tool lets you create curved lines and shapes.

The Pen tool includes a pop-out containing three additional tools for reshaping lines and frames: Add Anchor Point (shortcut +), Delete Anchor Point (shortcut –), and Convert Direction Point (no shortcut).

Cross-Reference For more information about using line reshaping tools, see Chapters 24 and 25.

Type tool

The Type tool, shortcut T, is the one and only tool you can use for entering, editing, or formatting text. The Type tool also lets you create rectangular text frames as you need them.

QuarkXPress users: Think of the Type tool as a combination of the Rectangle Text Box tool and the Content tool for text — except remember that it doesn't let you do anything else such as resizing a frame.

To use the Type tool:

✦ To create a rectangular text frame, click and drag; hold the Shift key to create a perfect square.

✦ To begin typing or editing text, click in a text frame or in any empty frame.

✦ To highlight text so you can format it, cut and paste it, and so on, click and drag.

✦ To select a word, double-click it; to select a paragraph, triple-click.

✦ To select all the text in a frame or story (a series of threaded text frames), choose Edit ➪ Select All or press ⌘+A or Ctrl+A.

You can place or drag-and-drop text files, and you can thread (link) text frames with either of the selection tools, but they won't let you touch the text.

Ellipse and Rectangle tools

The Ellipse tool, shortcut L, lets you create empty frames in oval or circular shapes. The Rectangle tool, shortcut M, lets you create empty frames in rectangular and square shapes. To create frames with these tools, click and drag using the rulers or the Transform pane to judge the size and position. To create a perfect circle with the Ellipse tool or a perfect square with the Rectangle tool, press the Shift key while you click and drag.

You can fill and stroke the empty frames for use as design elements or you can import text and graphics into them using the Place command (File ➪ Place, or ⌘+D or Ctrl+D). You can also click in an empty frame with the Type tool to begin typing in it.

If you'd rather create actual graphics frames, distinguished by a large X in the frames, use the pop-out tools available from the Ellipse tool and the Rectangle tool. The shortcut for the Ellipse Frame tool is Shift+L and the shortcut for the Rectangle Frame tool is Shift+M.

Note   No matter what type of frame you create, you can always use the Content commands in the Object menu to change the frame type later.

Line tool

The Line tool, shortcut E, lets you draw straight, freestanding rules on your page. To use this tool, simply click and drag it. You can use the rulers or Transform palette to size and position the line precisely. Pressing the Shift key while you click and drag constrains the line angle to 45-degree increments, which is useful for creating horizontal and vertical lines.

Polygon tool

The Polygon tool, shortcut N, lets you create empty frames with multiple, straight edges of equal length such as octagons or starbursts. Fortunately, you don't have to draw polygons by hand — you tell InDesign how many sides you want and what they should look like, and then click and drag to indicate the size and placement.

Steps: Creating a Polygon Frame

1. Double-click the Polygon tool to display the Polygon Settings dialog box, shown in Figure 2-19.

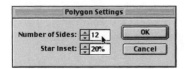

Figure 2-19: Double-clicking the Polygon tool displays the Polygon Settings dialog box, which you can use to specify the number of sides on a polygon.

2. Enter a value between 3 and 100 in the Number of Sides field to specify how many sides you want on your polygon.

3. If you want to create a star shape, use the Star Inset field to specify the size of the spikes. The percent value specifies the distance between the polygon's bounding box and the insides of the spikes — for example, 50% creates spikes that are halfway between the bounding box and the center of the polygon.

4. Click OK to close the Polygon Settings dialog box. The settings are saved with the active document for the next time you use the Polygon tool.

5. Click and drag to create the polygon, using the rulers or Transform pane to judge the size and position.

To create a symmetrical polygon in which all the sides are the same size, press the Shift key while you click and drag the Polygon tool.

The empty polygon frame can be converted to a text frame or graphics frame the same way you convert elliptical or rectangular frames. If you know you're going to import a graphic into the frame, however, you can create a polygonal graphics frame: Use the Polygon Frame pop-out tool, shortcut Shift+N.

Rotate tool

The Rotate tool, shortcut R, lets you change the angle of selected items visually. To use the Rotate tool, first select an item with the Selection tool or the Direct Selection tool, and then select the Rotate tool. Or ⌘+click or Ctrl+click an object with the Rotate tool. Click and drag in a circular motion.

The Rotate tool works as follows:

✦ The object rotates from the default location of the anchor point, which is the upper-left corner of the selected object.

✦ You can drag the anchor point to a new location, as shown in Figure 2-20.

✦ To rotate an object in 45-degree increments, press the Shift key while you click and drag.

✦ To rotate a copy of an object, press Option or Alt while you click and drag.

Figure 2-20: You can drag the anchor point for rotating items from the upper-left corner of an object to a different location.

Scale tool

The Scale tool, shortcut S, lets you grab any object and resize it horizontally, vertically, or both. When you scale text or graphics frames, the size of the text and image are resized as well. As with the Rotate tool, the Scale tool doesn't let you select items to scale. You either need to select an object first with a selection tool, or ⌘+click or Ctrl+click it with the Scale tool.

The Scale tool works as follows:

✦ To make an object wider, drag to the left; to make it narrower, drag to the right.

✦ To make an object taller, drag down; to make it shorter drag up.

✦ To resize an object both horizontally and vertically, drag diagonally.

✦ To resize an object proportionally, press the Shift key while you drag.

✦ To scale a copy of an object, press Option or Alt while you click and drag.

When you scale a text frame, the actual formatting of the text does not change. If you scale a frame containing 12-point type to cover the entire page, the Character pane still reports that the text is 12 points. Even though the text is obviously now larger because of the scaling.

Shear tool

The Shear tool, a pop-out of the Scale tool with the shortcut of Shift+S, works much the same way as the Scale tool. Rather than resizing the object and contents, the Shear tool slants selected objects and their contents (text or pictures) in the direction you drag. To shear a copy of an object, press Option or Alt while you click and drag.

Scissors tool

The Scissors tool, shortcut C, lets you cut a path into separate, smaller paths. When you cut an open path (a line), you get two separate lines. When you cut a closed path in one place, you get an open path. When you cut a closed path (a frame) in two places, you get two paths containing the same contents. You cannot cut paths containing text.

The Scissors tool works as follows:

✦ ⌘+click or Ctrl+click an object to select it.

✦ Click anywhere on a path to cut it. The path will not appear to be cut until you drag an anchor point with a selection tool.

✦ Click at two different locations on a path to divide a frame into two separate frames, as shown in Figure 2-21.

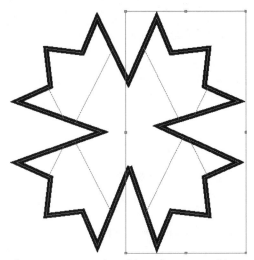

Figure 2-21: Cutting this polygon graphics frame in half results in two separate picture frames.

Gradient tool

The Gradient tool, shortcut >, lets you change the direction of existing gradient fills or strokes applied to objects. To apply gradients to objects, you use the Gradient pane (accessible via Window ➪ Gradient), as discussed in Chapter 27.

To change the gradient direction, first select an object. Click the Fill or Stroke button (a little below the Gradient tool — refer to Figure 2-15) to indicate where the gradient you want to change is. Then, select the Gradient tool, click within the object at the start point, and then drag to the end point. You can drag from the inside out, from top to bottom, from left to right, and so on, depending on the effect you want to achieve.

Hand tool

The Hand tool, shortcut H, lets you scoot pages around within the document window to view a different portion of a page or another page entirely. The Hand tool is an entirely visual method of scrolling, enabling you to see the page contents at all times. To use the Hand tool, click and drag in any direction. You can access the Hand tool temporarily without actually switching tools by pressing the spacebar. When the Type tool is selected, press Shift+spacebar.

Zoom tool

The Zoom tool, shortcuts Z for zooming in and Option+Z or Alt+Z for zooming out, lets you increase and decrease the document view scale. You can highlight a specific area on a page to change its view or you can click onscreen to change the view scale within InDesign's preset increments (shown in the view pop-up menu in the lower-left corner of the document window).

The Zoom tool works as follows:

✦ To increase the view scale by a preset increment, click onscreen.

✦ To increase the view scale of an area, click and drag around it.

✦ To decrease the view scale by a preset increment, Option+click or Alt+click onscreen.

✦ To decrease the view scale of an area, press the Option key or Alt while you click and drag around it.

Tip You can access the Zoom tool temporarily without actually switching tools by pressing ⌘+spacebar of Ctrl+spacebar.

Color buttons

The bottom portion of the Toolbox contains buttons for applying colors to the edges of objects (strokes) and the backgrounds of objects (fills). You use these tools with the Stroke, Color, Gradient, and Swatches panes to apply and experiment with the colors applied to objects (see Figure 2-22).

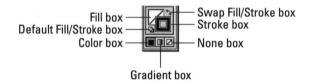

Figure 2-22: You use the color buttons at the bottom of the Toolbox to specify whether to stroke or fill an object, and to change the strokes and fills quickly.

Here's how these buttons work:

✦ To modify the fill (or background) of the selected object, click the Fill button. To modify the stroke (or outside edges) of the selected object, click the Stroke button. The shortcut X toggles between the Fill and Stroke buttons. Use the Colors, Swatches, or Gradient panes to change the stroke or fill.

✦ To switch the color and/or gradient of the stroke and fill, click the Swap Fill/Stroke button or use the shortcut Shift+X.

✦ To revert the selected object to InDesign's default of a white fill and a black stroke, click the Default Fill/Stroke button or press the shortcut D.

✦ To apply the last color used in the Swatches or Colors palette, click the Color button or use the shortcut <.

✦ To apply the last gradient pattern used in the Swatches or Gradient palette, click the Gradient button or use the shortcut G.

✦ To remove the stroke or fill from an object, click None or use the shortcut /.

Working with Palettes and Panes

Initially, software developers used floating palettes to provide convenient access to commonly used options such as colors, fonts, and styles. Palettes provide a more interactive method of working with features because the screen is not obscured by a large dialog box and you can access the controls quickly. Eventually, palettes started to move away from serving as a convenient alternative to commands, and became the primary method — often the only method — for performing many tasks.

InDesign has so many palettes that users might want to consider hooking up a second monitor for displaying them. And break out the computer glasses and your decoder ring because the palettes are small and laden with mysterious icons.

As with the tools, if you make sure Show ToolTips is checked in the General pane of the Preferences dialog box (File ➪ Preferences, or ⌘+K or Ctrl+K), you'll get some pretty good hints as to what the palette icons and fields do.

Note

Using an approach pioneered by Photoshop, InDesign's palettes are often composed of multiple panes. Each pane has a tab (like a file folder) that you click to switch to that pane. InDesign lets you drag panes from one palette to another, as well as to anywhere onscreen (creating a new palette with just the one pane). Being able to do this makes the distinction between a palette and a pane somewhat artificial. In this book, we use *palette* to refer a) to the entity that holds one or more panes, or b) for entities such as the Toolbox that are self-contained floating objects containing commands. We refer to *panes* for anything that can be made a pane, even if you might have made it into its own palette (such as the Transform pane, rather than the Transform palette).

Managing palettes

Because InDesign has so many palettes — a dozen standard palettes including the Toolbox, as shown in Figure 2-23, and *not* including library or color swatch palettes or any of the seven panes you might make into their own palettes — you're not going to want them all open all the time. You might have some palettes you leave open all the time, some you open only while formatting text, and some that you open and close for one-time uses. As you become familiar with the palettes, you'll find which ones you want to keep open.

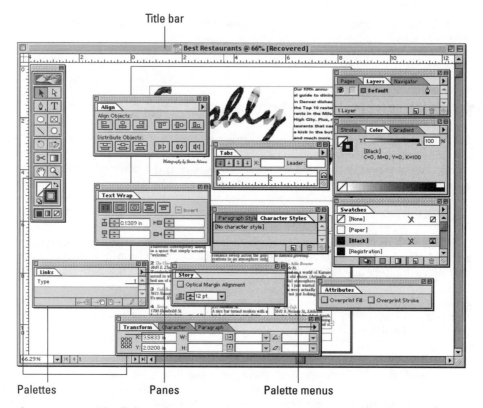

Figure 2-23: With all the palettes open in InDesign, it's impossible to work on a document.

Many palettes actually consist of multiple panes, such as the default combination of the Transform, Character, and Paragraph panes that mimic the QuarkXPress Measurements palette. You can create different combinations of panes to customize the palettes. Palettes have the following characteristics in InDesign:

✦ To open a palette or pane, choose its menu command (such as Window ⇨ Colors). Some have keyboard shortcuts, as indicated in the menu.

✦ To close a palette, click its Close box in the upper-left corner (Macintosh) or upper-right corner (Windows). This action closes all the panes in the palette.

✦ To close all open palettes, hit the Tab key (except when the Type tool is selected).

✦ To shrink a palette down to the names of the panes within it, click its Zoom box (Macintosh) or Minimize box (Windows).

✦ On the Mac, to collapse a palette down to its title bar, which doesn't actually contain a title, click the WindowShade box (or double-click the title bar).

✦ To move a palette, drag its title bar.

✦ A few palettes contains arrows in the lower-right corner that you can drag to resize the palette, and some palette menus let you change the orientation of the palette from horizontal to vertical.

✦ To select a different pane in a palette, click its tab.

✦ To combine the panes of different palettes, drag and drop a pane's tab into another palette as shown in Figure 2-24. To pull a pane out of a palette into its own, drag and drop its tab out of the palette.

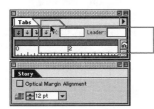

Figure 2-24: Dragging the Story pane up to the Tabs palette combines the two panes into a single palette.

Marrying and Divorcing Palette Panes

Although it may seem as if combining and splitting panes is the antidote to InDesign's palette-itis, the resulting palettes can be difficult to work with. Combined palettes can become cumbersome: If you combine palettes that have different default sizes or orientation, each time you click a different pane, the entire palette changes its size — this can be fairly disorienting. Plus you can't see and reach for different types of options as easily because you have to activate different panes. On the other hand, splitting panes into too many separate palettes can leave you with an overwhelming number of palettes.

Continued

(continued)

In general, you'll want to split panes that you use often, and combine or close panes that you use rarely. And you might change the pane/palette configuration based on the type of document you're working on. If you're working on a movie poster, you'll definitely want the Navigator pane, but might have little use for the Pages pane. Or if you're laying out a newsletter that is formatted exclusively with styles, you might as well close the Character and Paragraph panes.

We do suggest you make the following change. InDesign has combined the Transform, Character, and Paragraph panes into a single palette to mimic the QuarkXPress Measurements palette and PageMaker Control palette. We suggest you split these three panes into separate palettes (see the following figure). Use the Transform palette while performing layout tasks, and then keep both the Character and Paragraph palettes open separately while formatting text so you can see all the attributes at once. (You might combine the Character pane with the Character Styles pane and the Paragraph pane with the Paragraph Styles pane. If you do this, use the menus on the Paragraph and Character panes to change their orientation to vertical to match the Styles panes.)

Splitting the default combination of the Transform, Character, and Paragraph panes into the palettes shown may provide easier access to typesetting and layout features.

Using palettes

To use a palette, first you need to activate its pane. You can do this by clicking its tab or by choosing its menu command. You'll need to be on the lookout here — if a menu command brings a pane forward in a palette, you might not even notice. Once a pane is active, controls in palettes have the following characteristics:

✦ Click a pop-up menu to display and select an option; changes take effect immediately.

✦ Highlight a value in a field to enter a new value. To implement the value, press Shift+Return or Shift+Enter. Or, you can Tab to the next field or Shift+Tab to the previous field. Or just click in a different field or elsewhere in the document. To get out of a field you've modified, leaving the object unscathed, hit Escape.

✦ Some fields include up and down arrows that you can click to increase or decrease the value in the field.

✦ Fields accept values in all different measurement systems. (Chapter 3 discusses this in detail.)

✦ In addition to entering values in fields, you can enter calculations. You can add, subtract, multiply, and divide values in fields using the following operators +, –, * (multiply), and / (divide). For example, to reduce the width of a frame by half, you might type /2 next to the current value of 4.5 in. in the Width field. Or, to increase the length of a line by 6 points, you can type +6 next to the current value in the Length field.

✦ Some palettes include a full menu that you can display by clicking the arrow in the upper-right corner. The *palette menu* provides commands related to the palette's or pane's contents — for example, the palette menu for the Character Styles pane provides a command for creating a New Style, as shown in Figure 2-25.

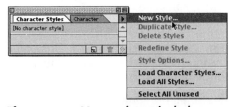

Figure 2-25: Many palettes include menus that provide access to related features.

Checking out the palettes

Like the tools in InDesign, each palette has a distinct function. The use of each palette is covered in detail in the appropriate chapters throughout this book (for example, Chapter 30 covers the Layers palette). But with the help of ToolTips and a quick introduction to the primary purpose of various palettes and panes, you can start using many of the palettes to perform basic functions.

✦ **Links palette (File ➪ Links, or Shift+⌘+D or Ctrl+Shift+D):** The Links palette shows the original location of imported graphic and text files (see Figure 2-26). Note that this is the closest thing you'll find to the Picture Usage feature in QuarkXPress. For PageMaker users, this is very similar to the PageMaker Links palette.

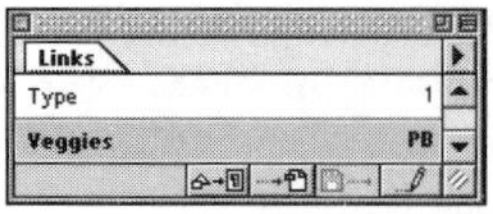

Figure 2-26: The Links palette.

✦ **Character pane (Type ➪ Character, or ⌘+T or Ctrl+T):** Use this pane to change common attributes of highlighted text such as the font, size, leading, kerning, tracking, and scaling.

✦ **Paragraph pane (Type ➪ Paragraph, or ⌘+M or Ctrl+M):** Use this pane to change common attributes of selected paragraphs such as the alignment, indents, space before and after, and hyphenation. Figure 2-27 shows the Character and Paragraph panes.

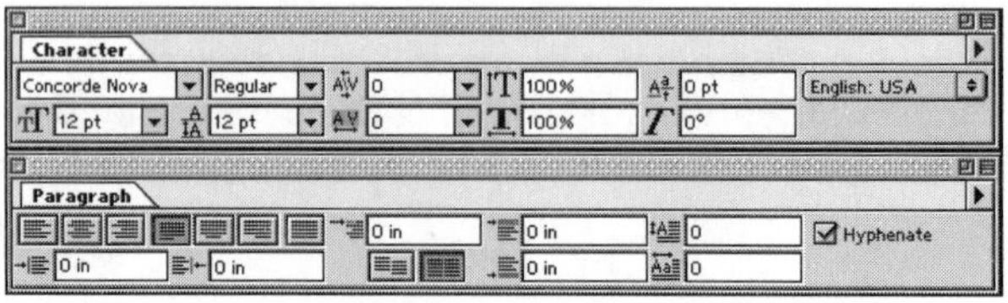

Figure 2-27: The Character and Paragraph panes.

✦ **Tabs pane (Type ➪ Tabs, or Shift+⌘+T or Ctrl+Shift+T):** This pane lets you create tab stops for selected paragraphs; you can also specify alignment, position, and leader characters for the tabs.

✦ **Story palette (Type ➪ Story):** It's small but important — the Story palette lets you specify hanging punctuation for all the frames in a story by checking Optical Margin Alignment. You can also change type size if the need strikes you. Figure 2-28 shows the Tabs and Story panes.

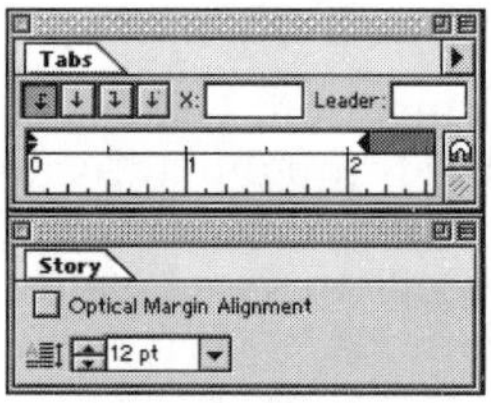

Figure 2-28: The Tabs and Story panes.

✦ **Character Styles pane (Type ➪ Character Styles, or Shift+F11):** Use this pane to create and apply styles consisting of character-level formats.

✦ **Paragraph Styles pane (Type ➪ Paragraph Styles, or F11):** Use this pane to create and apply styles consisting of paragraph-level formats. Figure 2-29 shows the Character Styles and Paragraph Styles panes.

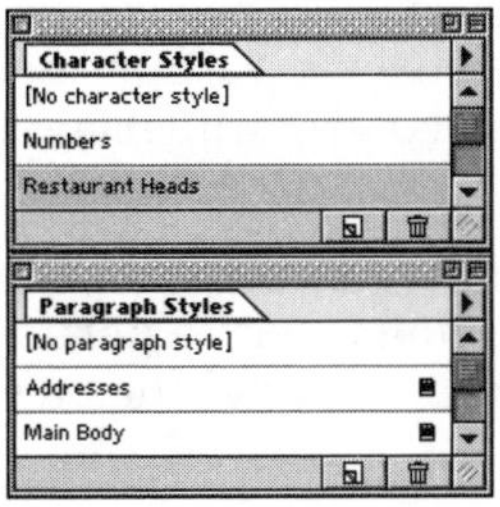

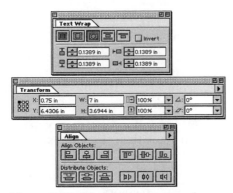

Figure 2-29: The Character Styles and Paragraph Styles panes.

✦ **Text Wrap pane (Object ➪ Text Wrap, or Option+⌘+W or Ctrl+Alt+W):** The Text Wrap pane provides intuitive buttons for controlling how text runs around selected objects.

✦ **Transform pane (Window ➪ Transform, or F9):** You can specify size, placement, scale, rotation, and shear of selected objects with the Transform pane.

✦ **Align pane (Window ➪ Align, or F8):** The Align pane provides buttons that let you evenly distribute or realign multiple-selected objects with one click. Figure 2-30 shows the Text Wrap, Transform, and Align panes.

Figure 2-30: The Text Wrap, Transform, and Align panes.

✦ **Pages pane (Window ➪ Pages, or F12):** Use this pane to create master pages and to add, rearrange, and delete document pages. You can also create independently numbered sections of pages using the Pages palette menu.

✦ **Layers pane (Window ➪ Layers, or F7):** Use this pane to manipulate layers, which act like clear plastic overlays of document pages. You can use layers to control the stacking order of objects, to isolate specific portions of a design, or to store revisions of the same document. You control which layers display and print through the Layers pane.

✦ **Navigator pane (Window ➪ Navigator):** The Navigator pane shows a miniature color proxy version of pages and lets you isolate a portion of any page to display in the document window. Figure 2-31 shows the Pages, Layers, and Navigator panes.

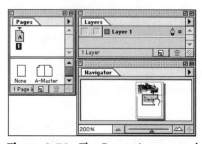

Figure 2-31: The Pages, Layers, and Navigator panes.

✦ **Swatches pane (Window ➪ Swatches, or F5):** The Swatches pane lets you create named colors such as those using Pantone, Focoltone, and Toyo inks, and apply the colors to text, strokes, and fills.

✦ **Stroke pane (Window ➪ Stroke, or F10):** Use the Stroke pane to outline the edges of frames and lines; you have control over the thickness and the pattern of the outlines.

✦ **Color pane (Window ➪ Color, or F6):** The Color palette lets you create LAB, CMYK, and RGB colors, and it lets you apply the colors to text, strokes, and fills.

✦ **Gradient pane (Window ➪ Gradient):** Use this pane to create a stroke or fill consisting of a graduated blend between two colors.

✦ **Attributes pane (Window ➪ Attributes):** The Attributes pane lets you specify that the stroke or fill in selected objects overprints the background. Figure 2-32 shows the Swatches, Stroke, Color, Gradient, and Attributes panes.

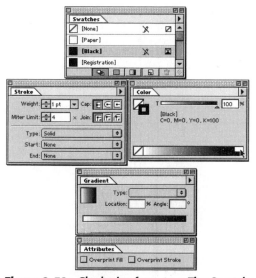

Figure 2-32: Clockwise from top: The Swatches, Color, Gradient, Attributes, and Stroke panes.

Reviewing Menu Commands

With so many palettes and panes, menu commands take on a more secondary function in InDesign. As we said before, many menu commands do nothing but display a palette or bring a pane of a palette forward. But to get comfortable in InDesign, you do need to know the basic function of each menu.

Tip   If you're switching from PageMaker or QuarkXPress, you might get lost in the menus, but don't despair—a chart in Appendix D, which covers how to make the move from QuarkXPress or PageMaker to InDesign, shows the equivalent menus.

File menu

The File menu lets you perform actions on entire documents, including creating, opening, saving, closing, and printing. The Place command lets you import graphic and text files, and the Export command lets you save documents in different formats such as EPS, HTML, and PDF. Commands in the File menu also let you set document-wide preferences, modify keyboard shortcuts, and set up color management. See Figure 2-33.

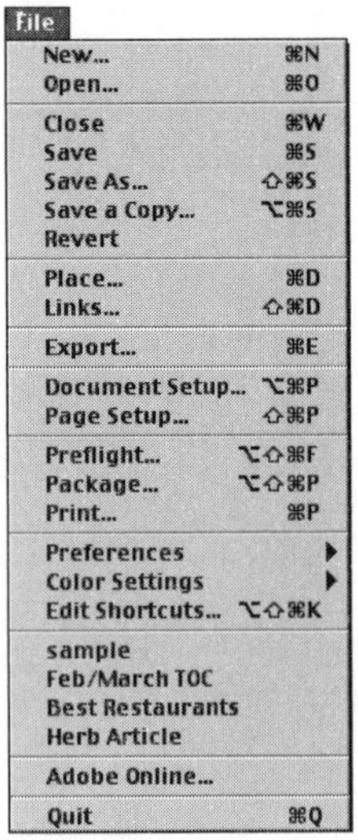

Figure 2-33: The File menu.

File	
New...	⌘N
Open...	⌘O
Close	⌘W
Save	⌘S
Save As...	⇧⌘S
Save a Copy...	⌥⌘S
Revert	
Place...	⌘D
Links...	⇧⌘D
Export...	⌘E
Document Setup...	⌥⌘P
Page Setup...	⇧⌘P
Preflight...	⌥⇧⌘F
Package...	⌥⇧⌘P
Print...	⌘P
Preferences	▶
Color Settings	▶
Edit Shortcuts...	⌥⇧⌘K
sample	
Feb/March TOC	
Best Restaurants	
Herb Article	
Adobe Online...	
Quit	⌘Q

Edit menu

InDesign's Edit menu provides access to the program's invaluable multiple undo and redo features, as well as the standard Cut, Copy, Paste, and Clear commands. You'll find Duplicate and Step and Repeat here, even though you might be searching the Object menu for them. The Edit menu also provides commands for searching and replacing text and formats, checking spelling, and editing spelling and hyphenation dictionaries. See Figure 2-34.

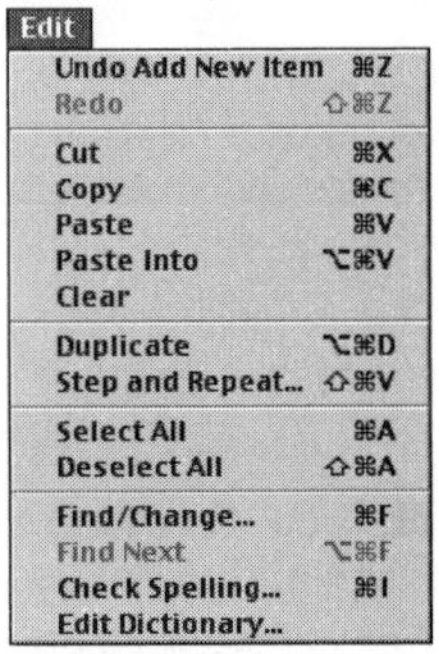

Figure 2-34: The Edit menu.

Edit	
Undo Add New Item	⌘Z
Redo	⇧⌘Z
Cut	⌘X
Copy	⌘C
Paste	⌘V
Paste Into	⌥⌘V
Clear	
Duplicate	⌥⌘D
Step and Repeat...	⇧⌘V
Select All	⌘A
Deselect All	⇧⌘A
Find/Change...	⌘F
Find Next	⌥⌘F
Check Spelling...	⌘I
Edit Dictionary...	

Layout menu

With the Layout menu, you can change the position of the column and margin guides you established in the New Document dialog box, create guides at specific locations, and resize an entire document proportionally. You can also turn pages in a document and insert automatic page numbers using Layout menu commands. See Figure 2-35.

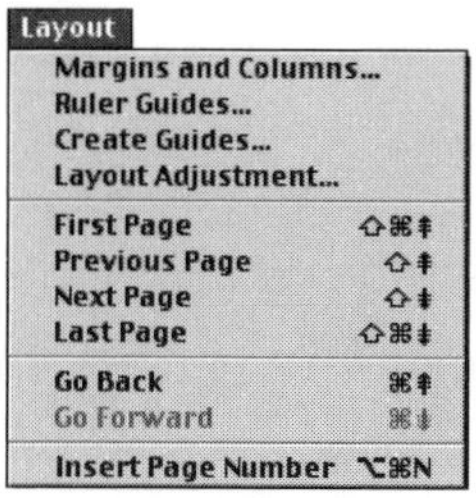

Figure 2-35: The Layout menu.

Type menu

The Type menu provides all the controls for formatting text — character formats, paragraph formats, tabs, and styles. The Story command lets you specify hanging punctuation for all the frames in a story. You can also convert text to a frame and insert special characters using a dialog box rather than keyboard shortcuts. If you're expecting to use the View menu to show and hide invisible characters such as spaces and tabs, stop and look in the Type menu instead. See Figure 2-36.

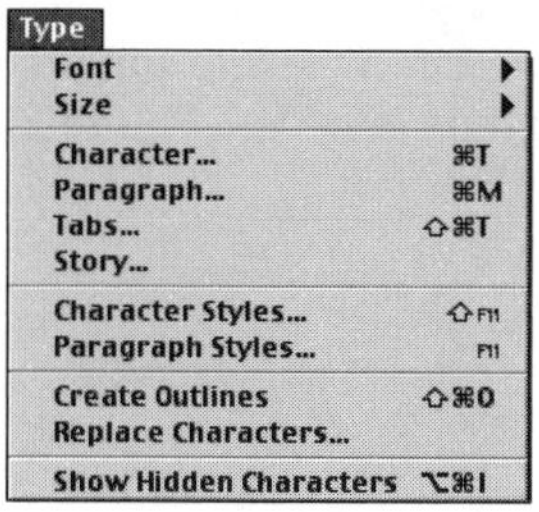

Figure 2-36: The Type menu.

Object menu

Use the Object menu for layout functions such as controlling the stacking order of lines and frames, grouping objects together, locking objects to the page, and wrapping text around objects. You can manipulate objects, such as changing the number of columns and text inset in the Text Frame Options dialog box or fine-tuning the corners of a frame using the Corner Effects dialog box. For working with graphics, the Object menu lets you fit graphics to frames and frames to graphics, create clipping paths, apply colors to some types of images, and merge paths. See Figure 2-37.

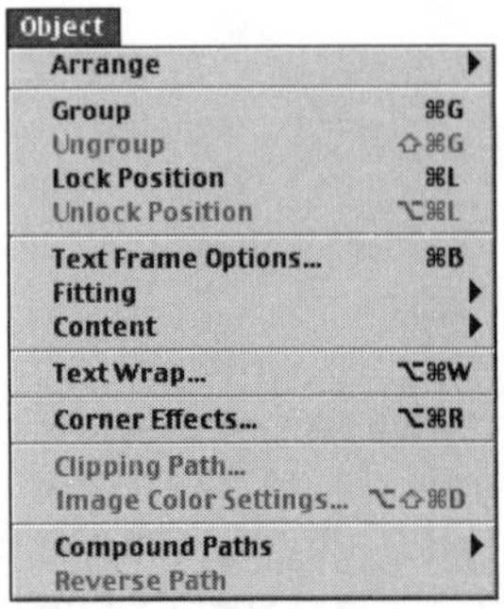

Figure 2-37: The Object menu.

View menu

With the View menu, you can change the view scale of the document, choose whether objects placed by master pages display, and specify which layout tools display: threads (links between text frames), the edges of frames, rulers, guides, the baseline grid, and the document grid. You can also specify whether guides are locked, and whether items snap to guides and the document grid. See Figure 2-38.

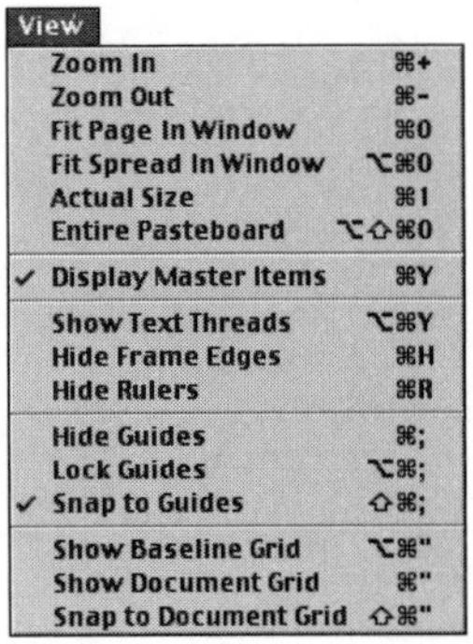

Figure 2-38: The View menu.

Window menu

For the most part, the Window menu opens palettes or brings panes of palettes forward. Other commands let you manage document windows, opening additional windows for the same document and redistributing document windows onscreen. The Libraries command lets you create and open library palettes, which store frequently used objects, text, and graphics. See Figure 2-39.

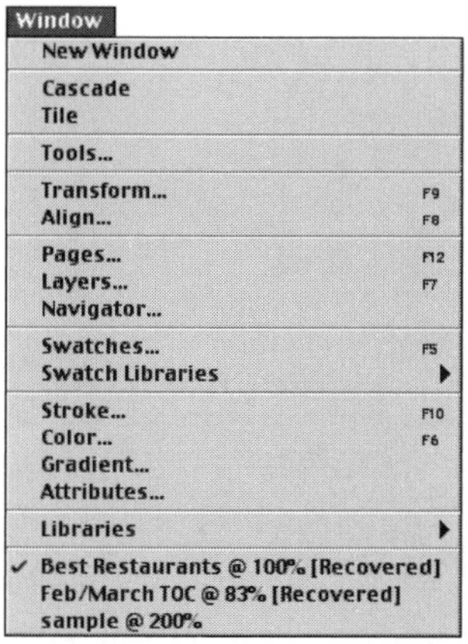

Figure 2-39: The Window menu.

Contextual menus

The last interface element you'll find useful in InDesign is the contextual menu. By Ctrl+clicking or right-clicking the document, an object, the rulers, and so forth, you can display a menu of options for modifying whatever it is you're clicking. See Figure 2-40 for an example of several contextual menus.

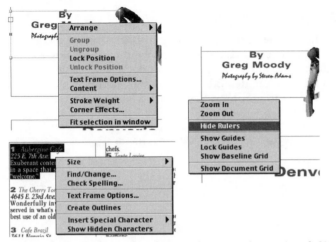

Figure 2-40: The contextual menu for a text frame (top left), for highlighted text (bottom left), and the document (right).

Summary

Inside the InDesign application folder, you'll find a variety of important files that, in most cases, you should leave alone. If you will be using InDesign constantly, create an alias or shortcut to it, and consider having your operating system launch the program automatically every time you restart your machine.

A standard, InDesign document window provides rulers, guides, a view scale field, and a page number field to assist you with layout. In the Toolbox, you'll find tools that let you create and manipulate objects such as lines, text frames, and picture frames. InDesign provides many controls in the form of panes, which can be combined into floating palettes. Reviewing the controls in these panes and reviewing the menu commands helps orient you to InDesign.

✦   ✦   ✦

Getting InDesign Ready to Go

◆   ◆   ◆   ◆

In This Chapter

Setting preferences
for documents and
the application

Customizing
keyboard shortcuts

Setting defaults for
documents, text, and
objects

Modifying defaults
for views

Creating default
colors and styles

Reverting preferences
and defaults

Changing the view
scale

Opening multiple
document windows

◆   ◆   ◆   ◆

Although you may not realize it, Adobe has made a variety of educated guesses about the way you work. For example, it assumes you work in picas, that you prefer low-resolution previews of images, and that you use typographers' quotation marks. Adobe has also made decisions about the default properties of text, the default color swatches included with documents, and the default attributes of some objects. In all cases, Adobe tried to make the defaults appropriate for most publishers.

But no matter how much thought Adobe put into making these educated guesses, they won't work for everybody. In fact, it's unlikely that every single setting will work for you. So no matter how tempted you are to jump in and start working, take a minute to prepare InDesign for the way you actually work. Otherwise, you'll end up conforming the way you work to InDesign's decisions, making it more difficult to learn the program and get your work done; or you'll end up making the same changes to document after document, wasting time in the process. Think of the software like a car — when you get in, you may need to adjust the seat, mirror, and steering wheel before you start driving comfortably.

Setting Preferences

Preferences are settings that affect an entire document — such as what measurement system you're using on the rulers, what color the guides are, and whether substituted fonts are highlighted. In InDesign, you access these settings through the Preferences dialog box (File ⇨ Preferences, or ⌘+K or Ctrl+K). They are stored in the InDesign Defaults and the InDesignSavedData files in your InDesign application folder.

InDesign has two methods for changing preferences. First, you can change preferences when no documents are open to create new settings for all future documents. Second, you can change preferences for the active document, which affects only that document. Your strategy for changing preferences depends on the way you work and the needs of specific documents. For example, if you generally prefer to work in points, you might change the default measurement system to points with no documents open. However, you might have a design such as an envelope that makes more sense in inches, so you can change the measurement system for that specific document.

The Preferences dialog box provides seven different types of settings divided into panels: General, Text, Composition, Units & Increments, Grids, Guides, and Dictionary. The steps for setting preferences stay the same, regardless of the changes you need to make.

Steps: Using the Preferences Dialog Box

1. Determine whether the preference you want to set is for a specific document or for all future documents. Close all documents to set preferences for all future documents; open a document to set preferences just for that document.

2. Choose File ➪ Preferences ➪ General or press ⌘+K or Ctrl+K to open the General pane. Alternately, you can choose a specific command from the Preferences submenu of the File menu. For example, you might choose File ➪ Preferences ➪ Composition. (These submenus have no shortcuts.)

3. To switch to a specific pane, choose an option from the pop-up menu at the top of the dialog box, as shown in Figure 3-1. To move one panel forward, click the Next button or ⌘+click or Ctrl+click the down arrow on the keyboard. To move one panel backward, click the Prev button or ⌘+click or Ctrl+click the up arrow on the keyboard.

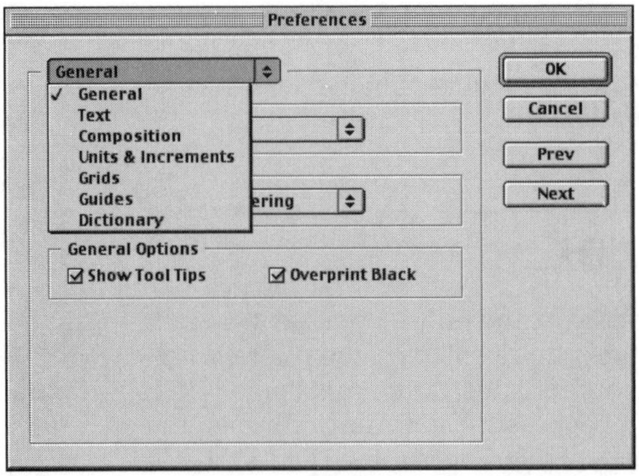

Figure 3-1: To display different panes of preferences, choose an option from the pop-up menu at the top of the Preferences dialog box or click the Next and Prev buttons.

4. Change any settings in any of the panes, and then click OK. The changes are saved with the active document or in the InDesign Defaults and InDesignSavedData files.

Note

This section takes a comprehensive look at all the preferences in InDesign. Preferences that affect specific features are often discussed again in the relevant chapters. For example, dictionary preferences are covered in the section on spell-checking in Chapter 10.

Caution

Unlike most actions you perform in InDesign, you cannot reverse changes to preferences using the Undo command (Edit ➪ Undo, or ⌘+Z or Ctrl+Z). If you change your mind about a preference setting, open the Preferences dialog box and change the setting again.

Setting General preferences

Options in the General pane, shown in Figure 3-2, affect the way several features in InDesign work. Two preferences in this pane deserve careful consideration: the setting for image display and the setting for viewing page numbers.

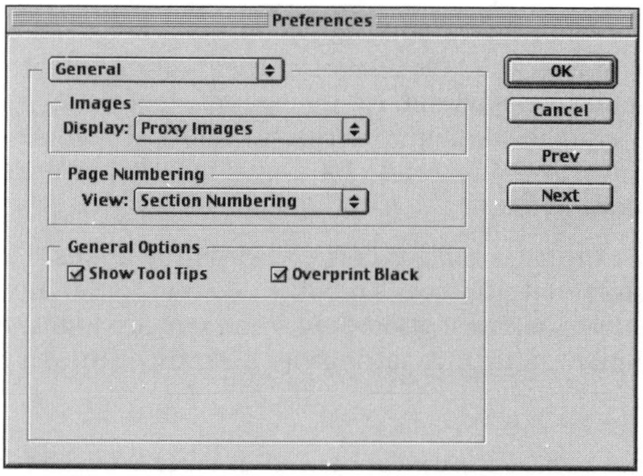

Figure 3-2: The General pane of the Preferences dialog box.

Display pop-up menu

The Display pop-up menu in the Images area of the Preferences dialog box controls the resolution of the previews that display for imported graphics. Whether you paste, place, or drag in a graphic, its display is controlled by this setting. Here are the options:

✦ By default, Display is set to Proxy Images, which are low-resolution previews of 36 dpi. Many users prefer proxies because they redraw faster onscreen and they keep the file size of documents smaller. In addition, if you choose Proxy Images, you can change the preview resolution for display while placing the image. (Check Show Import Options in the Place dialog box, and then enter a value in the Proxy Image Resolution field.) The drawback to Proxy Images is that they can look very blocky, making it difficult to judge colors and place other objects in relation to the image. As an example, see the difference between a Proxy Image and Full Resolution Image in Figure 3-3.

Figure 3-3: The coffee cup on the left is a Proxy Image, while the one on the right is a Full Resolution Image.

✦ The Full Resolution Images option displays images at their actual resolution and is required for using color management. No matter how fast your computer is, Full Resolution Images are likely to redraw noticeably more slowly than Proxy Images. However, images do look significantly better, letting you see more colors and more detail.

✦ The Gray Out Images option replaces images entirely with gray boxes that contain a large black X. Unfortunately, images display this way under any condition, even when selected, making it good only when you are focusing solely on the text in a document. Still, this setting significantly reduces screen redraw time.

Tip

Screen redraw of large images can be frustrating because it takes time, and low resolution can be frustrating because it looks bad. To counteract these problems, change the Image Display according to the type of work you're doing and the speed of your machine. For example, while you're initially designing a document, you might use Full Resolution Display. Then, as you flow in text you might opt for Gray Out Images, and finally back to Full Resolution Display when making the final layout adjustments. By contrast, an editor with a lower-end computer might use Proxy Images while writing captions for photos.

View pop-up menu

In the Page Numbering area of the Preferences dialog box, the View pop-up menu controls how page numbers display in the fields such as the Page Number box on the document window. (See Chapter 2 for information about the difference between section page numbers and absolute page numbers.) Here are the controls:

✦ The default setting, Section Numbering, means that InDesign shows the page numbers according to the information in the Section Options dialog box accessed via the Pages pane's palette menu. When Section Numbering is selected, by default you need to enter section page numbers, such as "Sec2:3," in fields.

If you choose Section Numbering, the page numbers displayed at the bottom of the InDesign window and in the Pages pane won't show the section prefixes, making it hard to remember what section a page is in.

✦ The Absolute Numbering option, which we prefer, shows page numbers according to each page's position in the document. For example, the first page is 1, the second page is 2, and the third page is 3, even if the pages display roman numerals i, ii, and iii. When this option is selected, you can always jump to the first page in a document by entering **1** in the Page Number box.

InDesign's method for entering section page numbers is extremely difficult. Say you create a section on the third page of a document, changing the page numbering to A, B, C format and starting the numbering for that section at page 5, making it page E. The page number that displays on the page is E. But to jump to that page, you'll have to enter "Sec2:5" in the Page Number box rather than "E" or even "Sec2:E." This forces you to not only know your Section Prefix, which is not displayed, but also to translate the letter to a number. We highly recommend that you simply enter absolute page numbers — just precede the number with a plus sign, such as +5 for the fifth page — or that you change your View preference for Page Numbering to Absolute Numbering.

Show ToolTips checkbox

When Show ToolTips is checked, as it is by default, InDesign gives you the names of tools and palette options as the mouse hovers over them. In the Toolbox, the tips include the keyboard shortcut for accessing each tool. This information is invaluable for looking up information in help files and books (it shows the InDesign names for tools, such as "Direct Selection tool" rather than the casual term, such as "the hollow arrow," that most people are likely to use), so you'll want to leave it checked in most cases.

Overprint Black checkbox

By default, Overprint Black is checked so that any black text, strokes, or fills overprint. This usually results in clearer text and lines. (This option applies to the Black color in the Swatches pane, rather than, say, a black that you create.) If you uncheck Overprint Black, all black text, strokes, and fills knock out of their backgrounds, which results in a lighter black and could cause some misregistration when printing. (See Chapters 27 and 33 for more details on creating colors and trapping colors, respectively.)

Setting Text preferences

Options in the Text pane of the Preferences dialog box, shown in Figure 3-4, affect how several character formats work, whether you use typographer's quotes, and how text displays onscreen.

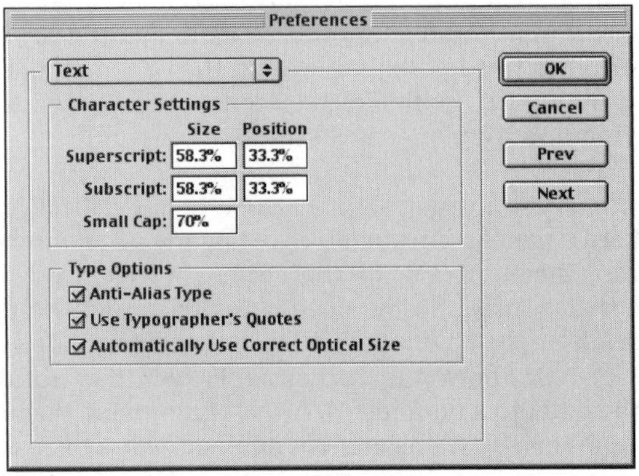

Figure 3-4: The Text pane of the Preferences dialog box.

Character Settings area

The palette menu on the Character pane (Type ➪ Character, or ⌘+T or Ctrl+T) lets you format highlighted characters as Superscript (reduced in size and raised above the baseline), Subscript (reduced in size and dropped below the baseline), or Small Caps (smaller versions of capital letters). Note that Superscript, Subscript, and Small Caps characters do not need to be reduced—they can actually be enlarged instead. The controls in the Character Settings area govern how these characters are placed and resized.

✦ The Size fields in the Superscript and Subscript areas let you specify how much to scale these characters. The default is 58.3%, but you can enter a value ranging from 1 to 200 percent. We prefer 60% or 65%, depending on the type size and font.

✦ The Position fields let you specify how much to shift Superscript characters up and Subscript characters down. The default is 33.3% of the baseline, but you can enter a value ranging from –500 to 500 percent. We prefer 30% for subscripts and 35% for superscripts.

✦ The Small Cap field lets you specify the scale of Small Caps characters in relation to the actual capital letters in the font. The default is 70%, but you can enter a value ranging from 1 to 200 percent.

Cross-Reference

See Chapter 16 for information about using the "true small caps" variation of a typeface, when available, rather than the Small Cap character format.

Type Options area

The three Type Options, which control different aspects of InDesign's character handling, are all checked by default.

✦ When Anti-Alias Type is checked, InDesign's smoothes the edges of characters so they appear less jagged. Although this makes the type look better onscreen, anti-aliased type is harder for some users to read, so they can uncheck this option.

✦ When you press the quote key on the keyboard with Use Typographer's Quotes checkbox, InDesign inserts the correct typographer's quotes for the current language in use. For example, for U.S. English, InDesign inserts curly single quote (' ') or double quotes (" ") rather than straight quotes. For French, InDesign inserts double angle brackets (« »). InDesign knows what language's characters to use based on the Language pop-up menu in the Character pane (Type ⇨ Character, or ⌘+T or Ctrl+T) or in the Paragraph Style and Character Style dialog boxes' Advanced Character Formats pane (Type ⇨ Paragraph Styles, or F11, and Type ⇨ Character Styles, or Shift+F11, respectively).

✦ Automatically Use Correct Optical Size, when checked, automatically accesses Multiple Master fonts that include an optimal size axis, which ensures optimal readability at any size.

Setting Composition preferences

In general, preferences in the Composition pane, shown in Figure 3-5, affect entire paragraphs rather than individual characters.

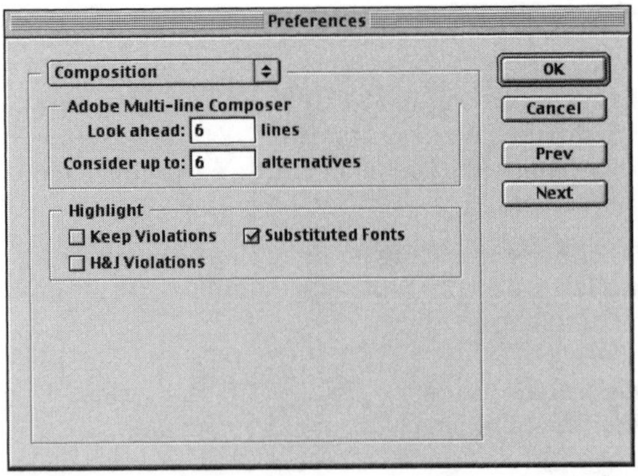

Figure 3-5: The Composition pane of the Preferences dialog box.

Adobe Multi-line Composer area

When InDesign hyphenates and spaces text in paragraphs for which you have selected Adobe Multi-line Composer from the Paragraph pane's palette menu, it consults these settings to determine exactly how to flow the text (see Chapter 13 for a complete explanation of these settings):

✦ The Look Ahead field, set to 6 lines by default, specifies the number of lines after each line that the composer looks at while flowing text. You can consider from 3 to 30 lines.

✦ The Consider Up To field, set to 6 alternatives by default, specifies the maximum number of possible hyphenation points the composer evaluates while flowing text. You can consider from 3 to 30 options.

Note The higher you set the Look Ahead and the Consider Up To values, the longer it will take InDesign to compose text.

Highlight area

The Highlight checkboxes control whether InDesign calls attention to possible typesetting problems by drawing a highlighter pen effect behind the text.

✦ Keep Violations, which is unchecked by default, highlights the last line in a text frame when it cannot follow the rules specified in the Keep Options dialog box in the Paragraph pane's palette menu (Type ➪ Paragraph, or ⌘+M or Ctrl+M). For example, if the Keep Options settings require more lines to stay together than fit in the text frame and thus bump all the text in a frame to the next text frame in the chain, the Keep Options rules are violated and the last line of text is highlighted so you know to change the frame size or the Keeps Options rules for that text.

✦ When checked, H&J Violations uses three shades of yellow to mark lines that might be too loose or too tight due to the combination of spacing and hyphenation settings. The darker the shade, the worse InDesign considers the problem to be. H&J Violations is unchecked by default; you might wish to check it while fine-tuning type, and then uncheck it when you're finished.

✦ Substituted Fonts is checked by default, and uses pink highlight to indicate characters in fonts that are not available to InDesign. InDesign actually uses Adobe Sans MM or Adobe Serif MM to create a replacement for missing fonts, so the text looks close to the actual font. For editing purposes, the substituted fonts work fine, although the pink highlight can be distracting. But, for output purposes, it's important that you have the correct fonts (so you may want to live with the irritation and have InDesign highlight Substituted Fonts for you).

Note

Remember: InDesign is hypersensitive to fonts (see Chapter 10), so you'll get such highlighting even when you have the correct font installed but the wrong face applied to it (such as Normal rather than Regular); in these cases, the font style will have brackets ([ ]) around it in the Character pane.

Setting Units & Increments preferences

The measurement systems you use for positioning items and the way the arrows on the keyboard increase or decrease settings are controlled by settings in the Units & Increments pane shown in Figure 3-6.

Preferences	
Units & Increments ⬍	OK
Ruler Units	Cancel
Horizontal: Picas ⬍ ☐ points	Prev
Vertical: Picas ⬍ ☐ points	Next
Keyboard Increments	
Cursor Key: 0p1	
Size/Leading: 2 pt	
Baseline Shift: 2 pt	
Kerning: 20 /1000 em	

Figure 3-6: The Units & Increments pane of the Preferences dialog box.

Ruler Units area

The Ruler Units area affects the measurement system displayed on the horizontal and vertical ruler on the document window as well as the default values in fields used for positioning objects. For example, if you choose Inches for both the Horizontal and Vertical Ruler Units, not only will the rulers display inches, but the X, Y, W, and H fields on the Transform pane (Window ➪ Transform or F9) display values in inches as well.

Note   To display the document ruler, choose View ➪ Show Ruler, or press ⌘+R or Ctrl+R.

Tip   The default horizontal and vertical measurement systems are picas. If you are not accustomed to working in picas, be sure to change the default Horizontal and Vertical Ruler Units when no documents are open. This ensures that all future documents use your preferred measurement system.

You can specify one measurement system for the horizontal ruler and measurements, and specify another measurement system for the vertical ruler and measurements. For example, you might use points for horizontal measurements so you can use the rulers to gauge tab and indent settings, while using inches for vertical measurements. To specify the measurement systems you want to use, choose an option from the Horizontal pop-up menu and from the Vertical pop-up menu. You have the following options:

✦ **Points:** A typesetting measurement equal to $1/72$ of an inch. To enter values in points, type a **p** before the value or **pt** after the value: *p6* or *6 pt.*

✦ **Picas:** A typesetting measurement equal to $1/6$ of an inch. To enter values in picas, type a **p** after the value.

✦ **Inches:** An English measurement system, in which an inch is divided into 16ths. To enter values in inches, type **i**, **in**, or **inch** after the value — but don't try the obvious abbreviation of quote marks (") because it doesn't work.

✦ **Inches Decimal:** Inches divided into 10ths on the ruler rather than 16ths. To enter values in decimal inches, include a decimal point as appropriate and type **i**, **in**, or **inch** after the value.

✦ **Millimeters:** A metric measurement that is $1/10$ of a centimeter. To enter values in millimeters, type **mm** after the value.

✦ **Centimeters:** A metric measurement that is about $1/3$ of an inch. To enter values in centimeters, type **cm** after the value.

✦ **Ciceros:** A European typesetting measurement that is slightly larger than a pica. To enter values in ciceros, type **c** after the value.

✦ **Custom:** This option actually gives you points, which places a labeled tick mark at every five points. You get to customize the number of tick marks between the labeled marks by entering a value in the Points field. For example, if you enter **12** in the field, you'll get a tick mark at each pica, because there are 12 points in a pica.

Tip Despite the Ruler Units you specify, you can enter values in any fields using any supported measurement system. For example, if you're working in picas, you can enter an inch value in the Width field by typing **1 in**. InDesign automatically converts the value to picas for you. You can enter values in picas and points by placing a **p** between the two values. For example, 1p2 indicates 1 pica and 2 points.

Keyboard Increments area

The arrow keys on the keyboard let you move selected objects right, left, up, or down. You can also use the arrow keys and other keyboard shortcuts to change some text formatting. You can customize the way these shortcuts work, such as by specifying how far each click of an arrow key moves an item.

Oddity These preferences are not actually used consistently to modify the arrow keys or keyboard shortcuts. Basically, the Cursor Key field works with all four arrow keys. The Size/Leading value works with the up and down arrow keys for leading, while the Kerning field works with the left and right arrows. Meanwhile, the Size value works with a keyboard shortcut using the greater than (>) and less than (<) symbols on the keyboard, and the Baseline Shift field works only while clicking the arrow keys when the Baseline Shift field is highlighted on the Character pane.

✦ **Cursor Key field:** When you select an object with the Selection tool or the Direct Selection tool, you can move it up, down, left, or right using the arrow keys on the keyboard. By default, the item moves one point. You can change the increment to a value ranging from 0 (which would be useless) to 1.3889 inches. For example, if you're using a document grid, you might change the increment to match the gridlines. If you press the Shift key while you click an arrow, the object moves 10 times the amount specified in the Cursor Key field.

✦ **Size/Leading field:** The value you enter in this field, which is 2 points by default, specifies how much point size or leading is increased or decreased when implemented with keyboard commands. You can enter a value ranging from 1 to 100. To increase the point size of selected text, press Shift+⌘+> or Ctrl+Shift+>; to decrease the point size, press Shift+⌘+< or Ctrl+Shift+<. Add Option or Alt to the combination to multiply the increment by 5. To modify leading for selected text, Option+click or Alt+click the up or down arrow on the keyboard.

✦ **Baseline Shift field:** You can shift the baseline of highlighted text up or down by clicking in the Baseline Shift field on the Character pane, and then clicking the up or down arrow on the keyboard. You can change the default value of 2 points to any value ranging from 1 to 100. If you press the Shift key while clicking, the increment is multiplied by 5.

✦ **Kerning field:** To kern text with keyboard commands, you position the cursor between two letters, and then Option+click or Alt+click the right-hand arrow button to increase kerning or the left arrow to decrease kerning. By default, each click changes kerning by $20/1000$ of an em. You can change the value of the kerning denominator to anything from 1 to 100. Add the ⌘ or Ctrl key to multiply the increment by 5.

Note that the arrow buttons appear only if you have selected a vertical orientation for the Character pane, through its palette menu.

Setting Grids preferences

Grids preferences let you set up a baseline grid, commonly used to space text evenly across columns, and a document-wide grid, which you can use for positioning or drawing objects. If you're planning a structured design that uses a grid, you'll want to set it up before you start working in the document. It's likely that each design you create will have different grid settings based on its content, so you probably won't change Grids preferences with no documents open. The Grids pane is shown in Figure 3-7.

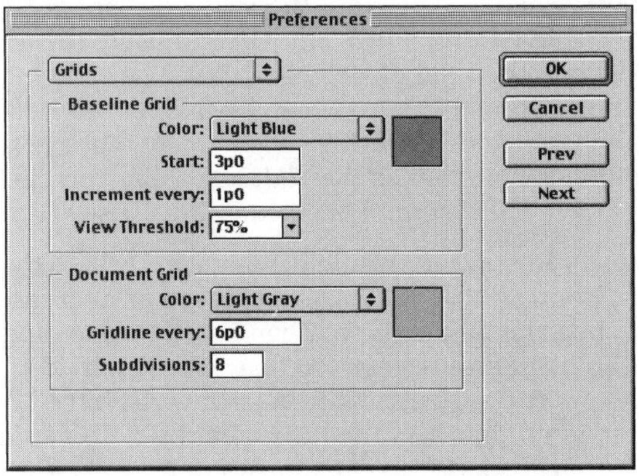

Preferences	
Grids ⬍	OK
	Cancel
Baseline Grid	Prev
Color: Light Blue ⬍	Next
Start: 3p0	
Increment every: 1p0	
View Threshold: 75% ▾	
Document Grid	
Color: Light Gray ⬍	
Gridline every: 6p0	
Subdivisions: 8	

Figure 3-7: The Grids pane of the Preferences dialog box.

Both the baseline grid and the document grid display on every spread behind all objects; the document grid displays on the pasteboard as well. Both grids cover the entire document and cannot be associated with a specific master page or layer.

Baseline Grid area

You can specify the color of the baseline grid, where it starts, how far apart each gridline is, and when it displays. To display the baseline grid for a document, choose View ➪ Show Baseline Grid, or press Option+⌘+" or Ctrl+Alt+".

✦ **Color pop-up menu:** The default color of the baseline grid is Light Blue. If this color is difficult for you to see, or if you're accustomed to the pink lines in QuarkXPress, you can choose a different color from the Color pop-up menu. Choose Other to access the system color picker and create your own color.

✦ **Start field:** This value specifies how far down from the top of the page the grid starts. The Start value, which defaults to 3p0, usually matches the top margin or the top of the page.

✦ **Increment every field:** The amount of space between gridlines is specified in the Increment every field. The default value of 1p0 is usually changed to match the leading of your body text so text aligns with the grid.

✦ **View Threshold field:** You can prevent the baseline grid from displaying when you decrease the view percentage. If you're using the default setting, the baseline grid will not display at views below 75%. You can enter a value ranging from 5 to 4,000 percent.

Tip You might want to change the View Threshold to match the document's most common Fit in Window view. For example, a magazine page on a 15-inch monitor in a full window might display at around 65 percent when you choose View ➪ Fit in Window. Usually you use Fit in Window to get an overall look at the page, and the baseline grid would simply be in the way.

Document Grid area

The document grid consists of intersecting horizontal and vertical gridlines, forming a pattern of small squares that you can use for object placement and for drawing symmetrical objects. You can customize the color and spacing of the gridlines. To display the document grid, choose View ➪ Show Document Grid, or press ⌘+" or Ctrl+".

✦ **Color pop-up menu:** The default color of the document grid is Light Gray. While this light shade is unobtrusive, you might want to change it to something brighter or darker so you can see it better. You can choose a different color from the Color pop-up menu or choose Other to create your own.

✦ **Gridline every field:** The major gridlines, which are slightly darker than minor gridlines, are positioned according to this value. The default value is 6p0; in general, you'll want to specify a value that's appropriate for the measurement system you're using. For example, if you're working in inches, you might enter **1 inch** in the Gridline every field. This way, the gridlines match up with the major tick marks on the ruler.

✦ **Subdivisions field:** Although this is a number and not a measurement, it ends up specifying the amount of space between gridlines. The major gridlines established in the Gridline every field are divided according to the value you enter here. For example, if you entered **1 inch** in the Gridline every field, and you enter **4** in the Subdivisions field, you will get a gridline at each quarter inch. The default number of Subdivisions is 8.

Setting Guides preferences

When you create a new document, you set up margins in the New Document dialog box (File ➪ New, or ⌘+N or Ctrl+N). For more alignment options within a document, you can create guidelines by dragging them off the rulers or using the Layout ➪ Create Guides command. Settings in the Guides pane, shown in Figure 3-8, control the color and other attributes of the margins and guides.

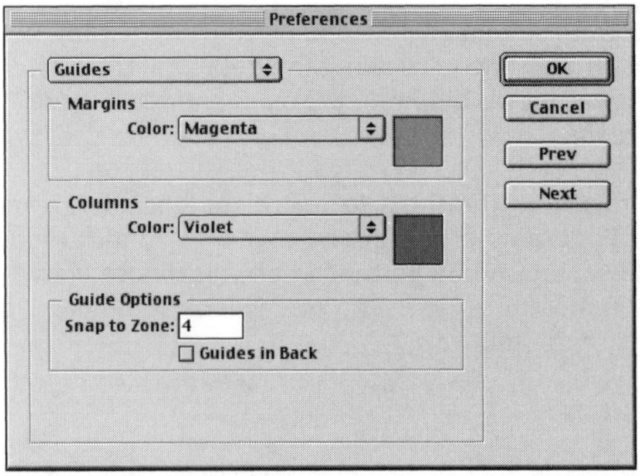

Figure 3-8: The Guides pane of the Preferences dialog box.

✦ The Color pop-up menus for Margins and Columns let you choose another color. If you want to make your own color, choose Other or double-click the colored box to access the system color picker. The Margins color, Magenta by default, displays on all horizontal guides; the Columns color, Violet by default, displays on all vertical guides. To display guides in a document, choose View ➪ Show Guides, or press ⌘+R or Ctrl+R.

✦ Snap to Zone field: When checked, the Snap to Document Grid and Snap to Guides commands in the View menu make gridlines and guide lines "magnetic." When you drag an object near a gridline or guide line, the object automatically aligns with it (or "snaps" to it). The Snap to Zone value specifies how close you need to drag an object to a gridline or guide line to make it snap (think of it as the size of the line's magnetic field). The default Snap to Zone value is 4 pixels, but you can enter a value ranging from 1 to 36.

✦ By default, margins and guides display in front of all objects. If you prefer to have objects obscure margins and guides, check Guides in Back. This feature is for those QuarkXPress 3.3 users who never figured out how to change the unfortunate default of placing guides in back, and are therefore accustomed to working with guides this way. Note that baseline grids and document grids always display behind all objects, regardless of this setting.

Setting Dictionary preferences

Eventually, you may be able to purchase third-party spelling or hyphenation dictionaries for InDesign. For example, you might be able to purchase a different Traditional German dictionary with more words than the one InDesign has. In such a case, when you check the spelling of a word with Traditional German as its Language format, InDesign would consult the third-party dictionary rather than the default. If you do purchase a third-party dictionary, you will need to install it and then choose it in the Dictionary pane, shown in Figure 3-9.

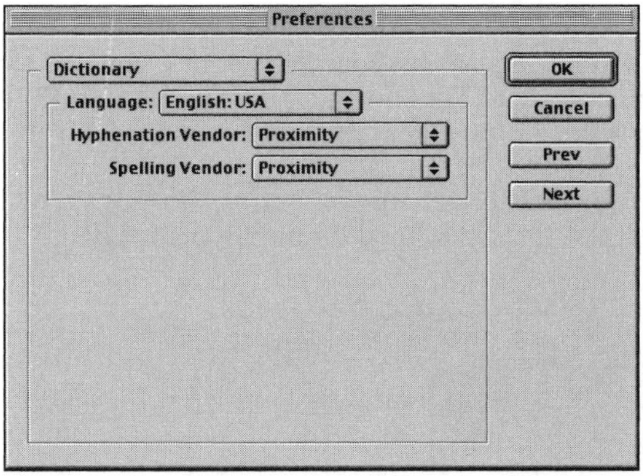

Figure 3-9: The Dictionary pane of the Preferences dialog box.

Cross-Reference

See Chapter 10 for more information about the default dictionaries that ship with InDesign.

Here are the options for Dictionary preferences:

✦ The Language pop-up menu lets you choose a language for which you want to choose a different hyphenation or spelling dictionary.

✦ The Hyphenation Vendor pop-up menu lets you choose from any hyphenation dictionaries installed for the selected language.

✦ The Spelling Vendor pop-up menu lets you choose from any spelling dictionaries installed for the selected language.

Note

To install different dictionaries, place them in the Dictionaries folder inside the Plug-ins folder (inside your InDesign folder). Press Option+⌘+/ or Ctrl+Alt+/ to update the pop-up menus in the Dictionary pane without restarting InDesign. Remember, in a workgroup it's important that everyone use the same dictionary.

Customizing Keyboard Shortcuts

InDesign provides keyboard shortcuts for accessing most tools and menu commands, and for many pane options. For the most part, the keyboard shortcuts selected by Adobe either match platform standards — such as ⌘+X and Ctrl+X for Edit ⇨ Cut — or they're based on keyboard shortcuts in PageMaker, Photoshop, and Illustrator. Fortunately, you're not stuck with the keyboard shortcuts Adobe decided on, and we say "fortunately" because a few decisions and omissions are a little odd.

You have several methods for customizing the keyboard shortcuts: You can modify a copy of the default set, you can choose to use shortcuts based on QuarkXPress 4.x shortcuts, or you can modify a copy of the QuarkXPress set and modify it.

The Edit Shortcuts dialog box (File ⇨ Edit Shortcuts, or Option+⌘+K or Ctrl+Alt+K), shown in Figure 3-10, provides all the tools you need for modifying keyboard shortcuts.

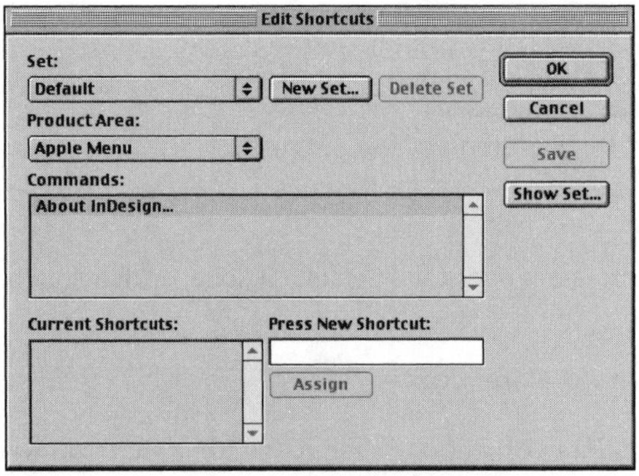

Figure 3-10: The Edit Shortcuts dialog box lets you create new sets of keyboard shortcuts.

To Customize or Not to Customize

The ability to customize keyboard shortcuts is great, letting you work the way you want. Or is it great? Maybe only if you work alone and never talk to anyone about your work or their work. Modified keyboard shortcuts can lead to confusion when discussing techniques, reading documentation, or sharing computers. While modifying keyboard shortcuts—or even while considering it—keep the following in mind:

✦ You can specify keyboard shortcuts for specific fonts and faces, such as a shortcut for Gill Sans Bold Italic. For the font to be listed in the Commands area, you'll need to make sure it's available to InDesign when you open the Edit Shortcuts dialog box.

✦ Don't change system-wide conventions such as the shortcuts for New, Open, Save, and Print.

✦ Don't change common keyboard commands to shortcuts that will unexpectedly change your design—for example, don't use ⌘+F or Ctrl+F for changing leading rather than invoking Find/Change.

✦ If you share computers in any way—even just another user reaching over your shoulder to provide assistance—it's safer to add keyboard shortcuts than to change them. Your shortcuts will be slightly customized, but other users will be able to use your copy of InDesign without unexpected results.

✦ If you're at a 24-hour shop in which two or three people share computers, each person can have his or her own set of named keyboard shortcuts. But this requires each user to remember to activate his or her own set.

✦ You can't export keyboard shortcuts to share with other users. If consistency is important, make sure everyone creates the same set.

✦ Don't modify keyboard shortcuts for computers in public places such as training centers or photocopy centers.

✦ QuarkXPress users coming to InDesign have to learn new software anyway, so they might benefit—in the long run—from learning new keyboard shortcuts, as well. Even though using your old shortcuts will ease the initial transition, the frustration caused by missing or different shortcuts can be worse than learning new ones.

✦ When you're specifying keyboard shortcuts, remember to use a modifier key or keys: ⌘, Option, Shift, or Control on the Mac and Ctrl, Alt, or Shift on Windows. Single letter or number commands (which Adobe uses for selecting tools) obviously can't be used while you're editing text.

If the preceding comments make us seem negative about customizing keyboard shortcuts, we're really not. Just consider all the ramifications before you do any customizing.

Using and modifying default shortcuts

When you first launch InDesign, you're using the Default set of shortcuts, which you can view in menus, in some ToolTips, and in your documentation. (This book lists default shortcuts as well.) You cannot modify the default set, but you can create a new set based on it, and then modify the shortcuts in that set.

The Edit Shortcuts dialog box (File ➪ Edit Shortcuts, or Option+Shift+⌘+K or Ctrl+Alt+Shift+K), already shown in Figure 3-10, provides all the tools you need for modifying keyboard shortcuts. To use the standard keyboard shortcuts after switching to another set, choose Default from the Set pop-up menu at the top of the dialog box and then click OK.

Steps: Modifying the Default Shortcuts

1. Choose File ➪ Edit Shortcuts, or press Option+Shift+⌘+K or Ctrl+Alt+Shift+K.

2. Click New Set.

3. In the New Set dialog box, shown in Figure 3-11, choose Default from the Based On Set pop-up menu.

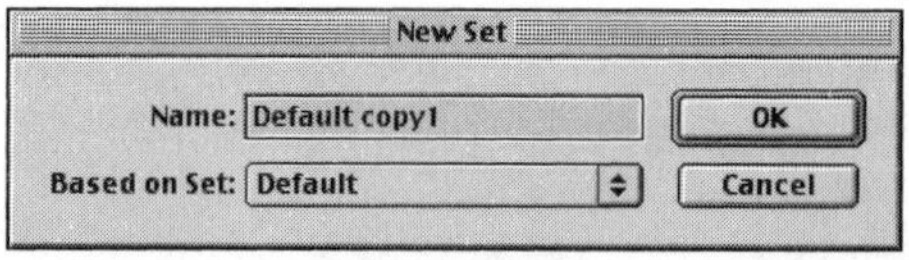

Figure 3-11: Use the New Set dialog box to create a new set of keyboard shortcuts based on an existing set.

4. Enter a different name for the set in Name field, and then click OK to create the set.

5. To start modifying the commands, select a menu or type of shortcut to change from the Product Area pop-up menu. For example, you can choose File Menu, Object Editing, or Typography.

6. Scroll through the Commands area, and click to select a command so you can change its shortcut. The Current Shortcuts area shows you the command's existing shortcut (if there is one).

7. Click in the Press New Shortcut field. You have three options at this point:

   • If a keyboard shortcut exists for this command, you can click Remove to delete it and free it up for another command.

   • If no keyboard shortcut exists for this command, you can press the actual modifier keys and command, and then click Assign.

• If a keyboard shortcut exists for this command, but you want to override it, you can press the actual modifier keys and letter or number, and then click Assign, as shown in Figure 3-12. (The shortcut you are overriding is shown below the Assign button.)

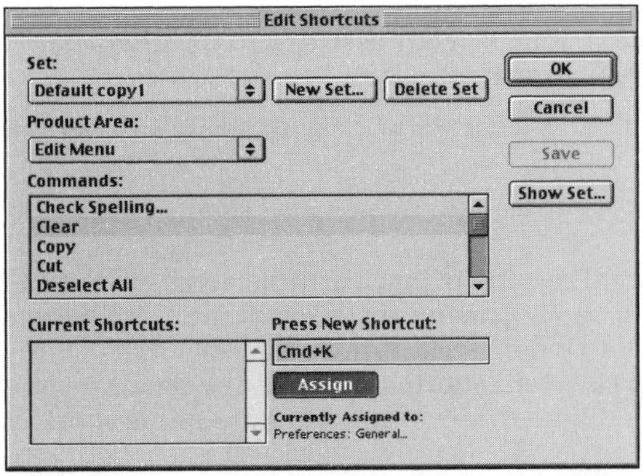

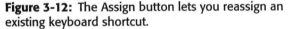

Figure 3-12: The Assign button lets you reassign an existing keyboard shortcut.

8. Click Save after modifying a shortcut.

9. When you finish editing keyboard shortcuts, click OK to save them. For the shortcuts that don't show in menus, you can print a list to use as a reference. See "Viewing and printing shortcuts" later in this chapter.

Tip

You might consider adding a keyboard shortcut for Layout ⇨ Create Guides, such as the unused Shift+G. Although you'll still get a capital "G" while typing, when any other tool is selected you'll be able to create a guide. Another command sorely in need of a keyboard shortcut is Type ⇨ Insert Character. Try the unused ⌘+U or Ctrl+U.

Using and modifying QuarkXPress shortcuts

If you're switching to InDesign from QuarkXPress — and are not accustomed to using Photoshop or Illustrator — the keyboard shortcuts in InDesign may seem odd. To ease the transition to InDesign, Adobe has provided a set of keyboard shortcuts based on those in QuarkXPress 4.0. We say "based on" because they either couldn't or didn't get them all right. And they couldn't really include them all, because some QuarkXPress commands don't have equivalents and some work so differently. And commands unique to InDesign still have their own keyboard shortcuts — for example, you can still select tools with the single letters shown in the ToolTips.

Among the shortcuts you'll miss or be confused by:

✦ Option or Alt for the Page Grabber Hand is missing (use the Navigator pane instead).

✦ ⌘+K or Ctrl+K for deleting selected objects is missing (you can always use the Delete key unless the Type tool is selected).

✦ Shift+⌘+F or Ctrl+Shift+F is incorrectly assigned to the Character formats rather than to Paragraph formats.

✦ Shift+⌘+D or Ctrl+Shift+D is incorrectly assigned to Tabs rather than to Character formats.

✦ Shift+⌘+T or Ctrl+Shift+T is incorrectly assigned to Align rather than to Tabs.

If you want to use the QuarkXPress set of keyboard shortcuts, choose Set for QuarkXPress 4.0 from the Set pop-up menu at the top of the Edit Shortcuts dialog box (File ⇨ Edit Shortcuts, or Option+Shift+⌘+K or Ctrl+Alt+Shift+K). You might want to print out the list of keyboard shortcuts and review them so you know what's available and what's different. (See "Viewing and printing shortcuts" following this section.)

If you decide to use the QuarkXPress set of keyboard shortcuts, you might want to create a copy and modify some of them. For example, you can assign ⌘+K or Ctrl+K to Clear because you're used to it deleting items (and it's not used in Adobe's QuarkXPress set anyway). You can also repair the incorrect commands, although in many cases they're assigned to other commands and must be replaced.

Viewing and printing shortcuts

After you modify keyboard shortcuts, you may need a list for reference. In addition, it's helpful to review the entire QuarkXPress set before you start editing it. (There's little need for a list of default shortcuts because they're well-documented by Adobe.)

Click Show Set in the Edit Shortcuts dialog box (File ⇨ Edit Shortcuts, or Option+Shift+⌘+K or Ctrl+Alt+Shift+K) to view a list of shortcuts for the currently selected set. The shortcuts are displayed in SimpleText (on the Macintosh) as shown in Figure 3-13 or in WordPad (in Windows). You can then print the list from that application.

Caution When you view a list of keyboard shortcuts, InDesign lists every single font and face available, regardless of whether it has a shortcut assigned. When you print, you could end up with pages and pages that list nothing but your fonts. If you're not assigning shortcuts to fonts, you might want to view and print this list when only the system fonts are available.

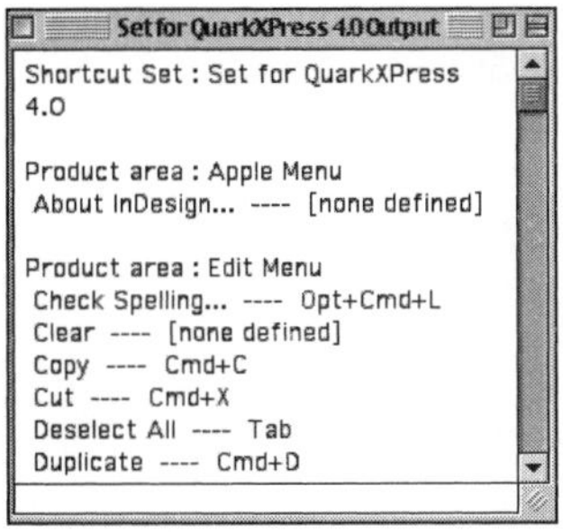

Figure 3-13: The QuarkXPress 4.0 keyboard shortcuts as displayed in SimpleText.

Modifying Defaults for Documents, Text, and Objects

When you create a new document, start typing, or create a new object, the attributes of the document, text, or object are based on default settings that you can change. For example, by default a new document is always letter-sized, but if you design only CD covers, you can change the default.

You may need to work with InDesign for a while to determine which of these settings to change and what settings you prefer. Once you identify a problem — say you realize that you always end up changing the inset for text frames — jot down a note about it or close all documents right then. When no documents are open, change the setting for all future documents.

Modifying document defaults

You can modify the default size, margins, and columns in new documents; the default attributes of guides; and the way layouts are adjusted. To modify document defaults, choose the following with no documents open:

✦ **File ⇨ Document Setup (Option+⌘+P or Ctrl+Alt+P):** The Document Setup dialog box, shown in Figure 3-14, lets you modify the default settings in the New Document dialog box for the Number of Pages, Page Size, Facing Pages, and Master Text Frame.

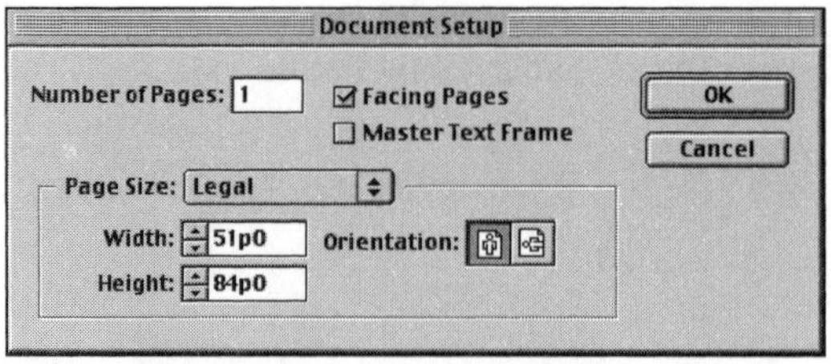

Figure 3-14: When no documents are open, the Document Setup dialog box lets you customize default settings in the New Document dialog box.

✦ **Layout ⇨ Margins and Columns:** The Margins and Columns dialog box, shown in Figure 3-15, lets you modify the default settings in the New Document dialog box for the Margins and Columns areas.

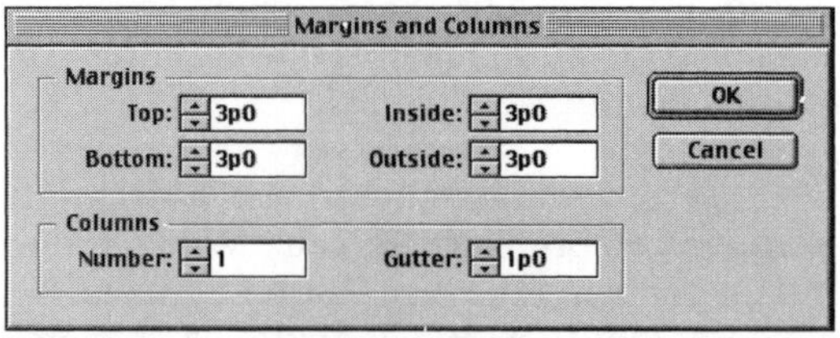

Figure 3-15: Use the Margins and Columns dialog box — when no documents are open — to establish default margins and columns.

✦ Use **Layout ⇨ Ruler Guides** to adjust the View Threshold and Color for all new guides.

✦ Use **Layout ⇨ Layout Adjustments** to enable the resizing of entire layouts and customize how they are resized.

Modifying text defaults

When you start typing in a new text frame, the text is formatted with default Character formats, Paragraph formats, and Story attributes. You can also choose to show invisible characters such as spaces and tabs by default, otherwise you'll need to activate them in each text-heavy document. To modify text defaults, choose:

✦ **Type ⇨ Character (⌘+T or Ctrl+T):** Choose default options for character formats such as Font, Size, and Leading from the Character pane.

✦ **Type ➪ Paragraph (⌘+M or Ctrl+M):** Choose defaults for paragraph formats such as alignment, indents, spacing, and so forth. from the Paragraph pane.

✦ **Type ➪ Story** lets you activate Optical Margin Alignment by default. (Because Optical Margin Alignment works best for display type rather than body type, it's unlikely that you'll do this.)

✦ **Type ➪ Show Hidden Characters (⌘+Option+I or Ctrl+Alt+I):** Check this if you edit in InDesign a great deal and always end up turning on Show Hidden Characters.

You can also edit the spelling and hyphenation dictionaries while no documents are open by choosing Edit ➪ Edit Dictionary. However, because all the edits are saved in the same file, it doesn't matter whether documents are open or not.

Modifying object defaults

When you create new objects, they are based on several default settings. For example, you can specify how text wraps around objects. To modify object defaults, use the following commands:

✦ **Object ➪ Text Frame Options (⌘+B or Ctrl+B):** The Text Frame Options dialog box, shown in Figure 3-16, lets you specify the default Columns, Inset Spacing, First Baseline, and Ignore Text Wrap settings for new text frames.

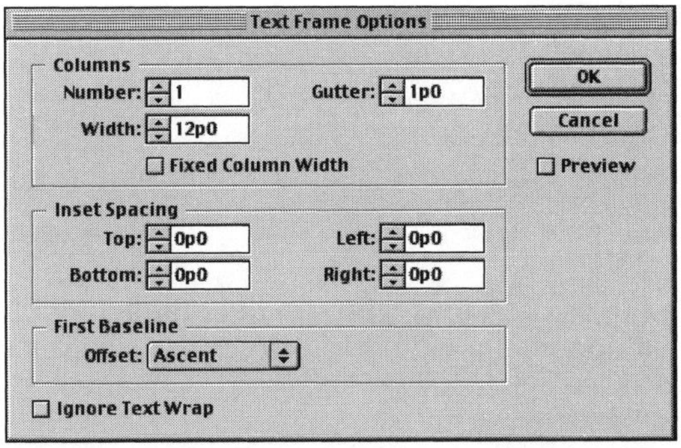

Figure 3-16: Use the Text Frame Options dialog box to specify default attributes of new text frames.

✦ **Object ➪ Text Wrap (⌘+Option+W or Ctrl+Alt+W):** The Text Wrap pane lets you specify how text will wrap around all new objects.

✦ **Object ➪ Corner Effects (⌘+Option+R or Ctrl+Alt+R):** The Corner Effects dialog box lets you choose a style for the corners of all new frames except those created with the Type tool.

✦ **Object** ➪ **Clipping Path:** The Clipping Path dialog box lets you specify the default attributes of clipping paths imported into graphics frames.

✦ Use **Window** ➪ **Stroke (F10), Window** ➪ **Color, Window** ➪ **Gradient (F6), or Window** ➪ **Attributes** to specify other default properties of objects. For example, if all objects you create are stroked (framed), specify a weight in the Stroke pane.

✦ **The Polygon Settings dialog box,** which you access by double-clicking the Polygon tool, lets you specify the default number of sides and the inset for the points on a starburst shape.

Modifying Defaults for Views

Another way to customize your copy of InDesign is to specify which layout tools display by default. The lower two-thirds of the View menu, shown in Figure 3-17, let you do this.

Figure 3-17: The View menu commands that are available when no documents are open.

If you'd prefer not to view the edges of frames, you can hide them by default. Or if you always want to start with a document-wide grid, you can show it by default. To modify viewing defaults, choose:

✦ **View** ➪ **Show Text Threads (Option+⌘+Y or Ctrl+Alt+Y)** to show the links between text frames.

✦ **View** ➪ **Hide Frame Edges (⌘+H or Ctrl+H)** to hide the edges of frames.

✦ **View** ➪ **Hide Rulers (⌘+R or Ctrl+R)** to hide the horizontal and vertical rulers.

✦ **View** ➪ **Hide Guides (⌘+; or Ctrl+;)** to hide margin, column, and layout guides.

✦ **View ➪ Show Baseline Grid (⌘+Option+" or Ctrl+Alt+")** to show the baseline grid established in the Grids pane of the Preferences dialog box (File ➪ Preferences ➪ Grids).

✦ **View ➪ Show Document Grid (⌘+" or Ctrl+")** to show the document-wide grid established in the Grids pane of the Preferences dialog box (File ➪ Preferences ➪ Grids).

In addition to changing which layout tools display by default, you can control some of their default behavior. Check or uncheck the following:

✦ **View ➪ Lock Guides (⌘+Option+; or Ctrl+Alt+;):** Unchecked by default, when you check this option all new guides are locked in place.

✦ **View ➪ Snap to Guides (⌘+Shift+; or Ctrl+Shift+;):** Checked by default, when you uncheck this option, it's more difficult to align objects with guides but makes it easier to position objects *near* guides.

✦ **View ➪ Snap to Document Grid (⌘+Shift+" or Ctrl+Shift+"):** Unchecked by default, when you check this option, objects align with document gridlines whether or not the gridlines are showing.

Although not specifically for viewing, you can also customize the way color management works. The File ➪ Color Settings options let you customize the default color transformations used for viewing and outputting colors (see Chapter 28)

Adding Default Colors and Styles

If you find yourself creating the same colors, paragraph styles, and character styles over and over again, create them with no documents open. They will be available to all future documents. To create these, use the New command in the palette menus for the following panes: Swatches (F5), Character Styles (Shift+F11), and Paragraph Styles (F11). You can also use the palette menus' Load commands to import colors and styles from existing documents rather than creating them from scratch. See the New Style and Load Character Styles shown in Figure 3-18.

Figure 3-18: The Character Styles pane's palette menu lets you create default character styles.

Reverting Preferences and Defaults

If you inherit a copy of InDesign from another user, or if you've been changing preferences and defaults at random and are unhappy with the results, you can revert InDesign to all its default settings. You will particularly want to do this if you're learning InDesign using tutorial files or in a class setting.

To revert all preferences and defaults, quit InDesign. Locate the InDesign application folder, and then delete the InDesign Defaults and InDesignSavedData files. (You can also move or rename these files for future use if you think you'll need them again.) The next time you launch InDesign, it will create new InDesign Defaults and InDesignSavedData files.

Tip If you revert to the default preferences, you will not lose sets of keyboard shortcuts that you created. And because InDesign doesn't let you modify the default keyboard sets, you never have to revert to them.

Changing Views

Customizing also involves the way you look at your work. InDesign provides a variety of options for magnifying and displaying your work. Understanding these views ahead of time and memorizing the ones that work best for your type of work, your eyesight, and your monitor will help you get started with InDesign.

Desktop publishing pioneers in the late 1980s often worked on publications using 9-inch black-and-white monitors, and they spent as much time zooming in, zooming out, and pushing oversized pages around on undersized screens as they did formatting text and modifying pictures. The best present you — or your employer — could give you is a large monitor (two large monitors aren't bad, either). In this era of proliferating panes, there's no such thing as too much screen space. But even if you have a huge monitor, you're going to find yourself zooming in and out and using InDesign's other display-related features to control what you see onscreen and help you work more efficiently.

Zooming and scrolling

When you begin building a page, it's often easiest to display the entire page (View ⇨ Fit Page In Window; ⌘+0 or Ctrl+0) or spread (View ⇨ Fit Spread in Window) and work somewhat roughly — creating the required objects and positioning them more or less where you want them. After you add text and pictures to your frames, you'll probably want to begin polishing the page by modifying individual objects. At this point, seeing a reduced view of an entire page or spread isn't the best way to work. If you need to work on details, it's best to pull out a magnifying glass. With InDesign, this means tapping into the program's view magnification capabilities.

You can zoom in to magnifications up to 4,000 percent and zoom out to magnifications as small as 10 percent. As with many other features, you have several options for changing view magnification. You can zoom in and out using:

✦ The Zoom tool

✦ The zoom commands in the View menu

✦ The Zoom pop-up menu or the accompanying box at the bottom-left corner of the document window

The Zoom tool

If you're the type of designer who prefers the click-and-drag solution when it's available, you will probably use the Zoom tool to enlarge a portion of a page.

Steps: Using the Zoom Tool

1. Select the Zoom tool or press Z if the Type tool is not selected.

2. At this point you have two options:

• You can move the Zoom pointer over the area you want to see and click the mouse. Each click enlarges the view to the next preset magnification percentage. (To display these percentages, click the pop-up menu next to the Zoom field at the bottom-left corner of the document window.)

• You can also click and drag a rectangle that encloses the area you want to see. When you release the mouse, the area is centered in the document window. (Note: When you hold down the Option or Alt key, the plus sign in the Zoom pointer changes to a minus sign. Clicking or clicking and dragging in this situation zooms out instead of in. Figure 3-19 shows an example of the Zoom tool in action.

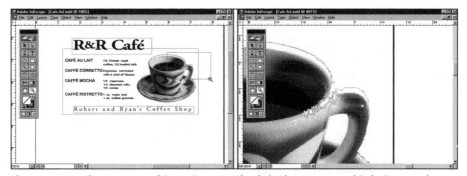

Figure 3-19: The Zoom tool in action. On the left, the Zoom tool is being used to click and drag a rectangle around a small portion of the page. The results appear on the right.

Tip   You never have to actually select the Zoom tool. Instead, use its keyboard short-cuts: ⌘+spacebar or Ctrl+spacebar (for zooming in) and ⌘+Option+spacebar or Ctrl+Alt+spacebar (for zooming out).

Zoom options in the View menu

The first six commands in the View menu, shown in Figure 3-20 let you change the view magnification.

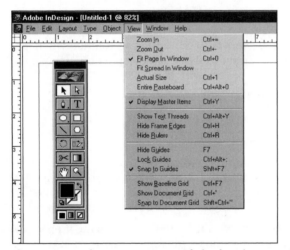

Figure 3-20: The zoom commands in the View menu.

Here's a brief description of each View menu command:

✦ **Zoom In (⌘+= or Ctrl+=):** Enlarges the display magnification to the next highest percentage. (When no objects are active, the Zoom In command is available in the Context menu.)

✦ **Zoom Out (⌘+- [hyphen] or Ctrl+- [hyphen]):** Reduces the display magnification to the next lowest percentage. (When no objects are active, the Zoom Out command is available in the Context menu.)

Tip   If an object is active when you choose Zoom In or Zoom Out or use the Zoom field or pop-up menu, the object is centered in the document window after the view changes.

✦ **Fit Page In Window (⌘+0 or Ctrl+0):** Reduces or enlarges the display magnification of the currently displayed page (the current page number is displayed in the page number field at the lower-left corner of a document window) so that the entire page is visible (and centered) in the document window.

✦ **Fit Spread in Window:** Similar to Fit Page In Window, except that if you're working on a facing-page document, the entire spread is displayed.

✦ **Actual Size (⌘+1 or Ctrl+1):** Displays the document at 100-percent magnification. When you choose Actual Size, a pica is a pica and an inch is an inch — if your monitor is appropriately configured.

Tip Double-clicking the Zoom tool is the same as choosing View ➪ Actual Size; it displays a document at 100-percent magnification.

✦ **Entire Pasteboard (⌘+Option+0 or Ctrl+Alt+0):** Reduces the display magnification so that the current page or spread and its surrounding pasteboard are visible within the document window.

Tip To switch back and forth between the two most recent magnification percentages, press ⌘+Option-2 or Ctrl+Alt+2.

The Zoom box

The Zoom box in the bottom-left corner of the document window and its accompanying pop-up menu, shown in Figure 3-21, offer two additional methods for changing display magnification. To use the box, simply enter a value ranging from 5% to 4,000%, and then press Return or Enter. To use the pop-up menu, click the arrow, and then choose one of the preset magnification values.

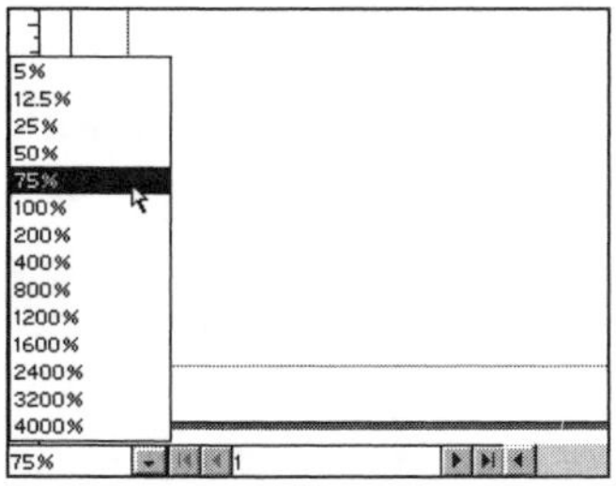

Figure 3-21: The Zoom box and its pop-up menu.

Tip If an object is active when you choose Zoom In or Zoom Out (from the View menu) or use the Zoom box or pop-up menu, the object is centered in the document window after the view changes.

Pushing a page around with the Hand tool

Sometimes after you've zoomed in to work on a particular object, you'll want to work on a portion of the page that's not currently displayed. You can always zoom out, and then use the Zoom tool or the zoom commands to zoom back in, or you "push" the page around within the window until you can see the portion of the page you want to work on. To scroll, you can use the scroll bars and boxes on the right and bottom of the document window, or you can use the Hand tool (H). Simply select it and then click and drag to move the currently displayed page or spread around within the document window. When you can see what you want, release the mouse.

Tip To temporarily access the Hand tool, press the spacebar (if the Type tool is selected, press Option or Alt along with the spacebar). The hand pointer is displayed. Click and drag to move the page within the document window. (This is one of InDesign's most useful keyboard shortcuts!)

Changing the view with the Navigator pane

The Navigator pane (Window ➪ Navigator), shown in Figure 3-22, is the home of several display-related features, most of which are available elsewhere (and which we've already covered in this chapter). The Navigator pane is covered in detail in Chapter 31.

Zoom box   Zoom tool   Zoom Out button | Zoom In button
Zoom slider┘ Document window rectangle

Figure 3-22: The Navigator pane.

Tip If you choose View All Spreads from the Navigator pane's pop-up menu, the page area at the top of the pane displays all of the document's spreads. The more spreads in a document, the smaller each one will appear in the Navigator pane when View All Spreads is selected.

Object display options

Generally, you're going to want to display the objects you've placed on your pages. After all, what's displayed onscreen is what gets printed, right? Not exactly. For example, text and graphic frames are displayed onscreen with blue borders, even if they're empty, but the borders don't print. In addition to the six zoom commands (covered earlier in this chapter), the View menu includes two other commands that affect how objects are displayed:

✦ **View ➪ Display Master Items:** When this command is checked, any objects on the currently displayed document page's master page are displayed. When unchecked, master objects on the currently displayed page are hidden. This command is page-specific, which lets you show or hide master objects on a page-by-page basis.

✦ **View ➪ Show/Hide Frame Edges (⌘+H or Ctrl+H):** When you choose Hide Frame Edges, text and graphics frames are not displayed with a blue border. Additionally, an X is not displayed in empty graphics frames when frame edges are hidden. You might want to hide frame edges to see how a page will look when printed. Figure 3-23 shows how hiding frame edges affects selected and unselected text and graphics frames.

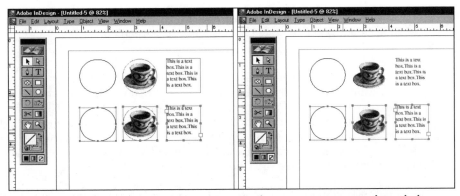

Figure 3-23: In both examples, the objects in the top row are not selected; the objects in the bottom row are selected. The page on the left is displayed with frame edges showing; the page on the right is displayed with frame edges hidden.

Tip

When you move an object by clicking and dragging, you have the choice of displaying the entire object (including the contents of a frame) or displaying only the bounding box. If you begin dragging immediately after clicking to select an object, only the bounding box is displayed as you drag. If you pause after clicking an object until the stem of the arrow pointer disappears and then begin dragging, the entire object is displayed.

Opening Multiple Document Windows

As with most programs, InDesign lets you open several documents at once. It also takes this concept one step further by letting you open multiple windows simultaneously for individual documents. Earlier in this chapter we recommended using the largest monitor you can get your mitts on. A large monitor makes this feature even more useful. By opening multiple windows, you can:

✦ Display two (or more) different pages or spreads at once and work on them at the same time (well, you still have to work on them one at a time, but no navigation is required — you have only to click within the appropriate window).

✦ Display multiple magnifications of the same page. For example, you can work on a detail at high magnification in one window and display the entire page — and see the results of your detail work — at actual size in another window.

✦ Display a master page in one window and a document page based on that master page in another window. When you change the master page, the change is reflected in the window in which the associated document page is displayed.

Platform Difference

Mac users of InDesign can open as many as 28 windows (documents, templates, and libraries) at one time; Windows users can open 60.

To open a new window for the active document, choose Window ➪ New Window. The new window is displayed in front of the original window. To show both windows at once, choose Window ➪ Tile. When you choose the Tile command, all open windows are resized and displayed side by side. (If you choose Window ➪ Cascade, all open windows are displayed stacked and staggered on top of each other. The front-most document window is visible; the title bars of the other windows are visible above the front-most document.)

When multiple windows are open, clicking a window's title bar or anywhere within the window activates it. Also, the names of all open documents are displayed at the bottom of the View menu. Choosing a document name from the View menu brings that document to the front. If multiple windows are open for a particular document, each window is displayed (they're displayed in the order in which you created them) in the View menu. Figure 3-24 shows how three open windows look after choosing View ➪ Tile.

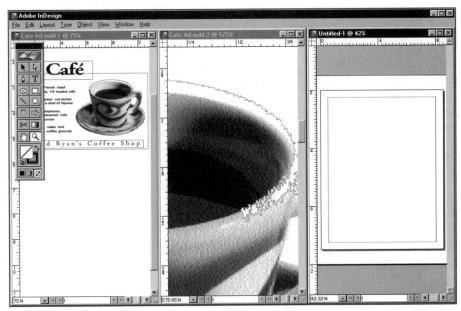

Figure 3-24: The two document windows on the left display different magnifications of the same document. The window on the right is a newly created document. Choosing View ➪ Tile displays all open document windows side by side as you see here.

> **Tip** When you open a document, it is displayed in the window you used most recently before you last saved it. Any other windows that were open when you saved the document are not saved.

> **Tip** To close all windows for the currently displayed document, press Shift+⌘+W or Ctrl+Shift+W. To close all windows for all open documents, press Option+Shift+⌘+W or Ctrl+Alt+Shift+W.

Summary

Although you can jump right in and start working, you'll save time in the long run by customizing InDesign to suit your needs. Preferences (Edit ➪ Preferences, or ⌘+K or Ctrl+K) let you customize the default measurement system, spelling dictionaries, and guide colors for example. Using the Edit Shortcuts command (File ➪ Edit Shortcuts, or Option+Shift+⌘+K or Ctrl+Alt+Shift+K), you can modify the keyboard shortcuts used by your copy of InDesign. If you're switching to InDesign from QuarkXPress, you can even choose to use a set of keyboard shortcuts similar to QuarkXPress 4.0.

When no documents are open, you can specify characteristics of all new documents. For example, you can change the default font, create new paragraph styles, change the default tab stops, and add color swatches. Simply choose available commands from the Layout, Type, Object, and Window menus and change their settings. To actually see what you're working on, InDesign provides a variety of methods for changing the view scale and navigating through a document. Reviewing the methods — and then memorizing your favorite options before you get started — prevents you from getting hung up on logistics while modifying a design.

✦   ✦   ✦

Creating, Opening, and Saving Documents

You're pumped up. You've purchased a copy of InDesign, installed it, checked out the interface, and now you're ready to put the program to work. So, what's next? Launch the application and start clicking? Hardly. Creating a publication with InDesign is much like going on a trip. You won't reach your destination unless you've prepared a plan for getting there. And you'll reach your destination more quickly and more easily if your plan is a sound one.

Remember, too, that most trips don't go exactly according to plan. InDesign is both versatile and forgiving. As you create a publication, you should feel free to change your mind, experiment, and let your creativity roam. As long as you reach your destination (on time!), taking a few detours is acceptable, and encountering a few roadblocks (hopefully, small ones) is inevitable.

Before You Begin

Before you launch InDesign, open a new document, and begin working, you must answer several fundamental questions about the publication you'll be producing.

What is the basic nature of the piece? Will it be printed, or will it be distributed over the Internet or an intranet? If you're creating a printed publication, what are its dimensions? How many pages will it have? If it will be a multipage publication, will it have facing pages, like a book or a catalog, or will it be single-sided, like a flip chart? How many columns will each page have? How wide will the margins be? Does the budget allow for the use of color? If so, how many colors? What kind of paper will it be printed on? What kind of printer or printing press will be used? How will the publication be distributed? Under what circumstances will it be read? What's the life expectancy of the publication? If the publication is bound for the Internet, will you create an HTML file (which can be viewed by anybody with a Web browser) or a PDF file (which requires viewers to have the free Acrobat Reader application)? And what about the content of your publication? What programs were used to create the text files and graphic files your publication will contain? Did you create the content yourself, or did others? What file formats were used for text and graphic files? What is the most effective way to present the content given the production requirements and budget?

As you answer these questions, a rough image of your publication will begin to take shape in your mind. When you're ready to begin turning your ideas into an actual publication, you have a couple of choices. Many (older?) designers whose skills date back to the days of traditional paste-up still prefer to use traditional tools — a drawing pad and colored markers or pencils in this case — to create rough sketches before they fire up their page layout or illustration program. Other (younger?) designers who were never exposed to such archaic tools are comfortable doing their brainstorming and sketching "on the fly" using their favorite software. Whatever method suits you is fine. Keep in mind that, at this early stage, you shouldn't be spending much time fine-tuning details. You can do that later with InDesign.

An overly careful person can plan forever. In which case, nothing actually gets done. At some point, when the image you have of the publication you're creating is clear enough in your mind to begin work, it's time to create a new InDesign document.

Setting Up a New Publication

After you launch InDesign, you have two options: You can choose the Open command (File ➪ Open, or ⌘+O or Ctrl+O) to open a previously created document or template (more on opening documents and templates later in this chapter). Or, you can choose the New command (File ➪ New, or ⌘+N or Ctrl+N) to create a new document.

When you create a new document, the New Document dialog box, shown in Figure 4-1, is displayed. Here is where you implement many of the decisions — including page size, number of pages, number of columns, and margin width — you arrived at during the planning stage. Although you are free to change your mind later, you'll save yourself time and potential headaches by sticking with the basic page parameters you establish in the New Document dialog box.

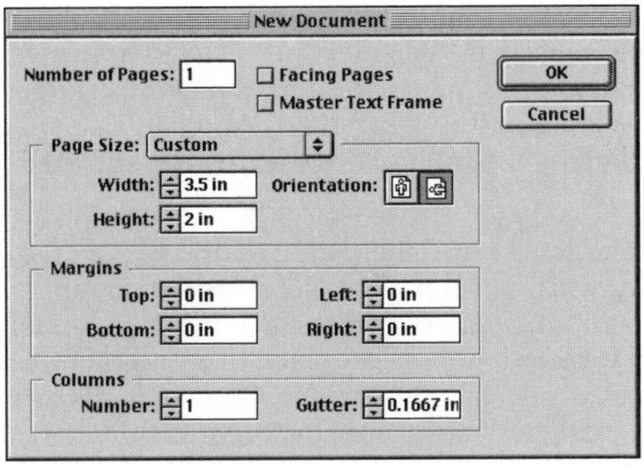

Figure 4-1: The settings you make in the New Document dialog box establish the basic framework for the pages in your publication. This example shows the settings used to create a standard 3.5" × 2" business card. Notice that Facing Pages and Master Text Frame are not checked because they're not necessary for a one-page document.

Steps: Creating a New Document

1. Choose File ➪ New or press ⌘+N or Ctrl+N.

2. If you know exactly how many pages your publication will have, enter the number in the Number of Pages field. (If you don't know for sure, you can always add or delete pages later as needed.)

3. If you're creating a multipage publication that will have a spine, such as a book, catalog, or magazine, check Facing Pages. If you're creating a one-page document, such as a business card, an ad, or a poster, don't check Facing Pages. Some publications, such as flip charts, presentations, and three-ring bound documents, have multiple pages but use only one side of the page. For such documents, don't check Facing Pages, either.

4. If you want to flow text from page to page in a multipage document, such as a book or a catalog, check Master Text Frame. (See Chapter 11 for more information about using master text frames.) If you check this box, InDesign automatically adds a text frame to the document's master page and to all document pages based on this master page. This saves you the work of creating a text box on each page and manually threading text through each frame.

5. In the Page Size area you can choose one of the predefined sizes from the pop-up menu—Letter (8.5" × 11"), Legal (8.5" × 14"), Tabloid (11" × 17"), Letter Half (5.5" × 8.5"), Legal Half (7" × 8.5"), A4 (210mm × 297mm), A3 (297mm × 420mm), A5 (148mm × 210mm), B5 (176mm × 250mm), Compact Disc (4.7222" × 4.5"), or Custom. If you choose Custom, you can enter values in the Width and Height fields. The minimum height and width is 1 pica (0.1667"); the

maximum is 216". Clicking the Portrait icon next to Orientation produces a vertical page (the larger of the Height and Width values is used in the Height field); clicking the Landscape icon produces a horizontal page (the larger of the Height and Width values is used in the Width field). You can also specify Height and Width values by clicking the up and down arrows associated with these fields.

6. Specify margin values in the Margins area. (The margin is the white area around the outside of the page within which page elements — text and pictures — are placed.) A document doesn't have to have margins (you can enter 0 into these fields), and if you want you can place text and pictures in the margin area. If Facing Pages is checked, Inside and Outside fields are available in the Margins area. Designers often specify larger inside margins for multipage publications to accommodate the spine. If Facing Pages is not checked, Left and Right fields replace the Inside and Outside fields. You can also specify margin values by clicking the up/down arrows associated with the fields.

7. To specify how many columns your pages have, enter a value in the Number field of the Columns area. You can also specify the number of columns by clicking the up/down arrows associated with the Number field.

8. Specify a gutter distance (in InDesign, the *gutter* is the space between columns) in the Gutter field. You can also specify a gutter width value by clicking the up/down arrows associated with the Gutter field.

9. Click OK to close the New Document dialog box. When you do, your new, blank document is displayed in a new document window. Figure 4-2 shows the window of a newly created document (a business card) that uses the settings shown in Figure 4-1.

Tip

You can bypass the New Document dialog box by pressing Shift+⌘+N or Ctrl+Shift+N. When you use this method, the most recent settings n the New Document dialog box are used for the new document.

Tip

To change the measurement units displayed in the New Document dialog box, choose File ⇨ Preferences ⇨ Units & Increments, or ⌘+K or Ctrl+K, and then choose the measurement system you want from the Horizontal and Vertical pop-up menus in the Ruler Units area. If you change preferences when no documents are open, your changes are applied to all subsequently created documents.

Tip

When you specify page size, make sure the values you enter in the Width and Height fields are the size of the final printed piece — and not the size of the paper in your printer. For example, if you're creating a standard-sized business card, enter 3.5" in the Width field and 2" in the Height field. If you want to print "multi-up" business cards on an 8.5" × 11" sheet of paper, you can create a letter-sized document (8.5" × 11"), but you'll have to arrange the business cards within the page boundary and add your own crop marks.

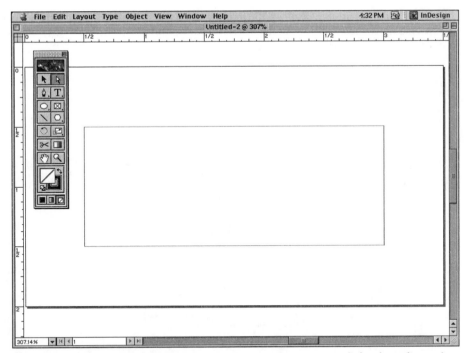

Figure 4-2: The business card settings in the New Document dialog box shown in Figure 4-1 resulted in the document you see here. The view percentage field in the lower-left corner of the document window shows that the business card is currently displayed at 307.14 percent of actual size.

Opening Documents and Templates

Opening documents with InDesign is pretty much the same as opening documents with any program. Simply choose File ➪ Open or press ⌘+O or Ctrl+O, locate and click the document you want to work on, and then click the Open button. In addition, InDesign offers a few options for opening documents you don't find in every program. For example, you can:

✦ Open more than one document at a time

✦ Open a copy of a document instead of the original

✦ Open a template under its own name (which makes editing templates easier than it is with other programs, specifically QuarkXPress)

✦ Open documents created with PageMaker and QuarkXPress, as well as PDF files

Tip

InDesign's File menu displays the names of the five most recently saved documents right above the Adobe Online and Exit options. You can open any of these documents by choosing its name from the menu.

Steps: Opening One or More Documents

1. Choose File ⇨ Open, or press ⌘+O or Ctrl+O. The Open a File dialog box, shown in Figure 4-3, is displayed.

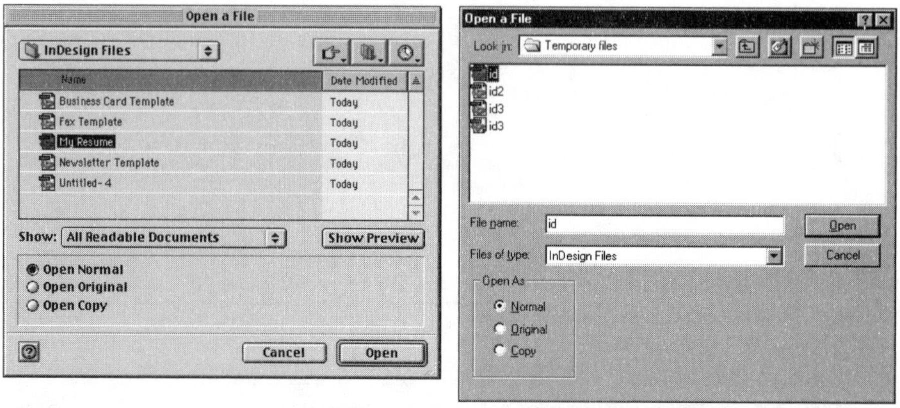

Figure 4-3: The Mac (left) and Windows (right) versions of the Open a File dialog box differ slightly. When you open a file, you have the option to open it normally (Open Normal), to open the original copy of a template (Open Original), and to open a copy of the file (Open Copy).

2. Locate and open the folder than contains the document(s) you want to open. Click a file name or hold down the ⌘ or Ctrl keys and click multiple file names. The Files of Type pop-up menu offers the option to display PageMaker 6.5 files, QuarkXPress 3.3x or 4.04 files, InDesign files, PDF files, and All Files. Choose any of these options to display a specific file format in the file list. On a Mac, the Open a File dialog box includes a Preview button that displays a thumbnail version of the selected file.

3. If you want to open the original document (rather than a copy of the document), click Normal under Open As. To open a copy of a document, click Open Copy. When you open a copy of a document, it's assigned a default name (Untitled-1, Untitled-2, and so on). (If you want to use a template to create a new version of a publication, click Normal; InDesign creates a document based on the template. To open a template under its own name so that you can edit it, click Open Original. Templates are explained later.)

4. Click OK to close the dialog box. Each document you opened is displayed in a separate document window. The page and view magnification displayed when a document was last saved is used when you open the document.

Tip   You can also open an InDesign document or template by double-clicking its file icon. If InDesign is not running, double-clicking a document or template file — as long as it has the proper icon on the Mac or file extension (.INDD for documents and .INDT for templates) in Windows — launches the application and open the document/template. If InDesign is already running, the document is displayed in a new window.

Tip   You can open up to 28 InDesign documents and libraries at one time on a Mac and up to 60 documents and libraries on a PC.

Opening documents versus opening templates

Whenever you save a document, you have the option of saving a standard document file or a template (more on saving templates later in this chapter). A *template* is an InDesign file that's used to create multiple iterations of the same publication. For example, if you produce a monthly newsletter, you'll save gobs of time and ensure consistency from issue to issue by using a template as the starting point for each edition of the newsletter. A template is essentially the shell of a publication that contains the basic framework — page layout, master pages, styles, and so on — but doesn't contain any actual content.

Cross-Reference   For more information about creating templates, see Chapter 29.

When you open a template, you have two choices: You can either open a copy of the file and use it to create a new publication, or you can open the original file, make changes, and then save an updated version of the template. If you want to use a template as the starting point for a new publication, choose File ➪ Open or press ⌘+O or Ctrl+O, locate and select the template, and make sure Open Normal is selected in the Open a File dialog box (shown in Figure 4-3) before you click Open. If you want to modify a template, click Open Original. If Normal is selected, clicking OK opens a new document window and assigns the document a default name, such as Untitled-1, Untitled-2, and so on. If Open Original is selected, the original file is opened and the original name is displayed in the title bar.

Tip   The names of the five documents or templates that you have worked on most recently are displayed below the Edit Shortcuts command in the File menu. You can open any of these documents/templates by choosing its name.

Converting documents created with other programs

One of InDesign's hallmarks is its capability to open documents from other programs and convert them to InDesign documents. You can open PageMaker, Portable Document Format (PDF), and QuarkXPress documents.

Note   Well, *most* of the time you can open PageMaker, PDF, and QuarkXPress documents. Because the other programs' formats are so different from InDesign's, and their capabilities differ as well, the chances of being able to import a foreign document and have it flawlessly convert to InDesign are small. So use this feature to do the first step in the conversion process, but expect to spend time cleaning up the converted files by hand. In some cases, you may see that the amount of cleanup work is more than simply re-creating the document in InDesign from scratch—don't panic when that's the case. And be happy when your documents convert effortlessly.

PageMaker

InDesign can read PageMaker 6.5 files (sorry, not earlier versions). Because PageMaker and InDesign offer many of the same features, you'll encounter fewer translation issues between them. Some issues to take note of include:

✦ Hyperlinks are ignored when converting from PageMaker to InDesign. The text and graphics that had the links are retained.

✦ Book, indexing, and other long-document features are ignored.

✦ Libraries won't convert.

✦ Printer styles won't convert.

 Cross-Reference   Appendix D covers other issues in moving from PageMaker to InDesign.

PDF

When you open a Portable Document Format (PDF) file, InDesign creates a new document based on that file. It gives you the option of importing all pages, a range of pages, or just one page. When it's done, you have an InDesign document whose layout and contents approximates as closely as possible that of the original PDF file. (You'll rarely get an exact match because of differences in how the two programs structure their elements.) And you can edit, delete, add, and otherwise manipulate the document's elements as you could in any InDesign document.

Note   While the text will be formatted to approximate the formatting in the PDF file, the InDesign version won't have any paragraph or character styles applied, so you'll need to create these styles and apply them to the text, as well as to any new text you add to the InDesign document. This is because PDF files don't use character or paragraph styles, so InDesign has none to import. (See Chapter 15 for more on styles.)

You may find the capability to convert PDF documents to InDesign less than compelling, because of an oddity in how InDesign handles text from the PDF file: Each line of text is in a separate text frame, unlinked to the rest of the text. That means each line is an independent element, and so you cannot edit the text and have it reflow from line to line as you add and delete. What you can do to get around this is to convert the PDF file by opening it in InDesign, and then open the original PDF file in Adobe Acrobat, select the text blocks, and copy the text to an InDesign text frame you create over the series of individual lines' frames. Then delete the individual lines' frames when you're done. That lets you preserve the layout and images in the original PDF file and create frames for text that match the original layout.

In either case, some PDF elements won't import: movies, sounds, hyperlinks, annotations, and buttons. They are stripped out of the document during import.

QuarkXPress

InDesign can read QuarkXPress files from version 3.0 through 4.04. Because so many differences distinguish QuarkXPress from InDesign files, it's impossible to predict all the conversion issues that may arise. The good news is that a great many conversions work well, but some don't. Here are some common issues to pay attention to:

✦ If your QuarkXPress document relies on XTensions (a type of plug-in) to add capabilities (such as table creation), it will not convert correctly into InDesign and may not even import at all. Examples include any documents built with QuarkXPress's indexing and book features.

✦ QuarkXPress's leading model is different than InDesign's, so expect leading to sometimes vary significantly, especially if you use additive leading as the automatic leading method in QuarkXPress.

✦ The customizable dashes and stripes in QuarkXPress are converted to solid and dashed lines.

✦ Special gradient blends, such as diamond-pattern, are converted to linear blends or circular blends.

✦ Text on a curved path is converted to regular text in a rectangular frame.

✦ Libraries won't convert.

✦ Printer styles won't convert.

Appendix D covers other issues in moving from QuarkXPress to InDesign.

Importing text files

In addition to letting you open InDesign, PageMaker, PDF, and QuarkXPress files, InDesign also lets you work with text files created with word processing programs. However, you can't open word processing files using the Open command (File ⇨ Open, or ⌘+O or Ctrl+O). Instead, you must place, or import, text files using the Place command (File ⇨ Place, or ⌘+D or Crtl+D).

You can use the Place command to import RTF (Rich Text Format), Excel 97/98/2000, Word 97/98/2000, WordPerfect 6/7/8/2000, Text-only (ASCII), and tagged text created with QuarkXPress, PageMaker, and InDesign.

Cross-Reference   For more information about importing text files, see Chapters 9, 10, and 11.

In addition to the capability to import text files, InDesign also lets you export text files. See the "Saving text, EPS, HTML, PDF, and prepress files" section later in this chapter for more information.

Recovering a document after a crash or power failure

InDesign includes an automatic recovery feature that protects your documents in the event of a power failure or a system crash. As you work on a document, any changes you make after saving it are stored in a separate, temporary file. Under normal circumstances, each time you choose Save, the information in the temporary file is applied to the document. The data in the temporary file is important only if you weren't able to save a document before crashing.

Caution   A word of warning: Although InDesign's automatic recovery feature is a nice safety net, you should still be careful to save your work often.

Steps: Recovering a Document after a Failure

1. Relaunch InDesign or, if necessary, restart your computer and then launch InDesign.

2. If automatic recovery data is available, InDesign automatically opens the recovered document and displays the word "Recovered" in the document's title bar. This lets you know that the document contains changes that were not included in the last saved version.

3. If you want to save the recovered data, choose File ⇨ Save; "Recovered" is removed as part of the file name, and InDesign asks if you want to overwrite the old file. (This is easier than using File ⇨ Save As and entering a name — unless you do want to save a copy of the file in case you want to go back to the old version later.) If you want to use the last saved version of the document (and disregard the recovered data), close the file (File ⇨ Close,

or ⌘+W or Ctrl+W) without saving, and then open the file (File ➪ Open, or ⌘+O or Ctrl+O).

Note
Sometimes, InDesign can't automatically recover the documents for you. Instead, it gives you the choice of recovering any files open during a crash or power outage, of saving the recovery data for later, or deleting the recovery data. You'll typically want to recover the files immediately.

Saving Documents and Templates

When you open a new document, it's assigned a default name — Untitled-1, Untitled-2, and so on — and the first page is displayed in the document window. At this point, you're like a painter standing in front of a blank canvas. But painters don't have to worry about system crashes and power failures. You do. Make sure that when you work on InDesign documents you follow the first rule of safe computing: Save early and often.

The second group of commands — Close, Save, Save As, Save a Copy As, and Revert — in InDesign's File menu provide options for saving the active/front-most document. Here's a rundown of what each command does:

✦ **Close (⌘+W, or Ctrl+W or Ctrl+F4)** closes the active document. If the document has never been saved or if it's been changed since it was last saved, a dialog box lets you save, close without saving, or cancel and return to the document.

✦ **Save (⌘+S or Ctrl+S)** saves changes you've made to the active document since you last saved. If you choose Save for a document that's not yet been saved, the Save As dialog box is displayed. This dialog box lets you name and choose a storage folder for the document.

Tip
If you have more than one document open, you can save them all at once by pressing Option+Shift+⌘+S or Ctrl+Alt+Shift+S.

✦ **Save As (Option+⌘+S or Ctrl+Alt+S)** lets you save a copy of the active document in a different (or in the same) folder using a different (or the same) name. When you choose Save As — and when you choose Save for an unsaved document — the Save As dialog box appears, as shown in Figure 4-4.

✦ **Save a Copy As** lets you create a copy of the active document in a different (or in the same) folder using a different (or same) name. When you use the Save a Copy As command, the original document remains open and retains its original name. It differs from Save As only in that it keeps the original document open.

✦ **Revert** undoes all changes you've made to a document since you last saved it.

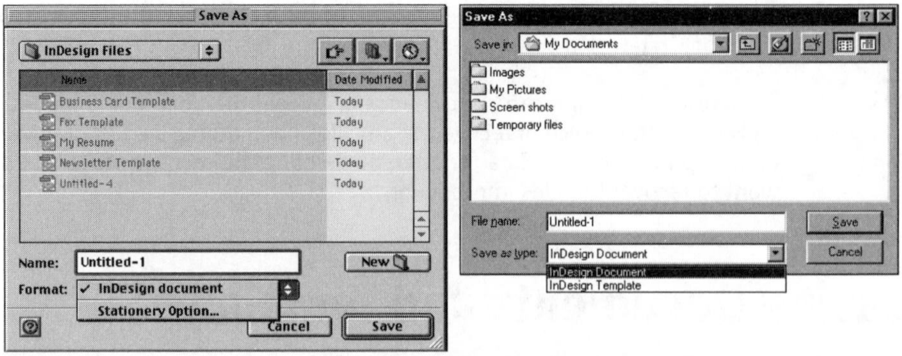

Figure 4-4: The Mac version of the Save As dialog box (left) and the Windows version (right) are slightly different.

Tip   InDesign's Save, Save As, and Save a Copy As commands let you save only InDesign documents and templates. If you want to save a document as an HTML, EPS, Prepress (PostScript), or PDF file, you should use the Export command (File ➪ Export), which is explained later in this chapter.

Saving documents versus saving templates

Whenever you save a document for the first time or you use the Save As or Save a Copy As command, the Save As dialog box lets you save a file as a standard InDesign document file or as a template.

Platform Difference   Figure 4-5 shows the Mac and Windows versions of the Save As dialog box and the differences between the Stationery option (Mac) and the InDesign Template option (Windows). To save a template on a Mac, you must choose the Stationery option from the Save As dialog box's Format menu, and then click the Stationery button in the Stationery Option dialog box (see Figure 4-6). On a PC, the Save as Type pop-up menu in the Save As dialog box lets you choose either InDesign Document or InDesign Template.

In an ideal world, you would create a finished template, save it, and then open a copy of the template and use it to create an actual publication. In the real world, however, templates are often created by yanking the content out of a finished publication and then saving the gutted file as a template. Regardless of how you create your templates, make sure you remember to select the Stationery/Template option in the Save As dialog box. If you forget to save a document as a template, it opens under its actual name. If you then make any changes and choose File ➪ Save (⌘+S or Ctrl+S), the changes are saved with the original document. If this happens, simply save the document again and choose the Stationery/Template option.

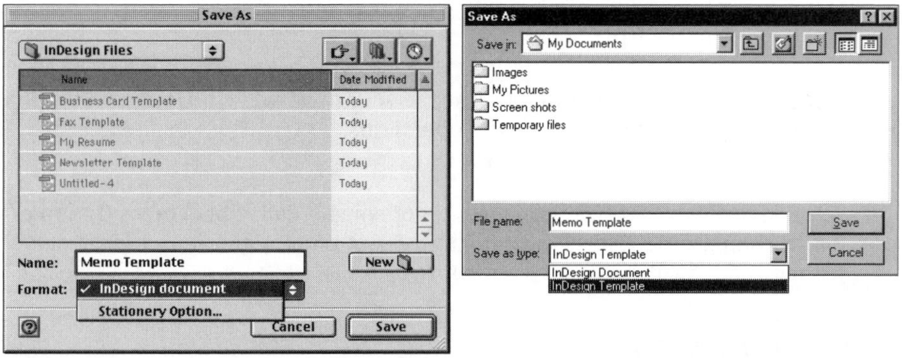

Figure 4-5: Saving InDesign templates is slightly different on a Mac (left) than on a PC (right). Mac users must choose the Stationery Option from the Format pop-up menu, which displays the Stationery Option dialog box. PC users can simply choose InDesign Template from the Save as Type pop-up menu.

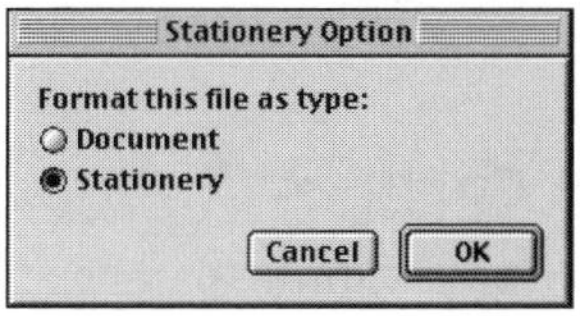

Figure 4-6: Mac users must choose the Stationery option in this dialog box to create a template.

> **Tip**
>
> The Package command in the File menu lets you save a copy of a document along with all files — linked graphics, fonts, and ICC color profiles — required to print the document. This feature is particularly handy if you intend to send an InDesign document to an output provider. (See Chapter 32 for more information about the Package command.)

How not to save changes

As mentioned earlier in this chapter, InDesign is a very forgiving program. If you make a mistake, change your mind, or work yourself into a complete mess, you don't have to remain in your predicament or save your mistakes. InDesign offers several escape routes. You can do any of the following:

✦ Undo your last action by choosing Edit ➪ Undo or by pressing ⌘+Z or Ctrl+Z. (Some actions, particularly actions such as scrolling that do not affect any items or the underlying document structure, are not undoable.)

✦ Redo an action you've undone by choosing Edit ➪ Redo or pressing Shift+⌘+Z or Ctrl+Shift+Z. Alternately choosing Undo and Redo is a handy way of seeing a before/after view of a particular change.

✦ To undo all changes you've made since last saving a document, choose File ➪ Revert.

Tip   If you perform an action and then change your mind while InDesign is completing the action, pressing Esc cancels the operation.

Tip   To undo any changes you've made after opening a dialog box, press Option or Alt, which changes the Cancel button into a Reset button, and then click Reset. (This feature is not available in all dialog boxes.)

The History palette

One of InDesign's most powerful features is the option to undo or redo as many as 300 of your most recent actions. (The number of undoable actions is limited by the amount of RAM available to InDesign and the kind of actions you have performed). The History palette (Window ➪ Show History) keeps track of every action you perform and lets you revert back to the state the document was in after any of the listed actions. The list of actions in the History palette is cleared each time you save a document and when you quit InDesign.

Steps: Using the History Palette to Undo Changes

1. If the History palette is not displayed, choose Window ➪ Show History.

2. To undo your most recent action, choose Undo Selection from the History palette menu or click the Undo button.

3. To redo an action that you've undone, choose Redo Selection from the menu or click the Redo button.

4. To undo or redo multiple actions, click the most recent action you want to save.

5. To delete an action from the list, click the action, and then click the Trash button or drag the action to the Trash button. Hold down the ⌘ or Ctrl key to select and remove multiple actions.

Saving text, EPS, HTML, PDF, and prepress files

InDesign's Save commands (File ➪ Save, File ➪ Save As, and File ➪ Save a Copy As) let you save documents and templates using InDesign's native file format. The Export command (File ➪ Export) lets you save the stories in InDesign documents as text files and save InDesign documents as HTML, PDF, EPS, or Prepress files.

Exporting text files

Unfortunately, the Export command doesn't support all of the text file formats that the Place command (File ➪ Place) does: Only InDesign Tagged Text, Rich Text Format, and text-only (ASCII) are supported. Here's a quick rundown on the three text formats:

✦ When you export a text-only (ASCII) file, all formatting information — fonts, leading, style, and so on — are stripped out; only the raw text remains. The good news is that every word processing program lets you open ASCII files; the bad news, of course, is that any formatting you've applied gets tossed, including bold and italics.

✦ The RTF format, developed by Microsoft, saves the text plus some basic style information (such as bold, italic, font, and text size). If you want to save formats, RTF is a step above ASCII and is supported by most word-processing and page-layout programs.

✦ If you export an InDesign Tagged Text file, all of InDesign's text-formatting codes are included along with the text. A tagged-text file is actually an ASCII file, which means you can open it in with any word processor. The embedded formatting codes will look a little strange, but you can edit the text — and the codes if you're the adventurous type — as you would any text file. (Chapter 9 shows some example tagged-text code.)

Tip   You can save only one text file at a time. If you need to export several stories from the same document, you must do so one at a time.

Steps: Saving a Text File

1. Select the Type tool or press T, and then click anywhere within the story you want to export. If you want to export only a portion of the text, highlight it. If you want to export the entire story, don't highlight any text.

2. Choose File ⇨ Export. The Export dialog box, shown in Figure 4-7, is displayed.

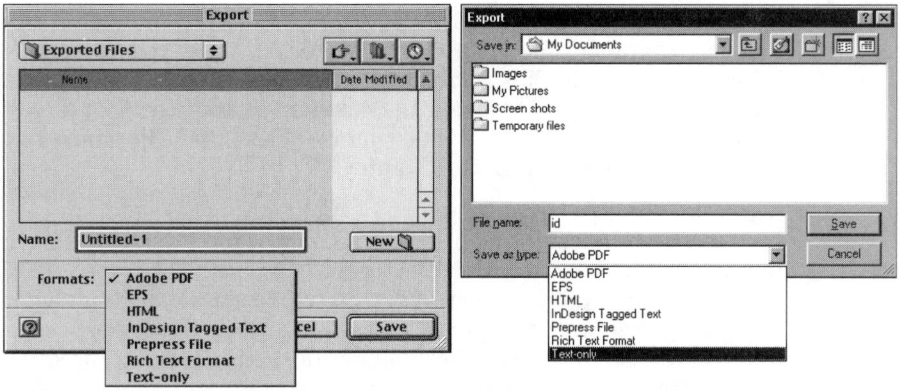

Figure 4-7: When exporting a text file, choose a text format from the Formats (Mac, at left) or Save as Type (Windows, at right) pop-up menu in the Export dialog box.

3. Choose a folder, specify a file name, and then choose any of the available text formats from the Formats (Mac) or Save as Type (Windows) pop-up menu.

4. Click Save to export the story in the selected format.

Tip
If you want to export a text file, make sure the Type tool is selected and a text frame is active. Otherwise, the text file formats are not available in the Export dialog box. The HTML, EPS, PDF, and Prepress File options are always available.

Exporting other document formats

If you create only print publications, you'll probably use InDesign's native file format for the majority of your documents. However, if you intend to produce electronic publications for distribution over the Internet, an intranet, or via CD-ROM, you'll use File ➪ Export to save HTML or PDF files. You can also export documents as EPS and prepress files. Here's a quick description of InDesign's document export options, all of which are covered in more detail elsewhere in this book:

✦ HyperText Markup Language, or HTML, is the primary language used to create World Wide Web pages. Although InDesign lets you export documents as HTML pages, it's not a full-blown Web-page layout program. If you want to do serious Web publishing, you'll need additional software. See Part X for a complete explanation of InDesign's Web publishing capabilities.

✦ Adobe's Portable Document Format, or PDF, is a multiplatform — Mac, Windows, and Unix — electronic document file format that can be opened and printed using the free Acrobat Reader application from Adobe. PDF files have two primary uses: 1) Reviewers and clients can use the Acrobat application to edit and add comments to PDF versions of InDesign documents; and 2) output providers can print a PDF version of an InDesign document more quickly and reliably than they can output the same document saved as a PostScript file. (For more information about exporting PDF files, see Chapter 34.)

✦ The Encapsulated PostScript (EPS) format is used to transfer PostScript-language graphics among applications. For example, you could export an InDesign page as an EPS graphic, and then import the EPS file into another page layout program, such as PageMaker or QuarkXPress, or into an illustration program, such as Illustrator or FreeHand. (For more information about exporting EPS files, see Chapter 34.)

✦ If your InDesign documents will be output with high-resolution imagesetters — either in-house or at an output provider — you have the option to save two flavors of PostScript files. The Print command (File ➪ Print) lets you create standard PostScript (.PS) files, which includes all information required to print the document, while the Export command lets you create a prepress .SEP file, which is optimized for post-processing work, such as trapping and imposition. For more information about creating PostScript and prepress files, see Chapter 33.

Summary

When you're ready to begin working on a new document, choose the New command (File menu) and then use the controls in the New Document dialog box to specify the page size, margins, and column format for the document. After opening a new document, use the Save command (File menu) to save a standard InDesign document file or a template file. (A *template* is a preconstructed document that you use to create multiple versions of a publication.) You can choose Save As (File menu) to save a copy of the current document, or you can choose Revert (File menu) to discard your most recent round of changes. If you want to work on a document you've previously saved, use the Open command (File menu). In addition to opening InDesign documents and templates, you can open QuarkXPress 3.3*x* and 4.04 documents, as well as PageMaker 6.5 documents. The Export command (File menu) lets you save InDesign documents as EPS, HTML, Prepress (PostScript), or PDF files.

✦   ✦   ✦

Frame and Line Fundamentals

P A R T

II

✦ ✦ ✦ ✦

In This Part

Chapter 5
Adding Text Frames,
Picture Frames, and
Lines

Chapter 6
Manipulating Frames
and Lines

Chapter 7
Orchestrating
Objects

Chapter 8
Time-Saving
Techniques

✦ ✦ ✦ ✦

The basic objects in InDesign are frames and lines. With these building blocks, you construct almost all the components in a layout: from the frame containers that hold text and pictures to original artwork you create in InDesign. The chapters in Part II explain how the frame and line tools work so you can create and manipulate layout objects.

First, **Chapter 5** explains how to create frames and lines using the various shapes available in InDesign, from rectangles to curved lines. Once you create frames and lines, you'll need to modify and embellish them. **Chapter 6** explains how to reshape, resize, color, rotate, skew, and do other manipulations to your frames and lines.

With your frames created to your liking, you'll find that you'll want to act on them even further, using InDesign's orchestration tools. For example, you may want to change the position of an object relative to another, to create a layered effect or have something appear on top of something else. You'll also want to group objects, so you can work on them simultaneously. **Chapter 7** shows you how to do all of these tasks.

As you get more proficient in creating and modifying objects, you'll find yourself copying existing objects to reuse previous work. InDesign's step-and-repeat and other copy tools can help you do that. **Chapter 8** shows you how to copy and precisely position objects.

Adding Text Frames, Picture Frames, and Lines

When you create a new InDesign document, you make several important decisions — including the page size, number of columns, and gutter width — that determine the basic structure of your publication. After you click OK in the New Document dialog box (File ⇨ New, or ⌘+N or Ctrl+N), you're greeted with a blank first page. Much like an artist confronting an empty canvas, it's now time for you to add the text, pictures, and graphic elements (shapes and lines) that will make up the final piece.

InDesign uses *shapes* (also referred to as *paths*) as the building blocks you manipulate to create finished pages. A shape is a graphic much like one you might create in an illustration program, such as Adobe Illustrator, Macromedia FreeHand, or CorelDraw. When a shape contains an imported graphic or text, or if a shape was created as a placeholder for a graphic or text, it's referred to as a *frame*. A frame looks and behaves much the same as a shape but has some additional properties:

   ◆ If you change the size or shape of a frame that contains text, you affect the flow of text in the frame and in any subsequent frames of a multiframe story.

   ◆ If you change the size or shape of a frame that contains an imported graphic, you also change the portion of the graphic that's visible.

Designing pages in InDesign is largely a matter of creating and modifying frames and modifying the text and graphics the frames contain. If, for example, you're creating a simple, one-page publication such as a business card, an advertisement, or a poster, you'll likely add several text frames to the page; each text frame will hold a different piece of textual information. In the case of a business card, text frames would contain the company name, the name and title of the cardholder, the company address and phone numbers, and so on. If you want to include pictures or computer-generated illustrations in your piece — maybe you want to add an EPS version of a corporate logo to your business card or a scanned image to an ad — you must also add graphics frames. A graphics frame serves as the cropping shape for the image within.

In this chapter, we'll examine how to create and modify basic text frames, graphics frames, and straight lines. After you create a text frame, you can enter text directly into it or you can place a text file from a word processing program. (For information about importing, formatting, and flowing text through a document, see Part III.) After you create a graphics frame, you can import a graphic into it and then crop, scale, or apply other effects to the graphic. (For more information about importing and modifying graphics, see Part V.)

Cross-Reference

This chapter focuses on creating simple frames and straight lines. You can also create complex shapes and convert them to frames for holding text and pictures. For more information about using InDesign's Pen tool to create free-form shapes and curved lines, see Part VI.

Creating a Text Frame

All the text blocks in an InDesign document are contained in text frames. Unlike a word-processing program, which doesn't let you do much more than enter text, InDesign requires you to create a text frame before you can add text to a page using the keyboard. If you want to import the text from a word-processing file onto a page, you don't have to create a text frame before you import. For information about importing text, see Chapters 9 and 11. After you create a new text frame, you can enter and format text, move or resize the frame, and add graphic effects to the frame edge and the frame background.

The Toolbox palette contains several tools for creating both shapes and graphics frames, and because any shape or graphics frame can be converted into a text frame, you can use any of these tools to create a container that you intend to fill with text. However, in most cases, your text will be contained within simple, rectangular text frames, and the quickest and easiest way to create such a frame is with the Type tool (it's the tool with a big T on it).

Tip

If you want to place a particular piece of text on every page in a multipage publication (for example, the title of a book or the name of a magazine), you should place the text frame on a master page.

Cross-Reference For more information about placing text frames on master pages, see Chapter 11.

Steps: Using the Type Tool to Add a New Text Frame

1. Select the Type tool by clicking it or by pressing T.

2. Move the I-beam pointer anywhere within the currently displayed page or on the pasteboard.

3. Click and hold the mouse button, and while holding down the mouse button, drag in any direction. As you drag, a crosshair pointer is displayed in the corner opposite your starting point and a blue rectangle indicates the boundary of the frame, as shown in Figure 5-1. You can look at the width and height values displayed in the Transform pane as you drag to help you get the size you want. Holding down the Shift key as you drag creates a square.

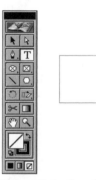

Figure 5-1: Creating a text frame with the Type tool is a simple matter of clicking and dragging until the rectangle that's displayed as you drag is approximately the size and shape of the intended text block.

4. When the frame is the size and shape you want, release the mouse button. The flashing cursor is displayed in the finished frame, indicating that you can enter new text via the keyboard. Don't worry too much about being precise when you create a text frame — you can always go back later and fine-tune its size and position.

Tip When you create a text frame with the Type tool, you can align the frame edge with a guideline by clicking within the number of pixels specified in the Snap to Zone in the Guides pane of the Preferences dialog box (File ➪ Preferences, or ⌘+K or Ctrl+K).

At this point, you can begin typing, or you can click and drag elsewhere on the page or pasteboard to create another text frame. To add text to the frame, you can also:

✦ Use the Place command (File menu) to import a word processing file.

✦ Paste in text that you've copied from another InDesign document or from a document created with another program. (Note: If you paste text that's been copied from another program, you'll lose any formatting applied to the text. If you paste text copied from within InDesign, formatting is retained.)

✦ Drag and drop text highlighted from text from another document.

Tip

You have a couple of other ways to place text on a page: 1) You can drag the icon of a text file or a supported word-processing file directly from the Windows Explorer (desktop or folder) or from the Mac Finder (desktop or folder) onto an InDesign page; and 2) You can use your operating system's drag-and-drop text feature to drag highlighted text from a document created with another program (Microsoft Word, for example) into an InDesign document window. In both cases, a new text frame is created.

Whenever the Text tool is selected, you can create as many new text frames as you want. Just make sure not to click in an existing text frame when your intention is to create a new one. If you click within an existing frame when the Type tool is selected, the flashing cursor is displayed and InDesign assumes you want to enter text.

In addition to adding text to a newly created text frame, you can also move, resize, delete, or add a border (called a *stroke*) or a colored background. But you can't do any of these tasks when the Type tool is selected. You have to switch to the Selection tool or the Direct Selection tool.

Cross-Reference

See Chapter 6 for more details about modifying frames and Chapter 27 for more on creating colors.

Tip

If you accidentally use the Type tool to create a frame that you want to use as a container for a graphic, you can change it to a graphics frame by choosing Object ➪ Content ➪ Graphic.

Oddity

Because InDesign lets you convert any empty shape into a text frame or a graphics frame and convert any text or graphics frame into an empty shape, it doesn't really matter what tool you use to create a particular shape. However, you have to be careful when working with shapes and frames. For example, using the Place command (File ➪ Place, or ⌘+D or Ctrl+D) to place an imported image into a text frame produces different results (placing an image in a text frame creates an anchored graphic within text, which limits your ability to size, position, and otherwise modify it) than placing an image within a graphics frame (where you have nearly unlimited control over its attributes).

Creating a Graphics Frame

Although you can use InDesign's illustration features to create the kind of vector graphics that can be created with dedicated illustration programs such as Illustrator, FreeHand, and CorelDraw, you may find yourself needing to import an illustration that you or somebody else created using another program. You may also want to add other kinds of digital images to a publication, such as a scanned photograph, a piece of clip art stored on a CD-ROM, or a stock photograph that you've downloaded from the Internet.

In InDesign, all imported images are contained within graphics frames. The Toolbox palette contains three tools for drawing graphics frames:

✦ The **Ellipse Frame tool** lets you create oval and round frames.

✦ The **Rectangle Frame tool** lets you create rectangular and square frames.

✦ The **Polygon Frame tool** lets you create equilateral polygons and starburst-shaped frames.

The first time you use InDesign, the regular Ellipse, Rectangle, and Polygon tools are displayed in the Toolbox palette, but the frame-creating variations of these tools are not. Clicking and holding on any of these tools displays a pop-up menu with the frame-creating version of the tool. Drag and release to select a frame tool. When you do so, it replaces the nonframe version of the tool in the Toolbox. All of the frame-creation tools include an X within to distinguish them from the regular Ellipse, Rectangle, and Polygon tools, which behave the same but which aren't designed specifically for creating containers for pictures.

Tip   If you accidentally use the Ellipse, Rectangle, or Polygon tool (instead of the frame version of these tools) to create a shape that you subsequently want to use as a graphics frame (or a text frame for that matter), you can change the frame's contents via Object ⇨ Content.

You can create a graphics frame using any of the frame tools, and then use the Place commands (File ⇨ Place, or ⌘+D or Ctrl+D) to import an image into the selected frame, or you can use the Place command to import an image directly onto a page without first creating a graphics frame. In this chapter, you learn how to create basic graphics frames into which you can then import an image. (See Part V for more information about importing images using the Place command and modifying images.)

Tip   Whether you use the Place command to import an image into a selected frame or you place an image directly onto a page, the results are similar: a frame surrounds the picture and also serves as the picture's cropping shape.

Steps: Using the Frame Tools to Add a New Graphics Frame

1. Select the Ellipse Frame tool (or press L), the Rectangle Frame tool (or press M), or the Polygon Frame tool (or press N).

2. Move the crosshair pointer anywhere within the currently displayed page or on the pasteboard.

3. Click and hold the mouse button, and while holding down the mouse button, drag in any direction. As you drag, the crosshair pointer is displayed in the corner opposite your starting point and a blue shape indicates the boundary of the frame. You can look at the width and height values displayed in the Transform palette as you drag to help you get the size you want. Holding down the Shift key as you drag creates a circle if the Ellipse Frame tool is selected, a square if the Rectangle Frame tool is selected, and an equilateral polygon or starburst if the Polygon Frame tool is selected.

4. When the frame is the size and shape you want, release the mouse button. Don't worry too much about being precise when you create a frame—you can always go back later and fine-tune it. Figure 5-2 shows an oval graphics frame.

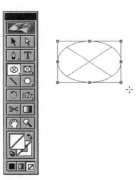

Figure 5-2: Creating a graphics frame with any of the frame-creation tools is the same as creating a text frame with the Type tool. Choose the appropriate frame tool, and then click, drag, and release. In this example, an elliptical graphics frame has just been created; its bounding box is displayed with resizing handles.

When you release the mouse button after creating a graphics frame, the frame you created is active. If the Selection tool was previously selected, the frame is displayed within its bounding box, which contains eight resizing handles. If the Direct Selection tool was previously selected, movable anchor points are displayed at each vertex of the frame. In both cases, you have to change tools if you want to change the shape or size of the bounding box or the frame. The Selection tool lets you change the shape of the frame's bounding box by dragging any of the resizing handles; the Direct Selection tool lets you change the shape of the frame itself by moving the frame's anchor points. Chapter 6 explains how to resize a frame with the Selection tool; see Part VI for information about modifying the shape of a frame using the Direct Selection tool.

Tip   When you create a graphics frame with any of the frame tools, you can align the frame edge with a guideline by clicking within the number of pixels specified in the Snap to Zone in the Guides pane of the Preferences dialog box (File ➪ Preferences, or ⌘+K or Ctrl+K). When the crosshair pointer is near a guideline, a small, hollow arrowhead is displayed below and to the right of the crosshair.

Modifying the shape of a frame

When a frame is active, you can modify it by adding a stroke to its edges or a background color, by rotating, skewing, or shearing it, and so on. You'll also notice that an empty graphics frame (like the frame-creation tools) contains a large X within, as already shown in Figure 5-2. Graphics frames, when selected, are displayed with eight resizing handles, as shown in Figure 5-3.

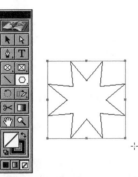

Figure 5-3: After you create a new frame, it's displayed with eight handles. If you create an oval or a polygon frame, as in this example, the handles are displayed around the frame's bounding box. To create this shape, the Number of Sides was 8 and the Star Inset was 50% in the Polygon Settings dialog box.

Caution   Don't try to click a frame handle when a frame-creation tool is selected. Instead of moving the handle you click, you'll end up creating a new frame. You have to switch to one of the Selection tools to move or resize a graphics frame.

Tip   You can configure the Polygon tool and the Polygon Frame tool to create either regular polygons or starburst shapes. Double-click either of the Polygon tools to display the Polygon Settings dialog box, shown in Figure 5-4. The value in the Number of Sides field determines how many sides your polygons will have. If you want to create a starburst shape, specify a value in the Star Inset field. As you increase the percentage value, the spikes become longer and pointier. When you change the values in the Polygon Settings dialog box, the new values are used for both versions of the polygon tool.

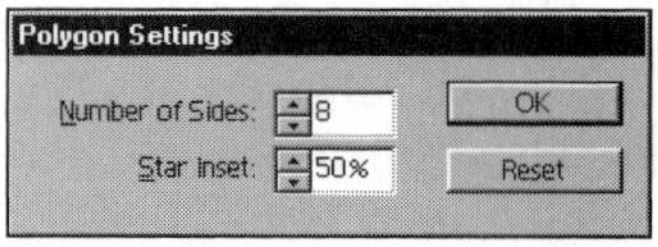

Figure 5-4: The Polygon Settings dialog box lets you specify the number of sides your polygons will have and, optionally, create starburst shapes by specifying a Star Inset value.

When any of the frame-creation tools is selected, you can create as many new frames as you want. Simply keep clicking, dragging, and releasing. After you create a graphics frame, you can modify it (without changing tools) by adding a border or a colored background or by applying any of the effects — such as rotation, shear, and scale — in the Transform palette. You can also move or resize a graphics frame, but you have to switch to the Selection tool or the Direct Selection tool to do so.

 Cross-Reference See Chapter 6 for more information about modifying frames.

Placing an image inside a frame

If you've gone to the trouble of creating a graphics frame, chances are that sooner or later you'll want to place an image within it. To add a picture to a graphics frame, you can:

✦ Use the Place command (File ➪ Place, or ⌘+D or Ctrl+D) to import a graphics file in any supported format.

✦ Paste in a graphic that you've copied from within InDesign.

Tip You can also place an image on a page — and automatically create a new graphics frame — by dragging a supported graphics file directly from Windows Explorer (desktop or folder) or the Mac Finder (desktop or folder) onto an InDesign page.

Cross-Reference See Part V for more information about importing images and modifying imported images.

Drawing Straight Lines

Although they're not as flashy or versatile as graphics shapes and frames, lines (also called *rules*) can serve many useful purposes in well-designed pages. For example, you can use plain ol' vertical rules to separate columns of text in a multicolumn page or the rows and columns of data in a table. Dashed lines are useful for indicating folds and cut lines on brochures and coupons. And lines with arrowheads are handy if you have to create a map or a technical illustration.

InDesign lets you create straight lines with the Line tool and zigzag lines, curved lines, and free-form shapes with the Pen tool. In this chapter, we keep things simple and limit the discussion to the Line tool. For information about using the Pen tool, see Chapter 24.

Steps: Using the Line Tool to Draw a Straight Line

1. Select the Line tool (or press E).

2. Move the I-beam pointer anywhere within the currently displayed page or on the pasteboard.

3. Click and hold the mouse button, and while holding down the mouse button, drag in any direction. As you drag, a thin, blue line is displayed from the point where you first clicked to the current position of the crosshair pointer. Holding down the Shift key as you drag constrains the line to horizontal, vertical, or a 45-degree diagonal.

4. When the line is the length and angle you want, release the mouse button. Don't worry too much about being precise when you create a line—you can always go back later and fine-tune it. Figure 5-5 shows a diagonal line.

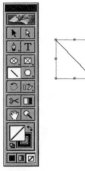

Figure 5-5: After you create a line with the Line tool, the active line is displayed either within a rectangular bounding box that has eight resizing handles (if the Selection tool was previously selected, as shown) or with anchor points at both ends (if the Direct Selection tool was previously selected).

When you release the mouse button after creating a line, the line is active. If the Selection tool was previously selected, the line is displayed within a rectangular bounding box, which contains eight resizing handles. If the Direct Selection tool was previously selected, movable anchor points are displayed at end of the line. In both cases, you have to change tools if you want to change the shape or size of the bounding box or the line. The Selection tool lets you change the shape of the line's bounding box (which also changes the angle and length of the line) by dragging any of the resizing handles. The Direct Selection tool lets you change the length and angle of the line itself by moving anchor points on the frame. Chapter 6 explains how to resize lines with the Selection tool; see Part VI for information about modifying shapes using the Direct Selection tool.

Tip

When you create a line, it takes on the characteristics specified in the Stroke pane (Window ⇨ Stroke, or F10). When you first open a document, the default line width is 1 point. If you want to change the appearance of your lines, double-click the Line tool and adjust the Weight in the Stroke pane that appears. If you make this adjustment when no document is open, all new documents will use the new line settings.

When the Line tool is selected, you can create as many new lines as you want. Simply keep clicking, dragging, and releasing. After you create a line, you can modify it (without changing tools) by changing any of the attributes — including weight, style, and start/end shapes — in the Stroke pane.

Cross-Reference

See Chapter 6 for more information about modifying lines.

Summary

Empty graphic shapes, frames that hold text and pictures, and lines are the fundamental building blocks of pages. InDesign's Toolbox palette contains several tools for creating these objects. The easiest way to create a text frame is by clicking and dragging a rectangle with the Type tool. After you create a text frame, you can enter text directly into it or import a text file, and then modify the appearance of the frame or the text within. Similarly, after you create a graphics frame, you can import a picture into it and then crop, scale, or apply other effects to the graphic or modify the frame. The Line tool lets you draw straight lines, which you can modify by changing color, width, and style.

✦   ✦   ✦

Manipulating Frames and Lines

✦ ✦ ✦ ✦

In This Chapter

Selecting, moving, resizing, and deleting objects

Adding strokes and fills to frames

Applying other graphic effects to frames

Changing the appearance of lines

✦ ✦ ✦ ✦

The primary purpose of the text frames and picture frames that you add to the pages of your InDesign documents is to hold text and pictures. Much of the time you spend using InDesign will involve modifying the appearance of the text and pictures that you put in your frames. However, like real-world containers — bags, boxes, cartons, and cans — text frames and picture frames exist independently of their contents (they don't even have to have any contents), and you can modify the position, shape, and appearance of frames without affecting the text and pictures within.

In this chapter, you learn how to manipulate the frames and lines that you add to your pages. If you've ever worked with a page-layout or illustration program, you will find many of the basic techniques for manipulating objects very familiar:

✦ If you want to move or modify an object, you must first select it.

✦ If you want to select an object, you must first choose a selection tool. InDesign offers two tools for selecting objects — the Selection tool (the solid arrow pointer; shortcut S) and the Direct Selection tool (the hollow arrow pointer; shortcut A). These tools are explained later in this chapter.

✦ When an object is selected, commands and controls for changing its position and appearance become available.

Cross-Reference For information about working with the text within a frame, see Part III; for information about working with imported pictures, see Part V.

Selecting Objects

All InDesign objects—unassigned shapes, text and picture frames, and straight and curved lines—have at least two levels of selection. You can select the object itself, or you can select the rectangular bounding box that encloses the object. (For rectangular objects, the bounding box and the shape are the same.) The tool that you choose—either the Direct Selection tool or the Selection tool—determines what you can do to the object you select:

✦ The Direct Selection tool lets you select any of the individual anchor points (and direction handles of freeform shapes and curved lines) on an object. If you click with the Direct Selection tool on an object that has a bounding box, the shape within is selected; the bounding box is not selected. You can also move an object with the Direct Selection tool by clicking within the object and dragging.

✦ The Selection tool lets you select an entire object by clicking anywhere in the object. This is the best tool to use if you want to move or resize an object. (You can also move objects with the Direct Selection tool.) When you click an object with the Selection tool, the object's bounding box is selected.

Cross-Reference

You'll find more information about using the Direct Selection tool to select and change the shape of objects by dragging anchor points and direction handles in Chapter 25.

Steps: Selecting a Frame or Line with the Selection Tool

1. Select the Selection tool by clicking it or, if the Type tool is not selected, by pressing V.

2. Move the pointer anywhere within an object, and then click and release. (To select an unassigned shape with no background color, you must click its edge. If you click within the shape, the object is not selected.)

When you release the mouse button, the object you clicked—or its bounding box if it has one—is displayed with a blue outline and eight resizing handles (four on the corners and four on the midpoints of the sides), as shown in Figure 6-1.

Tip

You can also select an object with the Selection tool by clicking and dragging a rectangle. Simply click an empty portion of the page or pasteboard near the object you want to select and drag out a rectangle that intersects the object (you don't have to enclose the entire object). Clicking and dragging is a handy way to select multiple objects.

Figure 6-1: When you select a frame with the Selection tool, in this case an oval text frame, the bounding box is displayed with eight resizing handles.

Selecting multiple objects

When an object is selected, you can move or modify it. When several objects are selected, you can move or modify all the objects at once, saving you the time and drudgery of selecting and performing the same modification to several objects one at a time. You have several options for selecting multiple objects. You can

✦ Choose the Selection tool and hold down the Shift key while clicking in succession on the objects you want to select.

✦ Choose either the Selection tool or the Direct Selection tool, and then click an empty portion of the page and drag a rectangle around any portion of each object you want to select, as shown in Figure 6-2. (Make sure you don't click an item or you'll move it when you drag.) If you use the Selection tool, the bounding box of each item is selected. You can resize any of the bounding boxes, but the anchor points and direction lines of the shapes within are not selected and cannot be moved. If you use the Direct Selection tool, the anchor points and direction handles of the shapes in the bounding boxes are selected. You can change the shape of any of the objects by dragging an anchor point or direction handle. Figure 6-3 shows the difference between selecting multiple objects with the Selection tool and the Direct Selection tool.

✦ If you want to select all items on a page or spread, choose Edit ➪ Select All or press ⌘+A or Ctrl+A. (Warning: If the Type tool is selected and a text frame is active when you choose Select All, you'll highlight all the text, if any, in the frame.) If the Direct Selection tool is selected when you choose Select All, the anchor points and direction handles of the shapes in the selected objects' bounding boxes are selected. If any other tool is selected when you choose Select All, the bounding boxes of the objects are selected.

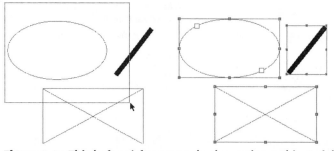

Figure 6-2: This before/after example shows three objects fully or partially enclosed by a rectangle created by clicking and dragging with the Selection tool (left). After releasing the mouse button, the bounding boxes of the selected objects are displayed with resizing handles (right).

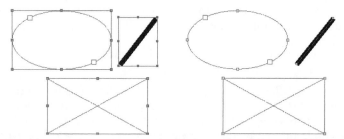

Figure 6-3: The objects on the left were selected with the Selection tool; the bounding box of each object is displayed with eight resizing handles. The objects on the right were selected with the Direct Selection tool; the anchor points of each object are displayed and available for dragging/reshaping.

Tip

To select a master item on a document page, you must hold down ⌘+Shift or Ctrl+Shift as you click it. For more information about using master pages, see Chapter 29.

Deselecting objects

A selected object remains selected until you cause it to become deselected, and there are many reasons you might want to deselect an item. For example, you may want to deselect a text frame if you want to see how it looks when displayed without in and out ports. Or you might want to simply "let go" of an object you just finished working on. You can deselect a selected object in several ways:

✦ Click an empty portion of the page with either of the selection tools selected.

✦ Hold down the Shift key with either of the selection tools selected and click the object you want to deselect.

✦ Choose any of the object-creation tools (the Pen tool, the Line tool, or any of the shape/frame-creation tools), and then click and drag to create a new object.

✦ If you want to deselect all items on a page or spread, choose Edit ➪ Deselect All or press Shift+⌘+A or Ctrl+ Shift+A. (Warning: If the Type tool is selected and a text frame is active when you choose Deselect All, you'll deselect any text that's highlighted in the frame.)

Moving, Resizing, and Deleting Objects

One of the great things about using computers to create publications is that it's easy to change your mind. For example, if you don't like where you've placed an object, it's easy to move it or remove it altogether. When you combine this flexibility with InDesign's option to undo as many previous actions as you want, you're free to experiment to your heart's content.

Moving objects

Before you can move an object, you must first select it. When an object is selected, InDesign provides several methods for moving it. You can move a selected object by:

✦ Clicking and dragging it to a different location. When you drag an object, you can move it anywhere within the current page or spread, into an open library (see Chapter 29 for more information about libraries), or into another document (if another document is open and its window is visible). If you drag an object from one document to another, a copy of the object is placed in the target document and the original object remains unchanged in the source document.

Tip Hold down the Shift key as you drag to restrict the angle of movement to multiples of 45 degrees.

Tip You can create a clone (that is, an exact duplicate) of an object when you move it by pressing the Option or Alt key as you drag with a selection tool. Not only is this a handy way to create a duplicate, it's also a great way to experiment. You can practice on a clone without jeopardizing the original.

✦ Pressing any of the arrow keys. Each time you press an arrow key, the object is nudged by the distance specified in the Cursor Key field in the Units & Increments Preferences dialog box (File ➪ Preferences ➪ Units & Increments, or ⌘+K or Ctrl+K). The default nudge value is 1 point. If you hold down the Shift key when using arrow keys, the nudge increment is 10 points.

Tip   If you hold down the Option or Alt key as you nudge an object with the arrow keys, a clone of the selected object is created.

✦ Changing the X and Y values in the Transform pane. These values determine the distance between an object's point of origin and the ruler origin, where the horizontal and vertical rulers intersect (usually the upper-left corner of a page or spread). (If the Transform pane is not displayed, activate it by choosing Windows ⇨ Transform or pressing F9.) Figure 6-4 shows the Transform palette and its controls. If you want, change the object's point of origin—to where the X and Y coordinates refer. The small, white squares in the upper-left corner of the Transform pane let you specify the point on the object used to position the object relative to the page origin. If a shape or curved line is selected, eight small squares are displayed; if a straight line is selected, three squares are displayed. The black square indicates the current point of origin. Click a white square to change the point of origin.

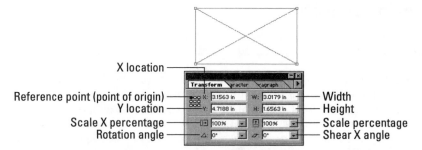

Figure 6-4: If you prefer modifying values in Palette fields to clicking and dragging, you can use the Transform palette to move objects and perform other modifications.

Tip   To create a clone of an object, use Option+Return or Alt+Enter after changing the X and/or Y value in the Transform pane.

Each of the methods above has its merits. The method you choose will depend on how you prefer to work.

Resizing objects

After you create a shape, frame, or line, you may find that it's too big or too small for your design. No problem. Resizing objects is as easy as moving them. And as is the case with repositioning objects, you have multiple options for resizing. You can

✦ Click and drag an object's bounding box using the Selection tool. To change the width and height, drag a corner handle. To change only the width or height, drag a midpoint handle. If you hold the Shift key as you drag, the object's original proportions are retained.

Note

If the Direct Selection tool is selected when you click an object, the object's anchor points and direction handles are displayed. Clicking and dragging a point or a handle changes the shape of the object. (For more information about changing the shape of objects, see Chapter 25.)

Tip

When you resize a picture frame by clicking and dragging a handle, the picture within isn't affected unless you hold down ⌘ or Ctrl as you drag. Holding down ⌘ or Ctrl and dragging changes the picture's scale as well as the size of the frame.

✦ After selecting the object with either selection tool, modify the horizontal and/or vertical scales by changing the width and/or height values in the Transform pane. If you want, change the object's point of origin. The small, white squares in the upper-left corner of the Transform pane let you specify the point on the object used to position the object relative to the page origin. If a shape or curved line is selected, eight small squares are displayed; if a straight line is selected, three squares are displayed. The black square indicates the current point of origin. Click a white square to change the point of origin.

Tip

You can flip the contents of a picture frame or text frame by dragging a bounding-box handle across and beyond the opposite corner or edge.

More about Scaling Frames

You can also resize an object by selecting it and then changing the values in the Scale X percentage and Scale Y percentage fields in the Transform pane. If you scale a picture frame with the Selection tool, both the frame and the picture within are scaled. If you scale a picture frame with the Direct Selection tool, only the frame size changes. If you scale a text frame with either selection tool, both the frame and its text are scaled. (By the way, if you resize an object by scaling it, you can return to its original size by choosing 100% from the Scale X percentage and Scale Y percentage pop-up menus.) The distinction in InDesign between a frame and its contents and between the Selection and Direct Selection tools can be a little confusing. The option to resize an object by changing its scale only adds to the confusion. The simplest method is to resize an object by dragging bounding box handles or changing width and height values in the Transform pane.

Tip If you drag immediately after clicking a handle, only a frame's bounding box is displayed as you drag. If you click and then pause until the pointer changes, the contents within are displayed as you drag.

Deleting objects

Alas, not all the objects you create will survive all the way to the final version of your publication. Some will wind up on the cutting room floor, so to speak. You can always move an object to the pasteboard if you're not sure whether you want to get rid of it altogether (objects on the pasteboard won't print). But when it's time to ax an object, oblivion is just a keystroke or two away. If you delete a text or picture frame, the contents are removed as well as the frame.

Steps: How to Delete Objects

1. Using either selection tool, click the object you want to delete.

2. Press the Delete key (Mac) or Backspace key (Windows). You can also delete a selected item by choosing Edit ➪ Clear.

Note QuarkXPress users may find themselves instinctively pressing ⌘+K or Ctrl+K to delete an object. In InDesign, this shortcut displays the Preferences dialog box. Even if you use File ➪ Edit Shortcuts to switch to InDesign's built-in QuarkXPress shortcuts, the ⌘+K or Ctrl+K shortcut won't work to delete items. However, you can create a new set of shortcuts (by making a copy of the QuarkXPress set if you want) and assigning ⌘+K or Ctrl+K to the Clear command.

Tip Choosing Edit ➪ Cut, or ⌘+X or Ctrl+X, also removes a selected object. However, in this case a copy of the object is saved to the Clipboard (and can be pasted elsewhere with Edit ➪ Paste, or ⌘+P or Ctrl+P) until you cut or copy something else or you shut down your computer.

Adding Strokes, Fills, and Other Effects

When you create a new frame, it has no content, no color (it's transparent — or "None-colored" in InDesign's vocabulary), and no border. If you print a page with an empty frame, you'll get a blank page. Of course, when you place text or a picture into a frame, it springs to life. But whether a frame is empty or filled, InDesign lets you change its appearance in several ways. You can

✦ Add a border, or stroke, around a frame's perimeter and apply a solid color, a tint, or a gradient to the stroke.

✦ Add a solid color, a tint, or a gradient to the frame's background.

✦ Apply any of several corner effects.

✦ Scale, rotate and/or shear the frame using tools or the Transform pane.

Note   View ➪ Show Frame Edges must be checked if you want to see frame edges.

Adding strokes

In the old days of traditional paste-up, adding a simple, black border around a sidebar or a thin keyline around a picture was a tedious and time-consuming process of laying out adhesive tape and then hoping that your meticulously placed rules remained straight and your perfectly square corners remained tight long enough to make it to the printer. If you were unlucky, your rules wound up on the floor or stuck to somebody's elbows. Nowadays, computers make adding borders to shapes an easy task. InDesign lets you quickly apply strokes to the shapes you create and modify the thickness, color, and style of strokes.

Steps: Adding a Stroke to a Frame

1. Select either of the selection tools and click the frame to which you want to add a stroke, and then click the Stroke box in the Toolbox palette (see Figure 6-5).

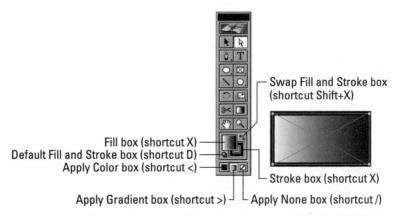

Swap Fill and Stroke box (shortcut Shift+X)

Fill box (shortcut X)
Default Fill and Stroke box (shortcut D)
Apply Color box (shortcut <)

Stroke box (shortcut X)

Apply Gradient box (shortcut >) — Apply None box (shortcut /)

Figure 6-5: The color tools at the bottom of the Toolbox offer the quickest and easiest method of applying the last-used color or gradient to objects, or to remove a color, tint, or gradient.

2. You now can click a color, tint, or gradient from the Swatches pane, or click one of the three boxes at the bottom of the Toolbox, which (from left to right) let you use the last-selected color, last-selected gradient, or None (this removes the stroke's color, tint, or gradient).

Cross-Reference   For information about adding colors to the Swatches pane, see Chapter 27.

When you add a stroke to a frame, it's assigned a width of 1 point. You can change the width and several other characteristics of a stroke using the controls in the Stroke palette. Figure 6-6 shows a graphics frame to which a black stroke has been added, while Figure 6-7 shows a graphics frame whose stroke is a gradient.

Figure 6-6: In this illustration, a 10-point black stroke has been added to the text frame.

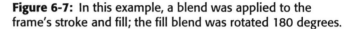

Figure 6-7: In this example, a blend was applied to the frame's stroke and fill; the fill blend was rotated 180 degrees.

> **Tip**   The controls in the Color palette (Window ➪ Color, or F6) let you change the tint of the color applied to a stroke. The Gradient palette (Windows ➪ Gradient) gives you the option to apply either a linear or radial gradient. For linear gradients, you can specify the angle via the Angle field.

Steps: Using the Stroke Pane to Modify a Stroke

1. Select either of the selection tools and click the object whose stroke you want to modify.

2. If the Stroke pane is not displayed, show it by choosing Window ➪ Stroke or pressing F10.

3. To change the width of stroke, enter a new value in the Weight field. You can also change the Weight value by choosing a new value from the field's pop-up menu or by clicking the up and down arrows. (Each click increases or decreases the stroke by one point.)

4. Click any of the three Cap icons to specify how dashes will look if you create a dashed stroke (covered in Step 7 below). Figure 6-8 shows how each of the cap styles affect a dashed stroke.

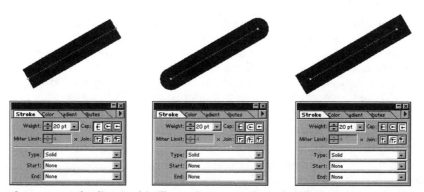

Figure 6-8: The line in this illustration was selected with the Direct Selection tool. Each of the three available endcap styles — butt (left), round (center), and projecting (right) is shown.

5. Click any of the three Join icons to specify how corners are handled. Figure 6-9 shows how each of the join styles affects a corner.

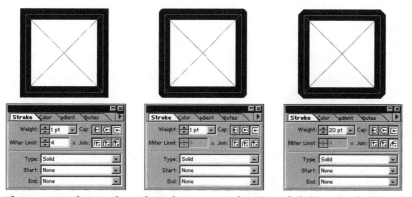

Figure 6-9: The Stroke palette lets you apply mitered (left), rounded (center), and beveled (right) corners to shapes.

6. To create a dashed line instead of a solid line, choose Dashed from the Type pop-up menu. When you choose Dashed, six dash and gap fields are displayed at the bottom of the Stroke palette. Enter values in these fields to create custom dashes.

Note

The value in the Stroke pane's Miter Limit field determines when a corner point switches from mitered (squared off) to beveled. You'll rarely use this feature; it's useful when you have thick lines joining at sharp angles. In such cases, the lines may extend further than needed, and the miter value (1 to 500, with 1 being the most conservative setting and 500 the most forgiving) tells InDesign when to change the squared-off corner to a beveled one, which prevents the problem.

Adding fills

The option to add a stroke to any shape becomes even more powerful when combined with the option to fill any shape with a color or tint. For example, adding a stroke around a text frame is an effective way to draw attention to a sidebar. Adding a fill to a shape is much like adding a stroke, and the options available for specifying color and tint are identical. The only difference is that you click the Fill box in the Toolbox palette rather than the Stroke box. Figure 6-10 shows an example frame with a gradient fill.

Figure 6-10: A frame with a gradient fill.

Design Advice

If you really want to turn heads, you can create reversed text within the frame by adding a fill color and lightening the text. But remember: Reversed text is harder to read, so keep the text size on the large side, and use this effect sparingly.

Adding special effects to corners

Any time you're working on an object that has any sharp corners, you have the option to add a little pizzazz to the corners via InDesign's Corner Effects feature (Window ➪ Corner Effects). Five built-in corner styles, shown in Figure 6-11, are available. Note that if the shape contains only smooth points, any corner effect you apply won't be noticeable.

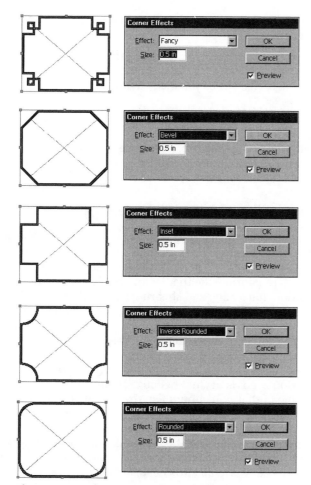

Figure 6-11: The Corner Effects dialog box lets you apply any of five effects to frame corners.

 A word of caution about adding fancy corners: These effects are handy for such things as certificates and coupons, but don't get carried away and use them for everyday tasks such as frames for pictures and text unless you have a good reason. Few things kill a design like too much graphic embellishment.

Steps: Adding a Corner Effect

1. Select either of the selection tools and click the shape to which you want to add a corner effect, and then choose Object ➪ Corner Effects to display the Corner Effects dialog box.

2. Choose an option from the Effect pop-up menu.

3. Enter a distance in the Size field. The Size value determines the length that the effect extends from the corner.

4. Click OK to close the dialog box and apply your changes.

Tip Click the Preview button to view changes as you make them.

Tip If you can't see a corner effect after applying one, make sure that a color is applied to the stroke or try making the object's stroke thicker. Increasing the Size value in the Corner Effects dialog box can also make a corner effect more visible.

Performing other transformations on frames

Earlier in this chapter we explained how to change the size of an item by clicking and dragging bounding box handles with the selection tools and by changing the values in the Transform pane's width (W) and height (H) fields. InDesign also provides some tools and several controls in the Transform pane that let you perform more dramatic effects on objects, such as rotation, mirroring, and shearing (which distorts a shape by applying a combination of rotation and slant). Keep in mind that if you press Option or Alt as you drag, you'll work on a copy of the object. To get finer control as you drag, click farther from the active object's point of origin.

How you use these special effects is up to you and is limited only by your imagination. As always, discretion is advised. Just because InDesign has some pretty cool features it doesn't mean that you should use them in every publication you create.

Tip If you drag immediately after clicking an object, the object is displayed in its original location and the object's bounding box moves as you drag. If you click and then pause until the crosshair changes to an arrowhead, the object is displayed as you drag.

Using the Rotation tool

If you need to rotate an object, and you prefer to accomplish such tasks by clicking and dragging rather than by entering values in fields, you'll want to use the Rotation tool. Here's how:

Steps: Rotating an Object Manually

1. Select the Rotation tool. If the Type tool isn't selected, you can also press R to select the Rotation tool.

2. If it's not already selected, click the object you want to rotate. If you want, you can drag the point of origin from its default location in the upper-left-hand corner of the bounding box to a different location. The object rotates around the point of origin. Figure 6-12 shows a text frame being rotated around the default point of origin (the upper-left corner).

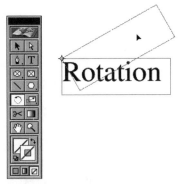

Figure 6-12: When you rotate an object with the Rotation tool, a moving bounding box is displayed along with the original object if you drag immediately after clicking, as in this example. If you pause before dragging, the moving object and its contents are displayed as you drag.

3. Move the pointer away from the point of origin, and then click and drag with a circular motion, clockwise or counterclockwise. Hold the Shift key as you drag to constrain rotation increments to 45 degrees.

4. Release the mouse button when the object is at the angle you want.

Using the Scale tool

The easiest way to scale an object is to drag a bounding box handle, as described earlier in this chapter.

Steps: Scaling an Object Manually

1. Select the Scale tool. (It's in a pop-up menu with the Shear tool). If the Type tool isn't selected, you can also press S to select the Scale tool (if it's displayed) or Shift+S (if the Shear tool is displayed).

2. If it's not selected, click the object you want to scale. If you want, you can drag the point of origin from its default location in the upper left-hand corner of the bounding box to a different location. When the object grows or shrinks, the point of origin doesn't move.

3. Move the pointer away from the point of origin, and then click and drag. Hold the Shift key and drag horizontally to apply only horizontal scale, vertically to apply only vertical scale, and diagonally to apply horizontal and vertical and keep the object's original proportions.

4. Release the mouse button when the object is the size you want. Figure 6-13 shows a before and after example of an object that's been scaled with the Scale tool.

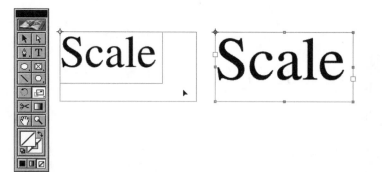

Figure 6-13: Clicking and dragging with the Scale tool enlarges or reduces a frame and its contents. In this example, the Scale tool is being used to enlarge a text frame (left). The results of the scale operation are shown on the right.

If you use the Scale tool on a text frame, the text within is scaled as well. However, if you use the Scale tool on a picture frame, the picture is not scaled. Even weirder: Text that's been enlarged by scaling its frame still shows its original font size and horizontal/vertical scale in the Character pane.

Using the Shear tool

When you shear an object with the Shear tool, you actually perform two transformations at once: rotation and slant. Because the contents within text frames and picture frames are distorted along with the frames when you shear an object, you'll probably use this tool only for special effects. The following steps show you how you can use sheared text boxes to create an interesting shadow effect and a 3D effect.

Steps: Shearing an Object Manually

1. Select the Shear tool. (It's in a pop-up menu with the Scale tool). If the Type tool isn't selected, you can also press S to select the Shear tool (if it's displayed) or Shift+S (if the Scale tool is displayed).

2. If it's not selected, click the object you want to shear. If you want, you can drag the point of origin from its default location in the upper left-hand corner of the bounding box to a different location. When you shear an object, the point of origin doesn't move.

3. Move the pointer away from the point of origin, and then click and drag. Hold the Shift key and drag to constrain rotation increments to multiples of 45 degrees. Figure 6-14 shows a before and after example of a sheared text box, and Figure 6-15 shows the use of the Shear tool.

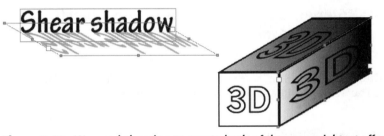

Figure 6-14: We used shearing to create both of these special text effects. The shadow on the left was done by shearing a copy of the original text frame, applying a tint of black to the sheared version, and then using the Flip Vertical command in the Transform palette's pop-up menu to create a mirror image. The slanted sides of the 3D shape on the right are sheared versions of the square text frame that have also been scaled.

Figure 6-15: In this example, a text frame was sheared using the Shear tool. By holding down Option or Alt as you click and drag with the Shear tool, a copy of the selected object is transformed, as shown here.

Modifying objects using the Transform palette

If you prefer to modify objects by specifying values in fields rather than by clicking and dragging, you can use the Transform pane (Window ⇨ Transform, or F9). Some designers prefer the click-and-drag approach when modifying objects because it more closely mimics traditional paste-up techniques: You put objects onto a page, and then you move them around until you're satisfied. Others prefer the precision that entering transformation values into fields offers. Chances are, you'll do a little of both.

For example, if you want to rotate a block of text exactly 45 degrees, entering a rotation value in the Transform palette is probably the quickest method. If you want to rotate a block of text to match the angle of a shape in an imported picture, you might decide that clicking and dragging is the best approach.

Steps: Rotating, Scaling, or Shearing an Object Using the Transform Pane

1. If it's not selected, click the object you want to modify.

2. If the Transform pane is not displayed, choose Window ➪ Transform or press F9. The Transform pane and its fields are shown in Figure 6-16.

Figure 6-16: The Transform pane's pop-up menu provides several commands for modifying objects.

3. Highlight the appropriate field in the Transform pane, enter a new value, and then press Return or Enter (or press Shift+Return or Shift+Enter to apply changes without leaving the pane). When an object is selected, you can also highlight fields in the pane by double-clicking the corresponding transformation tools. Double-click the Rotation tool to highlight the Rotation field, the Scale tool to highlight the Horizontal scale field, and the Shear tool to highlight the Shear X angle field.

Tip   Use Option+Return or Alt+Enter to apply a transformation value to a copy of the selected item.

Note   The Transform pane contains separate fields for horizontal scale (Scale X percentage) and vertical scale (Scale Y percentage). You can distort an object by applying different scale values. Applying equal horizontal and vertical scale values maintains an object's original proportions.

Modifying a shape using Transform palette commands

Like all of InDesign palette's, the Transform pane includes a palette menu (shown in Figure 6-16) that contains additional commands for modifying objects. Before you try to apply any of the effects in the pop-up menu, make sure the object you want to change is selected.

Tip   If you select a text or picture frame with the Selection tool and then apply a transformation, both the contents and the frame are affected. If you select a frame with the Direct Selection tool and then apply a transformation, only the frame is affected.

Here's list of the commands and a brief description of what each one does:

✦ **Scale Content:** Select this option before changing a picture or text frame's horizontal and/or vertical scale if you don't want to change the scale of the picture or text within.

✦ **Rotate 180°, Rotate 90° CW, and Rotate 90° CCW:** These commands provide an alternative to the Rotation field. You can rotate an object 180 degrees, 90 degrees clockwise, or 90 degrees counterclockwise.

✦ **Flip Horizontal, Flip Vertical, Flip Both:** These commands let you create a mirror version of the original.

✦ **Dimensions Include Stroke Weight:** Check this option if you want an object's height and width to be calculated from the outer edge of the object's stroke. Uncheck this option if you want to calculate an object's height and width from the center of the object's stroke. (In this case, a stroked object will actually be larger — by the width of the stroke — than the values in the width and height fields.)

✦ **Transformations are Totals:** When this option is selected, the angle of rotation of a nested object is calculated relative to the horizontal/vertical orientation of the page. If Transformations are Totals is checked, the angle of a nested object is calculated relative to the angle of the frame that contains it. For example, if Transformations are Totals is selected and you paste an unrotated item into a frame that's been rotated 30 degrees, the angle of rotation for the nested item is 0 degrees; if you then uncheck Transformations are Totals, the nested object's angle of rotation is –30 degrees.

✦ **Horizontal/Vertical Palette:** This option switches from horizontal orientation to vertical orientation, and vice versa, when you choose it. Use this to make the pane fit better on your screen.

Note   When an object is selected, the context menu (Control+clicking or right-clicking) includes commands that let you change stroke weight and display the Corner Effects dialog box.

Modifying Lines

When you create a line with the Line tool, there's not much to it. It's plain, black, and 1-point wide. But, like a frame, you can modify the color, tint, and thickness of a line, and you can optionally apply a custom dashed style and doodads to the endpoints.

Steps: Using the Stroke Palette to Modify a Line

1. Select either of the selection tools click the line whose stroke you want to modify.

2. If the Stroke palette is not displayed, show it by choosing Window ➪ Stroke or by pressing F10.

3. To change the width of stroke, enter a new value in the Weight field. You can also change the Weight value by choosing a new value from the field's pop-up menu or by clicking the up and down arrows. (Each click increases or decreases the stroke by one point.)

4. Click any of the three Cap icons to specify how dashes will look if you create a dashed stroke (covered in Step 6).

5. To create a dashed line instead of a solid line, choose Dashed from the Type pop-up menu. When you choose Dashed, six dash and gap fields are displayed at the bottom of the Stroke palette. Enter values in these fields to create custom dashes.

6. If you want, you can apply fancy endcaps to a line by choosing options from the Start and End pop-up menus. Not all of the available styles are particularly attractive, and some are downright clunky. Use with discretion. Figure 6-17 shows a line to which a custom dashed stroke and endcaps have been added.

Figure 6-17: A custom dash style has been applied to this 10-point line. Clicking the Round Cap icon in the Transform palette produces the rounded ends on the dashes.

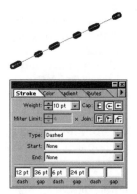

Steps: Changing the Color of a Line

1. Select either of the selection tools and click the line whose color you want to change, and then click the Stroke box in the Toolbox. (The color controls in the Toolbox are shown in Figure 6-5.)

2. You now can click a color, tint, or gradient from the Swatches pane, or click one of the three boxes at the bottom of the Toolbox, which (from left to right) let you use the last-selected color, last-selected gradient, or None (this removes the stroke's color, tint, or gradient).

Tip

The controls in the Color pane (Window ➪ Color, or F6) let you change the tint of the color applied to a stroke. The Gradient palette (Windows ➪ Gradient) gives you the option to apply either a linear or radial gradient. For linear gradients, you can specify the angle via the Angle field.

Summary

After you create an object, you can move, modify, or delete it. If the object is a frame, you also have the option to modify the text or picture within. Before you can modify an object, you must select it. When an object is selected, commands and controls for changing its position and appearance become available. To select an object, you must first choose either the Selection tool or the Direct Selection tool. If a frame is selected, you can add a stroke around its border, a color to its background, or you can change its shape using the Rotate, Scale, or Resize tools or the corresponding fields in the Transform palette. If a line is selected, you can change its width, color, and style.

✦ ✦ ✦

Orchestrating Objects

Text frames, picture frames, graphic shapes, and lines are the building blocks from which you construct InDesign pages. Becoming familiar with creating and modifying individual objects, which is the focus of Chapters 5 and 6, is the first step in learning how to create publications with InDesign. The next step is to learn how to use several features that let you manipulate multiple objects at once and quickly adjust the relationships among the various objects that make up a page. A good InDesign user can handle individual objects one at a time with ease; a virtuoso user can simultaneously juggle several objects with equal ease.

Think of it this way: As an InDesign user, you are much like an architect. You begin with a blueprint — perhaps a rough, felt-tip pen sketch; maybe just a picture in your mind's eye — open a new document, and start construction. The settings you establish in the New Document dialog box (File ➪ New, or ⌘+N or Ctrl+N) — the page size, margin placement, column arrangement, and number of pages — serve as the foundation as you begin adding objects to your pages. You must then construct your building — or rather, your publication — using four basic components: text frames, picture frames, shapes, and lines. Each of those components can be tweaked and twisted in a nearly endless variety of ways while retaining basic properties. After all, a sheared and mirrored text frame with a purple dashed stroke, a gradient background, and magenta text outlined in cyan is still just a text frame.

As a publication evolves, plans invariably change: An advertiser pulls out and a magazine article needs to be stretched an extra half page by enlarging an InDesign-created illustration. A client loves his company's newsletter, but wants the front-page picture cropped differently. A new product is added to a catalog and half the pages reflow. If you build your documents soundly from the ground up and use the features covered in this chapter, you'll be prepared to handle even the most challenging page building — and rebuilding — tasks.

Stacking Objects

Each time you begin work on a new page, you start with a clean slate (unless the page is based on a master page, in which case the master objects act as the page's background; see Chapter 29 for more on master pages). Every time you add an object to a page — either by using any of InDesign's object-creation tools or via the Place command (File ➪ Place, or ⌘+D or Ctrl+D), the new object occupies a unique place in the page's object hierarchy, or *stacking order*.

The first object you place on a page is automatically positioned at the bottom of the stacking order; the next object is positioned one level higher than the first object (that is, on top of and in front of the back-most object); the next object is stacked one level higher; and so on for every object you add to the page. (It's not uncommon for a page to have several dozen or even several hundred objects.)

Tip   When building pages, always try to keep the number of objects to a minimum. For example, instead of putting a headline in one text frame and a subhead in a separate text frame directly below the one that contains the headline, use a single text frame. The leaner your pages, the leaner your documents. Lean documents save and print more quickly and are less problematic to modify than bloated documents.

Although each object occupies its own level, if the objects on a page don't overlap, and then the stacking order is not an issue. But some of the most interesting graphic effects you can achieve with InDesign involve arranging several overlapping objects, so it's important to be aware of the three-dimensional nature of a page's stacking order.

Because objects are added in back-to-front order, it makes sense to build your pages from back to front. For example, if you want to use a lightly tinted version of a scanned image as the background for a page, you would first place the image on the page, and then add other objects on top of or in front of the picture frame.

Changing the stacking order of objects on a page

In an ideal world, the first object you place on a page would remain forever the back-most, the last object would be the front-most, and every object in between — created in perfect order from back to front — would relate correctly with every other object. In this perfect world, you would never have to worry about moving objects backward or forward.

But the world is not perfect, and you may change your mind about what you want to achieve in your layout after you've already placed objects in it. To change an object's position in a page's stacking order, use the Arrange command (Object ➪ Arrange), which offers four choices: Bring Forward, Bring to Front, Send Backward, Send to Back. For example, you might want to see how a piece of text looks in front of an illustration. But, if you created the text frame before you created or placed the illustration, you'll have to move the text frame forward (or the illustration backward) in the stacking order.

Cross-Reference
In addition to letting you change the stacking order of objects on a page, InDesign also lets you create document-wide layers. Each layer contains a separate collection of stacked objects. For more information about using layers, see Chapter 30.

Steps: Changing the Stacking Order of Objects

1. Use any of the object creation tools to create four overlapping shapes, as shown in Figure 7-1. (The numbers in parenthesis indicate the order in which you should create the shapes.)

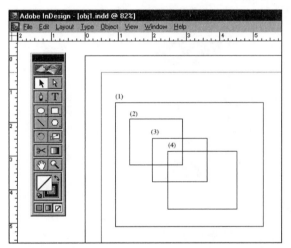

Figure 7-1: The first shape you create is the back-most, the second is one level above, and so on. In this example, the three smaller boxes partially overlap each other and they are all in front of the large box.

2. If it's not already displayed, open the Color pane by choosing Window ➪ Color or by pressing F6. (You'll use this pane to change the shade of each object so you can easily tell them apart.)

3. Click the Selection tool, click the last object you created, and then use the color tools in the Toolbox or the Color pane to fill the object with black. (See Chapter 6 for more information about applying strokes and fills to objects.)

4. Use the Color pane to fill each of the remaining boxes with a successively lighter tint of black, as shown in Figure 7-2. In the example, the remaining shapes are tinted with 75%, 50%, and 25% black, respectively.

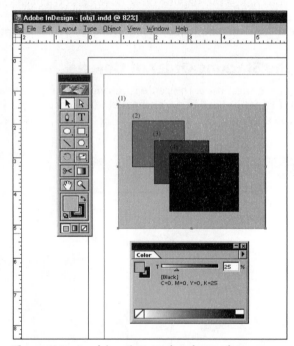

Figure 7-2: Applying tints to the shapes lets you see the stacking order of the four rectangles. Every InDesign object occupies one level in the stacking order.

5. Click the front-most shape (the last one you created), and then choose Object ⇨ Arrange ⇨ Send Backward or press ⌘+[or Ctrl+[. Notice that the Bring to Front and Bring Forward commands are not available. That's because you can't move the front-most object any farther forward in the stacking order.

6. Click the back-most shape (the first one you created), and then choose Object ⇨ Arrange ⇨ Bring Forward or press ⌘+] or Ctrl+]. When you bring the object forward, one of the objects becomes obscured.

7. Choose Object ⇨ Arrange ⇨ Bring to Front or press Shift+⌘+] or Ctrl+Shift+]. The smaller shapes are now obscured by the largest one.

8. Choose Object ⇨ Arrange ⇨ Send to Back or press Shift+⌘+[or Ctrl+Shift+[. The hidden objects are once again visible.

Tip To select an object that's hidden behind one or more other objects, hold down the ⌘ or Ctrl key, and then click anywhere within the area of the hidden object. The first click selects the top-most object; each successive click selects the next lowest object in the stacking order. When the bottom object is selected, the next click selects the top object. If you don't know where a hidden object is, you can simply click the object or objects in front of it, and then send the object(s) to the back.

Tip To select an object that's hidden behind one or more other objects without clicking, click the Selection tool, and then move the pointer over the hidden object. Hold down Option+⌘ or Ctrl+Alt and press [. The first time you press [, the top object is selected. Each successive press selects the next lowest object. If the bottom object is selected, the next click selects the top object as the top-to-bottom selection cycle begins to repeat itself.

Combining Objects into a Group

InDesign lets you combine several objects into a group. A group of objects behaves like a single object, which means that you can cut, copy, move, or modify all the objects in a group in a single operation. Groups have many uses. For example, you might create a group to:

✦ Combine several objects that make up an illustration so you can move, modify, copy, or scale all objects in a single operation.

✦ Keep a picture frame and its accompanying caption (text) frame together so that if you change your mind about their placement, you can reposition both objects at once.

✦ Combine several vertical lines that are used to separate the columns of a table so you can quickly change the stroke, color, length, and position of all lines.

Tip If you want to manipulate a group, choose the Selection tool, and then click any object in the group. The group's bounding box is displayed. Any transformation you perform is applied to all objects in the group. If you want to manipulate an object that's part of a group, select it using the Direct Selection tool.

Steps: Creating a Group

1. Select the Selection or Direct Selection tool.

2. Select all of the objects you want to include in your group. (See Chapter 6 for more information about selecting multiple objects.) Figure 7-3 shows several objects ready to be grouped.

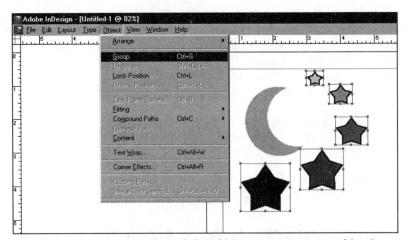

Figure 7-3: After you've selected the objects you want to combine into a group, choose Object ➪ Group or press ⌘+G or Ctrl+G. In this example, the five stars are being grouped.

3. Choose Object ➪ Group or press ⌘+G or Ctrl+G.

That's all there is to it. When you create a group from objects that do not occupy successive levels in the stacking order, the objects are shuffled as necessary so that the grouped objects are stacked on adjacent layers directly below the top-most object. If you create a group from objects on different layers, all objects are moved to the top layer and stacked in succession beneath the top-most object. (See Chapter 30 for more about layers.)

Tip You cannot create a group if some of the selected objects are locked and some are not locked. All selected objects must be locked or unlocked before you can group them. (Locking and unlocking objects is covered later in this chapter.)

Groups within groups

One nifty thing about groups is that you can include a group within a group. For example, all the objects in Figure 7-4 — five stars and two circles (a gray circle and a white circle form the moon) — have been grouped, making it easy to manipulate the whole illustration. But that's not all. The stars within the group are also a group. That is, first the stars were grouped together, and then the group of stars was grouped with the circles that form the moon to create a larger group. Grouping the stars makes it easy to change all of them at once, as shown in Figure 7-5. A group can contain as many levels of subgroups, or *nested* groups, as you want, but it's best to keep things as simple as you can. The more levels of nested groups you have within a group, the more work it is to ungroup the objects.

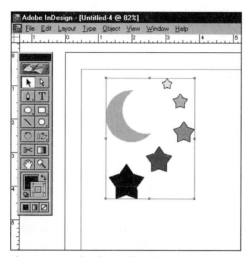

Figure 7-4: The bounding box indicates that all of the objects within have been grouped. What you can't tell from this illustration is that the five stars are a group within the larger group, which lets you move or modify all of them in a single operation, as shown in Figure 7-5.

Figure 7-5: The group selection tool (explained in the next section), lets you select a nested group. In this example, the nested group of stars was selected, and then a radial blend was applied to all of them.

Selecting objects within groups

The main reason you create groups in the first place is so you can delete, copy, move, or modify all the objects at once. But sometimes, you'll want to modify an object within a group. No problem. You don't have to ungroup objects to modify an individual object. InDesign offers several options for selecting objects — and nested groups — within groups. You can:

✦ Select an individual object by clicking it with the Direct Selection tool.

✦ Select the bounding box of an individual object by clicking it with the Direct Selection tool, and then switching to the Selection tool.

✦ Select multiple objects within a group by Shift+clicking each object with the Direct Selection tool.

✦ Select the bounding box of multiple objects within a group by Shift+clicking each object with the Direct Selection tool, and then switching to the Selection tool.

✦ Select a nested group by clicking any object within the nested group with the Direct Selection tool, and then holding down the Option or Alt key and clicking again on the object. Holding down the Option or Alt key in this situation temporarily accesses the Group Selection tool, indicated by a small plus sign (+) below and to the right of the arrow pointer.

Ungrouping

After creating a group, you may eventually decide that you want to return the objects to their original, ungrouped state. To do so, simply click any object in the group with the Selection tool, and then choose Object ➪ Ungroup or press Shift+⌘+G or Ctrl+Shift+G. If you ungroup a group that contains a group, the contained group is not affected. To ungroup this subgroup, you must select it, and then choose Ungroup again.

Nesting Objects within Frames

Not only does InDesign let you combine several objects into a group, you can also place an object within the boundaries of a frame. Just as a group that's embedded within a larger group is said to be a *nested* group, an object that's been placed within another frame is said to be a *nested* object. When you place an object within a frame, the containing frame acts as the cropping shape for the object within.

One of the most common uses of nested frames is for cropping imported graphics. When you place a graphic onto a page, the graphic is automatically placed within a frame. (You can also place a graphic within an existing frame.) You can reveal and hide different areas of the graphic by resizing or reshaping the container frame. Figure 7-6 shows an imported picture that's been placed within a circular frame. (For more information about importing and modifying pictures, see Part V.)

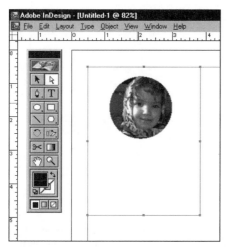

Figure 7-6: In this example, the rectangle displayed with handles indicates the border of a picture that's been placed into a round frame. Clicking the picture with the Direct Selection tool selects the picture rather than the round frame. To select the frame's bounding box instead of the picture, you would click the picture with the Direct Selection tool.

Nesting frames within other frames

As you can with groups, you can place a frame within a frame within a frame, and so on, to create as many nested levels as you want. The same caveat applies: Keep things as simple as possible to achieve the desired effect.

Steps: Nesting a Frame within a Frame

1. Use either the Selection tool or the Direct Selection tool to select the frame you want to nest within another frame.

2. Choose Edit ➪ Copy or press ⌘+C or Ctrl+C.

3. Select the frame into which you want to place the copied object, and then choose Edit ➪ Paste Into or press Option+⌘+V or Ctrl+Alt+V. Figure 7-7 shows a before/after example of a zigzag line that's been pasted into an oval frame, which serves as the cropping shape for the line.

Tip Selecting nested objects can be tricky. In general, the same selection techniques that work with groups work with nested frames. If you need to modify text within a nested — or grouped — text frame, simply click within the frame with the Type tool.

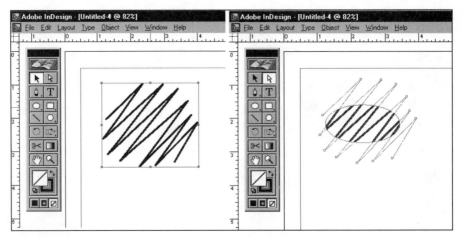

Figure 7-7: The zigzag line (left) was created with the Pen tool. It was then copied and pasted into (Edit ➪ Paste Into) an oval frame (right). Selecting the line with the Direct Selection tool shows the visible portion of the line within the oval cropping frame, as well as the parts of the line that are cropped.

Creating Inline Frames

In most cases, you'll want the objects you place on your pages to remain precisely where you put them. But sometimes you'll want to place objects relative to related text in such a way that the objects move when the text is edited. For example, if you're creating a product catalog that's essentially a continuous list of product descriptions and you want to include a picture with each description, you can paste pictures within the text to create inline graphic frames.

An inline frame is treated like a single character. If you insert or delete text that precedes an inline frame, the frame moves forward or backward along with the rest of the text that follows the inserted/deleted text. You have two ways to create an inline frame: Using the Paste command and using the Place command.

Caution

Inline graphics may interfere with line spacing in paragraphs with automatic leading. If the inline graphic is larger than the point size in use, the automatic leading value for that line is calculated from the graphic. This leads to inconsistent line spacing in the paragraph. To work around this, you can either apply a fixed amount of leading to all characters in the paragraph, adjust the size of inline graphics, place inline graphics at the beginning of a paragraph, or place inline graphics in their own paragraphs.

Creating an inline frame with the Paste command

If you want to create an inline frame from an object you've already created, all you have to do is copy—or cut—the object and then paste it into text as you would a piece of highlighted text. Here's how:

Steps: Using the Paste command to create an inline frame

1. Use the Selection tool to select the object you want to paste within text. Any type of object can be used: a line, an empty shape, a text or picture frame, even a group of objects.

2. Choose Edit ➪ Copy or press ⌘+C or Ctrl+C. If you don't need the original item, you can use the Cut command (Edit ➪ Cut; ⌘+X or Ctrl+X) instead of the Copy command. An object that you cut or copy remains on the clipboard until you cut or copy something else or you turn off your computer. If you intend to use the original object elsewhere, it's better to use the Copy command when creating an inline frame.

3. Select the Type tool (or press T), and then click within the text where you want to place the copied object. Make sure the cursor is flashing where you intend to place the inline frame.

4. Choose Edit ➪ Paste or press ⌘+V or Ctrl+V. Figure 7-8 shows a before/after example of an inline frame.

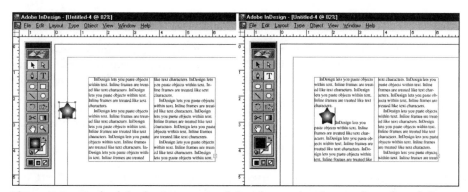

Figure 7-8: On the left, the frame containing the star has been selected, and then cut and pasted into the text. The result on the right is an inline frame of the star that is treated like a text character.

> **Tip**
>
> Inline graphics often work best when placed at the beginning of a paragraph. If you place an inline frame within text to which automatic leading has been applied, the resulting line spacing can be inconsistent. To fix this problem, you can resize the inline frame.

Creating an inline frame with the Place command

In addition to using the Paste command to create an inline frame from an existing object, you can use the Place command to create an inline graphic from an external picture file.

Steps: Using the Place Command to Create an Inline Frame

1. Select the Type tool (or press T), and then click within a text frame to establish the insertion point.

2. Choose File ➪ Place or press ⌘+D or Ctrl+D.

3. Locate and select the graphics file you want to place within the text, and then click Choose or Open.

After you create an inline frame, you can adjust its position vertically or horizontally. To move an inline frame vertically:

✦ Use the Type tool to highlight the inline frame as you would highlight an individual text character. In the Character pane, enter a positive value in the Baseline Shift field to move the inline frame up; enter a negative value to move the frame down.

✦ Use the Selection tool or Direct Selection tool to select the inline frame, and then drag the frame up or down.

To move an inline frame horizontally:

✦ With the Type tool selected, click between the inline frame and the character that precedes it, and then use the kerning controls in the Character pane to enlarge or reduce the space between the inline frame and the preceding character.

Tip   You can use the transform tools (Rotate, Scale, and Shear) and the Transform pane to modify an inline frame the same way you modify any other frame.

Tip   To delete an inline frame, you can select it, and then choose Edit ➪ Clear or Edit ➪ Cut, or you can position the cursor next to it and then press the Delete or Backspace key.

Locking Objects

If you're certain that you want a particular object to remain where it is, you can use Object ➪ Lock Position, or ⌘+L or Ctrl+L, to prevent the object from being moved. Generally, you'll want to lock repeating elements such as headers, footers, folios, and page numbers so that they're not accidentally moved. (Such repeating elements are usually placed on a master page; you can lock objects on master pages, too.) A locked object can't be moved whether you click and drag it with the mouse or change the values in the X and Y fields in the Transform pane. Not only can you *not* move a locked object, you can't delete one, either. However, you can change other attributes of a locked object, including its stroke and fill.

To unlock an object, use Object ➪ Unlock Position, or Option+⌘+L or Ctrl+Alt+L.

Summary

Most InDesign pages are made up of several objects. Each object occupies a separate level in a page's stacking order. The first object you place on a page occupies the bottom layer, and each new object you create or place occupies a new layer that's on top of all other layers. You can change a page's stacking order by moving individual items forward or backward in the stacking order. InDesign also provides options for working with several objects at once. When multiple items are selected, you can combine them into a group that behaves like a single item. You can also place an object within a frame to create a nested object, and you can insert objects within a text thread to create inline frames that flow with the surrounding text.

✦　　✦　　✦

Time-Saving Techniques

One of the advantages of using a computer for publishing is that it can do a lot of the work for you. That's particularly true of detail-oriented work or repetitive work. InDesign has several features that save you time by handling repetitive, exacting chores for you. For example, if you're creating a checkerboard pattern as a page background, there's no need to create, modify, and place 20 or more frames by hand. You might start with one or two, and then automatically duplicate and distribute the copies on your page.

Creating Copies of Objects

Once you've created something — a simple, rectangular frame or a complicated graphic made up of several dozen objects — InDesign makes it easy to reuse the original. Here are your options:

+ **Copy and Paste commands (Edit ⇨ Copy, or ⌘+C or Ctrl+C; Edit ⇨ Paste, or ⌘+V or Ctrl+V).** This is a good choice if you have to copy something from one page to another or from one document to another, but if you need a duplicate on the same page as the original, the Duplicate command is quicker.

+ **Duplicate command (Edit ⇨ Duplicate, or Option+⌘+D or Ctrl+Alt+D).** When you duplicate an object, the copy is placed one pica below and to the right of the original.

+ **Manual cloning.** When you click and drag an object while holding down the Option or Alt key, a copy of the selected object is created. If you're a click-and-dragger, you may prefer this manual method to the Duplicate command.

+ **Cloning with the Transform tools.** If you hold down the Option or Alt key while using any of the Transform tools (Rotate, Shear, and Scale), a copy of the selected object is transformed. The selected item remains unchanged.

✦ **Transform pane cloning.** If you hold down the Option or Alt key when you exit from the Transform pane (by pressing Return or Enter or releasing the mouse after choosing an option from a menu), the transformation is applied to a copy of the selected item.

✦ **Step and Repeat command (Edit ➪ Step and Repeat, or Shift+⌘+V or Ctrl+Shift+V).** Think of the Step and Repeat dialog box, shown in Figure 8-1, as the Duplicate command on steroids. It lets you create multiple duplicates of selected objects and specify the horizontal and vertical offset of the duplicates. This command is handy if you have to create, for example, a vertical and/or horizontal grid of lines on a page. Simply draw a horizontal line at the top of the page or a vertical line along the left edge of the page. With the line selected, use the Step and Repeat command to place — and evenly space — as many additional lines as you need.

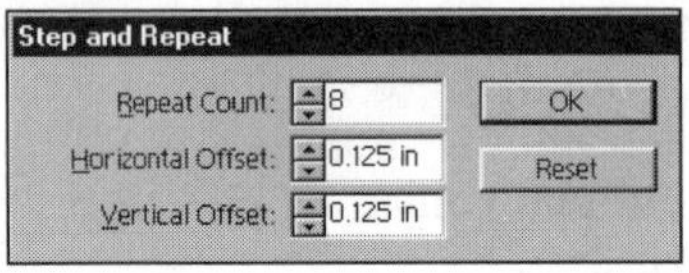

Figure 8-1: The Step and Repeat dialog box.

Figure 8-2 shows a typical task that's easily handled with the Step and Repeat command. First, the top row was built by creating three copies of the original with an inch of space between each duplicate; the second row was created by step-and-repeating three squares in the top row; and finally the bottom six rows were created by step-and-repeating the top two rows. Voilà!

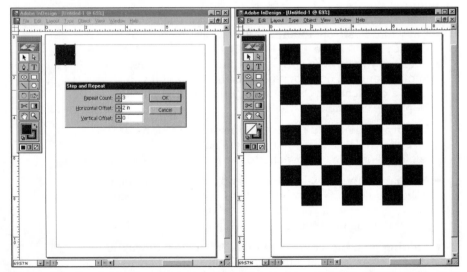

Figure 8-2: Starting with a single one-inch square shape (left), the finished checkerboard (right) was created with three trips to the Step and Repeat dialog box.

Tip If you need to use an object or a group of objects repeatedly, it's a good idea to store them in a library. For example, if you've used InDesign to create a logo or a house ad, copy the objects into a library. Once you place something in a library, you can drag-copy as many clones as you want into any document. For more information about using libraries, see Chapter 29.

Copying Objects between Documents

At times you'll want to use something you've created in one InDesign document in another document. For example, maybe an ad that ran in last month's newsletter is needed again for this month's edition. Or perhaps you created a small illustration for an ad that you want to use in a companion brochure. InDesign offers several options for moving objects between documents. You can:

✦ Open the document that contains the objects you want to copy, select the objects, and then copy them to the clipboard with Edit ⇨ Copy, or ⌘+C or Ctrl+C. Open the target document and use Edit ⇨ Paste, or ⌘+V or Ctrl+V, to place the copied objects.

✦ If you need to use the object(s) in more than one document, you can copy them into a library, which lets you place as many copies as you want in any document.

✦ You can open the source document (the one that contains the objects) and the target document and drag-copy the object(s) from the source document to the target document. (Use Window ⇨ Tile to display both document windows side by side.) Figure 8-3 shows how to do this.

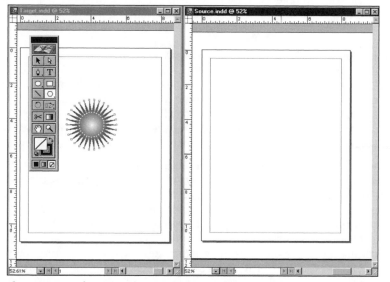

Figure 8-3: When two documents are open and visible, you can drag items between the documents. In this example, the starburst shape in the source document is ready to be drag-copied to the target document (right).

Aligning and Distributing Objects

InDesign lets you align and distribute objects, saving you the hassle of manually moving and placing each element, or figuring out the correct locations in the Transform pane to do so. The Align pane is where InDesign offers these time-saving capabilities.

The Align pane (Window ➪ Align, or F8), shown in Figure 8-4, has several buttons, described in the callouts, that let you manipulate the relative position of multiple objects in two ways.

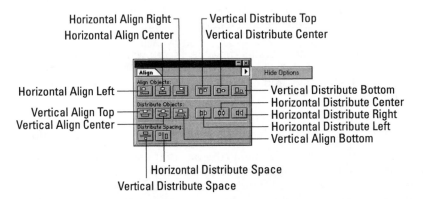

Figure 8-4: The Align pane contains 14 buttons that let you control the alignment and space between selected objects. If the two Distribute Spacing buttons are not displayed at the bottom of the palette, choose Show Options from the palette menu.

You can manipulate objects in the following ways:

✦ Line up objects along a horizontal or vertical axis. For example, if you've randomly placed several small graphic frames onto a page, you could use the alignment buttons in the Align pane to align them neatly — either horizontally or vertically. Figure 8-5 shows a before/after example of objects aligned with the Align pane.

✦ Distribute space evenly between objects along a horizontal or vertical axis. Here's a typical problem that's easily solved by using this feature: You've carefully placed five small pictures on a page so that the top edges are aligned across the page and equal space separates each picture. Then you find out one of the pictures needs to be cut. After deleting the unneeded picture, you could use the Align pane to redistribute the space between the remaining pictures so that they're again equally spaced. Figure 8-6 shows a before/after example of the Align pane's Distribute Spacing capability.

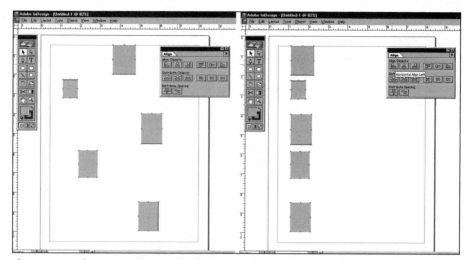

Figure 8-5: The rectangles on the left were aligned along the left edge of the left-most object by clicking the Horizontal Align Left button in the Align pane. The result of the alignment operation is shown on the right.

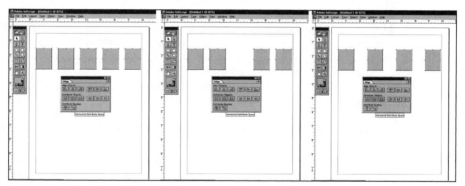

Figure 8-6: The five objects (left) are equally spaced. Deleting an object (center) and then selecting the remaining objects and clicking the Horizontal Distribute Space button in the Align pane repositions the center two objects so that the spaces between the objects are again equal (right).

Tip

The Align buttons don't work with objects that have been locked with the Lock Position command (Object ➪ Lock Position, or ⌘+L or Ctrl+L). If you need to align a locked object, you must first unlock it (Object ➪ Unlock Position, or Option+⌘+ L or Ctrl+Alt+L).

When you click a button in the Align pane, selected objects are repositioned in the most logical manner. For example, if you click the Horizontal Align Left button, the selected objects are moved horizontally (to the left in this case) so that the left edge of each object is aligned with the left edge of the left-most object. Along the same lines, if you click the Vertical Distribute Center button, the selected objects are moved vertically to create an equal amount of space between the vertical center of each object.

> **Tip**
>
> Sometimes the result of clicking a button in the Align pane isn't what you anticipate—or want. If this happens, simply choose Edit ➪ Undo or press ⌘+Z or Ctrl+Z and try another button. Another way to rectify unwanted results is to try clicking the corresponding horizontal/vertical spacing button. Spacing can appear uneven if you click the horizontal/vertical distribute buttons when objects of various sizes are selected.

Positioning Objects Precisely with Guides

Just as carpenters often use chalk lines to make sure things are straight when putting up the framework of a house, an InDesign user can use guidelines and gridlines to help achieve precise object placement and alignment when building documents. InDesign lets you show or hide three kinds of guides: user-created vertical and horizontal guidelines, document gridlines, and baseline gridlines. You can tell InDesign to automatically snap object edges to guidelines and gridlines when you create, resize, or move an object within a user-specified distance. (For more about creating and using guidelines and grids, see Chapter 29.)

Here's a quick rundown of what you can do in the way of creating, displaying, and snapping objects to guidelines and gridlines.

You can create horizontal and vertical guidelines whenever you want by clicking either the horizontal or vertical ruler and dragging the pointer onto the page or pasteboard. Choosing View ➪ Show Guides or ⌘+; or Ctrl+; turns guides on. The menu option name then changes to Hide Guides, so you can toggle guides on and off using the same shortcut. When guidelines are displayed and Snap to Guides (View ➪ Snap to Guides, or Shift+⌘+; or Ctrl+Shift+;) is checked, an object edge will snap to a guideline when you create, resize, or move the object within the number of pixels specified in the Snap to Zone preference (File ➪ Preferences ➪ Guides, or ⌘+K or Ctrl+K).

> **Note**
>
> When Snap to Guides is checked in the View menu, guidelines must be displayed (View ➪ Show Guides, or ⌘+; or Ctrl+;) for objects to snap to them. However, when Snap to Document Grid is checked, objects will snap to document gridlines (when Snap to Document Grid is checked) and to baseline gridlines (when Snap to Guides is checked) regardless of whether the document grid or the baseline grid is displayed.

All documents include a document-wide grid of vertical and horizontal lines that you can use for creating, resizing, and positioning objects. The View ➪ Show

Document Grid and Show ➪ Hide Document Grid commands, or ⌘+' or Ctrl+', toggle document grid display on and off. When displayed, the document grid looks much like graph paper. When guidelines are displayed and View ➪ Snap to Document Grid, or Shift+⌘+' or Ctrl+Shift+', is checked, an object edge will snap to a document gridline when you create, resize, or move the object within the number of pixels specified in the Snap to Zone preference (File ➪ Preferences ➪ Guides, or ⌘+K or Ctrl+K).

Tip   If you want to align objects with text baselines and text baselines with the baseline grid, use the Grids preferences (File ➪ Preferences ➪ Grids, or ⌘+K or Ctrl+K) to specify the same vertical spacing for the Document Grid as for the Baseline Grid. For example, specify an Increment Every value of 1 pica in the Baseline Grid area, and specify a Subdivisions value of 6 in the Document Grid area.

In addition to the document grid, all documents have a built-in baseline grid that represents the leading increments of body text. The View ➪ Show Baseline Grid and View ➪ Hide Baseline Grid commands, or Option+⌘+' or Ctrl+Alt+', toggle the baseline grid display on and off. When the baseline grid is displayed and Snap to Guides is checked, an object edge will snap to a baseline gridline when you create, resize, or move the object within the number of pixels specified in the Snap to Zone preference (File ➪ Preferences ➪ Guides, or ⌘+K or Ctrl+K). You can use the Align to Baseline Grid option in a paragraph style or via the Paragraph pane (Type ➪ Paragraph) to lock the baselines of text in selected paragraphs to baseline gridlines, and you can modify a document's baseline grid via the Grids pane in the Preferences dialog box (File ➪ Preferences ➪ Grids, or ⌘+K or Ctrl+K).

Tip   In addition to aligning objects with guides, you can also use the arrow keys to nudge items when precise positioning is required. This method works well when you're positioning an object relative to another object rather than aligning the object with a gridline. Each press of an arrow key moves the selected objects one point. If you hold down the Shift key when nudging, the increment is 10 points. You can set alternative nudge settings via the Cursor Key field after selecting File ➪ Preferences ➪ Units & Increments, or ⌘+K or Ctrl+K. Holding the Shift key when nudging moves the selected object(s) 10 increments of whatever Cursor Key is set to.

Summary

When it comes to working with the objects you've placed on a page, InDesign provides several time-saving features. You can create a single copy of any object using the Copy and Paste commands (Edit menu), the Duplicate command (Edit menu), or by Option+dragging or Alt+dragging a clone of the original. The Step and Repeat command (Edit menu) — the Duplicate command on steroids — lets you create multiple copies of objects and position the copies relative to the originals. The Align pane (Window ➪ Align) lets you align multiple objects and control the amount of space between them, while vertical and horizontal ruler guides help you accurately position and align items.

✦   ✦   ✦

Text Fundamentals

The chapters in Part III show you how to prepare, import, and format your text. First, you need to understand how to prepare your text. Today's word processors are very powerful, and many people are tempted to use their many capabilities in files destined for InDesign. Don't be. Today's word processors do too much for files destined for a page-layout program, and the key to effective preparation is to do just the basics in your word processor, as **Chapter 9** explains.

With your text ready to use, you need to bring it into InDesign, as well as enter some text directly into InDesign. **Chapter 10** shows you how to do so, as well as how to edit text, check its spelling, and set its hyphenation rules. **Chapter 11** explains how InDesign flows text from page to page and column to column, and how you can control the way text flows.

With your text in place, you'll want to apply the appropriate formatting—fonts, size, justification, alignment, and so on—to it. **Chapters 12 and 13** show how to format your text so it takes on the visual character you want in your layout. A special type of formatting involves tabs, which let you align text to specific locations. These are particularly handy for creating tables and charts, as **Chapter 14** explains.

Finally, you'll want to automate your text formatting wherever possible. That's what styles do, and **Chapter 15** explains how to create styles.

Preparing Text Files for Import

◆ ◆ ◆ ◆

CHAPTER 20

In This Chapter

Determining which formatting tasks to do in InDesign

Working with files across platforms

Preparing files for import from word processors and spreadsheets

Working with special file formats

◆ ◆ ◆ ◆

You can import text into your InDesign documents in several ways. InDesign is particularly adept at importing documents created in popular Macintosh and Windows formats. And through the use of the Macintosh and Windows clipboards (copy and paste), you can import file formats — to a limited degree — that are not directly supported by InDesign.

Determining Where to Format Documents

InDesign import capabilities may tempt you to do a lot of your text formatting outside the program; however, it's not always wise to do so. Here are some reasons why you *shouldn't* work outside the program:

◆ A word processor's styles won't match all InDesign typographic features, so it's often not worthwhile to do extensive formatting in your word processor. This is particularly true of layout-oriented formatting. Multiple columns and page numbers, for example, will be of a much higher standard in your final InDesign document than you could hope to create in a word processor. After all, even the sophisticated formatting features in today's word processors don't begin to approach those needed for true publishing.

✦ Similarly, formatting tables in your word processor or spreadsheet is typically a wasted effort because you have to re-create the tables using InDesign tab settings (see Chapter 14). If you turn your spreadsheet or chart into a graphic before importing it, you cannot edit the data. Nor can you resize the picture to fit a changing layout without winding up with different-size numbers among at least some charts — a definite no-no.

The bottom line is to use InDesign for your layout and complex text formatting (fonts, leading, and hyphenation). Use your word processor for basic text editing, style-sheet assignments (identifying headlines, body copy, and so forth), and basic character formatting (boldface, italics, and other meaning-oriented formatting).

Working with Files Across Platforms

It's increasingly common for people in publishing to work in a cross-platform (Mac and Windows) environment. Even if you do all your InDesign work on one platform, chances are high that you'll receive files created on the other platform. (Most text editing is done on PCs, while most graphics and publishing work is done on the Mac, for example.)

Even with the improved compatibility between Macs and PCs (mostly thanks to additions to the Mac OS that makes it easier to share files with PCs), you may still encounter some trip-ups in dealing with something as simple as file names when sharing files across platforms.

Both Windows and the Mac use icons to show you (and tell programs) what format a file is in. But how those icons are created differ between the two platforms, and when you move files from one platform to another, you can easily lose those icons.

On the Mac, a set of hidden files tells the Mac what kind of format the file has. These files have two pieces of key data: the *creator ID* for the program that created the file and the *type ID* for the type of format the file is in. When you save a file on the Mac, this hidden information is created automatically.

In Windows, the icon is based on the file name extension at the end of the file, such as .DOC in the file name *How to Import.doc*. (Note that the capitalization doesn't matter: .DOC is the same as .Doc is the same as .doc.) For InDesign, the extension is .INDD for documents and .INDT for templates. But by default, Windows hides the extension from users, so you may not realize that all file names have these extensions after the name. You can see them in DOS, but in Windows you have to disable the feature that hides them. You do that by using View ➪ Options and then select the View tab to get the pane shown in the following figure. (You have to have a disk or folder open to have the View menu.)

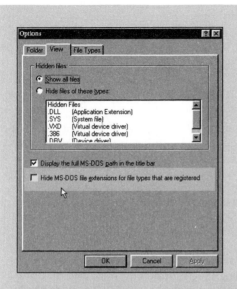

On the Mac, InDesign doesn't usually need those icons — it displays icon-less files with a PC icon (shown below) in its Place and Open dialog boxes, and let you import them, as long as what's in those files is in a format supported by InDesign.

In Windows, the PC icon and file extension are important for InDesign, because InDesign filters out files with icons and extensions it doesn't recognize. Fortunately, you can force it to see all files by making sure that All Files is the selected option for the Files of Type pop-up menu for the Open and Place dialog boxes.

The easiest way to keep files working on both platforms is to use the PC extension on all file names, even those created on the Mac. That way, you're assured that Windows users will see the correct icon (at least for formats that exist on both Windows and the Mac — some formats have no PC equivalents and thus no PC extension.) Macintosh users will have to remember to look at files that have the PC icon.

Some programs automatically map the Mac creator and type IDs to the PC extensions and vice versa, as described in Chapter 38, so files always look like native ones no matter where they were created. If you move files back and forth a lot, these programs are a wise investment.

Importing Text Files

What preparation do you possibly need to do for your word processor files? They should just load into InDesign as-is, right? Not necessarily, even if your word processor supports one of the InDesign text-import formats. Actually, the key to preparing text files is to not *over*-prepare them.

Most of today's major word processors include basic graphics and layout features to help users format single-document publications. Avoid using these features in files you intend to bring into InDesign. Do your sophisticated formatting in InDesign — that's one of the reasons you invested in such a powerful tool. This approach also enables you to do formatting in the context of your layout, rather than in a vacuum. Much of the graphics and layout formatting you do in a word processor is all for naught anyway because such nontextual formatting does not import into InDesign. Remember, you're importing text, not documents.

Tip Limit your word processor formatting to the type of formatting that enhances reader understanding or conveys meaning. Such formatting may include using italic and boldface to emphasize a word, for example, or using styles to set head-lines and bylines in different sizes and typefaces. (See Chapter 15 for tips on using styles in word processor text.) Let your editors focus on the words; leave presen-tation tasks to your layout artists.

Translating text files

One type of file preparation you may need to do is to translate text files into formats supported by InDesign. Table 9-1 shows what popular text formats are supported by InDesign.

<table>
<tr><td colspan="4">Table 9-1
Text Formats Supported by InDesign</td></tr>
<tr><td></td><td>*PC File Name Extension*</td><td>*Macintosh InDesign*</td><td>*Windows InDesign*</td></tr>
<tr><td colspan="4">**Macintosh Word Processors**</td></tr>
<tr><td>AppleWorks 5.0*</td><td>.CWK</td><td>▲</td><td>▲</td></tr>
<tr><td>ASCII (text-only)</td><td>.TXT</td><td>■</td><td>■</td></tr>
<tr><td>ClarisWorks 4.04/5.0*</td><td>.CWK</td><td>▲</td><td>▲</td></tr>
<tr><td>HTML</td><td>.HTM</td><td>❑</td><td>❑</td></tr>
<tr><td>MacWrite II</td><td>none</td><td>❑</td><td>❑</td></tr>
<tr><td>MacWrite Pro</td><td>none</td><td>❑</td><td>❑</td></tr>
<tr><td>Microsoft Word 4.0/5.x/6.0/98 (7.0)</td><td>.DOC</td><td>■</td><td>■</td></tr>
</table>

	PC File Name Extension	Macintosh InDesign	Windows InDesign
Macintosh Word Processors			
Microsoft Word 3.0	.DOC	❑	❑
Microsoft Works 2.0/3.0	none	❑	❑
Nisus Writer 5.1	none	❑	❑
Rich Text Format (RTF)	.RTF	■	■
WriteNow 3.0/4.0	none	▲	▲
WordPerfect 3.x	.WP3	▲	▲
WordPerfect 2.x	.WPD	❑	❑
Windows Word Processors			
Ami Pro 2.0/3.0	.SAM	❑	❑
AppleWorks 5.0*	.CWK	▲	▲
ASCII (text-only)	.TXT	■	■
ClarisWorks 4.04/5.0*	.CWK	▲	▲
HTML	.HTM	❑	❑
Microsoft Word 2000	.DOC	▲	▲
Microsoft Word 6.0/95 (7.0)/97 (8.0)	.DOC	■	■
Microsoft Word 2.0	.DOC	❑	❑
Rich Text Format (RTF)	.RTF	■	■
WordPerfect 6.x/7.0/8.0/2000	.WPD	■	■
WordPerfect 4.x/5.x	.WP	❑	❑
Word Pro 96 (7.0)/97 (8.0)/9.0	.LWP	▲	▲
WordStar	.WS	❑	❑
XyWrite III Plus	.XY	❑	❑

■ = Imports directly into InDesign.

❑ = Cannot import into or export for use in InDesign.

▲ = Can export or save as a format supported by InDesign.

* AppleWorks 5.0 and ClarisWorks 5.0 are the same format; the name was changed in 1998.

The following tips can help you work with popular word processors:

✦ Be sure that you installed the necessary import filters when you installed InDesign — you may have trouble importing a supported format because the filter was not installed. Appendix A shows you how to do this.

✦ Look for new and updated filters on Adobe's Web site at www.adobe.com.

✦ If your text files come from a word processor that InDesign doesn't support, see if your word processor can save as or export to a file format that InDesign does support.

Note

InDesign supports ASCII (text-only) files, however you should avoid using them. ASCII files cannot handle any character formatting, so you must do a lot of clean-up work in InDesign. Although programs must continue to support ASCII text because it is the only universally supported format, use ASCII as a last resort. A better option, if available in your word processor, is to export to Rich Text Format (RTF), a Microsoft file format it has promoted with some success as a universal text-file format.

Preserving special features in text files

Today's word processors let you do much more than enter and edit text. You can also create special characters, tables, headers and footers, and other document elements. Some of these features work when imported into a publishing program, but others don't. Table 9-2 shows which character formatting is preserved for the two most popular word processors: Word and WordPerfect.

Table 9-2 Character Formatting Imported by InDesign		
	Macintosh Word 6.0/98 (8.0)	**Windows Word 6.0/95 (7.0)/97 (8.0)**	**WordPerfect 6.x/ 7.0/8.0/2000**
Character Formatting *			
All caps	■	■	NA
Boldface	■	■	■
Color	■	■	■
Condense/expand	■	■	NA
Double strikethrough	❏ [1]	❏ [1]	NA
Double underline	❏ [2]	❏ [2]	❏ [2]
Emboss	❏ [3]	❏ [3]	NA
Engrave	❏ [3]	❏ [3]	NA
Font change	■	■	■
Hidden	❏ [4]	❏ [4]	❏ [4]
Italics	■	■	■
Outline	■	■	❏

	Macintosh Word 6.0/98 (8.0)	Windows Word 6.0/95 (7.0)/97 (8.0)	WordPerfect 6.x/ 7.0/8.0/2000
Character Formatting *			
Point size	■	■	■
Shadow	❏	❏	❏
Small caps	■	■	■
Strikethrough	■	■	■
Subscript	■	■	■
Superscript	■	■	■
Underline	■	■	■
Word-only underline	❏ [2]	❏ [2]	❏ [2]
Other Formatting *			
Annotations/comments	❏	❏	❏
Bulleted lists	■	■	■
Drop caps	■	■	❏
Footnotes	■ [5]	■ [5]	■ [5]
Indents	■	■	■
Numbered lists	■	■	■
Page breaks	❏	❏	❏
Pictures	■	■	❏
Redlining/revisions	■ [6]	■ [6]	❏
Section breaks	❏	❏	❏
Special characters	■	■	■
Subscribed/OLE items	❏	❏	❏
Tables	❏ [7]	❏ [7]	❏ [7]

* Not all formatting listed may be available in every supported version of Word and WordPerfect.

■ = Can import into InDesign.

❏ = Cannot import into InDesign or can import only with severe restrictions.

NA = Not available in this program.

[1] Double strikethrough is converted to single strikethrough.

[2] All underlining is converted to single underlines.

[3] Embossed and engraved text is made into paper color (usually white).

[4] Hidden text is deleted.

[5] Footnote text is placed at end of text.

[6] Revisions are converted to underline for additions and strikethrough for deletions.

[7] Table text is converted to tabbed text.

Tables

Word processors have developed very capable table editors, letting you format tabular information quickly and easily—and often rivaling dedicated spreadsheet programs. Unfortunately, page layout software has not kept up, and the result is that you can usually do more with tables in your word processor than in a page layout program. Therefore, it's best to use simple tabs between items in a table in your word processor and to use InDesign to do the actual formatting to ensure column alignment and so forth.

Note

When you use your word processor's table tools, don't expect much to survive when the file is imported into InDesign. Your text will be retained, and InDesign will place tabs between text from the table's cells, so you can set up tab stops in InDesign to duplicate the original text's cell spacing. You'll also keep basic formatting such as font, size, color, and attributes such as boldface and italics. But most cell formatting will be lost—such as borders and shading. In some cases, InDesign tries to replicate the original table's cell borders, but we've found that it usually cannot do so anywhere near accurately. So expect to redo most of your table formatting within InDesign. (See Chapter 14 for details.)

Tip

There's a slightly better way to bring tables into InDesign, and that's by importing them from Microsoft Excel. InDesign reads versions 95 (5.0) and 97/98 (6.0) of the popular spreadsheet—formats other spreadsheet programs can also save their own files as. Although InDesign ignores text and cell formatting (font, point size, cell borders, cell shading, and so forth), InDesign does do a much better job of replicating your Excel table's column spacing and alignment than it does when converting a word processor file's tables.

Headers and footers

Headers and footers are a layout issue, not a text issue, so you have no reason to include these elements in your word processor document if it's destined for InDesign. Because page numbers will change based on your InDesign layout, there's no point in putting the headers and footers in your word processor document anyway. Note that if you do use them, they will not import into InDesign. Chapter 31 explains how to add these elements to your layout.

Footnotes and endnotes

If you use a word processor's footnote or endnote feature and import the text file, the notes are placed at the end of the imported text. The superscripted numerals or characters in the notes usually translate properly.

Hyperlinks

Word processors such as Word and WordPerfect let you include hyperlinks in their text, so when you export to HTML or PDF format, the reader can click the link and jump to a Web page or to another PDF file. When you import text files with such hyperlinks, InDesign retains their visual formatting — hyperlinks usually display as blue underlined text — but that's all. The actual link is not retained, so any HTML or PDF files you create from InDesign will simply show the blue underlined text but not let readers click them to jump elsewhere.

Therefore, it's best to not use the hyperlinking feature in your word processor. To turn it off in Word, use Tools ➪ AutoCorrect, and then choose the AutoFormat as You Type pane and uncheck the Internet and network paths with hyperlinks option. To turn it off in WordPerfect, use Tools ➪ QuickCorrect, and then choose the QuickLinks pane and uncheck the Format words as hyperlinks when you type them option.

Inline graphics

Modern word processors typically support inline graphics, enabling you to import a picture into your word processor document and embed it in text. Word and WordPerfect, for example, both let you import graphics, and InDesign, in turn, can import the graphics with your text. But graphics embedded in your word processor document via Publish and Subscribe or via OLE will *not* import into InDesign.

Inline graphics will import as their preview images, not as the original formats. This means that in most cases you'll get a lower-resolution version in your InDesign layout.

Tip Despite their limitations, the use of inline graphics in your word processor can be helpful when putting together an InDesign document: Use the inline graphics whose previews are imported into InDesign as placeholders so that the layout artist knows you have embedded graphics. He or she can then replace the previews with the better-quality originals. If you find yourself using several graphics as characters (such as a company icon used as a bullet), use a font-creation program such as Macromedia's Fontographer to create a symbol typeface with those graphics. Then both your word processor and layout documents can use the same, high-quality versions.

Using Special Characters

The Mac and Windows both have built-in support for special characters, such as symbols, accented characters, and non-English letters. You have several ways to access these characters:

✦ On both platforms, using keyboard shortcuts (see Chapter 18).

✦ On the Mac, using Apple's KeyCaps program, which comes with the Mac OS and is accessible via the Apple menu. The following figure shows the KeyCaps utility. The two sets of special characters are found by holding Option and Option+Shift (each results in a different set). Some fonts also have symbols accessible by using the Control key. Use the Fonts menu, as shown in the figure, to change fonts in KeyCaps, in case a symbol you want is available in a font other than the current one in use.

Apple's KeyCaps

✦ On the Mac, using a shareware utility such as Günther Blaschek's PopChar Pro control panel. The following figure shows PopChar Pro. Notice how the keyboard shortcut for each special character is shown at the upper-right corner as a character is highlighted.

PopChar Pro

✦ On Windows, using the Character Map utility that comes with Windows. The following figure shows the program. Just as KeyCaps is usually installed in the Mac's Apple menu, Character Map is usually installed in the Windows Start menu.

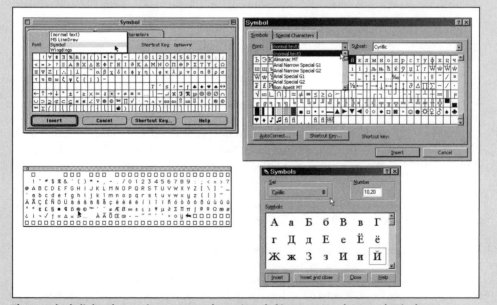

Window's Character Map

✦ On both platforms, you can use a word processor's own feature for special-character access. Microsoft Word, for example, has such an option via Insert ⇨ Symbol or via the toolbar (if you added this command to your toolbar, look for the button with the Ω character). WordPerfect has a similar dialog box accessed via Insert ⇨ Symbols (Mac) or Insert ⇨ Character (Windows), as shown in the following figure. (InDesign has its own dialog box like this for when you're adding symbols to your text from within your layout; access it via Type ⇨ Insert Character.)

The symbol dialog boxes in Mac Word 6.0 (top left), Mac Word 98 and Windows Word 95 and 97 (top right), WordPerfect 3.5 for Mac (bottom left), and WordPerfect 6.0 through 8.0 for Windows (bottom right).

Continued

(continued)

Note that the Windows and Mac versions of the symbol features often act differently: Windows Word 6.0 and 95 let you get symbols from any font, while the Mac's version 6.0 does not. (But Word 97 on Windows and Word 98 on the Mac do behave the same way, letting you access symbols from any font.) Likewise, WordPerfect 6.0 through 8.0 for Windows has its own symbol fonts, while Mac WordPerfect 3.x uses standard Mac fonts.

Not all fonts may have all special characters available. Typically, fonts from major type foundries such as Adobe and Bitstream have all the characters in each font, but custom-made fonts and those from other foundries may use different characters or have fewer. Also, fonts translated from Windows to the Mac, or vice versa, through a program such as Macromedia's Fontographer will likely have special characters in different locations than a native Mac or Windows font; Windows fonts generally have fewer special characters in the font.

Avoiding text-file pitfalls

Sometimes, issues not related to the contents of a word processor file can affect how files are imported into InDesign.

Fast save

Several programs (notably Microsoft Word) offer a fast-save feature, which adds information to the end of a word processor document. The added information notes which text has been added and deleted and where the changes occurred. You can use this feature to save time because the program doesn't have to write the entire document to disk when you save the file. When you use the fast-save feature, however, text-import into publishing programs — including InDesign — becomes problematic. We suggest that you turn off fast save, at least for files you import into InDesign. With today's speedy hard drives, the time you gain by using fast save is barely noticeable, anyway. The vast majority of file corruption problems and bugs in Word are related to the fast-save feature and that its use makes file recovery in the event of a crash problematic at best.

Figure 9-1 shows the Options dialog box for Word 97/98 (Tools ➪ Options ➪ Save); Word 6 and Word 95 use the same dialog box. You turn fast save on and off in this dialog box. You don't need to worry about whether fast save is enabled if you use Save As or Export options to save the file either in a format other than the word processor's native format or to a different name or location.

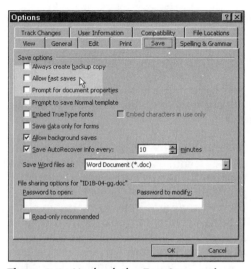

Figure 9-1: Uncheck the Fast Save option in Microsoft Word to ensure that InDesign can accurately import your text files.

Software versions

Pay attention to the version number of the word processor you use. This caution may seem obvious, but the issue still trips up a lot of people. Usually, old versions (two or more revisions old) or new versions (newer than the publishing or other importing program) cause import problems. The import filters either no longer recognize the old format (something has to go to make room for new formats) or were written before the new version of the word processor was released. Refer back to Table 9-1 to see which text formats and versions are compatible with InDesign.

Using Tagged Text

InDesign offers a file format of its own: Adobe InDesign Tagged Text. Tagged Text actually is ASCII (text-only) text that contains embedded codes to tell InDesign which formatting to apply. You embed these codes, which are similar to macros, as you create files in your word processor.

InDesign also imports the Tagged Text format from Adobe PageMaker 6.5 and the XPress Tags format used by version 3.*x* of the rival QuarkXPress. XPress Tags is similar to Adobe InDesign Tagged Text in that it is ASCII text with embedded codes that describe text and layout formatting.

PageMaker imports word processor files that have tagged text. Thus, you can use the word processor's boldface as well as tags at the same time, saving the file in a format such as Word, RTF, or WordPerfect and importing it into PageMaker. But InDesign can import only ASCII files that have tags — whether they are in InDesign Tagged Text, PageMaker Tagged text, or XPress Tags format. So Word files with PageMaker Tagged Text codes will not import properly into InDesign (the tags will be imported as if they were part of your text), but ASCII files using PageMaker Tagged Text codes will import correctly.

No matter what layout program they use, most people do not use the tagged-text option because the coding can be tortuous. Because you cannot use tagged-text codes with your word processor's formatting, you must code everything with tagged text and save the document as an ASCII file. So why have Tagged Text at all? Because this format is the one format sure to support all the formatting you do in InDesign. Its usefulness is not in creating text for import, but in transferring files created in InDesign to another InDesign user (including someone working on another platform) or to a word processor for further work. You can export an InDesign story or piece of selected text in the Tagged Text format and then transfer the exported file to another InDesign user or to a word processor for further editing. Similarly, you can retain much of a PageMaker 6.5 or QuarkXPress 3.*x* file's formatting by exporting it to the PageMaker Tagged Text or XPress Tags format and then importing the tagged text file into InDesign.

Exporting a Tagged Text file into a word processor makes sense if you want to add or delete text without losing special formatting — such as fonts, kerning, or style tags — that your word processor doesn't support. After you edit the text, you can save the altered file (make sure that it is saved as ASCII text) and reimport it into your InDesign layout.

The best way to understand the Tagged Text format is to export some of your own documents to it, and open the resulting file in a word processor to see how InDesign coded the file. A warning: the Tagged Text format can be complex, especially because most codes have two forms, a short (abbreviated) one and a long (verbose) one — you choose which InDesign exports from the Export dialog box in InDesign (File ➪ Export, and then choose InDesign Tagged Text as the file format). Note that a Tagged Text file is simply an ASCII text file, so it will have the extension .TXT on the PC and use the standard text-only file icon in Windows and on the Mac.

Here's an example of verbose coding (because the code is so long, we had to add line breaks; slightly indented lines are actually part of the same code segment):

```
<ASCII-WIN>
<DefineParaStyle:Normal=<Nextstyle:Normal><cTypeface:Regular>
 <cSize:10.000000><pHyphenationLadderLimit:0><pHyphenation:0>
 <pHyphenationZone:18.000000><cFont:Times New Roman>
```

```
<cColorTint:100.000000>
<DefineCharStyle:Default Paragraph Font=<Nextstyle:
Default Paragraph Font>
<DefineCharStyle:Hyperlink=<BasedOn:Default Paragraph Font>
 <Nextstyle:Hyperlink><cColor:Blue><cTypeface:Regular><cSize:
 10.000000><cHorizontalScale:1.000000><cBaselineShift:0.000000>
 <cCase:Normal><cStrokeColor:><cUnderline:1><cFont:
 Times New Roman><cPosition:Normal><cStrikethru:0>
 <cColorTint:100.000000>
<ColorTable:=<Black:COLOR:CMYK:Process:0.000000,0.000000,
 0.000000,1.000000><Blue:COLOR:RGB:Process:0.000000,0.000000,
 1.000000>
<ParaStyle:Normal><pHyphenation:1><CharStyle:
 Default Paragraph Font> <CharStyle:><CharStyle:
 Hyperlink>www.adobe.com<CharStyle:><CharStyle:
 Default Paragraph Font>. <CharStyle:><pHyphenation:>
```

Here is the same text with abbreviated tags:

```
<ASCII-WIN>
<dps:Normal=<Nextstyle:Normal><ct:Regular><cs:10.000000>
 <phll:0><ph:0><phz:18.000000><cf:Times New Roman>
 <cct:100.000000>
<dcs:Default Paragraph Font=<Nextstyle:Default Paragraph Font>
<dcs:Hyperlink=<BasedOn:Default Paragraph Font>
 <Nextstyle:Hyperlink><cc:Blue><ct:Regular><cs:10.000000>
 <chs:1.000000><cbs:0.000000><ccase:Normal><csc:><cu:1>
 <cf:Times New Roman><cp:Normal><cstrike:0><cct:100.000000>
<ctable:=<Black:COLOR:CMYK:Process:0.000000,0.000000,0.000000,
 1.000000><Blue:COLOR:RGB:Process:0.000000,0.000000,1.000000>
<pstyle:Normal><ph:1><cstyle:Default Paragraph Font> <cstyle:>
 <cstyle:Hyperlink>www.adobe.com<cstyle:><cstyle:
 Default Paragraph Font>. <cstyle:><ph:>
```

What does all that coding mean? Well, that's for a one-page document with one frame that has simply one line of text:

```
This is a hyperlink to www.adobe.com.
```

The text is black, except for the Web address, which is in blue underline.

As you can see, there's a lot to Tagged Text codes. InDesign comes with a complete list of codes in a PDF file called tagged text.pdf that you'll find in the Tagged Text folder within the Adobe Technical Info folder on the InDesign CD-ROM.

In practical terms, you may not mind editing Tagged Text slightly or leaving the codes in a file when you alter its text. But you're not likely to forgo the friendly formatting available in your word processor and in InDesign to apply Tagged Text coding to everything in your text files.

Summary

Because today's word processors are so powerful, there's a temptation to do a lot of sophisticated, layout-oriented formatting in them before bringing the files into a layout program such as InDesign. But don't. No word processor has the typographic or layout ability of InDesign, and doing a lot of work in your word-processing file is simply a waste of time — you'd need to do it over again in InDesign in the context of your layout anyhow.

Focus on the meaning-oriented formatting in your word processor: use of styles to indicate headlines, bylines, quotation blocks, and so on, as well as local formatting such as italics, superscripts, and font changes.

When you're done preparing your text, be sure to save it in a format compatible with InDesign. Even if your word processor format is not compatible with InDesign, chances are it can save in one that is.

Finally, consider using the Tagged Text format to specify sophisticated formatting, such as defining paragraph and character styles in InDesign, in your word processor. This requires a familiarity with programming or coding in formats such as HTML, but can be a powerful way to add formatting for highly predictable, structured documents in your word processor before importing the file into InDesign.

✦　　✦　　✦

Working with Text

While you can use InDesign as your primary word processor, doing so is a little like buying an SUV for suburban errands — glamorous but unnecessary. In publishing, at least the first draft of text is generally written in Microsoft Word or WordPerfect because these word processing programs offer many editorial bells and whistles. Text is then imported into an InDesign publication. If you prefer, you can use InDesign's basic word processing features for entering text. Once text is in a publication, you can use InDesign's editing capabilities, search and replace functions, and spelling checker to refine it.

Adding Text

No matter where your text originates — in your mind, in e-mail, on the Web, or in a word processor — you can add it to an InDesign publication easily. You can type text directly in InDesign, paste it, drag-and-drop it, or import it. InDesign works with text inside frames — holders for the copy — that you can create in advance or let InDesign create for you when you begin typing or when you import text.

Chapter 5 covers frames in detail.

Typing text

First, you can't do anything with text without the Type tool. Once the Type tool is selected, as shown in Figure 10-1, you can click in an existing block of text, or click and drag to create a new text frame. You can even click in any empty frame with the Type tool to convert it to a text frame. From this point, start typing to enter text.

Figure 10-1: When the Type tool is selected,
you can click in a text frame and start typing.

Note

What you can't do is simply click in your document and begin typing, as you can in
PageMaker. InDesign is like other page-layout programs in that the text must be in
a frame. Fortunately, you can create that frame just by clicking and dragging with
the Type tool.

Tip

You can't click in master text frames — text frames that are placed on the page by
the master page in use — and simply start typing. To select a master text frame and
add text to it, press Shift+⌘+click (Mac) or Ctrl+Shift+click (Windows) to select it.
You'll need to click in it again to start typing. (For more on master pages, see
Chapter 29.)

Keeping Characters to a Minimum

If you're new to professional publishing, you'll find a few things to learn about the difference between typing on a typewriter or into a word processor and entering text for a high-
end publication:

✦ Remember that there's no need to type two spaces after a period or colon. In fact, it
  causes awkward spacing and perhaps even text-flow issues.

✦ Don't enter extra paragraph returns for space between paragraphs and don't enter
  tabs to indent paragraphs — you'll accomplish both more consistently with
  paragraph formats (Type ⇨ Paragraph, or ⌘+M or Ctrl+M).

✦ When you need to align text in columns, don't enter extra tabs; place one tab
  between each column, and then position the tabs (Type ⇨ Tabs, or Shift+⌘+T or
  Ctrl+Shift+T).

To see where you have placed tabs, paragraph breaks, spaces, and other such invisible
(nonprinting) characters, use the command Option+⌘+I or Ctrl+Alt+I, or use Type ⇨ Show
Hidden Characters, as the following figure shows.

Shrimp·Enchiladas¶
with·jalapeño·cream·sauce·¶

EG's·Garden·Grill¶
1000·Grand·Ave.,·Grand·Lake·¶

The·Food .... »............................ A ·¶

The·Atmosphere .... »........................ B·+¶

Kids .... »...................... A ·¶

Menu·Variety .... »...................... A ·¶

When you choose Type ⇨ Show Hidden Characters,
you can see paragraph returns, spaces, tabs, and other
invisible characters while you're editing text.

Pasting text

When text is on the Mac or Windows clipboard, you can paste it at the location of
the cursor or replace highlighted text with it. If no text frame is active, InDesign
creates a new rectangular text frame to contain the pasted text.

Note   Text that is cut or copied from InDesign retains its formatting, while text pasted
from other programs loses its formatting. But text pasted from other programs
does retain its special characters such as curly quotes, em dashes, and accented
characters.

InDesign uses standard menu commands and keyboard commands for cutting and
copying text to the clipboard, and for pasting text. On the Mac, press ⌘+X to cut,
⌘+C to copy, and ⌘+V to paste. In Windows, press Ctrl+X to cut, Ctrl+C to copy,
and Ctrl+V to paste.

Dragging and dropping text

If you're the kind of person who likes to juggle many open windows and
applications, you can drag highlighted text from other programs — or, as Figure 10-2
shows, even text files from the desktop or a folder — into an InDesign publications.
As with pasted text, text that you drag-and-drop is inserted at the location of the
cursor, replaces highlighted text, or is placed in a new rectangular text frame. (Text
files that are dragged onto a page must be in a supported format; Chapter 9 covers
this in detail.)

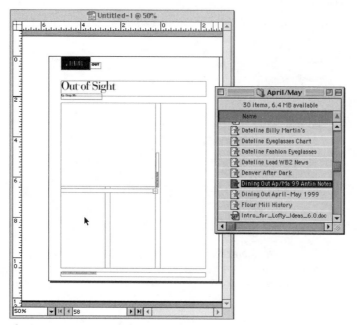

Figure 10-2: You can drag a word-processing file into an InDesign document to import it.

When you drag-and-drop a text selection, its formatting is lost. However, when you drag-and-drop a text file, the process is treated more like a text import: The text retains its formatting and it brings its styles with it. Unlike using the Place command (File ➪ Place, or ⌘+D or Ctrl+D) to import text, drag-and-drop does not give you the option to specify how some of the formatting and styles in the text file are handled.

Note   To drag-and-drop text into InDesign, the application you're dragging from must also support drag-and-drop. Most of the newer word processing, spreadsheet, e-mail, and browser programs support drag-and-drop. For example, you can drag-and-drop from any Microsoft Office 97/98 and 2000 application.

Importing text

If the text for your InDesign publication was written in a word processor, you can import it, with many styles intact, into a publication. InDesign provides import filters for Microsoft Word 4.x, 5.x, 6.0/95, and 8.0/97/98 and 2000; WordPerfect 6.1, 7.0, and 8.0; and Rich Text Format. You can also import ASCII text files, ANSI text files, and text tagged with InDesign, QuarkXPress, or PageMaker formatting codes. See Chapter 4 for more details.

Note The text import filters are located in the Filters folder within the Plug-ins folder inside your InDesign application folder—where they should remain. If you find updated or additional import filters on the Web or from other sources, be sure to add them to the Filters folder.

When you import text using the Place dialog box, it's placed according to your current selection:

✦ If the cursor is within text in a text frame, the text is inserted at that location.

✦ If an empty text frame is selected, the text is imported into the frame.

✦ If no text frames are selected, a loaded-text icon (shown in Figure 10-3) lets you draw a rectangular text frame to contain the text or click in an existing empty frame or text frame.

Figure 10-3: The loaded-text icon lets you create a new text frame or click a text frame to fill with text.

Steps: Placing Text

1. Choose File ➪ Place, or press ⌘+D or Ctrl+D.

2. Locate the text file you want to import.

3. If you want to specify how to handle current formatting in the file, check the Show Import Options checkbox, shown in Figure 10-4. (If you prefer memorizing keyboard commands to simply checking boxes, press Shift while you open the file to display the import options.)

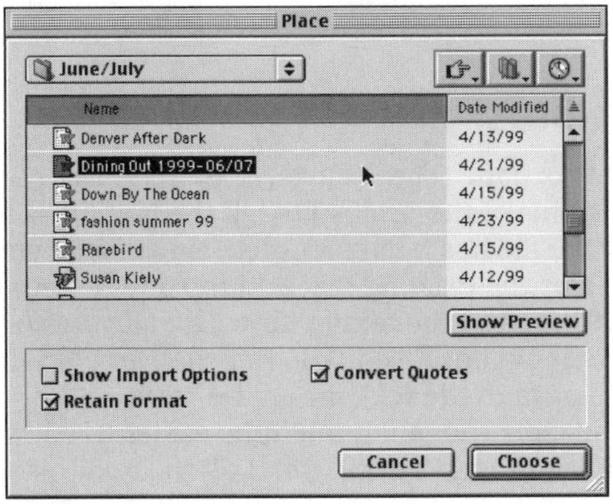

Figure 10-4: Use the Place dialog box to select a word-processing file you want to import.

Tip   If you're importing a text-only file that contains paragraph returns at the end of each line, be sure to check the Show Import Options as it will give you the option to remove them.

4. Check Retain Format to maintain paragraph and character attributes in the text and to import styles. If the text contains styles with the same names but different attributes than styles already in the InDesign publication, the styles in the publication override those in the imported text. (See Chapter 15 for more on setting up styles, which let you apply formatting to whole paragraphs or selections of text in one easy step.)

5. Check Convert Quotes to convert straight quotes (" ") to curly quotes (" ").

6. Click Choose (Mac) or Open (Windows) to import the text.

Oddity   Unlike other layout programs, InDesign does *not* translate two consecutive hyphens (--) into an em dash (—), even if you check the Convert Quotes option. Fortunately, many modern word processors do this, so the chances of having two consecutive hyphens from recently created documents are slim. (In Word, use Tools ➪ AutoCorrect to enable this feature; in Word Perfect, use Tools ➪ QuickCorrect.)

7. If you had not selected a frame before starting the text import, specify where to place the text by clicking and dragging the loaded-text icon to create a rectangular text frame, clicking in an existing frame, or clicking in any empty frame. To cancel the text import, just select a different tool.

Note   If you click a frame that holds a graphic when importing text, the text will replace the graphic.

If all the text you import doesn't fit in the selected text frame, see "Threading Text Frames" in Chapter 11 for more information on how to make it flow to other text frames.

Updating linked text files

When you place a text file, the Links pane (File ➪ Links, or Shift+⌘+D or Shift+Ctrl+D) keeps track of the location and status of the original file. If the text file is modified, the Links pane notifies you that the file has been modified. However, if you update the text file, InDesign simply deletes the existing text and replaces it with the updated text file. If you already formatted the text in InDesign, all your formatting will be lost. In general, text files should not be edited after they are imported into an InDesign document; any final changes to the text should be made in the InDesign document. If the text changes radically though, it might be easier to edit the text in a word processor, update it in InDesign, and then reformat all the text.

Handling Import Options

If you check Show Import Options in the Place dialog box, InDesign displays a set of options for handling formatting in the selected text file. These options vary based on the kind of file you are importing:

✦ **Text files:** You can choose a character set (ASCII or ANSI; ANSI supports different special symbols that the more common ASCII character set doesn't) and a language dictionary to associate with the text file, so InDesign will know how to check the spelling and hyphenate it. In addition, you can specify how extraneous paragraph returns and spaces are handled. The following figure shows this dialog box.

For text files, the Text Import Options dialog box lets you filter out paragraph returns at the end of each line and multiple spaces rather than tabs.

✦ **Tagged text:** You will receive options only when importing text containing InDesign tags — you have no options when importing QuarkXPress or PageMaker tagged-text files. Options include specifying whether to use styles from the tagged text or those in InDesign when styles conflict, and whether to preview problem tags.

✦ **Word 6.0/95 and earlier:** You can import a table of contents and index as text; convert Condensed/Expanded Spacing into scaling, kerning, or tracking; convert page breaks before paragraphs to column or page breaks; and convert tables to tabbed text.

✦ **Word 8.0/97/98 and 2000, RTF:** You can import an automatic table of contents, an index, hyperlinks (formatting only — the actual links are removed), tables, footnotes, and endnotes as text. Tables are imported as tabbed text and footnotes/endnotes are placed at the end of the story. You can also convert Condensed/Expanded Spacing to tracking or scaling, and you can either remove user-defined page breaks or convert them to column or page breaks.

✦ **WordPerfect:** No options exist, so you will not get an options dialog box even if Show Import Options is checked.

Continued

(continued)

✦ **Excel 97/98:** You can specify whether to import custom views, the worksheet you want to import, and a rectangular range of cells to import (separate the range with a colon, such as A1:C9 to import cells A1 through C9). Formatting options let you determine whether to use Excel's default spreadsheet styles or to specify the cell alignment and number of decimal places in a cell yourself. You can also specify whether cells expand to fit their contents and whether hyperlink formatting is included (again, the actual links are removed).

Exporting text files

Unfortunately, the Export command doesn't support all the text file formats that the Place command (File ➪ Place) does. Only InDesign Tagged Text, Rich Text Format, and text-only (ASCII) are supported. Here's a quick rundown on the three text formats:

✦ When you export a text-only (ASCII) file, all formatting information — fonts, leading, style, and so on — are stripped out; only the raw text remains. The good news is that every word-processing program lets you open ASCII files; the bad new, of course, is that any formatting you've applied gets tossed.

✦ The RTF format, developed by Microsoft, saves the text plus some basic style information (bold, italic, bold/italic). If you want to save formats, RTF is a step above ASCII and is supported by most word processing and page layout programs.

✦ If you export an InDesign Tagged Text file, all of InDesign's text-formatting codes are included along with the text. A Tagged Text file is actually an ASCII file, which means you can open it in any word processor. The embedded formatting codes may look a little strange, but you can edit the text — and the codes if you're adventurous — as you would any text file.

Tip   You can save only one text file at a time. If you need to export several stories from the same document, you must do so one at a time. (A story is contained by a series of linked text frames.)

Steps: Saving a Text File

1. Select the Type tool or press T, and then click anywhere within the story you want to export. If you want to export only a portion of the text, highlight it. If you want to export the entire story, don't highlight any text.

2. Choose File ➪ Export. The Export dialog box is displayed.

3. Choose a storage folder, specify a file name, and then choose any of the available text formats from the Formats (Mac) or Save as Type (Windows) pop-up menu.

4. Click Save to export the story in the selected format.

Tip
If you want to export a text file, make sure the Type tool is selected and a text frame is active. Otherwise, the text file formats are not available in the Export dialog box. The HTML, EPS, PDF, and Prepress File options are always available.

Editing Text

InDesign gives you the basic editing capabilities found in a word processor: cutting and pasting, deleting and inserting text, searching and replacing text and text attributes, as well as help in checking spelling.

Before you begin to edit text, however, you need to see it. In many layout views, the text is too small to work with. Generally, you'll zoom in around the block of text using the Zoom tool. For quick access to the tool, press Z (except when the cursor is in a block of text — in that case, you'll need to click the Zoom tool). Then click to zoom in. (To zoom out, hold the Option or Alt key when clicking.)

Another way to zoom in is to use the keyboard shortcut ⌘+= or Ctrl+=. Each time you use it, the magnification increases. (Zoom out via ⌘+- [hyphen] or Ctrl+- [hyphen].)

Tip
Choose the ⌘+= or Ctrl+= method when your text pointer is already on or near the text you want to zoom into — the pointer location is the centerpoint for the zoom. Use the Zoom tool when your pointer is not near the text you want to magnify; then move the Zoom pointer to the area you want to magnify, and click once for each level of desired magnification.

In addition to seeing the text larger, it also helps to see the spaces, tabs, and paragraph returns in the text. Choose Type ➪ Show Hidden Characters or press Option+⌘+I or Ctrl+Alt+I. In addition to seeing the text, you have to be able to access it, so choose the Type tool.

Navigating text

To work at a different text location, click in a different text frame or another location in the current text frame. You can also use the four arrow (cursor) keys on the keyboard to move one character to the right, one character to the left, one line up, or one line down. Add ⌘ or Ctrl to the arrow keys to jump one word to the right or left, or one paragraph up or down. The Home and End keys let you jump to the beginning or end of a line; add ⌘ or Ctrl to jump to the beginning or end of a story. (A story is text within a text frame or that is linked across several text frames, as described in Chapter 11.) Note that if your story begins or ends in a text frame on another page, InDesign takes you to that page.

Tip
As with most text editors, you can't enter text below the existing text in a frame. You'll need to click directly after the last character in the frame to start typing again.

Highlighting text

To highlight text, you can always rely on the old click-and-drag method. Or, you can add the Shift key to the navigation commands in the previous section. For example, while ⌘+right arrow moves the cursor one word to the right (on a Mac), Shift+⌘+right arrow highlights the next word to the right. Likewise, ⌘+Shift+End highlights all the text to the end of the story. In Windows, press Ctrl+Shift+right arrow or Ctrl+Shift+End.

For precise text selections, double-click to select a word and its trailing space (this will not select its punctuation) and triple-click to select a paragraph. If you need the punctuation trailing a word, double-click, and then press Shift+⌘+right arrow or Ctrl+Shift+right arrow to extend the selection. To select an entire story, choose Edit ➪ Select All, or press ⌘+A or Ctrl+A.

To deselect text, choose Edit ➪ Deselect All or press Shift+⌘+A or Shift+Ctrl+A. More simply, you can select another tool or click another area of the page.

Cutting, copying, and pasting text

Once you highlight text, you can press ⌘+X or Ctrl+X to remove it from its story and place it on the clipboard for later use. Use ⌘+C or Ctrl+C to leave the text in the story and place a copy on the clipboard. Click anywhere else in the text — within the same story, another story, or another publication — and press ⌘+V or Ctrl+V. If you're menu-driven, the Edit menu provides Cut, Copy, and Paste commands as well.

Deleting and replacing text

To remove text from a document, you can highlight it and choose Edit ➪ Clear or press Delete or backspace on the keyboard. Or you can simply type over the highlighted text or paste new text on top of it.

If text is not highlighted, you can delete text to the right or left of the cursor. On the Mac, press Delete to delete to the left and press Del to delete to the right. In Windows, press backspace to delete to the left and Delete to delete to the right.

Undoing text edits

Remember to take advantage of InDesign's multiple undos while editing text. Choose Edit ➪ Undo and Edit ➪ Redo any time you change your mind about edits. The Undo and Redo keyboard commands are definitely worth remembering: ⌘+Z and Shift+⌘+Z or Ctrl+Z and Ctrl+Shift+Z.

Searching and Replacing

InDesign's Find/Change dialog box (Edit ➪ Find/Change, or ⌘+F or Ctrl+F) lets you do everything from finding the next instance of "curry" in an article so you can insert "extra spicy" in red to finding all instances of a deposed chef's name in six different documents. If you know how to use the search and replace feature in any word processor or page-layout application, you'll be comfortable with InDesign's Find/Change in no time.

Searching and replacing text

The Find/Change dialog box comes in two forms: reduced for finding and changing only text, and expanded for including formats in a search. The More button expands the dialog box and the Less button reduces it.

Before starting a Find/Change operation, determine the scope of your search:

✦ To search within a text selection, highlight it.

✦ To search from a certain location in story to the end of it, click the cursor at that location.

✦ To search an entire story, select any frame or click at any point in a frame containing the story.

✦ To search an entire document, simply have that document open.

✦ To search multiple documents, open all of them (and close any that you don't want to search).

Steps: Searching for Text

1. Determine the scope of your search (as just described), open the necessary files, and insert the text cursor at the appropriate location.

2. Choose Edit ➪ Find/Change or press ⌘+F or Ctrl+F.

3. Use the Search pop-up menu, as shown in Figure 10-5, to specify the scope of your search: Document, All Documents, Story, To End of Story, or Selection. (The options available are based on your current text selection in InDesign. Unavailable options are grayed out.)

Tip   As you're using the Find/Change dialog box to search and replace text, you can jump into a text frame (just click it with the Type pointer) and edit it as you please, and then return to Find/Change by clicking its dialog box.

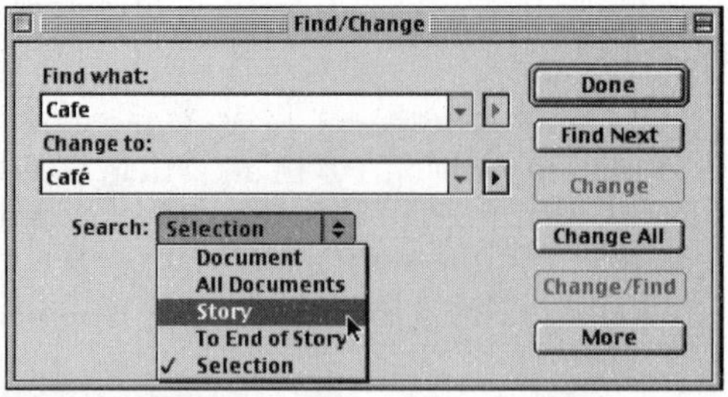

Figure 10-5: Use the Search pop-up menu in the Find/Change dialog box to specify the scope of the text to search.

4. Type or paste the text you want to find in the Find What field.

5. Type or paste the replacement text into the Change To field.

6. Specify whether to find the word within other words (for example, "cafe" within "cafeteria" or just "cafe") by checking or unchecking Whole Word. When checked, Find/Change locate only standalone instances of the Find What text.

7. Specify whether to consider capitalization patterns in the Find/Change operation by checking or unchecking Case Sensitive. When checked, Find/Change follows the capitalization of the text in the Find What and Change To fields exactly.

8. Click Find Next to start the search. Thereafter, click Find Next to skip instances of the Find What text, and click Change, Change All, or Change/Find to replace the Find What text with the Change to text. (Change simply changes the found text, Change All changes every instance of that found text in your selection or story, and Change/Find changes the current found text and moves on to the next occurrence of it — it basically does in one click the actions of clicking Change and then Find Next.)

Note   If you use the Change All feature, InDesign reports how many changes were made. If the number looks extraordinarily high and you suspect the Find/Change operation wasn't quite what you wanted, remember you can use InDesign's undo function (Edit ⇨ Undo, or ⌘+Z or Ctrl+Z) to cancel the search and replace, and then try a different strategy.

9. Click Done when you're all done. Note that you can do several search-and-replace operations, which is why the dialog box stays open after completing a search — and that's why there is a Done button for you to tell InDesign to close the dialog box.

Tip   InDesign records your last 15 entries in the Find What and Change To fields, so you can repeat previous Find/Change operations. That's why each field is a pop-up menu. Click the menu to open it, and use the down arrow key to scroll through those recorded operations.

Finding special characters

You're not limited to finding and changing words and phrases. You can search and replace spaces, tabs, paragraph returns, and other invisible characters along with special characters such as bullets, em dashes, and nonbreaking spaces. Searching and replacing these types of characters is often helpful for repair jobs: fixing imported text that contains double spaces after periods, extra returns between paragraphs, and double hyphens instead of em dashes.

If you want to search for or replace other characters that are not in InDesign's special-character menu, just enter their codes or paste them into the field. You can paste them by first copying them to the clipboard from your document text or from a utility such as PopChar Pro or KeyCaps on the Mac or Character Map in Windows. (See Chapter 16.)

InDesign also provides three wild cards that let you search for unspecified characters, numbers, or letters in other text. For example, if you want to change all the numbered steps in a document to bulleted lists, you might search for Any Digit and replace it with a bullet. Or you can search for variations of a word to find, say, "cafe" and "café" at the same time.

To enter invisible characters, special characters, or wild cards in the Find What or Change To fields, click the arrow buttons to the right of the fields. You'll get a menu that offers options such as Bullet Character, Hair Space, and Discretionary Hyphen, as shown in Figure 10-6. You can select any combination of these characters and combine them with other text and formatting attributes. The InDesign help file lists codes under the "Finding and changing text" entry.

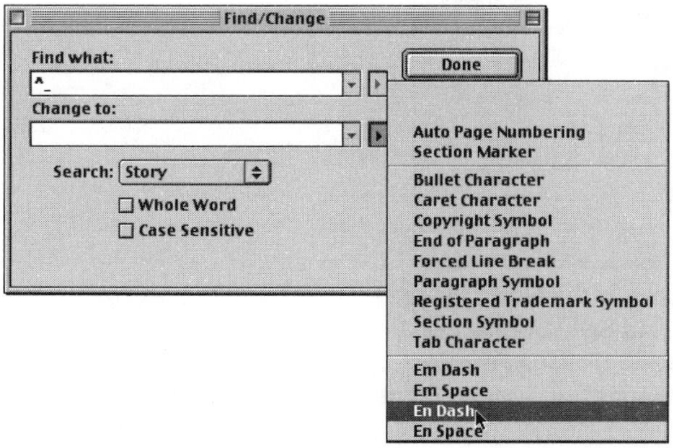

Figure 10-6: Click the right-facing arrow on the Find What and Change To fields to display a list of special characters. The example shown will find an em dash and change it to an en dash.

Note   To search and replace regular spaces, type the number of spaces you want to find and change in the Find What and Change To fields — as if they were any other regular character.

Searching and replacing formatting

To find and change formatting or text with specific formatting, you can use the expanded Find/Change dialog box. For example, you might find all the blue-colored words in 14-point Futura Extra Bold and change them to 12-point MrsEaves Bold. Or, you might find all instances of the words "hot and spicy" in 10-point body text, and then resize the text to 12 point and apply Red Litterbox.

Steps: Replacing Text Formatting

1. To add formats to a Find/Change operation for text, click the More button in the Find/Change dialog box (if it was not clicked earlier). The dialog box expands to include the Find Style Settings and Change Style Settings areas, as shown in Figure 10-7.

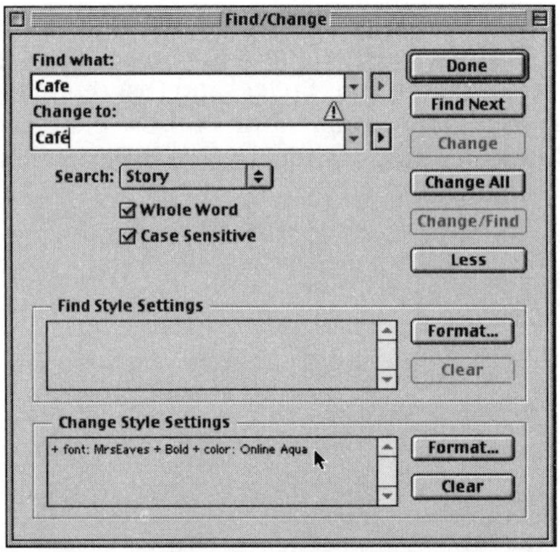

Find/Change

Find what:
`Cafe`

Change to:
`Café`

Search: `Story`

☑ Whole Word
☑ Case Sensitive

Done
Find Next
Change
Change All
Change/Find
Less

Find Style Settings

Format...
Clear

Change Style Settings

+ font: MrsEaves + Bold + color: Online Aqua

Format...
Clear

Figure 10-7: Clicking More in the Find/Change dialog box displays the Find Style Settings and Change Style Settings areas. Clicking Format opens the Find Format Settings or Change Format Settings dialog box.

2. Use the Format buttons to display the Find Format Settings and Change Format Settings dialog boxes, which let you specify the formats you want to find. (The two dialog boxes are identical, except for their names; Figure 10-8 shows the Find Format Settings one.)

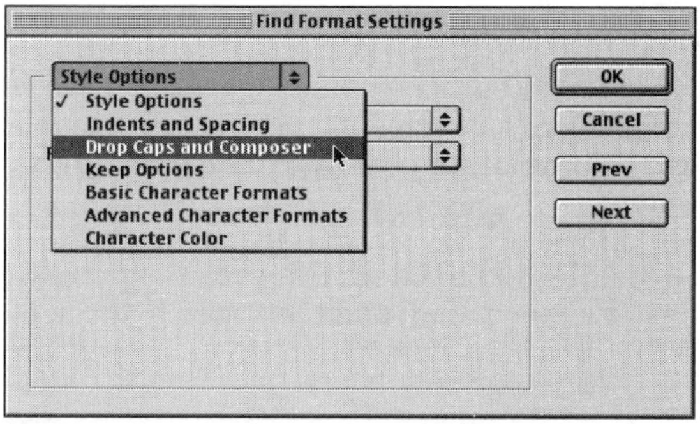

Figure 10-8: The Find Format Settings dialog box, with its pop-up menu of available option groups open.

3. Use the menu at the top to specify the type of formatting: Style Options (styles), Indents and Spacing, Drop Caps and Composer, Keep Options, Basic Character Formats, Advanced Character Formats, and Character Color. The Prev and Next buttons will move you from one pane to the next—remember, you can change multiple attributes at once by making selections from as many panes as needed.

Tip To search and replace formatting only—regardless of the text to which it is applied—leave the Find What and Change To fields blank.

Locating and specifying all the formatting you want to find and change requires you to dig deeper and deeper into the Find Format Settings and Change Format Settings dialog boxes. Unfortunately, you can't really get a picture of all the formats you're selecting at once, and you have to keep jumping from one pane to the next. Fortunately, when you're finished selecting formats, the selected options are summarized in the Find Style Settings and Change Style Settings areas (refer to the bottom of Figure 10-7).

Checking Spelling

Search and replace can help fix mistakes in your text, but it's usually not enough. Another helpful tool is a spelling checker, which reads through your text to look for misspelled words. While you'll still want to proofread your documents, it's a good idea to use the spelling checker both in your word processor and in InDesign to reduce the chances of errors in your final document.

InDesign's Check Spelling feature flags three types of possible editorial problems: repeated words such as "an an," words with odd capitalization such as the internal capitalization (called *intercaps*) in software and company names (InDesign), and words that are not found in the spelling dictionary and may be spelled wrong. You can customize the spelling dictionary, and you can purchase other companies' spelling dictionaries to add words from disciplines such as horticulture or gourmet cooking, as well as for other languages.

Specifying the text to check

InDesign lets you control which text is checked for spelling so you can concentrate on a new story or paragraph added to a document, check all the text in a document toward the end of the publishing process, or check multiple documents on similar subject matter at the same time.

As with Find/Change, specifying the text to check is a two-step process: first set up the spelling-check scope in the document, and then specify the scope in the Search menu.

To set up the scope, highlight text, click in a story to check from the cursor forward, select a frame containing a story, or open multiple documents. Just as in search and replace, what you choose to open and select determines the scope options InDesign offers for checking the spelling.

Then, open the Check Spelling dialog box (Edit ⇨ Check Spelling, or ⌘+I or Ctrl+I) and choose an option from the Search pop-up menu: Document, All Documents, Story, To End of Story, and Selection. Figure 10-9 shows the dialog box. Depending on how you set up the scope, not all the options are available in the Search pop-up menu. For example, if you did not highlight text, the Selection option is not available. However, you can change the scope setup in the document while the Check Spelling dialog box is open — for example, you can open additional documents to check.

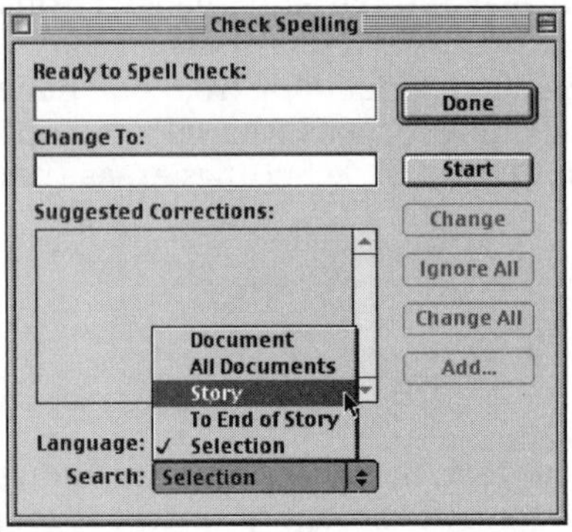

Figure 10-9: Use the Search pop-up menu in the Check Spelling dialog box to specify which text to check for spelling.

Tip   To check the spelling of a single word, double-click to highlight it and then open the spelling checker — the Check Spelling dialog box's Search pop-up menu is automatically set to Selection.

Tip   On the Mac, use Control+click, and in Windows, use right-click on a word or point
           in a text frame (using the Type tool) to get the contextual pop-up menu shown in
           Figure 10-10, and then choose Check Spelling.

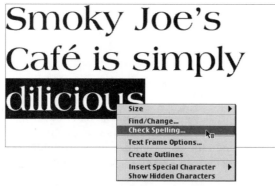

Figure 10-10: You can use a contextual menu to quickly
invoke the spelling checker. On the Mac, Control+click
the text, and in Windows, right-click it.

Using the Check Spelling dialog box

When you first open the Check Spelling dialog box, it displays "Ready to Spell
Check" near the top. To begin checking the text scope you specified in the Search
pop-menu, click Start. When the spelling checker encounters a word without a
match in the dictionary or a possible capitalization problem, the dialog box
displays "Not in Dictionary" near the top and shows the word. When the spelling
checker encounters a repetition such as "me me," the dialog box displays
"Duplicate Word" and shows the repeated words. Figure 10-11 shows the dialog box.

Use the buttons along the right side of the dialog box to handle flagged words
as follows:

✦ To leave the current instance of a Not in Dictionary word or Duplicate Word
   unchanged, click Ignore. To leave all instances of the same problem
   unchanged, click Ignore All.

✦ To change the spelling of a Not in Dictionary word, click a word in the
   Suggested Corrections list or edit the spelling or capitalization in the Change
   To field. To make the change, click Change.

✦ To correct an instance of a Duplicate Word, edit the text in the Change To
   field, and then click Change.

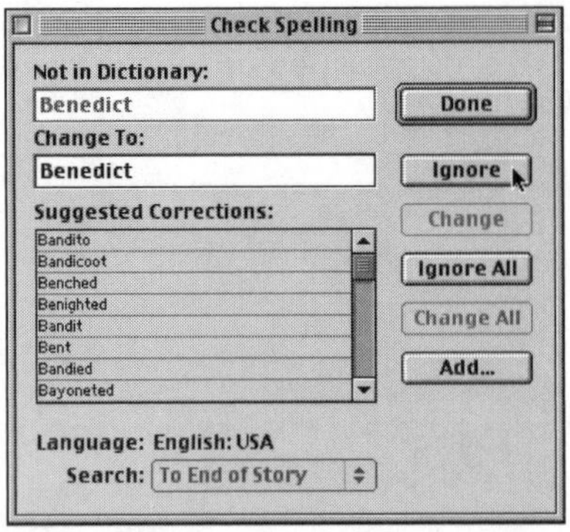

Figure 10-11: InDesign's spelling checker provides a list of possible alternatives for words it has flagged as possibly misspelled. You can choose to ignore its suggestions (the word may be correct but unknown to InDesign), add the word to InDesign's dictionary, correct it with one of InDesign's suggestions, or correct it with a word of your own choosing.

✦ To change all occurrences of a Not in Dictionary word or a Duplicate Word to the information in the Change To field, click Change All.

✦ To add a word flagged as incorrect — but that you know is correct — to InDesign's spelling dictionary, click Add.

✦ To close the Check Spelling dialog box after checking all the specified text, click Done.

While you're using the spelling checker, you can jump between the dialog box and the document at any time. This lets you edit a possibly misspelled word in context or edit surrounding text as a result of changed spelling. So if you find an instance of "a a" in front of "apple," you can change the entire phrase to "an apple" rather than just replace the duplicate "a a" with "a" in the dialog box and have to remember to later fix "a apple" to "an apple."

Working with multiple languages

Each word in InDesign can have a distinct language assigned to it (English, French, Spanish, German, and so on). The word's language attribute tells InDesign which dictionary to consult when checking the spelling or hyphenating the word. For example, if you have the word "Français" in an English sentence, you can change the language of that word so it is no longer flagged by the English spelling checker — the French spelling checker would be used on it to recognize that the word is correctly spelled.

The ability to control language at the word level doesn't necessarily mean that you have to. In general, even when publishing to an international audience, full paragraphs or stories will be in the same language. For example, if you have the same packaging for a product sold in the United States and France, you might have one descriptive paragraph in English and the other in French. The English dictionary also contains many common words with foreign origins such as "jalapeño," "mélange," and "crêpe."

To assign a language to text, highlight the text and choose an option from the language pop-up menu on the Character palette, as shown in Figure 10-12. You can also set the language as part of a character or paragraph style (see Chapter 15 for more details). In the Check Spelling dialog box, a field above the Search pop-up menu (at the bottom) shows the language of each word as it's checked. Unfortunately, you cannot change the language in that dialog box.

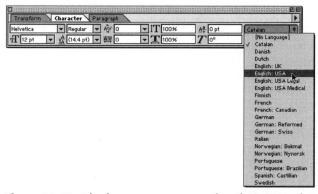

Figure 10-12: The language menu on the Character palette lets you choose a different language for hyphenating and checking the spelling of highlighted text.

There's a language option called [No Language] — selecting it prevents spelling checks and hyphenation.

Customizing the Spelling and Hyphenation Dictionaries

A spelling dictionary can never cover all the bases — you'll always have industry-specific words and proper nouns not found in the dictionary in use. In addition, some editors have their own preferences for how to hyphenate words. What they consider correct hyphenation may vary, and some word breaks are preferred over others. To solve both of these problems, you can customize InDesign's dictionaries by adding words and specifying hyphenation. InDesign handles both spelling and hyphenation in one dictionary for each language, so you use the same controls to modify both spelling and hyphenation.

Changes made to a dictionary file are saved only in the dictionary file, not with an open document. So if you add words to the English: USA dictionary, the modified dictionary is used for checking spelling and hyphenating all text in documents that use the English: USA dictionary.

Tip
If you're in a workgroup, be sure to share the edited dictionary file so everyone is using the same spelling and hyphenation settings. (The file is located in the Dictionaries folder inside the Plug-ins folder inside your InDesign folder.) You can copy it to other users, who must then restart InDesign or press Option+⌘+/ or Ctrl+Alt+/ to reflow the text according to the new dictionary's hyphenation.

Customizing the spelling dictionary

While you're checking spelling, you'll often find words that don't match those in the dictionary. If you know the word is spelled correctly and likely to appear in your publications often, you can add it to the dictionary. In the future, this word will not be flagged and you won't have to click Ignore to repeatedly skip it — and you can be sure that when it's used it is spelled as it is in the dictionary.

While adding words to the dictionary, you can specify their capitalization. For example, InDesign's dictionary prefers "E-mail." You can add "e-mail" if you prefer a lowercase "e" or "email" if you prefer to skip the hyphen. If you're adding a word that may have variations (such as "emailing") be sure to add those words separately.

Steps: Adding Words to the Dictionary

1. Choose Edit ➪ Edit Dictionary. Figure 10-13 shows the dialog box.

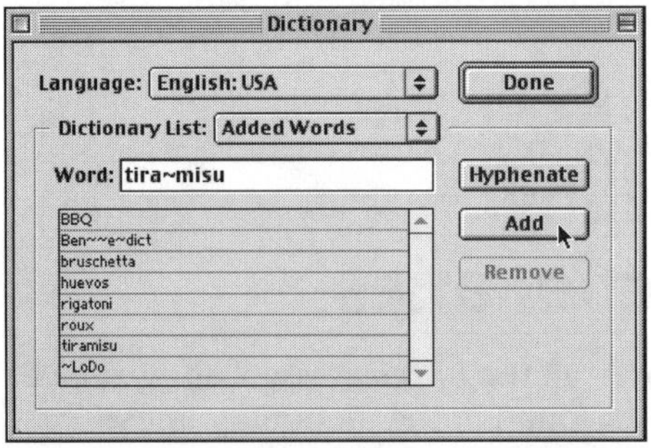

Figure 10-13: Enter new terms in the Word field and then click Add to include them in the spelling dictionary.

2. Choose the dictionary that you want to edit from the Language menu.

3. Type or paste a word in the Word field. The word can include special characters such as accents and hyphens, spaces, and a capitalization pattern to follow.

4. Click Add.

5. Continue to add words, and then click Done.

Tip When you're adding variations of words, you can double-click a word in the list to place it in the Word field (so you don't have to retype it all).

In addition to adding words through the Edit Dictionary dialog box, you can click Add in the Check Spelling dialog box when InDesign flags a word that you know is correct.

To delete a word that you added to the dictionary, select it in the list and click Remove. To change the spelling of a word you added, delete it and then re-add it with the correct spelling.

Customizing hyphenation points

Industries and publications usually have internal styles that specify how words hyphenate — especially if the text is justified. For example, a bridal magazine that uses the term "newlywed" often may prefer that it breaks at the end of a line as "newly-wed." But if that hyphenation would cause poor spacing, the publisher might let it break at "new-lywed" as well. InDesign lets you modify the hyphenation dictionary by specifying new, hierarchical hyphenation points.

Note When you customize the hyphenation points, be sure to add variations of words (such as the plural form "newlyweds") — InDesign sees each word as wholly unrelated, and thus won't apply the hyphenation of, say, "newlywed" to "newlyweds."

Steps: Specifying Hyphenation Points

1. Choose Edit ➪ Edit Dictionary.

2. Choose the dictionary that you want to edit from the Language menu.

3. Type or paste the word in the Word field; you can also double-click a word in the list.

4. If you wish, click Hyphenate to see InDesign's suggestions for hyphenating the word. You can then change the hyphenation according to Steps 5 and 6.

5. Type a tilde (~, obtained via Shift+`, the open single quote at the upper left of the keyboard) at your first preference for a hyphenation point.

Note   If you don't want a word to hyphenate at all, type a tilde in front of it in the Word field.

6. Type tildes in other hyphenation points as well. If you want to indicate a preference, use two tildes for your second choice, three tildes for your third choice, and so on. InDesign will first try to hyphenate your top preferences (single tildes), and then it will try your second choices if the first ones don't work out, and so on.

7. Click Add.

8. Continue to add words, and then click Done.

To revert a word to the default hyphenation, select it in the list and click Remove. To change the hyphenation, double-click a word in the list to enter it in the Word field, change the tildes, and then click Add. Again, when you're adding variations of words, you can double-click a word in the list to place it in the Word field.

Tip   If a word actually includes a freestanding tilde (not as an accent, as in ñ), type \~ to indicate the character is part of the word. These are rare, and happen mostly in World Wide Web addresses.

Setting spelling and hyphenation dictionary preferences

By default, when checking spelling and hyphenating text, InDesign consults dictionaries created by a company called Proximity. Because spelling and hyphenation points vary from dictionary to dictionary, and you may prefer one dictionary over another, you can purchase and install other companies' dictionaries to use instead of Proximity's.

The spelling and hyphenation in Proximity's dictionaries has the following origins: Catalan (Collins), Danish (IDE), Dutch (Van Dale), English: UK (Collins), English: USA (Franklin), English USA Legal (Merriam-Webster), English: USA Medical (Merriam-Webster), Finnish (IDE), French (Hachette), French: Canadian (Hachette), German: Traditional (unknown by Adobe at press time), German: Reformed (Bertelsmann), German: Swiss (Bertelsmann), Italian (Collins), Norwegian (IDE), Norwegian: Nynorsk (IDE), Portuguese (Collins), Portuguese: Brazilian (Collins), Spanish: Castilian (Collins), and Swedish (IDE).

Steps: Replacing the Dictionary

1. Place the new dictionary file in the Dictionaries folder in the Plug-ins folder inside your InDesign folder.

2. Choose File ➪ Preferences ➪ Dictionary to get the dialog box shown in Figure 10-14.

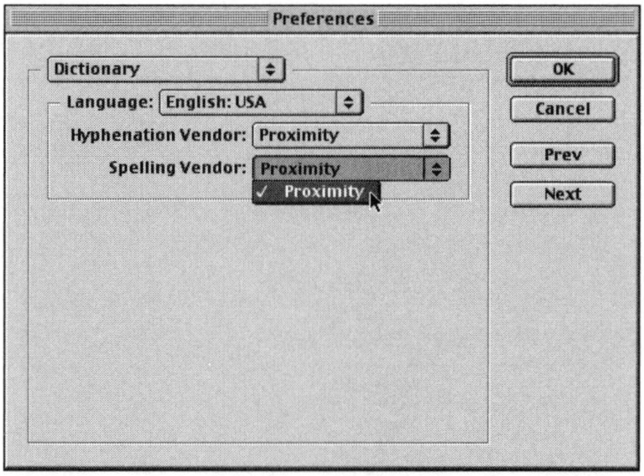

Figure 10-14: If you purchase and install different hyphenation and spelling dictionaries, you can select them in the Dictionary pane of the Preferences dialog box.

3. In the Language pop-up menu, choose which language's dictionary you want to replace.

4. Choose the new dictionary from the Hyphenation Vendor and/or Spelling Vendor pop-up menu.

5. Click OK.

Tip   If you change dictionary preferences with no documents open, the new dictionary becomes a program default and applies to all new documents. If a document is open, the change applies only to that document.

Summary

InDesign provides a variety of methods for getting text into your documents, including typing directly into a text frame, placing or dragging and dropping files generated in a word processor, and pasting text from other sources.

You can export formatted text from InDesign for editing in a word processor or for use in another application.

Once text is in InDesign, you can use the Find/Change feature to search and replace text and formatting in highlighted text, in a story, to the end of a story, in an entire document, or across several documents. You have the same scope options for checking spelling.

You can customize the spelling and hyphenation dictionary to include industry-specific words or proper nouns, and to specify your preferences for the way certain words are hyphenated. InDesign provides dictionaries for many different languages for international publishing.

✦   ✦   ✦

Flowing Text Through a Document

It doesn't take much experience with InDesign to discover that all your text doesn't fit into the finite space provided by individual frames. Consider these scenarios:

✦ If you're laying out a newsletter, you might receive an article in the form of a Microsoft Word document that you need to flow into several columns across a spread.

✦ Or, a magazine might have an article that starts on page 21 and continues on page 198, with the text originating from WordPerfect.

✦ And with catalogs, you might have a continuous file exported from a database that contains different product descriptions, which are positioned below the items' pictures.

✦ In book publishing, each chapter may be imported as a separate word processing file and flowed continuously through many pages.

✦ Even the text of a simple advertisement, delivered by a client via e-mail, might flow through several text frames.

In all these cases, the benefits of frames — the ability to size, resize, reshape, and place them with precision — seem limiting. When the text doesn't fit in a frame, what are you supposed to do? Well, don't resort to cutting and pasting text into different frames. You need to keep the imported text together and link the frames that will contain the text. InDesign refers to the process of linking frames as *threading* and considers linked frames to be *threaded*. You can link frames on a single page, link frames from any page to any other page no matter how many pages are in between, and you can link frames automatically to quickly flow text while adding new pages with frames.

The text flowing through a series of threaded frames is considered a *story*. When you edit text in a story, the text reflows throughout the columns and threaded frames. You can also check the spelling and search and replace text for an entire story even though you have a single text frame active. Similarly, you can select all or some of the text in the story and change its formatting, copy it, or delete it.

Chapter 5 explains how to create frames, while Chapter 9 explains what kind of text can be imported. Chapter 10 explains how to select, spell-check, and search-and-replace text. Chapters 12 through 15 explain how to format text.

Creating Text Frames

On a simple layout such as a business card or advertisement, you might simply create text frames as you need them. In a newsletter scenario, you might drag text frames for an article in from a library. But with a book or even a text-heavy magazine, text frames are usually placed on master pages — a template for document pages — so they automatically appear on document pages. Many publications combine master frames, individual frames, and threaded frames, as shown in Figure 11-1.

For detailed information about master pages, see Chapter 29 and for information about libraries see Chapter 37.

Creating text frames on master pages

Master pages — predesigned pages that you can apply to other pages to automate layout and ensure consistency — can contain several types of text frames. You can have:

✦ Text frames containing standing text such as a magazine's folio.

✦ Text frames containing placeholder text for elements such as figure captions or headlines.

✦ An automatically placed text frame for flowing text throughout pages. The automatically placed text frame is called the *master text frame* and is created in the New Document dialog box (File ➪ New, or ⌘+N or Ctrl+N).

Figure 11-1: In this magazine spread, a text frame on a document page contains the headline "It's Thyme" and a text frame placed by the master page contains the folios. The body of the article is in a master text frame, which has been shortened to contain only the article introduction; the master text frame is threaded to other master text frames, which contain the body of the article, on the following pages.

Creating a master text frame

A master text frame is an empty text frame on the default master page that enables you to automatically flow text through a document. When you create a new document, you can create a master text frame, which fits within the margins and contains the number of columns you specify.

Steps: Creating a Master Frame

1. Choose File ➪ New or press ⌘+N or Ctrl+N.

2. Check Master Text Frame at the top of the New Document dialog box, as shown in Figure 11-2.

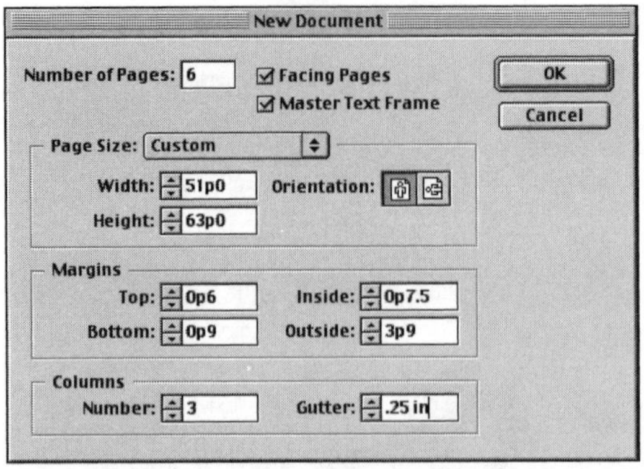

Figure 11-2: Checking Master Text Frame in the New Document dialog box places a text frame on the default master page within the Margins you specify.

3. Use the Page Size area to set up the size and orientation of the pages, and check Facing Pages if your pages will have a different inside and outside margin (as a book would).

4. Specify the size and placement of the master text frame by entering values in the Top, Bottom, Inside, and Outside (or Left and Right if Facing Pages is unchecked) fields. InDesign places guides according to these values and places a text frame within the guides. The text frame fits within the boundaries of these values and the guides on the master page.

5. Enter a value in the Number field in the Columns area to specify the number of columns in the master text frame. To specify the amount of space between the columns, enter a value in the Gutter field. InDesign places guides on the page to indicate the columns.

6. Click OK to create a new document containing a master text frame.

Once you create a document with a master text frame, you'll see guides on the first document page indicating the placement of the frame. (You cannot create a master text frame after creating a document.)

Modifying master text frames

Although you set up the master text frame in the New Document dialog box, you're not confined to those settings. As you design a publication, you may need to change the size, shape, and/or number of columns in the master text frame. To display the master page, choose Window ➪ Pages or press F12. In the Pages pane, double-click the A-Master icon in the lower portion of the pane. Use the Selection tool to click the master text frame within the guides and modify it using the following options:

✦ The Transform palette lets you change the placement of a selected master text frame using the X and Y fields, the size using the W and H fields, the angle using the Rotation field, and the skew using the Shear field. You can also enter values in the Scale fields to increase or decrease the width and height of the text frame by percentages.

✦ The Text Frame Options dialog box (Object ➪ Text Frame Options, or ⌘+B or Ctrl+B), shown in Figure 11-3, lets you change the number of columns and the space between them, specify how far text is inset from each side of the frame, and specify the placement of the first baseline. If you don't want text within this box to wrap around any items in front of it, check Ignore Text Wrap.

✦ The Direct Selection tool lets you drag anchor points on the frame to change its shape.

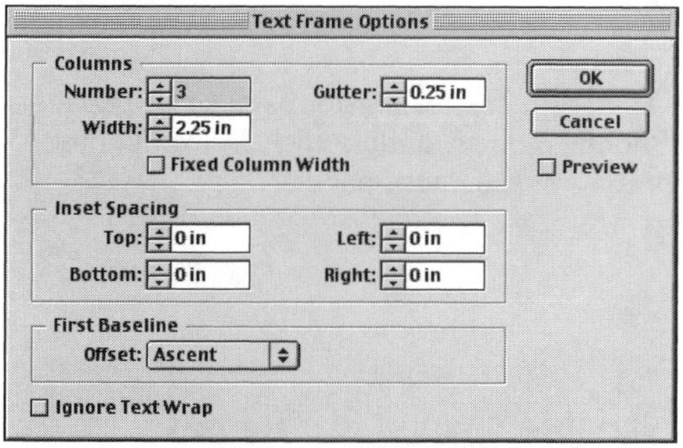

Text Frame Options

Columns
Number: 3   Gutter: 0.25 in   OK
Width: 2.25 in   Cancel
☐ Fixed Column Width   ☐ Preview

Inset Spacing
Top: 0 in   Left: 0 in
Bottom: 0 in   Right: 0 in

First Baseline
Offset: Ascent

☐ Ignore Text Wrap

Figure 11-3: To change the properties of a master text frame, select it on the master page and use the Text Frame Options dialog box.

Settings that relate to text formatting are not maintained by the master text frame. For example, if you click in the master text frame with the Type tool and choose a style from the Paragraph Styles pane or a font from the Character pane, this information is not retained in the master text frames placed on document pages. Settings in the Story palette are not maintained by the master text frame, either.

If you change the master text frame, you'll notice that guides remain on the page in the same position originally specified in the New Document dialog box. You can change these guides to align with the master text frame using the Margins and Columns dialog box (Layout ➪ Margins and Columns). The guides can align only with rectangular boxes.

Drawing additional text frames

The master text frame is helpful for containing body text that flows through a document. You're likely to need plenty of other text frames, on both master pages and document pages. Generally, these are smaller text frames intended to hold headlines, captions, or short paragraphs of descriptive copy.

Creating text frames on master pages

If you're going to add text frames to a master page for repeating elements such as headers and footers, you need to display the master page. Choose Window ⇨ Pages or press F12 to display the Pages pane. Then double-click the A-Master icon in the lower portion of the pane, as shown in Figure 11-4. Any text frames you add to master pages will appear on document pages based on that master page. To switch back to the document and view the text frames, double-click a page icon in the upper portion of the Pages pane.

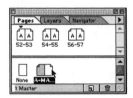

Figure 11-4: To access a master page so you can add or modify objects, double-click an icon in the lower portion of the Pages pane.

Creating rectangular and variable-shaped text frames

To create rectangular text frames on document pages or master pages, select the Type tool. Click and drag to create text frames, and use the Transform pane to fine-tune the placement and dimensions. Figure 11-5 shows a rectangular text frame used for a magazine folio.

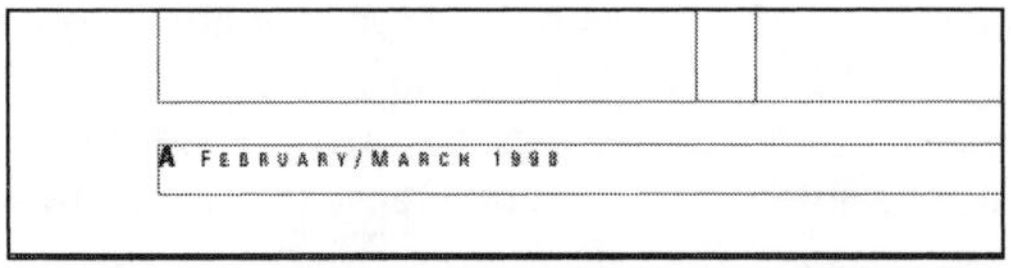

A FEBRUARY/MARCH 1998

Figure 11-5: To automatically place a folio on each page of a magazine, create a text frame containing the appropriate information on each master page in use.

For variable-shaped text frames such as circles or Bézier shapes, use the Pen tool, Ellipse tool, or Polygon tool to create an empty frame. (See Chapters 5 and 24 for more information about creating frames.) Then, convert the frame to a text frame by clicking it with a loaded text icon or choosing Object ➪ Content ➪ Text. (You get the loaded text icon when you place a text file or when you flow text from an existing frame, described later in this chapter.)

Tip If you're working on a document page and want to type in a text frame placed on the page by a master page, select the Type tool and Shift+⌘+click or Ctrl+Shift+click the frame.

Getting the Text

While you can type the text of a book or article directly into threaded text frames in InDesign, in most cases you will import text from a word processor. Most writers and editors will not have page-layout software, and will therefore provide the story in an importable form such as Microsoft Word or WordPerfect. Depending on your production workflow, they may have applied styles to the text in the word processor to indicate how the text should be formatted in InDesign.

Importing text files

The process of importing text files — and otherwise adding text to a document — is explained in full in Chapter 10. When working with documents that require threaded text frames, text is generally imported according to a few simple steps.

Steps: Importing Text for Threading

1. Using the Type tool, select the first text frame that will contain the imported story. If you need to select a master text frame, Shift+⌘+click it or Ctrl+Shift+click it.

2. Choose File ➪ Place or press ⌘+D or Ctrl+D.

3. Use the controls at the top of the Place dialog box to locate the word processing file, and then click it.

4. Check Convert Quotes to convert any straight quotes to curly, typesetter's quotes; check Retain Format to import styles with the text; and check Show Import Options if the text contains any special elements such as tables that need to be converted.

5. Click Choose (Mac) or OK (Windows) to import the text into the selected text frame. Text is likely to overflow the first frame, as shown in Figure 11-6.

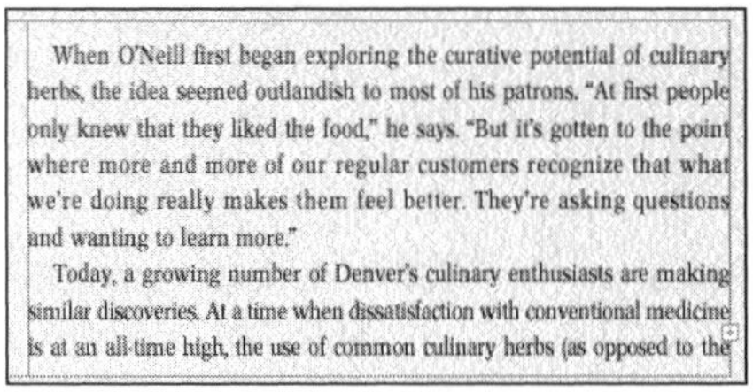

When O'Neill first began exploring the curative potential of culinary herbs, the idea seemed outlandish to most of his patrons. "At first people only knew that they liked the food," he says. "But it's gotten to the point where more and more of our regular customers recognize that what we're doing really makes them feel better. They're asking questions and wanting to learn more."

Today, a growing number of Denver's culinary enthusiasts are making similar discoveries. At a time when dissatisfaction with conventional medicine is at an all-time high, the use of common culinary herbs (as opposed to the

Figure 11-6: The plus sign in the lower-right corner of this text frame indicates there is more text than the frame can hold (called *overset text*).

Handling word processor styles

Whether writers are working on a 1,000-word story or a 40-page chapter of a book, chances are they're using some sort of formatting or styles in their word processing files. This might be as little as bold on headlines and space between paragraphs, or as sophisticated as different styles for each level of heading and type of paragraph in the manuscript.

When you import a word processing file into InDesign, you can bring the formatting and styles with it. (See Chapter 9 for a complete list of formatting options that will import from WordPerfect and Microsoft Word.)

Isolated formatting might be used to indicate which styles should be applied in InDesign — for example, the writer might apply bold to one-line paragraphs that should be formatted as a subhead. However, if the writer applies appropriate paragraph styles to text in his or her word processor, much of the formatting in InDesign can be automated by importing the styles. (Note that word processors' character styles are not imported.)

Other Text-Importing Techniques

InDesign lets you place text in several ways, not just by using the Place command:

✦ If your word processor supports drag and drop, you can drag a text selection directly from your word processor into an InDesign page. This creates a new text frame containing the selected text.

✦ You can copy and paste text from a word processor to an InDesign frame (note that the text's formatting will not be copied).

✦ Finally, you can drag a text file's icon from the desktop or folder into an InDesign page. This results in a loaded-text icon that you then use either to click the text frame you want to add it to or to click and drag to draw a new text frame in which to place the text.

You can use these imported paragraph styles in two different ways, depending on whether styles with the same name already exist in the InDesign document. Remember: To import styles with a word processing file, check Retain Format in the Place dialog box (File ⇨ Place, or ⌘+D or Ctrl+D).

Editing imported paragraph styles

If you import paragraph styles with text, you can simply use the styles specified in the word processor to format the text. This method works well for designs that do not follow a template — for example, brochures and feature stories. You might import the text, experiment with formatting it, and then edit the imported styles in InDesign to reflect your design.

For example, say you import a magazine feature article that is formatted with three paragraph styles (Headline, Byline, and Body Copy) into an InDesign document that does not contain styles with those names. The three styles are added to InDesign's Paragraph Styles list and have the same specifications they had in the word processor. However, because InDesign offers more formatting options, you might edit those styles to fine-tune the text formatting. To edit a paragraph style, select it in the Paragraph Styles pane, click the palette menu arrow, and choose Style Options, as shown in Figure 11-7.

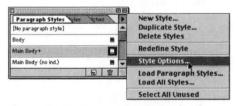

Figure 11-7: You can import styles from a word processor, and then edit them in InDesign using the Style Options command in the Paragraph Styles pane.

Overriding imported paragraph styles

In documents based on a standard design, you can provide writers with style names that must be applied to their text. For example, say you're working on a tri-fold brochure that is part of an entire series of similar tri-folds. The writer might format the text with five paragraph styles that also exist in your InDesign document: Heads, Subheads, Body Copy, Bullets, and Quotes. The style specifications in the word processor don't matter — only the names count — because InDesign document styles override imported styles.

For example, the writer's styles could use standard fonts such as Times and Helvetica along with bold and italic type styles to distinguish the types of text. But when the word-processing file is imported into InDesign, the styles are overridden with InDesign styles that have the same name but specify the actual fonts used by the designer and the many formatting options available in InDesign. See Figure 11-8 to compare the same styles in Microsoft Word and InDesign.

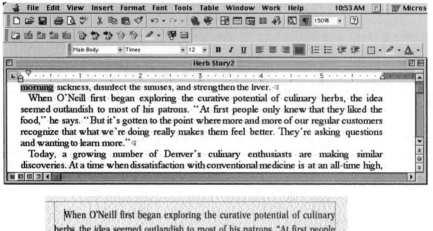

Figure 11-8: In Microsoft Word (top), the paragraph style Main Body specifies 12-point Times — fonts the writer is likely to have at a size that it's amenable to writing and editing (top). When the Word file is placed in InDesign, it is overridden by a paragraph style with the same name — except in InDesign the style specifies 9-point Concorde Nova (bottom).

You can supply writers either with actual styles or with only style names:

✦ To supply styles, export text from a similar story in RTF format, which writers can open in their word processor; the word processor adds the style names in the RTF file to its own style list. The writers can then save these style names to a template file and use that template for future documents. To export text, use the Export dialog box (File ⇨ Export, or ⌘+E or Ctrl+E) and choose Rich Text Format from the Formats menu.

✦ Or, you can simply give writers a list of style names that they can create themselves to their own specifications. In this case, it's particularly important that the styles created in the word processor have exactly the same names as those in the InDesign document.

Threading Text Frames

InDesign provides three options for *threading* (or linking) text frames: manual, semi-autoflow, and autoflow. Each has its own icon, as shown with the description of each method. The method you choose depends on how much text you're dealing with and the size and quantity of your text frames:

✦ You might use the **manual method**, in which you click the first and second text frame, to link two text frames across several pages for an article continuation.

✦ The **semi-autoflow method**, which enables you to click a series of text frames to flow text, works well for linking a succession of text frames in something like a catalog layout.

✦ The **autoflow method** adds text frames and pages as you import text, and is intended for flowing long text files such as a book chapter or annual report.

Text Frame Anatomy

Before you start threading text frames, you need to understand what a text frame is trying to tell you about its text. To get the message, you need to select the text frames with one of the selection tools — when the Type tool is selected, all you can see is overset text. The text frame provides the following indicators, as shown in the following figure.

✦ **In port (empty):** A small white square near the upper-left corner of a text frame is the in port, indicating where a story will enter the frame.

✦ **In port (with arrow):** Within a chain of threaded text frames, the in port contains a right-facing arrow indicating that the story is continuing into this frame.

✦ **Out port (empty):** A small white square near the lower-right corner of a text frame is the out port, indicating that the story fits comfortably within the frame.

✦ **Out port (with arrow):** Within a chain of threaded text frames, the out port might contain a right-facing arrow indicating that the story is continuing into another frame.

✦ **Out port (with + sign):** A small red plus sign in the out port indicates that more text exists than can fit in the text frame or chain of threaded text frames.

✦ **Threads:** When you choose View ➪ Show Text Threads (or press Option+⌘+Y or Ctrl+ Alt+Y), you can view threads, or lines, indicating the direction in which frames are threaded. (To see multiple text chains, Shift+click to select text frames from different threads.)

Continued

(continued)

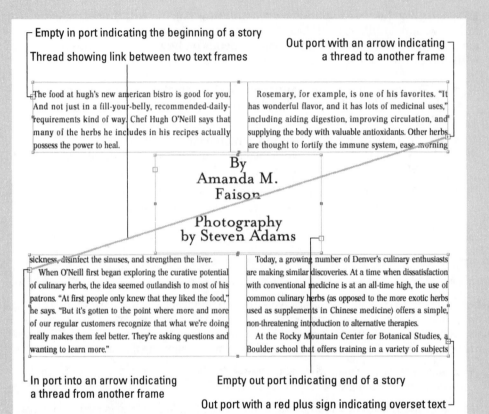

Empty in port indicating the beginning of a story

Thread showing link between two text frames

Out port with an arrow indicating a thread to another frame

The food at hugh's new american bistro is good for you. And not just in a fill-your-belly, recommended-daily-requirements kind of way. Chef Hugh O'Neill says that many of the herbs he includes in his recipes actually possess the power to heal.

Rosemary, for example, is one of his favorites. "It has wonderful flavor, and it has lots of medicinal uses," including aiding digestion, improving circulation, and supplying the body with valuable antioxidants. Other herbs are thought to fortify the immune system, ease morning

By Amanda M. Faison

Photography by Steven Adams

sickness, disinfect the sinuses, and strengthen the liver.

When O'Neill first began exploring the curative potential of culinary herbs, the idea seemed outlandish to most of his patrons. "At first people only knew that they liked the food," he says. "But it's gotten to the point where more and more of our regular customers recognize that what we're doing really makes them feel better. They're asking questions and wanting to learn more."

Today, a growing number of Denver's culinary enthusiasts are making similar discoveries. At a time when dissatisfaction with conventional medicine is at an all-time high, the use of common culinary herbs (as opposed to the more exotic herbs used as supplements in Chinese medicine) offers a simple, non-threatening introduction to alternative therapies.

At the Rocky Mountain Center for Botanical Studies, a Boulder school that offers training in a variety of subjects

In port into an arrow indicating a thread from another frame

Empty out port indicating end of a story

Out port with a red plus sign indicating overset text

In the small text frame containing the byline, you can see an empty in port (upper-left corner) and an empty out port (lower-right corner), indicating that the text fits comfortably in the box. In the text frame at the top right, the lower-right corner displays an out port with an arrow, indicating that text is flowing to another box. A thread shows exactly where the text enters the next text frame at its in port, which contains another arrow. The lower-right corner of the last text frame shows overset text (the plus sign in the out box), indicating that all the text still doesn't fit.

Threading frames manually

To thread text frames manually, you simply use a selection tool to link out ports to in ports. You can prethread existing text frames by linking empty text frames, and then add text later, or you can create threads from a text frame that contains overset text.

Oddly, you cannot thread frames while the Type tool is selected, so remember to switch to a selection tool.

Steps: Threading Text Frames

1. Create a series of text frames that you intend to flow text through. You can also create empty frames of other shapes; the frames do not need to be on the same page.

2. Click either the Selection tool or the Direction Selection tool.

3. Click the out port of the first text frame in the thread, as shown in Figure 11-9. If the port contains a plus sign indicating overset text, the pointer becomes the loaded text icon.

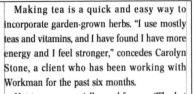

Figure 11-9: Clicking an out port containing a plus sign—which indicates overset text—lets you flow the text into another text frame.

4. Click the in port of the second text frame in the thread. You can also click any empty frame or click and drag to draw a new text frame. Any overset text will flow into the second text frame.

5. Use the Pages pane to add or switch pages as necessary while you continue clicking out ports and in ports until your chain of threaded text frames is complete.

6. When you finish threading text frames, select another object on the page or another tool. When you import a story into any text frame in this chain, it starts in the upper-left corner of the first frame and flows through the frames in same order as the threads.

Linking manually from out port to in port works well for continuing a magazine article from one page to the next, as shown in Figure 11-10.

Figure 11-10: In a magazine article that continues from one page to the next, you can simply thread the two text frames by clicking an out port, and then an in port.

Tip

To see text threads easily while threading text across pages, change the document view to 20 percent or so. You can also display two views of the same document by choosing Window ➪ New Window. The original window might be at 100% view so you can easily select the port indicating overflow text and the text frame you want to link it to. The second window might show a reduced version of the page that contains the text frame to which you are linking.

Note

Text flows through frames in the order in which you select the frames. If you move a frame, its order in the text flow remains unchanged, so if you're not careful, you could, for example, accidentally have text flow from a frame at the top of page to one at the bottom of a page and then to one in the middle of a page.

Threading frames semi-automatically

InDesign's semi-autoflow method of threading text frames varies only slightly from the manual method. Follow the same steps for threading text frames manually, except hold down the Option or Alt key each time you click in the next text frame. This lets you bypass the in ports and out ports, and simply click from text frame to text frame to establish links.

While first placing a word processing file, you can also Option+click or Alt+click in the first text frame to begin a semi-autoflow process. Threading frames semi-automatically works well for a series of small boxes on the same page, as shown in Figure 11-11.

Figure 11-11: To quickly flow text from one frame to the next as in this table of contents, you can use InDesign's semi-autoflow method.

Note Remember to Option+click or Alt+click each text frame or you'll revert to manual threading.

Threading frames and adding pages automatically

The autoflow method for threading frames is what lets you flow a lengthy story quickly through a document. You can either autoflow text into the master text frame or into automatically created text frames that fit within the column guides. InDesign flows the text into any existing pages, and then adds new pages based on the current master page. You can initiate autoflow before or after placing a word processing file.

Placing text while autoflowing

If you haven't imported text yet, you can place a file and have it automatically flow through the document. This method works well for flowing text into several pages that are all formatted the same way, such as a book.

Steps: Autoflowing

1. Confirm that the master page in use has a master text frame or appropriate column guides.
2. With no text frames selected, choose File ➪ Place or press ⌘+D or Ctrl+D.

3. Locate and select a word-processing file, and then click Choose (Mac) or OK (Windows).

4. When the loaded text icon displays, Shift+click in the first column that will contain the text, as shown in Figure 11-12. InDesign adds all the necessary text frames and pages, and flows in the entire story. (You must flow text into the right-most column of the text frame.)

Figure 11-12: The introduction to this story is in a short, two-column text box, which will be autoflowed into pages that follow the magazine's standard, three-column grid.

Autoflowing after placing text

If you've already placed a text file into a single text frame or even a threaded chain of text frames, you can still autoflow text from the last text frame. To do so, click the overset icon in the out port, and then Shift+click any page to indicate where to start the autoflow. You might use this method if you're placing the introduction to an article in a highly designed page (as in Figure 11-12), and then flowing the rest of the article into standard pages.

Threading Icons

While you're threading text, several icons provide visual cues as to the type of threading you're doing and what the results will be. Remember, to view threads from a text frame selected with the Selection tool or Direct-Selection tool, choose View ➪ Show Text Threads or press Option+⌘+Y or Ctrl+Alt+Y.

✦ **Manual text flow icon.** The loaded text icon contains text that needs to be placed or overset text that needs to be threaded into a new text frame.

✦ **Manual text frame flow icon.** When the loaded text icon is over a text frame, the icon changes so the icon is displayed in parentheses. The same change happens for the semi-autoflow icon.

✦ **Thread icon.** This icon, which looks like two links in a chain, appears while you're threading text frames manually. Specifically, the loaded text icon changes to this icon when it's over an empty text frame into which you can thread the current text frame.

✦ **Semi-autoflow icon.** This icon appears when you Option+click or Alt+click text frames while threading a series of text frames.

✦ **Autoflow icon.** This icon appears when you Shift+click a page to initiate the autoflow process, in which InDesign adds text frames and pages to contain the entire story.

Breaking and rerouting threads

Once text frames are threaded, you have three options for changing the threads: You can break threads to stop text from flowing, insert a text frame into an existing chain of threaded text frames, and remove text frames from a thread:

✦ To break the link between two text frames, double-click either an out port or an in port. The thread between the two text frames is removed and all text that had flowed from that point is sucked out of the subsequent text frames and stored as overset text.

✦ To insert a text frame after a specific text frame in a chain, click its out port. Then, click and drag the loaded text icon to create a new text frame. That new frame is automatically threaded to the previous and next text frame. (See Figure 11-13.)

Figure 11-13: To add a text frame between two existing threaded frames, click the first frame's out port. Click and drag the loaded text icon to create a new text frame. The new frame is automatically inserted into the thread and the text reflows.

✦ To reroute text threads — for example, to drop the middle text frame from a chain of three — click the text frame with the Selection tool and press Delete or backspace. The text frame is deleted and the threads are rerouted. You can Shift+click to multiple-select text frames to remove them as well. Note that you cannot reroute text threads without removing the text frames.

Adjusting Columns

The placement of columns on the page and the amount of space between them has significant impact on readability. Column width, in general, works with type size and leading to create lines and rows of text that you can read easily. This means you're not getting lost from one line to the next, that you're not accidentally jumping across columns, and that you're not getting a headache while squinting at the page.

Design Advice

As a rule of thumb, as columns get wider, the type size and leading should increase. For example, you might see 9-point text and 11-point leading in 2.5-inch columns, while 11-point text and 13-point leading might work better in 3.5-inch columns.

InDesign lets you place columns on the page automatically, create any number of columns within a text frame, and change columns at any time.

Specifying columns in master frames

If you choose to create a master text frame — an automatically placed text frame within the margin guides — when you create a new document, you can specify the number of columns in it at the same time.

In the Columns area at the bottom of the New Document dialog box shown in Figure 11-14, use the Number field to specify how many columns and the Gutter field to specify how much space to place between the columns. (The *gutter* is the space between columns.) Whether or not you check Master Text Frame (which makes the frame appear on all pages), guides for these columns will still be placed on pages based on the default master page (A) and can be used for placing text frames and other objects.

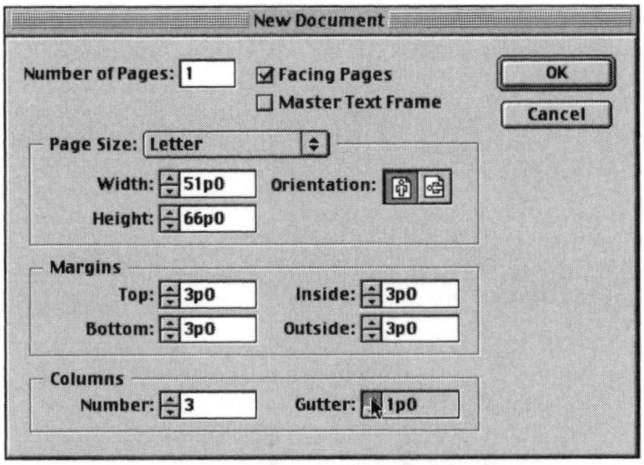

Figure 11-14: When you create a master frame in the New Document dialog box, specify the number of columns and the amount of space between them using the Columns area.

Adjusting columns in text frames

Once you've created a text frame and even flowed text into it, you can change the number of columns in it. First, select the text frame with a selection tool or the Type tool (or Shift+click to select multiple text frames and change all their columns at once). Then choose Object ➪ Text Frame Options or press ⌘+B or Ctrl+B. Note that each column in a text frame must be the same width; use threaded text frames of different widths to create columns of different widths.

Note that the options in the Columns area work differently depending on whether Fixed Column Width is checked or unchecked. Check Preview to see the effects of your changes before finalizing them.

Automatically adjusting columns

When Fixed Column Width is unchecked, InDesign automatically adjusts column widths within the boundaries of the text frame, as follows:

✦ When you change the value in the Number field, InDesign creates the requested number of columns and gives them all the same width.

✦ When you change the value in the Gutter field, InDesign reduces the width of the columns and expands or contracts the space between them per the new gutter value.

✦ When you change the value in the Width field, the text frame expands or contracts to accommodate the width and the gutter, as shown in Figure 11-15.

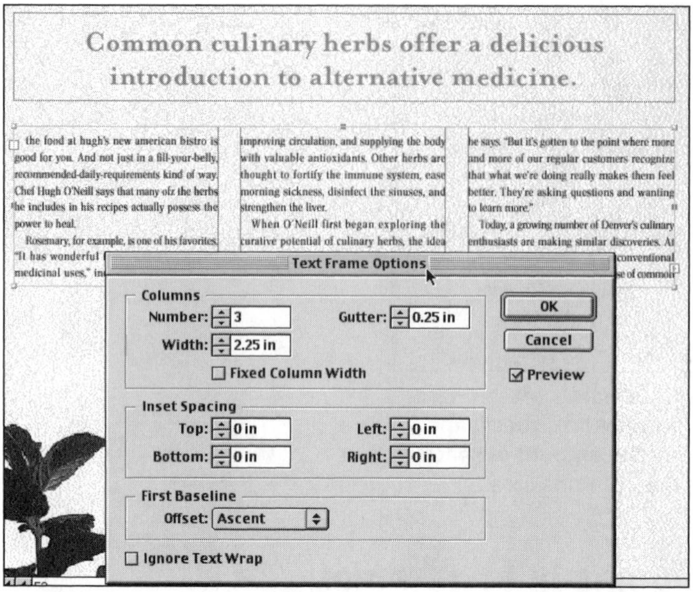

Figure 11-15: Because Fixed Column Width is unchecked in the Text Frame Options dialog box, changing the number of columns in the selected text frame from two to three resulted in narrower columns in the same-size frame.

Similarly, when you increase or decrease the width of a text frame for which Fixed Column Width is unchecked, InDesign adjusts the width of the columns proportionally. The gutter width is not affected.

Adjusting fixed columns

When Fixed Column Width is checked, InDesign increases or decreases the width of the text frame to accommodate the values you enter for the columns, as follows:

- ✦ When you change the Number of columns, InDesign creates columns according to the value in the Width field. For example, if you enter **3** in the Number field and **1in** in the Width field, InDesign creates three 1-inch columns, and makes the text frame wide enough to accommodate those columns and the gutters.

- ✦ When you change the value in the Gutter field, InDesign changes the width of the text frame as needed to accommodate the new gutter size.

- ✦ The Width field actually works the same regardless of whether Fixed Column Width is checked: When you change the value, the text frame expands or contracts to accommodate the width and the gutter.

Similarly, when you increase or decrease the width of a text frame with Fixed Column Width, InDesign automatically adds columns of the selected width, as shown in Figure 11-16.

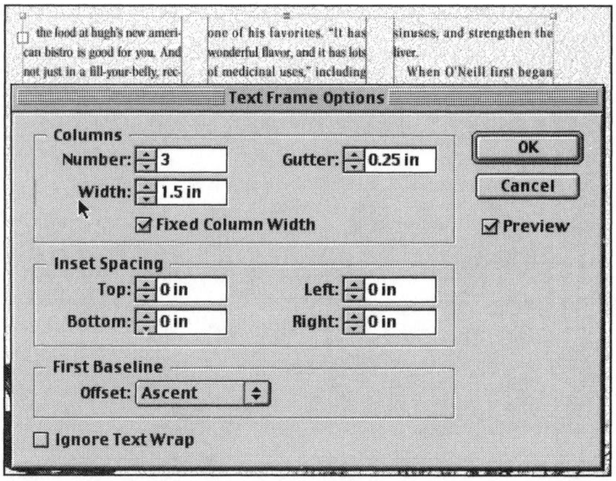

Figure 11-16: In this example, Fixed Column Width is checked in the Text Frame Options dialog box. When the designer changed the number of columns from two to three, InDesign created columns to match the values in the Width and Gutter fields, and altered the size of the text frame accordingly.

Placing rules between columns

Unfortunately, InDesign does not provide an automatic method for creating intercolumn rules. To get around this lack, you need to draw lines on the page—in the center of the gutters—with the Line tool. Because you might resize text frames or change the number of columns while designing a document, you should add the vertical rules at the end of the process. In a structured document, you can place the rules between columns in text frames on the master page.

When drawing rules between columns, use the rulers to precisely position the lines. After you've drawn the lines, Shift+click to select all the lines and the text frames, and then choose Object ➪ Group, or ⌘+G or Ctrl+G (see Figure 11-17). When the lines are grouped to the text frame, you can move them all as a unit. This also prevents someone from accidentally moving a vertical rule later.

Design Advice

The use of vertical rules (thin lines) between columns—called intercolumn rules— is an effective way to separate columns with small gutters (this is often done in newspapers, whose columns and gutters are usually thin). It can also add visual interest and a sense of old-fashioned authority—it was a common technique for newspapers early in the 20th century and is still used by the august *Wall Street Journal*, for example. Keep the width of intercolumn rules thin: usually a hairline (¹/₄ point) or ¹/₂ point. Larger than that is usually too thick and can be confused with the border of a sidebar or other boxed element.

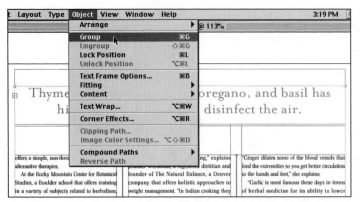

Figure 11-17: When drawing vertical intercolumn rules, group them to the text frame so they will move with the frame.

Summary

When text doesn't fit within a single frame—the case in almost any multipage publication—you need to link (or thread) the text frames. You can do this manually, threading one text frame to the next, or you can have InDesign automatically add pages containing threaded text frames. Once frames are threaded, you can still reflow text by breaking text threads and rerouting the threads.

In addition to flowing text through threaded frames, you can flow it through multiple columns within each frame. You can change the number of columns or their width within a frame at any time, and text reflows. To distinguish columns visually, you can draw vertical lines between columns and group them to the text frames.

✦   ✦   ✦

Specifying Character Formats

Type is the visual representation of the spoken word. A *typographer* is a person who designs with type. As a user of InDesign, chances are you're going to be making lots of decisions about the appearance of the text in the publications you produce. You are, whether you consider yourself one or not, a typographer. And not only are InDesign users typographers, they're typographers who have an extensive arsenal of text-formatting tools that let them tweak and polish their type in a nearly infinite variety of ways.

Of all the decisions an InDesign user makes when designing a publication, decisions about type are arguably the most important. Why? Because a publication can't be effective if the text is hard to read. The difference between good typography and bad typography is the same as the difference between clear speaking and mumbling. The intent of a clear speaker and a mumbler may be the same, but the effect on the listener is quite different. In publishing, the printed words are the containers in which the writer's message is transported to the reader. As the caretaker of those words, you hold great power. Whether or not the message is successfully transported depends largely on your typographic decisions.

As you learn to use InDesign's powerful type-formatting features, you should always remember the cardinal rule of typography: Type exists to honor content. By all means, you should take full advantage of the available tools, but sometimes knowing when not to use a fancy typographic feature is as important as knowing how to use the feature in the first place.

Cross-Reference This chapter focuses on modifying character-level typographic formats; the next chapter focuses on modifying paragraph-level formats. Part IV offers a broader look at using InDesign to design with type.

Character Formats versus Paragraph Formats

Before we begin looking at InDesign's character-formatting features, you should be clear about a fundamental InDesign type-formatting concept: InDesign lets you modify the appearance of highlighted characters *or* selected paragraphs.

When characters are highlighted (or the text cursor is flashing), you can use the Character pane (Type ⇨ Character, or ⌘+T or Ctrl+T), shown in Figure 12-1, to change their appearance in several ways.

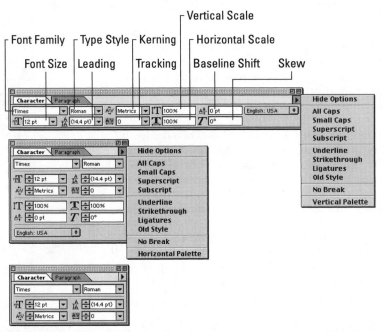

Figure 12-1: You can display the Character pane in a vertical (top) or horizontal (middle) window by choosing the corresponding option (Vertical Pane or Horizontal Pane) from the pane's palette menu. You can also hide some options (bottom).

When paragraphs are selected, the Paragraph pane (Type ⇨ Character, or ⌘+M or Ctrl+M) lets you change how the paragraphs are constructed.

Cross-Reference In addition to the Character and Paragraphs panes, InDesign's Story pane (Type ⇨ Story) lets you adjust the left and right margins for an entire story. See Chapter 17 for more information about the Story pane.

Both the Character and Paragraph panes are shown in Figure 12-1. If you choose Hide Options from the palette menu, the Vertical Scale, Horizontal Scale, Baseline Shift, and Skew fields and the Language pop-up menu are not displayed, as shown in the bottom example. As is the case in the figure, you might want to combine the Character and Paragraph panes into a single text-formatting pane. (For more information about the Paragraph pane, see Chapter 13.)

Tip If the Type tool is selected and no objects are active, the controls in the Character pane are available. In this situation, any changes you make in the Character pane become the default settings for the document and are automatically used when you create new text frames.

Tip If you change character formats when the cursor is flashing and no text is selected, your changes are applied at the insertion point. When you begin typing, you'll see the results of your changes.

Two ways to apply character formats

InDesign lets you apply character formats to highlighted text in two ways: You can:

✦ Use the controls in the Character pane or their keyboard shortcuts.

✦ Create and apply character-level styles.

Note In InDesign (and most programs), you can select only contiguous text. So if you have, for example, several subheads you want to apply a font to, you can't select them all and apply the formatting in one fell swoop. You'll have to do each text segment separately.

A character-level style is essentially a text-formatting macro that lets you apply several character formats to highlighted text in a single operation. If you are working on a simple, one-page publication, such as a business card, a poster, or an ad, you'll probably use the Character pane to format the text elements. However, if you're producing a multipage publication—a newsletter, magazine, catalog, or newspaper, for example—you should take advantage of styles. Using them will save you time and make your job a whole lot easier.

 Cross-Reference For details about creating and applying character and paragraph styles, see Chapter 15.

Even if you do use styles for a particular publication, it's likely that you'll also do some local formatting. For example, you would probably use the Character pane to format the type on the opening spread of a feature magazine article, and then use styles to quickly format the remainder of the article.

Here's the bottom line: If you understand InDesign's character-formatting options, you'll have no trouble getting the hang of character-level styles. (The same is true for paragraph formats.) The process of modifying the character formats applied to highlighted text is the same regardless of the formats you change.

The Character pane provides access to all of InDesign's character-formatting options. Three of the options — Font Family, Type Style, and Size — are also available in the Type menu, and several options have keyboard shortcuts.

Cross-Reference   Some of the controls in the Transform pane let you change the appearance of all the text within a text frame. For more information about the Transform pane, see Chapter 6.

Tip   You can change the default character formats associated with the Type tool by making changes in the Character pane when no text is selected or the text-insertion cursor isn't flashing.

Changing Font Family, Type Style, and Size

These days, the terms *font, face, typeface, font family,* and *type style* are often used interchangeably. When you're talking with friends or colleagues about typography, it doesn't matter which term you use as long as you make yourself understood, but if you're going to be setting type with InDesign, you should be familiar with the font-related terms you'll find in the menus and panes.

The term *font,* or *typeface,* usually refers to a collection of characters — including letters, numbers, and special characters — that share the same overall appearance, including stroke width, weight, angle, and style. For example, Helvetica Plain, Arial Bold, Adobe Garamond Semibold Italic, and ITC Beesknees Plain are well-known fonts. A *font family* is a collection of several fonts that share the same general appearance but differ in stroke width, weight, and/or stroke angle. Some examples of font families are Adobe Caslon, Berthold Baskerville, Times New Roman, and Tekton.

In InDesign each of the fonts that make up a font family is referred to as a *type style.* For example, the Berthold Baskerville font family is made up of four type styles: Regular, Medium, Italic, and Medium Italic, as shown in Figure 12-2. When you choose a font family from the Character pane's Font Family menu, InDesign displays the family's type style variations in the accompanying Type Styles pop-up menu.

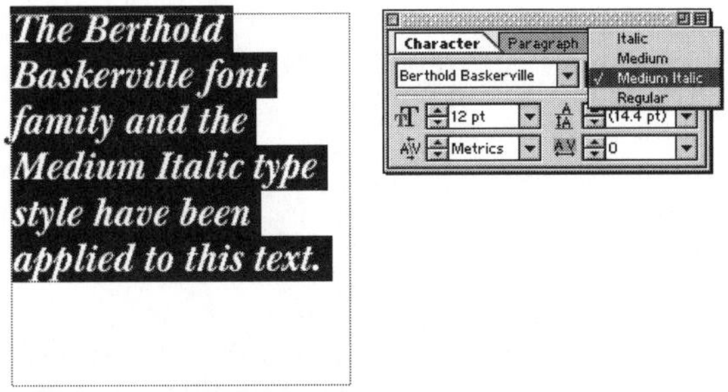

Figure 12-2: The Berthold Baskerville font family includes four type styles — Regular, Italic, Medium, and Medium Italic — as shown here.

When you change from one font to another in InDesign, you can choose a new font family and type style independently. For example, changing from Arial Bold to Times Bold or from Arial Regular to Berthold Baskerville Regular is a simple change of font family. However, if you switch from Bookman Light to Century Schoolbook Bold Italic, you're changing both family and type style.

When you change the font family applied to selected text, InDesign tries to maintain the applied type style. If, for example, you switch from Adobe Garamond Bold Italic to Adobe Caslon, InDesign automatically uses Adobe Caslon Bold Italic, which is one of several type styles that make up this font family. But if you switch from Arial Bold Italic to Avant Garde, which doesn't include a bold italic variation, Avant Garde Book will be used instead.

Unlike most word-processing and desktop-publishing programs, InDesign doesn't include built-in shadow and outline styles. (These styles are available only if a font includes them.) Most programs create these stylistic variations artificially by modifying plain characters. If you want to create outline text, you can use the Stroke pane (Window ⇨ Stroke, or F10) to apply a stroke, as covered in Chapter 19. If you want to create a drop shadow for text, you can stack and offset two text frames. (See Chapter 17 for more about creating special typographic effects.)

Similarly, bold and italic variations are available only for font families that include these type styles. This prevents you from applying, for example, italic to Trajan, a font family that doesn't include an italic variation. (InDesign does let you create false italics by skewing text, which is covered later in this chapter. However, you should avoid such heavy-handed shape twisting unless it's absolutely necessary.)

Changing font family

The Character pane offers two methods for changing the font family applied to highlighted text. You can:

✦ Click the Font Family menu, and then choose a name from the list of available font families, as shown in Figure 12-3.

✦ Click in front of or highlight the font name displayed in the Font Family field, type in the first few letters of the font family you want to apply, and then click Return or Enter. For example, entering **Ari** selects Arial (if it's available on your computer).

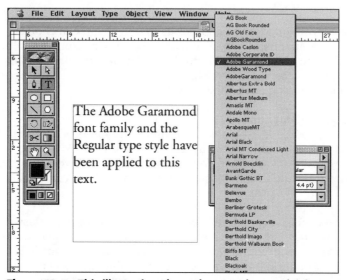

Figure 12-3: This illustration shows how to change the font family applied to highlighted text using the Font Family menu in the Character pane.

You can also change the font family by choosing Type ➪ Font and then selecting a name in the Font submenu. If a particular font family includes a submenu with type style variations, you must also choose a type style. If you choose only a font family when type styles are available in an accompanying submenu, no changes are applied to the selected text.

Note   InDesign displays the names of all fonts installed on your computer in the Font submenu and the Font Family menu in the Character pane.

One advantage of using the Font submenu instead of the Character pane is that you can reliably change the font family and the type style at the same time. If a corresponding type style does not exist when you change the font family via the Character pane, the base style (such as plain, book, or regular) of the new family is used. In this case, the Character pane's Type Style menu confusingly displays the name of the original type style in brackets.

Changing type style

Changing type styles is much like changing font families. You can choose a type style from the Type Style menu in the Character pane, click in front of or highlight the name in the Type Style field and enter the first few characters of the new style, or choose a font family and type style at the same time using the Font submenu (Type ➪ Font).

Changing font size

InDesign lets you specify font sizes from 0.1 point to 1296 points (108 inches) in increments as fine as 0.0001 point. Of course, even if it were possible to clearly print type as small as a tenth of a point (that is, one seven-hundred-and-twentieth of an inch), which is beyond the capabilities of most printers, nobody could read it without a microscope anyway. Use good judgment when choosing font sizes. For example, headlines should be larger than subheads, which in turn are larger than body text, which is larger than photo credits, and so on.

InDesign offers several methods for changing the font size of highlighted text. You can:

✦ Choose one of the predefined sizes from the Font Size menu in the Character pane, as shown in Figure 12-4.

✦ Highlight the currently applied font size displayed in the accompanying editable field, enter a new size, and then press Return or Enter.

✦ Use the up and down cursor keys to increase or decrease the size in 2-point increments. You can change the default increment of 2 points in the Size/Leading field in the Units and Measurements pane of the Preferences dialog box (File ➪ Preferences ➪ Units & Increments, or ⌘+K or Ctrl+K). Holding Shift multiplies the increment by 5.

✦ Choose Type ➪ Size, and then choose one of the predefined sizes listed in the Size submenu. If you choose Other from the submenu, the Font Size field is highlighted in the Character pane. Enter a custom size, and then press Return or Enter.

✦ Control+click (on the Mac) or right-click (in Windows), and then choose a size from the Size submenu. If you choose Other from the submenu, the Font Size field is highlighted in the Character pane. Enter a custom size, and then press Return or Enter.

✦ Hold down Shift+⌘ or Ctrl+Shift and press > to enlarge highlighted text in increments (usually 1-point increments, but you can set the increment in the Units & Measurements pane in the Preferences dialog box, accessed via File ➪ Preferences, or ⌘+K or Ctrl+K). Press < to reduce highlighted text. Option+Shift+⌘+> or Ctrl+Alt+Shift+> increases the text size at 5 times the increment, whereas Option+Shift+⌘+< decreases the text size at 5 times the increment.

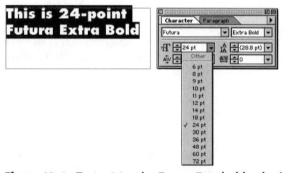

Figure 12-4: Text—24-point Futura Extrabold—that's been resized using the Font Size field's pop-up menu.

You can also shrink or enlarge all the text in a text frame with the Scale tool or by changing the values in the Scale X percentage and/or Scale Y percentage fields in the Transform pane. Beware: Changing the size of text by scaling a text frame does not actually change the font size applied to the text. This can be confusing. For example, 12-point text in a frame that's been enlarged to 200 percent of its original size will appear to be 24 points, but if you check its size in the Character pane's Font size field or the Size submenu (Type ➪ Size), it will show that the font size is 12 points. Keep things simple; don't resize text by scaling its frame unless you have a good reason to do so.

If text is highlighted and the Font Size field is empty, it means that more than one font size is used in the selected text.

Applying Other Character Formats

Font family, type style, and font size are the most commonly modified character formats, but the Character pane contains several other controls for managing the appearance of type. Some of these controls are displayed in the pane window; others are available in the pane's pop-up menu.

Pane controls

In the Character pane, you can adjust horizontal and vertical scale, baseline shift, skew, and language.

Note
You must choose Show Options from the Character pane's pop-up menu to display the Vertical Scale, Horizontal Scale, Baseline Shift, Skew, and Language options.

Horizontal Scale and Vertical Scale

...e font families include condensed (that is, slightly squeezed) and/or expanded ...htly stretched) stylistic variations, but most don't. InDesign's Horizontal Scale ...on lets you create artificially condensed and expanded type by squeezing or ...ching characters. Similarly, the Vertical Scale option lets you shrink or stretch ...vertically.

...graphers have two schools of thought about scaling type. One camp contends ...uch distortions of letterforms are taboo and should be avoided. The other ...ontends that a small amount of scaling doesn't adversely affect the original ...nd is acceptable. There's general agreement that overscaling should be avoided. For the most part, if you need to make text bigger or smaller, you should adjust font size; if you need to squeeze or stretch a range of text a bit, it's better to use InDesign's kerning and tracking controls (covered later in this chapter) because the letterforms are not affected. Only the space between letters changes when you kern or track text.

Unscaled text has a horizontal and vertical scale value of 100 percent. You can apply scaling values from 1 to 1000 percent. If you apply equal horizontal and vertical scale values, you're making the original text proportionally larger or smaller. In this case, changing font size is a simpler solution. As already mentioned, keep in mind that when you scale text, you are not changing the font size. For example, 24-point type scaled vertically to 200 percent is 48 points tall, but its font size is still 24 points.

To change the scale of highlighted text, enter new values in the Horizontal and/or Vertical Scale fields in the Character pane. You can also use the up and down cursor keys to increase and decrease the shift in 1-percent increments; hold Shift to increase or decrease in 10-percent increments. Figures 12-5 and 12-6 show examples of vertical and horizontal scaling, respectively.

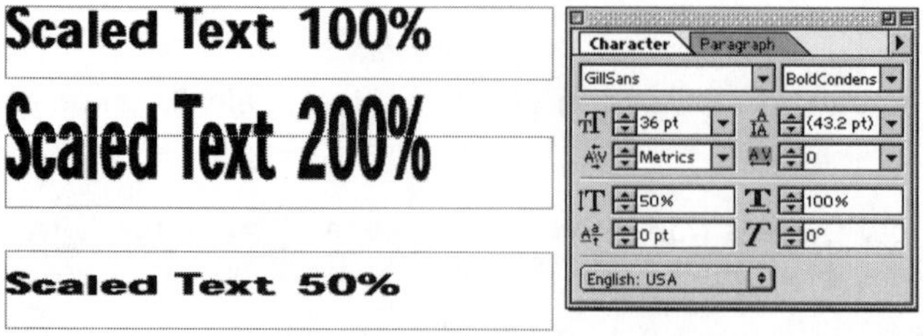

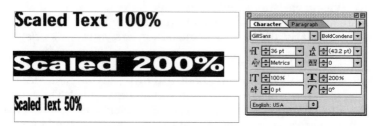

Figure 12-5: The original text (top) has been vertically scaled to 200 percent (center) and to 50 percent (bottom).

Figure 12-6: The original text (top) has been horizontally scaled to 200 percent (center) and to 50 percent (bottom).

Baseline Shift

The baseline is an invisible horizontal line on which a line of characters rests. The bottom of each letter (except descenders, such as in *y, p, q, j,* and *g*) sits on the baseline. InDesign's Baseline Shift feature lets you move highlighted text above or below its baseline. This feature is useful for carefully placing such characters as trademark and copyright symbols and for creating custom fractions.

To baseline-shift highlighted text, enter new values in the Horizontal and/or Vertical Scale fields in the Character pane. You can also use the up and down cursor keys to increase the shift in 2-point increments. You can change the default increment of 2 points in the Baseline Shift field in the Units and Measurements pane of the Preferences dialog box (File ➪ Preferences ➪ Units & Increments, or ⌘+K or Ctrl+K). Hold Shift to increase or decrease in 5 times the normal increment.

Figure 12-7 shows the Baseline Shift feature in action.

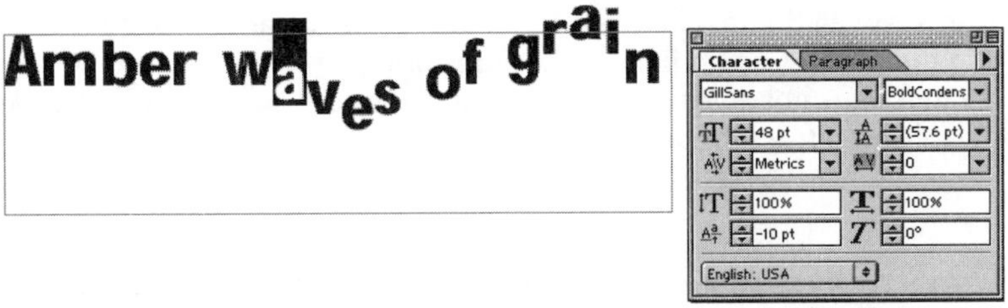

Figure 12-7: The characters in this example have been baseline shifted — some up; some down — to create a wavy effect. The first word has not been shifted and rests on the original baseline.

Skew (false italic)

For fonts that don't have an italic type style, InDesign provides the option to skew, or slant, text to create an artificial italic variation of any font. Like horizontal and vertical text scaling, skewing is a clunky way of creating italic-looking text. Use this feature to create special typographic effects, such as the shadow text shown in Figure 12-8, or in situations where a true italic style is not available.

Skewed shadow

Figure 12-8: Skewing, shading a copy of the black text, and then flipping the frame vertically (via the Flip Vertical command in the Transform pane's pop-up menu) created this backlit shadow effect.

Skewing as a form of italics typically works better for sans serif typefaces than for serif typefaces.

To skew highlighted text:

1. Enter an angle value from –85 to 85 in the Skew field in the Character pane. Positive values slant text to the left; negative values slant text to the right.

2. Click the accompanying up/down cursors to skew text in 1-degree increments. Holding down the Shift key while clicking the cursors changes the increment by 4 degrees.

Tip   You can also skew all the text in a text frame using the Shear tool or by changing the value in the Shear X angle field in the Transform pane. Slanting text by shearing a text frame does not affect the skew angle of the text. You can specify a skew angle for highlighted text independently from the frame's shear angle.

Language

The ability to correctly hyphenate and check the spelling of text in several languages is one of InDesign's most powerful features. The program uses Proximity dictionaries to accomplish these tasks. These dictionaries, each of which contains several hundred thousand words, also let you specify a different language for text on a character-by-character basis, although chances are that a single word will be the smallest text unit to which you will apply a separate language.

For example, an article about Spanish cooking might include the word "albóndigas" (the Spanish term for meatballs). By applying the Spanish: Castilian language to this word, as shown in Figure 12-9, InDesign will not flag it when you check spelling. However, if you were to apply U.S. English to albóndigas, it would show up as a misspelled word (unless you had added it to your dictionary; see the Tip that follows).

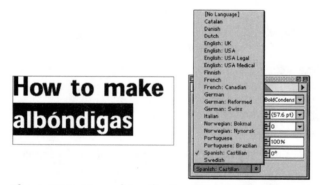

Figure 12-9: By applying the Spanish: Castilian language to albóndigas, as shown here, InDesign uses the associated dictionary when checking the spelling of this word.

To assign a different language to highlighted text, choose the appropriate language from the Language menu in the Character pane, as shown in Figure 12-9.

Tip   If you discover any correctly spelled words that are not included in a particular language dictionary, you can add the words to the dictionary. Choose Edit ⇨ Edit Dictionary and choose the appropriate dictionary in the Language pop-up menu, to customize any dictionary.

Cross-Reference For more information on checking a document's spelling, see Chapter 10.

Pane menu options

When you display the Character pane's palette menu, shown in Figure 12-10, nine additional character-format options are available. All of these options are on/off choices. An enabled option has a check mark next to its name. Choosing a checked option removes the applied format from highlighted text and unchecks the menu entry.

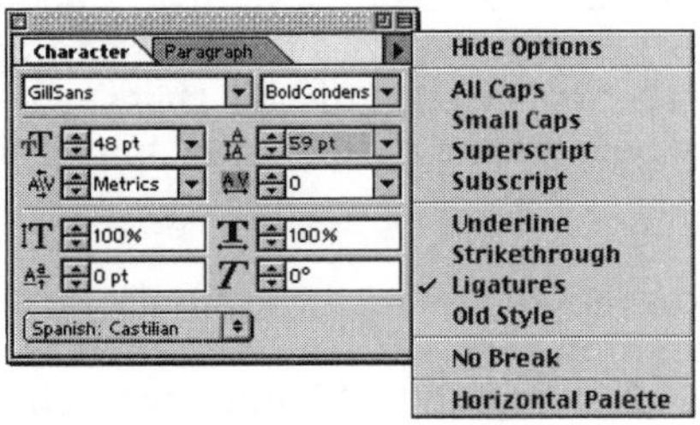

Figure 12-10: The Character pane and its palette menu.

All Caps and Small Caps

When you choose All Caps, the uppercase version of all highlighted characters is used: lowercase letters are converted to uppercase, and uppercase letters remain unchanged.

Similarly, the Small Caps option affects just lowercase letters. When you choose Small Caps, InDesign automatically uses the Small Caps type style if one is available for the font family applied to the highlighted text (few font families include this style). If a Small Caps style is not available, InDesign generates small caps from uppercase letters using the scale percentage specified in the Text pane of the Preferences dialog box (File ➪ Preferences ➪ Text, or ⌘+K or Ctrl+K). The default scale value used to generate small caps text is 70 percent (of uppercase letters).

Tip You should never enter text in all capital letters, even if you think you want all caps. If you enter lowercase letters, you can easily change them to uppercase by applying the All Caps format, but if you enter uppercase letters, you can't change them to lowercase nor to small caps — except by retyping them.

Superscript and Subscript

When you apply the Superscript and Subscript character formats to highlighted text, InDesign applies baseline shift to the characters, lifting them above (for Superscript) or lowering them below (for Subscript) their baseline, *and* reduces their size.

The amount of baseline shift and scaling that's used for the Superscript and Subscript formats is determined by the Position and Size fields in the Text pane of the Preferences dialog box (File ➪ Preferences ➪ Text, or ⌘+K or Ctrl+K). The default Position value for both formats is 33.3 percent, which means that characters are moved up or down by one-third of the applied leading value. The default Superscript and Subscript Size value is 58.3 percent, which means that superscripted and subscripted characters are reduced to 58.3 percent of the applied font size. The Text Preferences pane lets you specify separate default settings for Superscript and Subscript.

Design Advice

For most newspaper and magazine work, we prefer a size of 65 percent for superscripts and subscripts, as well as a position of 30 percent for subscripts and 35 percent for superscripts. These values work better in the small text sizes and tight leading of such publications than the InDesign defaults. If you change these settings when no document is open, they become the default for all future new documents.

You can use the Superscript and Subscript formats to create, for example, custom fractions or numbers for footnotes or to reposition special characters such as asterisks. To apply the Superscript or Subscript format to highlighted text, choose the appropriate option from the Character pane's pop-up menu. Figure 12-11 shows examples of text to which the default Superscript and Subscript settings have been applied.

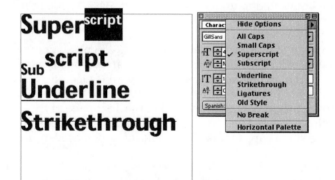

Figure 12-11: In this example, the Superscript character format has been applied to the "script" in "Superscript"; the "Sub" in "Subscript" bears the Subscript format. The Underline and Strikethrough formats have been applied to "Underline" and "Strikethrough," respectively.

Underline and Strikethrough

The Underline and Strikethrough formats, shown in Figure 12-11, are generally used for editing purposes. They are not considered typographically acceptable for indicating emphasis in text, which is better accomplished by using bold and/or italic type styles.

Note The weight of an underline is relative to font size. The larger the font, the thicker the underline. The horizontal line created by the Strikethrough format is one-half point thick regardless of the text's size.

Ligatures

A ligature is a special character that combines two letters. Most early typefaces included five ligatures — *ff, fi, fl, ffi,* and *ffl.* These days, most Mac fonts include just two ligatures — *fi* and *fl.* When you choose the Ligature option, InDesign automatically displays and prints a font's built-in ligatures — instead of the two component letters — if the font includes ligatures.

One nice thing about the Ligature option is that even though a ligature looks like a single character onscreen, it's still fully editable. That is, you can click between the two-letter shapes and insert text if necessary. Also, a ligature created with the Ligatures option will not cause InDesign's spelling checker to flag the word that contains it.

Platform Difference Windows doesn't support automatic ligatures, even for fonts that have the characters. If you transfer files from the Mac to Windows and back, however, your ligatures will be restored when the file is opened on the Mac.

To use ligatures within highlighted text, choose Ligatures from the Character pane's palette menu. Figure 12-12 shows a before-and-after example of text to which the Ligature option has been applied.

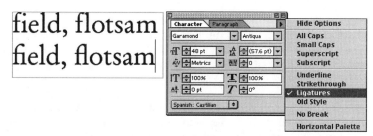

Figure 12-12: Ligatures are not used in the top line. Notice the space between the "fi" and "fl" letter pairs. Ligatures are used in the second line.

Caution For fonts that don't include ligatures, such as some sans serif fonts, InDesign creates artificial ligatures. Creating artificial ligatures with InDesign is a hit-and-miss affair depending on the font. For some fonts, the results aren't bad; for others, well, use your own judgment. Typographically, it's best to use ligatures only for fonts that include them.

For most Mac fonts that include ligatures, pressing Option+Shift+5 inserts the *fi* ligature, whereas Option+Shift+6 inserts the *fl* ligature. In Windows, you'll have to use the Alt code (hold the Alt key and press the character's four-digit code from the numeric keypad) or a program such as Character Map that comes with Windows to access the ligature characters in fonts that support them. Either way, if you enter ligatures yourself, InDesign's spelling checker will flag any words that contain them. For this reason, you may want to let the program handle the task of inserting ligatures.

Old Style

Much like alphabetic letters have uppercase and lowercase variations, numerals (0 through 9) have two variations:

✦ **Titling figures** — also called modern figures — are much like uppercase letters in that they are all the same size and the bottom of each numeral rests on the baseline. Titling figures are often used within uppercase text.

✦ **Old-style figures** — also called text figures, hanging figures, and lowercase figures — are not uniform in size. In old-style figures, parts of the numerals 3, 4, 5, 7, and 9 usually hang below the baseline like descenders in letters such as *g* and *y*. Similarly, the numerals 6 and 8 are taller than the others, and rise above the x-height like ascenders in letters such as *b* and *l*.

The new OpenType font standard developed by Adobe and Microsoft supports both titling and old-style numerals in one font. For OpenType fonts with both types of numerals, you can choose the Old Style option in the Character pane's menu to automatically use old style figures to display and print numerals in highlighted text.

But for the vast majority of fonts in use today, this feature has no effect because today's fonts don't support both types of numerals. Some fonts, such as Adobe Caslon, were designed with old-style figures rather than titling figures. Other fonts, such as Avant Garde, include only titling figures. Either way, InDesign's Old Style option has nothing to work with.

Note A type of font called an *expert font* includes old-style numerals, fractions, true small caps, and other special characters. It is used as an adjunct to the regular version of the font, letting you manually apply the special characters. For example, if you used Garamond as your font, you could apply Garamond Expert to the numerals to get old-style numerals. This is a lot of work, so most people don't bother except for typographically sophisticated — and short — documents such as ads. Unfortunately, InDesign's Old Style option won't use these expert fonts to provide old-style numerals, so you'll still have to apply them manually.

Figure 12-13 shows the difference between titling figures and old-style figures.

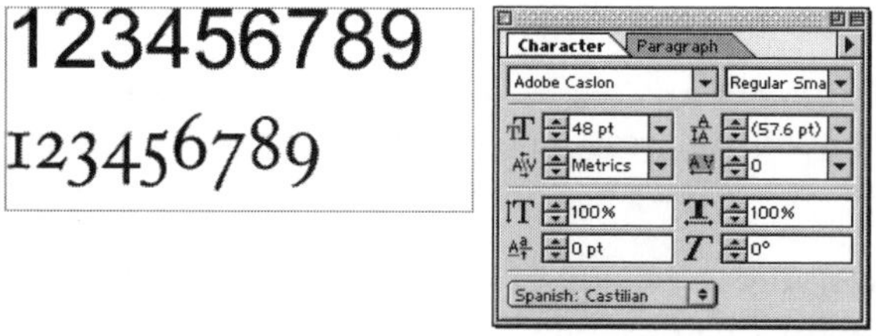

123456789
123456789

Figure 12-13: The top row of numbers uses typical titling figures — all are the same height. The bottom row uses old-style numerals. (Note that the fonts are different also.)

No Break

InDesign lets you prevent individual words from being hyphenated or a string of words from being broken at the end of a line. For example, you may decide that you don't want to hyphenate software names, such as "InDesign," "CorelDraw," or "FreeHand." Or perhaps you don't want to separate the *J* and the *P* in "J. P. Morgan." The No Break option was created for situations such as these.

To prevent a word or a text string from being broken, highlight it, and then choose No Break from the Character pane's palette menu.

Caution
If you apply the No Break option to a range of text that's longer than the width of the current column, InDesign tracks the text so that it fits on a single line — squeezing it unacceptably.

Tip
You can also prevent a word from being hyphenated by placing a discretionary hyphen (Shift+⌘+- [hyphen] or Ctrl+Shift+- [hyphen]) in front of the first letter.

Space between Characters and Lines

Typographers often pay as much attention to the space between characters, words, and lines of text as they do to the appearance of the characters themselves. Their concern about space is well justified. The legibility of a block of text depends as much on the space around it — called *white space* — as it does on the readability of the font. InDesign offers two ways to adjust the space between characters:

✦ **Kerning** is the adjustment of space between a pair of characters. Most fonts include built-in kerning tables that control the space between pesky character pairs, such as *LA*, *Yo*, and *WA*, that otherwise could appear to have a space between them even when there's not. Particularly at small font sizes, it's safe to use a font's built-in kerning information to control the space between letter pairs. But for large font sizes, such as the front-page nameplate of a newsletter or a magazine headline, you may want to manually adjust the space between certain character pairs to achieve consistent spacing.

✦ **Tracking** is similar to kerning but applies to a range of highlighted text. Tracking is the process of adding or removing space among all letters in a range of text.

InDesign lets you apply kerning and/or tracking to highlighted text in $1/1000$ em increments. An em is as wide as the height of the current font size (that is, an em for 12-point text is 12 points wide), which means that kerning and tracking increments are relative to the applied font size.

In addition to letting you adjust space between characters, InDesign also lets you adjust space between lines. The program's Leading (rhymes with *sledding*, not with *pleading*) format lets you control the vertical space between lines of type. It's traditionally an attribute of paragraphs, but InDesign lets you apply it on a character-by-character basis.

Cross-Reference   Chapter 13 explains how to control the spacing between words, which is part of paragraph formatting.

Kerning

The Kerning controls in the Character pane, already shown in Figure 12-13, provide three options for kerning letter pairs: Metrics kerning, Optical kerning, and Manual kerning:

✦ **Metrics kerning** uses a font's built-in kerning pairs to control the space between character pairs in the highlighted text.

✦ **Optical kerning** has InDesign "look" at each letter pair in highlighted text and add or remove space between the letters based on the shapes of the characters.

✦ **Manual kerning** is adding or removing space between a specific letter pair in user-specified amounts.

The kerning method you use will depend on the circumstances. For example, some fonts include a large set of kerning pairs. Such fonts, especially at text font sizes (9 to 12 points) and lower, may look fine using the default Metrics kerning option, which uses built-in kerning pairs. On the other hand, if the font applied to highlighted text has few or no built-in kerning pairs or if several different fonts are mixed together, the text may benefit from the Optical kerning method. At display type sizes (36 points and larger), you may want to manually kern individual letter pairs to suit your taste. Figure 12-14 shows a manually kerned letter pair.

OTTOWA

Figure 12-14: In this example, the "WA" letter pair has been manually kerned −30 to close up the space.

When the flashing text cursor is between a pair of characters, the Kerning field displays the pair's kerning value. If Metrics or Optical kerning is applied, the kerning value is displayed in parentheses.

To apply Metrics or Optical kerning to highlighted text, choose the appropriate option from the Kerning pop-up menu. To apply manual kerning, click between a pair of letters, and then enter a value in the Kerning field or choose one of the predefined values. Negative values tighten; positive values loosen.

Tip

You can also use a keyboard shortcut to apply manual kerning. Press Option+left cursor or Alt+left cursor to decrease the kerning value in increments of 20; Press Option+right cursor or Alt+right cursor to increase the kerning value in increments of 20 (known as a *unit*). If you add the ⌘ or Ctrl keys to these keyboard shortcuts, the increment is increased to 100. If you use the up and down cursor keys in the Kerning field in the Character pane, you change the kerning in increments of 10, and holding the Shift key changes the increments to 25.

InDesign users, especially QuarkXPress converts, may be surprised at the seemingly large kerning values produced by all the program's kerning methods (the same is true for tracking values). Keep in mind that InDesign lets you adjust space in 0.0001-em units. In QuarkXPress, for example, the kerning unit is 0.005 em. So QuarkXPress users should not be surprised to see kerning and tracking values that are 10 to 20 times greater than you're used to.

Design Advice

A warning about kerning and tracking. InDesign will happily let you tighten or loosen text to the point of illegibility. If this is the effect you're after, go for it. But as a general rule, when letter shapes start to collide, you've tightened too far.

Tracking

If you understand kerning, you can think of tracking as uniform kerning applied to a range of text. You might use tracking to tighten character spacing for a font that you think is too spacey or loosen spacing for a font that's too tight. Or you could track a paragraph tighter or looser to eliminate a short last line or a *widow* (the last line of a paragraph that falls at the top of a page or column).

To apply tracking to highlighted text, enter a value in the Character pane's Tracking field, shown in Figure 12-15, or choose one of the predefined values. Negative values tighten; positive values loosen (in 0.0001-em increments). Use the same keyboard techniques as for kerning.

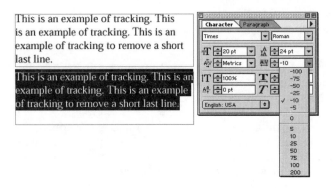

Figure 12-15: The text in the bottom frame has been tightened by applying a tracking value of –10 to fix a short last line. The original text is at top.

Leading

In the days of metal type, typesetters would insert thin strips of metal — specifically, lead — between rows of letters to aid legibility. In the world of digital typography, leading refers to the vertical space between lines of type as measured from baseline to baseline. Leading in InDesign is a character-level format, which means that you can apply different leading values within a single paragraph. InDesign looks separately at each line of text in a paragraph and uses the largest applied leading value within a line to determine the leading for that line.

Note

Leading as a character format is a carryover from PageMaker. QuarkXPress users may find InDesign's leading method to be odd at first because leading is a paragraph-level format in that program. In most cases, you'll apply a single leading value to entire paragraphs, in which case leading behaves like a paragraph-level format.

By default, InDesign applies Auto Leading to text. When Auto Leading is applied, leading is equal to 120 percent of the font size. For example, if Auto Leading is applied to 10-point text, the leading value is 12 points; for 12-point text, Auto Leading is 14.4 points; and so on. As long as you don't change fonts or font sizes in a paragraph, Auto Leading works pretty well. But if you do change fonts or sizes, Auto Leading can result in inconsistent spacing between lines. For this reason, it's safer to specify a leading value.

Generally, it's a good idea to use a leading value that is slightly larger than the font size, which is why Auto Leading works in many cases. When the leading value equals the font size, text is said to be set *solid*. That's about as tight as you'll ever want to set leading, unless you're trying to achieve a special typographic effect. As is the case with kerning and tracking, when tight leading causes letters to collide — ascenders and descenders are the first to overlap — you've gone too far.

Tip

You can change InDesign's preset Auto Leading value of 120 percent. To do so, choose Type ⇨ Paragraph, or ⌘+M or Ctrl+M, to display the Paragraph pane. Choose Justification in the palette menu, enter a new value in the Auto Leading field, and then click OK. (Why a character format setting is accessed via the Paragraph pane and what Auto Leading has to do with Justification are both mysteries.)

Oddity

Another mystery is why you cannot specify Auto Leading amounts in anything other than percentages. This causes many QuarkXPress documents to flow incorrectly because QuarkXPress lets you set the Auto Leading to a specific value, such as +2 (which adds 2 points to the text size rather than use a percentage that results in awkward leading amounts such as 14.4 points). Being able to specify a specific additive value such as +2 makes sense for many kinds of layouts, so the inability to specify such values is an unfortunate omission in InDesign.

To modify the leading value applied to selected text, choose one of the predefined options from the Leading pop-up menu in the Character pane or enter a leading value in the field. You can enter values from 0 to 5000 points in 0.0001-point increments. You can also use the up and down cursor keys to change leading in 1-point increments. Figure 12-16 shows the Leading controls in action.

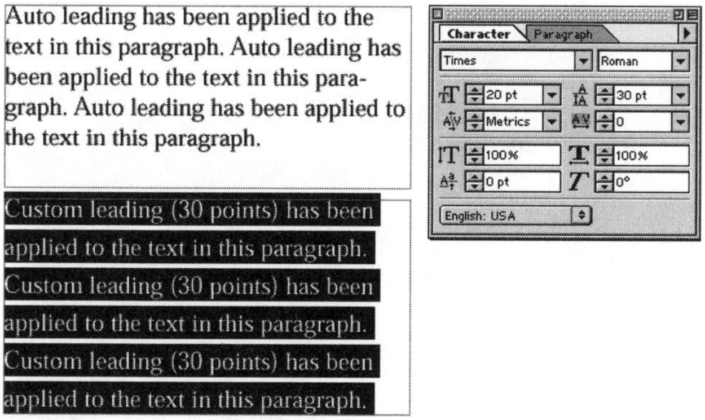

Auto leading has been applied to the text in this paragraph. Auto leading has been applied to the text in this paragraph. Auto leading has been applied to the text in this paragraph.

Custom leading (30 points) has been applied to the text in this paragraph. Custom leading (30 points) has been applied to the text in this paragraph. Custom leading (30 points) has been applied to the text in this paragraph.

Figure 12-16: Auto leading has been applied to the text in the top frame. The same font, type style, and size (24-point Times Roman) were used in the bottom frame, but with a custom leading of 30 points.

Summary

As a user of InDesign, modifying the appearance of type is one of the most common tasks you'll perform. InDesign lets you modify the appearance of highlighted characters or selected paragraphs. When text is highlighted, you can use the controls in the Character pane to change any of several character attributes: font family, font size, type style, leading, kerning, tracking, vertical and horizontal scale, baseline shift, and skew. You can also hyphenate and check spelling in several languages. The Character pane's pop-up menu provides additional character formatting options, including the option to apply all caps or small caps, superscript or subscript, underline and strikethrough, and to use ligatures in fonts that contain them.

✦   ✦   ✦

Specifying Paragraph Formats

Much like an individual character, a paragraph in InDesign is a basic typographic unit. When you create a new text frame and begin typing, you create a paragraph each time you press Return or Enter. A paragraph can be as short as one character or word on a single line or many words strung out over many lines. When you press Return or Enter, the paragraph formats of the preceding paragraph are automatically used for the subsequent paragraph (unless you've created styles that automatically change paragraph formats).

In general, paragraph formats control how the lines in the paragraph are constructed. Changing paragraph formats doesn't change the appearance of the individual characters within the paragraph. To do that, you must highlight the characters and modify character-level formats.

Cross-Reference This chapter focuses on modifying paragraph-level typographic formats; Chapter 12 focuses on modifying character-level formats. Part IV offers a broader look at using InDesign to design with type. Chapter 15 covers the creation and use of styles for both characters and paragraphs.

Applying Paragraph Formats

To select a paragraph, simply click within it. Any change you make to a paragraph-level format will be applied to all the lines in the paragraph. (Unlike character-level formats, you don't have to highlight all the text in a paragraph to modify a paragraph-level format.) If you need to change the paragraph formats of several consecutive paragraphs, you can highlight all the text in all the paragraphs; you can click anywhere in the first paragraph, drag anywhere within the last paragraph, and then release the mouse button; or you can click in the first paragraph and then Shift+click in the last paragraph (or vice versa).

Just as you can't apply two different colors to a single character, you can't apply conflicting paragraph formats within a single paragraph. For example, you can't specify for one line in a paragraph to be left-aligned and the rest right-aligned. All lines in a paragraph must share the same alignment, indents, tab settings, and all other paragraph-level formats.

As is the case with character formats, you have two ways to apply paragraph formats:

✦ Use the controls in the Paragraph pane, shown in Figure 13-1, or their keyboard shortcuts.

✦ Create and apply paragraph-level styles.

A paragraph-level style is essentially a text-formatting macro that lets you apply several paragraph formats to selected paragraphs in a single operation. If you're working on a multipage publication such as a book, newspaper, magazine, or catalog that repeatedly uses the same basic text formats, you will definitely want to use paragraph styles to handle the bulk of your formatting chores. But even if you use styles, you'll probably also use the Paragraph pane to do some manual paragraph formatting.

Cross-Reference Tab settings are also a paragraph-level format. See Chapter 14 for a detailed explanation of InDesign's Tabs feature.

Figure 13-1 shows the Paragraph pane. It can have several appearances: If you choose Hide Options from the pop-up menu, the Space Before/After, Drop Cap, and Hyphenate controls are not displayed, as shown in the bottom example in the figure. You might want to combine the Character and Paragraph panes into a single text-formatting pane.

Tip If the Type tool is selected and no objects are active, any changes you make in the Paragraph pane become the default settings for the document and are automatically used when you create new text frames.

The Paragraph pane provides access to most of InDesign's paragraph-formatting options. (You must open the Tabs pane — by choosing Type ➪ Tabs, or ⌘+Shift+T or Ctrl+Shift+T — to set tabs.) Several of the options have keyboard shortcuts.

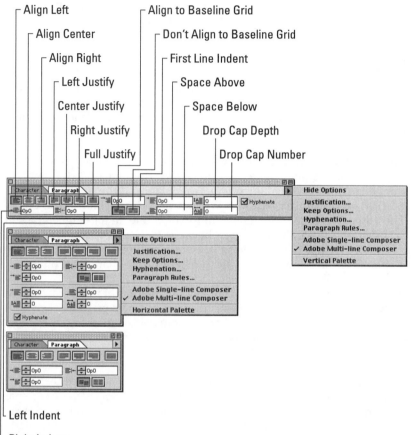

Figure 13-1: You can display the Paragraph pane in a horizontal (top) or vertical (middle) window by choosing the corresponding option (Horizontal Pane or Vertical Pane) from the palette menu. You can also hide some options (bottom).

Controlling Alignment and Indents

The seven alignment icons at the top of the Paragraph pane and the three fields and two icons just below are always displayed; the four additional fields and the Hyphenate checkbox are also displayed when you choose Show Options from the palette menu. InDesign refers to the top set of options as Basic Paragraph Formats; the additional five options are Advanced Paragraph Formats.

The top set lets you control a paragraph's alignment and indents (left, right, and first line) and lock text baselines to the document's baseline grid.

Alignment

The seven alignment icons at the top of the Paragraph pane control how line beginnings and endings in selected paragraphs are placed relative to the left and right margins. Here's a description of each alignment option (the icons do a pretty good job of showing what they do):

✦ **Align Left (Shift+⌘+L or Ctrl+Shift+L):** Places the left edge of every line at the left margin (the margin can be the frame edge, frame inset, left indent, or column edge) and fits as many words (or syllables if the hyphenation is turned on) on the line as possible. When a word (or syllable) won't fit at the end of a line, it's placed (flush left) on the next line. In left-aligned paragraphs, the right margin is said to be *ragged* because the leftover space at the right end of each line differs from line to line and produces a ragged edge. If you don't justify left-aligned paragraphs, you'll fit fewer characters on a line.

Some designers prefer to use left alignment for columns of text because they like the irregular, somewhat organic shapes that result; others prefer to align both left and right edges (justify), which produces a more rigid, vertical look. Similarly, left-aligned text is sometimes hyphenated, sometimes not. (You'll find more about hyphenation and justification later in this chapter.)

✦ **Align Center (Shift+⌘+C or Ctrl+Shift+C):** To create centered text, the leftover space of each line is divided in half. One-half of the leftover space is placed on the left end of the line; the other half is placed on the right end. The result is that both the left and right edges of the paragraphs are ragged, and the text is balanced along a vertical axis.

✦ **Align Right (Shift+⌘+R or Ctrl+Shift+R):** This is a mirror opposite of Align Left. The right edge is straight; the left edge is ragged. Columns of text are seldom set flush right because it's not as easy to read as flush-left text. Right-aligned text is sometimes used for such things as captions placed to the left of a picture, blurbs on magazine covers, and advertising copy.

✦ **Left Justify (Shift+⌘+J or Ctrl+Shift+J):** In justified text, the left and right ends of each line are flush with the margins. The flush left/flush right results are produced by evenly distributing the extra space of each line between characters and/or words or by reducing space between characters and/or words to accommodate additional characters (more about justification later in this chapter). Justified text is nearly always hyphenated (if you don't hyphenate justified text, spacing between letters and words is very inconsistent). Aligning the last line flush left is the traditional way of ending a paragraph.

✦ **Center Justify (Option+Shift+⌘+C or Ctrl+Alt+Shift+C):** This is the same as Left Justify except that the last line is center-aligned.

✦ **Right Justify (Option+Shift+⌘+R or Ctrl+Alt+Shift+R):** This is the same as Left Justify except that the last line is right-aligned.

✦ **Full Justify (Shift+⌘+F or Ctrl+Shift+F):** This is the same as Left Justify except that the last line is forcibly justified. This option can produce very widely spaced last lines. The fewer the characters on the last line, the greater the spacing.

These last three options are rarely used, and for good reason. People expect justified text to have the last line aligned left, and the space at the end of the line is a marker that the paragraph has ended. By changing the position of that last line, you can confuse your reader. So use Center Justify, Right Justify, and Full Justify options sparingly, in special situations where the reader won't be confused — typically in brief copy such as ads and pull-quotes.

To apply a paragraph alignment to selected paragraphs, click one of the icons. (The hand pointer is displayed when the pointer is over a pane button.) You can also use the keyboard shortcuts listed previously.

Indents

You can move the edges of paragraphs away from the left and/or right margins and indent the first line using the indent controls in the Paragraph pane. Figure 13-2 shows a paragraph to which all of these formats have been applied.

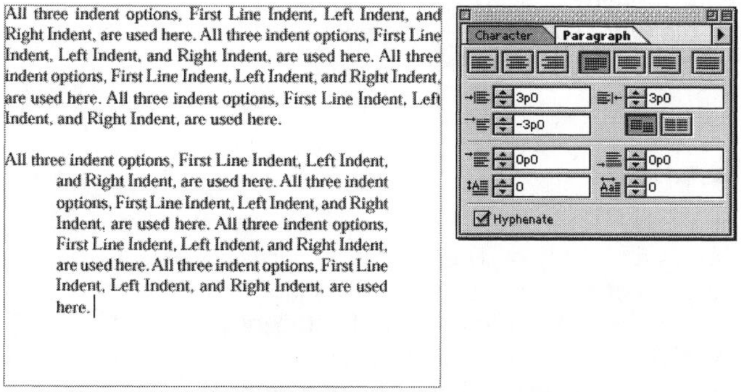

Figure 13-2: All three types of indents — First-Line Indent, Left Indent, and Right Indent — were applied to the second paragraph, which is a copy of the first, to create a hanging indent. The Paragraph pane shows the values used for each indent.

Left and right indents are often used for lengthy passages of quoted material within a column of text. Using indents is also a handy way of drawing attention to pull quotes and moving text away from a nearby picture.

The options are:

✦ **Left Indent:** Enter a value in this field to move the left edge of selected paragraphs away from the left margin. You can also use the up and down cursor keys. Each click increases the value by 1 point; holding down the Shift key while clicking increases the increment to 1 pica.

✦ **Right Indent:** Enter a value in this field to move the right edge of selected paragraphs away from the right margin. You can also use the up and down cursor keys.

✦ **First-Line Indent:** Enter a value in this field to move the left edge of the first line of selected paragraphs away from the right margin. You can also click the up and down cursor keys. The value in the First-Line Indent field is added to any Left Indent value. For example, if you've specified a Left Indent value of 1 pica and you then specify a 1-pica First-Line Indent value, the first line of selected paragraphs will be indented 2 picas from the left margin. If you've specified a Left Indent value, you can specify a negative First-Line Indent value to create a *hanging indent* (also called an *outdent*). You cannot specify a First-Line Indent value that would cause the first line to extend past the left edge of the text frame (that is, the First-Line Indent value can't exceed the Left Indent value).

Note

It's usually not a good idea to use a tab or spaces to indent the first line of a paragraph, which is what was done in the age of typewriters. You're better off specifying a First-Line Indent. Similarly, it's possible to indent an entire paragraph by inserting a tab or multiple word spaces at the beginning of every line, but both are typographic no-nos. Use the indent controls.

Lock to Baseline Grid

Every document includes a grid of horizontal lines, called the baseline grid, that can be displayed or hidden (View ➪ Show/Hide Baseline Grid, or ⌘+Option+" or Ctrl+Alt+") and used to help position objects and text baselines. A document's baseline grid is established in the Grids pane of the Preferences dialog box (File ➪ Preferences ➪ Grids, or ⌘+K or Ctrl+K). Generally, a document's baseline grid interval is equal to the leading value applied to the body text. You can ensure that lines of text align across columns and pages by locking their baselines to the baseline grid.

Although you can use InDesign's Lock to Baseline Grid feature to align text baselines across columns and pages, you can produce the same results by combining uniform body text leading with other paragraph formats (Space Before and Space After). Some designers like the certainty and simplicity of the Lock to Baseline Grid feature; others prefer to control text alignment across columns themselves. Whichever works best for you is fine.

Note Keep in mind that when paragraphs are aligned to the baseline grid, the applied leading values are ignored.

To align the baselines of text in selected paragraphs with a document's baseline grid, click the Align to Baseline Grid button (it's the one on the right) in the Paragraph pane. Click the Don't Align to Baseline Grid button if you don't want to align text baselines with baseline grid lines.

Adding Space Between Paragraphs

When you choose Show Options from the Paragraph pane's palette menu, four additional fields are displayed, as shown earlier in Figure 13-1. Two of these fields let you insert space before and/or after paragraphs.

When you need to format a lengthy chunk of text with multiple paragraphs, you have two ways to indicate a new paragraph: You can:

✦ Indent the paragraph's first line (by specifying a First-Line Indent value).

✦ Insert some extra space between the new paragraph and the preceding one.

There's no rule that says you can't use both methods, but generally you'll use one or the other. What you don't want to do is insert extra returns between a paragraph, which is what was done in the days of typewriters.

To insert space before selected paragraphs, enter a value in the Space Before field in the Paragraph pane. You can also use the up and down cursor keys; each click increases the value by 1 point, whereas holding down Shift increases the increment to 1 pica.

The Space After field works the same as the Space Before field but inserts space below selected paragraphs. Generally, you'll use Space Before or Space After to separate paragraphs. Combining both can be confusing.

Figure 13-3 shows the difference between using a First-Line Indent and space between paragraphs to indicate new paragraphs.

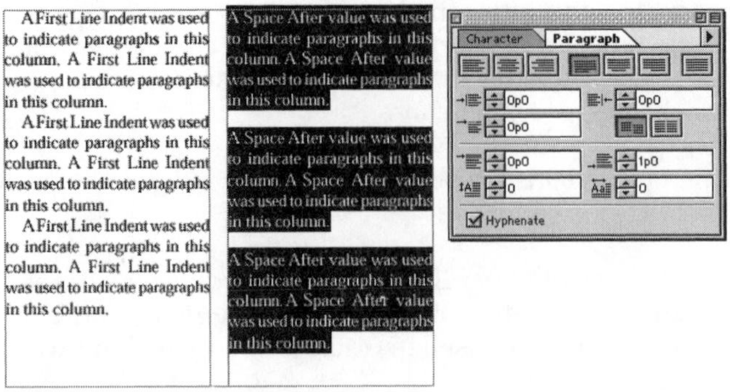

Figure 13-3: A 1-pica First-Line Indent has been applied to the paragraphs in the column on the left. The paragraphs in the column on the right are separated by a 1-pica Space After value, which you can see in the Paragraph pane's Space After field.

Adding Drop Caps

A drop cap is created by notching a paragraph's first letter — or letters — into the upper-left corner of the paragraph. Drop caps are often used to embellish the first paragraph of a story, to draw attention to paragraphs, and to interrupt the grayness in columns of text. In the Paragraph pane, InDesign lets you specify the number of letters you want to include in a drop cap and the number of lines you want to notch them.

To add one or more drop caps to selected paragraphs, enter a number in the Drop Cap Number field in the Paragraph pane. That's how many characters will be made into drop caps. You can also use the up and down cursor keys; each click increases the value by 1.

To specify the number of lines a drop cap will extend into a paragraph, enter a value in the Drop Cap Depth field in the Paragraph pane. You can also use the up and down cursor keys; each click increases the value by 1.

After you've created a drop cap, you can modify it by highlighting it and then changing any of its character formats — font, size, color, and so on — using the Character pane and other panes (such as Stroke and Swatches). Figure 13-4 shows some examples of drop caps.

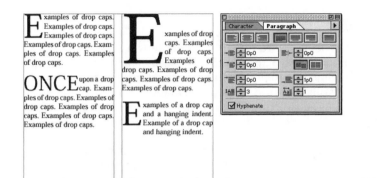

Figure 13-4: The values in the Paragraph pane were used to create the drop cap in the top-left example. The bottom-left paragraph has a two-line, four-character drop cap. In the top-right example, the font size of a one-letter, four-line drop cap has been enlarged to raise it above the first line of text. In the bottom-right example, a Left Indent value combined with a negative First-Line Indent value produced the one-character, three-line drop cap's hanging indent.

Controlling Hyphenation and Justification

Hyphenation is the placement of hyphens between syllables in words that don't completely fit at the end of a line of text — a signal to the reader that the word continues on the next line. InDesign gives you the option to hyphenate or not hyphenate paragraphs, and if you choose to hyphenate, you can customize the settings that determine when and where hyphens are inserted.

Justification is the addition or removal of space between words and/or letters that produces the flush left/flush right appearance of justified paragraphs. InDesign's justification controls let you specify how space is added or removed when paragraphs are justified.

If your pages will contain columns of text, you'll have to decide whether to use left-aligned or justified paragraphs and whether you want to hyphenate words that don't entirely fit at the end of a line. As mentioned earlier, if you justify paragraphs, you'll almost certainly want to hyphenate them, too. If you opt for left-aligned paragraphs, whether to hyphenate is a personal choice.

InDesign offers two hyphenation methods: manual and automatic.

Manual hyphenation

If you want to break a particular word differently from how InDesign would normally break the word, you can place a *discretionary hyphen* in the word. If the word falls at the end of a line in a hyphenated paragraph, InDesign uses the discretionary hyphen to split the word if the first syllable fits on the line. To insert a discretionary hyphen, use the shortcut Shift+⌘+- (hyphen) or Ctrl+Shift+- (hyphen) in the text where you want the hyphen to appear.

Tip

If you place a discretionary hyphen in a word, InDesign breaks the word only at that point (or doesn't break it at all). But you can place multiple discretionary hyphens within a single word. InDesign will use the one that produces the best results.

Note

InDesign uses discretionary hyphens only if the Hyphenate checkbox in the Paragraph pane is checked. If Hyphenate is not checked, neither manual or automatic hyphenation is applied.

Automatic hyphenation

To automatically hyphenate selected paragraphs, all you have to do is check the Hyphenate checkbox in the Paragraph pane. (The Hyphenate checkbox is displayed only if you choose Show Options from the palette menu.)

If you choose to hyphenate paragraphs, you can control how hyphenation is accomplished via the Hyphenation option in the palette menu. When you choose Hyphenation, the Hyphenation dialog box, shown in Figure 13-5, is displayed.

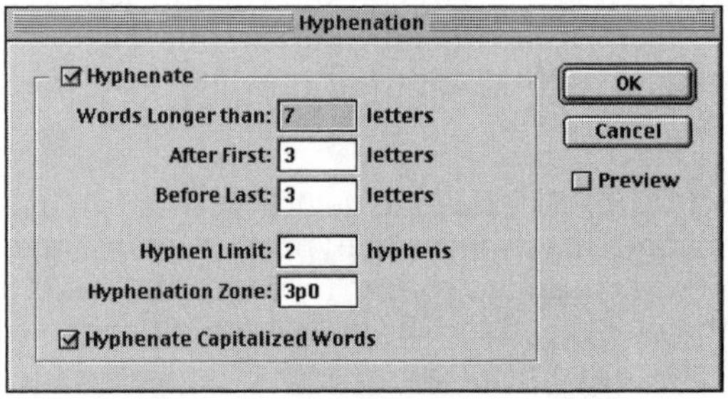

Figure 13-5: The Hyphenation dialog box.

Here's a brief description of each option in the Hyphenation dialog box:

✦ **Hyphenate checkbox:** This is a duplicate of the Hyphenate checkbox in the Paragraph pane. If you didn't check it in the pane before opening the Hyphenation dialog box, you can check it here.

✦ **Words Longer Than __ Letters:** Here, you specify the number of letters in the shortest word you want to hyphenate. For example, if you specify 4 letters, "mama" can be hyphenated, but "any" can't be.

✦ **After First __ Letters:** Here, you specify the minimum number of characters that can precede a hyphen. If you enter 2, for example, the word "atavistic" can be broken after "at." If you specify 3, "atavistic" cannot be broken until after "ata."

✦ **Before Last __ Letters:** This field is similar to After First __ Letters, but it determines the minimum number of characters that can follow a hyphen.

✦ **Hyphenation Limit:** Specify the number of consecutive lines that can be hyphenated in this field. Some designers limit the number of consecutive hyphens to 2 or 3 because they believe that too many consecutive hyphens produce an awkward, ladder-like look. If the Hyphenation Limit value you enter prevents hyphenation in a line that would otherwise be hyphenated, the line may look more spaced out than surrounding lines.

✦ **Hyphenation Zone:** This field applies only to nonjustified text and only when the Adobe Single-line Composer option is selected (in the Paragraph pane's palette menu). A hyphenation point must fall within the distance specified in this field to be used. Otherwise-acceptable hyphenation points that do not fall within the specified hyphenation zone are ignored.

✦ **Hyphenate Capitalized Words:** Select this option to break capitalized words, such as proper names and the first word of sentences. If you don't check this box, a capitalized word that would otherwise be hyphenated will get bumped to the next line, possibly producing excessive spacing in the previous line.

When you're done specifying hyphenation settings in the Hyphenation dialog box, click OK to close the dialog box and return to your document.

Tip

You can prevent a particular word from being hyphenated by highlighting it and choosing No Break from the Character pane (Window⇨Character, or ⌘+T or Ctrl+T) or by placing a discretionary hyphen (Shift+⌘+- [hyphen] or Ctrl+Shift+- [hyphen]) in front of the first letter.

Justifications controls

InDesign provides three options for controlling how justification is achieved: You can:

✦ Condense or expand the width of spaces, or *spacebands*, between words.

✦ Add or remove space between letters.

✦ Condense or expand the width of characters, or *glyphs*.

The options in the Justification dialog box, shown in Figure 13-6, let you specify the degree to which InDesign adjusts normal word spaces, character spacing, and character width to achieve justification. Although you can use the Justification controls on selected paragraphs, in most cases you will specify Justification settings when you create styles, particularly your body text styles.

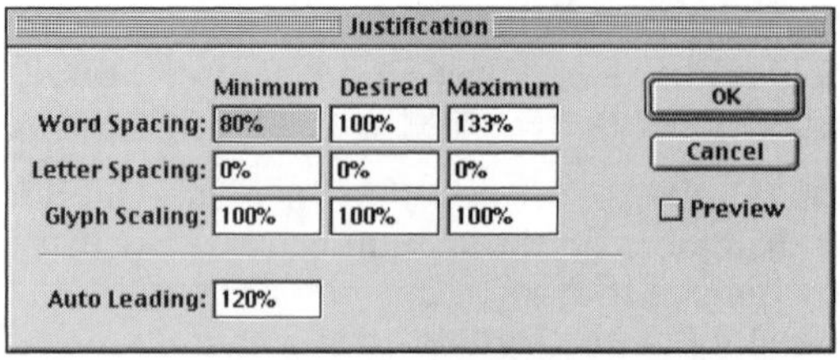

Figure 13-6: The Justification dialog box.

Here's a brief description of each option in the Justification dialog box:

✦ **Word Spacing:** Enter the percentage of a spaceband character that you want to use whenever possible in the Desired field. (The default value is 100%, which uses a font's built-in width.) Enter the minimum acceptable percentage in the Minimum field; enter the maximum acceptable percentage in the Maximum field. The smallest value you can enter is 0%; the largest is 1000%. Some designers are adamant that only word spaces — not letter spaces — should be adjusted when justifying text. Others tolerate small adjustments to letter spacing, as well.

✦ **Letter Spacing:** The default value of 0% in this field uses a font's built-in letter spacing. In the Desired field, enter a positive value to add space (in increments of 1% of a spaceband) between all letter pairs; enter a negative value to remove space. Enter the minimum acceptable percentage in the Minimum field; enter the maximum acceptable percentage in the Maximum field.

✦ **Glyph Scaling:** The default value of 100% uses a character's normal width. In the Desired field, enter a value greater than 100% to expand all character widths; enter a value less than 100% to condense character widths. Enter the minimum acceptable percentage in the Minimum field; enter the maximum acceptable percentage in the Maximum field. Some designers adamantly contend that scaling characters is even more unacceptable than letter spacing, whereas others see no harm in scaling characters, as long as it's kept to a minimum. If you do apply glyph scaling, it's best to keep it to a minimum of –2 to 3 percent at most.

Tip   When specifying values in the Justification dialog box, Minimum values must be smaller than Desired values, which in turn must be smaller than Maximum values.

If you use the Multi-line Composer option (explained in the next section) for justified paragraphs, specifying a narrow range between minimum and maximum Word Spacing, Letter Spacing, and Glyph Scaling will generally produce good-looking results. However, if you choose the Single-line Composer option, a broader range between Minimum and Maximum gives the composer more leeway in spacing words and letters and hyphenating words and can produce better-looking results. The best way to find out what values work best for you is to experiment with several settings. Print out hard copies and let your eyes decide which values produce the best results.

Tip A paragraph's justification settings are applied whether the paragraph is justified or not. However, for nonjustified paragraphs, only the Desired values for Word Spacing, Letter Spacing and Glyph Scaling are used.

Oddity The Auto Leading field in the Justification dialog box lets you specify a custom value for Auto Leading (see Chapter 12). Why this character-level default is hidden in a dialog box accessed via the Paragraph pane is a mystery.

Composing text

The Paragraph pane's palette menu offers two choices for implementing the hyphenation and justification settings you've established: the Single-line Composer and the Multi-line Composer.

Single-line Composer

In the past, programs such as QuarkXPress and PageMaker have used single-line composition methods to flow text. This method marches line by line through a paragraph and sets each line as well as possible using the applied hyphenation and justification settings. The effect that modifying the spacing of one line has on the lines above and below is not considered in single-line composition. If adjusting the space within a line causes poor spacing on the next line, tough luck. When you use the Single-line Composer, the following rules apply:

✦ Adjusting word spacing is preferred over hyphenation.

✦ Hyphenation is preferred over glyph scaling.

✦ If spacing must be adjusted, removing space is preferred over adding space.

Multi-line Composer

InDesign's Multi-line Composer, which is selected by default, takes a broader approach to composition by looking at several lines at once. If a poorly spaced line can be fixed by adjusting the spacing of a previous line, the Multi-line Composer reflows the previous line. The Multi-line Composer is governed by the following principles:

✦ The evenness of letter spacing and word spacing is the highest priority. The desirability of possible breakpoints is determined by how much they cause word and letter spacing to vary from the Desired settings.

✦ Uneven spacing is preferred to hyphenation. A breakpoint that does not require hyphenation is preferred over one that does.

✦ All possible breakpoints are ranked, and good breakpoints are preferred over bad ones.

Tip   You can customize the way the Multi-line Composer works using the controls in the Composition pane of the Preferences dialog box (File ➪ Preferences ➪ Composition, or ⌘+K or Ctrl+K). You can specify how many lines ahead you want the composer to look when applying hyphenation and justification settings to a line of text and how many possible alternatives you want to consider. The default is 6 lines in both directions.

To specify the composition method used to flow text in selected paragraphs, select either Adobe Single-line Composer or Adobe Multi-line Composer from the Paragraph pane's palette menu. One (and only one) of these options is always checked; Multi-line Composer is the default.

Setting Other Paragraph Formats

The Paragraph pane's palette menu contains two additional paragraph-formatting options:

✦ **Keep Options** lets you determine how and when paragraphs can be split when they fall at the bottom of a column or page.

✦ **Paragraph Rules** lets you place a horizontal line in front of or after a paragraph. Lines placed using the Paragraph Rules feature become part of the text and move along with surrounding text when editing causes text reflow.

Keep Options

A *widow* is the last line of a paragraph that falls at the top of a column (the poor thing has been cut off from the rest of the family). An *orphan* is the first line of a paragraph that falls at the bottom of a column (it, too, has become separated from its family). InDesign's Keep Options feature lets you prevent widows and orphans; it also lets you keep paragraphs together when they would otherwise be broken at the bottom of a column.

When you choose Keep Options from the Paragraph pane's palette menu, the Keep Options dialog box, shown in Figure 13-7, is displayed.

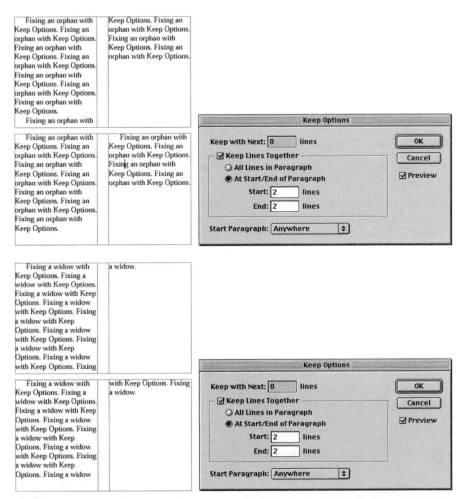

Figure 13-7: In the top example, a Start value of 2 in the Keep Options dialog box eliminates an orphan. An End value of 2 in the bottom example eliminates a widow.

The following are the options in the Keep Options dialog box:

✦ **Keep with Next __ Lines:** This option applies to two consecutive paragraphs. Specify the number of lines of the second paragraph that must stay with the first paragraph if a column break occurs within the second paragraph. This option is useful for preventing a subhead from being separated from the paragraph that follows.

✦ **Keep Lines Together:** Click this checkbox to prevent paragraphs from breaking and to control widows and orphans. When this box is checked, the two radio buttons below it become available. (The radio buttons present an either/or choice. One must be selected; At Start/End of Paragraph is selected by default.)

✦ **All Lines in Paragraph:** Select this option to prevent a paragraph from being broken at the end of a column. When a column break occurs within a paragraph to which this setting has been applied, the entire paragraph moves to the next column.

✦ **At Start/End of Paragraph:** Click this button to control widows and orphans. When this button is selected, the two fields below it become available.

✦ **Start __ Lines:** This field controls orphans. The value you enter is the minimum number of lines at the beginning of a paragraph that must be placed at the bottom of a column when a paragraph is split by a column ending. Figure 13-7 shows an example of an orphan being eliminated by a Start __ Lines value of 2. Keep in mind that when you eliminate an orphan using Keep Options, the orphan line is bumped to the next column or page, which can produce uneven column endings on multicolumn pages.

✦ **End __ Lines:** This field controls widows. The value you enter is the minimum number of lines at the end of a paragraph that must be placed at the top of a column when a paragraph is split by a column ending. Figure 13-7 shows an example of a widow being eliminated by an End __ Lines value of 2. Keep in mind that when you eliminate a widow using Keep Options, the line that precedes the widow line is bumped to the next column or page, which can produce uneven column endings on multicolumn pages.

✦ **Start Paragraph:** From this pop-up menu, choose In Next Column to force a paragraph to begin in the next column or frame; choose On Next Page to force a paragraph to begin on the next page (such as for chapter headings).

To specify Keep Options for selected paragraphs, choose Keep Options from the Paragraph pane's palette menu, enter the desired settings, and then click OK to close the Keep Options dialog box and return to your document.

Paragraph Rules

Usually, the easiest way to create a horizontal line is to use the Line Tool. But if you want to place a horizontal line within text so that the line moves with the text when editing causes the text to reflow, you need to create a paragraph rule. A paragraph rule looks much like a line created with the line tool, but behaves like a text character. Paragraph rules have many uses. For example, you can place one above or below a subhead to make it more noticeable or to separate the subhead from the paragraph that precedes or follows it. Or you could place paragraph rules above and below a pull quote so that the rules and the pull quote text move if editing causes text reflow.

Steps: Applying a Paragraph Rule

1. Select the paragraph(s) to which you want to apply a rule above and/or a rule below, and then choose Paragraph Rules from the Paragraph pane's pop-up menu. The Paragraph Rules dialog box, shown in Figure 13-8, is displayed.

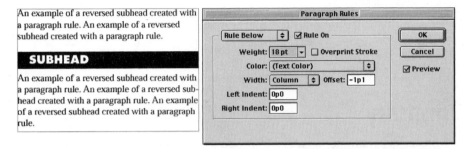

Figure 13-8: The settings in the Paragraph Rules dialog box helped produce this reversed subhead. A Rule Below has been applied to the subhead. The subhead text is white; a Left Indent value was used to indent the text.

2. Choose Rule Above or Rule Below, and then click Rule On. You can add either a rule above, below, or both. If you want to add rules above and below, you must click Rule On for both options and specify their settings separately. (Note: If you want to see the rule as you create it, click the Preview button.)

3. For Weight, choose a predefined thickness from the pop-up menu or enter a value in the field.

4. Choose a color from the Color pop-up menu, which lists the colors displayed in the Swatches pane (Window ⇨ Swatches, or F5). If you choose Text Color, InDesign automatically uses the color applied to the first character in the paragraph.

5. From the Width pop-up menu, choose Column if you want the rule to extend from the left edge of the column to the right edge of the column; choose Text if you want the rule to extend from the left edge of the frame or column to the line ending on the right.

6. To indent the rule from the left and/or right edges, enter values in the Left Indent and/or Right Indent fields.

7. To control the vertical position of the rule, enter a value in the Offset field. For a rule above, the offset value is measured upward from the baseline of the first line in a paragraph to the bottom of the rule; for a rule below, the offset is measured downward from the baseline of the last line in a paragraph to the top of the rule.

8. Click the Overprint Stroke box if you want to print a rule on top of any underlying colors. This ensures that any misregistration during printing will not result in white areas around the rule where the paper shows through. You typically use this for black or other dark colors.

9. Click OK to close the dialog box, implement your changes, and return to your document.

To remove a paragraph rule, click in the paragraph to which the rule is applied, choose Paragraph Rules from the Paragraph pane's pop-up menu, uncheck the Rule On box, and then click OK.

Summary

Much like character formats, InDesign's paragraph formats let you control the appearance of selected paragraphs. For example, you can control a paragraph's alignment and specify left, right, and/or first-line indents, and you can add drop caps and space between paragraphs. If you want to hyphenate a paragraph, you can add hyphens manually to individual words, or you can have InDesign automatically add hyphens where appropriate. If you choose to use justified columns of text, you can use InDesign's justification controls to specify how space is added or removed between characters and words to achieve justification, and you also have the option to condense or expand character shapes. InDesign offers two options for composing text: the multi-line composition method looks at several lines at a time, whereas the single-line method looks at only one line at a time.

✦　　　✦　　　✦

Setting Up Tabs and Tables

If you ever used a typewriter, you may remember hitting the tab key to indent each paragraph. And you may have pounded on it repeatedly to align columns of data. In InDesign, you use first-line indents to distinguish the first line of a new paragraph, and you reserve tabs for separating columns of data. There is no table editor built into InDesign, but you can create simple tables by combining an effective use of tabs with rules below paragraphs and vertical lines between columns.

In InDesign, tabs are part of paragraph formats — meaning that when you set them they apply to all the text in selected paragraphs rather than to selected characters within a paragraph. By default, when you start typing in a paragraph or you create a new paragraph style, invisible tab stops are set automatically every half inch. Regardless of the measurement system your rulers are set to use, when you hit tab you'll jump to the next 0.5-inch increment on the ruler.

As soon as you set a tab stop of your own, it overrides any of the automatic tab stops to its left. The automatic tab stops remain to the right until you override all of them.

Tip　Any tabs you set in the Tabs pane when no document is open are added to all future documents you create. Therefore, if tabs at every quarter-inch would be more useful to you, add them with no documents open.

InDesign provides four different types of tabs so you can do the following:

✦ Left-align text at a tab stop (the default setting, and the one you'll use most often)

✦ Center text on either side of the tab stop (very useful in column headers)

✦ Right-align text at a tab stop (useful for columns of integers)

✦ Align a specific character in the text with the tab stop (such as a comma or period in a number)

Figure 14-1 shows example tabs.

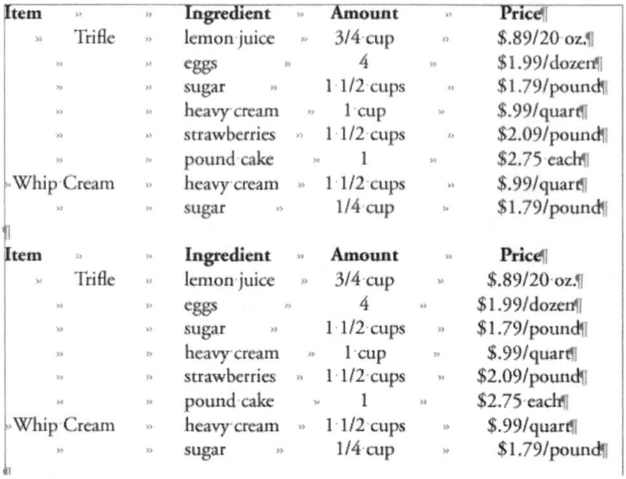

Item			Ingredient		Amount		Price
»	Trifle	»	lemon juice	»	3/4 cup	»	$.89/20 oz.
	»	»	eggs	»	4	»	$1.99/dozen
	»	»	sugar	»	1 1/2 cups	»	$1.79/pound
	»	»	heavy cream	»	1 cup	»	$.99/quart
	»	»	strawberries	»	1 1/2 cups	»	$2.09/pound
	»	»	pound cake	»	1	»	$2.75 each
Whip Cream		»	heavy cream	»	1 1/2 cups	»	$.99/quart
	»	»	sugar	»	1/4 cup	»	$1.79/pound
Item			Ingredient	»	Amount	»	Price
»	Trifle	»	lemon juice	»	3/4 cup	»	$.89/20 oz.
	»	»	eggs	»	4	»	$1.99/dozen
	»	»	sugar	»	1 1/2 cups	»	$1.79/pound
	»	»	heavy cream	»	1 cup	»	$.99/quart
	»	»	strawberries	»	1 1/2 cups	»	$2.09/pound
	»	»	pound cake	»	1	»	$2.75 each
Whip Cream		»	heavy cream	»	1 1/2 cups	»	$.99/quart
	»	»	sugar	»	1/4 cup	»	$1.79/pound

Figure 14-1: Under the Item column, Trifle and Whip Cream are positioned with right-aligned tabs. The three other column headings — Ingredient, Amount, and Price — are positioned with center tabs. In the chart, the ingredients are left-aligned, the amounts are center aligned, and the prices are aligned on the dollar sign (top chart) and the decimal point (lower chart).

Using the Tabs Pane

To set tabs in InDesign you use the Tabs pane, which floats above your text so that you can keep it open until you're finished experimenting with tabs. To open the Tabs pane, choose Type ➪ Tabs or press Shift+⌘+T or Ctrl+Shift+T. Figure 14-2 shows the Tabs pane.

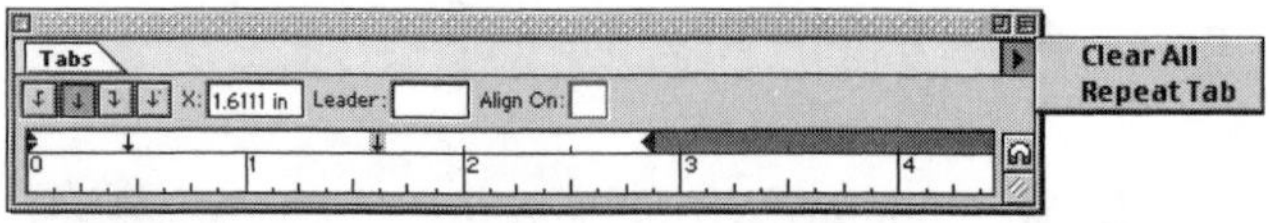

Figure 14-2: The Tabs pane and the Tabs menu.

Tip

If you find yourself adjusting tab settings and indents at the same time, you might wish to combine the Tabs pane and the Paragraph pane. Simply drag the Tabs pane into the Paragraph pane or vice versa. Use the palette menu on the

Paragraph pane to change its orientation to vertical so the palettes work together better. (By default, InDesign combines the Paragraph, Character, and Transform panes — we recommend you split the Paragraph and Character panes into separate palettes so you can see all your text formatting at once.)

Tab style buttons

Four buttons on the Tabs pane let you control how the text aligns with the tab you're creating:

✦ **Left:** The default tab stops are left-aligned, which means that the left side of the text touches the tab stop as if it were a left margin. Most tabs you create for text will be left-aligned.

✦ **Center:** Centered tab stops are like the centered paragraph alignment, with text balanced evenly on either side of the tab stop. Center tabs are often used for table headings.

✦ **Right:** When you set right-aligned tabs, the right edge of text touches the tab stop. This tab setting is commonly used for aligning numbers that do not include decimals or for the last column in a table.

✦ **Special:** By default, the last tab style button is for decimal tabs, which means that a period in the text aligns on the tab stop. If there's no period in the text, InDesign pretends that one exists after the last character. Rather than aligning on a period, you can specify a different character — such as a comma or dollar sign — for a Special tab, and text aligns to that character. You do this using the Align On field, covered later in this section.

Tip

If you need a tab flush with the right margin — for example, to position a dingbat at the end of the story — click the Right tab style button and position it on the right side of the tab ruler. Then, drag the right-aligned tab on top of the right indent arrow. (You can't actually click to place a tab on top of the arrow, but you can drag a tab on top of it.)

Tip

Rather than clicking a new tab style button for a selected tab, you can Option+click or Alt+click the tab on the ruler. This cycles through the four different styles; stop clicking when the style you need is displayed.

X (position) field

The X field of the Tabs pane lets you specify a position for a new tab stop. You can enter a value in this field in 0.01-point increments, and then press Shift+Return or Shift+Enter to create a tab. InDesign positions tabs relative to the left edge of the text frame or column. Or you can just click the mouse on the ruler where you want the tab to be, as described later.

Tip Why enter numbers when you can just use the mouse? The reason is to get more accurate positioning than using the mouse usually provides, especially when you know exactly where the tab stop should be. Of course, you can add a tab via the mouse then click it and enter a more precise value in the X field.

Note If a text frame has Inset Spacing specified for its left edge in the Text Frame Options dialog box (Object ➭ Text Frame Options, or ⌘+B or Ctrl+B), InDesign measures tabs from the text inset rather than from the frame.

As with other fields in InDesign, the X field can perform mathematical computations for you. Consequently, you can set a tab at half of 0.125 without figuring out that value, or you can move a tab by adding to or subtracting from its current value. It may seem unlikely that you would ever do this, but it's extremely handy for changing tab settings so they're, say, half as far apart as they used to be. Or half as far apart plus 2 points to the right.

Note The operands for performing math in fields are + (addition), - (subtraction), * (multiplication), and / (division). If you want to combine these operands, such as adding 5 and then subtracting 2, you'll have to remember back to middle school and Algebra I to enter the operands in the correct order. Or read on: Computations are performed in the following order: multiply, divide, add, and then subtract.

Leader field

A tab leader is a character or series of characters that fills the white space between tabs — like the periods you see between a table of contents entry and its page number. They got the name *leader* because they lead your eyes across the page.

InDesign lets you specify up to eight characters, including special characters, that will repeat to fill any white space. When you set a leader for a tab stop, the leaders actually fill any space prior to that tab stop (between the previous text and the tab location).

To spread out the leader characters, type spaces between the characters you enter. Don't enter spaces before and after a single character though, because that results in two spaces between the characters when the pattern repeats (unless that's the look you're going for). You can't enter special types of spaces — such as thin spaces or hair spaces — in the Leader field; you will always get em spaces.

Design Advice The reason to use tab leaders is to help the reader. Unless the design is more important than the content, you probably shouldn't use eight-character tab leaders even though you can. A cacophony of characters draws too much attention to itself and can be confusing. Because the pattern of leaders repeats, one space and a period is usually sufficient.

To enter special characters in the Leader field, use keyboard commands or a utility such as PopChar Pro or Character Map. If you use InDesign's Insert Character command (Type ➪ Insert Character), you'll insert a character into your text, which you'll have to copy and paste into the Leader field. It won't be inserted directly in the Leader field as you would expect.

Align On field

The Special tab style defaults to a period, but you can replace the period with any character, including special characters. When that character is found in tabbed text, it aligns on the tab stop. If that character is not found, InDesign pretends that it follows the last character in the tabbed string. The most common characters entered in the Align On field include a comma (,), dollar sign ($), cents symbol (¢), and opening or closing parentheses ((and)).

Tab ruler

Rather than entering values in the X field, you can position tabs by clicking the ruler at the bottom of the Tabs pane. The Tab ruler has the following characteristics:

✦ It displays in the same measurement system as the document, with 0 specifying the edges of the column. If Inset Spacing is specified for the left edge of the text frame in the Text Frame Options dialog box (Object ➪ Text Frame Options, or ⌘+B or Ctrl+B), the ruler starts after the text inset in the first column.

✦ The ruler provides arrows for controlling and displaying the selected paragraph's first-line, left, and right indents. Dragging the two left arrows changes both the paragraph's first line and left indent, whereas dragging the top arrow changes only the first-line indent. Dragging the arrow at right changes the right indents. These arrows help you see indents in relation to tabs that you're setting.

✦ Icons that match the tab styles display on the rulers to show you where and what type of tabs are already set. You can drag these around to reposition existing tabs, and you can drag them off the ruler to delete tabs.

Magnet icon

Under the right circumstances, clicking the Magnet icon near the lower-right corner of the Tabs pane snaps the pane and the ruler to the selected text frame or column. The idea is to make it easier to see the tab stops in relation to an actual area of text.

For this to work, you need to make sure the top of the text frame is visible onscreen, the Type tool is selected, and you've placed the cursor in text or highlighted text. If you don't meet all these prerequisites, you either get a "no deal" icon (shown below) or nothing happens at all.

⊘

Once you manage to get the Tabs pane positioned correctly, as shown in Figure 14-3, it's quite useful. You can add and adjust tabs in relation to the text (provided that the text is at the top of the text frame!) and you can always see from where the tabs are measured. Even better, if you move the cursor to another column in the text frame, you can click the Magnet again to position the Tabs pane over that column.

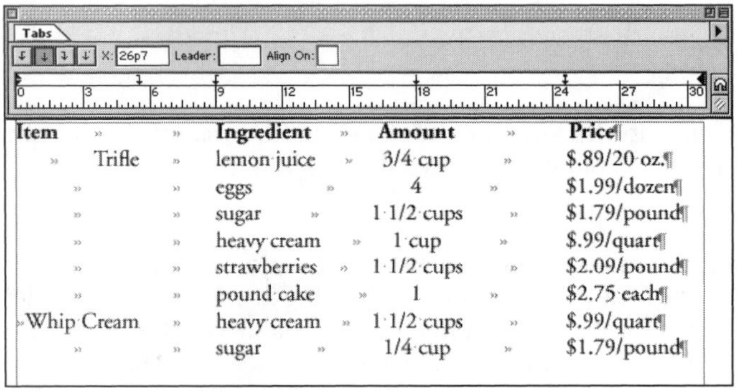

Figure 14-3: Clicking the Magnet icon snaps the Tabs pane above the active text frame or column.

Tabs pane menu

In addition to setting tabs in the Tabs pane, InDesign provides two additional options through the palette menu: Clear All and Repeat Tab:

✦ The **Clear All** command deletes any tabs you've created, and any text positioned with tabs reverts to the position of the default tab stops. (You can delete an individual tab stop by dragging its icon off the ruler.)

✦ The **Repeat Tab** command lets you create a string of tabs across the ruler that are all the same distance apart. When you select a tab on the ruler and choose this command, InDesign measures the distance between the selected tab and the previous tab (or if it's the first tab on the ruler, the distance between the selected tab and the left indent/text inset). The program then uses this distance to place new tabs, with the same alignment, all the way across the ruler. InDesign repeats tabs only to the right of the selected tab, but it will insert tabs between other tab stops.

Preparing Text Files for Setting Tabs

Before you start setting tabs in InDesign, take a look at the tabs already entered in the text. You can check this out in your word processor or in text that has been placed in InDesign. To view tab characters in InDesign, choose Type ⇨ Show Hidden Characters, or press Option+⌘+I or Ctrl+Alt+I. The light-blue double greater-than symbols (>>) are tabs.

To set effective tabs for columns of data, each line or row of information should be its own paragraph, and each column of data should be separated by only one tab character. If there's only one tab between each column, you need to set only one tab stop per column, and you can more carefully control a single tab stop rather than several.

The following figure shows an example of a "table" typed into Microsoft Word by a novice publisher for the publication *Buzz in the 'Burbs*. Although each row of the table is its own paragraph, the columns of information are separated by varying numbers of tabs as well as spaces. Although the text lines up somewhat onscreen, it will not align at all when printed or imported into InDesign.

```
Apriltidbits.doc

Eat your veggies!

Want to maximize the benefits you receive from the fruits and vegetables you eat? Include the
"top ten" fruits and veggies in your diet for the highest levels of antioxidants, which protect
against cancer and heart disease.

Fruit/Vegetable        Vit C       Beta carotene      Vit E
                       (mg)        (mg)               (mg)

Broccoli (1half c. cooked)    49        0.7        0.9
Cantaloupe (1 cup)            68        3.1        0.3
Carrot (1 med.)               7         12.2       0.3
Kale (1half c. cooked)        27        2.9        3.7
Mango (1 med)                 57        4.8        2.3
Pumpkin (1 half c. cooked)    5         10.5       1.1
Red bell pepper (1 half c)    95        1.7        0.3
Spinach (1 half c. cooked)    9         4.4        2.0
Strawberries (1 cup)          86        --         0.3
Sweet Potato (1 med)          28        14.0       5.5

Runners-up: Brussels sprouts, all citrus fruits, tomatoes, potatoes, other berries, leafy green
vegetables, cauliflower, green pepper, asparagus, peas, beets and winter squash.
```

Most of the writers for this publication are volunteers and therefore follow no file-preparation standards. The graphic designer received this original Microsoft Word file—which does look something like a table when invisible characters are not showing in Word—but is full of extraneous tabs and spaces that will wreak havoc in InDesign.

Continued

(continued)

The first step with a file such as this is to use a search/replace function in the word processor, or Edit ⇨ Find/Change, or ⌘+F or Ctrl+F, in InDesign to replace multiple spaces with tabs and replace multiple tabs with single tabs. The resulting word-processing file actually looks worse, as shown in the following figure, but will work significantly better in InDesign.

Ironically, cleaning out the extra spaces and tabs in this chart makes it look like nonsense in Microsoft Word. Nonetheless, this is the correct form for submitting tabular text for formatting in InDesign. If necessary, the writer can change tab settings in Word to align the columns for proofreading or editing purposes.

Because the text is not in its final font or text frame, the current tab placement does not matter. But if necessary, the writer can change tab settings in Word to align the columns for proofreading or editing purposes.

As with multiple tabs stops, if extra paragraph returns exist between the rows or information or if each line ends in a soft return or line break (Shift+Return or Shift+Enter) rather than a paragraph return (Return or Enter), you should fix these with search and replace in your word processor or Find/Change (Edit ⇨ Find/Change, or ⌘+F or Ctrl+F) in InDesign.

Creating Tables

Whether you're working on yesterday's box scores for the sports pages, an annual report, or a fun, little parenting magazine, you've got numbers. Numbers with dollar signs, numbers with decimals, numbers intermixed with text. You have to line the columns up correctly, not only so the information looks good but so it's easy to read as well. Then you often need to add ruling lines to help separate the material visually for the reader.

Note InDesign does not have a table editor for creating flexible rows and columns. You're limited to adjusting tabs and tab alignments to position text in columns and using rules to indicate rows. If you need to use more sophisticated tables, try the PowrTable plug-in from PowrTools Software Inc. (www.powrtools.com). You also have the option of saving tables from other applications as EPS graphics, and then importing the graphic into an InDesign picture frame. This can cause problems because the look or information in the table cannot be modified in InDesign.

Creating columns

Remember the "Eat your veggies!" word-processor chart shown in the sidebar "Preparing Text Files for Setting Tabs"? The text is now imported into an InDesign text frame with a gray fill, and formatted with Univers font on the heads and Adobe Garamond on the body text. First, we roughed in left-aligned tabs just to get a feel for how much space each column needed. After approximating the columns, we fine-tuned the tab alignment for the headings and the body text as follows:

✦ To position the column headings over each column, we highlighted the two lines, selected each tab, and clicked the Center tab style button. The column headings in Figure 14-4 are centered over each column.

✦ To position the columns of numbers, we used decimal tabs. First, we selected each tab, and then we clicked the Special tab style button. By default, the alignment character is a period, which works well for this chart because many of the values include a decimal point. (The values that do not have a decimal point align as if a period followed the value.) Notice in Figure 14-5 that the Beta Carotene and Vitamin E columns have been changed to decimal alignment, whereas the Vitamin C column is still aligned to the left of the tab stop. Because none of the Vitamin C values have decimals, right alignment would work just as well as decimal alignment in this case.

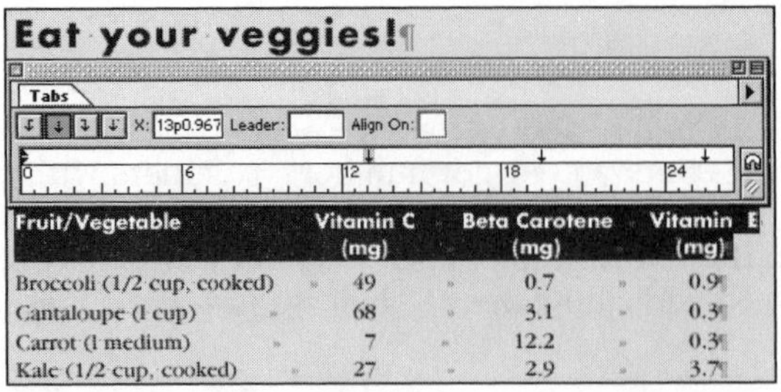

Figure 14-4: Column heads are often centered over each column after you rough out the initial tab placement.

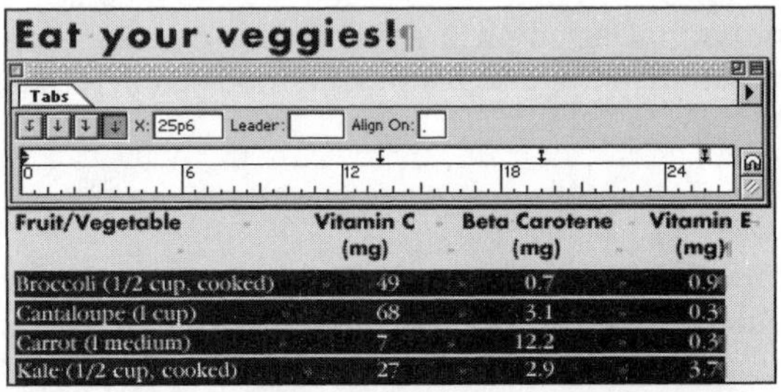

Figure 14-5: Using the Special tab alignment lets you align a decimal point or other character in text with a tab stop. The last two columns in this chart are aligned on decimal tabs.

Figure 14-6 shows the final chart. Notice the Beta Carotene value listed for Strawberries — there is none. The dash is aligned as if it were followed by a decimal point. To fix this, we can click in that line and change that tab to centered alignment. Sometimes you have to do such local overrides because not all data you're trying to align is always of the same format and thus can't have the same tab settings applied.

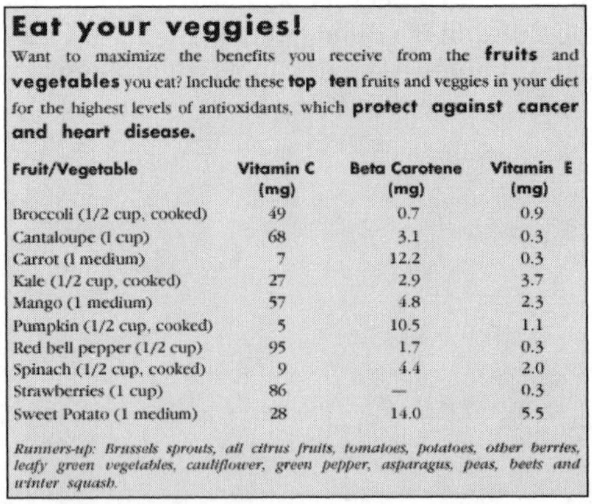

Eat your veggies!

Want to maximize the benefits you receive from the **fruits** and **vegetables** you eat? Include these **top ten** fruits and veggies in your diet for the highest levels of antioxidants, which **protect against cancer and heart disease.**

Fruit/Vegetable	Vitamin C (mg)	Beta Carotene (mg)	Vitamin E (mg)
Broccoli (1/2 cup, cooked)	49	0.7	0.9
Cantaloupe (1 cup)	68	3.1	0.3
Carrot (1 medium)	7	12.2	0.3
Kale (1/2 cup, cooked)	27	2.9	3.7
Mango (1 medium)	57	4.8	2.3
Pumpkin (1/2 cup, cooked)	5	10.5	1.1
Red bell pepper (1/2 cup)	95	1.7	0.3
Spinach (1/2 cup, cooked)	9	4.4	2.0
Strawberries (1 cup)	86	—	0.3
Sweet Potato (1 medium)	28	14.0	5.5

Runners-up: Brussels sprouts, all citrus fruits, tomatoes, potatoes, other berries, leafy green vegetables, cauliflower, green pepper, asparagus, peas, beets and winter squash.

Figure 14-6: Even after the tabs are aligned, the final chart needs a little fine-tuning. The dash in the Beta Carotene column for Strawberries would look better if it were center aligned.

Applying rules to tables

Because InDesign doesn't have a table editor that chunks information into nicely framed cells, you need to fake the effect by separating columns of data with tabs and separating rows with space, horizontal lines, shading or other design techniques. Depending on how close together the columns are, how tight the rows are spaced, and how many rows you have, it can be difficult to read across an entire row.

Designers often solve this problem by placing a thin line after each row or by placing a thick, shaded line behind every other row. Or sometimes the problem is solved with reverse type — by placing a dark line behind every other row and making the text lighter. The same techniques are used to separate columns from each other.

Tip

If you want vertical lines between columns in a table, wait until you're sure the text is final. Then, draw vertical lines between the columns of the length, weight, and color you want. Using the Selection tool, Shift+click to multiple-select the lines and the text frame, and then choose Object ➪ Group, or press ⌘+G or Ctrl+G. This glues the objects together so they can be moved and resized as one unit, although the objects can still be modified individually (such as changing their size and color). To place a frame around the table, select the frame, and use the Stroke palette (Window ➪ Stroke, or F10) to pick the stroke thickness (weight). Then select the Stroke button in the Toolbox palette and apply a color from the Swatches palette. Use the same technique to put vertical bands of color, tints, or gradients behind entire columns rather than lines between them.

Placing rules below table rows

The chart in Figure 14-7 is a little difficult to read, with 15 rows containing three columns of tightly spaced information. One way to help busy people read the chart is to add thin lines under each row. What might seem like the obvious way to accomplish this — drawing a line under each row and positioning it carefully — is absolutely the wrong way. Not only would positioning the lines be difficult, but if the font size changed or information was added to the table, all the lines would need to be repositioned.

InDesign provides a feature called Paragraph Rules for automatically placing lines of any width and style above or below selected paragraphs. As mentioned before, each row in your table should be its own paragraph, separated by a paragraph return rather than a line break. When you place rules above or below paragraphs, the rules flow with the text, are deleted when a paragraph is deleted, and can be added as paragraphs are added.

Figure 14-7: For a newspaper targeted at busy parents, this chart is a little crowded and difficult to read.

Steps: Using the Paragraph Rules Feature

1. If the Paragraph pane is not open, choose Style ⇨ Paragraph, or press ⌘+M or Ctrl+M.

2. With the Type tool, highlight the range of paragraphs that you want to position a rule above or below.

3. Click the Paragraph pane's palette menu to display the Paragraph menu. Choose Paragraph Rules from the menu, as shown in Figure 14-8.

Figure 14-8: To place rules above and/or below highlighted paragraphs, select the Paragraph Rules command from the menu on the Paragraph pane.

4. In the Paragraph Rules dialog box, shown in Figure 14-9, select Rule Above or Rule Below from the pop-up menu at the top. It's best to stick with just one choice, a rule above or a rule below. For a table, you'll generally be using rules below. To activate the rule, check Rule On.

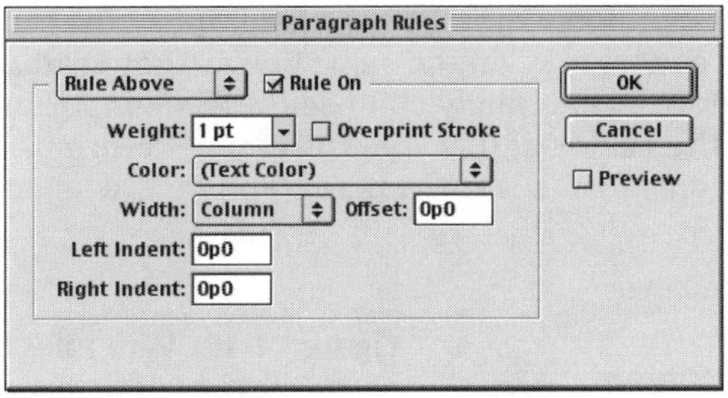

Figure 14-9: The Paragraph Rules dialog box lets you specify the weight, color, width, and offset of rules applied to highlighted paragraphs.

5. To specify the thickness of the rule, enter a value in the Weight field.

6. To specify the color of the rule, choose an option from the Color pop-up menu. You can choose Text Color, which colors the rules according to the color of the first character in the paragraph. Or you can choose one of the color, tint, or gradient swatches you created in the Swatches pane. If you want a different swatch, you'll need to close the Paragraph Rules dialog box, create the swatch, and then reopen the dialog box.

7. To specify the length of the rule, choose an option from the Width field. If you choose Text, the rule length varies depending on the length of each paragraph. If you choose Column, the rule spans the width of the text frame or column. If Inset Spacing is specified for the left edge of a left-hand column or the right edge of a right-hand column, the rule is measured according to the inset value rather than the edges of the text frame or column.

8. Regardless of the Width you choose, you can further control the length of the rule using the Left Indent and Right Indent fields. Positive values indent the rule in from the edges of the column or text; negative values extend the rule beyond the edges of the column or text.

9. Check the Preview box, and then tab to the Offset field. You'll notice the rule is placed at the baseline and is uncomfortably close to the text. Type a value in the Offset field to move a rule above up or a rule below down. (A positive number moves a Rule Above up, whereas it moves a Rule Below down; negative numbers do the opposite.) To preview the results, click in another field in the dialog box. Adjust this value until you're satisfied with it.

10. Selected paragraphs can have either or both a rule above and a rule below. If you want both, choose the other option from the pop-up menu at the top of the Paragraph Rules dialog box and use the controls to set it up. When you're finished, click OK.

Tip   Create these ruling lines as part of a paragraph style (see Chapter 15), so you can use them in other tables in your document. To create a new paragraph style based on selected text that's already been formatted, click the arrow on the Paragraph Styles pane to display the menu, and then choose New Style.

Figure 14-10 shows the results of 1-point rules below paragraphs offset three points from the text. The rules help readers stay on the same line as they read across the chart, ensuring that readers don't accidentally confuse these all-important venues. If you need to add a row into the center of this chart, pressing Return or Enter inserts a paragraph with the same formats as the paragraph before — including the same tabs and rules.

Bead-it	Create your own unique jewelry designs	303-706-1888
Champion Gymnastics	Gymnastics, club champs' birthday parties, wacky sports, weird games	303-843-0711
Children's Museum	Hands-on exhibits and activities for kids	303-433-7444
Denver Zoo	Special tours, Wild Nights	303-331-4110
Discovery Zone	Climbing mazes, arcade games, party rooms	303-649-1831
Fit Kids	Tea parties, Olympic birthday games, western horse party, more	303-338-9118
Funplex	Bowling, laserstorm, rollerskating, mini-golf	303-972-4344
Goodson Rec. Center	Swim parties, gymnastics	303-798-2476
Grand Golf	Party room, miniature golf, outdoor driving range	303-470-9300
Jungle-Quest	Indoor climbing, ropes challenge course, outdoor sports, field trips	303-738-9844
Kids Skits	Musical theater, play production, movie-making	303-446-8200
Laser Quest	Laser tag	303-796-0707
Mad Science	Hands-on fun science activities brought to you	303-403-0432
Sega City	Video arcade	303-708-1091
S. Suburban Ice Arena	Ice skating	303-794-6522

Figure 14-10: With rules below each paragraph, the text can be resized and rows can be added or deleted, all without repositioning lines.

Creating stripes

Rather than placing rules above or below paragraphs, you can actually place rules behind paragraphs to create a striped effect, or a band of color. As with the rules below, the stripes help lead the readers' eyes across the row. If the rules are a darker color, you can make the type pop out by making it a lighter color. Or, if the rules are a light color or tint, you can overprint the text on them. In a table or chart, you might place a rule behind every other paragraph so the rows are easy to distinguish. Striping a chart with this method, rather than drawing colored lines behind the text frame, gives you all the benefits of using the Paragraph Rules feature — the stripes flow with the text, are deleted as paragraphs are deleted, and can be added as new paragraphs are added.

To place a stripe behind a paragraph, follow the same steps given for "Using the Paragraph Rules Feature" earlier in this chapter The key to creating the stripe is to specify a line weight several points larger than the text's point size. For example, the 12-point rule shown in Figure 14-11 is placed behind 8.5-point text. Because the rule sits on the baseline of the text, it extends above the text. To move the line down slightly, you can enter an Offset value. (In the figure, we used an offset of 0.125 inch down from the baseline.)

Birthday Party Buzz

Where to go for that special day!

Bead-it	Create your own unique jewelry designs	303-706-1888
Champion Gymnastics	Gymnastics, club champs' birthday parties, wacky sports, weird games	303-843-0711
Children's Museum	Hands-on exhibits and activities for kids	303-433-7444
Denver Zoo	Special tours, Wild Nights	303-331-4110
Discovery Zone	Climbing mazes, arcade games, party rooms	303-649-1831
Fit Kids	Tea parties, Olympic birthday games, western horse party, more	303-338-9118
Funplex	Bowling, laserstorm, rollerskating, mini golf	303-972-4344
Goodson Rec. Center	Swim parties, gymnastics	303-798-2476
Grand Golf	Party room, miniature golf, outdoor driving range	303-470-9300
Jungle Quest	Indoor climbing, ropes challenge course, outdoor sports, field trips	303-738-9844
Kids Skits	Musical theater, play production, movie making	303-446-8200
Laser Quest	Laser tag	303-796-0707
Mad Science	Hands-on fun science activities brought to you	303-403-0432
Sega City	Video arcade	303-708-1091
S. Suburban Ice Arena	Ice skating	303-794-6522

Figure 14-11: Combining a 12-point, light-colored rule below with 8.5-point body text creates horizontal stripes that flow with the text.

Design Advice

In addition to placing stripes within a chart, you might simply use thin rules below in the chart, but reverse the headings out of thick rules.

Tip

Create color bands as part of a paragraph style (see Chapter 15), so you can use them in other tables in your document. To create a new paragraph style based on selected text that's already been formatted, click the arrow on the Paragraph Styles pane to display the menu, and then choose New Style.

Reusing Table Formatting

Creating a table by setting tabs, placing rules, stroking text frames, and adding vertical lines can be a tedious and manual process. Fortunately, you don't need to do all the work from scratch over and over again. You can save time on future tables by saving your tab and rule settings as paragraph styles, and even saving text frames that contain tables in libraries for easy access.

Cross-Reference For specific information about creating and applying styles, see Chapter 15. For detailed information about using libraries to store frequently used objects, see Chapter 29.

Saving tabs and rules in paragraph styles

Once you've created a table format you like, you can save the tabs, paragraph rules, font, size, and other characteristics in a paragraph style. You can use the New Paragraph Style dialog box to specify a keyboard command for the style.

Once you have a paragraph style, you can simply apply that style to tabbed text, and then adjust the tabs and rules according to the content. Or you can edit the styles as necessary. Because you can import paragraph styles from other documents (use the Load Paragraph Styles option in the Paragraph pane's palette menu), you can easily bring in the table styles any time you need them.

Saving table frames in libraries

The text frame you place in the table may represent as much work as the table text itself. You might have the text frame stroked and filled with a gradient, and you might have the Inset Spacing adjusted in a certain way. If you prefer vertical lines separating columns in a table, you might have those grouped to the text frame.

To preserve this work, you can drag the table into a library palette. Once the table is in a library, you can drag it into any open document — and the table will bring its paragraph styles and colors along with it. Then you can simply modify the content and design for the specific publication.

Summary

Unlike typewriter days, creating tabs in a page-layout application provides various options for aligning text with a tab and creating tab leaders. The Tabs pane (Type ⇨ Tabs, or ⌘+Shift+T or Ctrl+Shift+T) provides an interactive ruler for positioning tabs along with all the other controls you need. Your ultimate success with using the tabs feature depends on how well you prepared the text in the first place — the key is to position one tab correctly rather than entering several tabs to achieve what looks like the correct placement.

To create tables in InDesign, you use tabs to position text in columns, draw vertical lines to separate columns, and use rules to separate rows. (The rows should be one-line paragraphs.) To apply rules to paragraphs, use the Paragraph pane's palette menu (Type ⇨ Paragraph, or ⌘+M or Ctrl+M) to create rules above or below rows, or to create stripes behind rows. Once you've set up your basic table formatting, save it as a paragraph style (Type ⇨ Paragraph Styles or F11).

✦　　✦　　✦

Setting Up Styles

If you were assigned the task of making 500 star-shaped cookies, the first thing you'd do is find a star-shaped cookie cutter. Of course, you could shape each cookie by hand, but not only would this take considerably more time than using a cookie cutter, no two cookies would look exactly the same. Think of styles as cookie cutters for formatting text. They save you time and ensure consistency. If you'll be using InDesign to create long documents that require considerable text formatting, styles are indispensable.

InDesign lets you create two types of styles:

◆ A *character style* is a set of character-level formats you can apply to a range of highlighted text in a single step.

◆ A *paragraph style* is a set of both character- *and* paragraph-level formats you can apply to selected paragraphs in a single step.

In one respect, styles are far superior to cookie cutters. If you've used a cookie cutter to create hundreds of cookies and then find out your cookies are the wrong shape, you're out of luck. But if you use styles to format hundreds of pieces of text and then decide you don't like the look of the styled text, you can simply modify the styles. Any text you've formatted with a style is automatically updated if you modify the style.

Tip When it comes to using styles, it's as important to know when *not* to use them as it is to know *when* to use them. For short documents — especially one-pagers such as business cards, ads, and posters — that contain relatively little text and don't use the same formats repeatedly, you're probably better off formatting the text by hand.

Tip If you create multiple editions of a particular publication — for example, a form, a daily newspaper, a monthly magazine, or a corporate business card — you'll want to create a *template* (called *stationery* on the Mac). A template is a shell of a document that contains all the layout elements necessary to create the document—including styles if it's a multipage publication—but no content (except content that appears in every issue). You use a template as the starting point each time you need to create a new version of a publication. For more information about templates, see Chapter 29.

Creating and Applying Styles

Before you can use a style to format text, you must create it. You can create styles whenever you want, but usually, creating styles is one of the first tasks you'll tackle when working on a long document. Also, you may want to create your paragraph styles first and then, if necessary, add character styles. In many cases, character styles are used to format text within paragraphs to which paragraph styles have already been applied.

Paragraph styles

Let's say you've been given the job of creating a newsletter. It will be several pages long and contain several stories. Each story will have the same text elements: a big headline, a smaller headline, an author byline, and body text. The stories will also include pictures, and each picture requires a caption and a credit line. Before you begin laying out pages and formatting text, you should create styles for all of these repetitive text elements. The Paragraph Styles pane (Type ➪ Paragraph Styles, or F11), shown in Figure 15-1, is where you need to go for both creating and applying styles.

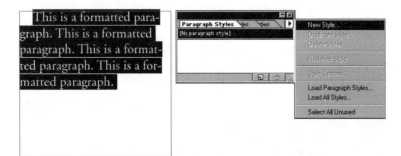

Figure 15-1: The Paragraph Styles pane and its pop-up menu. In this example, a new paragraph style is being created from the sample paragraph.

Tip   You may want to combine the Character Styles and Paragraph Styles panes into a single palette by click-dragging the tab of one pane on top of the other pane and then releasing the mouse. Similarly, you may want to combine the Character

(Type ⇨ Character, or ⌘+T or Ctrl+T) and Paragraph panes (Type ⇨ Paragraph, or ⌘+M or Ctrl+M). If you're really into combining panes, you may want to combine all four panes into a single text-formatting palette.

Creating paragraph styles

The easiest way to create a paragraph style is to manually apply character- and paragraph-level formats to a sample paragraph and then — with the sample paragraph selected — work through the following steps. (See Chapter 12 for information about specifying character-level formats; see Chapter 13 for information about paragraph-level formats.) If no text is selected when you create a style, you'll have to specify character- and paragraph-level formats as you create the style, which is more difficult than formatting a paragraph in advance. Here's how you create a paragraph style from a preformatted paragraph:

Steps: How to Create a Paragraph Style

1. If it's not displayed, show the Paragraph Style pane by choosing Type ⇨ Paragraph Styles or pressing F11.

2. Make sure you've highlighted a paragraph that's been styled with all the character and paragraph formats you want to include in your style, and then choose New Style from the Paragraph Styles pane's palette menu, as shown in Figure 15-1. The New Paragraph Style dialog box, shown in Figure 15-2, is displayed.

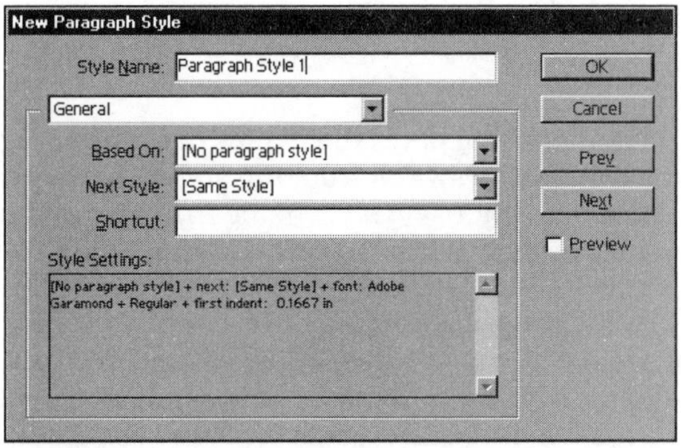

Figure 15-2: The New Paragraph Style dialog box.

3. Enter a name for the style in the Style Name field.

4. The pop-up menu beneath the Style Name field displays 11 options, as shown in Figure 15-3. If you want to change any character- or paragraph-level formats, choose the appropriate option, and then make your changes.

(Character formats and paragraph formats are explained in Chapters 12 and 13, respectively.)

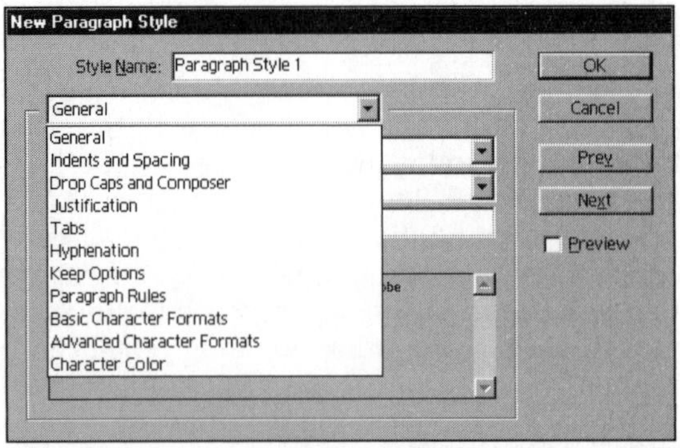

Figure 15-3: If you want to modify any character or paragraph formats when creating a style, choose the appropriate option from this pop-up menu, and then make your changes.

5. The Based On pop-up menu displays the names of other paragraph styles. You can use this feature to create families of styles. For example, you could create a style called "Body Copy/Base" for the bulk of your body text, and then create variations such as "Body Text/Drop Cap," "Body Text/No Indent," and "Body Text/Italic." If you used the Based On pop-up menu to base each of the variations on "Body Text/Base" and you then modified this "parent" style, your changes are applied to all the variations.

6. The Next Style pop-up menu also displays the names of other paragraph styles. If you want to automatically switch from the style you're creating to another style as you enter text, choose a style name from the pop-up menu. If you specify a Next Style for a style, it's automatically applied to a new paragraph when you press Return or Enter. If you choose Same Style (the default), the style you're creating will continue to be applied to new paragraphs when you press Return or Enter while typing. Typically, you'd use Next Style for items such as headlines that are always followed by a specific kind of paragraph (such as a byline). And you'd typically use Same Style for body text, where the next paragraph usually has the same formatting.

7. If you want (and you should), you can assign a keyboard shortcut to a style. (Windows users: Make sure Num Lock is on.) Hold down any combination of ⌘, Option, and Shift, or Ctrl, Alt, and Shift, and press any number on the keypad. (Letters and nonkeypad numbers cannot be used for keyboard shortcuts.)

8. When you're done specifying the attributes of your style, click OK.

You can also create a new style by clicking the Create New Style button at the bottom of the Paragraph Styles pane (to the left of the trash can). When you click this button, a new style with a default name (Paragraph Style 1, Paragraph Style 2, and so on) is added to the list. The formats applied to the selected paragraph are included in the new style; the New Paragraph Style dialog box is not displayed. If you want to modify any formats, double-click the new style name in the pane; the Modify Paragraph Style Options dialog box is displayed. This dialog box is identical to the New Paragraph Style dialog box.

Note   Assign your style names with care; be descriptive. Imagine that somebody else will be using the document and assign a name that conveys the purpose of the style. For example, anybody will know what a style called "Body Copy" is used for, but a style called "Really cool style" won't mean anything to anybody but you.)

Tip   You may want to consider using a naming scheme that displays families of related styles together in the Paragraph Styles pane. (You'll learn how to create a family of parent/child styles later in this chapter.) For example, you could use numbers (01, 02, 03, and so on) or letters (A. Body Copy/Base, A. Body Copy/Drop Cap, A. Body Copy/No Indent, and so on) in front of style names to group styles.

Applying paragraph styles

After you've created a paragraph style, applying it is easy. Just click within a paragraph or highlight text in a range of paragraphs, and then click the style name in the Paragraph Styles pane or press its keyboard shortcut. (Windows users: Make sure Num Lock is on when using shortcuts for styles.)

When you apply a style to selected paragraphs, all local formats and applied character styles are retained. All other formats are replaced by those of the applied style.

Tip   If you hold down Option or Alt when clicking a name in the Paragraph Styles pane, any character styles that have been applied within selected paragraphs are retained, as are the following character formats: superscript, subscript, underline, strikethrough, language, and baseline shift. If you hold down Option+Shift or Alt+Shift when clicking a style name, all local formatting within the selected paragraphs is removed.

Note   If a plus sign (+) is displayed to the right of a style name, it means that some of the text within the selected paragraphs has "local" formats that differ from those of the applied style. This can occur if you apply a style to text to which you've done some manual formatting or if you modify text formatting in a paragraph after applying a style to it.

A few last words about paragraph styles. No hard-and-fast rules govern how best to implement them. Like handwriting, you should develop your own style. How many styles you create, the names you use, whether you apply them with keyboard shortcuts or via the Paragraph Styles pane, and whether you use paragraph styles, character styles, or both are all matters of personal taste. One thing is indisputable: You should use styles whenever possible. They're a typesetter's best friends.

Managing paragraph styles

The Paragraph Style's pop-up menu, shown in Figure 15-4, displays eight options for managing styles; two buttons at the bottom of the pane let you create and delete paragraph styles.

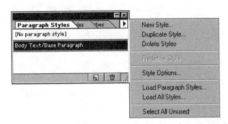

Figure 15-4: The Paragraph Styles pane's palette menu.

Here's a brief description of each option in the Paragraph Style's pop-up menu:

✦ **New Style:** Creates a new paragraph style. When you choose New Style, the New Paragraph Style dialog box is displayed.

✦ **Duplicate Style:** Click a style name, and then click this button to create an exact copy. If you want to create a style that's similar to one you've already created, you might want to choose New Style rather than Duplicate, and then use the Based On option to create a "child" of the original. If you choose Duplicate, the copy is identical to but not based on the original; if you modify the original, the copy is not affected.

✦ **Delete Styles:** Choose this to delete highlighted styles. To select multiple styles, hold down the ⌘ or Ctrl key as you click their names. To select a range of styles, click the first one, and then hold down the Shift key and click the last one.

✦ **Redefine Style:** This option lets you modify an existing style. Highlight text to which the style you want to modify has been applied, change the formats as desired, and then click Redefine Style. The newly applied formats are applied to the style.

✦ **Style Options:** This option lets you modify an existing style. When a style is highlighted in the Paragraph Styles pane, choosing Style Options displays the Modify Paragraph Style Options dialog box, which is identical to the New Paragraph Style dialog box.

✦ **Load Paragraph Styles:** Choose this option if you want to import styles from another InDesign document. (Importing styles is discussed in detail later in this chapter.)

✦ **Load All Styles:** This option lets you import both paragraph and character styles from another InDesign document. (Importing styles is discussed in detail later in this chapter.)

✦ **Select All Unused:** Select this option to highlight the names of all paragraph styles that have not been applied to any paragraphs. This is a handy way of identifying unused styles in preparation for deleting them (by choosing the Delete Styles option).

✦ **Create New Style:** Click this button to create a new style. If text is highlighted, the new style uses the applied formats. If no text is highlighted and the cursor is not flashing, the current formats in the Paragraph and Character panes are used.

✦ **Delete Selected Styles:** Clicking this button deletes any highlighted styles. You can also delete a style by clicking its name, and then dragging the pointer to the trash can button.

Character styles

Character styles are identical in nearly every way to paragraph styles, but instead of using them to format selected paragraphs, you use character styles to apply character-level formats a highlighted range of text. For example, you could use a character style to:

✦ Modify the appearance of the first several words in a paragraph. For example, some publications — particularly magazines — use a style variation such as small caps as a lead-in for a paragraph. You could use a character style to not only switch the font style to small caps, but you could change, size, color, font family, and so on, as well.

✦ Within body text you could use a character style to apply different formatting to such text elements as Web site, e-mail, and FTP addresses (URLs).

✦ Create other body text variations for such things as emphasis, book and movie titles, product and company names, and so on.

Creating and applying character styles

Using character styles is much the same as using paragraph styles. First you create them; then you apply them. And you use the Character Styles pane (Type ➪ Character Styles, or Shift+F11), shown in Figure 15-5, to do both.

Figure 15-5: The Character Styles pane
and its palette menu.

As is the case with paragraph styles, the easiest way to create a character style is
to apply the character-level formats you want to use in a style to some sample text,
and then complete the following steps. You can create a character style from
scratch (that is, without preformatting any text), but if you do, you'll have to set all
the character formats when you create the style. Here's how you create a character
style from highlighted text:

Steps: How to Create a Character Style

1. If it's not displayed, show the Character Style pane by choosing Type ➪
   Character Styles or pressing Shift+F11.

2. Make sure you've highlighted a paragraph that's been styled with all the
   character and paragraph formats you want to include in your style, and then
   choose New Style from the Character Styles pane's pop-up menu, as shown
   in Figure 15-5. The New Character Style dialog box, shown in Figure 15-6,
   is displayed.

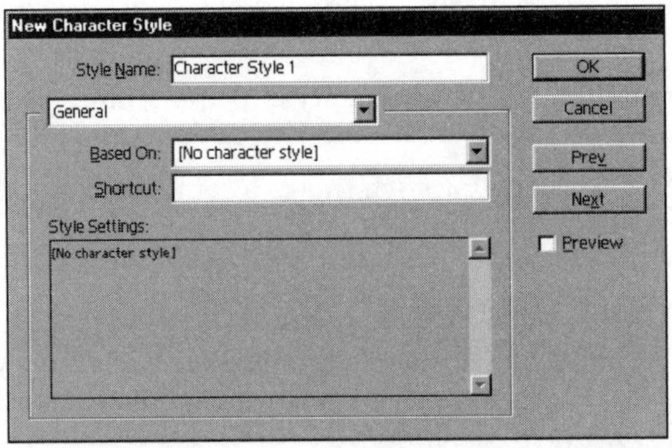

Figure 15-6: The New Character Style dialog box. In
this example, a new character style for URLs has been
created from the highlighted text. This new "child" style
is based on the Body Text/Base Character "parent" style.

3. Enter a name for the style in the Style Name field.

4. The pop-up menu beneath the Style Name field displays four options: General, Basic Character Formats, Advanced Character Formats, and Character Color. If you want to change any character-level formats, choose the appropriate option and then make your changes. (Character formats are explained in Chapter 12.)

5. The Based On pop-up menu displays the names of other character styles. You can use this feature to create families of styles. For example, you could create a style called "Body Copy/Base Character" that uses the same character attributes as your base Body Copy paragraph style and then create variations such as "Body Text/Emphasis," "Body Text/URL," and so on. If you used the Based On pop-up menu to base each of the variations on "Body Text/Base Character" and you then modified this "parent" style, your changes are applied to all the variations.

6. If you want (and you should), you can assign a keyboard shortcut to a style. (Windows users: Make sure Num Lock is on.) Hold down any combination of ⌘, Option, and Shift, or Ctrl, Alt, and Shift, and press any number on the keypad. (Letters and nonkeypad numbers cannot be used for keyboard shortcuts.)

7. When you're done specifying the attributes of your style, click OK.

Tip   You can also create a new style by clicking the Create New Style button at the bottom of the Character Styles pane (to the left of the trash can). When you click this button, a new style with a default name (Character Style 1, Character Style 2, and so on) is added to the list. The formats applied to the selected characters are included in the new style; the New Character Style dialog box is not displayed. If you want to modify any formats, double-click the new style name in the pane; the Modify Character Style Options dialog box is displayed. This dialog box is identical to the New Character Style dialog box.

Managing character styles

The options displayed in the Character Styles pane's palette menu are the same as those for the Paragraph Styles palette menu, which are explained earlier in this chapter. The only difference is that Load Character Styles is displayed in place of Load Paragraph Styles. This option lets you import Character Styles from other documents the same way you import paragraph styles.

Changing Styles

If you write your name into wet cement, you have only a few minutes to change your mind. After that, your formatting decisions are cast in stone, so to speak. Fortunately, styles are much more forgiving. Not only can you modify a style whenever you want, you are free to manually modify text to which styles have been applied.

Modifying styles

The most important thing to know about modifying a style is that all text to which a modified style has been applied is automatically updated. Additionally, if you modify a "parent" style, all "child" styles that were created by choosing Based On are also automatically updated.

You have two ways to modify an existing style. You can:

✦ Click the style name in the Character Styles or Paragraph Styles pane, and then choose Style Options from the pane's palette menu. The Modify Character Style Options or the Modify Paragraph Style Options dialog box is displayed. These dialog boxes are the same as the New Character Style and New Paragraph Style dialog boxes. Make whatever changes you want, and then click OK.

✦ Double-click a style name to display the Modify Character Style Options or Modify Paragraph Style Options dialog box. If text is highlighted, the style you double-click is applied to the text; if no text is selected, the style you double-click becomes the default style and is automatically applied when you enter text in a newly created box. If you hold down Shift+⌘ or Ctrl+Shift when you double-click a style name, the style is not applied to text.

Modifying text that's been styled with a style

If you need to change the appearance of text that's been formatted using a style, all you have to do is highlight the text — characters or paragraphs — and then use the Character pane (Type ⇨ Character, or ⌘+T or Ctrl+T) or Paragraph pane (Type ⇨ Paragraph, or ⌘+M or Ctrl+M) to change the formats.

When you change any formats in text to which a style has been applied, you are making "local" changes (to make "global" changes, you would modify the style). When you change formatting in style-formatted text, a plus sign is displayed next to the style name in the Character Styles or Paragraph Styles pane, as shown in Figure 15-7.

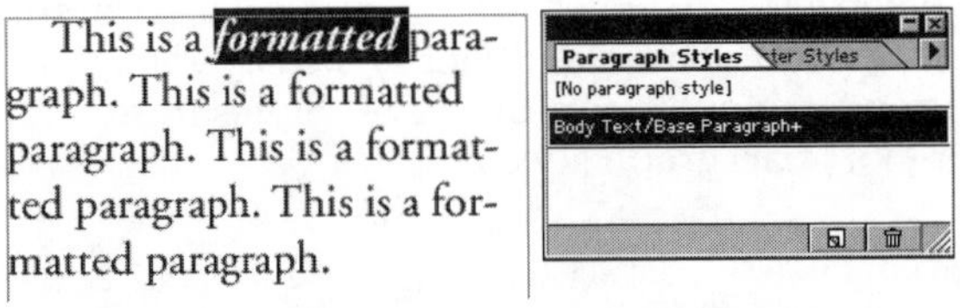

Figure 15-7: A "local" format (the Bold Italic type style) has been applied to the highlighted text, which was formatted with a style. The + sign at the end of the style name in the Paragraph Styles pane indicates that local formatting has been applied within the paragraph.

Unapplying styles

If you want, you can remove the link between style-formatted text and the assigned style. All you have to do is highlight the text — a range of characters if you want to dissociate them from the applied character style or one or more paragraphs if you want to dissociate it/them from the applied paragraph style — and then choose No Paragraph Style from the Paragraph Styles pane or No Character Style from the Character Styles pane. When you break the link between text and its applied style, any local formatting is retained unless you hold down the Option or Alt key when you choose No Paragraph Style or No Character Style. If you hold down the Option or Alt key, local formatting is removed.

Along the same lines, if you delete a style that's been applied to text, the formatting of that text remains unchanged, but if you click within or highlight the text, No Paragraph Style or No Character Style is displayed in the corresponding pane.

Importing Styles

If you've created a style, you never have to recreate it — assuming you've saved the document that contains the style. InDesign lets you import character and paragraph styles from one document into another. Also, when you import text files from word-processing programs that use styles, you can import the styles along with the text.

Importing styles from InDesign documents

The Paragraph Styles and Character Styles panes' palette menus contain commands that let you move styles between documents. The Paragraph Styles pane lets you import only paragraph styles or paragraph and character styles; the Character Styles pane lets you import only character styles or character and paragraph styles. Here's how you do it:

Steps: How to Import Styles

1. If it's not displayed, show the Paragraph Styles pane by choosing Type ➪ Paragraph Styles or pressing F11, or show the Character Styles pane by choosing Type ➪ Character Styles or pressing F11.

2. Choose Load Paragraph Styles from the Paragraph Styles pane's palette menu if you want to import only paragraph styles; choose Load Character Styles from the Character Styles pane's palette menu if you want to import only character styles; or choose Load All Styles from either pane's palette menu if you want to import both character and paragraph styles. Regardless of what kind of styles you choose to import, the Open a File dialog box, shown in Figure 15-8, is displayed.

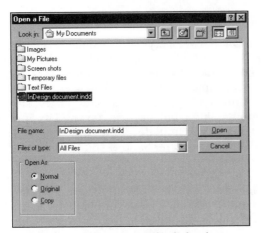

Figure 15-8: The Open a File dialog box.

3. Use the controls in the Open a File dialog box to locate the InDesign document that contains the styles you want to import.

4. Double-click the document name or click once on the document name, and then click Open.

Caution

If you import a style that has the same name as an existing style, the imported style replaces the existing one. Any text formatted with the original style will be reformatted using the imported style.

You can also use the Copy (Edit ➪ Copy, or ⌘+C or Ctrl+C) and Paste commands (Edit ➪ Paste, or ⌘+V or Ctrl +V) to move a style from one document to another. Simply copy some text in the source document to which the style you want to move has been applied. Then display the target document and use the Paste command to place the copied text into a text frame. The Character Styles and/or Paragraph Styles panes in the target document display the names of the new, "imported" styles.

Working with styles in imported text files

In most workgroup publishing environments, writers generate text using word-processing programs such as Microsoft Word and Corel WordPerfect, and InDesign users place the text in a layout and add other design elements — imported pictures, illustrations, lines, and so on — to create a finished publication. Whether writers are producing short magazine articles or lengthy book chapters, chances are they're doing some text formatting as they write — perhaps as little as applying occasional bold or italic characteristics or as much as using a complete set of styles, if their word processor supports them.

When you import a word-processing file into InDesign, you can bring the formatting and the styles along with the text. (See Chapter 4 for a complete list of formatting options that import from WordPerfect and Word.)

Tip If you're using InDesign in a workgroup environment and importing text generated by writers who use word processors, you're probably going to want to retain any formats they've applied. Most word processors let you save text files in several flavors. The native file format, of course, retains all formatting information, but InDesign may or may not be able to handle the file format depending on the program and the version number. Begin by experimenting a bit. Have the writers save text files in several formats and determine which works best. If writers use styles in their word processors, you'll have to save files in their program's native format (or any other format that retains style information and is recognized by one of InDesign's text import filters) if you want to import them into an InDesign document.

Isolated formatting might be used to indicate which styles should be applied in InDesign — for example, the writer might apply bold to one-line paragraphs that should be formatted as a subhead. However, if the writer applies appropriate paragraph styles to text in his or her word processor, much of the formatting in InDesign can be automated by importing the styles. (Note that word processors' character styles are not imported.)

You can use these imported paragraph styles in two different ways, depending on whether styles with the same name already exist in the InDesign document. Remember: To import styles with a word-processing file, check Retain Format in the Place dialog box (File ➪ Place, or ⌘+D or Ctrl+D).

 For more information about using the Place command to import text files, see Chapter 11.

Steps: Importing a Text File that Contains Styles

1. Choose File ➪ Place or press ⌘+D or Ctrl+D. The Place dialog box is displayed.

2. Locate the text file you want to import.

3. Select Show Import Options, and then double-click the file name or click Choose. The Import Options dialog box is displayed and offers several controls that let you retain or remove various formats within the text file. If Show Import Options is not checked, holding down the Shift key when double-clicking or clicking Choose also displays the Import Options dialog box. You can also import a text file without displaying this dialog box. Styles are retained and imported regardless of any Import Options you select.

4. Click OK in the Import Options dialog box or, if you didn't display this dialog box, click Choose in the Place dialog box.

5. Click the pointer on a page or on the pasteboard to place the text file in the document.

After you place a text file that contains styles, the Paragraph Styles pane displays the names of all the imported styles, and any text to which styles have been applied retain the style's formats as well as a link to the style.

Editing imported paragraph styles

If you import paragraph styles with text, you can simply use the styles specified in the word processor to format the text. This method works well for designs that do not follow a template — for example, brochures or feature stories. You might import the text, experiment with formatting it, and then edit the imported styles in InDesign to reflect your design.

For example, say you import a magazine feature article that is formatted with three paragraph styles (Headline, Byline, and Body Copy) into an InDesign document that does not contain styles with those names. The three styles are added to InDesign's Paragraph Styles list and have similar specifications to what they had in the word processor. However, because InDesign offers more formatting options, you might modify those styles to fine-tune the text formatting. To edit a paragraph style, select it in the Paragraph Styles pane, choose Style Options from the pane's palette menu, and then make your changes in the Modify Paragraph Style Options dialog box.

Overriding imported paragraph styles

In documents that follow a template, you can provide writers with style names that must be applied to their text. For example, say you're working on a tri-fold brochure that is part of an entire series of similar tri-folds. The writer might format the text with five paragraph styles that also exist in your InDesign document: Head, Subhead, Body Copy, Bullet, and Quote. The style specifications in the word processor don't matter — only the name counts — because the styles in an InDesign document override styles in imported text files.

For example, the writer's styles may use standard fonts such as Times and Helvetica along with bold and italic type styles to distinguish the types of text. But when the word-processing file is imported into InDesign, the styles are overridden with InDesign styles that have the same name but specify the actual fonts used by the designer and the many formatting options available in InDesign. See Figure 15-9 to compare the same styles in Microsoft Word and InDesign.

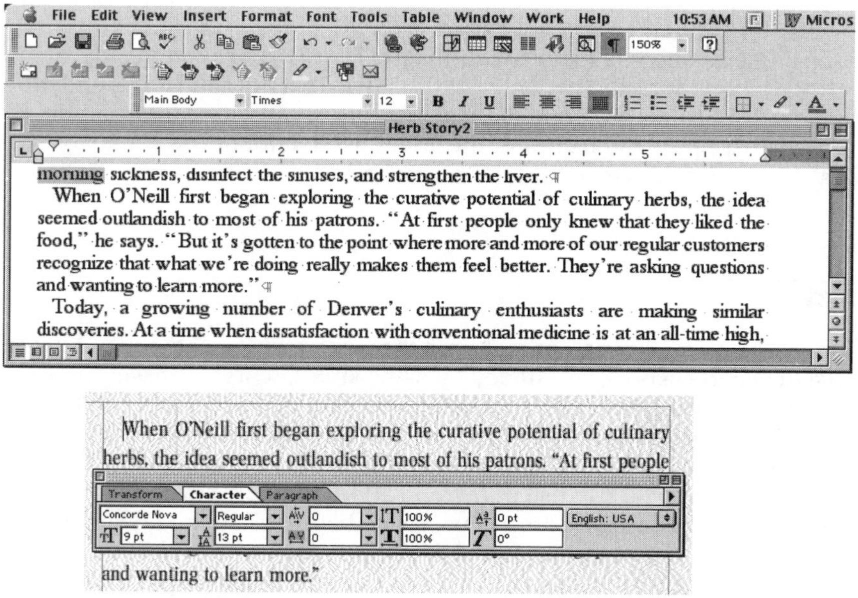

Figure 15-9: In Microsoft Word (top), the paragraph style Main Body specifies 12-point Times—fonts the writer is likely to have at a size that is amenable to writing and editing. When the Word file is placed in InDesign, a paragraph style with the same name overrides it—here, the InDesign style Main Body specifies 9-point Concorde Nova (bottom).

You can supply writers either with actual styles or with only style names:

✦ To supply styles, export text from a similar story in RTF format, which writers can open in their word processor; the word processor adds the style names in the RTF file to its own style list. The writers can then save these style names to a template file and use that template for future documents. To export text, use the Export dialog box (File ➪ Export, or ⌘+E or Ctrl+E) and choose Rich Text Format from the Formats pop-up menu.

✦ Or you can simply give writers a list of style names that they can create themselves to their own specifications. In this case, it's particularly important that the styles created in the word processor have exactly the same names as those in the InDesign document. The formatting doesn't have to match exactly, however.

Exporting styles

Although InDesign lets you export text (via the File ➪ Export command), only a few file formats are supported: Text only (ASCII), Rich Text Format (RTF), and InDesign Tagged Text. Unfortunately, none of these formats retains style information. (RTF and Tagged Text retain the names of the styles used, but not the actual formatting settings. ASCII doesn't even retain the style names.)

Summary

If you're working on a document that uses the same text formats repeatedly, you can save time and ensure consistency by using styles. A style is essentially a "macro" for formatting text. InDesign lets you create character-level styles and paragraph-level styles. Character styles let you apply several character attributes — such as font, size, leading, kerning, and tracking — to highlighted text all at once. Similarly, you can use paragraph styles to apply several paragraph formats — alignment, indents, drop caps, space before or after, and so on — simultaneously to selected paragraphs. After you apply a style to text, you can still manually modify the text by highlighting it and overriding the style's formats. If you're importing a text file from a word processing program that supports styles, such as Microsoft Word or Corel WordPerfect, you can import any applied styles along with the text.

✦ ✦ ✦

Typography Fundamentals

Text can be just the gray stuff that fills the page and anchors the graphics, or it can be part of the art of layout. We believe it's a key part of that art, and so do the makers of InDesign. In Part IV, you learn how to use typography effectively in any program, and then learn how to take advantage of InDesign's typographic power.

Chapter 16 covers the essentials of typography—everything from understanding typographic terms and what text is actually composed of to how to effectively use the many typeface variants available.

Once you understand how typography works, you'll be ready to use your knowledge to create innovative designs. **Chapter 17** shows you how to apply typographic effects to your layout to create truly standout documents. You can do a great deal with type and InDesign's typographic controls that add real pizzazz.

Text is more than just letters and numerals; hundreds of special characters are also available. Accented letters for multilingual publishing. Symbols for math and sciences. Icons for all sorts of hobbies and interests. And many more. But how do you find these characters and use them in your documents? **Chapter 18** reveals how.

Finally, text can actually be art. InDesign has several features to treat text as art, from colors and gradients to converting text to editable shapes. **Chapter 19** shows you how to use these features.

Fundamental Typography

The heart of a document is its typography—everything else can be well laid out and illustrated, but if the text is not legible and appealing, all that other work is for naught. That's why InDesign has such fine, flexible control over typography—arguably the best of any page layout program.

If you don't believe type is central, consider this: You've surely seen engaging documents with no artwork, but have you ever seen artwork carry the day if they type is ugly or scrunched? We didn't think so.

Desktop publishing has changed typography forever. In the old days, typefaces were available in a limited number, and they were available only in a limited number of sizes. You couldn't condense or expand them. And you certainly couldn't add drop shadows or make them print as outlines without hours of work in a darkroom. Desktop publishing has changed all that. By rendering type into a series of mathematical equations—curves and lines and angles—and manipulating that math with today's fast computers, type can be almost anything.

Working with Typefaces

A *typeface* is a set of characters designed with a particular look. The two basic types of typefaces are serif and sans serif. A *serif* typeface has horizontal lines (called serifs) extending from the edges of the character, such as at the bottom of a *p* or the top of an *I*. A *sans serif* typeface does not have these lines (*sans* is French for *without*).

More types of typefaces exist than just serif and sans serif, but they are all in the minority. And calligraphic, block, and other nonserif/nonsans serif typefaces usually have other elements that serve the purpose of serifs — extensions to the characters that add a distinctive character to the typeface.

Another distinct type of typeface is the *pi font*, which is a font made up of themed symbols (anything from math to Christmas ornaments). The name *pi font* comes from the Greek letter *pi* (π), a common mathematical symbol. They're also commonly called *dingbats*.

A typeface usually has several variations, the most common of which are *roman*, *italic*, *boldface*, and *boldface italic* for serif typefaces; and *medium*, *oblique*, *boldface*, and *boldface oblique* for sans serif typefaces. Other variations that involve type weight include *thin*, *light*, *book*, *demibold*, *heavy*, *ultrabold*, and *black*. *Compressed*, *condensed*, *expanded*, and *wide* describe type scale.

Italic and oblique differ in that italics are a curved variant of the typeface, with the serifs usually heavily curved, whereas an oblique is simply a slanted version of the typeface.

Note   In Web publishing, typography is usually extremely primitive. For text attributes, only boldface, underline, and italics survive most browsers. Similarly, font changes don't survive, although new technologies are being introduced that will change that over the next several years. Type sizes don't usually survive either, except for about a dozen styles that all popular browsers recognize, and they do have different text sizes — which means that you can vary the type size for a paragraph in some cases, and you can sometimes specify a type attribute such as "larger" to which the browser then assigns a size, but you cannot specify the specific type size for individual characters. Part X covers Web-publishing issues in detail.

Each of these variants, as well as each available combination of variants (for example, compressed light oblique), is called a *face*. Some typefaces have no variants; these are typically calligraphic typefaces, such as Park Avenue and Zapf Chancery, and symbol typefaces (pi fonts), such as Zapf Dingbats and Sonata. In Figures 16-1 through 16-7, you see samples of several typefaces and some of their variants. By using typeface variants wisely, you can create more attractive and more readable documents.

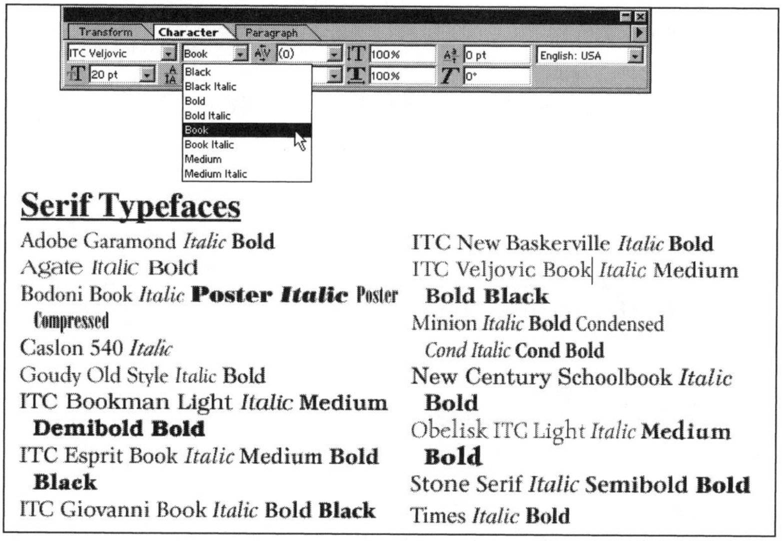

Figure 16-1: A sampling of serif typefaces, as well as the Character pane that shows available variations for the selected typeface.

Figure 16-2: A sampling of sans serif typefaces.

Figure 16-3: A sampling of block typefaces.

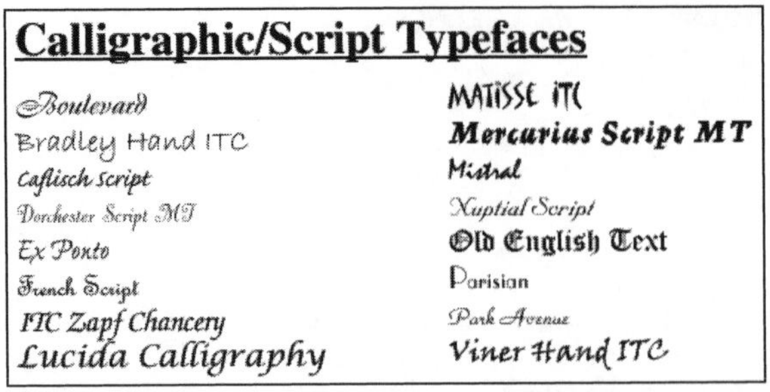

Calligraphic/Script Typefaces

Boulevard
Bradley Hand ITC
Caflisch script
Dorchester Script MT
Ex Ponto
French Script
ITC Zapf Chancery
Lucida Calligraphy

MATISSE ITC
Mercurius Script MT
Mistral
Nuptial Script
Old English Text
Parisian
Park Avenue
Viner Hand ITC

Figure 16-4: A sampling of calligraphic/script typefaces.

Monotype/Typewriter Typefaces

Andale Mono
Courier *Oblique* **Bold**
ITC American Typewriter Light
  Medium **Bold** Condensed Light Cond
  Medium **Cond Bold**

KEYSTROKES MT

Letter Gothic *Oblique* Bold
Monotype.com
OCR-A OCR-B

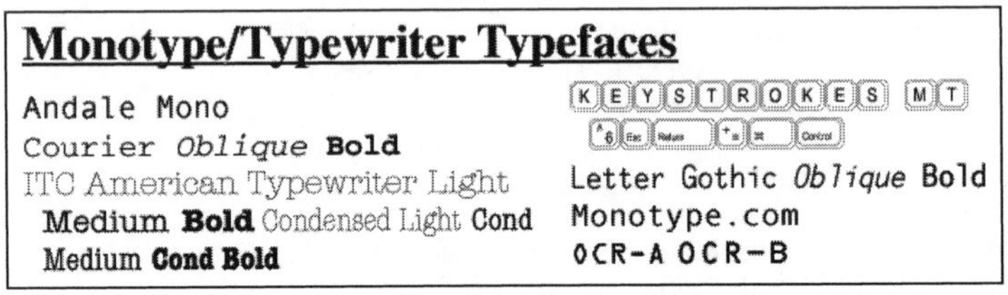

Figure 16-5: A sampling of monotype/typewriter typefaces.

Decorative Typefaces

ALGERIAN
Bodaccous
CRITTER
Flexure
Gradl
MATISSE ITC

MYTHOS
Ransom
ROSEWOOD
TRAJAN
UMBRA
Westminster

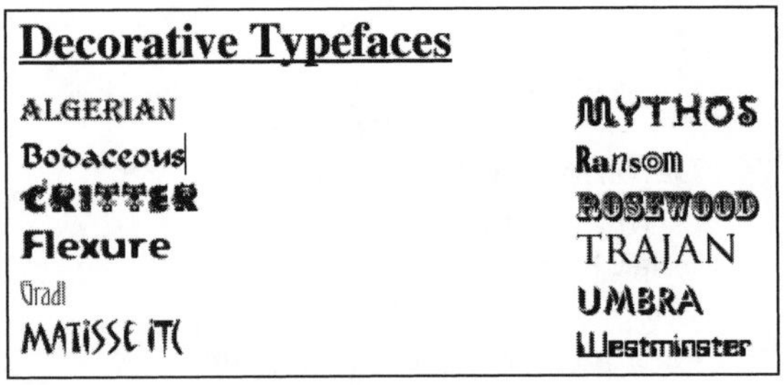

Figure 16-6: A sampling of decorative typefaces.

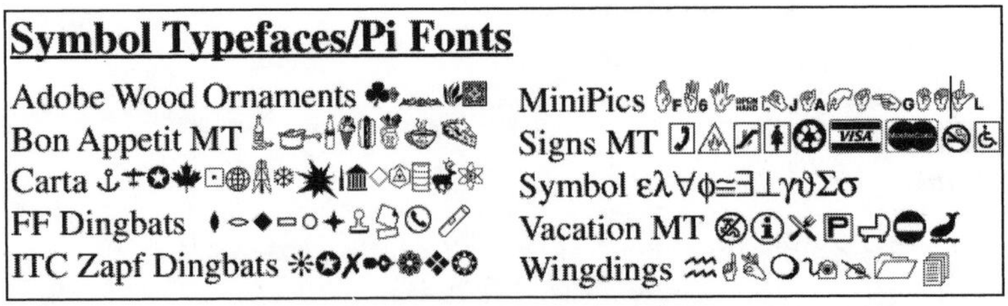

Symbol Typefaces/Pi Fonts

Adobe Wood Ornaments
Bon Appetit MT
Carta
FF Dingbats
ITC Zapf Dingbats

MiniPics
Signs MT
Symbol ελ∀φ≡⊥γϑΣσ
Vacation MT
Wingdings

Figure 16-7: A sampling of symbol typefaces/pi fonts.

Note

Desktop-publishing programs popularized the use of the term *font* to describe what traditionally was called a *typeface*. In traditional terms, a *typeface* refers to a set of variants for one style of text, such as Times Roman. A *face* is one of those variants, such as Times Roman Italic. A *font*, in traditional terms, is a face at a specific point size, such as 12-point Times Roman Italic. (Until electronic typesetting was developed, printers set type using metal blocks that were available only in a limited range of sizes.) The word *font* today means what *typeface* used to mean, and almost no one uses *font* any more in its original meaning.

Dealing with typeface variants

The many variants of typefaces confuse many users, especially because most programs use only the terms *normal* (or *plain*), *italic* (or *oblique*), *bold*, and *bold italic* (or *bold oblique*) to describe available variations. Here's how to handle the common issues.

Note

For information on font formats, how Windows and the Mac OS handle fonts, and other issues in making fonts work on your computer, see Chapter 39.

Extended font families

When a typeface has more than the basic normal/bold/italic/bold italic variations, programs usually split the typeface into several typefaces. For example, in some programs, Helvetica comes as Helvetica, with medium, oblique, boldface, and boldface oblique faces; Helvetica Light/Black, with light, light oblique, black, and black oblique faces; Helvetica Light/Black Condensed, with condensed light, condensed light oblique, condensed black, and condensed black oblique faces; Helvetica Condensed, with condensed medium, condensed oblique, condensed boldface, and condensed boldface oblique faces; and Helvetica Compressed, with compressed medium and condensed oblique faces. When this many variations exist, you have to choose from among several Helvetica typefaces, and you have to know that, for example, selecting bold for Helvetica Condensed results in Helvetica Condensed Bold type.

For some typefaces, the variants are even more confusing. For example, in text, ITC Bookman is usually printed in light face, which is lighter than the medium face. So when you select plain, you really select Bookman Light. And when you select bold, you really select Bookman Demibold. Bookman Medium and Bookman Bold are too heavy for use as body text, which is why the typeface comes in the light/demi combination of faces. Similarly, a variant exists called book, which is between a light and a roman weight.

Note *ITC* in front of a font name simply means the font comes from International Type Corp., a font designer. The company adds its name to its fonts (usually at the front of the name, but not always) to help people know where to buy them. Adobe does the same for the fonts it creates, adding "Adobe" to the beginning of the name, whereas Bitstream and Monotype tend to add "BT" and "MT," respectively, to the end of their fonts' names. An oddity in U.S. copyright law lets anyone duplicate a font as long as they don't copy the font computer files — so if you trace a font and create a new font file, you're legal. This has led to many almost-identical fonts with a variety of names — and sometimes the same name — coexisting, so adding the company name has become a popular way of highlighting ownership.

Different names, same font

The other area related to knowing your font names is that some fonts have more than one name. You usually encounter a problem in only one of the following situations:

✦ When you are working with a service bureau that has typeface names that are different, or whose staff uses the traditional names rather than the desktop-publishing names.

✦ When you are working with artists or typesetters to match a typeface. Typically, the problem is a lack of familiarity with the different names for a typeface. The best way to reach a common understanding is to look at a sample of the typefaces being discussed.

Platform Difference Macs and Windows fonts often have slight variations to their names, even when the fonts are identical. Mac names tend to have a space (such as Bookman Light), whereas PC names tend not to (such as BookmanLight).

✦ InDesign automatically translates most font-name variants as you move files across platforms. But for those it can't translate, InDesign gives you a message saying that specific fonts are missing. After you've let it continue opening the document, you can replace these missing fonts with InDesign's standard Find/Replace dialog box (Edit ➪ Find/Change, or ⌘+F or Ctrl+F). The dialog box can be confusing, so pay careful attention to the following steps:

Steps: Replacing Missing Fonts

1. Don't enter any text in the Find What and Change To fields.

2. Make sure Document is selected in the Search pop-up menu.

3. Click the More button in the dialog box to be able to change format attributes — doing so makes the dialog box deeper to display those normally hidden options.

4. Click the Format button in the Find Style Settings section to open the Find Format Settings dialog box.

5. In the pop-up menu at the top (which normally shows Style Options), change the setting to Basic Character Formats). You'll get the dialog box shown in Figure 16-8.

6. Scroll to the end of the list of fonts in the Fonts pop-up menu. The names of missing fonts are at the end, enclosed in bracket characters ([and]), as Figure 16-8 shows.

7. Select the font you want to replace and click OK.

8. Repeat Steps 4 through 7 but use the Format button in the Change Format Settings part of the dialog box, and select the font you want to use in place of the missing font.

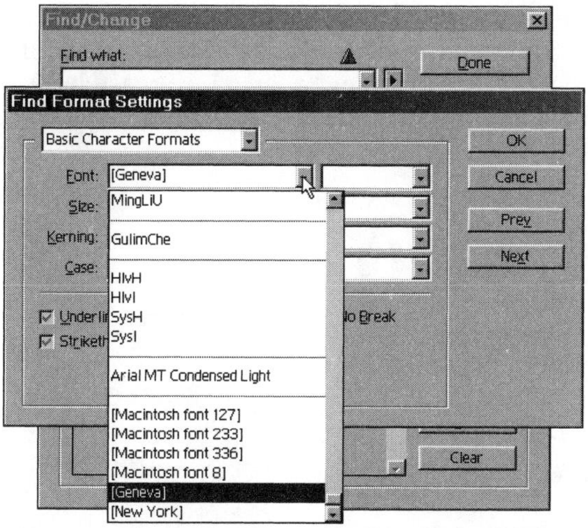

Figure 16-8: To replace missing fonts, use the standard Find/Change dialog box, and select the missing font (indicated in brackets).

9. Click the Change All button.

10. Repeat as necessary for other missing fonts. Click Done when finished.

Expert and alternate fonts

Finally, some fonts have a separate version called an *expert font* or an *alternate font*, which usually adds special symbols, ligatures, true small caps, and old-style numerals. For example, you might have Minion and Minion Expert appear on your font list — Minion is the font you use most of the time, whereas Minion Expert contains characters you use rarely, when exacting typography (such as in large headlines and in advertising and marketing materials) is crucial.

In typography, two kinds of numerals exist: modern and old style. *Modern* numerals are the same height as capital letters, and align to the baseline. *Old-style* numerals are more like lowercase letters and have ascenders and descenders.

For fonts that support both modern and old styles, you can select which type of numeral you want InDesign to use for selected text by checking the Old Style option in the Character pane's right-most pop-up menu. Figure 16-9 shows examples of old-style and modern numerals, as well as the pop-up menu.

In addition to old-style numerals, expert fonts contain true small caps. When you use the small-cap feature in a program such as InDesign, the program simply reduces the size of a regular capital letter. This usually reduces the width of the character, making it a little lighter in appearance than a lowercase letter. A true small cap, by contrast, is designed to have the same weight as a lowercase letter.

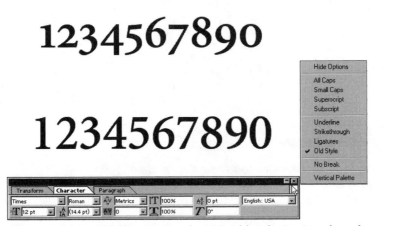

Figure 16-9: Two kinds of numerals exist: old-style (top) and modern (bottom). For fonts that support both, InDesign lets you choose which to use, through the pop-up menu in the Characters pane.

Note

Few fonts do support both modern and old-style numerals — more typical is that you'll have the regular font and the expert font as separate fonts. InDesign won't automatically switch between the fonts even if you use the Old Style option in the Character pane.

Finally, some expert fonts contain special symbols not found in the standard version, such as fractions, cent signs (¢), and stylized ampersands (&) and dollar signs ($). Figure 16-10 shows examples of these variations.

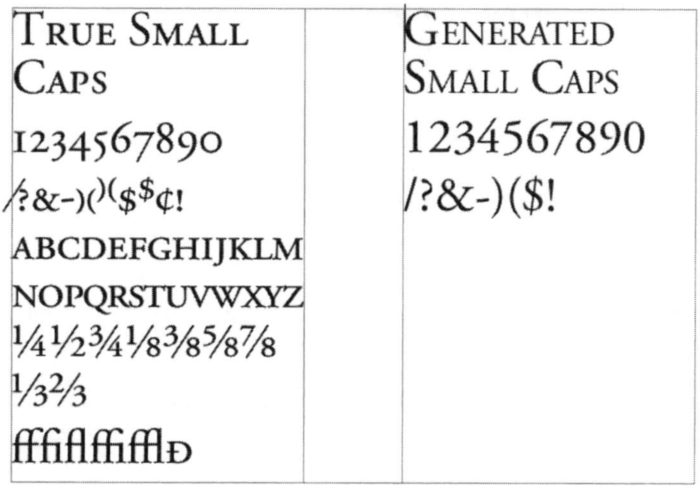

TRUE SMALL CAPS	GENERATED SMALL CAPS
1234567890	1234567890
/?&-)()($$¢!	/?&-)($!
ABCDEFGHIJKLM NOPQRSTUVWXYZ	
¼½¾⅛⅜⅝⅞	
⅓⅔	
ﬀﬁﬂﬃﬄĐ	

Figure 16-10: Variations in an expert font (left) of items in a regular font (right).

Multiple-master fonts

Adobe Systems has created a special type of PostScript font called *multiple master*. Multiple-master fonts are designed to be elastic, so you can change their characteristics — such as thickness, width, and optical scaling — on the fly by creating new versions (such as semicondensed semibold). Thus, a multiple-master font such as Minion or Myriad may have a dozen versions, not just the usual normal, bold, italic, and bold italic. (The font name usually ends with *MM* so you know it's a multiple-master font.) You use Adobe Type Manager Deluxe or a font editor such as Macromedia's Fontographer to create these variations, as described in Chapter 39.

As Figure 16-11 shows, a multiple-master font's faces have unusual names. They are coded to describe the variation in each face. Typical codes include RG for regular weight, SB for semibold weight, BD for bold weight, BL for black weight, LT for light weight, NO for normal width, CN for condensed width, SC for semicondensed width, SE for semiexpanded width, EX for expanded width, and OP for optical scaling. The numbers preceding the codes indicate the degree of attribute — for example, a font coded 485 SB is not as bold as one coded 500 SB, whereas 12 OP means the font has the optical scaling of a 12-point face while one with 24 OP has the optical scaling of a 24-point face.

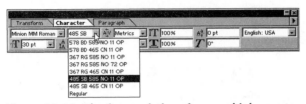

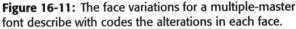

Figure 16-11: The face variations for a multiple-master font describe with codes the alterations in each face.

What is optical scaling? When you change font size, you're not just blindly enlarging or shrinking the typeface in direct proportion. As text gets smaller, any subtleties or embellishments would tend to muddy up how it prints, so smaller fonts actually have different designs that reduce such subtleties and embellishments. And larger fonts may have more of such features because they are more visible at large sizes. Optical scaling adjusts these subtleties and embellishments. But some multiple-master fonts let you override the optical scaling and dictate which is to be used at what size.

Note

Not all fonts support optical scaling — some of the ones created by amateurs or knock-off shops use one optical scaling for all sizes. But most professionally created fonts use optical scaling, and InDesign automatically adjusts optical scaling for those fonts if you check the Automatically Use Correct Optical Size option in the Text pane of the Preferences dialog box (File ➪ Preferences ➪ Text, or ⌘+K or Ctrl+K).

Changing typeface attributes

InDesign provides a simple set of tools to let you apply typeface variants and styles. In fact, you have only five places to set typeface attributes, and two of these are for rarely applied attributes:

✦ **The Character pane,** shown in Figure 16-12 with annotations as to what each item does, is the main area to set typeface attributes. Use this when you are applying attributes to selected text, such as when italicizing a word in a sentence, making a footnote's numeral superscripted, or adjusting character spacing for a more pleasing look. (If this pane is not visible, use Type ➪ Character, or ⌘+T or Ctrl+T, to open it.)

✦ **The Type menu,** which has menus for font and size, as well as other typography-oriented menu items that bring you to the Character pane.

✦ **The Swatches pane,** shown in Figure 16-13, for applying color to text.

✦ **The Strokes pane,** also shown in Figure 16-13, for applying color and other effects to the character outlines.

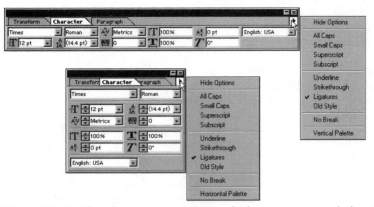

Figure 16-12: The Character pane, from which you can control almost every typographic specification, including tracking, typefaces, type size, and type style.

Figure 16-13: The Swatches pane (top), from which you apply colors, tints, and gradients, and the Strokes pane (bottom), from which you set attributes for text's outlines. (Examples of text with strokes applied are in the figure's lower-right corner.)

✦ **The New Paragraph Style and New Character Style dialog boxes,** which you use when you want to save formatting so you can apply it in the future without risk of inconsistency. The New Paragraph Style dialog box has all the options of the New Character Style dialog box, plus a host of others for paragraph formatting such as leading and tabs. Chapters 10 and 11 cover these dialog boxes in detail.

To select a typeface quickly, double-click the typeface name in the typefaces pop-up menu in the Character pane and enter the first letter or so of the typeface's name. The list jumps to the first typeface that begins with what you type. This method is faster than displaying the pop-up menu and scrolling if you have many typefaces available.

To the right of the typeface name is a pop-up menu of available faces—attributes such as italics, bold, and condensed—for the current typeface. You can use the double-click-and-navigate-via-typing-a-letter technique also in this pop-up menu.

Tip   Once you click in a field in the Character pane, you can move around the pane by using the Tab and Shift+Tab shortcuts, rather than selecting each one by mouse. Tab goes to the left, whereas Shift+Tab moves to the right.

How InDesign Handles Font Faces

InDesign is smart enough to know a demibold from a bold, and it adjusts the attribute labels in the Character pane accordingly, as Figure 16-1 illustrated earlier. But when you use the keyboard shortcuts to change faces, you'll still have to choose from Normal (Shift+⌘+Y or Ctrl+Shift+Y), Italic (Shift+⌘+B or Ctrl+Shift+B), and Bold (Shift+⌘+B or Ctrl+Shift+B), so you still should have a sense of your font's variations.

If the font has other faces in addition to normal (regular), bold (or something like demibold instead of—not in addition to—bold), and italic—such as light or ultrabold—note that they can't be accessed via shortcuts. For them, you'll need to use the Character pane.

If you see a face in brackets, such as [Light], InDesign is telling you that it is does not have the typeface available and so it is using Adobe Type Manager's substitution feature to simulate it onscreen. (A "light" version of ATM comes with the Mac OS. The $99 full Deluxe version is a must-have for any publisher on Windows or Macintosh. See Chapter 39 for more details.) Often, you get that simulation indication when you switch from a font to one that doesn't have the same styling. For example, you may have switched from a font with a semibold but no bold to one with bold but no semibold. InDesign is unsure whether you wanted to still apply a semibold in the new face, so it displays [Semibold] to indicate it is simulating the face. In this case, all you need to do is select Bold from the pop-up menu to get the intended boldface.

Finally, note that if a font doesn't support a particular face—such as italics—using the shortcut key for that face has no effect.

Note   If InDesign doesn't do any formatting when you use a shortcut for bold or italic, this means it can't tell which face to use. So you have to use the Character pane and select the face from there.

Tip   If you apply the plain formatting to a text selection, it undoes all attribute formatting except color and stroke attributes. So, for example, if you have bold italic type and want to make it just italic, apply bold again to the selection, which removes the bold and leaves the italic. This is easier than making the text plain and then reapplying italics.

If you want to apply other attributes—such as strikethrough, underline, small caps, all caps, superscript, subscript, ligatures, and old-style numerals—use the Character pane's palette menu or use the shortcuts in Table 16-1.

Table 16-1 **Shortcut Keys for Typeface Attributes**		
Attribute*	*Macintosh Shortcut*	*Windows Shortcut*
Plain	Shift+⌘+Y	Ctrl+Shift+Y
Bold	Shift+⌘+B	Ctrl+Shift+B
Italic	Shift+⌘+I	Ctrl+Shift+I
<u>Underline</u>	Shift+⌘+U	Ctrl+Shift+U
~~Strikethrough~~	Shift+⌘+/	Ctrl+Shift+/
ALL CAPS	Shift+⌘+K	Ctrl+Shift+K
SMALL CAPS	Shift+⌘+H	Ctrl+Shift+H
Superscript	Shift+⌘+=	Ctrl+Shift+=
Subscript	Option+Shift+⌘+=	Ctrl+Alt+Shift+=
Enlarge point size	Shift+⌘+>	Ctrl+Shift+>
Reduce point size	Shift+⌘+<	Ctrl+Shift+<

* No shortcut keys exist for enabling ligatures or old-style numerals, or for adjusting baseline shift or scaling—
you must access these options through the Character pane.

Selecting the Best Typefaces

If you've ever seen a type chart, you already know that thousands of typefaces are available, each with a different feel. Matching the typeface's feel to the effect that you want for your document is a trial-and-error process. Until you are experienced at using a variety of typefaces (and even then), experiment with different typefaces on a mock-up of your document to see what works best.

Tip

We recommend that you take the time necessary to define a standard set of typefaces for each group of publications. You may want all employee newsletters in your company to have a similar feel, which you can enforce by using common body text and headline typefaces, even if layout and paragraph settings differ.

The key to working with a standard set of typefaces is to avoid limiting the set to only a few typefaces. Selecting more typefaces than any one document might use gives you enough flexibility to be creative while providing an obviously standard appearance. You also can use the same typeface for different purposes. For example, you might use a newsletter's headline typeface as a kicker in a brochure. A consistent—but not constrained—appearance is a good way to establish an identity for your company.

You may have noticed that many people use serif typefaces for body copy and sans serif typefaces for headlines, pull-quotes, and other elements. But no rule exists that forces you to do this. You can easily create engaging documents that use serif typefaces for every element. All-sans-serif documents are possible, but they are rare because sans serif typefaces tend to be hard to read when used in many pages of text. (Exceptions include typefaces such as News Gothic and Franklin Gothic, which were designed for use as body text.) No matter which type-faces you use, the key is to ensure that each element calls an appropriate amount of attention to itself.

If you're feeling confused about which typeface is right for your project, here are some basic guidelines:

✦ Use a roman, medium, or book weight typeface for body text. In some cases, a light weight works well, especially for typefaces such as Bookman and Souvenir, which tend to be heavy in the medium weights.

✦ Output some samples before deciding on a light typeface for body text because many light typefaces are hard to read when used extensively. Also, if you intend to output publications on an imagesetter (at 1,270 dpi or finer resolution), make sure that you output samples on that imagesetter because a light font may be readable on a 300- or 600-dpi laser printer but too light on a higher resolution printer that can reproduce thin characters more faithfully than a laser printer. (The laser printer may actually print a light typeface as something a bit heavier: Because the width of the text's stroke is not an even multiple of the laser printer's dots, the printer has no choice but to make the stroke thicker than it should be.)

✦ Use a heavier typeface for headlines and subheads. A demibold or bold usually works well. Avoid using the same typeface for headlines and body text, even if it is a bolder variant. On the other hand, using the same typeface for subheads and headlines, even if in a different variant, helps ensure a common identity. (And if you mix typefaces, use those that have similar appearances. For example, use round typefaces with other round typefaces and squared-off typefaces with other squared-off typefaces.)

✦ If captions are long (more than three lines), use a typeface with the same weight as body text. If you use the same typeface as body text, differentiate the caption visually from body text. Using a boldface caption lead-in (the first words are boldface and act as a title for the caption) or putting the caption in italics distinguishes the caption from body text without being distracting. If captions are short (three lines or fewer), consider using a heavier face than body text or a typeface that is readily distinguished from your body text.

✦ As a general rule, avoid using more than three typefaces (not including variants) in the main document elements (headlines, body text, captions, pull-quotes, and other elements that appear on most pages). However, some typefaces are very similar, so you can use them as a group as if they were one. Examples include Helvetica, News Gothic, and Univers; Avant Garde, Bauhaus, and Futura; Eras, Myriad, and Syntax; Gill Sans and Stone Sans; Benguiat, Korinna, and Souvenir; Times and its many relatives (including Times

New Roman and Times Ten); Esprit, Galliard, New Baskerville, and Veljovic; Americana Condensed, Garamond, and Giovanni; Charter, Cheltenham, and Stone Serif; and Caslon 224, Century Old Style, Goudy Old Style. (Figure 16-14 shows these combinations.) You can treat the individual typefaces within these groups almost as variants of one another, especially if you use one of the individual typefaces in limited-length elements such as kickers (the text above a headline that is used as a label or as a secondary headline), pull-quotes (the large quotes set off as almost a small sidebar within a story), and bylines.

✦ Italics are particularly appropriate for kickers, bylines, sidebar headlines, and pull-quotes.

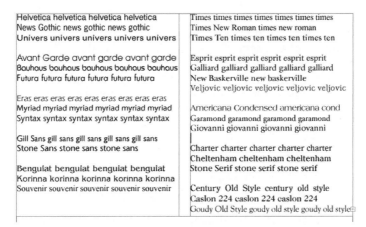

Figure 16-14: Examples of appropriate typeface groupings.

Taking Advantage of Type Styles

Typefaces have several faces — such as boldface and italics — to give publishers visual variety and content guides. Publishing programs (as well as some word processors) also offer special *typeface attributes*, such as small caps and underlines, to provide even more design and content tools.

Earlier in this chapter you learned how to access typeface attributes. This section gives you advice on how to use them effectively. Of course, these and other guidelines are meant to be ignored by those purposely trying to create a special effect.

Basic text styles

Most people are familiar with basic text styles such as boldface and italics. After all, we see them routinely in books, newspapers, magazines, ads, and television. Despite this familiarity, these styles can be misused, especially by people experienced in producing reports on typewriters and word processors rather than creating published (typeset-quality) documents in which these basic styles are used differently.

Italics

Italics are used to emphasize a word or phrase in body text — for example, "You *must* remember to fully extinguish your campfire." Italics are also used to identify titles of books, movies, television and radio series, magazines, and newspapers: "Public TV's *Discovery* series had an excellent show about the Rocky Mountains." Italics can also be applied to lead-in words of subsections or in lists (these instances are described in Chapter 17).

Note   In typewritten text, people often use underlines or uppercase as a substitute for italics, but do not substitute these effects in published text.

Boldface

Boldface is seldom used in body text because it is too distracting. When it is used, boldface is typically applied to the lead-in words in subsections. As a rule, do not use it for emphasis — use italics instead. However, when you have a lot of text and you want people to easily pick out names within it, boldfacing the names may be appropriate. If, for example, you create a story listing winners of a series of awards or publish a gossip column that mentions various celebrities, you may want to boldface people's names in order to highlight them.

Small caps and all caps

Capital letters have both functional and decorative uses. Functionally, they start sentences and identify proper names. Decoratively, they add emphasis or stateliness.

Capital letters have a more stately appearance than lowercase letters most likely because of the influence of Roman monuments, which are decorated with inscribed text in uppercase letters (the Romans didn't use lowercase much). These monuments and the Roman style have come to symbolize authority and officialism. Most government centers have a very Roman appearance, as a visit to Washington, D.C., quickly confirms.

Using all capital letters has two major drawbacks:

✦ Text in all caps can be overwhelming because uppercase characters are both taller and wider than lowercase. In typeset materials, as opposed to typewritten, all caps loom even larger because the size difference between a capital letter and its lowercase version is greater than it is in typewriter characters, which are all designed to fit in the same space. All caps can be thought of as the typographic equivalent of yelling: "READ THIS SENTENCE!" Now, read this sentence.

✦ People read not by analyzing every letter and constructing words but by recognizing the shapes of words. In all caps, words have the same rectangular shape — only the width changes — so the use of word shape as a reading aid is lost. All caps is therefore harder to read than regular text.

The use of small caps can result in elegant, stately text that is not overwhelming. The smaller size of the caps overcomes the yelling problem of all caps. Figure 16-15 shows an example of effective use of small caps. In the example, the kicker and byline are set in small caps.

SPRINGTIME IN PARIS

The Joy of French Baking

❦✦❀ BY ANITA EPLER ❧✦❀

Figure 16-15: Example of effective use of small caps.

The key to using small caps is to limit them to short amounts of text where it's OK not to give readers the aid of recognizable word shapes. Small caps are effective in kickers, bylines, and labels.

InDesign lets you set the proportional size of small caps (compared to regular caps) in the Text pane of the Preferences dialog box (File ➪ Preferences ➪ Text, or ⌘+K or Ctrl+K), as shown in Figure 16-16. (You can also set the relative size and position of superscripts and subscripts in this dialog box.) InDesign's default setting is 70 percent, and most small caps should be set between 70 and 80 percent. We prefer 75 percent in most cases. Remember also that some fonts have optional expert-font versions that have specially designed small-cap characters, as described earlier in this chapter (see Figure 16-10).

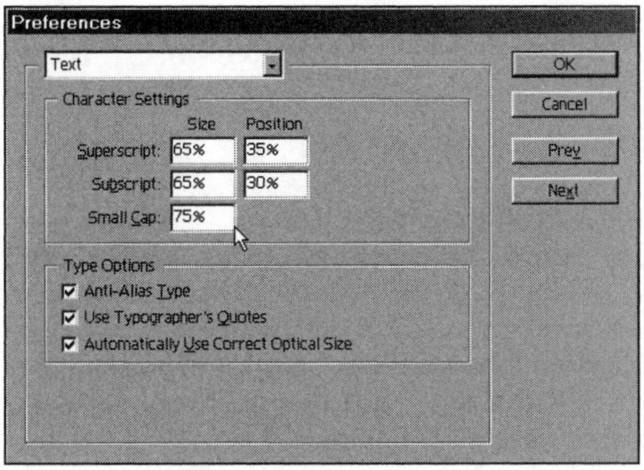

Figure 16-16: The Text pane of the Preferences dialog box lets you set small cap size.

Tip

If you want typographic settings to affect all documents, invoke the Text pane in the Preferences dialog box with no document selected. Any future documents use the new settings as the default settings.

Old-style numerals

If you look at books published early in this century or in previous eras, you'll notice that the numerals look very different from the ones you see today in books, magazines, and newspapers. Numerals used to be treated as lowercase letters, so some, such as the number *9*, had descenders, just as lowercase letters such as *g* do. Others, such as the number *6*, had ascenders, as do lowercase letters such as *b*. But this way of displaying numerals changed, and most modern typefaces treat numerals like capital letters: no descenders and no ascenders. This style keeps numerals from sticking out in headlines, but it also can make numerals too prominent in some text, especially in type-intensive documents such as ads, where individual character shapes are important to the overall look.

Although they often look more elegant, old-style numerals have three drawbacks that you should consider before using them routinely:

✦ In most cases, they reside in a separate font, so you must change the font for each and every numeral (or groups of numerals) — InDesign can switch between them for fonts that have both, as described earlier in this chapter. Even if you code this in your word processor, it can be a lot of extra work. In tables and other numerals-only text, using old-style numerals is less of an issue because you can have a separate style for text that uses the expert font.

✦ They do not have the same width as each other. Modern numerals are almost always the same width (that of an en space), so typographers and publishers don't have to worry about whether columns of numbers align. (Because all modern numerals are the same width, they align naturally.) But the old-style numerals in expert fonts have variable widths, just like most characters, so they can look awkward in columns of numbers even if you use decimal or comma alignment.

✦ They are unusual in modern typography, so they can call more attention to themselves than is appropriate. For design-intensive work, this extra attention is usually not an issue, but in commonplace documents such as reports and newsletters, they can look out of place.

Superscripts and subscripts

Superscripts and subscripts let you indicate notes in your text and set some mathematical notations.

The most common use is to indicate footnotes. Although numerals are typically used for these footnotes, you can also use special symbols such as asterisks and daggers. These footnote characters appear in a smaller size than the rest of the text and are positioned above or below the regular baseline.

Superscripts and subscripts are also typically used in math and other sciences. A superscript can indicate an exponent, such as a^2 for *a squared*, or a notation, such as U^{235} for *uranium-235*. A subscript can be used to indicate a position in a series, such as a_3 for the third value in the series *a*.

As it does for small caps, InDesign lets you set the relative size and spacing for superscripts and subscripts. You specify these sizes in the Text pane of the Preferences dialog box, accessed via File ⇨ Preferences ⇨ Text, or ⌘+K or Ctrl+K. (Figure 16-16 showed the dialog box.) You may need to experiment to derive a setting that works for all paragraph styles.

We prefer the following settings over InDesign's defaults: superscripts offset 35 percent and scaled 60 percent, and subscripts offset 30 percent and scaled 60 percent. Our settings tend to work better for body text used in magazines, newspapers, and other dense text — in books and manuals, where the leading and size tends to be larger, InDesign's settings are fine.

If you want typographic settings to affect all documents, invoke the Text pane in the Preferences dialog box with no document selected. Any future documents use the new settings as the default settings.

Baseline shift

Baseline shift is similar to superscripting and subscripting. Baseline shift lets you move text up or down relative to other text on the line. The biggest difference between baseline shifting and superscripting or subscripting is that with baseline shift, the text size does not change. This effect is rarely needed, but it can come in handy when you position text for ads and other design-intensive text.

Another use of the baseline shift feature is to change the text size to create superscripts or subscripts that differ from the normal settings in a document. Most people won't need this feature; among those who may are scientists and engineers whose documents require several levels of subscripting or superscripting. Because InDesign supports just one level, you would shift the baselines for the second and further levels of subscripts and superscripts.

You change baseline shift through the Character pane or as part of a character or paragraph style.

Underlines and rules

Underlines and rules are not typically used in body text in published documents. In fact, underlines are used in typewritten text as a substitute for italics. But underlines do have a place in published materials as a visual element in kickers, subheads, bylines, and tables. When used in such short elements, underlines add a definitive, authoritative feel.

InDesign's underlines affect all characters selected, including spaces and tabs. If you want to underline just the words (as many word processors and other programs let you do), you'll have to remove underlining manually for spaces and tabs.

Underlines are limited in line size and position — all underlines are fixed by InDesign. But you can create underlines and other types of lines meant to enhance text with the ruling line feature. InDesign offers a wide range of ruling lines through the Paragraph Rules pane (accessed from the Paragraph pane's palette menu, via

Type ➪ Paragraph, with the shortcuts ⌘+M or Ctrl+M, or when creating or editing paragraph styles). Figure 16-17 shows the dialog box and the example of a ruling line placed behind text.

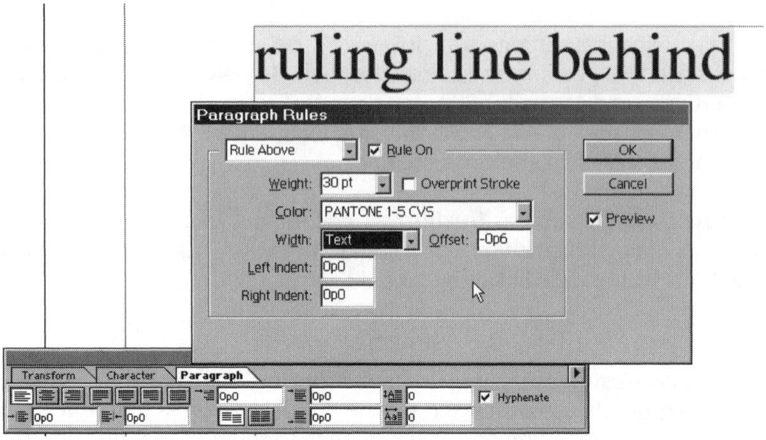

Figure 16-17: The Paragraph Rules pane and text with a ruling line behind it.

Note

Ruling lines can be applied only to paragraphs, not specific text selections.

Tip

In the Paragraph Rules pane, you can set a ruling line above and a ruling line below for the paragraph with totally different settings. It may not appear that way at first, but it's true: Use the pop-up menu to select Rule Below, make sure Rule On is checked, and make your settings. Then use the pop-up menu to select Rule Above, make sure Rule On is checked, and make your settings. Your text will have both rules applied. To undo a rule, just uncheck Rule On for Rule Above or Rule Below, as appropriate.

The first option available for the rule is the Weight option, where you determine the rule's thickness. Use the Color pop-up menu to select a color (it will use any defined in the Swatches pane). You also have the option of checking Overprint Stroke, which you should do if outputting to color separations (enabling this option ensures that the color of the rule will overlap slightly with whatever is next to it, in case during printing the color negatives shift slightly, which could cause an unsightly gap).

Now you set the width of the rule, in the Width pop-up menu. The choices are Text and Column, to make the rule the same width as the paragraph's text or as wide as the full column it is in. But you can adjust these settings by entering values in Left Indent and/or Right Indent. The indent settings move the ends of the rule as you indicate. Positive numbers basically make the rule narrower. Negative numbers make it wider — you can even make the rule extend past the text frame this way.

Use Indents when you want a rule to be a standard width, no matter how long the text is. An example is a series of centered labels in a menu—*Appetizers*, *Salads*, *Pasta*, and so on—whose lengths vary greatly. By making the rules the same width, you call more attention to the rules and to the fact that they indicate a major heading.

Finally, by selecting the Offset feature, you can specify the position of the rule relative to the text's baseline. A rule above starts at the baseline and goes up, whereas a rule below starts at the baseline and goes down. A positive number moves the rule away from the baseline (so for a rule above, it moves up, whereas for a rule below, it moves down). A negative number does the opposite.

Tip

You can use the Offset feature to create reversed type. To do this, you essentially move the rule into the text line associated with it. The key is to make the rule larger than the text. If the text is 28 points, we would set the rule to be 30 points, which provides a slight margin above and below the text. (Make your rule at least 2 points larger than the text to get an adequate margin.) We then offset the rule by −8 points, to move it below the baseline (to cover the descender such as in the *g* character).

Quotes

Several characters that are not used in traditionally typed business documents are used routinely in typeset documents. Do not ignore these symbols; readers expect to see them in anything that appears to be published, whether on the desktop or via traditional means. If you're used to working only with typewritten or word-processed documents, pay careful attention to the proper use of these characters.

The most common of these characters are *typographic quotation marks*. The typewriter uses the same character (") to indicate both open and closed quotation marks (" "), as well as the same character (') to indicate apostrophes (') and open and closed single quotation marks (' '). Using the " and ' marks (also called *straight quotes*) rather than typographic quotation marks (also called *curly quotes*) in a published document is a sign of an amateur.

Fortunately, an option in InDesign called Use Typographer's Quotes lets you turn on a feature that inserts typographically correct quotation marks. It even uses the right quotes for the language associated with the current text. Just go to the Text pane of the Preferences dialog box (File ➪ Preferences ➪ Text, or ⌘+K or Ctrl+K) and check the Use Typographer's Quotes option. Your word processor likely has a similar feature to generate typographic quotes in the first place: In Word, use Tools ➪ AutoCorrect; in WordPerfect, use Tools ➪ QuickCorrect.

InDesign also offers an option during text import that automatically changes quotes to their typographic equivalents. When you get text, make sure that you check the Convert Quotes box in the Place dialog box (File ➪ Place, or ⌘+D or Ctrl+D).

When you type text directly into InDesign, you can type in a command to get typographic quotes (instead of using the Use Typographer's Quotes option). You might do this if your text has both typographic quotes and keyboard quotes, which are often used for the foot, inch, prime, and double prime symbols. The commands are listed in Table 16-2.

Note

Although you can insert special characters such as quotes, spaces, and dashes via the Type ⇨ Insert Character menu, or by Control+clicking or right-clicking in text to get a contextual menu with the Insert Special Character option, it's faster to enter a code if you're using a special character repeatedly.

Table 16-2 Typographic Quote Shortcuts		
Character	*Macintosh Shortcut*	*Windows Shortcut*
" (open double quote)	Option+[	Alt+[
" (closed double quote)	Shift+ Option+[	Shift+Alt+
' (open single quote)	Option+]	Alt+]
' (closed single quote)	Shift+Option+]	Shift+Alt+]
« (open French quote)	Option+⌘+[	Ctrl+Alt+[
» (closed French quote)	Option+⌘+]	Ctrl+Alt+]

Punctuating text with quotes confuses many people, but the rules are not complicated for North American English:

✦ Periods and commas always go inside the quotation.

✦ Semicolons and colons always go outside the quotation.

✦ Question marks and exclamation marks go inside if they are part of the quote, outside if not. When the main clause is a question, but the quote is a declaration, the question mark takes precedence over the period, so it goes outside the quotes. When the main clause is a question, and the quote is an exclamation, the exclamation takes precedence, and it goes within the quotation. Look at the following examples:

- Did he really say, "I am too busy"?

- She asked, "Do you have time to help?"

- I can't believe she asked, "Do you have time to help?"

- She asked me, "Can you believe that he said, 'I am too busy'?"

- He really did yell, "I am too busy!"

When a single quote is followed immediately by a double quote, separate the two with a nonbreaking space (⌘+spacebar on the Mac and Ctrl+5 in Windows) or one of InDesign's narrow space characters (covered later in this chapter).

✦ He told me, "She asked, 'Do you have time to help?' "

✦ He told me, "Bob heard him say, 'I am too busy.' "

For more information on these rules, refer to a grammar guide.

Dashes and hyphens

Just as several types of quotation marks are designed for typographic use, so are several types of dashes and hyphens. When typing, most people use two hyphens (--) to indicate an em dash (—), which gets its name because it is the width of a capital *M* when typeset). Using two consecutive hyphens is fine on a typewriter, but not in a published document, so be sure to use the correct character.

Unlike other programs, InDesign does not translate consecutive hyphens to em dashes even if you the Use Typographer's Quotes option in the Preference dialog box's Text pane (File ➪ Preferences ➪ Text, or ⌘+K or Ctrl+K), or if you use the Convert Quotes option when importing a text file (File ➪ Place, or ⌘+D or Ctrl+D). Fortunately, most word processors will convert consecutive hyphens to dashes; use Tools ➪ AutoCorrect in Word and Tools ➪ QuickCorrect in WordPerfect.

Typographers are divided over whether you should put spaces around em dashes — like this — or not—like this. Traditionally, no spaces are used. But having spaces lets the publishing program treat the dash as a word, so that even space appears around all words in a line. Not having a space around dashes means that the publishing program sees the two words connected by the em dash as one big word, so the spacing added to justify a line between all other words on the line may be awkwardly large because the program doesn't know how to break a line after or before an em dash that doesn't have spaces on either side. Still, whether to surround a dash with spaces is a decision in which personal preferences should prevail.

There's also the en dash (–), so called because it is the width of a capital *N*. Traditionally, an en dash is used to:

✦ Separate numerals, as in a range of values (the en dash can be thought of as substituting for the word "to," as in "1776–1999").

✦ Label a figure.

✦ Indicate a multiple-word hyphenation (as in "Nouvelle Cuisine–inspired").

Finally, two special hyphen characters are used to control how text breaks at the end of columns:

✦ A *nonbreaking hyphen* prevents a compound word (such as *e-mail*) from breaking at the hyphen, with the text before at the end of one line and the rest at the beginning of the next line. A nonbreaking hyphen is typically used when the reader might misread the text if broken at that point.

✦ A *discretionary hyphen*—also called a *soft hyphen*—tells InDesign to consider this hyphen first in breaking a word. It is typically used for words such as *project* that hyphenate differently as a noun (*proj-ect*) than as a verb (*pro-ject*).

Note

All dashes in InDesign are nonbreaking—if no spaces exist on either side of the dash, the text will not break immediately before or after the dash.

If you want to enter dashes or special hyphens in text while typing directly into a InDesign document, you must use the Insert Special Character contextual menu (Control+click or right-click while in text) or enter special commands, as shown in Table 16-3.

Table 16-3
Keyboard Shortcuts for Dashes and Hyphens

Character	Macintosh Shortcut	Windows Shortcut
— (em dash)	Shift+Option+- (hyphen)	Shift+Alt+- (hyphen)
– (en dash)	Option+- (hyphen)	Alt+- (hyphen)
- (nonbreaking hyphen)	Option+⌘+- (hyphen)	Ctrl+Alt+- (hyphen)
discretionary hyphen*	Shift+⌘+- (hyphen)	Ctrl+Shift+- (hyphen)

* If you turn on Show Hidden Characters (Type ➪ Show Hidden Characters, or Option+⌘+I or Ctrl+Alt+I), you can see where such discretionary hyphens are in your text, as well as other invisible characters.

Special spaces

Several special spaces are available in InDesign to help you position text precisely—InDesign offers more than most publishing programs. These are typically used to align text in tables, as well as to give enough separation between characters that need to be near each other but not quite touching, such as between some letters and a parenthesis, or between single quotes and double quotes.

InDesign offers these special spaces:

✦ A **nonbreaking space** prevents a line from breaking at the space. Its width is the same as any other space on the line.

✦ An **em space** is the same width as the current point size, which is usually the same as the size of a capital *M* (thus the name). It is typically used to align items in tables and as an indent character.

✦ An **en space** is half as wide as an em space, and is usually the same width as a capital *N*. It too is used to align items in tables (it's the same width as most numerals), as well as to follow a bullet character in a list (because it helps make sure the text following the bullet aligns along all paragraphs).

✦ A **figure space** is the width of a zero (0), and is used in tables to ensure numerals align properly.

✦ A **thin space** is a quarter as wide as an em space, and is usually the same width as a lowercase *t*. It is used to align table elements as well as to separate single quotes from double quotes that immediately follow.

✦ A **hair space** is ½th the width of an em space, and is used to align text in tables (because it is about the width of a period or comma), as well as to put slight space between items that might otherwise touch (such as between some letters and parentheses). In many cases, it's easier to use kerning to adjust such spacing.

✦ A **flush space**, also called a punctuation space, is the width of a comma or period, making it used mostly to align items in tables. Not all fonts have this character, which is why the thin or hair space is commonly used in its place. InDesign substitutes a regular space if you specify a flush space for a font that doesn't have one.

Note

If you turn on Show Hidden Characters (Type ➪ Show Hidden Characters, or Option+⌘+I or Ctrl+Alt+I), you can see where such spaces are in your text, as well as other invisible characters. Figure 16-18 shows how InDesign indicates each such character, and shows the contextual menu's Insert Special Character menu as well.

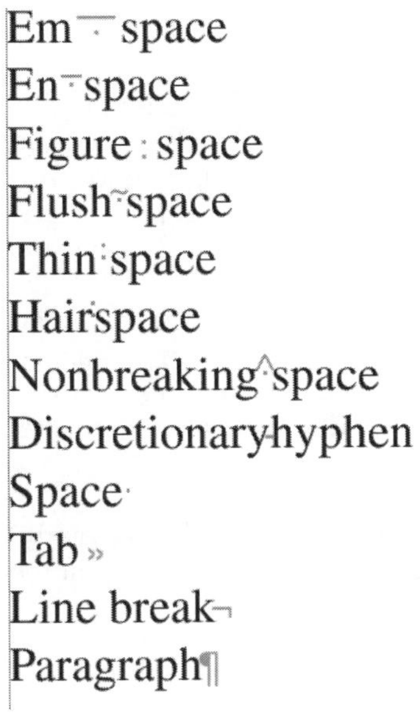

Em⁻space
En⁻space
Figure : space
Flush⁻space
Thin space
Hair space
Nonbreaking^space
Discretionary hyphen
Space·
Tab »
Line break⁻
Paragraph¶

Figure 16-18: How InDesign shows special characters onscreen.

If you want to enter special spaces in text while typing directly into an InDesign document, you must use the Insert Special Character contextual menu (Control+click or right-click while in text) or enter special commands, as shown in Table 16-4.

Table 16-4 Keyboard Shortcuts for Spaces		
Character	*Macintosh Shortcut*	*Windows Shortcut*
Nonbreaking space	Option+⌘+X	Ctrl+Alt+X
em space	Shift+⌘+M	Ctrl+Shift+M
en space	Shift+⌘+N	Ctrl+Shift+N
figure space	Shift+Option+⌘+8	Ctrl+Alt+Shift+8
flush space	Shift+Option+⌘+J	Ctrl+Shift+J
thin space	Shift+Option+⌘+M	Ctrl+Shift+Alt+M
hair space	Shift+Option+⌘+I	Ctrl+Shift+I

Summary

InDesign is designed with typography in mind, offering a full set of controls for manipulating font attributes. For novices, the number of typefaces and the variety of attributes among them can be overwhelming. But by choosing a set of complementary typefaces, you can create a consistent but not constrained design that is easily manageable.

InDesign offers the standard attribute controls — italics, boldface, underlining, strikethrough, all caps, small caps, superscripts, and subscripts — as well as some unique controls, including old-style numerals. It also offers a broader variety of fixed-size spaces than other programs do, while also offering the standard mix of special symbols such as dashes and quotes.

Now that you have seen the typographic range in InDesign, you're ready to learn some fancy techniques. Chapter 17 describes how to create many such effects.

✦   ✦   ✦

Creating Special Text Formatting

Once you learn the basics of typefaces, character formats, and paragraph formats, you can achieve just about any look with text. The trick is learning to combine and apply the skills you've learned to produce special effects that not only look professional but also enhance the meaning of the text. Glance at any professional publication — a national magazine, direct-mail catalog, cookbook, or product brochure — and you'll notice typographic techniques that set the publication apart from anything that can be easily produced in a word processor. (Even when word processors do offer a feature, they often lack the control necessary to really fine-tune an effect.) And skilled designers use these effects with a purpose — special bullet characters emphasize a theme, drop caps draw readers in, and pull-quotes tantalize. Throughout this chapter, we show you how standard InDesign features can produce typographic special effects, and more important, we show you when to use them.

Indenting Text

InDesign lets you indent paragraphs from the left side, right side, or both sides of the column or text frame. You can also indent the first line of a paragraph inde pendently of the rest of the paragraph. If Inset Spacing is specified in the Text Frame Options dialog box (Object ⇨ Text Frame Options, or ⌘+B or Ctrl+B), text is indented from the inset value.

First-line indents

To indicate a new paragraph, you might indent the first line or put a noticeable amount of space between paragraphs. If you opt to indent the first line, don't do it the typewriter way with tabs. Select the paragraphs, and then enter a value in the

First Line Left Indent field in the Paragraph pane as shown in Figure 17-1 (Type ➪ Paragraph, or ⌘+M or Ctrl+M). Press Shift+Return or Shift+Enter to see the results with the field still highlighted; press Return or Enter to get out of the pane and back into the document.

Restaurant sticker shock happens a lot in the mountains. People somehow get the idea that small towns equal small prices. But unless

piece of fish. Ser complemented th new potatoes with

out of your wallet. Consider it a scenery tax.

to be buried.

Figure 17-1: In this publication, body text paragraphs have a first-line indent of 0.125".

Once you have a setting that works, create a paragraph style using it, as explained in Chapter 15.

Hanging indents

In hanging indents, the first few characters of text (often a number or bullet) are aligned with the left margin while the remaining lines in the paragraph are indented. Notice the left-aligned menu items in Figure 17-2; the multiline coffee descriptions that make up the rest of the paragraphs "hang" to the right of the coffee names.

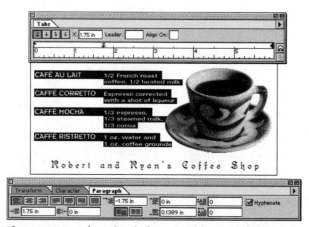

Figure 17-2: A hanging indent combines a tab and left indent at the same value with a negative first-line indent.

To create a hanging indent, first separate the textual items, bullets, or numbers from the text with a tab. Note the position of the tab, and then specify a left indent for the paragraphs at the same location. Use the Left Indent field in the Paragraph pane (Type ➪ Paragraph, or ⌘+M or Ctrl+M). Then, enter the same value in the first-line indent field — except make the value negative to pull the first line back. For example, if you have a tab at 1.75", use a left indent of 1.75", and a first line indent of –1.75".

Block indents

Publishers often offset quotes that are longer than a few lines by indenting the paragraph from both sides of the text frame or column. To do this, use the Left Indent and Right Indent fields in the Paragraph pane (Type ➪ Paragraph, or ⌘+M or Ctrl+M). In general, use the same values you use for first-line indents, and indent both sides the same amount.

Spacing Guidelines for Indents and Bullets

The easy part of creating first-line indents, hanging indents, bulleted lists, and numbered lists in InDesign is using the software. The hard part can be deciding how much space to use. How do you decide how deep to make a first-line indent? How much space goes between a bullet and the text following it? Amateur publishers or designers, who are likely to be thinking in inches rather than points or picas, are likely to use too much space. They're tempted to use 0.25", 0.125" or another nice dividend of an inch for spacing rather than a more appropriate value such as 6 points. When deciding on spacing, consider the following:

✦ First-line indents that indicate new paragraphs should generally be one or two em spaces wide. The width of an em space is equal to the point size in use — so 10-point text should have a 10- or 20-point first-line indents. Opt for less space in narrower columns to avoid awkward space and more space in wider columns so the spacing is evident.

✦ As you remember from grade-school outlines, indents help organize information, with deeper indents indicating more detail about a topic. Professional publications, though, have many organizational options — such as headlines, subheads, and run-in heads — so they rarely have a need for more than two levels of indents. You might use indents on lengthy quotes, bulleted lists, numbered lists, kickers, and bylines. If you do, stick to the same amount of indent for each so the reader's eyes don't wander.

✦ In bulleted lists, use a hanging indent for a succession of two- or three-line bulleted paragraphs in wider columns. If your bulleted items are five or six lines long, especially in narrow columns, it might work better to use run-in heads to break up the information.

Continued

(Continued)

✦ Generally, the amount of space between a bullet and its text is equal to half the point size of the text. So if you're working with 11-point text, place 5.5 points between the bullet and text.

✦ When it comes to numbered lists, you need to decide whether you're going to include a period or other punctuation after the number and whether you'll ever have two-digit numbers. Numerals in most typefaces are the width of an en space, and should be followed by the same amount of space the numbers and their punctuation take up. If you have a two-digit numeral, the numbers take up one em space and so should be followed by one em space.

Although these values give you a good starting point, you might need to modify them based on the typeface, font size, column width, design, and overall goals of the publication.

Adding Bullets and Formatting Lists

Unlike many word processors, InDesign does not have a "bullet me" feature. You can't just highlight paragraphs and add bullets or numbers. You have to type a bullet character or numeral at the beginning of each paragraph and insert spaces or tabs to offset the text. The good thing about this is you have complete control over the bullet or numeral's font, color, size, and placement. And once you set up the formatting, you can automate it with both paragraph and character styles.

Note   You apply spacing to lists using tabs and indents—paragraph formats—so you'll want to make sure each bulleted or numbered item is followed by a paragraph return. (Choose Type ➪ Show Hidden Characters or press Option+⌘+I or Ctrl+Alt+I to confirm the existence of paragraph returns, which are indicated with the ¶ symbol.) If bullets or numerals exist in the text, look for a single tab character between the bullet or numeral and the following text. This lets you adjust only one tab stop. If you need to strip out extra tabs or change line breaks to paragraph returns, use the Find/Change dialog box (Edit ➪ Find/Change, or ⌘+F or Ctrl+F).

Adding bullets or numerals

Chances are, you're not writing in InDesign. The text was delivered in the form of a word-processing file, and the writer or editor made some decisions about bullets or numerals. A lot of times, writers will simply enter an asterisk followed by a space to indicate a bullet. Or maybe an editor typed a numeral followed by a parenthesis in front of each step. Other times, writers or editors might use their word processor's automatic bullet or numbering feature. In many cases, you'll need to repair the bullets or numerals in the text using the Find/Change dialog box (Edit ➪ Find/Change, or ⌘+F or Ctrl+F). The way you enter a bullet or numeral depends on what you started with:

✦ If the writer or editor typed numerals or used an automatic numbering feature, the numbers and their punctuation arrive in InDesign intact. However, you might want to change or even remove the punctuation following the numeral. The look of the numerals is more of a design decision than an editorial decision. If numerals are in a different typeface and/or in a different color, a period following the numeral might just look cluttered. Using Find/Change on a text selection, you can easily change or remove punctuation in numbered lists.

✦ InDesign doesn't like word processors' automatic bullets, converting them to characters in the current font, which will need to be changed to bullets. Or rather than using automatic bullets, the writer might have typed in asterisks, hyphens, or another character to indicate bullets. Once you determine what characters indicate bullets in your text, use Find/Change to change it to the bullet character you want. For example, you can search for an asterisk and change it to an "n" in the Wingdings font, which looks like a square ■.

✦ If you're writing in InDesign, you can enter numerals and bullets as you type. If you're editing and decide to add bullets or numerals to existing paragraphs, you can paste completely formatted bullets followed by tabs or spaces at the beginning of each paragraph. You can also paste a numeral, and then edit the numeral's value as appropriate.

While you're adding bullet characters, decide on the font you're going to use. You can press Option+8 or Alt+8 for a simple, round en bullet (•) in the same typeface as the body text. You can choose a different character in the body text font, or pick a character in a symbol font such as Zapf Dingbats or Wingdings. Use the Insert Character command (Type ⇨ Insert Character) to see all the possibilities within a font, as explained in Chapter 18.

Deciding on initial formatting for bullets and numerals

Once your lists include bullets or numerals, use the Character pane (Type ⇨ Character, or ⌘+M or Ctrl+M) to experiment with the formatting of a bullet or numeral. For example, change the typeface of a numeral and increase the size slightly or horizontally scale the symbol used for a bullet. You can also apply a color to the stroke (outlines) or fill (inside) of the bullets or numbers; see the "Applying Color to Text" section later in this chapter.

Adding space between bullets or numerals

In addition to the formatting of bullets and numerals, you need to decide how text will follow them. Figure 17-3 shows three different options for bullets. The first column shows an en bullet followed by a tab; the second column shows an en bullet followed by a tab and hanging indent; the third column shows a Zapf Dingbats sideways heart used as a bullet followed by a tab and hanging indent.

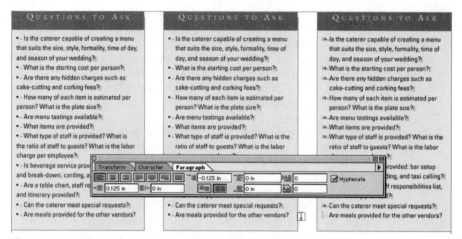

Figure 17-3: These three columns show the evolution of an en bullet to a fancy bullet followed by a hanging indent. In this case, the writer typed an en bullet followed by a tab in front of each paragraph in Microsoft Word (avoiding the automatic Bullets and Numbering feature). The designer flowed in the text, formatted it, and repositioned the tab. In the second column, the designer specified a hanging indent. The designer then decided to choose a different character for the bullet, so she highlighted the text and used Find/Change to change en bullets to a sideways heart shape in the Zapf Dingbats font.

The most consistent way to space a bulleted or numbered list is to separate the bullet or numeral from the text with a single tab, as shown in Figure 17-4. You can then create a hanging indent as described earlier in this chapter, and you can indent the paragraphs from the left and/or right as you wish.

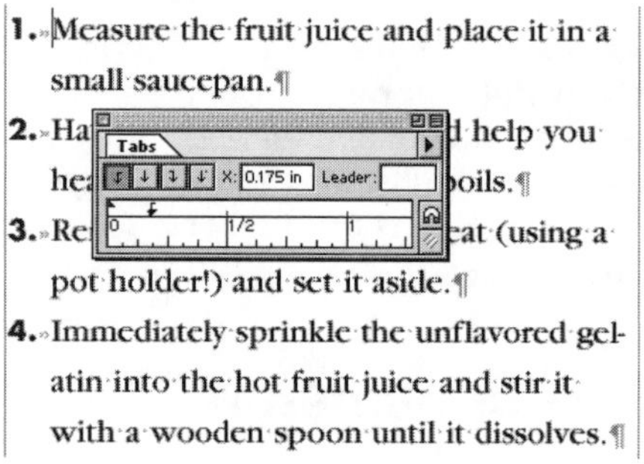

1. Measure the fruit juice and place it in a small saucepan.¶

2. Ha[...] help you he[...] oils.¶

3. Re[...] at (using a pot holder!) and set it aside.¶

4. Immediately sprinkle the unflavored gelatin into the hot fruit juice and stir it with a wooden spoon until it dissolves.¶

Figure 17-4: To achieve the most consistent spacing in bulleted and numbered lists, use a single tab to set off the bullets or numerals from the text.

Applying styles for numbered and bulleted lists

The combination of paragraph and character formats necessary to produce numbered and bulleted lists can be tedious to apply. You'll want to save the basic formatting as a paragraph style. If the bullets or numerals have different formatting, save that as a character style. Make sure to specify keyboard commands for the styles so you can apply them quickly (see Chapter 15).

To apply the styles to existing text, first highlight all the paragraphs, and then apply the paragraph style. Then you can highlight each numeral or bullet and apply the character style. With bullets, you can use Find/Change to locate all the bullets and apply the character style.

Tip   Make sure to apply the paragraph style first, and the character style second or the paragraph formatting will wipe out your special numeral or bullet formatting.

Bullet Character Options

Although you may not know what they're called, you're used to seeing *en bullets*, the small round bullet (•) included in most typefaces. But you're not limited to using this character. You can use any character in the body text font, or you can switch to a symbol or pi font and choose a more decorative character.

Zapf Dingbats and Wingdings are the most common symbol fonts, offering an array of boxes, arrows, crosses, stars, and check marks. These can be cute and effective, but cute isn't always a good thing. If you opt for a different bullet character, make sure you have a reason and that it works well with the rest of the design. Check mark bullets in an election flyer might make sense; square bullets in a to-do list for a wedding caterer might not make sense.

Note that you might want to reduce the size of the symbol slightly and that you might need to use different spacing values than you would use with an en bullet.

Don't limit yourself to Zapf Dingbats and Wingdings either. You can purchase many different symbol fonts to support different content. For example, you might see leaf-shaped bullets in an herb article and paw-print bullets in a pet training article. To use your own drawing or a logotype as a bullet, convert the drawing to a font using Macromedia Fontographer and Pyrus FontLab (a demo version of Pyrus FontLab is included on the CD-ROM that comes with this book).

Adding Drop Caps

Few things set off a professional publication from an amateur or word-processed document like the use of drop caps. Decorative characters at the beginning of paragraphs serve both editorial and design purposes, drawing readers into the content with their size and position, while emphasizing a theme with their style. You'll see drop caps ranging from a single four-line drop cap in the same typeface as the paragraph in a financial publication's letter from the editor to a 140-point word in a script face kicking off a feature article in a bridal magazine. Drop caps often use more decorative typefaces — you can even purchase fonts that consist only of ornate capital letters. A children's book might use a graphic of a letter formed from an animal's body, and a cooking magazine might use the outlines of a letter filled with an image of related foods. You can achieve all these effects with the typographic and layout features in InDesign.

 Don't forget that text is for reading. Heavily designed drop caps can become unrecognizable as text, leaving the reader with a disjointed word or sentence in the first paragraph of a story. No matter how gorgeous a 192-point "S" looks flowing behind a paragraph in rose-colored Kuenstler Script, if readers don't recognize the "S," they're left trying to make sense of the word "ensitivity." You would have been better off leaving "Sensitivity" to start the paragraph and drawing a nice curly shape behind the text.

Creating automatic drop caps

A *drop cap* is an enlarged capital letter at the beginning of a paragraph that drops down several lines into the text. In daily newspapers and weekly magazines, which are likely to have limited production time, the most common effect you'll see is a simple drop cap in the paragraph's font. Simple drop caps such as these can be created automatically — in two simple steps — in InDesign. Even though drop caps look like character formatting, they're actually created through a paragraph format. This ensures that drop cap formatting remains in the paragraph even if you edit or delete the original first characters.

Steps: Creating a Drop Cap

1. Select the Type tool and click in the paragraph to select it.

2. If the Paragraph pane isn't open, choose Type ➪ Paragraph, or press ⌘+M or Ctrl+M.

3. Specify how many lines down the character(s) should drop into the paragraph by typing a number from 2 to 25 in the Drop Cap Number of Lines field. Generally, you'll drop the character(s) 3 to 5 lines.

4. Specify how many characters in the first line should be enlarged as drop caps by typing a number from 1 to 150 in the Drop Cap One or More Characters field. Generally, it looks best to drop the first character or the first word in the story. If the columns are wide enough, you can drop the first phrase.

5. Press Return or Enter to see the drop caps.

Once you create a drop cap with the InDesign feature, you can highlight the enlarged characters and change the font, color, or any other character formats. See Figure 17-5 for an example of a four-line drop cap in a different font and color.

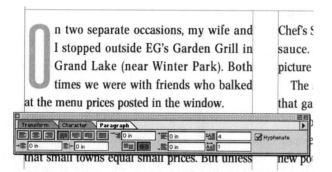

Figure 17-5: To create this drop cap, first we typed 4 in the Drop Cap Number of Lines field and 1 in the Drop Cap One or More Characters field. Then we highlighted the character, changed the font to Univers Light Ultra Condensed, and changed the color to violet.

For different drop caps effects, try the following:

✦ Tab after the drop caps, and then create a hanging indent so the text is aligned to the right of the characters.

✦ Kern between the drop caps and the paragraph text to tighten or expand the space.

✦ Baseline-shift the drop caps to move them up or down.

✦ Change the font size of the drop caps to enlarge them and raise them above the paragraph.

✦ Scale the drop caps to make them more dramatic.

Remember to save the drop cap as a paragraph style, and any modifications to the drop cap as a character style.

Note

If you decide to drop the first word or phrase in a story, you'll have to count the number of characters and change the value in the Drop Cap One or More Characters field for each paragraph. This means you can't apply the formatting automatically with a paragraph style—you'll have to give each introductory paragraph individual attention.

If the first character in a paragraph is a quotation mark (" or '), it can look odd as a one-character drop cap. If you don't like this look, you have a couple options: you can either delete the opening quotation mark, an acceptable but potentially confusing practice, or you can use the first two characters in the paragraph as drop caps instead. Some publications simply prefer not to start paragraphs with quotes, preventing the problem from the editorial side.

Creating raised caps

Raised caps are a variation of drop caps, enlarging and raising the first few characters of the paragraph above the first line in the paragraph. Creating raised caps is simple — highlight the characters you want to raise with the Type tool and enlarge them using the Font Size field on the Character pane (Window ➪ Character, ⌘+T or Ctrl+T).

If you raise a word or phrase, you might need to track the raised words to tighten them. You also might need to kern between the raised text and the remainder of the line. Other options for raised caps include changing the font, color, and scale of the characters. See Figure 17-6 for an example of raised caps used in a subhead. If you plan to repeat the raised cap formatting, save it as a character style.

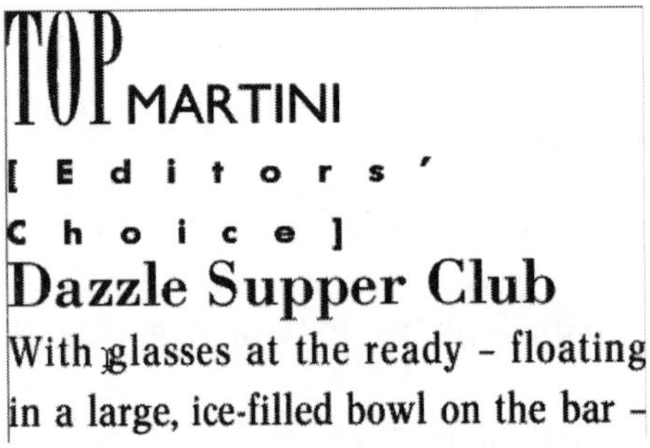

TOP MARTINI

[E d i t o r s '

C h o i c e]

Dazzle Supper Club

With glasses at the ready – floating in a large, ice-filled bowl on the bar –

Figure 17-6: Subheads in *5280* magazine's "Top of the Town" article call attention to each new category with a raised cap. The subhead is in all caps, with "Top" in 36-point Bordeaux typeface next to "Martini" (the category) in 12-point Bank Gothic Medium BT.

Converting text to outlines for drop or raised caps

You can convert drop caps, raised initial caps, or any character in any font to a frame. You can then resize, scale, shear, fill, and stroke the character-shaped frame. To do this, highlight the characters with the Type tool, and then choose Type ➪ Create Outlines, or press Shift+⌘+O or Ctrl+Shift+O. Frames are based on the size and outlines of the font in use and are automatically anchored in the paragraph so they flow with the text.

Note When you convert text to outlines, the characters no longer exist as text. If you converted part of a word, the remaining portions of the word may be flagged during a spelling check. If you need to edit the text, you will need to delete the outlines, retype the word, and convert the characters again.

Using graphics as drop caps

Rather than using text for drop caps, you can use special graphics. You can purchase clip-art collections that consist of nothing but ornate capital letters to use as drop caps. To use a graphic as a drop cap, first delete the characters you will replace with graphics. Then, use the Place command (File ⇨ Place, or ⌘+D or Ctrl+D) to import the graphic.

Size the graphic as appropriate, and then place it behind the paragraph, next to the paragraph, or anchored in the text of the paragraph. To anchor a graphic in text, select it with the Selection tool and choose Edit ⇨ Cut, or press ⌘+X or Ctrl+X. Select the Type tool and click at the beginning of the paragraph, and then choose Edit ⇨ Paste, or press ⌘+V or Ctrl+V. The graphic is now anchored to the text, so if text is reflowed, the graphical drop cap will flow with it.

In addition to importing graphics for use as drop (or initial) caps, you can create your own graphics in InDesign. For example, you can place the drop cap character in its own text frame and create reverse type from it as discussed later in this chapter. Or you can shade the character and place it slightly behind the paragraph.

Labeling Paragraphs

Along with initial caps, changing the formatting of the first few words in a paragraph can indicate the beginning of a story or a new topic. For example, in *Time* magazine, the first paragraph of a story often starts with a single drop cap, followed by the entire first line in small caps. This change in formatting is variously called a label, a lead-in, or a run-in head (see Figure 17-7). Used as subheads, labels offer a more subtle method — one that consumes less vertical space — for distinguishing content.

To experiment with label formatting, use the attributes available via the Character pane and its palette menu, such as font changes, horizontal scale, or small caps (Type ⇨ Character, or ⌘+T or Ctrl+T). Once you decide on the formatting for labels, you can apply it using character styles after paragraph styles are applied — and after the text is final.

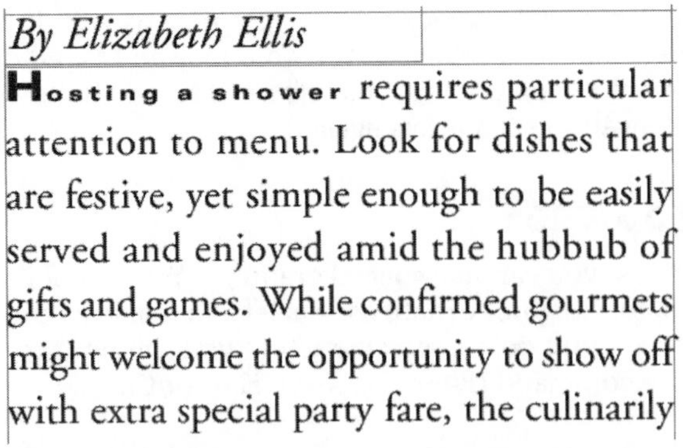

> *By Elizabeth Ellis*
>
> **H**osting a shower requires particular attention to menu. Look for dishes that are festive, yet simple enough to be easily served and enjoyed amid the hubbub of gifts and games. While confirmed gourmets might welcome the opportunity to show off with extra special party fare, the culinarily

Figure 17-7: The first paragraph of this story was enhanced with 10 points on the first letter and a 5-point label on the first few words, both in Univers Black. The body of the story is in 10-point Adobe Garamond.

Note   Depending on the formatting, applying a label style might reflow the text, causing a need for copyfitting.

Tip   To provide a little more space between the label and the text, you might want to use an en space rather than a normal space.

The following descriptions show frequently used label formatting:

✦ **Boldface:** Bold speaks the loudest, and is generally used for subheads in magazines, newspapers, and reports. To apply boldface in InDesign, you must select the bold version of the typeface from the Style pop-up menu on the Character pane.

✦ *Italics:* If bold shouts, italics tends to whisper. It's a good choice for tertiary heads and to label bulleted items within a list. To apply italics in InDesign, you must select the oblique version of the typeface from the Style pop-up menu on the Character pane.

✦ <u>Underlines</u>: For a typewriter effect, you might underline the text of a label. Use the Underline command available from the menu on the Character pane—you have no control over the style, thickness, or placement of the line.

✦ SMALL CAPS: For a subtle, classic look that blends well with the rest of the document, use small caps on labels. However, don't use small caps if you're using labels as subheads that let readers skim through a document and read only relevant portions. You have two choices for applying small caps from the Character pane: choose a small caps variation of a typeface from the Style pop-up menu or choose the Small Caps command from the palette menu.

✦ **Typeface change:** Rather than relying on different variations of a font, you can use a different font altogether, such as Futura as used to start this paragraph, for a label. To contrast with serif body text, you might choose a sans serif typeface that complements the look of your publication. Often, this will be a variation of your headline font. To apply a typeface, use the Font pop-up menu in the Character pane.

✦ Scaled text: Scaling text horizontally — up 10 or 20 percent — quietly differentiates it from the remainder of the paragraph. (More severe scaling will distort the typeface and could look unprofessional.) Unlike bold or underline, the text won't pop off the page at you, but it will be visually distinct. Scaling text vertically, however, can be too subtle unless combined with boldface or another style. Use the Horizontal Scale and Vertical Scale fields in the Character pane to scale text.

✦ Size change: Creating a label by simply bumping the size up a point or two is another subtle design choice. The labels blend well with the body text, but they don't announce their presence enough to be used as subheads for scanning. To change the size of type, use the Font Size field in the Character pane.

Adding Professional Touches

With today's word processors and low-end page layout programs offering predesigned templates for birthday cards and reports, almost anyone can claim to be a designer. But a closer look reveals the difference — skilled graphic designers plan their typography and layout around the content, using typographic techniques to call attention to and refine content. The use of reverse type, sidebars, and pull-quotes helps break up pages and organize text, while careful formatting of fractions, hanging punctuation, and end-of-story markers adds a professional touch.

Reversing type out of its background

This is the reverse of what you usually see — white type on a black background rather than black type on a white background. Of course, reverse type doesn't have to be white on black, but any lighter color on a darker color. You'll often see reverse type in table headings, kickers (explanatory blurbs following headlines), and in decorative elements as shown in Figure 17-8. Reverse type, which brightens text and pulls readers in, works best with larger type sizes and bold typefaces so the text isn't swallowed by the background.

Figure 17-8: This design element consists of white type in a rectangular text frame with a background of None. The text frame is placed on top of a red circle, which is on top of a black square. Because this element is used to indicate sections of a "Top of the Town" article, the designer planned the size to fit the other categories: shopping, services, spas, and so on.

InDesign doesn't have a reverse type command or type style — but using this effect involves just a simple combination of basic InDesign skills. To lighten the text, highlight it with the Type tool, click the Fill button on the Toolbox, and choose a light color from the Swatches pane (Window ⇨ Swatches, or F5). For a dark background, you have two options: filling the text frame with a darker color or making the text frame transparent and placing it on top of darker objects. For either option, select the text frame with the Selection tool or the Direct Selection tool, and then click the Fill button on the Toolbox. To fill the text frame with a color, click a darker color on the Swatches pane. To make the text frame transparent, click the Apply None button on the Toolbox. Then, place the text frame in front of a darker object or graphic.

When designing elements with reverse type, make sure the point size of the text is large enough to print clearly on the darker background. Consider the thinnest part of characters, especially in serif typefaces, when judging the size and thickness of reverse type.

Creating sidebars and pull-quotes

Pick up almost any publication, from *Time* magazine to your neighborhood newsletter, and you're almost guaranteed to see sidebars and pull-quotes. So basic that you can even create them with a modern word processor, these treatments aren't really typographic treatments — they're just page-layout techniques involving text elements you create by applying simple InDesign skills.

✦ A *sidebar* is supplemental text, formatted differently, and often placed within a shaded or outlined box. Sidebars help break up text-heavy pages and call attention to information that is often interesting but not essential to the main story. Even in technical publications, it's helpful to pull in-depth information or related text into sidebars to provide visual relief. To create a sidebar, you'll usually place the text in its own frame, and then stroke the frame and fill it with a tint. To inset the text from the edges of the frame, use the Text Frame Options dialog box (Object ⇨ Text Frame Options, or ⌘+B or Ctrl+B).

✦ A *pull-quote* is a catchy one- or two-line excerpt from a publication's text that is enlarged and reformatted to achieve both editorial and design objectives. On the editorial side, pull-quotes draw readers into articles with excerpts that do everything from summarize the content to provide shock value. On the design side, pull-quotes break up staid columns and offer opportunities for typographic treatment that emphasize the content (such as colors and typefaces that reflect the mood of an article). Although the use of and length of pull-quotes is often dictated by design, an editorial person should select the text and indicate it on hard copy or within text files. To create a pull-quote, copy and paste the relevant text into its own text frame, and then reformat the text and frame as you wish. Use the Text Wrap pane (Object ➪ Text Wrap, or Option+⌘+W or Ctrl+Alt+W) to control how text in columns wraps around the pull-quote.

Formatting fractions

If you're in a big hurry, it's fine to type "⅓ cup" and get on with your life. It looks like a fraction, but it's kind of big and ugly, and it calls a little too much attention to itself. Compare the first line in Figure 17-9, which is formatted appropriately for a fraction, to the last two lines, which are not. InDesign doesn't provide an automatic fraction maker, but you can use expert typefaces or character formats to achieve professional-looking fractions.

**¹/₃ espresso,
1/3 steamed milk,
1/3 cocoa**

Figure 17-9: In the first line of text here, the "1/3" text is formatted manually to look like an expert fraction.

Applying a fraction typeface

Some expert typefaces include a variation, appropriately called fractions, that include a number of common fractions such as ½, ⅓, ¼, and ¾. Adobe's Garamond Expert collection for both Macintosh and Windows includes a fractions face; examples of Mac typefaces with fraction variations include MrsEaves and New Century Schoolbook. To use an expert fraction, use the Insert Character command (Type ➪ Insert Character). Select the font and face from the pop-up menus at the bottom of the dialog box, and then select the fraction you want.

Tip If you're dealing with a wide range of fractions in something like a cookbook, you probably won't find all the fractions you need. Because it would be difficult to format fractions such as ³⁄₁₆ exactly the same as an expert font's ¼, you might opt for formatting all the fractions manually.

Formatting fractions manually

You'll notice that expert fractions are approximately the same size as a single character in that font. That's your eventual goal in formatting a fraction. Usually, you achieve this by decreasing the size of the two numerals, raising the numerator (the first number in the fraction), and kerning on either side of the slash as necessary.

For example, see the fraction in the first line of Figure 17-9. First, we reduced the 9-point Univers numerals in the denominator (the number after the slash in a fraction) to 6 points using the Font Size field on the Character pane. Then, we made the 1 a superscript using the Character pane's menu. Finally, we kerned by –50 units on either side of the slash. Remember: The font size and kerning that works for your font, size, and values will vary.

Note

InDesign's default superscript and subscript size is 58.3% of the character's size (this odd value actually equals $\frac{7}{12}$). The numerator and denominator in a fraction should be the same size, so if you use InDesign's superscripts at its default settings, multiply the text's point size by 0.583 (just highlight the denominator text, go to the Size field in the Character pane, and type ***0.583** in the Size field after the current point size). We think InDesign's superscript and subscript type styles benefit visually from a change to 65%. You can change these default settings in the Text pane of the Preferences menu (File ➪ Preferences, or ⌘+K or Ctrl+K).

Unless you're rarely confronted with fractions, by all means save your formatting as character styles. You'll be able to apply the formats with a keystroke or use Find/Change (Edit ➪ Find/Change, ⌘+F or Ctrl+F) to locate numbers and selectively apply the appropriate character style.

Platform Difference

Macintosh fonts provide another option for refining fractions. It's a special kind of slash called a *virgule*, which is smaller and at more of an angle than a regular slash. Press Option+Shift+1 to enter a virgule, and then kern around it as you would a slash. (Our fraction in the first line of Figure 17-9 uses a virgule rather than a regular slash.)

Hanging punctuation

When display type, such as a pull-quote or headline type in ads, is left-aligned or justified, the edges can look uneven due to the gaps above, below, or next to quotation marks, punctuation, and some capital letters. See the text frame at left in Figure 17-10, which does not have hanging punctuation. To correct the unevenness, graphic designers use a technique called *hanging punctuation*, in which they extend the punctuation slightly beyond the edges of the rest of the text, as shown in the text frame at right in Figure 17-10.

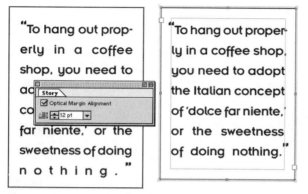

Figure 17-10: Notice the difference between the text frame at left, with standard alignment, and the text frame at right, with Optical Margin Alignment (otherwise known as hanging punctuation).

Note   The "edge" of text is defined by the edges of the text frame or any Inset Spacing specified in the Text Frame Options dialog box (Object ➪ Text Frame Options, or ⌘+B or Ctrl+B).

InDesign's Optical Margin Alignment feature automates hanging punctuation, extending punctuation and the edges of some glyphs (such as capital T's) slightly outside the edges of the text. (We assume Adobe bills it as margin alignment rather than hanging punctuation because of the addition of capital letters.) Unfortunately, you can't control how much the characters "hang" outside the text boundaries — InDesign decides that for you. And Optical Margin Alignment applies to all the text frames in a story rather than to highlighted text. This means you need to isolate any text for which you want hanging punctuation into its own text frame.

To specify Optical Margin Alignment, select any text frame in a story and choose Type ➪ Story. Check Optical Margin Alignment as shown in Figure 17-10.

Design Advice   In general, Optical Margin Alignment improves the look of display type whether it's left-aligned, centered, justified, or even right-aligned. However, Optical Margin Alignment will actually cause columns of body text to look uneven (as they are).

Choosing and placing end-of-story markers

In magazines, newsletters, and other publications with multiple stories, the text often continues from one page to the next. In news magazines, a story might meander from page to page, interrupted by sidebars and ads. In a fashion magazine, stories generally open on a splashy spread, and then continue on text-heavy pages at the back of the magazine. In either case, readers can get confused about whether a story has ended. Designers solve this by placing a *dingbat* (a special character such as a square) at the end of each story.

You can use any dingbat character — in Zapf Dingbats, DF Organics, Woodtype, or Wingdings, for example — or an inline graphic to mark the end of a story. The end-of-story marker should reflect the overall design and feel of a publication, or emphasize the content. You might see a square used in a financial publication, a heart in a teen magazine, or a leaf in a gardening magazine. A derivative of the company's logo might even be used to mark the end of a story — you can easily envision the Nike swoosh used in this way.

To place a dingbat, first decide on the character and create a character style for it. If you're using a graphic, you might consider converting it to a font with a utility such as Macromedia Fontographer so you can insert and format it automatically. If you're using an inline graphic, you might store it in an InDesign library (see Chapter 29) so it's easily accessible. Make sure everyone working on the publication knows the keystroke for entering the dingbat or the location of the graphic.

Once you have the character established, you need to decide where to place it. Generally, the dingbat will be flush with the right margin or right after the final punctuation in the last line. To place the dingbat flush with the right margin, set a right-aligned tab in the paragraph style you use for final paragraphs (see Chapter 14 for more details on setting tabs). To place the dingbat after the final punctuation, separate the two with an en space by typing Option+spacebar or Ctrl+Shift+6, or with an em space by typing two en spaces.

Applying Color to Text

Just because you're printing in four-color or have a color inkjet printer doesn't mean you should be getting carried away with coloring text. You want to keep your content legible and unified, but that doesn't have to mean it's all black on white. You'll commonly see color in headlines, banners, subheads, and pull-quotes. However, you'll rarely see color applied to body text.

Colors applied to text are often derived from colors within related graphics or from a publication's traditional palette. In general, the smaller the type, the darker its color should be — with pastels reserved for large text, bright colors for bold text, and dark colors for body text. InDesign lets you make an entire character one color, or make the fill (inside) and stroke (outlines) of a character two different colors, as shown in Figure 17-11. You can even apply gradients to fills and strokes.

Figure 17-11: The 192-point headline for this herb article is colored a light purple that complements the color of one of the flower pots on the same page. Because the headline is placed on top of an image, the headline is stroked with a dark green color derived from one of the herb images.

Steps: Coloring Text

1. Click the Type tool in the Toolbox or press T.

2. Highlight the text you want to color.

3. Click the Fill button or the Stroke button on the Toolbox to specify whether you're coloring the character or its outlines.

4. If necessary, open the color Swatches pane by choosing Window ➪ Swatches or pressing F5.

5. Click a color swatch to apply it to the stroke or fill, as shown in Figure 17-12.

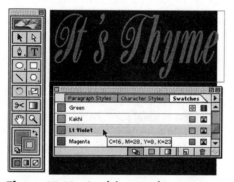

Figure 17-12: Applying a color to text consists of three easy steps: First, highlight the text with the Type tool. Second, click the Stroke or Fill button on the Toolbox. Third, click a color on the Swatches pane.

6. To specify the thickness of the stroke, use the Strokes pane (Window ➪ Stroke, or F10) and to apply a gradient to the stroke or fill, use the Gradient pane (Window ➪ Gradient).

Cross-Reference
For information about creating color swatches or working with gradients, see Chapters 19 and 27.

Rotating Text

You've seen newsletters with nameplates running horizontally down the first page and catalogs with "sale" splashed diagonally across pages. You do this by placing the text you want to rotate in its own frame, and then rotating the entire frame. InDesign lets you rotate any object from 180 degrees to –180 degrees — basically, full circle. You can rotate in increments as small as 0.01 degrees using the Rotate tool or 0.001 degrees using the Rotation Angle field on the Transform pane. Figure 17-13 shows the icons.

Figure 17-13: The Rotate tool (left) from the Toolbox palette and the Rotation Angle field from the Transform pane.

Using the Rotation Angle field

Use the Rotation Angle field on the Transform pane if you know the angle you need. For example, to run text along the left side of a graphic like the photo credit in Figure 17-14, you rotate the frame 90 degrees. To use the Rotation Angle field, select the object with the Selection tool. Then choose an option from the pop-up menu, which offers 30-degree increments, or enter a value in the field. Hit Return or Enter to rotate the object.

Figure 17-14: The Rotation Angle field on the Transform pane lets you rotate selected objects with 0.001 degrees of precision. Entering a value in the field is ideal for turning a photo credit 90 degrees to place it alongside a graphics frame.

Using the Rotate tool

Use the Rotate tool to experiment with different angles while designing. To rotate items freehand, select the Rotate tool by clicking it in the Toolbox or pressing R (unless the Type tool is selected). If the object you want to rotate isn't selected, ⌘+click it or Ctrl+click it. Drag in any direction to rotate the object, releasing the mouse button as necessary to check the placement and any text wrap. To restrict the rotation to 45-degree increments, press the Shift key while you drag. Figure 17-15 shows an example of a drop cap rotated and filled with a related graphic.

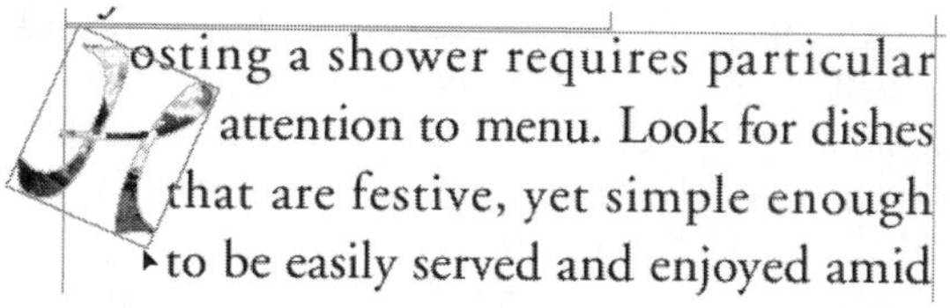

osting a shower requires particular attention to menu. Look for dishes that are festive, yet simple enough to be easily served and enjoyed amid

Figure 17-15: Using the Rotate tool, you can change the angle of objects freehand until they look just right in context. We created the drop cap by highlighting an "H" in Insignia font and selecting the Create Outlines command from the Type menu. This created a graphics frame, based on the outlines of the selected character, which we filled with a related graphic.

Scaling Text

While you're roughing out a design, you'll probably find yourself changing type sizes, object placement, and colors as you go. Changing the size of text can get a little tedious — especially if the text is tucked into its own frame. You have to select the Type tool, highlight the text, enter a new size, and then often switch to the Selection tool to resize the frame so the text doesn't overflow. For a more interactive method of resizing text, you can use the Scale tool (see Figure 17-16) to resize the text and its frame at the same time.

Figure 17-16: The Scale tool icon.

To use the Scale tool, click it in the Toolbox or press S (if the Type tool is not selected). If the text frame is not already selected you'll need to ⌘+click or Ctrl+click. Then, simply drag any frame edge or handle in any direction. To scale proportionally so the text is not distorted, press the Shift key while you drag, as shown in Figure 17-17. The amount of scaling is reported in the Scale X Percentage and Scale Y Percentage fields in the Transform pane.

Figure 17-17: In this menu in progress, the restaurant name is in its own text frame. To increase the type size without having to enlarge the text frame, drag a frame handle with the Scale tool.

When text is scaled, InDesign considers the text to be resized the same way a graphic is resized—by percent values. The Character pane still reports the text's original font size, leading, tracking, kerning, horizontal scale, and vertical scale. This can be confusing because you might scale 24-point type up to 3 inches tall (216 points) while the Font Size field claims it's still 24 points.

Because you can't determine the point size of scaled type, we don't recommend this technique for formatting that will be reused. For example, if you create a logotype for a company and achieve the size you want by scaling, you'll never know the font size of the logo. Or if you scale a headline for a strict newsletter template, you won't know the font size to create a paragraph style. However, the Scale tool works well for one-time uses, such as making a daily newspaper's headline fit.

Summary

InDesign gives you the power to embellish and manipulate text in almost infinite ways. It's your responsibility to format text in ways that clarify and reinforce the content rather than simply decorate it. Bulleted lists—often created with special character bullets, tabs, and hanging indents—help break out information. Drop caps and run-in heads call attention to the beginning of a story or to topic shifts within a story. You can pull readers into a story with sidebars and pull quotes, which also break up text-heavy areas. For display type, InDesign provides an automatic method for hanging punctuation outside the margins, and it enables you to rotate and scale text.

✦   ✦   ✦

Working with Special Characters

A typeface comes with dozens of special characters ranging from bullets to copyright symbols. Some characters are pretty much standard in all fonts, whereas others are available in just some fonts. Windows fonts and Mac fonts that are otherwise identical may have differences in what symbols they include.

And new font formats—OpenType and Unicode—promise to add hundreds of new characters to fonts, everything from foreign-language characters to specialty symbols. Already, new TrueType fonts include dozens of new characters, as Figure 18-1 shows. This common Windows TrueType font—Times New Roman—has several character sets inside it, as the figure shows. A program such as Microsoft Word 97 displays all these characters in its Symbol dialog box (Insert ➪ Symbols) and shows what set each character is from.

Macs and PCs differ in how they handle all special characters. Windows fonts and programs tend to show and support more characters than Mac programs do. For example, Word 98 on the Mac shows just the standard 256 characters available in most fonts in its Symbol dialog box, not the several hundred shown for the same font in Word 97's dialog box. And InDesign for the Mac tends to reveal fewer characters in Mac fonts than InDesign for Windows does for equivalent Windows fonts. However, Mac fonts and programs are more consistent in what special characters they use and how they make them accessible via keyboard shortcuts than Windows fonts and programs do.

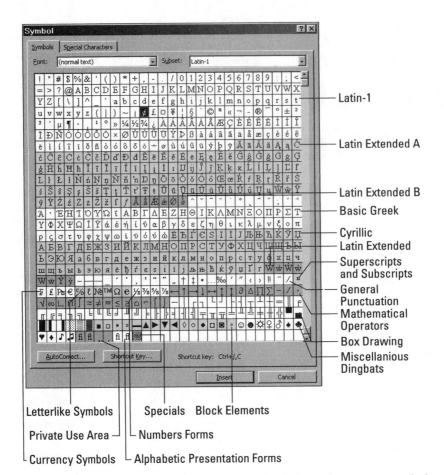

Figure 18-1: This dialog box from Microsoft Word shows how many symbols new TrueType fonts can have. (Note that we combined several screenfuls of the dialog box to show all its options in one window, and then highlighted each character section.) And more are coming with the Unicode and OpenType technologies.

Note

To be safe, use just characters from the Latin-1 set—chances are that most fairly recent fonts will have the vast majority of these characters. If your program doesn't specify character sets when displaying special characters—as InDesign does not—stick to the characters in Tables 18-1 and 18-2 (later in this chapter) unless you know the output device for your document has exactly the same fonts as you are using.

Of course, your existing fonts won't have all the new characters being added to TrueType and PostScript fonts with technologies such as Unicode and OpenType, so you'll live with uncertainty about what is supported in what font as long as you have a mix of fonts in your repertoire.

Using Special Characters on the Web

Web browsers don't support all the special symbols available in print publishing. But popular Web browsers such as Netscape Navigator and Microsoft Internet Explorer support most of the symbols listed in Tables 18-1 and 18-2 later in this chapter.

Here are the exceptions for both Mac and Windows browsers: Š, š, Ý, ý, Ÿ, Œ, œ, fi , fl , ffi , ffl , •, ™, †, ‡, ≠, ∞, ≈, — (em dash), – (en dash), and ... (ellipsis) are not supported. In addition, typographic quotes and apostrophes (', ', ", ") are converted to their keyboard equivalents (" and ').

In addition, Macintosh Web browsers don't support these characters: ¼, ½, ¾, √, and ×. And Windows Web browsers don't support these additional characters: Æ and æ.

Because of these complexities, there's no simple, all-inclusive list of special characters and how to access them. But we have gathered the most common characters and show how you can access them via menus and directly through codes.

Why use both options? Menus are great when you can't remember a code or need to see what options are available, but they're terrible if you have a lot of data entry to do. Codes are great for fast data entry, but require a lot of memorization and thus frequent use. Fortunately, you can use both techniques, mixing them however you like.

Cross-Reference In addition to the menus and dialog boxes in InDesign and in word processors to add special characters, both Windows and the Mac OS come with utilities that display and insert special characters into any program. Chapter 39 covers these in more detail.

Accessing Characters by Menu

InDesign provides two menu options for inserting special characters. The first is meant to insert any of a font's characters, whereas the second is meant to insert common special characters:

✦ Use Type ➪ Insert Character to get the Insert Character dialog box shown in Figure 18-2. You scroll through this dialog box. In the default view, the characters are usually too hard to read, so be sure to click the large mountain-like icon at the lower right to enlarge them. The small mountain-like icon reduces the characters' size. Note that you can select a font and face through the pop-up menus at the bottom. That's handy because it means you don't have to be in the typeface that contains the character you want to use. Double-click the characters you want to insert, or click one character and then click Insert to insert it. Click Done when you finish.

✦ When in a text box using the Type tool, Control+click or right-click to open the contextual menu in Figure 18-3, and select the Insert Special Character menu, as shown in the figure. This gives you quick access to the special typographic characters described in Chapter 14, but it also lets you get to common symbols such as trademark symbols (® and ™), copyright (©), bullet (•), degree (°), ellipsis (...), paragraph (¶), and section (§).

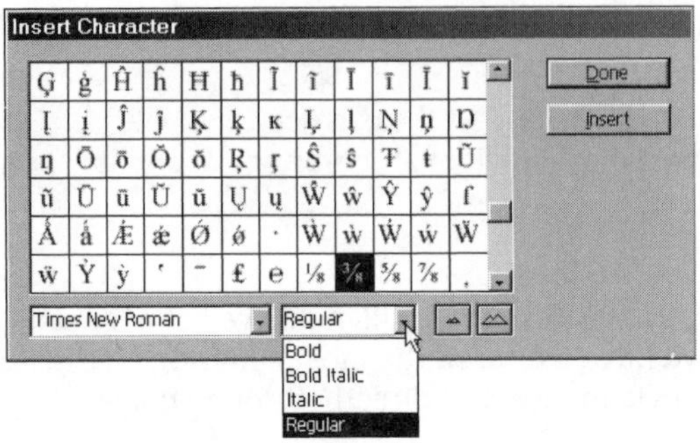

Figure 18-2: The Insert Character dialog box.

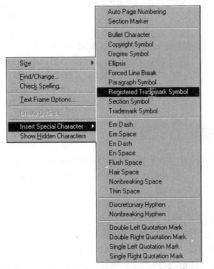

Figure 18-3: The Insert Special Character contextual menu.

Accessing Characters by Keyboard

The most common special characters are accessible from InDesign through the following commands:

- • **En bullet:** Press Option+8 or Alt+8. A bullet is an effective way to call attention to issues being raised. Typically, bullets are used at the beginning of each element in a list. If the sequence of the elements is important, as in a series of steps, use numerals instead of bullets.

- © **Copyright:** Press Option+G or Ctrl+Alt+C. A copyright symbol signifies who owns the rights to text or other visual media. The standard format is *Copyright © 2000 IDG Books Worldwide. All rights reserved.* For text, you must include at least the © symbol, the word *Copyright*, or the abbreviation *Copr*, as well as the year first published and the name of the copyright holder. (Note that only the © symbol is valid for international copyright.) Works need not be registered with the federal Copyright Office to be copyrighted—the notice is sufficient, but registering is best.

- ® **Registered trademark:** Press Option+R or Alt+R. This is usually used in advertising, packaging, marketing, and public relations to indicate that a product or service name is exclusively owned by a company. The mark follows the name. You may use the ® symbol only with names registered with the United States Patent and Trademark Office. For works whose trademark registration is pending, use the ™ symbol.

- ™ **Trademark:** Press Option+2 or Alt+2.

- § **Section:** Press Option+6 or Alt+6. This symbol is typically used in legal and scholarly documents to refer to sections of laws or research papers.

- ¶ **Paragraph:** Press Option+7 or Alt+7. Like the section symbol, the paragraph symbol is typically used for legal and scholarly documents.

- † **Dagger:** Press Option+T or Alt+0135. This symbol is often used for footnotes.

Keep in mind that you have many alternatives to using the regular en bullet (so called because it is the width of a lowercase *n*). Using special characters such as boxes, check marks, triangles, and arrows, you can create attractive bulleted lists that stand out from the crowd. More information on how to select such characters is in Chapter 15.

See Table 18-1 for other common symbols and Table 18-2 for foreign-language characters. Note that Windows shortcuts that involve four numerals (such as Alt+0157) should be entered from the numeric keypad with Num Lock on—not from the row of numbers at the top of the keyboard—while holding the Alt key.

Note   Sometimes, especially in Windows, programs change keyboard shortcuts, so the keyboard shortcuts shown in Tables 18-1 and 18-2 may not behave this way in all Windows programs. We provided the shortcuts that work in InDesign.

Table 18-1
Shortcuts for Common Special Symbols

Character	Macintosh Shortcut	Windows Shortcut
Legal		
Copyright (©)	Option+G	Ctrl+Alt+C *or* Alt+0169
Registered trademark (®)	Option+R	Alt+R *or* Alt+0174
Trademark (™)	Option+2	Alt+2 *or* Alt+0153
Paragraph (¶)	Option+7	Alt+7 *or* Alt+0182
Section (§)	Option+6	Alt+6 *or* Alt+0167
Dagger (†)	Option+7	Alt+0134
Double dagger (‡)	Option+Shift+T	Alt+0135
Currency		
Cent (¢)	Option+4	Alt+0162
Pound sterling (£)	Option+3	Ctrl+Alt+Shift+4 *or* Alt+0163
Yen (¥)	Option+Y	Ctrl+Alt+- (hyphen) *or* Alt+0165
Mathematics		
One-half fraction (½)	*not supported**	Ctrl+Alt+7 *or* Alt+0189
One-quarter fraction (¼)	*not supported**	Ctrl+Alt+6 *or* Alt+0188
Three-quarters fraction (¾)	*not supported**	Alt+0190
Infinity (∞)	Option+5	*not supported**
Multiplication (×)	*not supported**	Alt+0215
Division (÷)	Option+/	Alt+0247
Root (√)	Option+V	*not supported**
Greater than or equal (≥)	Option+>	*not supported**
Less than or equal (≤)	Option+<	*not supported**
Inequality (≠)	Option+=	*not supported**
Rough equivalence (≈)	Option+X-	*not supported**
Plus or minus (±)	Option+Shift+=	Alt+0177
Logical not (¬)	Option+L	Ctrl+Alt+\ *or* Alt+0172
Per mil (‰)	Option+Shift+R	Alt+0137

Character	Macintosh Shortcut	Windows Shortcut
Degree (°)	Option+Shift+8	Ctrl+Shift+; (semicolon) *or* Alt+0176
Function (ƒ)	Option+F	Alt+0131
Integral (∫)	Option+B	*not supported**
Variation (∂)	Option+D	*not supported**
Greek beta (ß)	Option+S	Alt+0223
Greek mu (µ)	Option+M	Ctrl+Alt+M *or* Alt+0181
Greek Pi (∏)	Option+Shift+P	*not supported**
Greek pi (π)	Option+P	*not supported**
Greek Sigma (∑)	Option+W	*not supported**
Greek Omega (Ω)	Option+Z	*not supported**
Punctuation and Typographic		
Apostrophe (')**	Shift+Option+]	Shift+Alt+]
Ellipsis (…)	Option+; (semicolon)	Alt+; (semicolon) *or* Alt+0133
En bullet (•)	Option+8	Alt+8 *or* Alt+0149
Thin bullet (·)	Option+Shift+9	Alt+0183
Em dash (—)	Shift+Option+- (hyphen)	Shift+Alt+- (hyphen)
En dash (–)	Option+- (hyphen)	Alt+- (hyphen)
Open double quote (")**	Option+[	Alt+[
Closed double quote (")**	Shift+ Option+[	Shift+Alt+
Open single quote (')**	Option+]	Alt+]
Closed single quote (')**	Shift+Option+]	Shift+Alt+]
fi ligature	Option+Shift+5***	*not supported**
fl ligature	Option+Shift+6***	*not supported**
ffi ligature	*not supported****	*not supported**
ffl ligature	*not supported****	*not supported**
Miscellaneous		
Light (¤)	Option+Shift+2	Ctrl+Alt+4 *or* Alt+0164
Open diamond (◊)	Option+Shift+V	*not supported**

* Character is available in a pi font, as are hundreds of other specialty symbols.

** Typographic quotes are generated automatically if Use Typographer's Quotes is checked in the Text pane of the Preferences menu (File ➪ Preferences ➪ Type, or ⌘+K or Ctrl+K).

*** Ligatures are automatically generated for fonts that support them on the Mac.

Table 18-2
Shortcuts for Common Foreign Characters

Character	Macintosh Shortcut	Windows Shortcut*
Á	Option+E A	' A *or* Alt+0193
á	Option+E a	' a *or* Alt+0225
À	Option+` A	` A *or* Alt+0192
à	Option+` a	` a *or* Alt+0224
Ä	Option+U A	" A *or* Alt+0194
ä	Option+U a	" a *or* Alt+0228
Ã	Option+N A	~ A *or* Alt+0195
ã	Option+N a	~ a *or* Alt+0227
Â	Option+I A	^ A *or* Alt+0194
â	Option+I a	^ a *or* Alt+0226
Å	Option+Shift+A	Alt+0197
å	Option+A	Alt+0229
Æ	Option+Shift+ '	Ctrl+Shift+Alt+Z *or* Alt+0198
æ	Option+ '	Ctrl+Alt+Z *or* Alt+0230
ß	Option+S	Alt+0223
Ç	Option+Shift+C	' C *or* Alt+0199
ç	Option+C	' c *or* Ctrl+Alt+, (comma) *or* Alt+0231
Ð	*not supported*	Alt+0208
e	*not supported*	Alt+0240
É	Option+E E	' E *or* Alt+0201
é	Option+E e	' e *or* Alt+0233
È	Option+` E	` E *or* Alt+0200
è	Option+` e	` e *or* Alt+0232
Ë	Option+U E	" E *or* Alt+0203
ë	Option+U e	" e *or* Alt+0235
Ê	Option+I E	^ E *or* Alt+0202
ê	Option+I e	^ e *or* Alt+0234
Í	Option+E I	' I *or* Alt+0205
í	Option+E i	' i *or* Alt+0237
Ì	Option+` I	` I *or* Alt+0204

Character	Macintosh Shortcut	Windows Shortcut*
ì	Option+` i	` i *or* Alt+0236
Ï	Option+U I	" I *or* Alt+0207
ï	Option+U i	" I *or* Alt+0239
Î	Option+I I	^ I *or* Alt+0206
î	Option+I i	^ I *or* Alt+0238
Ñ	Option+N N	~ N *or* Alt+0209
ñ	Option+N n	~ n *or* Alt+0241
Ó	Option+E O	' O *or* Alt+0211
ó	Option+E o	' o *or* Alt+0243
Ò	Option+` O	` O *or* Alt+0210
ò	Option+` o	` o *or* Alt+0242
Ö	Option+U O	" O *or* Alt+0214
ö	Option+U o	" o *or* Alt+0246
Õ	Option+N O	~ O *or* Alt+0213
õ	Option+N o	~ o *or* Alt+0245
Ô	Option+I O	^ O *or* Alt+0212
ô	Option+I o	^ o *or* Alt+0244
Ø	Option+Shift+O	Alt+0216
ø	Option+O	Alt+0248
Œ	Option+Shift+Q	Alt+0140
œ	Option+Q	Alt+0156
Þ	*not supported*	Alt+0222
þ	*not supported*	Ctrl+Alt+T *or* Alt+0254
ß	Option+S	Alt+0223
š	*not supported*	Alt+0138
š	*not supported*	Alt+0154
Ú	Option+E U	' U *or* Ctrl+Shift+Alt+U
ú	Option+E u	' u *or* Ctrl+Alt+U
Ù	Option+` U	` U *or* Alt+0217
ù	Option+` u	` u *or* Alt+0249
Ü	Option+U U	" U *or* Ctrl+Shift+Alt+Y

Continued

Table 18-2 *(continued)*

Character	Macintosh Shortcut	Windows Shortcut*
ü	Option+U u	" u *or* Ctrl+Alt+Y
Û	Option+I U	^ U *or* Alt+0219
û	Option+I u	^ u *or* Alt+0251
Ý	*not supported*	' Y or Alt+0221
ý	*not supported*	' y *or* Alt+0253
Ÿ	Option+U Y	" Y
ÿ	Option+U y	" y
French open double quote («)**	Option+\	Ctrl+Alt+[*or* Alt+0171
French close double quote (»)**	Option+Shift+\	Ctrl+Alt+] *or* Alt+0187
Spanish open exclamation (¡)	Option+1	Ctrl+Alt+1 *or* Alt+0161
Spanish open question (¿)	Option+Shift+/	Alt+0191

* See the "How to Type Accents Directly" sidebar in this chapter for setup information.

** Automatically generated if the Use Typographer's Quotes option is selected in the Preferences dialog box's Text pane (File ➪ Preferences ➪ Text, or ⌘+K or Ctrl+K) and the French language dictionary is applied to the text you're typing in.

How to Type Accents Directly

You don't need to use codes or dialog boxes to insert accented characters one at a time. Instead, you can use the built-in accent-generation features of your operating system.

Note that Mac and Windows differ in how they work with accents, and that Windows 98 and NT 4 have slightly different ways to set up accent generation.

✦ On the Mac, accents are built in. Just enter the shortcut for the accent and the type the letter to be accented (for example, to get é, type Option+E and then the letter e).

✦ In Windows 98, the keyboard layout must be set to United States-International before you can enter the accent signifier and then type the letter (for example, type ` and then the letter e to get è). You set the keyboard layout in the Keyboard control panel (Start ➪ Settings ➪ Keyboard), and then select the Language pane, select the language English (United States), click Properties, and select United States-International from the pop-up menu. (The normal keyboard layout is United States 101.)

✦ In Windows NT, the keyboard layout is also set to United States-International from the Keyboard control panel. But you'll need to select the Input Locales pane to select the language English (United States), click Properties, and select United States-International from the pop-up menu. (The normal keyboard layout is US.)

This scheme in Windows can be annoying in some cases, especially if you use quotation marks regularly. For example, under the regular United States keyboard layout, typing the sequence **"A** would generate "A, but with the US-International keyboard layout, it would generate Ä. You need to type a space after an accent signifier to prevent it from applying the accent. Of course, if you type an accent signifier and the next character is not legal to be accented, no accent is placed on it. Thus, typing **"W** simply generates "W, whether or not you type a space between the " and the W. But if you use lots of accented characters, the occasional aggravation is worthwhile.

Here's how to enter accents as you type:

Character	Macintosh Shortcut	Windows Shortcut
Acute (´)	Option+E *letter*	' *letter*
Cedilla (ˌ)	See Table 18-2	' *letter*
Circumflex (ˆ)	Option+I *letter*	^ *letter*
Grave (`)	Option+` *letter*	` *letter*
Tilde (~)	Option+N *letter*	~ *letter*
Trema (¨)	Option+U *letter*	" *letter*
Umlaut (¨)	Option+U *letter*	" *letter*

Summary

Fonts come in many formats with many variations — TrueType, PostScript, OpenType, Unicode, Macintosh, and Windows; unfortunately, there's no constant set of special characters you can count on from font to font. A good rule of thumb is that the newer the font, the more likely it is to have a wider variety of special characters.

Fortunately, InDesign, word processors, and both the Mac OS and Windows come with tools that let you insert special characters easily into your documents and see what characters a particular font has available.

In addition to using these menus and utilities, you can also use keyboard shortcuts and codes to enter special characters and accented letters. For frequently used characters, the keyboard approach is a significant timesaver.

✦   ✦   ✦

Treating Text as Artwork

CHAPTER

19

◆ ◆ ◆ ◆

In This Chapter

Understanding and using strokes with text

Using colors and gradients with strokes

Using color and gradients with text

Converting text into graphics

◆ ◆ ◆ ◆

Text can be beautiful, thanks to some of the innovative, engaging letterforms that type designers have created. So it makes sense to think of type as an art element, not just a medium with which to convey information. For centuries designers have used type as a design element, using beautiful letterforms to embellish the appearance of their layouts.

Desktop publishing quickly gave users much more control over typography, blurring the distinction between type and art. On a computer, type is represented mathematically as a series of curves, just as an illustration is. But it has taken almost 15 years for page layout programs to be capable of manipulating these curves, whether for type or illustrations. InDesign takes this to a whole new level.

Although InDesign will not replace such programs as Illustrator and CorelDraw, it gives you many tools to handle illustration (see Part VI). How does this relate to type? You can use many of those tools to transform letterforms — from the actual shapes to their use of color.

Applying Strokes to Type

Text is made up of a series of *outlines* — curves that form the shape, as Figure 19-1 shows. When printed or displayed, those outlines are filled in, giving the appearance of a solid shape. When you resize text, programs such as InDesign stretch these curves automatically, which is how InDesign lets you use almost any size imaginable for your text. Most programs keep those outlines hidden from you, using them only for their internal calculations.

Figure 19-1: Text is made up of invisible outlines that InDesign can then manipulate to change its size and create special effects.

Unlike most page-layout programs, InDesign lets you work with text outlines to create special effects called *strokes*. A stroke is an outline of the character that is made visible and given a thickness (called a *weight*) and often a color. The thicker the stroke, the fatter the character will appear. Figure 19-2 shows some examples of what you can do with strokes.

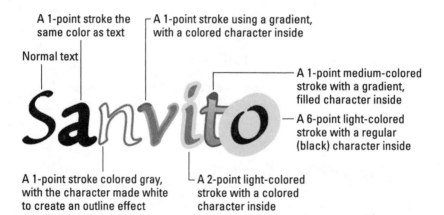

A 1-point stroke the same color as text

A 1-point stroke using a gradient, with a colored character inside

Normal text

A 1-point medium-colored stroke with a gradient, filled character inside

A 6-point light-colored stroke with a regular (black) character inside

A 1-point stroke colored gray, with the character made white to create an outline effect

A 2-point light-colored stroke with a colored character inside

Figure 19-2: Examples of how you can apply strokes to text — a process that makes the outlines visible and lets you change the stroke size and coloration.

Note   As you increase stroke size, the stroke grows outward from the letter. This can cause overlapping into adjacent text, as you see in the "o" in Figure 19-2.

At first, using strokes with text can be a little confusing. Several palettes and panes are involved, and you'll also need to have defined the colors, tints, and gradient fills you want to use before you apply them. (See Chapter 27 for information on defining colors, tints, and gradient fills.) Figure 19-3 shows the palettes and panes involved.

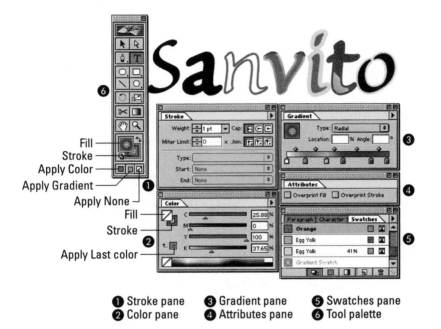

Fill
Stroke
Apply Color
Apply Gradient
Apply None
Fill
Stroke
Apply Last color

❶ Stroke pane ❸ Gradient pane ❺ Swatches pane
❷ Color pane ❹ Attributes pane ❻ Tool palette

Figure 19-3: The palettes and panes used to apply strokes to text. Note that all panes are showing all options (use the palette menu and Show Options to display all options).

In the same floating palette are usually four panes related to strokes: Stroke, Color, Gradient, and Attributes. Use these to apply the stroke's attributes. Note that the Color and Gradient panes display only existing color, tint, and gradient definitions — you cannot create them from here.

Note

Because InDesign lets you move panes to new palettes or to other existing palettes, these panes may not appear together on your system, but you can always access them through the Window menu. Note that the Stroke pane also has the keyboard shortcut F10 and the Color pane has the shortcut F6.

The Tool palette lets you switch between the stroke and the fill for text. (By default, the stroke is the active control in this palette.) It also lets you apply the last-used color and gradient to either the stroke or fill, saving you the hassle of switching to the Color pane.

You'll also need the Swatches pane open if you intend to define new colors, tints, or gradients for your strokes. Chapter 27 covers these tasks in detail; use Window ⇨ Swatches or F5 to access this pane. You can open this pane at any time; new colors, tints, and gradients defined here appear in the Color and Gradients pane immediately.

Note   If question marks (?) display on the Fill or Stroke icons in either the Color pane or the Tool palette, that means several colors and/or gradients are used in the selected text.

Steps: Creating a Stroke

1. Using the Type tool, highlight the text that you want to apply a stroke to. You can highlight as little as one character or as much as your entire story.

2. Go to the Stroke pane (use Window ⇨ Stroke or F10 if it is not on your screen). We suggest you move the pane so the text you are applying the stroke to remains visible onscreen and you can see the effects of your actions.

3. Use the Weight pop-up menu to select a thickness for the stroke, or just enter a value in increments as fine as 0.001 point. Note that the other controls in this pane do not apply to strokes on text and thus are grayed out.

 Oddity   Once you select a weight, you can adjust it with the arrow icons — the up arrow to increase and the down arrow to decrease — but you cannot use these icons to increase the weight if the weight is empty or 0.

4. Here's where you get choices that may initially be confusing. If you want to change the stroke color, you have several options:

   • To use the most recently used color, select the Stroke icon on the bottom of the Tool palette and then click the Apply Color button (see Figure 19-3).

   • To pick a different color, select the Stroke icon on the bottom of the Tool palette and then click an existing color for, or create a new color in, the Swatches pane.

   • You can also select the stroke icon in either the Tool palette or Color pane, and then drag the color onto either location's stroke icon or directly onto selected text.

   • Or you can use the Color pane. The small form of the pane shows just the None color and a range of tints (shades) for the last color used — select a tint by clicking the tint range at the location of the tint you want. The full version of the pane (use its palette menu and its Show Options) lets you create colors by showing a range of colors (pick the color model — LAB, RGB, or CMYK — from the palette menu) and letting you define the color with sliders or by specifying exact percentages of each color. Select the Stroke icon on the pane, and then select the color you want to apply.

Note The Color pane shows an additional item — the Last Color button, as shown in Figure 19-3 — only when the current stroke is set to either None or to a gradient. If you click the Last Color button, the last color selected (the button will be in this color) is applied to the stroke in place of None or of the gradient. You cannot use this to undo a color change — it works only if the stroke did not have a solid color applied to it.

5. If you want to use a gradient fill, you also have some choices:

   • To use the most recently used gradient, select the Stroke icon on the bottom of the Tool palette and then click the Apply Gradient button (see Figure 19-3).

   • Go to the Gradient pane and click the gradient — it will be the last-used color. (If no gradients are defined in your document, you will need to create one via the Swatches pane.) When you click the gradient, you will see gradient controls shown in Figure 19-3. The bottom ones (squares) display the colors used in the gradient, whereas the top ones (diamonds) show the gradation slope. You can slide the colors to change how the gradient looks. You can also add color controls by double-clicking in the gradient bar; the color at that point will appear as a control that you can then slide. You can also change the gradient slope — how quickly one color changes to the next by dragging the diamonds. Note that you cannot apply an angle to a gradient used on text. Chapter 26 covers this task in more depth.

   • If you want to pick a different gradient, select the Stroke icon on the bottom of the Tool palette and then click an existing gradient for, or create a new gradient in, the Swatches pane.

Note If you use the full Gradients pane (use the palette menu's Show Options item to display it, as shown in Figure 19-3), you can change the gradient type from radial (circular) to linear, or vice versa, as well as add exact percentages for the gradient controls (click a control and then change its location percentage; this percentage starts at 0 at the far right and ends at 100 percent at the far right of the gradient bar).

When you apply gradient to text, you'll find that InDesign makes some assumptions that you may not like. The gradient is centered in the text frame, so as your text moves, the gradient appears to move as well (see Figure 19-4 for examples). The same gradient is applied to any text, so you cannot have a gradient reset for each center. (For example, if you use a radial gradient, you might want an effect where each letter appears to have a circular halo created from a gradient. You can't do that if you apply a gradient to the stroke, as the center of the radial gradient will be the center of the text frame, not of each character. You'll have to convert each letter to a graphic, as described later in this chapter, and apply the stroke to achieve this halo effect.)

Figure 19-4: InDesign keeps the gradient centrally located in your text frame, which affects how the gradient appears in your text as the text moves within the frame. Here, you see three examples of how changes to the text frame's size — and thus to the text's relative position — affect the gradient for the 5-point strokes on this text.

6. In the Attributes pane, decide whether to enable Overprint Stroke. Normally, this option should not be checked. If checked, InDesign makes the stroke's color print on top of any object underneath it if you are making color separations for output to a printing press, which can make them appear wrong. For example, if you overprint blue on a yellow object, you get green where they overlap.

You may want to overprint black strokes because doing so ensures that no registration issues occur in four-color printing — no gap between the black stroke and the underlying color.

InDesign keeps the Overprint Stroke option even when you select None or white as your colors. This makes no sense because you cannot overprint these colors — white and None are the absence of color. When you have a None-colored object overlapping a colored option, you see the color where they overlap. When you have a white object overlapping a colored option, you see the white where they overlap. These options should be grayed out when White or None is selected.

The order in which you use the Color, Gradient, and Attributes pane doesn't matter, and you may find yourself jumping back and forth among those, the Stroke pane, and the Swatches pane as you experiment with various settings. In fact, expect to spend time experimenting—it's a crucial part of defining and applying special effects that enhance rather than disrupt.

Note

You can also apply these settings in character and paragraph styles via the Character Color pane in the New Character Style dialog box when creating or editing a style. Figure 19-5 shows the pane; Chapters 12 and 13 cover style creation in depth.

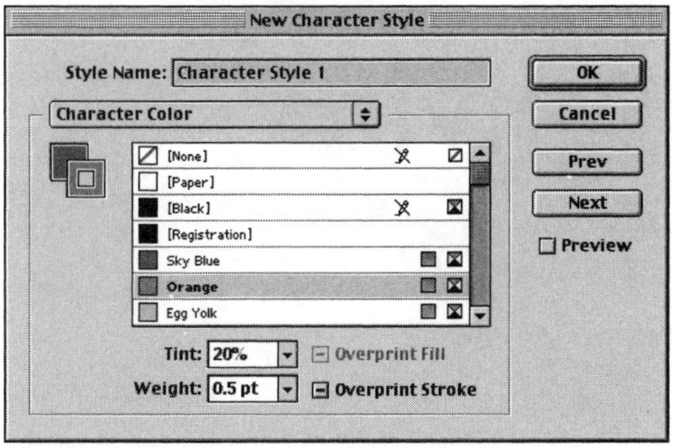

Figure 19-5: Applying strokes and fills when defining a style.

Applying Color to Type

Applying color and gradients is almost exactly the same as applying color to strokes, except you choose the Fill icon in the Tool palette or Color pane. Follow the steps for "Creating a Stroke" in the previous section, substituting "fill" for "stroke." The same tips, notes, and caveats apply for fills as for strokes.

Note

If you want to color text consistently—such as having all subheads be green—do so using styles, as covered in Chapter 15.

Although we recommended earlier a case where it makes sense, via the Attributes pane, to overprint black strokes rather than have them print cleanly, that case doesn't apply for black fills. The only time you want to overprint black on a color is to get a richer, deeper black, but in that case, it makes more sense to not use the Overprint option and instead create a "superblack" color from 100-percent black and either 100-percent magenta or 100-percent cyan, and use that as the fill color.

Tip

For gray text, use a tint of black.

You can mix the use of colors and gradients for strokes and text to get some unusual typography. Figure 19-3 showed some examples; Figure 19-6 shows some more exotic ones, using 30-point text in all cases.

Figure 19-6: Exotic examples of how you can apply strokes and fills to text.

Here are the techniques used in Figure 19-6:

✦ The top text frame uses a linear gradient for the 6-point text stroke and the same gradient — with the colors in the opposite order — as the fill for the text frame.

✦ The first frame in the second row uses a light gray fill with a radial gradient from white to black for the 2-point strokes. An optical illusion makes the gray fill appear to be a gradient as well because the progression of white to black next to gray makes the eye think the gray is changing as well.

✦ The second frame in the second row uses a 3-point gray stroke on just one letter to accentuate it.

✦ The first frame in the third row uses a 0.5-point, radial white-to-black gradient to soften the edges of the letters.

✦ The second frame in the third row uses a thicker gray stroke for each subsequent character, starting at 0.5 point and ending at 3.5 points.

Converting Text into Graphics

A technique prized by high-end designers has been to use text as the outline of an image — masking the image within the confines of a letter's shape. But the work to do that has historically been very great, limiting its use to publications with the time and money to achieve it. But the miracles of computer technology have taken what had been an arcane technique and made it commonplace.

InDesign has a simple way to create graphics from text: Select the text and use Shift+⌘+O, or Ctrl+Shift+O. (You can also use Type ➪ Create Outline.) In a few seconds, the selected text becomes a graphic, complete with any fills, gradients, and/or strokes you may have applied. The new graphics will be in their own frames, treated as inline graphics, so they will move with any surrounding text as if they were text. If you selected multiple lines of text to convert to graphics, each line will be put in its own frame.

Tip   If you don't want the converted text to be anchored within the text frame, you must cut and copy the text frame containing the converted text to make it an independent graphic.

Note   Be sure to format the text with the exact typeface, style, size, scale, tracking, kerning, and so forth *before* converting to outline — you cannot convert it back.

Now that the text is a graphic, you can do anything with it you would with a graphic you created in InDesign (see Part VI). For example:

✦ You can edit the shape of the text the same way you can edit any Bézier frame or graphic — after selecting the frame with the regular Selection tool, use the Direct Selection tool to display the Bézier control points.

✦ You can use it as a drop cap that is embellished, or simply wrap around the text's natural shape — just be sure to have the surrounding text wrap around the graphic, as described in Chapters 5 and 17.

✦ You can import a graphic inside the text, as Figure 19-7 shows. Select the frame with the Selection tool, and then the graphical text with the Direct Selection tool, and use ⌘+D or Ctrl+D, or File ➪ Place, to import the graphic into the outline. You can move, resize, or otherwise manipulate the placed image just as you could an image imported into any other frame, as Chapter 22 shows.

Note   Keep in mind that the entire set of characters within the frame is considered to be one frame, so a graphic imported into text can span them all. (In Figure 19-7, the graphic was not wide enough to span past the first letter.) If you want to repeat a graphic individually on several letters, convert each letter to an outline separately, so each appears in its own frame.

Tip   A popular text-as-graphic effect is to have text follow the path of a curve. InDesign does not support this effect, so use a program such as CorelDraw or Illustrator to create the effect, and then import the resulting graphic file into InDesign.

Figure 19-7: Text converted to a graphic has Bézier points that can be edited, plus the text can act as a mask in which to place graphics.

Summary

You can do more with text than adjust its font and size. In InDesign, you can color text and add strokes (outlines) that can also be colored. By using strokes and colors, you can create all sorts of text effects, from thickening the characters to creating a neon-glow effect.

InDesign also lets you convert text into graphics. These textual graphics can then be modified like any other drawing, and they can also hold text or pictures like any other frame.

✦   ✦   ✦

Picture Fundamentals

While text carries the message, it's a picture that gets your attention. Pictures can often say more than any collection of words. That's why working with pictures — photos, drawings, and other graphics — is so critical in layout. And that's why InDesign works closely with Adobe's picture programs, Photoshop and Illustrator. But no matter what programs you use to create your images, you'll find InDesign capable of working with all popular formats.

The first step is preparing your pictures for use in InDesign. **Chapter 20** explains the do's, don'ts, and the gotchas of all the image formats that InDesign can work with, showing you how to optimize the quality of your images and how to prevent font and color flaws when printing.

With your images ready to be used, the next step is actually importing them into InDesign. **Chapter 21** explains how to bring pictures into your layout, including how to position them within frames.

Chapter 22 explains in depth how to work with your imported pictures. You'll learn how to change the size, cropping, and other attributes of your pictures, as well as how to ensure your layout uses the latest version of your pictures.

Finally, InDesign offers sophisticated controls for using your pictures for fancy layout techniques. For example, you can do curve-hugging text wraps around images and even create outlines from the picture contents that become frames in which to hold text or other elements. **Chapter 23** explains these techniques.

Preparing Picture Files for Import

You can import graphics into your InDesign documents in several ways. InDesign is particularly adept at importing documents created in popular Macintosh and Windows formats. And through the Mac and Windows clipboards (copy and paste), you can import file formats — to a limited degree — that are not directly supported by InDesign.

Determining Where to Format Documents

Because InDesign has some built-in graphics features, as described in Part VI, you may be tempted to use InDesign as your graphics program. Don't. Its tools are fine for some work, such as creating shapes that text wraps around, borders, and gradations of color — but InDesign is not meant to be a professional graphics-creation tool. In fact, it is designed to work closely with such professional tools, especially Adobe's Illustrator and Photoshop.

Particularly for bitmap images such as scanned files and photographs, InDesign has few capabilities to apply special effects or otherwise manipulate the image's content, so you should do as much work as possible in your image editor before bringing the file into InDesign. For example, you can resize, crop, rotate, and slant an imported image in InDesign, but you can's convert it from a full-color image into a duotone or change its line screen or brightness and contrast.

The bottom line is this: Use your graphics program for creating and editing original images and photos. Use InDesign's graphics features to embellish your layout rather than create original artwork.

Preparing Graphics Files

InDesign offers support for many major formats of graphics files. Some formats are more appropriate than others for certain kinds of tasks. The basic rules for creating your graphics files are as follows:

✦ Save line art in a format such as EPS, PDF, Adobe Illustrator, or PICT. (These object-oriented formats are called *vector* formats. Vector files are composed of instructions on how to draw various shapes.) InDesign works best with EPS, PDF, and Illustrator files.

✦ Save bitmaps (photos and scans) in a format such as TIFF, MacPaint, Adobe Photoshop, PNG, JPEG, PCX, BMP, GIF, or PICT. (These pixel-oriented formats are called *raster* formats. Raster files are composed of a series of dots, or pixels, that make up the image.) InDesign works best with TIFF and Photoshop files.

Note   PICT files can be in vector or bitmap format depending on the original image and the program in which it was created or exported from. If you enlarge a PICT image and it begins to look blocky, it is a bitmap. Similarly, EPS and PDF files can contain bitmap images as well as vector ones.

Tip   If you output to high-end PostScript systems, make EPS and TIFF formats your standards because these have become the standard graphics formats in publishing. If you're working almost exclusively with Adobe software, you can add the PDF, Illustrator, and Photoshop formats to this mix. (The Illustrator and PDF formats are variants of EPS.)

Graphics embedded in text files

Modern word processors typically support inline graphics, letting you import a picture into your word-processor document and embed it in text. Word and WordPerfect, for example, both let you import graphics, and InDesign, in turn, can import the graphics with your text. But graphics embedded in your word-processor document via Publish and Subscribe or via OLE will not import into InDesign.

Inline graphics will import as their preview images, not as the original formats. This means that in most cases you'll get a lower-resolution version in your InDesign layout.

Tip

Despite their limitations, the use of inline graphics in your word processor can be helpful when putting together a InDesign document: Use the inline graphics whose previews are imported into InDesign as placeholders so that the layout artist knows you have embedded graphics. He or she can then replace the previews with the better-quality originals. If you find yourself using several graphics as characters (such as a company icon used as a bullet), use a font-creation program such as Macromedia's Fontographer to create a symbol typeface with those graphics. Then both your word processor and layout documents can use the same, high-quality versions.

Support formats for import

InDesign imports the following file formats. If your program's format is not one of these, chances are high it can save as or export to one. In the following list, italics indicate the file name extension common for these files on PCs. The file formats InDesign imports include:

✦ **BMP:** The Windows bitmap format. (*.BMP, .DIB*)

✦ **EPS:** The Encapsulated PostScript vector format favored by professional publishers. A variant is called DCS, a color-separated variant whose full name is Document Color Separation. (*.EPS, .DCS*)

✦ **GIF:** The Graphics Interchange Format common in Web documents. (*.GIF*)

✦ **JPEG:** The Joint Photographers Expert Group compressed bitmap format often used on the Web. (*.JPG*)

✦ **Illustrator:** The native format in Adobe Illustrator 5.5 through 8.0, similar to EPS. (*.AI*)

✦ **PCX:** The PC Paintbrush format that was very popular in DOS programs and common still in Windows. (*.PCX, .RLE*)

✦ **PDF:** The Portable Document Format that is a variant of EPS and is used for Web-, network-, and CD-based documents. (*.PDF*)

✦ **Photoshop 4.0 and 5.0:** The native format in Adobe Photoshop. (*.PSD*)

✦ **PICT:** Short for *Picture*, the Mac's native graphics format (it can be bitmap or vector) that is little used in professional documents but common for inexpensive clip art. (*.PCT*)

✦ **PNG:** The Portable Network Graphics format that Adobe introduced several years ago as a more capable alternative to GIF. (*.PNG*)

✦ **Scitex CT:** The continuous-tone bitmap format used on Scitex prepress systems. (*.CT*)

✦ **TIFF:** The Tagged Image File Format that is the bitmap standard for professional image editors and publishers. (*.TIF*)

✦ **Windows Metafile:** The format native to Windows but little used in professional documents. (*.WMF*)

Note InDesign does not support several somewhat popular formats, although it's possible someone may develop plug-in filters for them: AutoCAD Document Exchange Format (DXF), Computer Graphics Metafile (CGM), CorelDraw, and Eastman Kodak's Photo CD. DXF and CGM are vector formats used mainly in engineering and architecture, while CorelDraw is the native format of the leading Windows illustration program, and Photo CD is a bitmap format meant for electronically distributed photographs.

Issues with vector files

Vector images are complex because they can combine multiple elements — curves, lines, colors, fonts, bitmap images, and even other imported vector images. This means that you can unknowingly create a file that will cause problems when you try to output an InDesign layout file using it. Thus, when dealing with vector formats, you have several issues to keep in mind.

Embedded fonts

When you use fonts in text included in your graphics files, you usually have the option to convert the text to curves (graphics). This option ensures that your text will print on any printer.

Note If you don't convert text to curves in graphics files, make sure that your printer or service bureau has the fonts used in the graphic. Otherwise, the text will not print in the correct font (you will likely get Courier or Helvetica instead).

If your graphic has a lot of text, don't convert the text to curves — the image could get very complex and slow down printing. In this case, make sure that the output device has the same fonts as in the graphic.

PostScript files: EPS, DCS, Illustrator, and PDF

PostScript-based files come in several varieties — EPS, DCS, Illustrator, and PDF — and because the format is a complex one, you need to be aware of more issues up front.

EPS

The usual hang-up with Encapsulated PostScript (EPS) files is the preview header. The preview is a displayable copy of the EPS file. Because EPS files are actually made up of a series of commands that tell the printer how to draw the image, what you see onscreen is not the actual graphic. Most programs create a preview image for EPS files, but many programs have trouble reading them, especially if the EPS file was generated on a different platform. In such cases, they display an X or a gray box in place of the image (the EPS file still prints properly in such cases to a PostScript printer). That's why InDesign creates its own preview image when you import EPS files, lessening the chances of your seeing just an X or a gray box in place of the EPS preview.

Tip   In CorelDraw 6.0 and later, and in Adobe Illustrator 6.0 and later, be sure to set the EPS creation options to have no preview header—this keeps your files smaller. (In CorelDraw, export to EPS. In Illustrator 6.0 and later, save as Illustrator EPS. Note that Illustrator 5.*x*'s native format is EPS, so don't look for an export or save-as option.)

DCS

The Document Color Separation (DCS) variant of EPS is a set of five files: an EPS preview file that links four separation files (one each for cyan, magenta, yellow, and black). Use of this format ensures correct color separation when you output negatives for use in commercial printing. These files are often preferred over standard EPS files by service bureaus that do color correction.

Note   You should not use DCS files if you intend to create composite proof files or in-RIP separations from InDesign—InDesign will ignore the DCS separation files and just use the preview file for output. Use DCS files only if you are outputting separations (but not in-RIP separations). Chapter 33 covers this in detail.

Illustrator

Adobe Illustrator (AI) files are very similar to EPS, except they don't have a preview header. Illustrator files cause no special concerns; just be sure to note the font and color issues noted previously in this section.

PDF

InDesign has two ways to open a Portable Document Format (PDF) file: One is to imports PDF files similar to how it imports EPS and other graphics files (File ➪ Place, or ⌘+D or Ctrl+D). The other is to convert it into an InDesign document (via File ➪ Open, or ⌘+O or Ctrl+O). (See Chapter 4.)

When you import a PDF file, InDesign treats it as a graphic, placing just the first page of the PDF file (if it has more than one page) into your document as an uneditable graphic. You can crop, resize, and do other such manipulations common to any graphic, but you can't work with the text or other imported PDF file's components.

Special PDF features, such as sounds, movies, hyperlinks, control buttons, and annotations, are ignored in the imported file.

Other vector formats

If you're outputting to negatives for professional printing, you should avoid non-PostScript vector formats. But they're fine for printing to inkjet and laser printers.

PICT

The standard Macintosh format for drawings, PICT (which stands for *Picture*) also supports bitmaps and is the standard format for Macintosh screen-capture utilities. InDesign imports PICT files with no difficulty, but it cannot color-separate them for output to negatives. Because fonts in vector PICT graphics are automatically translated to curves, you need not worry about whether fonts used in your graphics are resident in your printer or available at your service bureau.

Windows Metafile

The standard Windows format for drawing, Windows Metafile (WMF) is similar to PICT in that it can contain bitmap images as well as vector drawings. But InDesign ignores any bitmap information in Windows Metafiles, stripping it out during import.

Issues with bitmap formats

Bitmap (also called *raster*) formats are simpler than vector formats because they are made up of rows of dots (*pixels*), not instructions on how to draw various shapes. But that doesn't mean that all bitmaps are alike.

Professional-level bitmap formats

Although InDesign supports a wide variety of bitmap formats, you should usually concern yourself with just one if you're producing professional documents for output on a printing press: TIFF. (You may also use the Scitex CT format if you are using Scitex output equipment to produce your negatives.) We suggest you convert other formats to it, using your image editor (Corel Photo-Paint and Adobe Photoshop, the two top image editors, import and export most formats, as do other current image-editing programs) or a conversion program such as the Mac shareware program GraphicConverter, Equilibrium's Debabelizer for Macintosh, or DataViz's Conversions Plus (for Windows) and MacLinkPlus (for Macintosh).

Photoshop

InDesign can import version 4.0 and 5.0 file formats of this popular image editor. When you place Photoshop files in InDesign, note that you lose the alpha channel information, so use clipping paths instead to create irregular runarounds or transparent backgrounds for your image. Also, all of your layers and layer masks will be flattened (just as happens when you export a Photoshop file to TIFF format). Your original Photoshop file is unaffected, but InDesign essentially converts to TIFF the copy of the Photoshop file it keeps in the layout.

Scitex CT

The continuous-tone Scitex CT format is used with Scitex output high-resolution devices, and is usually produced by Scitex scanners. If you are using this format, you should be outputting to a Scitex system. Otherwise, you're not going to get the advantage of its high resolution.

TIFF

The most popular bitmap format for publishers is TIFF, the *Tagged Image File Format* developed by Aldus (later bought by Adobe Systems) and Microsoft. TIFF supports color up to 24 bits (16.7 million colors) in both RGB and CMYK models, and every major photo-editing program supports TIFF on both the Macintosh and in Windows. TIFF also supports grayscale and black-and-white files.

The biggest advantage to using TIFF files rather than other formats that also support color, such as PICT, is that InDesign is designed to take advantage of TIFF. For example, in an image editor you can set clipping paths in a TIFF file, which act as a mask for the image. InDesign sees that path and uses it as the image boundary, making the area outside it invisible. That in turn lets you have nonrectangular bitmap images in your layout — the clipping path becomes the visible boundary for your TIFF image.

But TIFF comes in several variants, and no program, including InDesign, supports all of them. Here are our recommendations for how to save TIFF files for optimal use in InDesign:

✦ You should have no difficulty if you use the uncompressed and LZW-compressed TIFF formats supported by most Mac programs (and increasingly by most Windows programs). If you do have difficulty, we recommend that you use uncompressed TIFF files.

✦ Don't save the alpha channel for 24-bit TIFF images because InDesign doesn't pay attention to this feature. Instead, if you want to create a nonrectangular boundary around your image and have the rest of the background be transparent, set a clipping path in your TIFF file.

✦ Use the byte order for the platform that the TIFF file is destined for. Macs and PCs use the opposite byte order — basically, the Mac reads the eight characters that comprise a byte in one direction and the PC reads it in another. Although InDesign reads both byte orders, other programs may not, so why invite confusion? Of course, if only InDesign and Photoshop users will work on your TIFF files, the byte order doesn't matter.

Web-oriented bitmap formats

In recent years, several formats have been developed for use on the Web, in the HyperText Markup Language (HTML) documents found there. These formats — GIF,

JPEG, and PNG — achieve small size (for faster downloading and display on your browser) by limiting image and color detail and richness.

Although you can use any supported graphics format for documents you expect to export to the Web's HTML format (InDesign converts all images to GIF or JPEG when you export to HTML), if you know your document is bound for the Web, you might as well use a Web graphics format from the start.

GIF

The Graphics Interchange Format (GIF) is the oldest Web format. To help keep file size down, it is limited to 256 colors, reducing file size but also making it unsuitable for photographs. But its compression approach doesn't lose any image detail, so it works well for sketches, cartoons, and other simple images with sharp details.

JPEG

The Joint Photographers Expert Group (JPEG) compressed color-image format is used for very large images and the individual images comprising an animation or movie. Images compressed in this format may lose detail, which is why TIFF is preferred by publishers. But JPEG can be used effectively even on documents output to a printing press because you can set the level of loss to none during export.

Still, JPEG is more useful on the Web, where the limited resolution of a computer monitor makes most of JPEG's detail loss hard to spot — giving you an acceptable tradeoff of slightly blurry quality in return for a much smaller file size. It's particularly well suited for photographs because the lost detail is usually not noticeable because of all the other detail surrounding it.

If you do use JPEG for print work, note that you can provide a clipping path for it in programs such as Photoshop. The clipping path lets the image have an irregular boundary (rendering the rest of its background transparent) so you can use InDesign effects such as text wrap.

PNG

A newcomer format from Adobe, the Portable Network Graphics (PNG) format is meant to provide GIF's no-loss compression but support 24-bit color so it can be used for photography and subtly colored illustrations on the Web.

When importing PNG files, you can choose whether to retain the background color defined in the file or to substitute white — just be sure that Show Import Options is checked in the Place dialog box (File ⇨ Place, or ⌘+D or Ctrl+D) so that choice is presented. Similarly, you can also adjust the gamma value during import — the gamma is a setting that describes the color range of a device, and to ensure most accurate reproduction, you'd want the gamma setting for the PNG file to be the same as that of your output device (a printer or monitor).

Other bitmap formats

The other supported formats are ones that you should avoid, unless you're printing to inkjet or laser printers. If you have images in one of these formats and want to use it for professionally output documents, convert them to TIFF before using them in InDesign.

BMP

Like TIFF, the Windows bitmap (BMP) format supports color, grayscale, and black-and-white images.

PCX

Like TIFF, PCX supports color, grayscale, and black-and-white images.

PICT

PICT, the standard Macintosh format for drawings, also supports bitmaps and is the standard format for Macintosh screen-capture utilities. InDesign imports PICT files with no difficulty.

 For more information on working with files between platforms, refer to the sidebar, "Working with Files Across Platforms" in Chapter 9.

Color Issues

It used to be that importing color from graphics files into publishing programs was an iffy proposition—colors would often not print properly even though they appeared correct onscreen. Those nightmares are largely a thing of the past because modern page layout program such as InDesign can accurately detect color definitions in your source graphics, and current illustration and image-editing programs are better at making that information accessible to programs such as InDesign. So just note the following advice to ensure smooth color import.

If you create color images in an illustration or image-editing program, make sure that you create them using the CMYK color model or using a named spot color. If you use CMYK, the color is, in effect, preseparated. With InDesign, any spot colors defined in an EPS file are automatically added to the Colors palette for your document and set as a spot color.

 See Part VII for details on creating and editing colors.

If your program follows Adobe's EPS specifications (Adobe Illustrator, CorelDraw, and Macromedia FreeHand all do), InDesign color-separates your EPS file, no matter whether it uses process or spot colors. Canvas automatically converts Pantone spot colors to process colors in your choice of RGB and CMYK models. For other programs, create your colors in the CMYK model to be sure they will print as color separations from InDesign.

Color systems

Several color systems, or models, are in use, and InDesign supports the common ones, including CMYK (process), RGB, Pantone, Focoltone, Dainippon Ink & Chemical (DIC), Toyo, Trumatch, and Web. A color system defines either a set of individual colors that have specially mixed inks (shown on swatchbooks, which have small samples of each color) or a range of colors that can be created by combining a limited number of inks (such as RGB — for red, green, and blue — and CMYK — for cyan, magenta, yellow, and black).

Chapter 27 describes the various color models, but for file import, it's best to use just three — CMYK (process), RGB, and the Pantone Matching System — because they're universally used and tend to be the most reliable when passing information from one system to another.

Note   The advice on color systems applies to just vector images because bitmap programs use CMYK or RGB as their color models, even if they offer swatchbooks of other models' colors.

Tip   Most layout artists use Pantone to specify desired colors, so keep a Pantone swatch book handy to see which CMYK values equal the desired Pantone color. (One of the available Pantone swatch books — *The Pantone Process Color Imaging Guide CMYK Edition* — shows each Pantone color next to the CMYK color build used to simulate it.)

Of course, you can simply pick a Pantone color from the electronic swatchbook in InDesign, and InDesign will convert it to CMYK if you specify it to be a process color (the default setting). Many high-end illustration programs, including Adobe Illustrator, support Pantone and can do this instant conversion as well. If available (as it is in InDesign), use the Pantone Process color model because it is designed for output using CMYK printing presses. But remember: What you see onscreen won't match what you get on paper, so it's a good idea to have the printed Pantone swatchbook.

Note   The *CV* after the Pantone color number in the InDesign (and other programs') dialog boxes means *computer video*, which is Pantone's way of warning you that what you see onscreen may not be what you get in print. Because of the different physics underlying monitors and printing presses, colors cannot be matched precisely, even with color calibration. This is true for other color models, such as Focoltone and Trumatch.

Calibrated color

With InDesign's Color Management System (CMS) feature enabled, the program will calibrate the output colors (whether printed to a color printer or color-separated for traditional printing) based on the source device and the target output device in an attempt to ensure that what you see onscreen comes close to what you'll see on the printed page. Although color calibration is a tricky science that rarely results in exact color matches across all input and output devices, it can help minimize differences as the image travels along the creation and production path.

Today, most image-editing programs let you apply color profiles that conform with the International Color Committee (ICC) standards. If you are using color calibration, it's best to apply these ICC profiles in the images when you create them.

If you can't — or forget to — apply an ICC profile when creating your image, don't worry. You can add a profile (if you're creating images in a program that doesn't support ICC profiles) or apply a different one from InDesign.

Summary

If you work with publishing-oriented graphics formats — EPS, PDF, Illustrator, TIFF, and Photoshop — created by mainstay programs such as Adobe Photoshop, Adobe Illustrator, CorelDraw, Corel Photo-Paint, and Macromedia FreeHand, you'll likely have no difficulties importing graphics into or printing graphics from InDesign.

But be sure to stick with common color models, particularly CMYK and Pantone.

If you're producing documents for display on the Web or a computer screen, you can use native Web formats such as JPEG, GIF, and PNG — or keep using the print-oriented graphics formats because InDesign converts them to JPEG or GIF during HTML export anyhow.

Be sure to do any special effects in your graphics program — InDesign has limited capabilities to manipulate graphics beyond layout-oriented functions such as resizing, cropping, flipping, slanting, and text wrap.

✦   ✦   ✦

Importing Pictures

Although InDesign's shape-creation tools, type-formatting options, and object-manipulation features provide great flexibility when it comes to designing pages, you're probably going to want to use other graphic elements — particularly scanned images and computer-generated illustrations — in your publications. InDesign lets you import graphics files in a variety of formats (see Chapter 20 for details about supported graphics file formats), and once you've imported a graphic, you have several options for modifying its appearance (see Chapter 22 for information about modifying imported pictures).

Note   The terms *graphic* and *picture* are interchangeable, refer-ring to any type of graphic. An *image* is a bitmap graphic, such as that produced by an image editor or a scanner, whereas an *illustration* or *drawing* is a vector file produced by an illustration program.

It's important to understand that when you import a picture into a document, InDesign establishes a link between the graphics file and the document file and then sends the original graphics file to the printer when the document is output. (There is one exception to this scenario — when you copy and paste an Adobe Illustrator graphic into an InDesign document — that's explained later in this chapter.) InDesign links to graphics because a graphics file, particularly a high-resolution scanned picture, can be very large. If the entire graphics file were included in an InDesign document when you imported it, InDesign documents would quickly become prohibitively large. Instead, InDesign saves a low-resolution preview of an imported graphics file with the document, and it's this file that you see displayed onscreen. InDesign remembers the location of the original file (see Chapter 22 for information about managing links to imported graphics) and uses this information when printing.

Note If you place a graphic that's 48K or smaller, InDesign automatically embeds the full-resolution image rather than a low-resolution preview. See Chapter 22 for more information about embedding graphics.

When it's time to import a picture, you're responsible for knowing where the file is — whether it's stored on a floppy desk that your friend gave you, on your hard disk, on a networked file server, or on a local or networked CD-ROM.

Note If you import a graphics file that's stored on any kind of removable media, such as a floppy disk, Zip disk, or CD-ROM, the link between the document and the graphics file will be broken when the media is removed. Generally, it's best to copy graphics files to your hard disk or to a networked file server before importing them into an InDesign document.

Using the Place Command

Although you have several ways to add a graphics file to an InDesign document (all of which are explained in this chapter), the Place command (File ⇨ Place, or ⌘+D or Ctrl+D) is the method you should use most often. When you use the Place command, InDesign offers import options for various graphics file formats that are not available if you use other import methods.

Steps: Using the Place Command to Import a Picture

1. If you want to import a picture into an existing frame, select the frame using either of the selection tools, and then choose File ⇨ Place or press ⌘+D or Ctrl+D. The Place dialog box, shown in Figure 21-1, is displayed. If you want InDesign to create a new frame when you import the picture, make sure no object is selected when you choose Place.

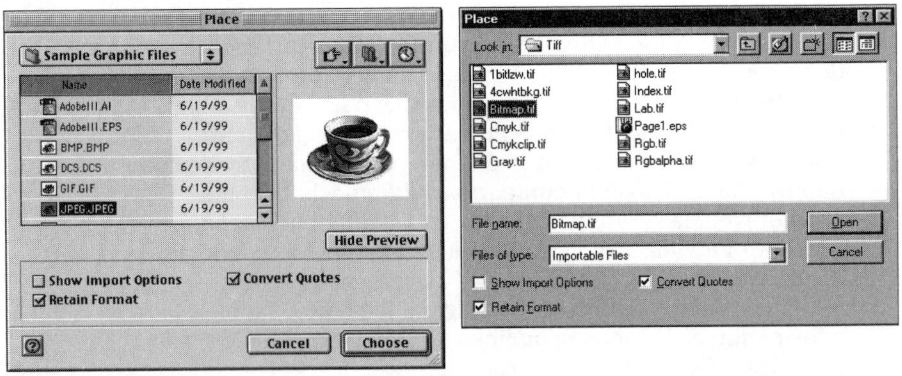

Figure 21-1: The Place dialog box. The File Name and Files of Type controls are available only in the Windows version (right); only the Mac version displays a preview (if the file includes one).

Note You can import a picture into any kind of frame or shape (including a curved line created with the Pen tool) except a straight line. Be careful: If the Type tool is selected when you use the Place command to import a picture into a selected text frame, you'll create an inline graphic at the text cursor's location (see Chapter 7 for information about creating inline graphics).

2. Use the controls in the Place dialog box to locate and select the graphics file you want to import.

3. If you want to display import options that let you control how the selected graphics file is imported, either select Show Import Options, and then click Choose or Open, or hold down the Shift key and double-click the file name or Shift+click Choose or Open. If you choose to Show Import Options, the Image Import Options dialog box, which is covered in the next section, is displayed — if, of course, import options are available for the selected graphics file's format. Specify the desired import options, and then click OK.

4. If a frame is selected, the graphic is automatically placed in the frame. The upper-left corner of the picture is placed in the upper-left corner of the frame, and the frame acts as the cropping shape for the picture.

To place the graphic into a new frame, click the loaded-graphic icon on an empty portion of a page or on the pasteboard. The point where you click establishes the upper-left corner of the resulting graphics frame, which is the same size as the imported picture and which acts as the picture's cropping shape.

To place the graphic in an existing, unselected frame, click in the frame with the loaded-graphic icon. The upper-left corner of the picture is placed in the upper-left corner of the frame, and the frame acts as a cropping shape.

Note As you can see in Figure 21-1, the Mac and Windows versions of the Place dialog box are slightly different. A preview display is available only in the Mac version, whereas the Windows version has a pair of controls the Mac version lacks: 1) the File Name field displays the name of a highlighted file; and 2) the Files of Type field displays a list of options for displaying specific text and graphics file formats or categories of file types in the scroll list of importable files. For example, if you choose Importable Files, both text and picture files are displayed — which is understandable because whenever you choose the Place command you can import either a text or picture file. If you want to display only supported graphics file formats, choose Images. And if you want to further limit the type of files displayed in the scroll list, choose a specific graphics file format. The choices are EPS, DCS, and PDF. Finally, use All Files to show files that don't use the Windows file name extensions InDesign uses to identify file types — you would use this option, for example, when importing a Mac-created file with no extension.

After you place a picture, it's displayed in the frame that contains it, and the frame is selected. If the Selection tool is selected, the eight handles of its bounding box are displayed; if the Direct Selection tool is selected, handles are displayed only in the corners. At this point, you can modify either the frame or the picture within, or you can move on to another task.

Tip   If you can store all of your graphics files in a single location — not necessarily in a single folder, but perhaps within a folder hierarchy on your hard disk or a file server — you can minimize link problems. If you move, rename, or delete the original file after importing a graphic, you'll break the link, which causes printing problems. Keeping all graphics files in a single, safe place — a place that's backed up regularly — is a good idea.

Specifying Import Options

If you've ever used a graphics application — for example, an image-editing program such as Adobe Photoshop or an illustration program such as Adobe Illustrator or Macromedia FreeHand — you're probably aware that when you save a graphics file, you have several options that control such matters as file format, image size, color depth, preview quality, and so on. When you save a graphics file, the settings you specify are determined by the way the image will be used. For example, you could use Photoshop to save a high-resolution TIFF version of a scanned picture for use in a slick, four-color annual report or a low-resolution GIF version of the same picture for use on a company Web page. Or you could use Illustrator or FreeHand to create a corporate logo that you'll use in various sizes in many of your printed publications.

If you choose to specify custom import settings when you import a graphics file, the choices you make will depend on the nature of the publication. For example, if it's bound for the Web, there's no need to work with or save pictures using resolutions that exceed a computer monitor's 72-dpi resolution. Along the same lines, if the publication will be printed, the image import settings you specify for a newspaper that will be printed on newsprint on a web-offset press will be different from those you specify for a four-color magazine printed on coated paper using a sheet-fed press.

If you choose Show Import Options when you place a picture, the options displayed in the Image Import Options dialog box, shown in Figures 21-2 and 21-3, depend on the file format of the selected graphic. When you set options for a particular file, the options you specify remain in effect for that file format until you change them. If you don't choose Show Import Options when you place a picture, the most recent settings for the file format of the selected graphic are used.

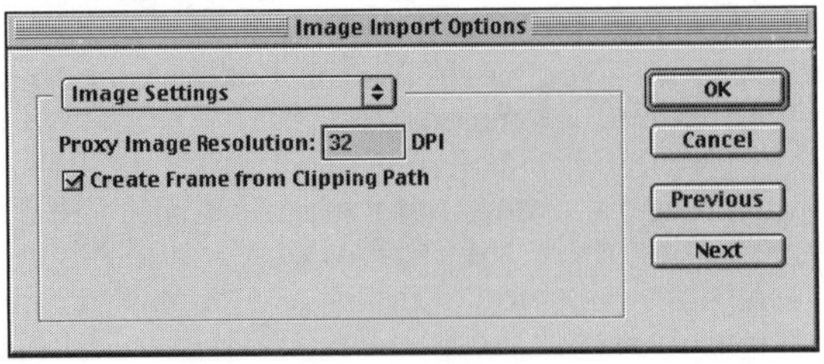

Figure 21-2: The Image Settings options in the Image Import Options dialog box. The Create Frame from Clipping Path checkbox is available because the graphic being placed contains a clipping path.

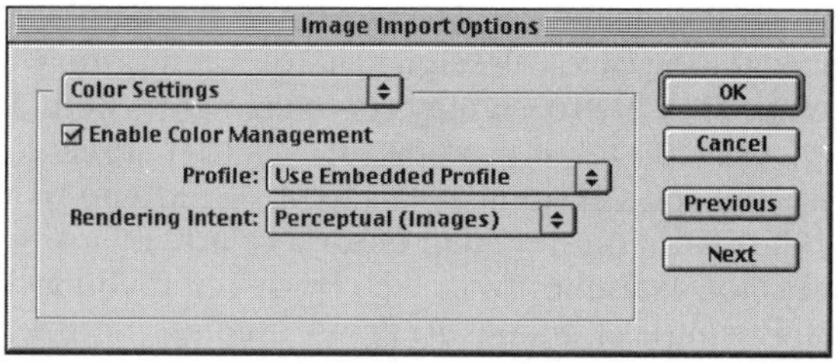

Figure 21-3: The Color Settings options in the Image Import Options dialog box. When you check Enable Color Management, the Profile and Rendering Intent pop-up menus become available.

Import options for all bitmap pictures

When you use the Place command to import a bitmap picture — TIFF, JPEG, Scitex CT, Photoshop (.PSD), and so on — and you choose to display import options, the Image Settings options let you specify a display resolution and let you create a frame using the selected picture's clipping path (if it has one). To display these options, choose Image Settings from the pop-up menu at the top of the Image Import Options dialog box. Figure 21-2 shows the options that are available for bitmap pictures when you choose Image Settings.

Proxy Image Resolution __ DPI

As mentioned earlier in this chapter, graphics files — particularly high-resolution bitmap files — can be very large. The Proxy Image Resolution field in the Show Import Options dialog box lets you specify the resolution, in dots per inch (dpi), at which an imported bitmap graphic is displayed onscreen. To view bitmaps at the resolution you specify, Proxy Images must be selected in the Display pop-up menu in the General Preferences dialog box (File ⇨ Preferences ⇨ General, or ⌘+K or Ctrl+K). (The value you specify in the Proxy Image Resolution field is also used when you select the Low Resolution option in the Send Image Data pop-up menu in the Print dialog box's Graphics pane; see Chapter 33 for details.)

Upping the Proxy Image Resolution value is a good news/bad news situation: Higher values produce better-looking pictures onscreen — especially when they're scaled up or magnified — but higher values also produce larger document files and pictures that take longer to draw onscreen. That's why it's your choice. It's important to note that the value you enter in the Proxy Image Resolution field does not affect the resolution of the original graphics file, which is used when you print the document. It controls only the resolution used for the low-resolution preview that InDesign generates and uses to display the picture onscreen. This preview is stored with a document along with the path name to the original file.

InDesign uses a default setting of 36 dpi, which is much coarser than what a computer monitor can display (72 dpi). Most people will prefer a setting of 72 dpi, which ensures that the image appears onscreen the same as it did in the image editor you used to create it. At 36 dpi, the image can be hard to make out, and if you have several similar images, that low resolution can make it hard to distinguish one from the other onscreen. So, although a 72-dpi preview takes four times the pixels of a 36-dpi image, most people will want the clarity of 72-dpi previews.

If Full Resolution Images (rather than Proxy Images) is selected in the Display pop-up menu in the General Preferences dialog box, InDesign creates a temporary file from the original and uses this temporary file to display the image at its actual resolution. The down side of displaying full-resolution pictures is that screen redraw is slower than when low-resolution versions are used. If you intend to display your bitmap pictures at full resolution, you can enter a relatively low value in the Proxy Image Resolution field (for example, 16 or 32). However, if you switch your preference settings from Full Resolution Images to Proxy Images, pictures with low-resolution proxies are going to look jagged.

Create Frame from Clipping Path

This checkbox is available if the selected bitmap file contains a clipping path. (Not all bitmap files contain clipping paths, and not all bitmap formats let you include clipping paths.) If you select Create Frame from Clipping Path, InDesign uses the clipping path as the frame instead of creating a rectangular frame — as it would if you don't check this box. If the selected bitmap file does not contain a clipping path, you can create one after you import the file using the Clipping Path command (Object ➪ Clipping Path). Chapter 23 covers clipping paths in more detail.

Import options for color bitmap pictures

When you choose Color Settings from the pop-up menu at the top of the Image Import Options dialog box, you have the option to turn on color management for the picture and to control how the image is displayed. Figure 21-3 shows the controls displayed in the Image Import Options dialog box when you choose Color Settings from the pop-up menu.

Enable Color Management

Check this box if you want to use InDesign's color management features with the selected graphics file. If consistent color across multiple devices — scanners, monitors, color printers, printing presses, and so on — is not a high priority, don't check this box. When Enable Color Management is checked, the Profile and Rendering Intent pop-up menus are available. (See Chapter 28 for more information about using InDesign's color-management features.)

Profile

From this pop-up menu, choose a color-source profile that matches the color gamut of the device (scanner, digital camera, and so on) or software used to create the file. InDesign will try to translate the colors in the file to the colors that the output device is capable of producing.

Rendering Intent

The option you choose from this pop-up menu determines how InDesign translates the color in the selected graphics file with the gamut of the output device. If the picture is a scanned photograph, choose Perceptual (Images). The other options — Saturation (Graphics), Relative Colorimetric, and Absolute Colorimetric — are appropriate for images that contain mostly areas of solid color, such as Illustrator EPS files that have been opened in Photoshop and saved as TIFFs.

Import options for various file formats

The Show Import Options dialog box displays different controls depending on the format of the selected graphics file and the settings applied when the file was saved. (See Chapter 20 for a brief description of the graphics file formats that InDesign lets you import.) Here's an explanation of the import options available for each format:

✦ **Adobe Illustrator (.AI).** You can import native Illustrator files created with version 5.5 or later via the Place command or by copying and pasting between applications, which is explained later in this chapter. When you use the Place command, the import options for native Illustrator files are the same as those for EPS files, which are also explained later in this section.

✦ **Adobe Photoshop (.PSD).** Native Photoshop files created with versions 4 and 5 are supported. When you import a Photoshop file, layers and layer masks are flattened and any transparency information in an alpha channel (if there is one) is not retained. If you want to create a transparent background for a Photoshop file, you should create a clipping path around the area(s) you want to reveal, and then save the file as a TIFF or EPS graphic. When you import a TIFF or EPS file that contains a clipping path, you can create a frame from the clipping path during import. Areas outside the path are, effectively, transparent.

✦ **BMP (.BMP), GIF (.GIF), JPEG (.JPG), PCX (.PCX), Scitex CT (.SCT), TIFF (.TIF), and Windows Metafile (.WMF).** The proxy resolution and clipping path options available for all bitmap images, which were explained earlier in this chapter, are available for these bitmap formats.

✦ **DCS (.DCS).** A Document Color Separation, or DCS, file is a variation of the EPS file format. The options available for EPS files are explained in the next paragraph.

✦ **EPS (.EPS).** Two checkboxes, shown in Figure 21-4, are available for EPS files. If you use an Open Prepress Interface–based proxy workflow — that is, if an OPI-based service bureau supplies you with low-resolution versions of graphics files that will eventually be replaced by high-resolution files during output, check Read Embedded OPI Image Links if you want InDesign rather than your service bureau to perform image replacement during output. You should also check this box if you import graphics files that contain OPI comments for other imported graphics files; for example, an EPS file that contains OPI information for an embedded TIFF picture. Don't check this box if you don't use an OPI-based workflow or if you want your service bureau to handle image replacement during output. When Read Embedded OPI Image Links is not checked, InDesign retains OPI comments but doesn't use them. When you print (or export) the document, the proxy image and the link information is sent.

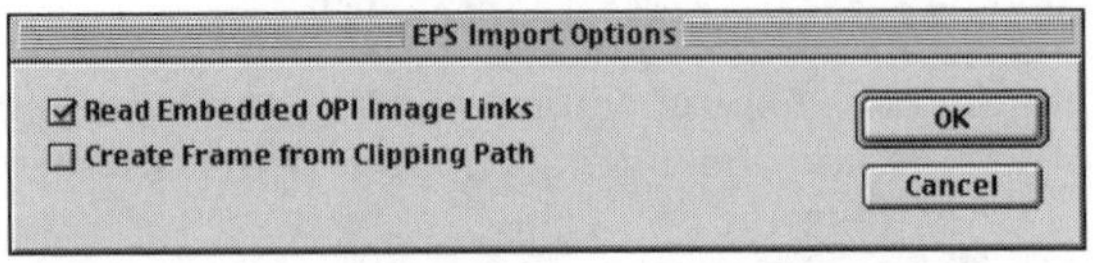

Figure 21-4: The EPS Import Options dialog box is displayed when you choose to show import options when placing an EPS file.

Check Create Frame from Clipping Path if you're importing a Photoshop-generated EPS file that contains a clipping path and you want to use the path to create the graphic frame.

✦ **PICT (.PICT).** Both the Mac and Windows versions of InDesign can import PICT files; however, no import options are available for this low-resolution file format that originated in the Mac world.

✦ **Portable Document Format (.PDF).** Importing PDF files and the options available for it are explained separately in the next section.

✦ **PNG (.PNG).** Several options are available for Portable Network Graphics, or PNG, files:

• Click Use Transparency Information (it's checked by default) to include transparency information in an alpha channel or in a grayscale or color image that contains a designated transparent color. When you select this option, two additional options are available: Click White Background if you want to use white as the background color when transparency is applied; click File Defined Background Color to use the background color saved with the file.

• If the PNG file was saved with a gamma value, click Apply Gamma Correction to adjust the midtones of the image so they match the colors that can be produced by your monitor and printer. If you select this option, you can specify a value from 0.01 to 3.0 in the Gamma Value field.

• The proxy-resolution and clipping-path options available for all bitmap images, which were explained earlier in this chapter, are available for these bitmap formats.

Import options for PDF files

When you use the Place command to import a PDF file and you choose to Show Options, the Place PDF file dialog box, shown in Figure 21-5, is displayed. It provides several controls for specifying how the file is imported. The following steps show how you import a PDF file with the Place command.

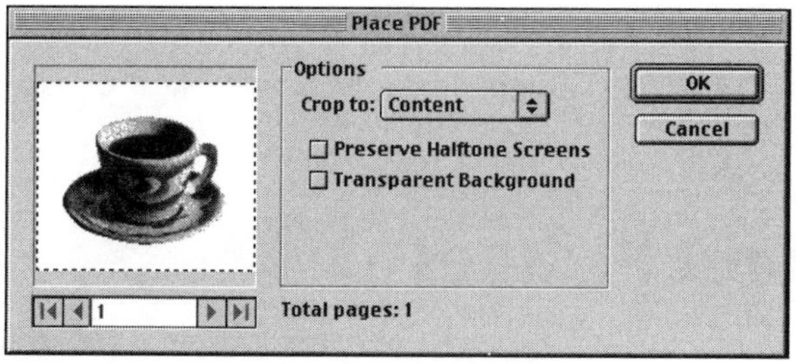

Figure 21-5: The Place PDF dialog box.

Steps: Using the Place Command to Import a PDF File

1. Choose File ➪ Place or press ⌘+D or Ctrl+D, and then locate and select the PDF file you want to import.

2. In the Place dialog box, select Show Import Options, and then click Choose or Open.

3. If prompted, enter the required password and click OK. If the selected file was saved with any security restrictions (no text editing, no printing, and so on), you can't place any pages of the file.

4. Use the controls below the preview image to select the page you want to place (you can place only one page at a time). You can enter a page number in the field or use the arrows to scroll to page.

5. Select one of the cropping options from the Crop To pop-up menu. If you choose Content, the page's bounding box or a rectangle that encloses all items, including page marks, is used to build the graphics frame. Choosing Art places the area defined by the file's creator, if any, as placeable artwork. For example, the person who created the file might have designated a particular graphic as placeable artwork. Choosing Crop places the area displayed and printed by Adobe Acrobat. Choosing Trim places an area equal to the final, trimmed piece. Choosing Bleed places the page area plus any specified bleed area. Media places an area defined by the paper size specified for the PDF document, including page marks.

6. Click Preserve Halftone Screens if you want to use the file's built-in halftone settings instead of InDesign's when printing the file. Uncheck this option if you want to use InDesign's settings. This setting is used only when you print to a PostScript printer.

7. Click Transparent Background if you want the white areas of the PDF page to be transparent. Uncheck this option if you want to preserve the page's opaque white background.

8. After you finish setting all the options, click OK.

9. Click the loaded-graphic icon within a page or on the pasteboard to place the selected PDF page into the document.

Other Ways to Import Pictures

If you want to specify custom import options for an imported graphics file, you must use the Place command. However, if you don't need this level of control, InDesign offers three other options for importing pictures:

✦ You can also use your computer's Copy (File ➪ Copy, or ⌘+C or Ctrl+C) and Paste (File ➪ Paste, or ⌘+V or Ctrl+V) commands to move a graphics file between two InDesign documents or from a document created with another program into an InDesign document.

✦ You can drag and drop graphics file icons from your computer's desktop into InDesign documents.

✦ For Illustrator files, you can drag objects directly from Illustrator into InDesign.

If you use these methods to add a graphic to an InDesign document, some of the attributes of the original graphic may not survive the trip. The operating system, the file format, and the capabilities of the originating application all play roles in determining which attributes are preserved. If you want to be safe, use the Place command.

Copy and paste

If you copy an object in an InDesign document and then paste it into a different InDesign document, the copy retains all the attributes of the original. In the case of a copied and pasted picture, all import settings, frame modifications, and picture modifications are retained, as is the link to the original graphics file.

Note
Macintosh users cannot use the Mac OS's Publish and Subscribe feature nor can Windows users use that operating system's Object Linking and Embedding (OLE) feature to import pictures into InDesign documents. (Neither of these technologies has earned a reputation for being universally reliable, and few production sites use them.) The Links pane (File ➪ Links, or Shift+⌘+D or Ctrl+Shift+D) helps you manage the links that are established between an InDesign document and a graphics file when you use the Place command. See Chapter 22 for more about managing links to graphics files.

When you copy and paste a graphic into an InDesign document, a link between the original graphics file and the InDesign document is *not* established. The graphic becomes part of the InDesign document, as though you created it using InDesign tools.

Drag and drop

When an InDesign document is open, you can import a graphics file in any supported file format by dragging the file's icon into the window of the InDesign document. When you drag and drop a graphics file into a document, a link between the original graphics file and the document is established, just as it would be if you had used the Place command.

Adobe Illustrator files

If you drag and drop an Illustrator file icon into an InDesign document window, the graphic behaves the same as it would if you had used the Place command. That is, individual elements within the graphic are not selectable or modifiable within InDesign. However, if you drag and drop Illustrator objects from an Illustrator document window into an InDesign document window, as shown in Figure 21-6, each object becomes a separate, editable InDesign object, as though you had created it in InDesign.

This is a handy way of moving objects that you may want to modify between Illustrator and InDesign. For example, you can create text along a path in an Illustrator document, and then drag and drop the object into an InDesign document. Each character is converted into an editable shape, which you can stroke, fill, distort, and so on, using InDesign features. However, you cannot edit text along a path after you've dragged and dropped it into InDesign. (You'd have to go back to Illustrator, edit the original text, drag and drop it again, and then redo all of your modifications.)

Using the Copy and Paste commands to add Illustrator objects to InDesign documents is the same as dragging and dropping objects between the programs. The copied objects behave the same as objects created in InDesign when you choose Paste, and no links are established.

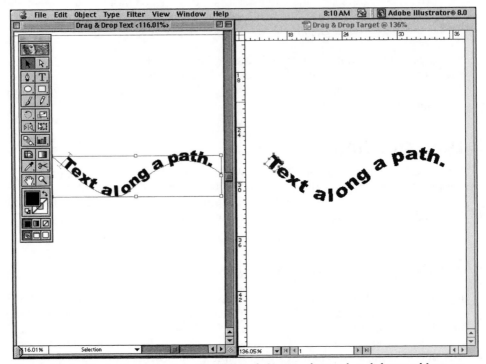

Figure 21-6: The text on a path in Illustrator (left) was dragged and dropped into an InDesign document (right). The text is editable in Illustrator. In InDesign, each character has been converted into a modifiable graphic shape.

Summary

InDesign lets you import pictures in any of several supported graphics file formats. The preferred method for importing pictures is the Place command (File ➪ Place, or ⌘+D or Ctrl+D) because it lets you customize various import settings that control how an imported picture is displayed and printed. You can also import pictures into an InDesign document by dragging and dropping graphics file icons into a document window or by copying and pasting objects between InDesign documents or between documents created with other programs and InDesign documents.

If you need to use Illustrator-generated objects or graphics files in your InDesign documents, several options are available: the Place command, the Copy and Paste commands, file drag and drop, and interapplication drag and drop.

Now that you know how to bring graphics into InDesign, you're ready to learn how to modify them, which is the subject of Chapter 22.

✦　　✦　　✦

Modifying Imported Pictures

Getting a picture into your layout is one thing, but adjusting that graphic to make it really work in your layout is quite another. In almost every case, you'll want to manipulate the pictures you bring into your layout — change the size, crop out part of the image, wrap text around the image, and perhaps change the image color or distort its appearance.

The modifications you make will depend on your layout needs and the attributes of the pictures themselves. But no matter what modifications you end up making, you'll find yourself regularly using the techniques covered in this chapter.

Basic Picture Modifications

After you import a picture into an InDesign document, you can modify either the picture or the frame that contains it. (For information about modifying frames, see Chapter 6.) The following options are available for modifying imported pictures:

♦ You can crop pictures in a rectangular or free-form frame.

♦ You can use tools or the Transform pane to rotate, scale, and/or shear pictures.

♦ You can flip pictures horizontally and/or vertically via commands in the Transform pane's pop-up menu.

✦ You can apply color and tint to imported grayscale and one-bit (black-and-white) bitmap pictures.

Caution   The border around an imported picture, the picture's clipping path, the frame that contains the picture, and the picture's bounding box are all displayed in blue, which can be confusing. When you're working on a picture, make sure you select it with the proper tool. In general, use the Selection tool if you want to modify the frame; use the Direct Selection tool if you want to modify the picture.

Whether you decide to modify a picture after importing it into a document or open the graphics file in its original program and modify it there is up to you. Here are some matters to consider in making this decision:

✦ InDesign lets you crop, rotate, scale, shear, and flip any imported picture regardless of format. Generally, you're safe applying any of these transformations on vector-based formats such as Illustrator-, Freehand-, and CorelDraw-generated EPS graphics — but not Photoshop EPS files, which are pixel-based images in an EPS shell. It's also safe to apply these transformations to DCS files. However, because EPS files are encased (thus the term *encapsulated*) in a sort of protective shell, you can't select or modify any of the component pieces in InDesign — you must use a dedicated application to make such modifications.

✦ For bitmapped images, such as TIFF, JPEG, GIF, and Photoshop-native files, all of the aforementioned transformations except increasing horizontal and/or vertical scale are safe to perform in InDesign. But we recommend doing as much as possible in the original program, to minimize unexpected distortions in your final output. For example, if your imported images are more than twice as large as the size you need them to be in your layout, resize the images in an image editor, and then reimport the resized image in InDesign. Doing so speeds printing and prevents moiré patterns that could result when InDesign takes the reduced pixels of the original image and creates new pixel for output — resizing the image in an image editor usually resizes the pixels in a way that outputs well. Similarly, enlarging an image in InDesign can cause a blocky look, whereas an image editor might let you resize it in a way that preserves image detail.

Tip   If you greatly increase the scale of an imported bitmap graphic, the image will look pixellated (jagged) onscreen, particularly at high magnifications, and the printed image will look blurrier than the same image printed at actual size or smaller. If you need to print a pixel-based image larger than actual size, you may want to consider rescanning and/or resaving the image at a higher resolution. (Vector-based images will display and print at the highest possible resolution regardless of any scaling you apply.)

Cross-Reference   You can apply a stroke to a graphics frame to add a border around a picture, and you can apply a color fill and, optionally, a tint to the frame's background. See Chapter 6 for more about adding strokes and fills to frames.

Cropping pictures

Remember, when you import a picture using the Place command (File ➪ Place, or ⌘+D or Ctrl+D) or by dragging a graphics file into a document window, the picture is contained in a graphics frame—either the frame that was selected when you placed the picture or the frame that is automatically created if a frame wasn't selected. The upper-left corner of an imported picture is automatically placed in the upper-left corner of its frame.

Cropping a picture by resizing its frame

The easiest way to crop a picture is to resize the frame that contains it. If you want to mask out (that is, hide) portions of an imported picture, you have the option to use an irregular shape as the frame, a picture's built-in clipping path (if it has one), or a clipping path generated in InDesign (via the Object ➪ Clipping Path command). Clipping paths are covered in Chapter 23.

To resize the frame, use the Selection tool to drag the frame's handles to reveal the portion of the picture you want to print (and to conceal the portion you don't want to print). Hold the Shift key as you drag to maintain the proportions of the frame. Figure 22-1 shows an imported picture before and after being cropped by resizing its frame.

 **Figure 22-1:** The original image (left) was cloned to create the copy (right), which has been cropped by dragging the midpoint handle on the right edge of the frame to the left.

Cropping a picture by moving it in its frame

You can also click a picture with the Direct Selection tool, and then drag the picture in its frame to reveal and conceal different parts of the picture. For example, you could crop the top and left edges of a picture by dragging the picture above and to the left of its original position (in the upper-left corner of the frame).

Of course, you could get the same result by selecting the frame with the Selection tool and dragging the upper-left corner down and to the right. The advantage of moving the image within the frame is that when you have positioned the frame in the desired location in your layout, resizing the frame to crop the image would then require you to move the resized frame back to the desired location.

Cropping a picture by using an irregular frame

If you want to use an irregular shape as the frame for a picture that's currently cropped by a rectangular frame, go through the following steps.

Steps: Cropping a Picture Using an Irregular Frame

1. Click the Direct Selection tool (or press A if the Type tool isn't selected).

2. Click the picture you want to place in a free-form shape (don't click its frame), and then choose Edit ➪ Copy or press ⌘+C or Ctrl+C.

3. Click the shape you want to use as a cropping frame (or create such a shape if you haven't already). It can be any kind of object except a straight line. (For more information about creating and modifying free-form shapes, see Chapters 24 and 25.)

4. Choose Edit ➪ Paste Into or press Shift+⌘+V or Ctrl+Shift+V. (See Figure 22-2.)

Figure 22-2: In this example, the coffee cup and saucer picture shown in Figure 22-1 has been copied and pasted into a free-form frame that reveals only the cup. The shape was created by tracing the contour of the cup using the Pen tool.

Note   If you select a frame with the Direct Selection tool instead of the Selection tool, handles are displayed only at the frame corners rather than at the bounding-box corners and midpoints. When you select a frame with the Direct Selection tool, you can reshape the frame, and thus crop the picture differently, by dragging corner points, adding and deleting points, and so on.

Of course, you could also create the irregular shape first, and then use the Place command to place the graphics file directly into the shape. Using an irregular shape to crop a picture is similar to using a clipping path except that you create the irregular shape yourself using InDesign's object-creation tools while a clipping path is either built into a graphics file or generated by InDesign (via the Object ➪ Clipping Path command).

Rotating, scaling, and shearing pictures

InDesign provides two methods for rotating, scaling, and shearing pictures: You can click and drag a picture using transformation tools, or you can use the Transform pane, which is explained in the next section, to enter numerical values into fields or to choose a preset value from a pop-up menu.

The method you use is up to you. If you're into the hands-on-mouse approach to object manipulation and page building, you'll probably prefer the click-and-drag method of modifying pictures. Others prefer the pane approach. You'll probably end up using both methods. Regardless of the tool you use, the steps for transforming a picture are pretty much the same:

Steps: Using the Transform Tools with Pictures

1. Click the Direct Selection tool (or press A if the Type tool isn't selected).

2. Click the picture you want to modify.

3. If you want, you can click and drag the object's point of origin (by default it's in the upper-left corner of a graphics frame). All transformations applied to an object are applied relative to the point of origin. For example, when you rotate an item, it rotates around its point of origin.

4. Click and drag to perform the transformation. Hold down the Shift key to constrain transformation increments to preset values. For example, holding down the Shift key while rotating a picture limits rotation increments to multiples of 45 degrees. If you pause for a moment between clicking and dragging — long enough for the crosshair pointer to change to the arrowhead pointer — the transformed picture is displayed while you drag. If you don't pause, only the picture boundary is displayed while you drag. If the Transform pane is open, the value in the field that's associated with the selected tool changes as you drag.

5. Release the mouse button when the picture looks the way you want it to look.

Tip If you hold down the Option or Alt key while using a transformation tool, the modification is performed on a clone of the selected object.

Tip If you double-click a transformation tool, the corresponding field in the Transform pane is highlighted. (Note that double-clicking the Shear tool highlights the Skew field.) Double-clicking a transformation tool also opens the Transform pane if it's not currently displayed

Each transformation tool has a few idiosyncrasies:

✦ **Rotation tool:** You can select this tool by pressing R if the Type tool isn't selected. Holding down the Shift key while dragging limits rotation increments to multiples of 45 degrees.

✦ **Scale tool:** This tool shares a pop-up menu with the Shear tool. If you hold down the Shift key while dragging with the Scale tool, only the horizontal scale of the selected picture changes if you drag horizontally, only the vertical scale changes if you drag vertically, and the original proportions are maintained if you drag diagonally.

✦ **Shear tool:** This tool applies a combination of rotation and skew to a picture. (The Transform pane includes separate Rotation and Skew controls, but no Shear-specific controls.) Holding down the Shift key constrains the selected picture's rotation value to increments of 45 degrees.

Modifying Pictures with the Transform Pane

In addition to duplicating the capabilities of the three transformation tools — the Rotation, Scale, and Shear tools — the Transform pane (Window ⇨ Transform or F9), shown in Figure 22-3, lets you perform several other modifications on a selected picture.

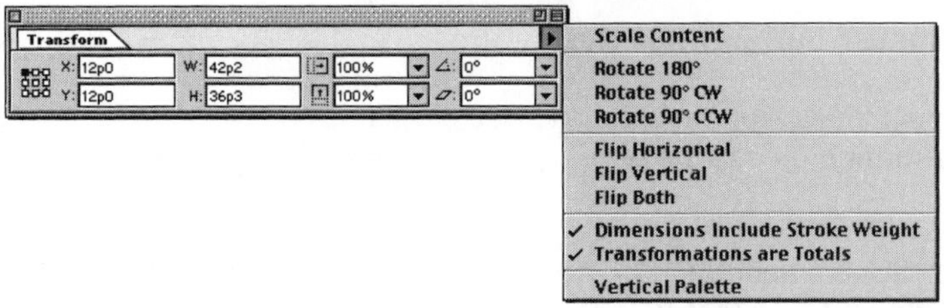

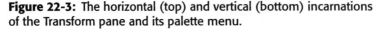

Figure 22-3: The horizontal (top) and vertical (bottom) incarnations of the Transform pane and its palette menu.

The Vertical Pane/Horizontal Pane option at the bottom of the pane's palette menu lets you specify the orientation of the pane. The X Location, Y Location, Width, and Height fields are displayed on top of a vertical pane and on the left side of a horizontal pane. The other four fields — Horizontal Scale, Vertical Scale, Rotation, and Skew — are displayed on the bottom of a vertical pane and on the right side of a horizontal pane.

To highlight a value in a Transform pane field, you can double-click a transformation tool (the value in the corresponding field is highlighted), or you can double-click directly on the field. If you enter a value in a field, press Return or Enter to apply it to the selected item.

> **Tip** If you hold down the Option or Alt key when you press Return or Enter to apply a value you've entered into a field in the Transform pane, the modification is applied to a clone of the selected object.

Changing an object's point of origin

The nine small, white squares at the top-left corner of the Transform pane let you specify the point of origin for the selected object. An object's point of origin is used to determine the values in the X Location (horizontal distance from left edge of page) and Y Location (vertical distance from top of page) field. When you apply a transformation, it's applied to the selected object relative to the fixed point of origin. By default, the point of origin of a graphics frame is in the upper-left corner.

A filled-in black square indicates the current point of origin. If no square is black, it means that a custom point of origin has been established by clicking and dragging the object's point of origin. In most cases, it's simplest to use the default point of origin, but you may want to click the middle square if, for example, you want to rotate a picture around its center, or you may use a different corner or midpoint in certain situations. To change the point of origin for a selected object, click one of the small white squares.

Moving a picture in its frame

You can move a picture in its frame by changing the values in the Transform pane's X Location and/or Y Location fields. The values in these fields indicate the distance between the upper-left corner of the page and the selected object's point of origin, which users of other graphics and publishing programs — particularly QuarkXPress — may find to be a little strange. In QuarkXPress, a picture's position is relative to the box that contains it, not the upper-left corner of the page. (We're assuming here that you have not moved the document's ruler origin, which by default is in the upper-left corner of a page or spread.)

Scaling a picture

You can scale a picture by changing the value in the Width and/or Height fields or by changing the value in the Horizontal Scale and/or Vertical Scale fields. Most graphics designers are familiar with the concept of scaling an object by specifying a percentage value. If you're one of them, you'll probably use the Scale fields. After all, horizontally scaling a 4-inch-wide picture to two-thirds of its original size by applying a Horizontal Scale value of 66.6% is easier than changing the picture's width to 2.667 inches.

You can enter scale values from 1% to 10,000%. If you want to maintain a picture's original proportions, make sure the values in the Horizontal Scale and Vertical Scale fields are the same. If you want to return a picture to the size it was when you first imported it, specify Horizontal Scale and Vertical Scale values of 100%.

In addition to specifying a value in the Horizontal Scale or Vertical Scale field, you can choose one of the predefined values from the fields' pop-up menus, or you can highlight a value and press the up or down arrow keys on the keyboard. Each press of an arrow key changes the value by 1%. If you hold down the Shift key while clicking an arrow, the increment is 10%. Figure 22-4 shows a picture before and after being scaled.

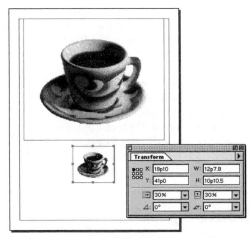

Figure 22-4: The full-sized (100% scale) picture on top was cloned and then scaled horizontally and vertically to 30% of its original size to create the bottom picture. The Horizontal Scale and Vertical Scale fields in the Transform pane show the applied scale values.

The Fitting options (Object ➪ Fitting), which are explained later in this chapter, also let you change the scale of a picture relative to the size of its frame.

Rotating a picture

You can change the angle of a selected picture by entering a different value in the Rotation field, choosing one of the predefined angles from the field's pop-up menu, or by choosing any of the three rotation options—Rotate 180°, Rotate 90° CW, and Rotate 90° CCW—in the Transform pane's palette menu. If you choose one of these options, the current angle of the selected object is added to the applied angle. For example, if you choose Rotate 90° CCW (counterclockwise), an object that's currently rotated 12 degrees will end up with a rotation angle of 102 degrees. If you choose to enter a value in the Rotation field, positive values rotate the selected item counterclockwise; negative values rotate it clockwise.

Note The Transformations are Totals option in the Transform pane's palette menu relates to the angle of rotation of a nested object. If Transformations are Totals is checked, the Rotation angle displayed for a nested item is calculated by adding its angle to the angle of the containing frame. For example, if Transformations are Totals is checked, a picture that's been rotated 30 degrees that's in a frame that's been rotated 30 degrees will display a Rotation value of 60 degrees. If Transformations are Totals were unchecked, the Rotation value would be 30 degrees.

Skewing a picture

You can skew, or slant, a picture in its frame by applying a Skew value in the Transform pane or by choosing a predefined value from the field's pop-up menu. Positive skew values slant an object to the right (that is, the top edge of the object is moved to the right), whereas negative values slant an object to the left (the bottom edge is moved to the right). You can enter skew values from 1 to 89 degrees (although values above 70 degrees cause considerable distortion).

To "unskew" a picture, enter a Skew value of 0 degrees. Figure 22-5 shows a picture that's been skewed.

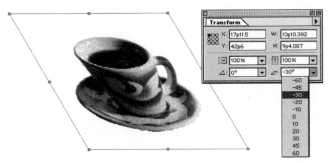

Figure 22-5: The applied Skew value of –30 degrees causes the picture to lean to the left.

Note When you use the Shear tool, you change the selected object's angle of rotation *and* skew angle simultaneously.

Flipping a picture

The three flipping commands—Flip Horizontal, Flip Vertical, and Flip Both—in the Transform pane's palette menu let you create a mirror image of a selected picture. If you choose Flip Horizontal, the picture is flipped along a vertical axis (that is, the right edge and left edge exchange places); if you choose Flip Vertical, the picture is flipped upside down; and if you choose Flip Both, the picture is flipped horizontally and vertically to produce an upside-down and backward version of the original.

Be careful when flipping pictures: Generally you'll want to flip both a picture and its frame. To do so, make sure you select the frame using the Selection tool (rather than the Direct Selection tool, which selects the picture). If you flip a picture that's been cropped in a frame, you'll probably have to recrop the picture.

 Note

When you flip a picture, the axis around which the picture flips runs through the frame's point of origin.

The Fitting Commands

If you've placed a picture in a frame that's either larger or smaller than the picture, you can use the Fitting options (Object ➪ Fitting) to scale the picture to fit the frame proportionally or disproportionally or to scale the frame to fit the picture. Another option lets you center the picture in the frame.

The Fitting commands for pictures are available only if you've used the Selection tool to select a graphics frame. Here's a description of each of the four options:

✦ **Fit Content to Frame:** To resize a picture to fill the selected frame, choose Object ➪ Fitting ➪ Fit Content to Frame or press Option+⌘+E or Ctrl+Alt+E. If the frame is larger than the picture, the picture is enlarged; if the frame is smaller, the picture is reduced. If the picture and the frame have different proportions, the picture's proportions are changed so that the image completely fills the frame.

✦ **Fit Frame to Content:** To resize a frame so that it wraps snugly around a picture, choose Fit Frame to Content or press Option+Shift+⌘+V or Ctrl+Alt+Shift+V. The frame will be enlarged or reduced depending on the size of the picture, and the frame's proportions will be changed to match the proportions of the picture.

✦ **Center Content:** To center a picture in its frame, choose Center Content or press Shift+⌘+E or Ctrl+Shift+E. Neither the frame nor the picture is resized when you center a picture.

✦ **Fit Content Proportionally:** To resize a picture to fit in the selected frame while maintaining the picture's current proportions, choose Object ➪ Fitting ➪

Fit Content Proportionally or press Option+Shift+⌘+E or Ctrl+Alt+Shift+E. If the frame is larger than the picture, the picture is enlarged; if the frame is smaller, the picture is reduced. If the picture and the frame have different proportions, a portion of the frame background will show above and below or to the left and right of the picture. If you want, you can drag frame edges to make the frame shorter or narrower and eliminate any portions of the background that are visible.

Note

For frames with strokes, the Fitting options align the outer edge of a picture with the center of the stroke. A stroke will obscure a strip along the picture's edge that's half the width of the stroke. The wider the stroke, the more of the picture that gets covered up.

Modifying Bitmap Graphics versus Vector Graphics

When it comes to working with bitmap and vector graphics in InDesign, there's not much difference. When you use the Place command, the import options for these two graphics formats are slightly different (see Chapter 21), but the transformation tools and the controls in the Transform pane are available and work the same for all imported pictures regardless of their file format.

Note

Some page layout programs, notably QuarkXPress, provide limited features for modifying the appearance of bitmap pictures. InDesign does not. (No matter what page-layout software you use, if you want to modify a vector-based graphic, such as an Adobe Illustrator–generated EPS file, you have to open and modify it using Illustrator or another compatible illustration program.) However, even in programs such as QuarkXPress, if you want to perform any serious pixel-level modifications to a bitmap graphic, you'll need to use a dedicated image-editing program such as Adobe Photoshop.

When it comes to performing picture modifications in InDesign, the only difference between bitmap graphics and vector-based graphics is that you can apply color and, optionally, tint to grayscale and one-bit (black-and-white) bitmaps. These options are not available for vector-based images and color bitmaps.

Applying color and tint to bitmap pictures

Remember, you can apply color and tint only to grayscale and black-and-white bitmap pictures. If you're unable to apply a color or tint to a bitmap picture that you think should be modifiable, check the picture's file type. To do so, open the Links pane (File ➪ Links, or Shift+⌘+D or Ctrl+Shift+D), and then double-click the picture's name or click its name once and choose Show Link Information from the pane's pop-up menu. The picture's color mode (CMYK, Grayscale, and so on) is displayed next to Color Space; the picture's file format is displayed next to File Type.

Steps: Applying Color to a Picture

1. Click the Direct Selection tool (or press A if the Type tool isn't selected).

2. Click in the picture's frame to select the picture.

3. If it's not displayed, show the Swatches pane by choosing Windows ➪ Swatches or pressing F5.

4. Click a color in the scroll list.

Cross-Reference   See Chapter 27 for information about defining colors.

You also apply color to a selected picture by dragging a swatch from the Swatches pane and dropping it onto the picture.

Applying a tint to a picture

Applying a color tint—that is, a shade or a percentage of the applied color—to a picture is the same as applying a color. You must create a tint of an available color before you can apply the tint to a picture. To create a tint of a color, click the color in the Swatches pane, and then choose New Tint Swatch from the Swatches pane's pop-up menu. Use the Tint controls in the New Swatch Tint dialog to specify the percent of the parent color you want to use. After you create a tint, you apply it to a picture following the same steps you would use if you were applying color.

Managing Links to Imported Pictures

As Chapter 21 explained, when you place a graphic into an InDesign document — either via the Place command (File ➪ Place, or ⌘+D or Ctrl+D) or by dragging and dropping a graphics file's icon directly into a document window — InDesign remembers the name and location of the original graphics file and uses this file when the document is printed.

If you always print your documents from your own computer, and your graphics never get modified, moved, renamed, or deleted, you won't have to worry much about managing the links between your InDesign documents and imported graphics files. But these days, that scenario is the exception rather than the rule. Graphics files are often modified while the InDesign pages that contain them are under construction, and at many publishing sites, the computer used to create a document is seldom the computer from which it's printed.

Note If you import a graphics file that's 48K or smaller in size, the entire full-resolution image is automatically embedded in the InDesign document. The Links pane, explained next, lets you manage links to these embedded graphics files and all other imported pictures.

Tip If you'll be taking your documents to a service provider for output, be sure to include all imported graphics files, as well. You can use InDesign's Preflight and Package features, which are covered in Chapter 32, to automatically collect graphics files in preparation for output.

The Links pane

The Links pane (File ➪ Links, or Shift+⌘+D or Ctrl+Shift+D), shown in Figure 22-6, displays link-related information about all imported graphics files, and the pane's accompanying pop-up menu provides tools for managing links. The scroll list displays the name of each imported graphic. A Missing-Link icon (a question mark) is displayed for graphics that have been moved, renamed, or deleted since they were imported into the document. A Modified-Link icon (an exclamation mark) is displayed for graphics that have been modified since being imported.

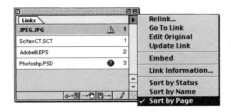

Figure 22-6: The Links pane and its palette menu. Note the Missing-Link icon displayed for the file named Photoshop.PSD and the Modified-Link icon displayed for the file named JPEG.JPG.

When you open a document that contains imported graphics files that have been modified, moved, renamed, or deleted since they were imported, the alert shown in Figure 22-7 is displayed. This alert tells you the number of files with "Missing" links (that is, the original graphics file has been moved, renamed, or deleted) and with "Modified" links (graphics files that have been opened and saved since they were imported). You don't have to update missing or modified links as soon as you open a document, but it's not a bad idea.

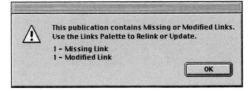

Figure 22-7: This alert appears when you open a document that contains imported pictures that have been modified, moved, renamed, or deleted.

If the status of a link to a particular graphics file changes while you're working on a document, a Missing-Link or Modified-Link icon is displayed in the Links pane. For example, if you import an illustration created with Illustrator or FreeHand into an InDesign document, and then open, modify, and resave the illustration using its original program, the Links pane will display the Modified-Link icon for that file.

Note   Generally, you'll want to keep all links up to date. If you don't update the link for a modified graphic, it will still print correctly, but what you see onscreen may be quite different from what prints. Remember that when you import a graphics file, InDesign creates and saves a low-resolution screen preview for display. If the graphics file is then modified, InDesign continues to use the old screen preview for screen display until you update the link.

If you try to print a document that contains a missing graphics file, the alert shown in Figure 22-7 is displayed. At this point, you can Cancel the print job and then use the Links pane to update the link, or you can click OK to print anyway. If you print anyway, InDesign sends the low-resolution screen preview to the printer instead of sending the original graphics file.

Cross-Reference   The Links pane also displays the names of imported text files. See Chapter 10 for more information about importing text files and managing links between text files and InDesign documents.

Note   If you import an EPS file that, in turn, contains OPI links to placed images in the file, the Links pane will display these links. You shouldn't change them. Doing so could cause printing problems.

The Links pane's palette menu has four groups of commands that let you manage links, embed the original graphics file of any imported graphic, display link information for individual graphics, and control how file names are displayed in the pane. If you want to update, relink, or view information about a specific file, click its name in the pane, and then choose a command from the palette menu or click a button at the bottom of the pane, all of which are explained next.

Managing links

The first four command in the Links pane's palette menu let you reestablish links to missing and modified graphics files, display an imported graphic in the document window, and open the program used to create a graphics file:

✦ **Relink:** This command, and the Relink button (the left-most at the bottom of the pane), lets you reestablish a missing link or replace the original file you imported with a different file. When you choose Relink or click the button, the Relink dialog box is displayed and shows the original path name and file name. You can enter a new path name and file name in the Location field, but it's easier to click Browse, which opens a standard Open file dialog box. Use the controls to locate and select the original file or a different file, and then click OK. (You can also drag and drop a file icon from the Mac OS Finder or Windows Explorer directly into the Relink dialog box.) If you want to restore broken links to multiple files, highlight their file names in the scroll list, and then choose Relink or click the Update Link button.

✦ **Go To Link:** Choose this option, or click the Go to Link button (second from left) to display the highlighted graphics file in the document window. InDesign will, if necessary, navigate to the correct page and center the image in the document window. You can also display a particular graphic by double-clicking its name in the scroll list while holding down the Option or Alt key.

✦ **Edit Original:** If you want to modify an imported graphic, choose Edit Original from the palette menu or click the Edit Original button (far right). InDesign will try to locate and open the program used to create the file. This may or may not be possible, depending on the original program, the file format, and the programs available on your computer.

✦ **Update Link:** Choose this option or click the Update Link button (third button from the left) to update the link to a modified graphic. Highlight multiple file names and then choose Update Link or click the Update Link button to update all links at once.

Note

When you update missing and modified graphics, any transformations—rotation, shear, scale, and so on—that you've applied to the graphics or their frames are maintained.

Embedding imported pictures

The Links pane's Embed command lets you embed the complete file of any imported graphic. (Remember, except for files that are 48K and smaller, you import only a low-resolution screen preview when you place a picture.) If you want to ensure that the graphics file will forever remain with a document, you can choose to embed it — however, by embedding graphics you'll be producing larger document files, which means it will take you longer to open and save them.

To embed a picture, click its name in the scroll list, and then choose Embed from the Links pane's palette menu. An alert is displayed and informs you about the increased document size that will result. Click Yes to embed the file.

Caution

When you embed a file, the file name is no longer displayed in the Links pane, nor is an embedded file automatically updated if you modify the original. Generally, you should avoid embedding files, especially large ones, unless you're certain that they won't be modified.

Displaying link information

Choosing Link Information from the Links pane's palette menu displays the Link Information dialog box, shown in Figure 22-8. This dialog box doesn't let you do much (the Previous and Next buttons let you display information about the previous and next files in the list, but that's about it), but it does display 11 useful items of information about the highlighted graphics file, including its name, status, creation date, file type, and location.

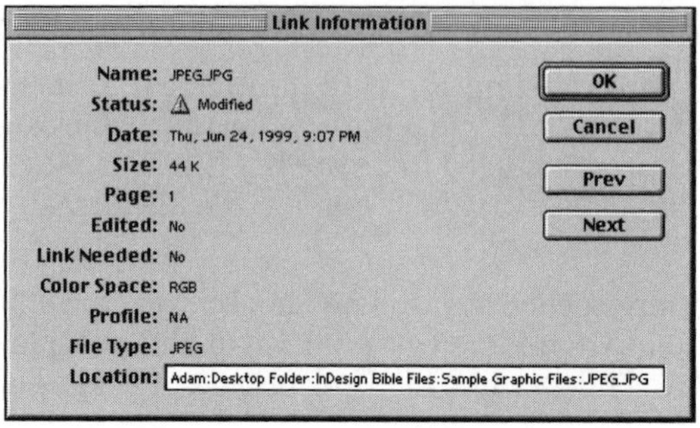

Figure 22-8: The Link Information dialog box.

Sorting imported files in the Links pane

The last three commands in the Links pane's palette menu let you control how the files in the scroll list are arranged.

✦ **Sort by Status** lists files with missing links first, followed by files that have been modified, and finally files whose status is okay.

✦ **Sort by Name** lists all files in alphabetical order.

✦ **Sort by Page** lists imported files on page 1 first, followed by imported files on page 2, and so on.

If you Ctrl+click or right-click an imported picture, the contextual menu displays two options that are also available in the Links pane's palette menu: Link Information and Edit Original. Keep in mind that the Links pane displays the names of all imported files — text and graphic. When you sort files, text files and graphics files are listed together according to the selected sort method.

Note   InDesign's Preflight command (File ➪ Fitting) displays link information and link-related problems and lets you fix these problems prior to printing. The Packaging command (File ➪ Packaging) lets you update broken graphic links and collect linked graphics prior to sending an InDesign document to an output provider. For more information about the Preflight and Package commands, see Chapter 32.

Summary

After you import a picture into a document, you have many options for changing its appearance. You can crop it in a rectangular or free-form frame or manipulate it with three transformation tools — the Rotation, Scale, and Shear tools. The Transform pane lets you perform the same modifications as the transformation tools and offers other choices for modifying pictures, including moving, scaling, skewing, and flipping. For grayscale and bitmap pictures only, you have the option to apply a color and a tint to the image.

The Fitting command (Object ➪ Fitting) provides four options for positioning and scaling a picture relative to its frame, whereas the Links pane displays link-related information about imported pictures and lets you update links for pictures that are missing or have been modified.

✦　　✦　　✦

Special Effects for Pictures

CHAPTER 23

T he options offered by the transformation tools and the Transform pane let you change the appearance of imported pictures in several ways, but that's not all you can do with your graphics.

InDesign provides several other picture-modification features that — among other things — let you wrap text around pictures, show and hide portions of pictures using clipping paths, place pictures within compound shapes, and place pictures within a text thread so that they move along with the surrounding text.

Wrapping Text around Pictures

In the "old" days before personal computers and page-layout software, wrapping text around a picture was a time-consuming and expensive task. Text runarounds were rare, found only in the most expensively produced publications.

Not any more. Not only do all page-layout programs let you create text runarounds, most programs, including InDesign, provide several options for controlling how text relates to pictures and other objects that obstruct its flow.

When a graphics frame is positioned in front of a text frame, InDesign provides the following options. You can:

- ✦ Ignore the graphics frame and flow the text behind it.
- ✦ Wrap the text around the frame's rectangular bounding box.
- ✦ Wrap the text around the frame itself.
- ✦ Jump the text around the frame (that is, jump the text from the top of the graphics frame to the bottom).
- ✦ Jump the text to the next column or page when the text reaches the top of graphics frame.

✦ ✦ ✦ ✦

In This Chapter

Creating text runarounds

Masking pictures with clipping paths

Other cool tricks for pictures

✦ ✦ ✦ ✦

✦ Specify the amount of distance between the text and the edge of the obstructing shape.

✦ Flow text within the obstructing shape rather than outside it.

Tip   If you want to wrap text around only a portion of a picture — perhaps you need to isolate a face in a crowd — the best solution is to open the graphics file in its original program, create a clipping path around that portion, and then resave the file and import it and its clipping path into an InDesign document (clipping paths are explained in the next section). (Another option is to use the Pen tool to create a free-form shape within InDesign and then use the shape as both a frame and a clipping path.)

The Text Wrap pane

The controls in the Text Wrap pane, shown in Figure 23-1, let you specify how a selected object affects the flow of text behind it. Remember, the flow of text around an obstructing object is determined by the text wrap settings applied to the obstructing object.

Figure 23-1: The Text Wrap pane.

Tip   You can override the text-wrap settings of objects that are in front of a text frame by telling the text frame to ignore them. To do so, click a text frame, and then choose Object ⇨ Text Frame Options, or press ⌘+B or Ctrl+B. In the Text Frame Options dialog box, select Override Text Wrap, and then click OK. Text in the frame will then flow behind any obstructing items regardless of the text-wrap settings applied to them.

Steps: Applying Text-Wrap Settings to a Graphics Frame

1. If the Text Wrap pane is not displayed, choose Object ⇨ Text Wrap, or press Option+⌘+W or Ctrl+Alt+W.

2. Click either of the selection tools. If the Type tool isn't selected, you can press V to select the Selection tool or press A to select the Direct Selection tool.

3. Click the graphics frame to which you want to apply text-wrap settings. (The frame can be anywhere, but you'll probably want to position it on top of a text frame that contains text so you can see the results of the settings you apply.)

4. Click one of the five text-wrap buttons at the top of the Text Wrap pane. Figure 23-2 shows how each of these options affects a graphics frame.

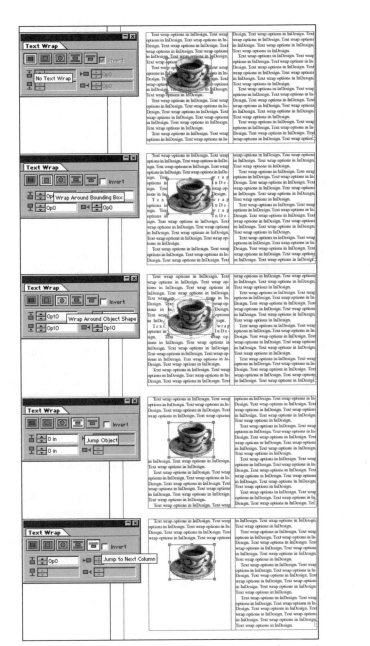

Figure 23-2: The five text-wrap options (top to bottom) — No Text Wrap, Wrap Around Bounding Box, Wrap Around Object Shape, Jump Object, and Jump to Next Column — are shown here applied to a picture that contains an embedded clipping path.

5. If you want, adjust the space between the surrounding text and the obstructing shape by entering values in the Top Outset, Bottom Outset, Left Outset, and Right Outset fields. (These fields are not available if you click the No Text Wrap button.) If the object is a rectangle, all four fields are available if you click the Wrap Around Bounding Box button or Wrap Around Object Shape. Only the Top Outset field is available if you click the Wrap Around Object Shape button for a free-form shape or the Jump to Next Column button. The Top Outset and Bottom Outset fields are available if you click the Jump Object button.

6. If you want to flow the text in the obstructing shape, select Invert.

Tip   If you specify text-wrap settings when no objects are selected, the settings are automatically applied to all new objects.

Tip   To apply text-wrap settings to a master item on a document page, hold down Shift+⌘ or Ctrl+Shift to select the item, and then use the controls in the Text Wrap pane as described previously.

Changing the shape of a text wrap

When you specify text-wrap settings for an object, an editable shape is created. If the text-wrap shape is the same shape as the object, the text-wrap boundary is superimposed on the object. You can modify a text-wrap boundary by clicking it with the Direct Selection tool and then moving, adding, deleting, and changing the direction of anchor points and by moving direction lines. Figure 23-3 shows a text wrap before and after being manually reshaped.

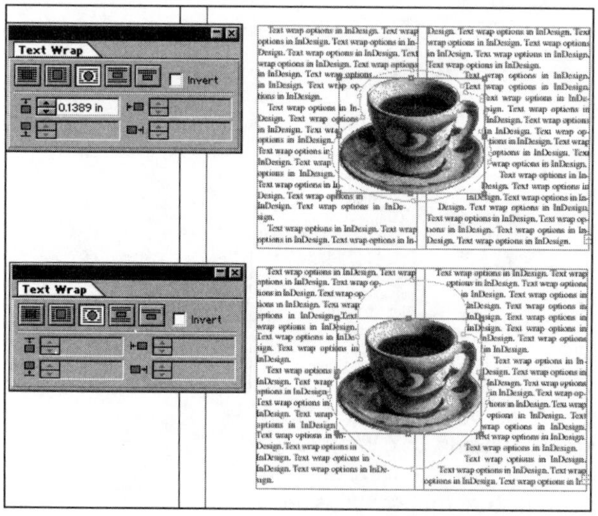

Figure 23-3: The example on the top shows a text wrap created by using the picture's built-in clipping path (Wrap Around Object Shape). The text wrap was modified, by dragging anchor points, to create the variation on the bottom.

Cross-Reference For more information about modifying free-form shapes, see Chapter 25.

Working with Clipping Paths

Some graphics file formats — including TIFF, JPEG, and Photoshop EPS, and Photoshop-native (.PSD) files — let you embed a clipping path in the file. A clipping path is used to mask certain parts of a picture and reveal other parts. For example, if you want to create a silhouette around a single person in a crowd of people, you could open the file in an image-editing program such as Photoshop, and then create and save a clipping path that isolates the shape of the person. (You could also erase everything except the person you want to silhouette, but not only can this be time consuming, but if you want to reveal other parts of the picture later, you're out of luck.)

If you want to use a clipping path to mask parts of a picture, InDesign offers three options. You can:

✦ Use a graphics file's built-in clipping path.

✦ Create a free-form shape that acts as your mask in InDesign and then place a picture in the shape.

✦ Create a clipping path in InDesign using the Object ⇨ Clipping Path command.

As with changing the shape of a text wrap, regardless of the method you use to clip an imported picture, you can modify a clipping path by moving, adding, deleting, and changing the direction of anchor points and by moving direction lines.

Placing graphics files that contain clipping paths

When you use the Place command (File ⇨ Place, or ⌘+D or Ctrl+D) to import a graphics file that contains a clipping path, you have the option to use the clipping path as the graphics frame or to ignore the clipping path and have InDesign create a rectangular frame.

Steps: Creating a Frame from a Clipping Path When Placing a Picture

1. With no object selected, choose File ⇨ Place, or press ⌘+D or Ctrl+D. (If an object is selected, you can still use a graphics file's clipping path and ignore the selected object.)

2. Locate and select the graphics file you want to import.

3. Select Show Import Options, and then click Choose or Open to display the Image Import Options dialog box. (You can also hold down the Shift key and double-click the file name to display the Image Import Options dialog box.)

4. Select Create Frame from Clipping Path — and set other import options if you want — and then click OK. If this option is not available, the selected graphics file doesn't have a recognizable clipping path or the file format doesn't support clipping paths.

Figure 23-4 shows a picture that's been imported with and without its clipping path.

Figure 23-4: The Use Embedded Clipping Path option was checked in the Import Options dialog box when the TIFF picture on the left was imported with the Place command. Unchecking the Use Embedded Clipping Path option for the same graphics file produced the unclipped version on the right.

Using a free-form shape to clip a picture

If you want to mask a portion of a picture that doesn't include a built-in clipping path, you can create a free-form shape and use it as a frame that functions like a clipping path. You have two ways to place a picture in a free-form shape:

✦ You can use the Pen tool to create the shape, and then use the Place command (File ⇨ Place, or ⌘+D or Ctrl+D) to place a picture in the shape.

✦ You can import the picture into a rectangular frame (by using the Place command with no object selected), use the Pen tool to create a free-form shape that surrounds the portion of the image you want to show, and then copy and paste the picture into the free-form shape. In this case, you must use the Paste Into command (Edit ⇨ Paste Into, or Option+⌘+V or Ctrl+Alt+V) to place the copied picture in the selected free-form shape. When you create the free-form shape, make sure that the default color for the Pen tool is set to None so that the shape you create is transparent. Otherwise, the colored area in the shape will obscure the picture behind it.

You're more likely to use the second method than the first because it's difficult to mask a portion of a picture without seeing it. Figure 23-5 shows a picture in a rectangular frame next to a copy of the same picture in a free-form shape.

Figure 23-5: The free-form frame used to clip the image on the right was created by tracing around a portion of the picture in the rectangular frame (left). The free-form shape was then moved and a copy of the picture was pasted into it.

> **Tip**
> The Pen tool lets you create one shape at a time. The Compound Paths command lets you combine multiple shapes to create more complex objects. For example, you could place a small circle on top of a larger circle and then use the Compound Paths command to create a donut-shaped object. A figure later in this chapter shows a picture in a compound path. (See Chapter 26 for more information about creating complex shapes with the Compound Paths command.)

Using InDesign's Clipping Path command

If you import a bitmap picture that doesn't have a clipping path, you can use the Clipping Path command (Object ➪ Clipping Path) to generate one automatically in InDesign. The clipping paths that InDesign generates are based on a picture's value. For this reason, the Clipping Path command works very will for images that have a white background but no clipping path. It's less useful for pictures whose background has not been erased and for images that contain a broad range of intermingling values.

> **Note**
> If you use the Clipping Path command to generate a clipping path for a picture that has a built-in clipping path, the one that InDesign generates replaces the built-in path.

Steps: Creating a Clipping Path Using the Clipping Path Command

1. Select either the Selection tool or the Direct Selection tool, and then click the picture to which you want to add a clipping path. If the Type tool isn't selected, you can press V to select the Selection tool or press A to select the Direct Selection tool.

2. Choose Object ➪ Clipping Path to display the Clipping Path dialog box, shown in Figure 23-6.

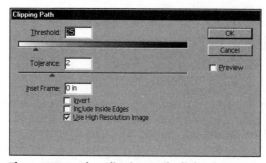

Figure 23-6: The Clipping Path dialog box.

3. Enter a value in the Threshold field or drag the field's slider to specify the value below which pixels will be placed outside the clipping path shape (that is, pixels that will become transparent). Pixels darker than the Threshold value remain visible and will thus be inside the clipping path shape. The lowest possible Threshold value (0) makes only white pixels transparent. As the value gets higher, less of the picture remains visible. The lightest areas are removed first, and then midtones, and so on. (Click Preview to see the results of your changes without closing the dialog box.)

4. The value you enter in the Tolerance field determines how closely InDesign looks at variations in adjacent pixels when building a clipping path. Higher values produce a simpler, smoother path than lower values. Lower values create a more complicated, more exact path with more anchor points.

5. If you want to enlarge or reduce the size of the clipping path produced by the Threshold and Tolerance values, enter a value in the Inset Frame field. Negative values enlarge the path; positive values shrink it. (The Inset Frame value is also applied to the path's bounding box.)

6. Click Invert to switch the transparent and visible areas of the clipping path produced by the Threshold and Tolerance values.

7. If you want to include areas in the perimeter shape InDesign generates based on the Threshold and Tolerance values, click Include Inside Edges. For example, if you have a picture of a donut and you want to make the hole transparent (as well as the area around the outside of the donut), click Include Inside Edges. If you don't click Include Inside Edges, InDesign builds a single shape (in the case of a donut, just the outside circle). The portion of the picture in the shape remains visible; the rest of the picture becomes transparent.

8. Click Use High Resolution Image if you want InDesign to use the high-resolution information in the original file instead of using the low-resolution

proxy image. Even though using the high-resolution image takes longer, the resulting clipping path is more precise than it would be if you didn't check Use High Resolution Image.

9. When you finish specifying clipping path settings, click OK to close the dialog box and apply the settings to the selected picture.

Figure 23-7 shows a picture before and after a clipping path was applied to it using the Clipping Path command.

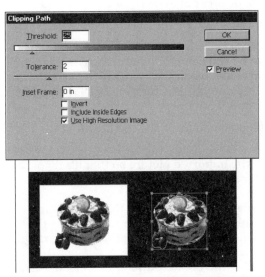

Figure 23-7: The image on the bottom left does not contain a clipping path. Notice how the frame background obscures the black object behind the picture. The Clipping Path dialog box shows the settings used to create the image on the bottom right. The background is visible outside the InDesign-generated clipping path.

Other Special Effects

When you combine your imagination with InDesign's picture-modification, page-layout, and typographic features, the possibilities for manipulating imported pictures become endless. Here are a few of our favorite tricks for adding pizzazz to your pictures.

Using text characters as graphics frames

InDesign's Pen tool lets you create any kind of shape for use as a graphics frame, but if you want to place a picture in the shape of a text character or in several characters, there's a much easier way than drawing the characters yourself: You can use the Create Outlines command (Type ➪ Create Outlines, or Shift+⌘+O or Ctrl+Shift+O) to convert highlighted text into editable outlines, and then place a picture in the character shapes. Here's how:

Steps: Creating a Clipping Path Using Character Shapes

1. Format and then highlight the text you want to use as a graphics frame. You can use a single character or a range of text.

2. Choose Type ➪ Create Outlines, or press Shift+⌘+O or Ctrl+Shift+O.

3. Choose either of the selection tools, and then click the highlighted text.

4. Choose File ➪ Place, or press ⌘+D or Ctrl+D, and then locate and select the graphics file you want to import. (You can also copy and paste a picture you've already imported. In this case, when you're ready to paste the copied picture, make sure you select the outlines and then choose Edit ➪ Paste Into, or press Option+⌘+V or Ctrl+Alt+V.)

5. Click OK or double-click the file name to place the picture into the selected outlines.

6. Adjust the size and position of the imported picture so that it's displayed the way you want it in the character shapes.

You can modify character outlines created with the Create Outlines command the same as you modify any shape — by adding a stroke and/or fill, by using the transformation tools or Transform pane to apply rotation, scale, or shear, and so on.

When you convert text to outlines using the Create Outlines command, the outlines replace the highlighted text and are embedded in the text. One handy aspect of the Create Outlines command is that the text remains editable. If you want to remove the outlines from the text and place them elsewhere, select the outlines with either of the selection tools, copy them (Edit ➪ Copy, or ⌘+C or Ctrl+C), and then click an empty portion of the page and choose Edit ➪ Paste, or press ⌘+V or Ctrl+V. Figure 23-8 shows a picture that's been placed in the outline of a single text character.

Figure 23-8: Converting the O character into an outline with the Create Outlines command and then using the Paste Into command to import the graphics file into the shape created this picture-in-a-character effect.

Using compound shapes as graphics frames

The Object ⇨ Compound Paths command lets you combine several paths into a single object. Once you create a multishape object, you can use the Place command or the Copy and Paste Into commands to put a picture in. In Figure 23-9, three paths have been placed in front of the cup and saucer picture:

1. A clipping path generated with the Clipping Path command surrounds the cup and saucer.

2. A path created with the Pen tool is in the cup handle.

3. A third, oval-shaped path — also created with the Pen tool — surrounds the coffee in the cup.

Figure 23-9: Three separate shapes (left) were combined to create the effect on the right. Notice how the areas in the two inner shapes on the left are transparent (that is, the blended background is visible in the shapes) in the example on the right.

In the image on the left, the picture — rather than the blended background shape — is visible in all three paths. The image on the right shows the results of creating a compound path out of the three paths. The blended background shows through in the two inner paths — areas that were previously obscured.

Cross-Reference For more information about working with compound paths and reversing the direction of paths, see Chapter 26.

Creating inline frames

In most cases, you place a picture into a graphics frame and then, if necessary, manually move the frame by clicking and dragging it with the Selection tool or by changing the frame's X Location or Y Location values in the Transform pane. If you want to place a picture relative to text in such a way that the picture moves — and thus remains close to its associated text — when editing causes the text to reflow, you can create an inline frame out of the graphics frame. Inline frames are particularly useful for publications such as catalogs that contain lengthy text threads that, in turn, contain pictures that must flow with the text. An inline frame behaves much like a single character, yet it retains all the attributes of a frame, which means you can add a stroke or fill, transform it with the transformation tools or the Transform pane, and so on.

If you want to create an inline frame from an object you've already created, all you have to do is copy the object and then paste it into text as you would a piece of highlighted text.

 Tip

Inline graphics often work best when placed at the beginning of a paragraph. If you place an inline frame in text to which automatic leading has been applied, the resulting line spacing can be inconsistent. To fix this problem, you can resize the inline frame

In addition to using the Paste command to create an inline frame from an existing object, you can use the Place command to create an inline graphic from an external picture file. The key is to use the Type tool to select an insertion point in your text before placing the graphic (using File ⇨ Place, or ⌘+D or Ctrl+D); the graphic will be placed in the text in an inline frame.

Cross-Reference

For more information about working with inline frames, see Chapter 7.

Slicing a picture with the Scissors tool

The Scissors tool is the InDesign equivalent of a utility knife. It lets you slice objects into two parts. Figure 23-10 shows a picture that's been cut into halves with the Scissors tool.

Figure 23-10: The Scissors tool was used to create the split image (right) from a clone of the original image (left).

Steps: Slicing a Picture

1. Select the Scissors tool. If the Type tool isn't selected, you can press C to select the Scissors tool.

2. Position the crosshair pointer anywhere over a graphics frame, and then click.

3. Move the pointer to a different position along the frame edge, and then click again.

After you click the frame edge twice, you can switch to either of the selection tools and then drag either of the two picture pieces that your scissors cut created.

Note   If you use the Scissors tool to split a frame to which a stroke has been applied, the resulting edges will not include the stroke.

Summary

After you import a picture into an InDesign document, you can use the Text Wrap pane to control how text flows when the picture is in front of a text frame.

To mask out certain areas of a picture, you can use a picture's built-in clipping path (if it has one), place the picture in a free-form shape created with the Pen tool, or use the Clipping Path command to have InDesign build a clipping path.

If you want to get even trickier with your imported pictures, you can place them in complex shapes created with the Compound Path command, paste them into a text thread so that they move along with the surrounding text, or slice them into two pieces with the Scissors tool.

✦   ✦   ✦

InDesign Color Techniques

Adobe InDesign offers a strong set of tools for color creation and control, as Part VII covers in detail. This special eight-page color section shows some of those tools in action, using InDesign's actual capabilities. Most images used in this section are color photographs scanned in as 24-bit RGB files at 600 dpi and converted to CMYK TIFF images in Adobe Photoshop 5.0. We also adjusted brightness, sharpness, and color balance as needed. (Chapters 27 and 28 show how to use the tools and accomplish the techniques illustrated here.)

Color Models

Color is made up of light, but the printing model and computer-monitor models act very differently. Color printing is based on how light reflects off paper through inks — ths standard inks in printing are cyan magenta, yellow, and black (CMYK), although there are specialty inks such as Pantone, Toyo, and Trumatch. The ink absorbs all colors but the one you see; for example, your eyes see cyan because the ink has absorbed all the other colors that light would normally pick up. That's why mixing several inks produces a dark brown or gray — most of the light is absorbed by the multiple inks. By contrast, computer monitors use a model based on how the three colors of light — red, green, and blue (RGB) combine. All three combine to make white, while having none gives you black. Because the physics of the two models is different, what you see on screen — or what your scanner or digital camera sees when capturing an image — won't necessarily match what is printed.

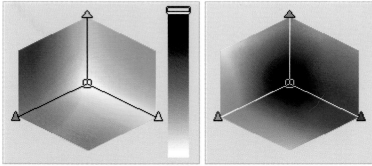

The CMYK model   *The RGB model*

CMYK color (far left) and RGB color (iimediate left). For CMYK, the cube shows how cyan, magenta, and yellow combine in various percentages; the slider at the cube's right adds black, which has the effect of darkening the combinations shown. In RGB, there's no slider since the three colors combine to produce all color shades (white is the absence of all colors). Below are example inks from specialty color libraries.

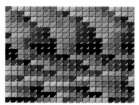
Pantone ink swatches

Pantone Process ink swatches

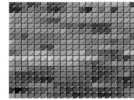
Toyo ink swatches

Trumatch ink swatches

Colors on the Web

Although the Hypertext Markup Language (HTML) supports thousands of colors, you can count only on 216 colors to display properly on popular Macintosh and Windows Web browsers. That's because most browsers play it safe and assume that people have just the basic video support on their computers: 8-bit color depth, which permits 256 colors. Of those 256, Windows reserves 40 for its interface, leaving 216 for the browser to use. Understanding this, InDesign comes with a Web swatch library that has only the Web-safe colors.

The InDesign swatch library at right shows all Web-safe colors; compare that to the very partial (about 2 percent) listing of print-oriented colors shown in the swatches on the preceding page.

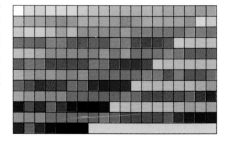

The examples below show how print-oriented colors are typically shifted when viewed in a Web browser.

Photograph in print

Photograph on the Web

Gradient in print

Gradient on the Web

Solid color in print

Solid color on the Web

Copying Colors from an Image

Even if you have an excellent sense of color, matching colors by eye can be difficult. Because you may want to use a color from an image in your document — as a text color or for lines or strokes — an accurate color-matching tool is a necessity. Unfortunately, InDesign doesn't include an eyedropper tool to sample a color and add it to the Swatches pane. However, Adobe Photoshop, Corel Photo-Paint, and other image editors do have such a tool. So use it to sample a color within an image and then define a color in InDesign with identical values. Remember to sample the image in the color model you'll use to define the color in InDesign. If you intend to print using a commercial printing press, you should convert the image to CMYK, then sample its color values, and finally recreate the color in InDesign using CMYK values.

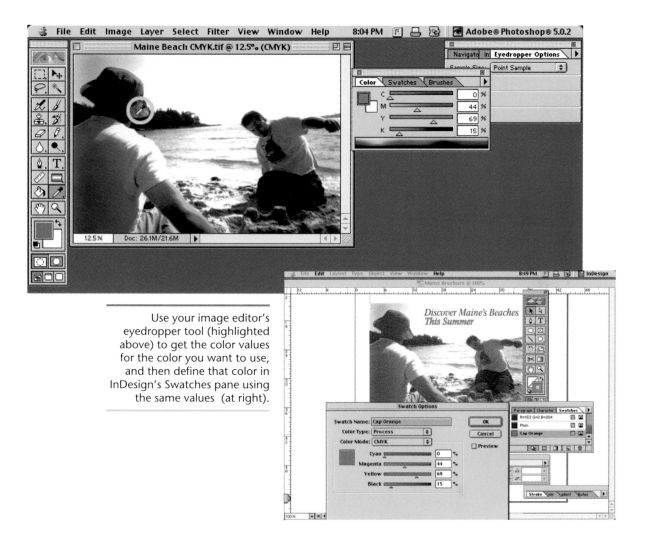

Use your image editor's eyedropper tool (highlighted above) to get the color values for the color you want to use, and then define that color in InDesign's Swatches pane using the same values (at right).

Applying Color Tints

Adding color to an image, whether at full strength or as a lighter tint, can greatly change its character. The examples here show how you can apply color to object to give your grayscale images a new look. To do more-complex colorizing, use an image editor like Adobe Photoshop or Corel Photo-Paint.

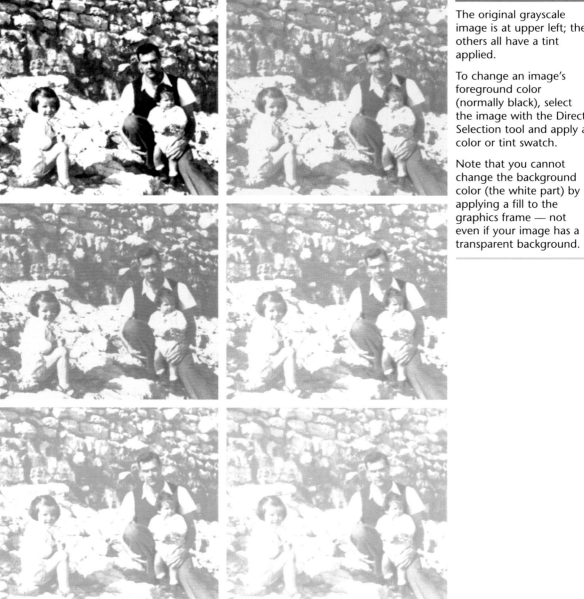

The original grayscale image is at upper left; the others all have a tint applied.

To change an image's foreground color (normally black), select the image with the Direct Selection tool and apply a color or tint swatch.

Note that you cannot change the background color (the white part) by applying a fill to the graphics frame — not even if your image has a transparent background.

Working with Gradients

Gradients (also called blends) add a sense of motion or depth to a background or image. An image editor or illustration program such as Photoshop, Photo-Paint, Illustrator, or CorelDraw gives you very ﬁne control over gradients, letting you control their shape and pattern. InDesign approaches the ability of such programs, and in some cases surpasses them.

Two-color linear gradient **Two-color radial gradient**

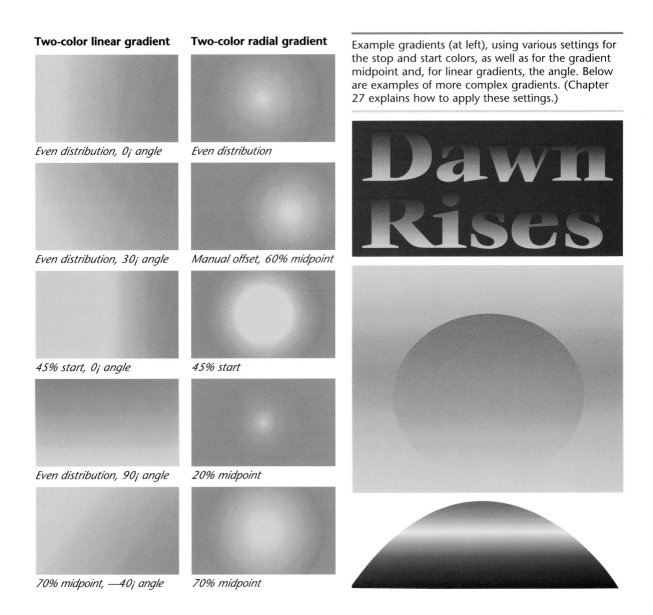

Even distribution, 0¡ angle *Even distribution*

Example gradients (at left), using various settings for the stop and start colors, as well as for the gradient midpoint and, for linear gradients, the angle. Below are examples of more complex gradients. (Chapter 27 explains how to apply these settings.)

Even distribution, 30¡ angle *Manual offset, 60% midpoint*

45% start, 0¡ angle *45% start*

Even distribution, 90¡ angle *20% midpoint*

70% midpoint, —40¡ angle *70% midpoint*

The Effects of Color Profiles

Like most professional design tools, InDesign uses color profiles to help ensure that your output will match as closely as possible the original image's colors (the capabilities and limits of your output device ultimately determine how close you can get). By applying color profiles and using InDesign's Rendering Intent color settings, you can change the output character of your images.

Compare the original image against the modified insets. The original uses the Generic CMYK color profile and is set with a Rendering Intent of Perceptual (Images), the default for photograph-like images.

In the top row, the insets all use the Generic CMYK profile but different Rendering Intent settings: from left to right, Saturation (Graphics), Relative Colorimetric, and Absolute Colorimetric.

The remainder of the inset images use the Rendering Intent setting of Perceptual (Images), but different profiles. In the second row, we applied the three Kodak SWOP Proofer CMYL profiles: from left to right, Coated, Uncoated, and Newspaper.

Finally, we applied the Color LW 12/600 PS profile (for an Apple color laser printer) in the third row and the 3M Color Matchprint Euro profile to the inset image in the final row.

Working with Traps

If you don't have your InDesign documents output to negatives or directly to plate and have them printed on a standard web offset press (SWOP), you don't need to worry about trapping. But if you do such professional output, trapping is an issue you should be aware of. InDesign lets you control trapping in some situations, based on what kind of output device you are using. These controls are global — affecting everything in the document — so if you want to set specific trapping settings for graphics, for example, you'll need to do so as part of creating the illustration in a program like Illustrator or CorelDraw. The one local control InDesign does offer is whether strokes and fills overprint or traps.

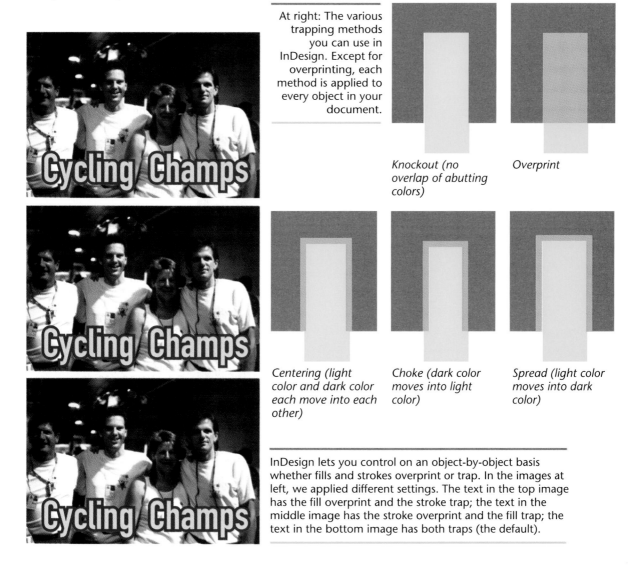

At right: The various trapping methods you can use in InDesign. Except for overprinting, each method is applied to every object in your document.

Knockout (no overlap of abutting colors)

Overprint

Centering (light color and dark color each move into each other)

Choke (dark color moves into light color)

Spread (light color moves into dark color)

InDesign lets you control on an object-by-object basis whether fills and strokes overprint or trap. In the images at left, we applied different settings. The text in the top image has the fill overprint and the stroke trap; the text in the middle image has the stroke overprint and the fill trap; the text in the bottom image has both traps (the default).

Working with Clipping Paths

InDesign can import clipping paths — (invisible outlines) — in images created in such programs as Photoshop. It can also create clipping paths from images placed in InDesign. However they are generated, the clipping paths become InDesign frame boundaries. Using clipping paths, you can create close-fitting text wraps or create masks in images through which other objects can appear.

At top left is a picture imported with the clipping path ignored, while at top right is the same image with the path enabled. That let us put a gradient in the frame behind it to create a new background.

The set of bottom images is similar, except that in this case we created a clipping path that excluded the soccer ball so we could colorize it in InDesign by having a colored frame behind it.

InDesign can also create its own clipping paths by ignoring image areas that have less than a certain hue (see Chapter 23). This is less exact than in a program like Photoshop where you can specify the actual path, but it does work for simpler images.

Drawing Fundamentals

For many years, drawing was something you did in an illustration program separate from your page-layout work. But slowly, page-layout programs have incorporated drawing tools, and InDesign is no exception. Although you'll still rely on an Adobe Illustrator, CorelDraw, or Macromedia FreeHand for creating your artwork, you can use the tools in InDesign to create a variety of shapes that you can use as original artwork or as specialty containers for text and images.

InDesign's Pen tool uses a technique called Bézier curves that is both powerful and complex. **Chapter 24** shows you how to use the Pen tool and its several methods of creating lines, curves, and shapes.

Whether you create a shape yourself or are working with an existing object — whether created in InDesign, imported from Illustrator or Photoshop as the frame of a graphic, or created from an imported image using InDesign's clipping-path function — chances are that you'll want to edit the shape. You might want to fine-tune the shape, make it simpler, or adjust boundaries for a more pleasing text wrap. With InDesign's shape-modification tools, you can do all this and more. **Chapter 25** explains how.

Some of the more complex graphics just can't be easily drawn as one object. That's where compound paths come in — they let you merge several objects to create a new object from them. **Chapter 26** shows you how to use InDesign's compound-path features to create a new level of drawing or frame in your documents.

Drawing Free-Form Shapes and Curved Paths

InDesign's basic drawing tools let you create basic shapes, such as straight lines, rectangles and squares, circles and ellipses, and equilateral polygons. But what about when you need to create shapes that aren't so basic? An amoeba, perhaps, or a cursive version of your first name? That's where InDesign's Pen tool comes in. You can use the Pen tool to create any kind of line or closed shape. And anything you create with the Pen tool can be used as an independent graphic element or as a frame for text or a picture.

If you've ever used an illustration program such as Illustrator, FreeHand, or CorelDraw, or a page layout program such as PageMaker or QuarkXPress 4, you may already be familiar with Bézier drawing tools. (Bézier tools are named after Pierre Bézier, a French engineer and mathematician, who developed a method of representing curved shapes on a computer in the 1970s.) If you aren't familiar with Bézier tools, you should know in advance that getting the hang of using them takes a little time and patience. Even if you're a virtuoso when drawing with a piece of charcoal or a Number 2 pencil, you'll need to practice with the Pen tool for a while before your drawing skills will kick in. The good news is that once you get comfortable using the Pen tool, you can draw any shape you can imagine. (Of course, if you can't draw very well in the first place, using the Pen tool won't magically transform you into an illustrator!) If this is new terrain for you, start simply and proceed slowly.

Tip   If you intend to use InDesign extensively as a drawing tool, you might want to consider purchasing a drawing tablet, which can make working with the Pen tool a bit easier than using a mouse or trackball.

All about Paths

Every object you create with InDesign's object-creation tools is a path. This includes:

✦ Straight lines created with the Line tool

✦ Basic shapes created with the Ellipse, Rectangle, and Polygon tools

✦ Basic frames created with the Ellipse Frame, Rectangle Frame, and Polygon Frame tools

✦ Lines and shapes created with the Pen tool

All of InDesign's object-manipulation features are available for all paths. This includes the transformation tools and the Transform pane, the Stroke and Color panes, and—except for straight lines—the option to place a text file or graphics file within the path.

Properties of a path

Regardless of the tool you use to create a path, you can change its appearance by modifying any of four properties that all paths share: closure, stroke, fill, and contents.

Closure

A path is either *open* or *closed*. Straight lines created with the Line tool and curved and zigzag lines created with the Pen tool are examples of open paths. Basic shapes created with the Ellipse, Rectangle, and Polygon tools and free-form shapes created with the Pen tool are examples of closed shapes. A closed free-form shape is an uninterrupted path with no endpoints. Figure 24-1 shows the difference between open and closed paths.

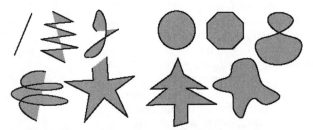

Figure 24-1: The five paths on the left are open; the five on the right are closed. A stroke and fill have been added to show how they affect open and closed paths.

Tip You can use the Scissors tool to convert a closed path into two (or more) open paths, and you can use the Pen tool to create a closed path from an open path. (See Chapter 25 for more information about creating a closed path from an open path and vice versa.)

Stroke

If you want to make a path visible, you can apply a *stroke* to it. (An unselected, unstroked path is not visible.) When you stroke a path, you can specify the stroke's width, color, tint, and style. Figure 24-2 shows a path before and after a stroke was added.

Figure 24-2: The original path (left) is selected. At right, a 2-point stroke has been added to a clone of the original path.

Fill

A color, color tint, or gradient applied to the background of an open path or a closed path is called a *fill*. Figure 24-3 shows some examples of fills.

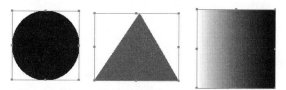

Figure 24-3: From left to right: a color fill (black), a color tint fill (50 percent black), and a gradient fill. The paths are selected and displayed in their bounding boxes.

Contents

You can place a text file or a graphics file in any path (with the exception of a straight line). When a path is used to hold text or a picture, the path functions as a *frame*. For users of other page-layout programs (specifically, QuarkXPress), the idea of placing text and pictures in lines (that is, in open paths), may seem strange at first. (In QuarkXPress lines cannot contain text or pictures.) Placing text and pictures in closed paths is far more common than placing them in open paths. Figure 24-4 shows some examples of pictures and text placed in open and closed paths.

Figure 24-4: Top: The same picture was imported into three different paths. (A stroke has been added to the paths to make them more visible.) Bottom: Text has been placed in clones of the paths on the top row.

The anatomy of a path

No matter how simple (a short, straight line) or complicated (a free-form shape with several straight and curved edges) a path is, all paths are made up of the same components. Figures 24-5 through 24-7 show the parts that make up a path, described as follows:

✦ A path contains one or more straight or curved *segments*, as shown in Figure 24-5.

Figure 24-5: From left to right, each path contains one more segment than the previous path. The two right-most paths each contain three segments.

✦ An *anchor point* is located at each end of every segment. The anchor points at the ends of a closed path are called *endpoints*. When you create a path of any kind, anchor points are automatically placed at the end of each segment. After you create a path, you can move, add, delete, and change the direction of anchor points.

Cross-Reference

See Chapter 25 for more information about modifying paths.

✦ Two kinds of anchor points exist: *smooth points* and *corner points*. A smooth point connects two adjoining curved segments in a continuous, flowing curve. At a corner point, adjoining segments — straight or curved — meet at an angle. The corners of a rectangular path are the most common corner points. Figure 24-6 shows some examples of smooth and corner points.

Figure 24-6: The path on the left has only corner anchor points; the path in the center has only smooth anchor points; and the path on the right has both kinds of anchor points.

✦ A *direction line* runs through each anchor point and has a handle at both ends. You can control the curve that passes through an anchor point by dragging a direction line's handles. Figure 24-7 shows how you can change the shape of a path by dragging a direction line handle.

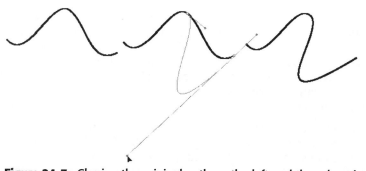

Figure 24-7: Cloning the original path on the left and then dragging the direction handle of the right endpoint created the path on the right.

Note

Anchor points and direction lines do not print.

Drawing Lines with the Pen Tool

Reading about riding a bike is one thing. Riding a bike is another. If you've read Chapter 5, you already know how to ride with training wheels — you can create basic shapes with the basic object-creation tools. Now that you know more about what paths are made of, you're ready to tackle more complex shapes. You're ready to wield the Pen tool.

The Pen tool is very versatile. With it you can create lines (open paths) and shapes (closed paths).

Straight and zigzag lines

The simplest kind of path is a straight line (that is, an open path) with a single segment, which you can create with either the Line tool (which is explained in Chapter 5) or the Pen tool. But the Pen tool is much mightier than the Line tool because it lets you draw zigzag lines with multiple straight segments, curvy lines, and lines that contain straight and curved segments. You can't draw those kinds of shapes with the Line tool, or any of the other object-creation tools, for that matter.

Steps: Drawing Lines with Straight Segments

1. Select the Pen tool or press P if the Type tool isn't selected.

2. Move the Pen pointer to where you want to place one of your line's endpoints, and then click and release the mouse button (make sure you don't drag before you release the mouse button). When you click and release the mouse button while using the Pen tool, you create a corner point. A small, filled-in square indicates the anchor point, which is also an endpoint of the open shape you're creating.

3. Move the Pen pointer to where you want to place the next anchor point, and then click and release the mouse button. When you create the second point, a straight line connects it with the first point, the first anchor point changes to a hollow square, and the second anchor point is filled in. (If you want to create a line with a single segment, you can stop drawing at this point by choosing another tool.)

4. For each additional anchor point, move the Pen pointer, and then click and release the mouse button. If you hold down the Shift key as you click, the angles you create are limited to multiples of 45 degrees. To reposition an anchor point after you click the mouse button but before you release it, hold down the spacebar and drag. (Be careful, if you drag before you press the spacebar, you'll create a smooth point and curved segments.)

5. To complete the path, hold down the ⌘ key or the Ctrl key and click an empty portion of the page or choose another tool. If you click the page, the Pen tool remains selected and you can continue creating additional paths. Figure 24-8 shows a path in various stages of being drawn.

Figure 24-8: As each anchor point was created (from left to right), a new, straight segment was added to the path. The finished open path is a zigzag line that contains four straight segments produced by clicking and releasing the mouse a total of five times.

You can also complete the path by clicking the first point you created, but it you do, you'll create a closed path (closed paths are covered at the end of this chapter).

Tip As you create a path, you can move any anchor point, direction line handle, or the entire path by holding down the ⌘ or Ctrl key, and then clicking and dragging whatever element you want to move.

Curved lines

If all you ever need to create are zigzag lines with corner points and straight segments, the preceding click-and-release method is all you need to know. But if you want to create curvy lines, you need to take the next step up the Bézier ladder and learn to add smooth points. Creating smooth points and curved segments is much like creating corner points and straight segments — with a twist. You have two ways of connecting curved segments when drawing a path: with smooth points and with corner points. The following steps demonstrate both methods.

Curved segments connected by smooth points

If you want to draw a continuously curvy path that contains no corner points and no straight segments, you should create only smooth points as you draw. Here's how:

Steps: Drawing Lines with Curved Segments and Smooth Points

1. Select the Pen tool or press P if the Type tool isn't selected.

2. Move the Pen pointer to where you want to place one of your line's endpoints, and then click and hold down the mouse button. The arrowhead pointer is displayed.

3. Drag the mouse button in the direction of the next point you intend to create. (Adobe suggests dragging about one-third of the way to the next point.) As you drag, the anchor point, its direction line, and the direction line's two handles are displayed, as shown in Figure 24-9. If you hold down the Shift key as you drag, the angle of the direction line is limited to increments of 45 degrees.

Figure 24-9: To create a smooth point when beginning a path, click and hold the mouse and drag in the direction of the next point. Here you see the direction line of a smooth endpoint created by clicking and dragging in the direction of the next anchor point.

4. Release the mouse button.

5. Move the Pen pointer where you want to establish the next anchor point — and end the first segment — and then drag the mouse. If you drag in approximately the same direction as the direction line of the previous point, you'll create an S-shaped curve; if you drag in the opposite direction, you'll create a C-shaped curve. Figure 24-10 shows both kinds of curves.

Figure 24-10: An S-shaped curved segment (left) and a C-shaped curved segment (right).

6. When the curve between the two anchor points looks how you want it to look, release the mouse button.

7. Continue moving the Pen pointer, clicking, dragging, and then releasing the mouse button to establish additional smooth points and curved segments.

8. To complete the path, hold down the ⌘ or Ctrl key and click an empty portion of the page or choose another tool. If you click the page, the Pen tool remains selected and you can continue creating additional paths.

You can also complete the path by clicking the first point you created, but it you do, you'll create a closed path (closed paths are covered at the end of this chapter). Figure 24-11 shows a finished line that contains several curved segments.

Figure 24-11: This line contains five anchor points — all smooth points — and four curved segments. The two segments on the left are both C-shaped curves; the two on the right are S-shaped.

Tip

The two segments that form a smooth point's direction line work together as a single, straight line. When you move a handle, the line acts like a teeter-totter; the opposite handle moves in the opposite direction. If you shorten one of the segments, the length of the other segment doesn't change. The angle and length of direction lines determine the shape of the segments with which they're associated.

Curved segments connected by corner points

Sometimes you may need to create a line with curvy segments that don't adjoin smoothly. Figure 24-12 shows an example of a line that's made up of several C-shaped curves that are connected with corner points. When adjoining segments — curved or straight — meet at a corner point, the transition is abrupt rather than smooth, as it is at a smooth point. To create this kind of shape, you need to be able to connect curved segments using corner points instead of smooth points.

Figure 24-12: Here, three corner points join four curved segments. The direction handles of the two right-most segments are visible. The direction handles of a corner point are joined like a hinge; moving one handle doesn't affect the other handle.

Steps: Drawing Lines with Curved Segments and Corner Points

1. Select the Pen tool or press P if the Type tool isn't selected.

2. Move the Pen pointer to where you want to place one of your line's endpoints, and then click and hold down the mouse button. The arrowhead pointer is displayed.

3. Drag the mouse button in the direction of the next point you intend to create. As you drag, the anchor point, its direction line, and the direction line's two handles are displayed. If you hold down the Shift key as you drag, the angle of the direction line is limited to increments of 45 degrees.

4. Move the Pen pointer to where you want to establish the next anchor point — and end the first segment — and then press Option or Alt and drag the mouse. As you drag, the anchor point's handle moves and the direction line changes from a straight line to two independent segments. The angle of the direction line segment that you create when you drag the handle determines the slope of the next segment.

5. Release the mouse button.

6. Continue moving the Pen pointer and repeat Steps 4 and 5 to add segments joined by corner points.

7. To complete the path, hold down the ⌘ or Ctrl key and click an empty portion of the page or choose another tool. If you click the page, the Pen tool remains selected and you can continue creating additional paths.

Note

A corner point that connects two curved segments has two direction lines; a corner point that connects two straight segments has no direction lines; and a corner point that connects a straight and curved segment has one direction line. If you drag a corner point's direction line, the other direction line, if there is one, is not affected. The angle and length of direction lines determine the shape of the segments with which they're associated.

Combining straight and curved segments

By combining the techniques for drawing straight segments and curved segments, you can create lines that contain both. Figure 24-13 shows three lines made up of straight and curved segments, as well as curved segments joined by smooth points and curved segments joined by corner points.

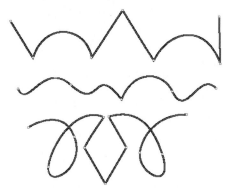

Figure 24-13: Here you see three paths with both curved and straight segments, as well as corner points and smooth points.

Steps: Drawing a Straight Segment Followed by a Curved Segment

1. While drawing a path, create a straight segment by clicking and releasing the mouse button, moving the Pen pointer, and then clicking and releasing the mouse button again.

2. Move the Pen pointer over the last anchor point you created in Step 1. The Convert-Point icon is displayed.

3. Click, drag, and then release the mouse button to create the direction line that determines the slope of the next segment.

4. Move the Pen pointer to where you want to establish the next anchor point, and then click and drag to complete the curved segment.

Figure 24-14 shows a step-by-step sequence of a curved segment being added to a straight segment. You can also follow a straight segment with a curved segment by simply clicking and dragging to create a smooth point. However, if you don't use the method explained previously, you'll be able to adjust the slope associated with only one of the curved segment's anchor points rather than both.

Move the pointer over the end point, and click and drag to establish the curve of the next segment.

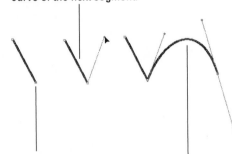

Figure 24-14: At left is a straight segment. In the center, one of the direction lines of the straight segment's endpoint is being dragged. At right, clicking and dragging creates a smooth anchor point, and a C-Shaped curve is added after the straight segment.

Draw a straight segment.

Move the pointer where you want to place the next anchor point, then click and drag to create a curved segment.

Steps: Drawing a Curved Segment Followed by a Straight Segment

1. While drawing a path, create a curved segment by clicking, dragging, and then releasing the mouse button, and then moving the Pen pointer, clicking, dragging, and releasing the mouse button again.

2. Move the Pen pointer over the last anchor point you created in Step 1. The Convert-point icon is displayed.

3. Click the anchor point to convert it from a smooth point to a corner point.

4. Move the Pen pointer to where you want to establish the next anchor point, and then click and release the mouse button to complete the straight segment.

Figure 24-15 shows a straight segment being added to a curved segment.

Tip   When creating paths, you should use as few anchor points as possible. As you become more comfortable creating free-form paths, you should find yourself using fewer anchor points to create paths.

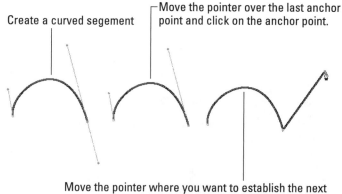

Create a curved segement

Move the pointer over the last anchor point and click on the anchor point.

Move the pointer where you want to establish the next anchor point, then click and release the mouse button.

Figure 24-15: At left is a curved segment. In the center, the curved segment's smooth endpoint has been changed to a corner point. At right, clicking and releasing the mouse creates a new corner anchor point, and a curved segment is added to the straight segment.

Drawing Free-Form Shapes with the Pen Tool

A closed path is an uninterrupted enclosure with no endpoints. When you apply a stroke to a closed path, there's no beginning or end. Generally, you'll create closed paths when you want to place text or pictures in free-form frames. Although you can place text or a picture in an open path, the result can look more than a little strange, especially if you add a stroke to the path. Then again, you can achieve some strange effects by using open paths as frames. If strange is your goal, go for it.

When it comes to creating closed paths with the Pen tool, the process is exactly the same as for creating open paths, as explained earlier in this chapter, with one difference at the end: If you click the first endpoint you created, you create a closed path:

✦ To create a straight segment between the endpoint and the last anchor point you created, click and release the mouse button.

✦ To create a curved segment, click and drag the mouse in the direction of the last anchor point you created, and then release the mouse button.

Just like an open path, a closed path can contain straight and/or curved segments and smooth and/or corner points. All the techniques explained earlier in this chapter for drawing lines with curved and straight segments and smooth and corner points apply when you're drawing closed paths. Figure 24-16 shows several closed paths used as graphic shapes, text frames, and graphics frames.

Figure 24-16: Paths of various shapes.

Cross-Reference

If you draw a path and it turns out to be a little (or a lot, for that matter) different from what you intended, don't worry. You can always modify it by moving, adding, deleting, and converting anchor points and by adjusting direction lines. See Chapter 25 for information about modifying lines and shapes. You can also use the transformation tools or the Transform pane to rotate, scale, shear, mirror, and change the position of the path. See Chapter 6 for more information about using InDesign's transformation features.

Summary

If you need to create free-form paths — zigzag or curvy lines or complex closed shapes — you must use the Pen tool. All paths are made up of one or more segments, which begin and end in anchor points. Direction lines control the behavior or anchor points, which in turn control the transition between adjoining segments. When you create an open or closed path using the Pen tool, you have the option to create straight segments or curved segments and corner points or smooth points.

✦   ✦   ✦

Modifying Shapes and Paths

CHAPTER

25

No matter how skillful you become using InDesign's Pen tool to create freeform paths, it's difficult to create exactly what you want on your first attempt. For example, after creating a path, you may want to add detail, smooth out a rough spot, or turn a straight segment into a curved one. No problem. InDesign lets you modify the paths you create in several ways. You can:

+ Add or delete anchor points

+ Move anchor points

+ Change corner points to smooth points and vice versa

+ Modify direction lines

+ Extend an open path

+ Change a closed path to an open path and vice versa

Note The path-manipulation techniques explained in this chapter apply to all types of paths, including open and closed paths created with the Pen tool and the object-creation tools, text and picture frames (which are simply paths that act as containers), clipping paths created with the Clipping Path command (Object ⇨ Clipping Path) or built into imported pictures, and text wrap paths created with the Text Wrap pane (Object ⇨ Text Wrap).

Generally, when you want to manipulate a path, you'll use one of the three variations of the Pen tool, all of which are displayed in a single pop-up menu in the Toolbox (shown in Figure 25-1):

✦ Both the Add Anchor Point tool and the Delete Anchor Point tool let you add and delete anchor points.

✦ The Convert Direction Point tool lets you change smooth points to corner points and vice versa.

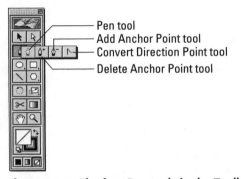

Pen tool
Add Anchor Point tool
Convert Direction Point tool
Delete Anchor Point tool

Figure 25-1: The four Pen tools in the Toolbox.

You can also use the Pen tool with keyboard shortcuts to perform all the functions of the Add Anchor Point, Delete Anchor Point, and Convert Direction Point tools.

Adding and Deleting Anchor Points

If you want to add detail to an existing path, you'll need to add anchor points that give you more precise control over a portion of the path. Perhaps you've drawn the profile of a face and you want to add detail to the lips. Or maybe you've written your name longhand and you need to add a flourish that your original attempt lacks. In both cases, you could add smooth or corner points and then manipulate the curves associated with those points by moving them or manipulating their direction lines. (The next section explains how to move anchor points and manipulate direction lines.)

On the other hand, maybe you've created a path that's more complicated than necessary. Perhaps you drew a hand with six fingers instead of five or a camel with one too many humps. In these instances, you need to simplify the path by removing anchor points. InDesign lets you add and delete as many anchor points as you want.

Tip   You should always try to use as few anchor points as possible in the paths you create. The fewer points a path has, the less likely it is to cause printing problems.

Note

When you want to modify the shape of a path, you should begin by selecting it with the Direct Selection tool rather than the Selection tool. If you select a path with the Selection tool, the path's bounding box is displayed with eight movable handles. In this situation, you can modify the bounding box (thereby resizing the path), but you can't modify the path itself.

Steps: Adding an Anchor Point

1. Select the path by clicking it with the Direct Selection tool. You can also select multiple paths and then modify them one at a time.

2. Select the Pen tool, the Add Anchor Point tool, or the Delete Anchor Point tool. You can use any of these tools to add and delete anchor points. If the Type tool is not selected, you can select the Pen tool by pressing P, the Add Anchor Point tool by pressing = or keypad +, and the Delete Anchor Point tool by pressing - (hyphen) on the main keyboard or on the numeric keypad.

3. Move the Pen pointer over the selected path at the point you want to add an anchor point.

4. Click and release the mouse button. A new anchor point is created where you click. If the Delete Anchor Point tool is selected, you must hold down the ⌘ or Ctrl key to add an anchor point. If you click a straight segment between two corner points, a corner point is created. If you click a curved segment between two smooth points or between a smooth point and a corner point, a smooth point is created. You can also click, drag, and then release the mouse button if you want to adjust the direction line of the point you create. Figure 25-2 shows a before and after example of a path to which a smooth anchor point is added.

Figure 25-2: The original path (left) is modified by adding a smooth point (second from left). Dragging the smooth point (third from left) produced the final shape (right).

After you add an anchor point, you can hold down the ⌘ or Ctrl key or switch to the Direct Selection tool and drag it or either of its direction handles to adjust the adjoining segments.

Tip
Whenever you're working on a path, you can hold down the ⌘ or Ctrl key and then click and drag any element of the path — an anchor point, a direction line, or the entire path.

Steps: Deleting an Anchor Point

1. Select the path by clicking it with the Direct Selection tool. You can also select multiple paths and then modify them one at a time.

2. Select the Pen tool, the Add Anchor Point tool, or the Delete Anchor Point tool. You can use any of these tools to add and delete anchor points. If the Type tool is not selected, you can select the Pen tool by pressing P, the Add Anchor Point tool by pressing = or keypad +, and the Delete Anchor Point tool by pressing - (hyphen) on the main keyboard or on the numeric keypad.

3. Move the pointer over the anchor point that you want to delete, and then click. If the Add Anchor Point tool is selected, you must hold down the ⌘ or Ctrl key to delete an anchor point. Figure 25-3 shows a before and after example of a path from which an anchor point has been deleted.

Figure 25-3: The curved segment of the original path (left) is removed by deleting the smooth anchor point (center) with the Delete Anchor Point tool. The resulting path is shown on the right.

Modifying Segments

In Chapter 24, you learned that a path is made up of one or more segments, and every segment is defined by a pair of anchor points. If you want to modify a segment, you can do so by dragging either or both of its anchor points, dragging the direction handles (if present) of the anchor points, or converting either of the anchor points from smooth to corner or vice versa. For example, you could drag an anchor point on a curvy path to increase or decrease the severity of a particular bump, as shown in Figure 25-4. Or you could convert a straight-edged polygon into a curvy shape by converting all its corner points to smooth points, as shown in Figure 25-5.

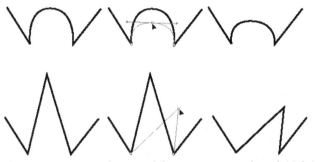

Figure 25-4: Top: The arc of the curve was reduced (right) by clicking and dragging the smooth anchor point at the top of the curve (center). Bottom: Dragging a corner point changes the two adjoining segments.

Figure 25-5: Top: The outer corner points of a straight-edged polygon path (left) were converted to smooth points to create the shape on the right. Bottom: The zigzag path (right) was created by converting all the smooth points in the path on the left into corner points.

Moving anchor points

When you select a path with the Direct Selection tool, its anchor points are displayed as small, hollow squares. When you click and drag an anchor point, the two adjoining segments change, but the direction handles, if present, are not affected. If you hold down the Shift key as you drag an anchor point, movement is restricted to increments of 45 degrees. Figure 25-4 showed how moving an anchor point affects adjoining curved and straight segments.

Tip　If all you need to do is resize a path — particularly a simple rectangle — rather than change its shape, you should select it with the Selection tool rather than the Direct Selection tool, and then drag one of its bounding box handles.

Converting anchor points

If you want to change a wavy path that contains only curved segments to a zigzag path that contains only straight segments, you can do so by converting the smooth anchor points of the wavy path into corner points. Similarly, by converting corner points to smooth points you can smooth out a path that contains straight segments. Figure 25-5 showed how straight and curved paths are affected by converting their anchor points.

Steps: Converting an Anchor Point

1. Select the path by clicking it with the Direct Selection tool.

2. Choose the Convert Direction Point tool. You can also perform the functions of this tool by holding down Option+⌘ or Ctrl+Alt when the Direct Selection tool is selected or by holding down Option or Alt when the Pen tool is selected.

3. Move the pointer over the anchor point you want to convert. Depending on the point you want to convert, do one of the following:

   • To convert a corner point to a smooth point, click the corner point, and then drag (direction lines are created and displayed as you drag).

   • To convert a smooth point to a corner point without direction lines, click and release the mouse on the smooth point.

   • To convert a smooth point to a corner point with independent direction lines, click and drag either of the smooth point's direction handles.

   • To convert a corner point without direction lines to a corner point with direction lines, click and drag the corner point to create a smooth point, and then release the mouse button. Then click and drag either of the direction lines.

Tip　When using the Convert Direction Point tool, you can temporarily switch to the most recently used selection tool by pressing the ⌘ or Ctrl key.

Manipulating direction handles

In addition to dragging and converting anchor points, you can adjust the shape of a curved segment by dragging any of the direction lines associated with the anchor points at either end of the segment. Figure 25-6 shows how moving direction lines affects a curved segment.

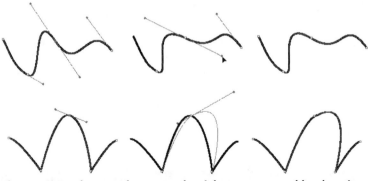

Figure 25-6: The two shapes on the right were created by dragging a direction line of a smooth point.

Note   Remember, corner points between straight segments don't have direction handles. If you want to modify the segments associated with a corner point, simply click and drag the point.

Steps: Dragging a Curved Segment's Direction Handle

1. Use the Direct Selection tool to select the path.

2. Click either of the two endpoints that define the curved segment. Handles are displayed at the ends of the two lines that make up the selected point's direction line (and the lines make up what appears to be a single, straight line). The direction lines of the two adjoining segments (if present) are also displayed.

3. Click and drag any available handle. Hold down the Shift key as you drag to constrain movement to multiples of 45 degrees. As you drag, the handle at the opposite end of the direction line moves in the opposite direction like a teeter-totter. However, if you lengthen or shorten one side of a direction line, the other side is not affected.

4. As you drag, the modified shape is displayed. Release the mouse button when the shape is the way you want it.

Note   If you use the Convert Direction Point tool to click and drag a smooth point's direction line handle, the opposite portion of the direction line remains unchanged. This lets you adjust the segment on one side of a smooth point without affecting the segment on the other side.

Working with Open and Closed Paths

If you've created an open path and subsequently decide that you want to extend the path at either or both ends, you can do so using the Pen tool. Along the same lines, you can use the Pen tool to connect two open paths and to close an open path. For example, if you've placed text or a picture into an open path, you may decide that the path would work better in a closed frame. And if you want to get even trickier, you can use the Scissors tool to split an open or closed path into two separate paths.

Extending an open path and connecting open paths

The steps required to extend an open path and to connect two open paths are very similar. Here's how you extend an open path.

Steps: Extending an Open Path

1. Use the Direct Selection tool to select the path you want to extend.

2. Move the Pen pointer over one of the path's endpoints. When the Pen pointer is over an endpoint, a small, angled line is displayed below and to the right of the Pen.

3. Click and release the mouse button.

4. Move the pointer to where you want to place the next anchor point. If you want to create a corner point, click and release the mouse button. If you want to create a smooth point, click and drag, and then release the mouse button.

5. Continue adding smooth and corner points until you're done extending the path.

6. Finish the path by holding down the ⌘ or Ctrl key and clicking an empty portion of the page or choosing another tool.

To connect two open paths, follow the preceding Steps 1 through 3, and then click the endpoint of another path (the other path doesn't have to be selected). Figure 25-7 shows a path before and after being extended; Figure 25-8 shows an open path produced by connecting two open paths.

Tip   If you hold down the Shift key when you click an endpoint with the Pen tool, an endpoint for a new path is created (that is, the selected path remains unchanged). In this situation, a small *x* is displayed below and to the right of the Pen pointer. This is useful if you want to create two paths that touch at a particular point. For example, you could draw a path and apply a 4-point black stroke to it and then create another path that shares an endpoint with the first path. By adding a different kind of stroke to the second path, the two paths would look like a single path to which two kinds of strokes have been applied.

Figure 25-7: The original path (left) was cloned to create the path on the right. The cloned path was then extended by clicking its right endpoint with the Pen tool and then clicking four more times to create four additional corner points.

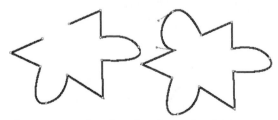

Figure 25-8: Connecting the two open paths on the left with the Pen tool produced the single path on the right.

Closing an open path

Closing an open path is much the same as extending an open path. The only difference is that you complete the path — that is, you close it — by clicking the other endpoint. For example, if you slice a graphics frame into two pieces using the Scissors tool (this is explained in the next section of this chapter), you create two open paths. If you add a stroke to these open frames, a portion of the picture edge (the nonexistent segment between the endpoints) will not be stroked. If you close the path, the stroke will completely enclose the picture within. Figure 25-9 shows an open path that's been converted into a closed path.

![Two star-like shapes, the left one an open path and the right one a closed path]

Figure 25-9: The closed path on the right was created from a clone of the open path on the left.

Using the Scissors tool

The Scissors tool does precisely what its icon suggests: It lets you slice items in two. Specifically, it lets you split paths — open and closed — into two pieces. Here are a few points to remember when using the Scissors tool:

✦ It takes only one click with the Scissors tool to split an open path, but it takes two clicks to completely split a closed path.

✦ You can split graphics frames, but you can't split text frames that contain text. If you want to split a text frame that contains text, you must first cut the text and paste it elsewhere.

✦ If you split a graphics frame, a copy of the picture is placed within both frames.

✦ When you split a path, all stroke and fill attributes of the original path are inherited by the two offspring. After you split a path, it looks the same as before you split it until you move or modify one of the resulting paths.

To split an open path, use the Scissors tool and move the crosshair pointer over a path, and then click and release the mouse button. You can click an open portion of a segment (that is, between anchor points) or on an anchor point. In both cases, two anchor points — endpoints of the two resulting paths — are created.

To split a closed path, use the Scissors tool and move the crosshair pointer over a path, and then click and release the mouse button. You can click an open portion of a segment or on an anchor point. In both cases, two anchor points — endpoints of the two resulting paths — are created. Move the crosshair pointer to a different position along the same path, and then click and release the mouse button.

After you split a path, you can switch to either of the selection tools and then select, move, or modify either of the two resulting paths as you wish. If you've split a closed path, you may want to close the two open paths (as described in the previous section). Figure 25-10 shows a pair of open paths that were created using the Scissors tool on an open path. Figure 25-11 shows a closed picture frame that's been split into two open frames.

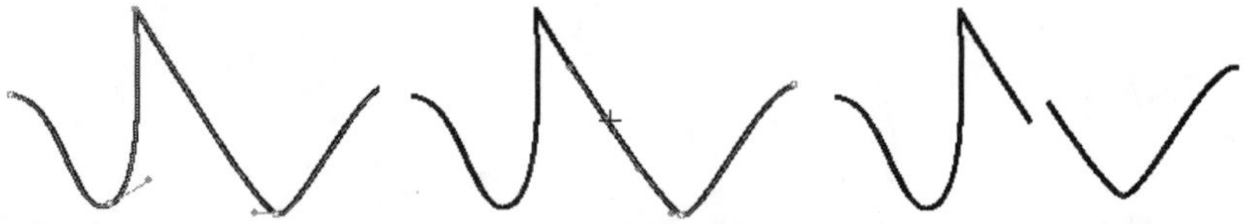

Figure 25-10: The original path (left) was split into two pieces by clicking it with the Scissors tool (center). On the right, you see the two resulting paths after the one on the right has been moved.

Figure 25-11: The closed path on the left was cut twice with the Scissors tool (center). On the right, one of the resulting open paths has been moved with the Selection tool.

Summary

When it comes to drawing with the Pen tool, close is plenty good enough. That's because InDesign lets you modify paths in many ways — by moving, adding, and deleting anchor points, by switching smooth points to corner points and vice versa, and by dragging direction lines. You also have the option to extend either end or both ends of an open path and to close open paths.

If a path requires more drastic surgery, you can use the Scissors tool, which lets you split any kind of path into two pieces.

✦   ✦   ✦

Special Effects for Drawings

InDesign is, first and foremost, a page-layout program. If you need a heavy-duty illustration tool, you're better off using a dedicated illustration program such as Adobe Illustrator, Macromedia FreeHand, or CorelDraw. All of these applications have many more drawing-related features than InDesign. That said, InDesign has a few wrinkles of its own that let you add special effects to paths. You can:

+ Use the Make (Compound Paths) command (Object ⇨ Compound Paths ⇨ Make, or ⌘+8 or Ctrl+8) to combine several paths into a compound path. A compound path, although made up of multiple paths, behaves like a single object.

+ Use the Create Outlines command (Type ⇨ Create Outlines, or Shift+⌘+O or Ctrl+Shift+O) to convert text characters into editable paths.

+ Use the Corner Effects command (Object ⇨ Corner Effects or Option+⌘+R or Ctrl+Alt+R) to add fancy effects to the corner points of any path.

Tip
If you find that you simply can't create a particular graphic effect within InDesign, you can always resort to your illustration program (assuming you have one). If you're an Illustrator user, it's easy to drag and drop objects from Illustrator into InDesign documents (see Chapter 21 for information about dragging and dropping Illustrator objects and files into InDesign documents). For example, InDesign doesn't let you flow text along a path, but Illustrator does. Simply create the text along a path in an Illustrator document, and then drag it directly into an InDesign document window.

Working with Compound Paths

When more than one path is selected, you can use the Make (Compound Path) command (Object ➪ Compound Paths ➪ Make, or ⌘+8 or Ctrl+8) to convert the paths into a single object. A compound path is similar to a group (Object ➪ Group, or Ctrl+G or ⌘+G), except that when you create a group out of several objects, each object in the group retains its original attributes, such as stroke color and width, fill color or gradient, and so on. By contrast, when you create a compound path, the attributes of the back-most path are applied to all the other paths (that is, the attributes of the back-most path replace the attributes of the other paths).

You can use a compound path to produce such results as:

✦ Creating transparent areas within a path. For example, by drawing a circular path in front of a picture, you could then use the Make (Compound Paths) command to "poke a hole" in the picture and reveal the objects or the empty page behind the picture. Figure 26-1 shows a compound path used as a picture frame.

Figure 26-1: We created the picture with the hole in it (right) by drawing a circular path (center) in front of a clone of the original picture frame (left), and then creating a compound path from the picture frame and the circular path. The background shape shows within the transparent hole.

✦ Applying a single background color or placing a single picture within several shapes. For example, you could use the Create Outlines command (Type ➪ Create Outlines, or Shift+⌘+O or Ctrl+Shift+O) to convert text characters into a compound path, and then place a blend behind the path so that it extends across all characters. (The Create Outlines command is explained in the next section.) Figure 26-2 shows an example of this.

Figure 26-2: We converted the text on the top into the editable outlines on the bottom. We then skewed the character outlines — which make up a compound path — by −30 degrees via the Skew field in the Transform pane and applied a gradient fill.

✦ Quickly creating complex shapes that would be difficult to create with the Pen tool. For example, you could create the complex shape in Figure 26-3 by drawing each of the shaded areas as a separate, closed path. Or you could simply create a square, place four circles in front of it so that they overlap the edges of the square, and then choose the Make (Compound Paths) command — a process that takes only a few seconds.

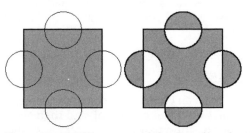

Figure 26-3: We converted the five closed paths on the left into a compound path via the Make (Compound Path) command to create the shape on the right. InDesign automatically applied the attributes of the original square path, which is the back-most path, to the resulting compound path. Notice that the four semicircular areas where the original shapes overlapped became holes after converting the shapes to a compound path.

That's only the beginning of what you can do with the Make (Compound Paths) command. Mix in a little bit of your imagination and InDesign's other path-, picture-, and text-manipulation features and the possibilities become endless.

Creating compound paths

You can create a compound path out of any kinds of paths, including open and closed paths as well as text and graphics frames. When you create a compound path, all the original paths become subpaths of the compound shape and inherit the stroke and fill settings of the path that's farthest back in the stacking order. After you create a compound path, you can modify or remove any of the subpaths.

Tip

If the results of choosing Make (Compound Path) are not what you expected or want, you can undo the operation (Edit ➪ Undo). In this case, try changing the stacking order and then choose Make (Compound Path) again.

Note

The direction of each subpath determines whether the subpath is filled or transparent. If a particular subpath is transparent instead of filled, or vice versa, you can use the Reverse Path command (Object ➪ Reverse Path) to switch the behavior of a subpath. (The Reverse Path command is explained more fully later in this chapter.)

If frames that contain text and/or pictures are selected when you choose Make (Compound Path), the resulting compound path retains the content of the frame that's closest to the bottom of the stacking order. If the bottom-most frame doesn't have any content, the content — text or picture — of the next highest nonempty frame is retained in the compound path. The content of all frames above the frame whose content is retained is removed.

Tip   To change an object's stacking order (to determine which path's attributes are used for the compound path), use Object ⇨ Arrange ⇨ Send to Back, or Shift+⌘+[or Ctrl+Shift+[.

Editing compound paths

After you create a compound path, you can change the shape of any of the subpaths by clicking on one with the Direct Selection tool, and then clicking and dragging any of its anchor points or direction handles. The Pen, Add Anchor Point, Delete Anchor Point, and Change Direction Line tools work the same for subpaths as for other paths, which means that you can reshape them however you want.

Cross-Reference   See Chapter 25 for more information on modifying paths.

The Stroke pane (Window ⇨ Stroke, or F10) and Fill pane (Window ⇨ Color or F6), as well as the transformation tools and the Transform pane (Window ⇨ Transform or F9) also let you change the appearance of a compound path. When you change the appearance of a compound path, the changes are applied uniformly to all subpaths.

Moving a subpath is a little tricky because you can't drag just that subpath. If you try, all the subpaths move. If you want to move an entire subpath, you must move each of the subpath's anchor points individually. In this case, it's probably easier to release the compound path, as described next, move the path as needed, and then recreate the compound path by choosing Make (Object ⇨ Compound Path ⇨ Make, or ⌘+8 or Ctrl+8).

If you want to delete a subpath, you must use the Delete Anchor Point tool to delete all its anchor points. If you delete an anchor point of a closed subpath, it becomes an open subpath.

Note   You can't delete anchor points using the Cut or Clear commands (Edit ⇨ Cut, or ⌘+X or Ctrl+X, or Edit ⇨ Clear) nor the Del or Delete key, all of which remove the entire path.

Changing a subpath's direction

When you create a path, it has a built-in direction—clockwise or counter-clockwise—that is generally not noticeable but affects a compound path. Generally, you can't determine the direction of a path by looking at it. However, you can tell if subpaths' directions differ by how subpaths interact:

✦ If a subpath in a compound path has the same direction as the back-most path, the area within the subpath is transparent.

✦ Conversely, if a subpath's direction is different from the back-most path, the area within the subpath will be filled.

If a subpath is filled in and you want it to be transparent, or vice versa, click the compound path with the Direct Selection tool, and then click one of the anchor points of the subpath whose direction you want to change and choose Object ⇨ Compound Path ⇨ Release, or Option+⌘+8 or Ctrl+Alt+8. Figure 26-4 shows how changing the direction of a subpath changes it from filled to transparent.

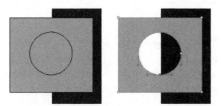

Figure 26-4: The gray square and circle on the left have been combined into a compound path, but the direction of the circular subpath causes it to be filled in instead of transparent. Changing the subpath's direction produced the results on the right: a transparent hole in the square shape.

Splitting a compound path

If you decide you want to "deconstruct" a compound path, you can do so by clicking anywhere within the compound path and then choosing Object ⇨ Compound Paths ⇨ Release, or Option+⌘+8 or Ctrl+Alt+8. The resulting paths retain the attributes of the compound path.

Note   The Release command is not available if the selected compound path contains text or if it's nested within a frame.

Converting Text into Editable Paths

If you want to use the shape of a letter, or the combined shapes of several letters, as a frame for text or a picture, you could test your skill with the Pen tool and create the letter shape(s) yourself. But getting hand-drawn characters to look just the way you want them can take lots of time. A quicker solution is to use the Create Outlines command (Type ➪ Create Outlines, or Shift+⌘+O or Ctrl+Shift+O) to convert text characters into editable outlines. The Create Outlines command is particularly useful if you want to hand-tweak the shapes of characters, particularly at display font sizes, or place text or a picture within character shapes.

You can create outlines from TrueType, OpenType, and PostScript (Type 1) format fonts. When you create outlines of highlighted characters, any hinting information in the font is removed. (*Hinting information* is used to adjust the space between characters, especially at small font sizes.) Therefore, you should adjust the appearance of any characters before you choose Create Outlines.

Note
The character shape information required to create outlines is not available in all fonts. If such information is not available when you choose Create Outlines, InDesign alerts you to this fact.

Tip
If all you need to do is apply a stroke or fill to characters within text, you don't have to convert the characters into outlines. Instead, simply highlight the characters and use the Stroke pane (Window ➪ Stroke or F10) and Color pane (Window ➪ Color or F6) to change their appearance. This way you'll still be able to edit the text.

When you use the Create Outlines command, you have the choice of creating an inline compound path that replaces the original text or an independent compound path that's placed directly on top of the original letters. If you want the text outlines to flow with the surrounding text, create an inline compound path. If you want to use the outlines elsewhere, create an independent compound path.

Steps: Converting Text into Outlines

1. Use the Type tool to highlight the characters you want to convert into outlines. (Generally, this feature works best with relatively large font sizes.)

2. Choose Type ➪ Create Outlines or press Shift+⌘+O or Ctrl+Shift+O. If you hold down the Option or Alt key when you choose Create Outlines or press Shift+Option+⌘+O or Ctrl+Alt+Shift+O, a compound path is created and placed in front of the text. In this case, you can use either of the selection tools to move the resulting compound path. If you don't hold down Option or Alt when you choose Create Outlines, an inline compound path is created. This object replaces the original text and flows with the surrounding text.

Tip If you hold the Option or Alt keys when creating text outlines, the text in the result-ing inline compound path will be editable.

Figure 26-5 shows text outlines created with the Create Outlines command and then modified using the Transform pane.

Figure 26-5: Top: We converted the highlighted characters into an independent compound path by holding down Option or Alt when applying the Make (Compound Path) command. Bottom: After moving the compound path with a selection tool, we placed the angled-line image in the path and added a 2-point stroke.

After you create text outlines, you can modify the paths the same as you can modify hand-drawn paths — by selecting them with the Direct Selection tool and then adding, deleting, or moving anchor points, dragging direction handles, and converting smooth points to corner points and vice versa. You can also use the transformation tools and the Transform pane (Window ➪ Transform or F9) to change the appearance of text outlines. You cannot, however, edit text after converting it to outlines. (See Chapter 6 for information about InDesign's transformation features.)

Additionally, you can use the Place command (File ➪ Place, or ⌘+D or Ctrl+D) to import text or a picture into text outlines. Figure 26-6 shows character outlines used as text and graphics frames.

Figure 26-6: Both character shapes were created with the Create Outlines command. We placed text into the shape on the left, and we placed a picture with a clipping path into the shape on the right and then filled the path with a gray tint.

Tip When you create outlines out of a range of highlighted characters, a compound path is created, and each of the characters becomes a subpath. You can use the Release (Compound Path) command (Object ➪ Compound Path ➪ Release, or Option+⌘+8 or Ctrl+Alt+8) to turn each of the subpaths into independent paths.

Adding Corner Effects to Paths

When a path is selected, the Corner Effects command (Object ⇨ Corner Effects, or Option+⌘+R or Ctrl+Alt+R) lets you apply any of several graphic embellishments to its corner points (if the path has any corner points). For example, you could use a corner effect to add pizzazz to the border of a coupon or a certificate. Generally, corner effects work best with rectangular shapes, but they can also produce interesting results when applied to freeform shapes, as shown in Figure 26-7.

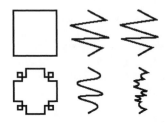

Figure 26-7: The original shapes are on the top row. The bottom row shows the same shapes after applying (from left to right) the Fancy, Rounded, and Inverse Rounded corner effects.

Steps: Applying a Corner Effect to a Path

1. Use either of the selection tools to select the path to which you want to apply corner effects.

2. Choose Object Corner Effects or press Option+⌘+R or Ctrl+Alt+R. The Corner Effects dialog box, shown in Figure 26-8, is displayed.

Figure 26-8: The Effect menu in the Corner Effects dialog box displays the names of five built-in corner effects.

3. Choose a Corner Effect from the Effect pop-up menu. If you want to see the effect as you create it, click Preview and, if necessary, move the dialog box out of the way so you can see the selected path.

4. In the Size field, enter the distance away from the corner point that the effect will extend.

5. After you've finished specifying the appearance of the corner effect, click OK to close the dialog box.

InDesign doesn't let you modify the built-in corner effects or add your own to the list of choices. Nor can you use the Direct Selection tool to modify the corner of a path to which a corner effect has been applied (anchor points are not displayed for the additional segments that are added when a corner effect is applied to a corner point). The only control you have over a corner effect is the value you specify in the Size field of the Corner Effects dialog box.

Summary

Because InDesign is primarily a page-layout program, it doesn't contain the breadth of illustration-specific features that you would find in a dedicated vector-based drawing program. Although you may decide that you need a dedicated illustration program to handle your industrial-strength drawing tasks, InDesign does have several features for creating complex shapes.

For example, the Compound Path command lets you combine several paths into a single object, whereas the Create Outlines command lets you create character-shaped paths from highlighted text. If you want to add a graphic flourish to the corners of a path, the Corner Effects command lets you apply any of several built-in corner styles and specify the size of the corner effect.

✦   ✦   ✦

Color Fundamentals

P A R T

VII

◆ ◆ ◆ ◆

In This Part

Chapter 27
Defining Colors and
Gradients

Chapter 28
Preparing for Color
Prepress

◆ ◆ ◆ ◆

Color is both natural and counterintuitive. We take colors for granted because we see in color as soon as we are born, but color is a difficult attribute to handle in printing.

Fortunately, color is easy to create. InDesign lets you create colors, tints of colors, and even blends of colors, so you'll have plenty of ways to jazz up your document's objects. **Chapter 27** shows you how to create colors in InDesign, as well as work with colors from other documents.

Monitors, paper, inks, printing presses, negatives, our eyes — they all use different physics to produce and recognize color, which means that what we see when we draw or take a picture often doesn't match what we see when we print. **Chapter 28** walks you through InDesign's tools for minimizing these differences and ensuring the best possible color reproduction.

Be sure to check out the eight-page color insert included with this book, as it shows InDesign's color controls in action. On these color pages you see real-world results and can get a feel for how you might take advantage of InDesign's color features.

Defining Colors and Gradients

Although color is most widely used by high-end publishers — people producing magazines and catalogs — color is becoming more accessible to all publishers, thanks to the recent emergence of inexpensive color printers, color copiers, and leading-edge desktop publishing programs. Whether you want to produce limited-run documents on a color printer, create newsletters using spot colors, or publish magazines and catalogs using process colors and special inks, InDesign offers the tools that you need to do the job well.

You can either use color in your graphics or apply colors to text and layout elements (such as bars along the edge of a page). Or you can use color in both ways. To a great extent, where you define and apply color determines what you can do with it.

Note   Chapter 28 covers color matching and other high-end color issues in depth. This chapter concentrates on how to create and apply colors within InDesign.

Defining Colors

InDesign comes with very few predefined colors: black, registration (black on each negative for the printing press), paper (white), and none (transparent). So you'll likely want to add a few of your own.

Before you can apply any colors — whether to bitmap images or to layout elements such as strokes, text, frames, and shapes — you must first define the colors.

Before you can define colors, you have a couple decisions to make first:

✦ Do you want to create your own color by mixing basic colors such as red, green, and blue (called RGB and typically used for screen display), or cyan, yellow, magenta, and black (called CMYK or process colors, and typically used for printing presses)?

✦ Do you want to use a color from an ink maker such as Pantone or Toyo? These colors — called *spot colors* — are typically used as an extra ink on your document, but can also be converted to the standard four colors and so are handy when you'll know the color you want when you see it.

The answers to the preceding questions will tell you where you need to go to create your new color. Figure 27-1 shows the various options all in one place. (Note that this is a composite screen shot — normally, only one submenu or palette menu can be active at one time.) After you create a color, it will be in the Swatches pane, accessible for future use.

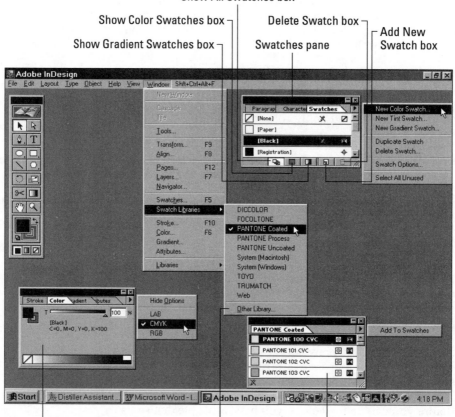

Figure 27-1: The various methods for creating colors: using the Swatches pane, the Color pane, or a spot color swatch library from the Swatch Libraries submenu.

Note If no document is open when you create, edit, or delete colors, the new color palette becomes the default for all future documents.

 InDesign has an Add New Swatch icon at the bottom of the Swatches pane. Avoid it. It simply duplicates the currently selected swatch. That's a hassle if you happen to have selected a gradient swatch and want to create a new color, for example.

Creating mixed colors

To create your own color, go to the Swatches pane (Window ➪ Swatches, or F5) and select New Color Swatch from the palette menu. You'll get the New Color Swatch dialog box shown in Figure 27-2.

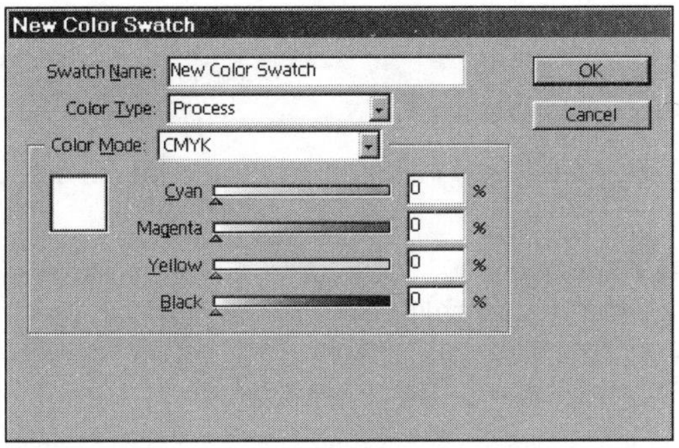

New Color Swatch

Swatch Name: New Color Swatch

Color Type: Process

Color Mode: CMYK

Cyan: 0 %
Magenta: 0 %
Yellow: 0 %
Black: 0 %

OK
Cancel

Figure 27-2: The New Color Swatch dialog box lets you define colors. An identical dialog box named Swatch Options lets you edit them.

Now follow these steps:

1. In the Swatch Name field, give your color a name that describes it, such as Lime Green or Bright Purple.

2. In the Color Type pop-up menu, choose from Process or Spot. (These are covered later in this chapter — leave the color type at Process if you're not sure.)

3. In the Color Mode, choose the mixing system (color model) you will use:

   • **CMYK:** Cyan, magenta, yellow, and black, the colors used in professional printing presses and many color printers.

   • **RGB:** Red, green, and blue, the colors used on a computer monitor, for CD-ROM–based or Web-based documents or for some color printers.

   • **LAB:** Luminosity, *A* axis, *B* axis, a way of defining colors created by the international standards group Comité International d'Éclairage (the CIE, which translates to International Lighting Committee in English).

4. Use the sliders to create your new color. A preview appears in the box at left.

5. Click OK when you're done, or click Cancel to abort the color definition.

Tip

You can give a color any name you want. To make it easier to remember what a defined color looks like, either use descriptive names (such as Grass Green) or use names based on the color settings. For example, if you create a color in the CMYK model, give it a name based on its mix, such as *55C 0M 91Y 0K* for that grass-green color — composed of 55 percent cyan, 0 percent magenta, 91 percent yellow, and 0 percent black. (Believe it or not, this naming convention is how professionals specify colors on paste-up boards.) The same system applies to the RGB, and LAB models. That way, you can look at the Swatches pane and immediately tell what color you'll get.

Design Advice

Because regular black can appear weak when it's overprinted by other colors, many designers create what printers call *superblack* by combining 100 percent black and 100 percent magenta. You can define superblack as a separate color or redefine the registration color as 100 percent of all four process colors, and use that as a superblack.

The Evils of the Color Pane's Colors

Many people will try to use the Colors pane (Window ➪ Color, or F6) to define colors, but that's a mistake.

At first, you may not realize you can create colors from the Color pane. It shows a gradation of the last color used, and lets you change the tint for that color on the current object, as shown here. But if you go to the palette menu and choose a color model (RGB, CMYK, or LAB), you'll get a set of mixing controls, as shown previously in Figure 27-1.

The Color pane lets you change the tint of an existing color applied to a selected object.

So what's the problem? Colors created via the Color pane won't appear in your Swatches pane and so can't be used for other objects. Called unnamed colors because they don't appear anywhere, these can be dangerous for publishers to use. (Adobe added them to InDesign to be consistent with how Illustrator defines colors — a foolish consistency.)

First, you can't modify them later in the Swatches palette if you want to adjust the color for all objects using them.

Second, you can't specify the color to print as a spot color, which you might later decide is how you want to print a particular color. They will print only as process colors, and will not show up in the list of colors in the Color pane of the Print dialog box (see Chapter 33 for more details on this).

Creating spot colors

To add a predefined color to your Swatches pane, use Window ⇨ Swatch Libraries and choose the desired swatch library from the submenu. Here are the color swatch libraries that InDesign comes with:

✦ **DIC (Dainippon Ink & Chemical)** Color, a spot-color model used in Japan.

✦ **Focoltone**, a CMYK-based spot-color model popular in Europe.

✦ **Pantone**, a spot-color model with a range of inks (of which three variants are supplied: one for coated paper, one for uncoated paper, and one for Pantone colors that can be accurately translated to CMYK).

✦ **System**, the native colors to Windows and the Macintosh (there's a separate swatchbook for each platform), used for creating documents to be displayed onscreen.

✦ **Toyo**, a Japanese color model.

✦ **Trumatch**, a CMYK-based set of spot colors designed for accurate color-separation.

✦ **Web**, the colors that will accurately display on a Macintosh or Windows Web browser.

Note
In the Swatch Libraries submenu, several of the swatchbook names are in all uppercase. That's because they're trademarked names, which some people (such as those at Adobe) like to indicate by using all caps. That's just a convention and means nothing per se.

If you have other swatch libraries bought as an add-on to InDesign or Illustrator (they use the same library format), choose Other Libraries and navigate through the resulting dialog box to the location containing that library (this dialog box works like a standard Mac or Windows Open dialog box). Any selected swatch libraries are added to the bottom of the Swatch Libraries submenu.

Oddity
Once you add a swatch library from the Swatch Libraries submenu, you cannot remove it.

Design Advice
Color swatches based on the CMYK colors — such as Focoltone, Pantone Process, and Trumatch — will accurately color-separate and thus print accurately on a printing press, because a printing press uses the CMYK colors. Other swatches' colors often do not color-separate accurately because they are supposed to represent special inks that may have elements such as metals and clays designed to give metallic or pastel appearances that simply can't be replicated by combining cyan, magenta, yellow, and black. Similarly, some colors (such as several hues of orange and green) can't be accurately created using the CMYK colors.

Understanding Pantone Variants

The most popular swatchbooks used by professional publishers are those from Pantone, whose Pantone Matching System (PMS) is the de facto standard for most publishers in specifying spot-color inks. The Pantone swatchbooks come in several variations, of which InDesign includes three:

✦ **Pantone Coated:** Use this when your printer will use actual Pantone inks (as spot colors) when printing to coated paper stock. Colors in this variant will have the code CV (Computer Video) appended to their names.

✦ **Pantone Uncoated:** This is the same as Pantone Coated but for uncoated paper. Colors in this variant will have the code CVU (Computer Video Uncoated) appended to their names.

✦ **Pantone Process:** Use this when you color-separate Pantone colors and your printer uses the standard Pantone-brand process-color inks. (These colors will reproduce reliably when color-separated, whereas the other Pantone swatchbooks' colors often will not.) Colors in this variant will have the code S (SWOP, or standard web offset printing) prefixed to their names.

Both PageMaker 6.5 and QuarkXPress support more Pantone color swatches—such as metallics and pastels in PageMaker 6.5 and Hexachrome in QuarkXPress. Let's hope that someone will make such swatch libraries available to InDesign users as well.

When printing on uncoated paper stock with any colors designed for use on coated stock (which is glossier and shinier), you will usually get weaker, less-saturated color reproduction. That's because the colors designed for uncoated stock are a little richer to make up for the fact that some of the ink gets absorbed into the paper. In coated stock, much less absorption occurs because the coating acts as a barrier.

Once you select a swatch library, InDesign creates a pane for it. Scroll through the list of colors and double-click the ones you want to add to the Swatches pane. (You can also use the palette menu's Add to Swatches command, but double-clicking is easier.)

Tip
For swatch libraries that you use a lot, drag them into the palette containing the Swatches pane. In fact, you might want to have a palette just for color-related panes: Swatches, any swatch libraries, Color, and Gradient.

Creating tints

A tint is a shade of a color. InDesign lets you create such tints as separate color swatches, so they're easy to use for multiple items. The process is easy:

1. In the Swatches pane, just select a color you want to create a tint from.

2. Using the palette menu, select New Tint Swatch. You'll get the New Tint Swatch dialog box shown in Figure 27-3.

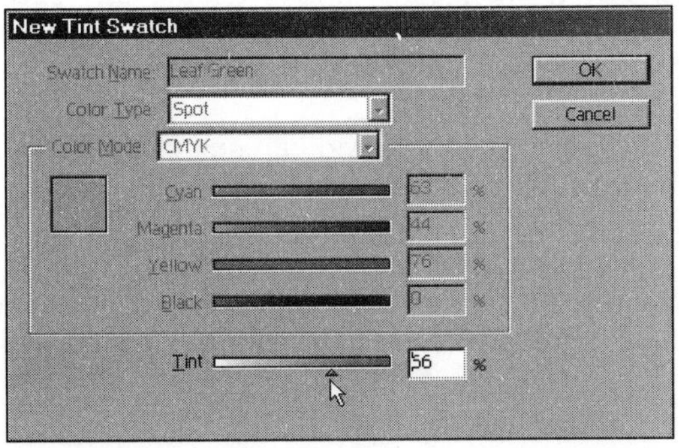

Figure 27-3: The New Tint Swatch dialog box lets you define colors. A nearly identical dialog box named Swatch Options lets you edit them — the difference is that, when editing, you can change all the other color values, not just the degree of tint.

3. Use the slider to adjust the tint, or enter a value in the field at right.

4. Click OK to save, Cancel to abort. Any new tint will have the same name as the original color and the percentage of shading, such as Leaf Green 66%.

Note   You can create a tint from a tint, which can be confusing. Fortunately, InDesign goes back to the original color when letting you create the new tint. Thus, if you select Leaf Green 66% and move the slider to 33 percent, you'll get a 33 percent tint of the original Leaf Green, not a 33 percent tint of the Leaf Green 66% (which would be equivalent to a 22 percent tint of the original Leaf Green).

Editing Colors and Tints

Editing colors is pretty easy in InDesign: For any color in the Swatches pane, just double-click the color or its name, and the Swatch Options dialog box (shown previously in Figure 27-2) appears. Make any adjustments and click OK when done. Voilà! Your color is now changed.

Similarly, if you double-click a tint swatch, you get the Swatch Options dialog box, which lets you change the tint percentage.

Caution   When editing a tint, the Swatch Options dialog box also lets you change other attributes of the color. It's key to remember that if you change those settings in the tint, all other tints based on the original color, as well as the original color, are changed accordingly. If you want to change a setting of just the tint — such as making it a spot color while leaving the original color a process color — you need to duplicate the original color and make a tint from that duplicate.

In addition to double-clicking a swatch to edit it, you can select Swatch Options from the palette menu, but why bother?

To help work with swatches, you can have InDesign show just color and tint swatches, just gradient swatches, or all swatches by using the icons at the bottom of the Swatches pane. Figure 27-1, shown earlier in the chapter, illustrates which icon does what.

Deleting and Copying Swatches

When you create colors, tints, and gradients (described later in this chapter), you'll find it easy to go overboard and make too many. You'll also find that different documents have different colors, each created by different people, and you'll likely want to move colors from one document to another. InDesign provides basic tools for managing colors in and across documents.

Note   Remember that when selecting swatches for deletion of duplication, you can ⌘+click or Ctrl+click multiple swatches to work on all at once. Note that Shift+clicking selects all swatches between the first swatch clicked and the swatch that you Shift+click, whereas ⌘+click or Ctrl+click lets you select specific swatches in any order and in any location in the pane.

Deleting swatches

InDesign makes it easy to delete swatches: Just select the color, tint, or gradient in the Swatches pane. Then choose Delete Swatch from the palette menu, or click the trash can icon (the Delete Swatch box) at the bottom of the Swatches pane.

Well, that's not quite it. You'll then get the dialog box shown in Figure 27-4, which lets you assign anything using the deleted swatch to a new color (the Defined Swatch option) or leave the color on any object that happens to be using it but delete the swatch from the Swatches pane (the Unnamed Swatch option). Remember: As explained in the sidebar "The Evils of the Color Pane's Colors," unnamed colors should be avoided, so if your document is using a color, keep its swatch.

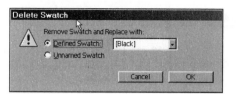

Figure 27-4: The Delete Swatch dialog box ets you replace a deleted color with a new one, or leave the color applied to objects using it.

You get the dialog box shown in Figure 27-4 regardless of whether anything is using the swatch you are deleting, so you have no way of immediately determining whether you need to keep it. A better way to delete unused colors is by using the Select All Unused option in the Swatches pane's palette menu.

If you delete a tint and have it replaced with another color, any object using that tint will get the full-strength version of the new color, not a tint of it.

InDesign offers a nice option to quickly find all unused colors in the Swatches pane: the palette menu's Select All Unused option. Then you can just delete them in one fell swoop. Note that you don't get the option to assign each deleted color separately to another color in the Delete Swatch dialog box—they are all replaced with the color you select or they are made into unnamed colors. Because no object uses these colors, choosing Unnamed Swatch in essence is the same as replacing them with a color using the Defined Swatch option.

Copying swatches

To duplicate a swatch, so you can create a new one based on it, use the Duplicate Swatch option in the Swatches pane. The word *copy* will be added to its name, and you can edit it — including its name — as you would any swatch.

You can also import colors from other InDesign, Illustrator, and Illustrator EPS files by using Window ➪ Swatch Libraries ➪ Other Library.

A quick way to import specific colors from another InDesign document or template is to drag the colors from that other file's Swatches pane into your current document or template.

Spot Color versus Process Color

Earlier in this chapter, we mentioned briefly that there are two types of colors that InDesign works with: spot and mixed. Understanding how these color types differ is vital to using them effectively and saving hassles and money when printing your documents.

Several forms of color are used in printing, but the two basic ones are *process color* and *spot color*.

Process color refers to the use of four basic colors — cyan, magenta, yellow, and black (known as a group as *CMYK*) — that are mixed to reproduce most color tones the human eye can see. A separate negative is produced for each of the four process colors. This method, often called *four-color publishing*, is used for most color publishing.

Note   Like CMYK, RGB and LAB are also created by mixing colors, so we refer to all such colors as *mixed colors*, leaving the term *process color* for CMYK because that's an industry standard term for CMYK.

Spot color refers to any color — whether one of the process colors or some other hue — used for specific elements in a document. For example, if you print a document in black ink but print the company logo in red, the red is a spot color. A spot color is often called a *second color* even though you can use several spot colors in a document. Each spot color is output to its own negative (and not color-separated into CMYK).

Tip   If you create spot colors, we suggest that you include the word *Spot* as part of the name, so you can quickly tell in a palette or menu whether a selected color will print on its own plate or be color-separated. InDesign does use an icon to tell you whether a color is process or spot, as well as what color model (CMYK, RGB, or LAB) it was defined in, as Figure 27-5 shows, but using the word is often more visible than looking for a tiny icon.

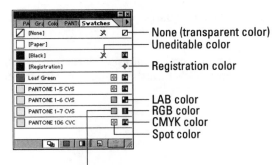

Figure 27-5: The Swatches pane uses several icons to show the settings for colors.

Using spot color gives you access to special inks that are truer to the desired color than any mix of process colors can be. These inks come in several standards, with Pantone being the most popular. Trumatch, Focoltone, Toyo, and DIC are less popular but still common standards, with Trumatch used mainly in the United States, Focoltone in Europe, and Toyo and DIC in Japan. InDesign supports all five spot-color standards.

Note   Adobe programs, including InDesign, show spot colors such as Pantone, Toyo, and DIC as being based on the CMYK color model, even though they are not. It doesn't really matter because if you print them as a spot color, they get their own plate, and your printer will use the actual Pantone, Toyo, or DIC ink. And if you color-separate them into process colors, you'll get the CMYK values shown in the Swatch Options dialog box or by holding the mouse over the color name in the Swatches pane (if the ToolTips option is enabled in the Preferences dialog box, as described in Chapter 2).

Spot-color inks can produce some colors that are impossible to achieve with process colors, such as metallics, neons, and milky pastels. You can even use varnishes as spot colors to give layout elements a different gleam than the rest of the page. Although experienced designers sometimes mix spot colors to produce special shades not otherwise available, it's unlikely that you will need to do so.

Design Advice   In most cases, you need not worry about spot-color output because most users of these colors apply them to solid objects or text. However, some designers use them more demandingly, such as mixing them with black to produce many variants or using them with scanned images. In these cases, the way that InDesign outputs them may lead to displeasing results. Be sure to test such mixes by creating a color proof first.

Some designers use both process and spot colors in a document — known as using a *fifth color*. Typically, the normal color images are color-separated and printed via the four process colors while a special element (such as a logo in metallic ink) is printed in a spot color. The process colors are output on the usual four negatives; the spot color is output on a separate, fifth negative and printed using a fifth plate, fifth ink roller, and fifth ink well. You can use more than five colors; you are limited only by your budget and the capabilities of your printing plant.

No matter whether you set a color to be a spot color, you still have the option when you output to convert all spot colors to process (see Chapter 33 for more details). What you can't do when printing is select specific spot colors to be output as process colors (to be color-separated) and let others remain spot colors. If you're going to color-separate some colors and have others print as spot colors, you must be sure to set them up properly in the Swatch Options dialog box.

Converting colors

InDesign can convert spot colors to process colors, and vice versa. This handy capability lets designers specify the colors they want through a system they're familiar with, such as Pantone, without the added expense of special spot-color inks and extra negatives.

You can convert a color defined in any model to the CMYK, RGB, or LAB models simply by selecting one of those models when editing the color: Just use the Color Mode pop-up menu in the Swatch Options dialog box.

Caution   Colors defined in one model and converted to another may not reproduce exactly the same because the physics underlying each color model differs slightly. Each model was designed for use in a different medium such as on paper or a video monitor.

Although conversions are almost never an exact match, guidebooks can show you in advance the color that will be created. With Pantone Process variation (which InDesign supports), designers can now pick a Pantone color that will color-separate predictably. And the Focoltone and Trumatch colors were created by mixing process colors, so all can reliably be color-separated into CMYK.

Tip   If you use Pantone colors, we suggest that you get a copy of the *Pantone Process Color Imaging Guide: CMYK Edition* swatchbook, available from several sources, including art and printing supply stores, mail order catalogs, and Pantone itself. This swatchbook shows each Pantone color and the CMYK equivalent so you can see how accurate the conversion will be and thus decide whether you want to use the actual Pantone ink on its own negative or convert to CMYK.

Where to Get Swatchbooks

Anyone who uses a lot of color should have a color swatchbook handy. You probably can get one at your local art-supply store or from your commercial printer (prices typically range from $50 to $100, depending on the color model and the type of swatchbook). But if you can't find a swatchbook, here's where to order the popular color models' swatchbooks.

✦ **Pantone:** This company has several swatchbooks, including ones for coated and uncoated paper, and those for spot-color output and process-color output. If you are converting (called *building* in publishing parlance) Pantone colors to CMYK for four-color printing, we particularly recommend the *Pantone Process Color Imaging Guide: CMYK Edition* or the *Pantone Process Color System Guide* swatchbooks.

Pantone
590 Commerce Boulevard
Carlstadt, NJ 07072-3098
Phone: (800) 222-1149 or (201) 935-5500
Fax: (201) 896-0242
Web: http://www.pantone.com

✦ **Hexachrome:** Pantone also created the Hexachrome standard and sells Hexachrome swatchbooks, as well as the HexWrench software that adds Hexachrome output capability to Adobe Photoshop.

✦ **Trumatch:** Based on a CMYK color space, Trumatch suffers almost no matching problems when converted to CMYK. You can get variants of the swatchbooks for coated and uncoated paper.

Trumatch
25 W. 43rd Street #802
New York, NY 10036
Phone: (800) 878-9100 or (212) 302-9100
Fax: (212) 302-0890
Web: http://www.trumatch.com

✦ **ANPA:** Designed for reproduction on newsprint, these colors also are designed in the CMYK color space. Although InDesign doesn't have an ANPA color library predefined, you can create these colors using the swatchbook's definitions.

Newspaper Association of America
1921 Gallows Road #600
Vienna, VA 22182
Phone: (703) 902-1600
Web: http://www.naa.org

✦ **Focoltone:** Like Trumatch, this color model (used primarily in Europe) is based on the CMYK color space.

Focoltone AND Systems
Springwater House, Taffs Well
Cardiff CF4 7QR, U.K.
Phone: 44 (222) 810-940
Fax: 44 (222) 810-962
Web: http://www.focoltone.com

✦ **Dainippon:** Like Pantone, this is a spot-color based system.

Dainippon Ink & Chemical Americas
222 Bridge Plaza South
Fort Lee, NJ 07024
Phone: (201) 592-5100
Fax: (201) 592-8232
Web: http://dicwww01.dic.co.jp/index-e.html

✦ **Toyo:** Similar to Pantone in that it is based on spot-color inks, this model is popular in Japan.

Toyo Ink Manufacturing Co. Ltd.
3-13 2-chome Kyobashi, Chuo-ku
Tokyo 104, Japan
Phone: 81 (3) 3272-5731
Fax: 81 (3) 3278-8688
Web: http://www.iandi.com/toyoink/ **(in Japanese)**

Simulating other color models

Although InDesign supports many color models—Trumatch, DIC, Toyo, Focoltone, and several variants of Pantone—other color models are also in use, such as the Pantone Hexachrome and ANPA color models. (*ANPA* stands for the American Newspaper Publishers Association, which several years ago renamed itself the Newspaper Association of America, but the color model's name hasn't changed.)

In some cases, you can still use these color models in InDesign by following these techniques. The key is that the color model must be a spot-color model, where each color is its own ink, or must be convertible into CMYK. For example, consider how to use the ANPA color model in InDesign:

✦ If you are using spot color, in which the color prints on its own plate, just define a color with the ANPA name you want the printer to use. The printer doesn't care if you actually had the right color onscreen—the fact that your printer knows what color you want and you have a plate for that color is all that's needed.

✦ If you are using process (CMYK) color for your output, you'll need to create the ANPA colors using the CMYK color model. This means you'll need to know the CMYK values for the ANPA colors you want to use; you can get these values from the swatch book you use to select colors or from your commercial printer. (You can also use RGB values to enter the colors and then switch the model with InDesign to CMYK. This may result in some altered colors because you are converting colors twice: once to RGB and then again to CMYK. Any conversion between color models may result in color differences because of the physics involved in reproducing color.)

✦ If you use certain ANPA colors repeatedly, create them in the Swatches pane with no document open—they'll then be available for all future documents. If different types of documents use different sets of colors, define them in the template for each type of document. Doing so will save a lot of redefinition.

Like PageMaker, InDesign does not support the Pantone Hexachrome colors, which are composed of six inks—the four CMYK inks plus green and orange—to reproduce a broader range of colors more accurately than can CMYK. Although Hexachrome printing—also called Hi-Fi Color—is costlier than CMYK and not available from all commercial printers, it is an important color set for a professional publishing program to have. And because it is made up of mixed colors, it can't be simulated like spot-color or CMYK-compatible color models such as ANPA.

Working with Color Pictures

When you work with imported graphics, whether they are illustrations or scanned photographs, color is part of the graphics file. So the responsibility for color controls lies primarily with the creator of the picture. It is best to use color files in

CMYK EPS or DCS format (for illustrations) or CMYK TIFF format (for scans and bitmaps). These standards are de facto for color publishing, so InDesign is particularly adept at working with them. (See Chapter 20 for details on preparing graphics files for import.)

Note
RGB is the standard color model used by scanners and graphics software because monitors use red, green, and blue electron guns to display images. The dilemma most designers face is that an RGB image displays properly onscreen but may appear with slightly adjusted hues in print, whereas a CMYK image may print correctly but appear incorrectly onscreen. Most designers get good at mentally shifting the colors from one model to another, as they see the results of their work in print over time. Until that happens to you, rely on color proofs from your printer to see what your images actually look like when printed.

Caution
Color files pasted via the clipboard should print properly after they are pasted into an InDesign picture box. But problems do sometimes occur, such as dropped colors or altered colors, depending on the applications involved and the amount of memory available. If you drag files from Photoshop or Illustrator directly into InDesign, rather than use copy and paste, you should have no such problems.

Working with EPS files

InDesign automatically imports color definitions from EPS files, so you'll see any spot colors in them show up in your Colors palette and in menus and dialog boxes that display color lists.

Note
If you create files in EPS format, do any required color trapping in the source application—InDesign offers only basic trapping capabilities (see Chapter 28).

Not all programs encode color information the same way. If you create EPS files in some illustration programs, colors may not print as expected. One of three things can happen:

✦ Each color prints on its own plate (as if it were a spot color), even if you defined it as a process color.

✦ A spot color is color-separated into CMYK even when you define it as a spot color in both the source program and in InDesign.

✦ A color prints as black.

There is no easy solution because the problem is in how the illustration program manages color internally. The only safe bet is to use a program that uses standard color-definition methods; these include the latest versions of Adobe Illustrator, CorelDraw, and Macromedia FreeHand.

Working with TIFF files

Color TIFF files do not cause such peculiarities because they don't use spot colors — by their very nature, they are broken down into RGB or CMYK when they are created.

InDesign can color-separate RGB TIFF files, as well as CMYK TIFF files. You may notice a color shift for color-separated RGB images, or for RGB images printed on a CMYK proofing printer. The degree of shift will depend on the device and whether any Color Management System (CMS) plug-ins were used in creating the image, and whether the same one is active in InDesign for printing. Chapter 28 covers this topic in more detail.

Working with PDF files

InDesign accurately imports any colors used in a PDF file. It also retains any Hexachrome colors in the PDF file and retains them for output *only* if you export the InDesign file to PDF format. Otherwise, the Hexachrome colors are converted to CMYK when you print or generate a PostScript file from InDesign. Many Hexachrome colors do not print properly when converted to CMYK, so you should always export InDesign files using Hexachrome PDF images to PDF for output. If that's not possible, edit the original image in the program that generated the PDF, or in a program such as Illustrator that can edit PDF files, and choose CMYK colors instead, and then re-export the PDF image.

Working with Gradients

A technique that has increased in popularity is the *gradient*, which blends two or more colors in a sequence, going from, say, green to blue to yellow to orange. InDesign has a powerful gradient creation feature that lets you define and apply gradients to pretty much any object you create in InDesign: text, lines, frames, shapes, and their outlines (strokes).

Note   Gradients go by several names among artists. Other names include *blends* and *graduated fills*.

Creating gradients

In the Swatches pane, where you define colors and tints you can also define gradients: Just use the New Gradient Swatch option in the palette menu. You'll get the dialog box shown in Figure 27-6.

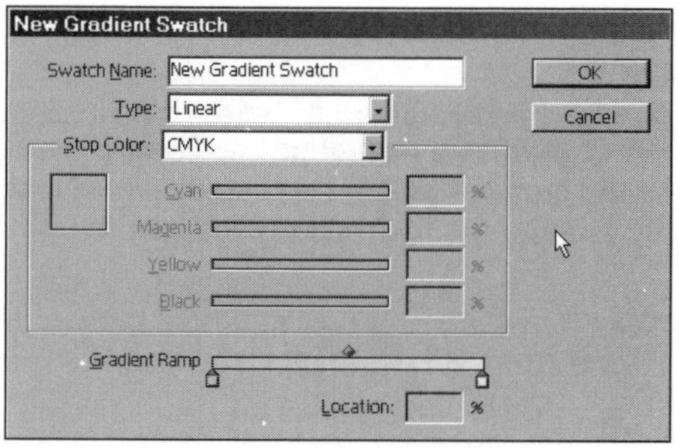

Figure 27-6: The New Gradient Swatch dialog box.

The first two options are straightforward:

✦ Enter a name for the gradient in the Swatch Name field. Picking a name is a bit more difficult than for a color, but use something like "Blue to Red" or "Bright Multihue" or "Logo Gradient" that has a meaning specific to the colors used or to its role in your document.

✦ In the Type pop-up menu, choose Linear or Radial. A linear blend goes in one direction, whereas a radial blend radiates out in a circle from a central point. (Later in this section you'll see some example gradients.)

Now it gets a little tricky. Follow these steps:

1. Select a stop point — one of the squares at the bottom of the dialog box, on either side of the gradient ramp that shows the gradient as you define it. The stop points are essentially the "from" and "to" colors, with the "from" being the stop point at the left, and the "to" being the stop point at the right.

2. With a stop point selected, you can now define its color. Choose what color model you want to define the color in — select from CMYK, RGB, LAB, and Named Color in the Stop color pop-up menu. The area directly beneath the pop-up menu changes accordingly, displaying sliders for CMYK, RGB, and LAB, and a list of all colors from the Swatches pane for Named Color.

3. Now create or select the color you want for that stop point.

4. Repeat Steps 1 and 2 for the other stop point. Note that the color models for the two stop points don't have to be the same — you can blend from a Pantone spot color to a CMYK color, for example.

You now have a simple gradient. But you don't have to stop there. Here are your options:

✦ You can change the rate at which the colors transition by sliding the diamond icon at the top of the gradient ramp.

✦ You can create additional stop points by clicking right below the gradient ramp. By having several stop points, you can have multiple color transitions in a gradient. (Think of them as tab stops in text — you can define as many as you need.) You delete unwanted stop points by dragging them to the bottom of the dialog box.

✦ Notice that there's a diamond icon between each pair of stop points — this means each pair can have its own transition rate. Figure 27-7 shows a complex gradient being defined.

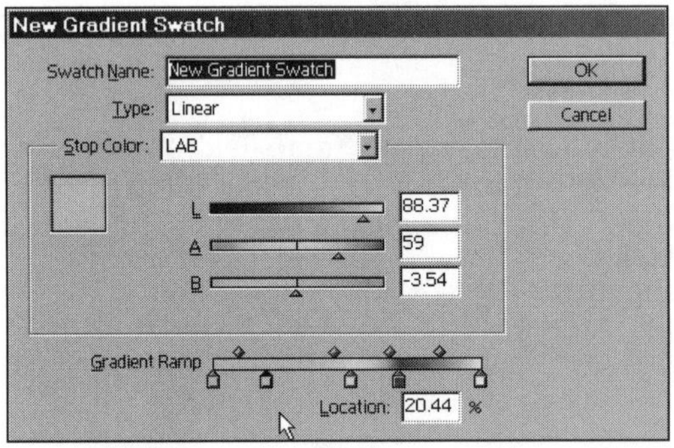

Figure 27-7: A complex, multihue gradient being defined.

Tip   When you create a new gradient, InDesign uses the settings from the last one you created. If you want to create a gradient similar to an existing one, click that existing gradient before selecting New Gradient Swatch from the palette menu. InDesign copies the selected gradient's settings to the new one, which you can then edit. One reason to use this method is to create, say, a radial version of an existing linear gradient.

The Swatches pane shows the actual gradient next to its name, as Figure 27-7 shows. You'll also see the pattern in the Fill box or Stroke box in the Toolbox palette if that gradient is currently selected as a fill or stroke, as well as in the Gradient box in that palette whether or not it's currently applied as a fill or stroke.

Note   If a gradient mixes spot colors and process colors, InDesign converts the spot colors to process colors.

Tip
If you want to share your settings, you can give colleagues the color definitions for each stop point, as well as the exact location of each stop point and transition control—notice the Location field at the bottom of the dialog box. As you click each control and stop point, it shows the current setting. You can also adjust the settings for the select control or stop point by changing the value in the field rather than sliding the control or point.

Unnamed gradients

Just as it does with colors, InDesign lets you create unnamed gradients—gradients that have no swatches. Our caution on using this feature for colors applies less for gradients because all colors in a gradient are converted to process colors. Here's how it works:

1. Select the object you want to apply the gradient to. Make sure the stroke or fill, as appropriate, is active in the Toolbox.

2. Go to the Gradient pane (Window ➪ Gradient), as shown in Figure 27-8.

Figure 27-8: Use the Gradient pane to create unnamed gradients and to adjust a linear gradient's angles.

3. Select a stop point.

4. Now go to the Color pane (it's usually in the same palette as the Gradient pane, but use Window ➪ Color or F6 to display it if not).

5. Create a color using the CMYK, RGB, or LAB models (use the palette menu to choose the model).

6. Repeat Steps 2 through 5 for the other stop point.

7. Create any additional stop points by clicking below the gradient ramp, and adjust the transition controls as desired.

Editing gradients

Editing a gradient is as simple as double-clicking its name in the Swatches menu or selecting it and choosing Edit Gradient Swatch. You'll get the Gradient Options dialog box, which is nearly identical to the New Gradient Swatch dialog box in Figures 27-6 and 27-7.

What's different in the Gradient Options dialog box is the Preview checkbox, which lets you see a gradient change in a selected object (if it's visible onscreen, of course) as you make changes in the Gradient Options dialog box.

The Gradient pane used to create unnamed gradients also has a use for gradient swatches. Once you apply a linear gradient — whether via a gradient swatch or as an unnamed gradient — you can change the angle of the gradient, as done with the bottom middle gradient in Figure 27-9 (compare it to the otherwise identical object at the bottom right). Just enter a value in the Angle field to rotate the gradient's direction.

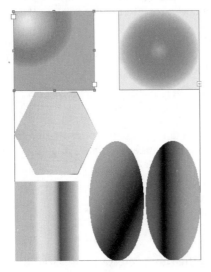

Figure 27-9: Examples of gradients.

You can't rotate a radial gradient because it's circular and thus any rotation will have no effect. That's why InDesign grays out the Angle field for radial gradients. But you still can adjust the location of a radial gradient — as well as that of a linear gradient — using the Gradient tool in the Toolbox.

 The gradient tool looks like this. After applying a gradient to an object, select the Gradient tool and draw a line in the object, as shown in Figure 27-10:

✦ For a linear gradient, the start point corresponds to where you want the first stop point of the gradient to be, whereas the end point corresponds to the last point. This lets you stretch or compress or the gradient, as well as offset the gradient within the object. Also, the angle at which you draw the line becomes the angle for the gradient.

✦ For a radial gradient, the line becomes the start and end point for the gradient, in effect offsetting it, as done in the upper-left gradient in Figure 27-9 (compare it to the standard gradient setting for the same object at the upper-right corner).

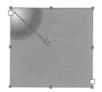

Figure 27-10: The Gradient tool lets you set the offset, adjust the gradient length, and (for gradient blends) adjust the gradient angle.

Summary

InDesign uses swatches to contain defined colors, tints, and gradient blends; the use of swatches lets you apply colors repeatedly with the assurance it's the same color each time, much as styles assure consistent text formatting. Although you can also apply colors without using these swatches, doing so can cause output problems, especially when you are using color separations.

Key to defining colors is choosing the appropriate color model: spot or process. A spot color prints on its own plate, whereas a process color is separated into the four basic colors used in traditional color publishing. If you define too many colors as spot colors, you're likely to create a document that's impossible or very expensive to print. InDesign lets you convert colors from spot to process and vice versa, so you can choose the right output options for each document. Similarly, it's best to create color images in the color model you intend to use for output: CMYK for traditional printing and RGB for onscreen display.

A powerful feature in InDesign is its ability to create gradient blends that can contain blends among multiple colors. No other layout program offers this level of control or flexibility on gradients, although image editors such as Photoshop go even further than InDesign does.

✦   ✦   ✦

Preparing for Color Prepress

Since their invention in the mid-1980s, desktop publishing programs have broadened their features to cover more and more color publishing needs. Many of the color-oriented features have caused consternation among professional color separators and printers who have seen amateurs make a tough job worse or ruin an acceptable piece of work. This situation is familiar to anyone in desktop publishing in the early years when the typographic profession looked on in horror as amateurs published documents without understanding tracking, hyphenation, and many other fundamentals of typography.

Some programs have added more and more high-end color prepress features. InDesign takes a different approach: It offers just the basics, such as relying on the creator of objects to handle what's known as *color trapping* (which ensures that adjacent colors don't print with awkward gaps between them) or a service bureau to adjust their equipment or work with a professional color-trapping application such as Adobe TrapWise.

As Adobe builds more color-management technology into its PostScript output language and its graphics-creation programs Photoshop and Illustrator, the company hopes that the need for a lot of color-management features in a page-layout program such as InDesign will decline. And because most competing programs to Photoshop and Illustrator tend to adopt the same color standards, Adobe may just be right.

The perfect scenario for InDesign color output is that you are using all Adobe software in their latest versions: Photoshop 5.0 or later, Illustrator 8.0 or later, a PostScript Level 3 output device, and perhaps PressReady (a new program that lets you output color proofs on popular ink-jet printers, a topic covered in Chapter 33). But most people won't have that perfect scenario, especially the PostScript Level 3 part, because it is new and the output devices that commercial printers use are expensive and not replaced often. And not everyone uses Illustrator; FreeHand is very popular among professional artists, and CorelDraw has established a toehold among that group as well, especially on Windows.

Having said this, don't panic if you're not using cutting-edge equipment and software. After years of user education and efforts by software developers such as Adobe to build in some of the more basic color-handling assumptions into their programs, most desktop publishers now produce decent color output by simply using the default settings, perhaps augmented by a little tweaking in Photoshop or an illustration program. To really use the color-management and trapping tools in InDesign effectively, you should understand color printing. But if you don't, you can be assured that the default settings in InDesign will produce decent-quality color output.

Note   Please note that the illustrations and figures in this chapter are in black and white. You'll need to look at your color monitor to see the effects of what's described here. Also take a look at the full-color examples in this book's special eight-page insert on color techniques.

Color Calibration

InDesign comes with several Color Management System (CMS) options. A CMS helps you ensure accurate printing of your colors, both those in imported images and those defined in InDesign. What a CMS does is track the colors in the source image, the colors displayable by your monitor, and the colors printable by your printer. If the monitor or printer does not support a color in your document, the CMS alters (recalibrates) the color to its closest possible equivalent.

Activating color calibration

To activate a CMS, make sure color management is enabled in your document. Do so by using File ➪ Color Settings ➪ Document Color Settings to get the dialog box shown in Figure 28-1. Be sure Enable Color Management is checked. (We'll get to the other options a bit later in this chapter.)

Note   We do not characterize InDesign's CMS capabilities as color *matching*. It is impossible to match colors produced in an illustration or paint program, or via a scanner, with what a printer or other output device can produce. The underlying differences in color models (how a color is defined) and the physics of the media (screen phosphors that *emit* light versus different types of papers with different types of inks that *reflect* light) make color matching impossible. But a calibration tool such as a CMS can minimize differences.

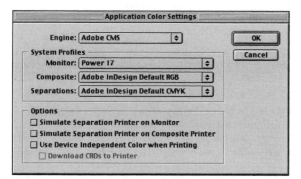

Figure 28-1: The Document Color Settings dialog box lets you activate color calibration and set document defaults.

The second step to activate color calibration is to choose a CMS. You do that in the Application Color Settings dialog box, accessed via File ➪ Color Settings ➪ Application Color Settings and shown in Figure 28-2.

Figure 28-2: The Application Color Settings dialog box lets you set your CMS and other application defaults.

In the Engine pop-up menu, you'll get a list of available CMSs. The options differ based on what platform you're using: Adobe CMS is available for all platforms, whereas Apple ColorSync and LinoColor CMM are available just for Macintosh, and Kodak Digital Science ICC CMS just for Windows. ICC (the International Color Committee's color standard) is the color-calibration system built into Windows, whereas ColorSync (developed by Apple Computer) is built into the Mac OS. LinoColor was designed by Linotype-Hell, a company that produces the popular Linotronic imagesetters. Choose a CMS that is compatible with your output equipment; if in doubt, choose Adobe CMS.

Setting up the monitor

To have color calibration in effect for a monitor, you must be displaying thousands of colors (16-bit color depth) or more colors (a higher color depth, such as 24-bit). On the Mac, use the Monitors & Sound control panel to change your monitor's bit depth. In Windows, use the Display control panel.

It's possible to have a different onscreen appearance than a CMS expects. For example, your brightness and contrast settings affect how colors display, but the CMS has no way of gauging their settings.

Likewise, you can change the color characteristics (the *gamma*) of your display in the Mac's Monitors & Sound control panel's Monitor pane by using the Calibrate option in the Color pane. The default is 1.8 Standard Gamma (this used to be called Mac Std Gamma in previous versions of Mac OS 8), which is the setting that CMSs expect. But you may want to select 1.0 Linear Gamma (previously called Uncorrected Gamma), which makes the monitor display colors as the manufacturer originally intended. Apple's monitors have a slight bluish cast to them (which makes whites appear whiter), but a monitor's display usually appears more vivid without the Mac gamma, so some people change the gamma to 1.0 Linear Gamma to get a more pleasing display.

Windows has no such built-in gamma controls, but many video cards come with one, so you may be able to set the monitor's gamma through one of those. A PC monitor usually is set to a gamma of 2.2, which the Mac calls 2.2 Television Gamma and used to call Paper White Gamma.

To have truly accurate color-calibration and display on your monitor, you should use a calibrated monitor, which is usually composed of a specially designed monitor and a calibration tool that senses the color output onscreen. Such displays — such as the Radius PressView now sold by Miro Displays (the monitor was first sold by SuperMac Technologies, which was then was bought by Radius, and is now sold by Miro) — are very expensive and must be used in a room with specially controlled lighting. For most users, the variances in monitor brightness, color balance, and contrast, coupled with the varying types of lighting used in their workspace, mean that true calibration is impossible for images created onscreen and displayed onscreen. Still, using the calibration feature makes the onscreen color closer to what you'll print, even if not a near-exact match.

You also want indirect lighting to reduce glare and keep the lighting even throughout the work area. Avoid fluorescent lights because they add a yellow cast to images — look for lights that have a color temperature of 5,000 degrees Kelvin. Keep shades closed to minimize the variations in light from changes in the sunlight outside. Avoid colored walls and carpets — they can change the room's color cast, as can patterned or colored screen backgrounds (in the Mac's Appearance control panel or the Windows Display control panel, use gray screen patterns such as the ones included on the CD-ROM that accompanies this book).

Understanding profiles

The mechanism that a CMS uses to do its calibration is the profile that contains the information on color models and ranges supported by a particular creator (such as an illustration program or scanner), display, and printer. InDesign includes dozens of such predefined profiles.

A CMS uses a device-independent color space to match these profiles against each other. A color space is a mathematical way of describing the relationships among colors. By using a device-independent color model (the CIE XYZ standard defined by the Comité International d'Éclairage — the International Lighting Committee), a CMS can compare gamuts from other device-dependent models (such as RGB and the others). What this means is that a CMS can examine the colors in your imported images and defined colors, compare them against the capabilities of your monitor and printer, and adjust the colors for the closest possible display and printing.

In the application's Color Settings dialog box, you should set the profiles for your monitor and output devices. Do so in the Systems Profiles section of the dialog box, as the following list explains.

Note that Windows InDesign has fewer built-in profiles than the Mac version, so you may not see all the following options.

✦ Use the Monitor pop-up menu to select your monitor. If your monitor is not listed, select one of the Generic EBU or P22 monitors or Adobe InDesign Default RGB. Note that EBU and P22 are types of phosphors — the elements on a monitor that glow — with EBU (electron beam unit) used in highly color-saturated displays (usually in more expensive, professional models) and P22 (phosphor level 22) used in most other displays. You'll notice several variations of these phosphors, which indicate the brightness-midpoint setting: The 1.8 setting is the default on the Mac (the Mac Std gamma), whereas 2.2 is standard on Windows (called Paper White on the Mac); this difference is why Mac screens tend to look cooler or bluer than Windows screens.

To create a monitor profile if InDesign doesn't support your monitor, use the Adobe Gamma control panel that is installed with InDesign — it very nicely walks you through the necessary steps. One tip: When asked to make the center box fade into the background to adjust the image's gamma, focus your eyes between the monitor and your head, to make the image fuzzy — this will help you better gauge when the colors become equivalent. You can also use commercial software tools such as Color Solutions' ColorBlind (a demo version of which is included in the CD-ROM that accompanies this book), as long as it creates an ICC profile. Remember to adjust the lighting in your work area so it's not too bright or dark; the lighting around you affects how you perceive the monitor display and affects the profile you create.

Windows users: You must use DOS-style names for your monitor profile (eight characters maximum, followed by the file extension .icc) — Adobe Gamma oddly doesn't support long file names for files it creates.

✦ Use the Composite pop-up menu to select a proofing printer for your color documents. This is usually a printer you have in-house, but it could be a color copier or other short-run color-printing device. If your printer is not listed, use Adobe InDesign Default RGB or Adobe InDesign Default CMYK — depending on whether your printer is an RGB or CMYK device.

✦ Use the Separations pop-up menu to select the device that generates your four-color negatives. If your device is not listed, use Adobe InDesign Default CMYK.

The settings here become your default profiles for all documents, but you can override any of these for a specific document using the same options in the Document Color Settings dialog box.

While in this dialog box, you can also set how InDesign handles color onscreen and when printing, through the Options section:

✦ Check Simulate Separation Printer on Monitor to have InDesign adjust the display of colors onscreen to match as closely as possible how they'll look when produced from color negatives using the device you chose in the Separations pop-up menu. Remember: This is a simulation and will not be an exact match, and perhaps not even a close match. This option should *not* be checked if you're producing pages that will be viewed onscreen (on the Web, CD-ROM, or via PDF files).

✦ Check Simulate Separation Printer on Composite Printer to have InDesign adjust the display of colors when printing to your proofing (composite) color printer, so they'll match as closely as possible how they'll look when produced from color negatives using the device you chose in the Separations pop-up menu. Remember: This is a simulation and will not be an exact match, and perhaps not even a close match. It will also slow printing time.

✦ Check Use Device-Independent Color when Printing to prevent InDesign from adjusting the document's colors when printing — instead, it sends the source profile information (from each image, or what is set in the Monitors pop-up menu) to the output device, which then does the color adjustments itself. The output device must support PostScript device-independent color for this to work; otherwise, it is the same as turning off color management. Similarly, you can have InDesign create and send the output device a PostScript Color Rendering Dictionary (CRD) based on your Separations profile by checking the Download CRDs to Printer. Only use these options after consulting with your service bureau — you need to make sure that its equipment supports these capabilities and that it is not doing any manipulation on your files that your use of these settings could mess up.

Note Other programs may have similar settings for calibrating their display against your type of monitor. For example, Adobe Photoshop offers such an option (via File ⇨ Color Settings ⇨ Profile Setup), whereas in Illustrator it's just File ⇨ Color Settings. If you're creating colors in a program and importing those colors into InDesign, it's important to have them calibrated the same way, or at least as closely as the different programs will allow.

Make sure that you use the same color profiles wherever possible in all the programs you use to create images and colors — InDesign, your image editor (Photoshop, Fractal Painter, and so on), and your illustration program (Illustrator, FreeHand, CorelDraw, and so on). Almost every professional program now uses the ICC color profiles that InDesign does, so such consistent color model use should be easy to achieve.

Note In Windows, color profiles are stored in the Color folder inside the System folder inside the folder that contains Windows (usually called Windows or Win98). On the Mac, color profiles are stored in folders within the System Folder: ColorSync Profiles for ColorSync profiles, and CMSCP and KPCMS for Kodak and ICC profiles.

Defining colors

Whether you define colors in InDesign or in your illustration or paint program, the method you use to define them is critical to ensuring the best possible output. It's best to define all colors in the same model as the target output device. Use the following guidelines:

✦ If your printer is RGB, use the RGB model to define colors.

✦ If your printer is CMYK (like an offset printer), use CMYK to define colors.

✦ If you are using Pantone colors for traditional offset printing, pick the Pantone or Pantone Uncoated models if using Pantone inks.

✦ If you are using Pantone colors for traditional offset printing, pick the Pantone Process model if you will color-separate those colors into CMYK.

✦ Trumatch and Focoltone colors were designed to reproduce accurately whether output as spot colors or color-separated into CMYK. Other models (such as Toyo and DIC) may or may not separate accurately for all colors, so check with your printer or the ink manufacturer.

✦ Never rely on the screen display to gauge any non-RGB color. Even with a CMS's monitor calibration, RGB monitors simply cannot match most non-RGB colors. Use the onscreen colors only as a guide and rely instead on a color swatchbook from your printer or the ink's manufacturer.

Calibrating imported colors

When you load an image into InDesign, the active CMS applies the default settings defined in the Application Color Settings dialog box or, if they're different, those in the Document Color Settings dialog box (these are described earlier in this chapter). But you can change those settings for specific images as follows:

✦ As you import each file, check Show Import Options when you place a graphic into InDesign in the Place dialog box (File ➪ Place, or ⌘+D or Ctrl+D). In the resulting dialog box, select Color Settings from the pop-up menu and select the profile, as shown in Figure 28-3. You also get the opportunity to turn color management on if it is set to off in the Application Color Settings dialog box.

✦ Any time after you place a graphic, select it with a selection tool and use Object ➪ Image Color Settings, or Shift+Option+⌘+D or Ctrl+Alt+Shift+D, to set a new profile. You get the same options as shown in Figure 28-3.

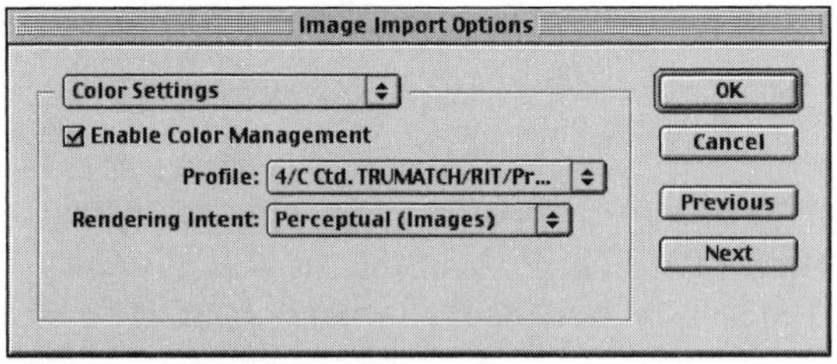

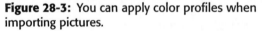

Figure 28-3: You can apply color profiles when importing pictures.

Note

Only profiles appropriate for the image type appear in these pop-up menus — for example, only CMYK profiles (generally these are output devices) appear for a CMYK TIFF file, even though the image may have been scanned in from an RGB scanner and later converted to CMYK with Photoshop. This limitation exists because InDesign assumes that the image is designed for output to that specific printer and thus calibrates it with that target in mind. For RGB files, InDesign lets you apply monitor-oriented profiles such as Sony CPD Series or scanner-oriented profiles such as Umax Astra 610S Reflective.

These dialog boxes also let you have InDesign adjust the colors based on other factors, via the Rendering Intent pop-up menu:

✦ **Perceptual (Images)** tries to balance the colors in an image when translating from the original color range to the output device's color range under the assumption that it is a photograph and thus needs to look natural. This is appropriate for photographs.

✦ **Saturation (Graphics)** tries to create vivid colors when translating from the original color range to the output device's color range—even if doing so means that some colors are printed inaccurately. This is appropriate for charts and other slide-like graphics whose colors are intended for impact rather than naturalness.

✦ **Absolute Colorimetric** makes no adjustments to the colors during output. As a result, it lets an image that uses two similar colors, for example, end up being output as the same color because of the printer's limited color range.

✦ **Relative Colorimetric** is the same as Absolute Colorimetric except that it shifts all the colors to compensate for the white point of the monitor as set in the Monitor profile (essentially, adjusting the brightness of the output to compensate for any dimness or excess brightness in the monitor).

Tip Depending on the kinds of documents you produce, you'll likely want Perceptual (Images) or Saturation (Graphics) as your document-wide default, which you set in the Document Color Settings dialog box.

Working with Color Traps

Color trapping controls how colors overlap and abut when printed. InDesign offers moderate controls over trapping—enough to set the basics document-wide without getting into the expertise level of a commercial printer. It's also a feature that novice users can abuse terribly, which is one reason InDesign hides these options. If you don't know much about trapping, leave the features of the program at the default settings. Before you use InDesign trapping tools, study some books on color publishing, talk to your printer, and experiment with test files that you don't want to publish. If you are experienced with color trapping—or after you become experienced—you'll find InDesign trapping tools easy to use.

You'll still want to use the trapping tools within the illustration product with which you create your EPS and PDF graphics because these tools help you to finely control the settings for each image's specific needs. Also, if you are using a service bureau that does high-resolution scanning for you and strips these files into your layout before output, check to make sure that the bureau is not also handling trapping for you with a Scitex or other high-end system. If it is, make sure you ask whether and when you should be doing trapping yourself.

Note If you're printing to a color laser, dye-sublimation, ink-jet, or thermal wax printer, don't worry about trapping. You're not getting the kind of output resolution at which this level of image fine-tuning is relevant. But if you're outputting to an imagesetter (particularly if you are outputting to negatives) for eventual printing using standard web offset printing (SWOP) or other printing method, read on.

Choking versus spreading

So what is trapping, anyway? Trapping adjusts the boundaries of colored objects to prevent gaps between abutting colors. Gaps can occur because of misalignment of the negatives, plates, or printing press — all of which are impossible to avoid.

Colors are trapped by processes known as *choking* and *spreading*. Both make an object slightly larger — usually a fraction of a point — so that it overprints the abutting object slightly. The process is called choking when one object surrounds a second object, and the first object is enlarged to overlap the second. The process is known as spreading when you enlarge the surrounded object so that it leaks (bleeds) into the surrounding object.

The difference between choking and spreading is the relative position of the two objects. Think of choking as making the hole smaller for the inside object (which in effect makes the object on the outside larger), and think of spreading as making the object in the hole larger.

 The object made larger depends on the image, but you generally bleed the color of a lighter object into a darker one. If you did the opposite, you'd make objects seem ungainly larger. Thus, choke a dark object inside a light one, and spread a light object inside a dark one. If the objects are adjacent, spread the light object.

Figure 28-4 shows the two types of trapping techniques. Spreading (at left) makes the interior object's color bleed out; choking (at right) makes the outside color bleed in, in effect making the area of the choked element smaller. The dashed lines show the size of the interior object; as you can see in the image at right, when you choke a darker object into a lighter one, the effect is to change its size (here, the interior object gets smaller). In the middle is an untrapped image whose negatives shifted slightly during printing, causing a gap.

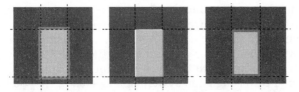

Figure 28-4: Two kinds of traps: spreading (left) and choking (right), with an untrapped image in the center that was misregistered during printing.

InDesign supports a third type of trapping technique: Called *centering*, it both chokes and spreads, splitting the difference between the two objects. This makes traps look nicer, especially between light and dark colors where regular choking and spreading can encroach on the light object, as shown in Figure 28-4.

In practice, trapping also involves controlling whether colors *knock out* or *overprint*. The default is to knock out — cut out — any overlap when one element is placed on top of another. If, for example, you place two rectangles on top of each other, they print like the two rectangles on the right side of Figure 28-5. If you set the darker rectangle in this figure to overprint, the rectangles print as shown on the left side of the figure. Setting colors to overprint results in mixed colors, as on the left, whereas setting colors to knock out results in discrete colors, as on the right.

Figure 28-5: The two kinds of untrapped options: overprint (left) and knockout.

In InDesign, you use the Attributes pane (Window ➪ Attributes) for individual objects — text, frames, shapes, and lines — to pick from the pane's two trapping options: Overprint Fill and Overprint Stroke. These are both normally unchecked because you usually want objects' fills and strokes to knock out. Figure 28-6 shows the Attributes pane.

Figure 28-6: The Attributes pane lets you set whether objects overprint or knock out (the default).

Specifying trapping styles

In InDesign, document-wide trapping settings are handled as part of the printing process (see Chapter 33). In the Print dialog box (File ➪ Print, or ⌘+P or Ctrl+P), select the Trapping pane from the pop-up menu; Figure 28-7 shows the pane.

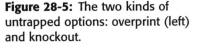

Figure 28-7: The Trapping pane in the Print dialog box.

To use these trapping settings, your output device must support Adobe's In-RIP Trapping feature (found only in some PostScript Level 3 devices), and Adobe In-RIP Trapping must be checked in the Trapping pane. Otherwise, your file will be output based on the settings of the output device or on any adjustments your service bureau or commercial printer may make to your files using a program such as Adobe TrapWise.

Note

You must use the Adobe PostScript driver that comes with InDesign (version 8.6 on Macintosh, 4.3 in Windows 95/98, and 5.1 in Windows NT 4.0). The trapping controls are actually part of the driver, not InDesign. Don't use printer drivers from other companies (such as Microsoft or Hewlett-Packard or Apple) with InDesign — even if they have the same version number). They do not offer these trapping controls. On the Mac, you will likely need to switch between using the AdobePS 8.6 driver with InDesign and the Apple LaserWriter 8.x driver with other programs because AdobePS crashes often with other programs and otherwise is less reliable with them.

Use the Styles button to create a reusable set of trapping settings. You'll get the Trapping Styles dialog box, in which you will see a list of existing styles (at the least you'll see a style called Default). You use three buttons to create and modify your styles: New Style, Edit Style, and Remove Style. When you click New Style or Edit Style, you get the View Trap Style dialog box shown in Figure 28-8.

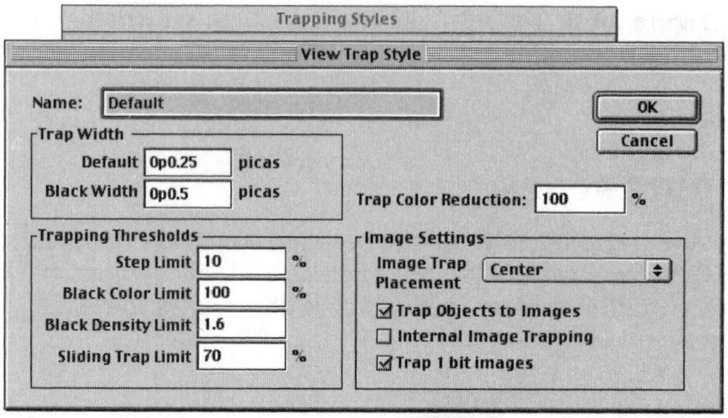

Figure 28-8: The View Trap Style dialog box.

Tip

If you click New Style after selecting a style from the Styles list, your new style inherits the selected style's options. This is a great way to create a variant of an existing style.

Note

Consult your service bureau or commercial printer before changing the default settings. They'll know what setting you should use based on the paper, inks, printing press, and image types you're using.

Follow these steps to create a new trapping style:

1. Give the trap style a name in the Name field.

2. Set your trap width — the amount of overlap you want between adjacent colors. The default is 0.25 point, a common setting. The Default field is for all colors except black and white. You set the trap width separately for black, using the Black Width field; this value is usually 1.5 to 2 times as much as the regular trap settings because it controls how colors spread into black objects. The value is higher because you have more leeway with black — spreading a color into it won't change it from being black, while, for example, spreading yellow into blue makes a green, so you want to minimize that spreading.

3. Now set your trapping thresholds, which guide InDesign in how to apply your trapping settings:

   • **Step Limit** gives InDesign the color-difference threshold before trapping is implemented. The default is 10 percent, a value that traps most objects. A higher value traps fewer objects. The way this works is that the value represents the difference in color variance between adjacent objects, and you're telling InDesign not to worry about colors that are within the percentage difference. This is usually a low setting when you don't care if traps are made between similar colors. Trapping is less of an issue between similar colors because the human eye notices misregistration less between them because of their similarity. In most cases, keep this value between 8 and 20 percent.

   • **Black Color Limit** defines at what point InDesign should treat a dark gray as black for the trap width in Black Width. For coarse paper, which usually absorbs more ink, dark tints and grays often end up looking like a solid color — 85 percent black appears as 100 percent black. Use Black Color Limit in such cases so that an 85 percent black object traps as if were a 100 percent black object.

   • **Black Density Limit** is similar to Black Color Limit, except that it treats dark colors (such as navy blues) as black, based on their ink density. You can enter a value from 0 to 10, with 1.6 being the default (0 is full black, and 10 is white).

   • **Sliding Trap Limit** adjusts the way a choke or spread works. The normal value is 70 percent, which tells InDesign, when the difference in ink density (a good measure of color-saturation) is 70 percent or more, not to move the darker color so much into the lighter color. The greater the contrast between two colors, the more the lighter object is distorted as the darker color encroaches onto it. At 0 percent, all traps are adjusted to the centerline between the two objects, whereas at 100 percent the choke or spread is done at the full trap width.

4. Set the Trap Color Reduction option. The default is 100 percent, which means that the overlapping colors in a trap are produced at 100 percent, which in

some cases can cause the trap to be darker than the two colors being trapped, due to the colors mixing. Choosing a lower value in Trap Color Reduction lightens the overlapping colors to reduce this darkening. A value of 0 percent keeps the overlap no darker than the darker of the two colors being trapped.

5. Finally, set the trap defaults for images (photographs and other imported bitmap images). The issue with images is that they are not solid objects but arrays of individual dots, so trapping is usually turned off for the image itself. Here are the options:

- **Image Trap Placement** determines how to handle trapping between an image and an abutting solid color. Your choices are Center, which has the trap straddle the edge between the image and the abutting color object; Choke, which has the abutting color object overprint the image by the Trap Width amount; Spread, which has the image overprint the abutting color object by the Trap Width amount; Neutral Density; and Normal, which traps each pixel in the image individually and thus can result in an uneven edge between the image and the abutting object.

- **Trap Objects to Images** turns on trapping for images and any abutting objects.

- **Internal Image Trapping** actually traps colors within the bitmap image. Use this only for high-contrast bitmaps, such as cartoons and computer screen shots, where the color has fewer gradations and more broad, consistent swaths.

- **Trap 1-Bit Images** traps black-and-white bitmaps to any abutting objects (including those underneath). This setting prevents the black portions from having a white ghost area around them if any misregistration occurs when printing.

Specifying trapping zones

Finally, InDesign offers trapping zones, in the Trapping pane. A trapping zone is simply a way to specify a range of pages that you apply a particular trapping style to. You may have one zone for a magazine's cover page because it uses different paper and perhaps special inks, for example, and another for certain ads that have special paper and ink characteristics.

To use trapping zones, click the Create button in the Trapping pane (see Figure 28-7) to get the New Trapping Zone dialog box shown in Figure 28-9. (When you later edit a trapping zone, the dialog box's name changes to Edit Trapping Zones, but it is otherwise identical.) Give your zone a name, pick a trapping style in the Trapping Style pop-up menu, and specify the pages you want to be in the trapping zone. You can specify a range of pages, such as "1, 3, 5, 10-13," or a section (if your document uses sections — see Chapter 31 for more information).

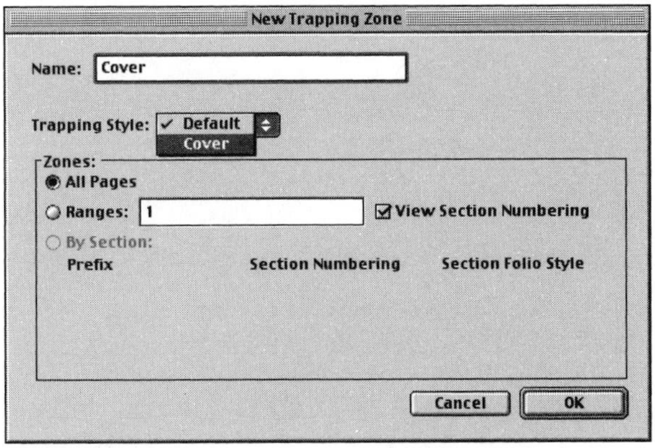

Figure 28-9: The New Trapping Zone dialog box.

If your document uses sections, you can enter page numbers in the Ranges field using the section numbering style (such as "A-2, D-3, F-5-G-10") or by using absolute page numbers ("+1, +5, +10-+16"). Check the View Section Numbering option to get a list of sections and corresponding page numbers for your document; uncheck it to get a list of sections and the absolute page numbers within them.

When you're done creating a trapping zone, you'll see it in the Trapping Zones section of the Trapping pane. Click the Enable box for all zones you want active.

Tip To change trapping styles for a document, create a trapping zone that is set for All Pages for each trapping style. Then you can just click Enable for the particular trapping style you want to be used for the current document rather than open the Trapping Styles dialog box and choose one there.

Summary

Although it's often impossible to precisely match colors from an electronic image when printing, InDesign can help make the color fidelity as high as possible through its support of color profiles and color management. It can also help make what you see onscreen and print on proofing devices look close to the final output so as to help you better gauge your actual colors.

If you use a compatible output device, InDesign also lets you control how adjacent colors print, in a process known as *trapping* that minimizes the chances of gaps appearing between colored objects. Fortunately, most users won't need to worry about fine-tuning trapping settings because InDesign's default settings handle most objects well.

✦ ✦ ✦

Page Fundamentals

It's easy to forget about pages — they're just the things that hold your text and pictures. But pages are a key part of your layout, and so InDesign comes with a set of tools to work with pages. Most of these tools help you automate repetitive work, applying common elements to a range of pages, for example, while others enable you to customize page settings such as numbering.

Although you typically work on document pages, there's a form of page called a *master page* that can function as a template for your document pages. With master pages, you can ensure that margins, headers and footers, and even standard text and graphics appear on each and every page — or selected pages. **Chapter 29** shows how these features work. The chapter also explains how to create document *templates*, which let you create a skeleton for documents that you create regularly using a common design but different content (such as newsletters), and *libraries*, which let you store commonly used objects for access by any layout artist in any document.

A layout feature unique to InDesign is its layers feature, which lets you place objects on separate electronic overlays. You can then hide and enable these overlays to change the contents of a document. For example, you may have a newsletter that has an English and Spanish version, so you would have one layer containing text frames with English content and another containing text frames with Spanish content — and you'd display each in turn to print the two version of your newsletter. **Chapter 30** explains how to use the layers feature.

Finally, InDesign gives you control over individual pages by enabling you to move, add, delete, number, and navigate through them. **Chapter 31** explains how to use these controls.

Creating Layout Standards

Think for a moment about the publications you produce. Chances are that most of your work involves creating multiple iterations of a basic set of publications, and each publication looks more or less the same from issue to issue. For example, periodicals such as newsletters, magazines, and newspapers don't change much from one issue to the next (disregarding the occasional redesigns that all publications undergo). The ongoing uniformity of such matters as page size, margins, page layouts, text formats, even the tone of the writing, gives each publication a unique look and feel.

If you had to start from scratch every time you created a publication, you'd spend the bulk of your time setting up your documents and have little time left to attend to the appearance of the content (and you'd probably get terribly bored, too). Few tasks are less rewarding than doing the same job over and over. Fortunately, InDesign includes several extremely useful features that let you automate repetitive tasks. This chapter focuses on three of them: master pages, templates, and libraries.

✦ A *master page* is a preconstructed page layout that you can use when adding pages to a multipage document. With master pages, you can design a single "background" page and then use it as the basis for as many document pages as you want. Without master pages, you would have to create every page from scratch.

✦ A *template* is a preconstructed document that's used to create multiple iterations of the same design or publication. A template is a shell of a document that contains everything in a publication — except content. Each time you need to create a new version of a repeatedly produced publication, you open its template, add the content (text and pictures), tweak as desired, and then print. Next issue, same thing.

✦ As its name suggests, a *library* is a place where you store things. Specifically, InDesign libraries are files for storing objects that you've created in InDesign and that you intend to use repeatedly in multiple documents.

When you combine master pages, templates, and libraries with the ability to create character and paragraph styles (covered in Chapters 12 and 13, respectively), you have a powerful set automation tools. Styles automate text formatting; libraries automate object creation; master pages automate page construction; and templates automate document construction.

How and to what extent you use these features depends on your personal preferences and the publications you produce. You might think that something as small as a business card wouldn't benefit from any of these features, but if it's a business card for a corporate employee, the chances are that, other than the personal information, it's exactly the same as business cards of every other employee. By creating and saving a business card template, you could quickly build cards for several or several hundred new employees. All you have to do is open the template, add the name, title, and phone number of the new employee, and then print.

For other publications, you might use several — perhaps all — of the afore-mentioned timesaving features. A good newsletter template, for example, would contain a set of styles for formatting text, probably a master spread or two (depending on whether all pages shared exactly the same design or not), and perhaps an associated library of frequently used objects — house ads, corporate logos, boilerplate text, and so on.

Tip

Although this chapter begins with master pages, this doesn't mean that you should begin work on a publication by creating master pages. You may prefer to work on text formatting tasks first and build styles before turning your attention to page layout and document construction tasks. One of the best features about InDesign is that it lets you perform tasks in whatever order makes most sense to you. Over time, you'll develop a personal modus operandi for creating publications. Whatever style you develop, make sure that you make full use of styles, libraries, master pages, and templates.

Note

In this chapter, the terms *master page* and *master spread* are used interchangeably. If you're working on facing-page documents, you'll use facing-page masters that have both left- and right-hand pages. These are master spreads. For single-sided documents, a master page has only a single page.

Creating and Applying Master Pages

Before the arrival of personal computers, publications were created by graphic designers who leaned over light tables and — armed with matte knives and waxing machines — stuck galleys of type, halftones, and plastic overlays onto paste-up boards. The paste-up boards were usually oversized sheets of white card paper on which was printed a grid of light blue lines. The blue guidelines indicated such items as the edge of the final, trimmed page, the margins in which text and pictures were placed, column boundaries, and so on. These guidelines helped the designer position elements on a page and also helped ensure consistent placement of repeating page elements, such as page numbers.

Although no paste-up boards exist in the electronic publishing world, the concept has survived in the form of *master pages*. A master page is a nonprinting page that you can use as the background (that is, as the starting point) for document pages. Typically, master pages contain text and graphic elements that appear on all pages of a publication, such as page numbers, headers, footers, folios, and so on. And like their paste-up board ancestors, master pages also include guidelines that indicate page edges, column boundaries, and margins, as well as other manually created guidelines to aid page designers in placing objects. By placing items on master pages, you save yourself the repetitive work of placing the same items one by one on each and every document page.

By default, every InDesign document you create contains a master page. Whether you use the master page or create and use additional master pages depends on the kind of publication you're creating. If it's a single-page document, such as a business card, or an advertisement, you don't need to worry about master pages at all. (Generally, master pages are of little use for one-page documents.) However, if you're creating a multipage document such as a newsletter, a book, or a catalog, using master pages will save you time and help ensure design consistency. It's impossible to overstate the importance of master pages. They're one of InDesign's most powerful features.

The Pages pane

When you work on multipage documents, you'll probably want to display the Pages pane (Window ⇨ Pages or F12), shown in Figure 29-1. The Pages pane displays an icon-based view of document pages (top) and master pages (bottom) in the current document. The controls in the Pages pane and its accompanying pop-up menu let you perform several master page–related tasks, including creating and deleting master pages, applying master pages to document pages, and creating master pages out of document pages. The Pages pane also lets you add and remove document pages. (See Chapter 31 for more information about adding and removing document pages.)

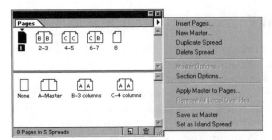

Figure 29-1: The Pages pane. The document page icons at the top of the pane show that the publication has eight pages. The master page icons at the bottom show the default masters—None and A-Master—and two custom masters (B-3 columns and C-4 columns), both based on A-Master.

Here's a quick rundown of the controls available in the Pages pane and the commands in its pop-up menu:

✦ The page icons at the top of the pane represent document pages. Dog-eared icons represent left and right pages in a facing-page document. The letter displayed on a page icon indicates the master page it's based on. (If no letter is displayed, the page is based on the blank master page.) The numbers below the page icons indicate the page numbers, including section numbering, if any (sections are covered in Chapter 31). If a page number is displayed in reverse type (that is, white characters on a black background), it means that it's currently displayed in the document window.

✦ The page icons at the bottom of the pane represent master pages. Every document includes a master page called None, which includes only margin guidelines, and Master Page A, which reflects the margin and column settings you specified in the New Document dialog box when you created the document. If a letter is displayed on a master page icon, it indicates that the master spread is based on another (parent) master page. A master page's name is displayed below its icon. If a master page name is displayed in reverse type, it's currently displayed in the document window.

✦ The Create new page button (notepad icon) at the bottom of the pane enables you to add a new page with a mouse click.

✦ The Delete selected pages button (Trash can) enables you to delete document and master pages.

✦ Insert Pages enables you to add pages to a document and specify the master page on which they're based.

✦ New Master enables you to add a new master page.

✦ Duplicate Spread, Duplicate Master Spread does exactly what it says. It enables you to duplicate the pages of a facing-page spread and add them to a document and duplicate a master page spread. The name of the command depends on what kind of spread is highlighted.

✦ Delete Page, Delete Spread, Delete Master Page, Delete Master Spread — these commands enable you to delete single pages and facing-page spreads (both document pages and master pages).

✦ Master Options is used for changing master page attributes, including name and parent master page (if you want to base a master page on another master page).

✦ Use Section Options to establish independently numbered sections in a single document. For example, you could create a section if you wanted to use a different numbering scheme (Roman numeral, perhaps) for the front matter of a book than for the body. (See Chapter 31 for more information about sections.)

✦ Apply Master to Pages is used for applying a master page layout to one or more document pages.

✦ Remove Selected Local Overrides, Remove All Local Overrides returns master objects that you've modified on document pages to their original condition.

✦ Save As Master lets you convert a document page into a master page.

✦ Set as Island Spread, Clear Island Spread — if you specify a facing-page spread to be an island spread, the pages will not be split apart and used singly in a spread with other pages.

Creating a new master page

If all the pages in the publication you're creating share essentially the same page design, you don't need to create a new master page. Instead, you can simply use the default master page called A-Master that every document has. But if you intend to use more than one page layout in your document — maybe you're building a magazine and you want some pages to use a three-column format and others to use a two-column format — you'll need to create additional master pages.

Before you create a new master page, you should have a general idea of how you want it to look. In particular, you should know where you want to place margins, column boundaries, and repeating elements, such as page numbers. (Laying out master pages is covered later in this section.) When you're ready to create a new master page, here's what you do:

Steps: Creating a Master Page

1. If the Pages pane is not displayed, choose Windows ➪ Pages or press F12.

2. From the Pages pane's palette menu, choose New Master. You can also press Option+⌘ or Ctrl+Alt and click the New page button at the bottom of the pane. The New Master dialog box, shown in Figure 29-2, displays.

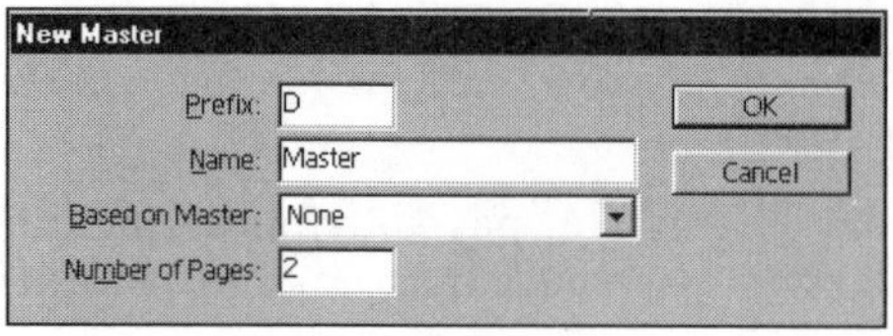

Figure 29-2: The New Master dialog box.

3. In the Prefix field, specify a one-character prefix that's attached to the front of the master page name and displayed on associated document page icons in the Pages pane.

4. In the Name field, enter a name for the master page. Use something descriptive, such as "3-column Layout," "Front Matter Layout," or "Chapter Title Pages."

5. If you want to base the master page on another master page you've already created, choose the parent master page from the Based on Master pop-up menu. (Basing a master page on another master page is covered in more detail later in this section.)

6. In the Number of Pages field, enter the number of pages you want to include in the master spread. Typically, you'll enter 2 for a facing-page document.

7. After you've finished specifying the attributes of the new master page, click OK to close the dialog box.

After you create a new master page, it's displayed in the document window. (When a master page is displayed, its name is displayed in the Page Number field in the bottom left corner of the document window.) You can modify any of a master page's attributes at any time by clicking its icon at the bottom of the Pages pane, choosing Master Options from the pane's palette menu, and changing any of the settings in the Master Options dialog box, which is identical to the New Master dialog box.

Basing a master page on another master page

If you find that a particular publication requires more than one master page, you may want to first lay out a base master page (you could use the default A-Master) and then create additional master pages that share the same basic layout but are slightly different. For example, if the magazine you're working on uses two-, three-, and four-column page layouts, you could create the two-column master spread first and include all repeating page elements. You could then create two additional master page spreads, base them on the two-column master, and specify different column formats. The two "children" masters would be identical to the parent except for the number of columns. If you subsequently decide to modify, move, or delete a repeating page element, you could make the change on the parent master, and it will automatically be applied to the children masters.

When you create a new master page, the New Master dialog box provides the option to base it on an existing master page. You can also choose or change a master spread's parent by:

✦ Choosing Master Options in the Pages pane's palette menu and then choosing a master page from the Based on Master pop-up menu.

✦ Dragging and dropping the icon of a master spread (the parent) onto the icon of another master spread (the child). Be careful if you use this method. It's possible to base only one page of a master spread on another, but in most cases you'll want to base both pages of the child master on both pages of the parent master. To do so, make sure that when you release the mouse button both pages of the child are highlighted.

✦ Clicking the master spread you want to be the child, and then pressing Option or Alt and clicking the master spread you want to be the parent.

When you base a master page on another master page, the prefix of the parent is displayed on the page icon of the child.

Tip   If you base a master spread on another master spread, you can still modify the master objects (that is, the objects inherited from the parent master) on the child master page.

Creating a master spread from a document spread

Generally, if you need a new master spread, you'll begin by choosing New Master from the Pages pane's palette menu. But you can also create a master spread from a spread of document pages. To do so, highlight the spread of document pages by clicking the page numbers below the page icons in the Pages pane, and then choose Save as Master from the Pages pane's palette menu. The new master is assigned a default name and prefix. If you want to modify any of its attributes, click its name in the Pages pane, and then choose Master Options from the pop-up menu.

Duplicating a master

You can create a copy of a master spread by clicking its icon and then choosing Duplicate Master Spread from the Pages pane's palette menu or by clicking its icon, dragging it onto the Create new page button, and releasing the mouse. If you duplicate a master spread, a parent/child relationship does not exist between the original master and the copy (as is the case when you base a master on another master).

Deleting a master

To delete a master page, click its name and then choose Delete Master Page from the Pages pane's palette menu. You can also click the master icon, and then click the Trash icon in the Pages pane or drag the icon directly to the Trash.

Laying out a master page

Because a master page is similar to a document page, you can use the same approach for building both master and document pages. Some designers prefer to do a preliminary sketch on paper and then recreate the design in InDesign. You may like to do your creative brainstorming at your computer, in which case you can use InDesign as your sketchpad. The main difference between document pages and master pages is that master pages don't contain any content (other than elements that appear on every page). So, when you're building a master page, you should be thinking more about the page's overall infrastructure rather than about details.

Here are a few observations to keep in mind when designing master pages:

✦ If you're working on a facing-page document (most multipage publications have facing-pages), you'll create facing-page master spreads. The left-hand page (used for even-numbered document pages) and right-hand page (used for odd numbered document pages) of the master spreads you create will be — more or less — mirror opposites of each other. For example, page numbers are generally placed near the outside edge of facing pages so that they're visible when a reader thumbs through the pages. Or you may decide to place the publication name on one side of a spread and balance it by placing the date of publication in the same position on the other side.

✦ If you want to automatically place page numbers on document pages, you should add a page number character on each page of your master spreads. To add a page number character, draw a text frame with the Type tool, and then choose Layout ➪ Insert Page Number or press Option+⌘+N or Ctrl+Alt+N. The prefix of the master page (A, B, C, and so on) is displayed on the master page, but on document pages, the actual page number is used. When you add a page number to a master page, make sure to format it as you want the actual page numbers to look on document pages.

✦ Perhaps the most important elements of a master page are the margins and column guides. To specify margins and columns for a master page, make sure the page is displayed in the document window, and then choose Layout Margins and Columns. The Margins and Columns dialog box, shown in Figure 29-3, is displayed. The controls in this dialog box enable you to specify the position of the margins, the number of columns, and the gutter width (space between columns).

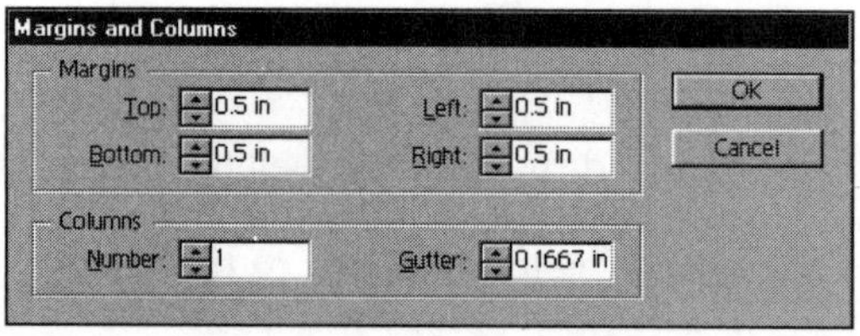

Figure 29-3: The Margins and Columns dialog box.

Tip

When placing text elements on master pages, you may want to use placeholder text instead of actual text. For example, if you produce a monthly magazine and you want to include the name of the month on each spread (perhaps opposite the name of the newsletter on the facing page), you could use placeholder text such as "[Name of month]," or "[Add month here]." If you use placeholder text, format it as you want the actual text to look on document pages.

✦ If you want to place additional guidelines on a master page, you can add as many custom guidelines as you want. (Guidelines are covered later in this chapter.)

✦ As with objects on document pages, the objects you place on master pages have a stacking order. On document pages, all master objects remain beneath any objects you add to the page.

Figure 29-4 shows a typical master page spread for a newsletter. Whenever you want to make a change to a master page, double-click its icon in the Pages pane to display it in the document window.

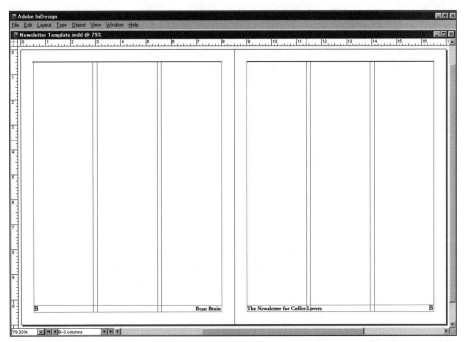

Figure 29-4: A typical three-column master layout for a newsletter. The footer at the bottom of the left- and right-hand pages includes a page number character (B) on the outside.

Tip   To copy a master spread from one document to another, display the source document, click the master's name in the Pages pane, drag it to the window of the target document and then release the mouse button.

Applying a master page to document pages

After you've built a master page, you can apply it to new document pages as you add them or to existing pages. (See Chapter 31 for information about adding and removing document pages.) For facing-page documents, you can apply both pages of a master spread to both pages of a document spread, or you can apply one page of a master spread to one page of a document spread. For example, you could apply a master page with a two-column format to the left-hand page of a document spread and apply a master page with a three-column format to the right-hand page.

To apply only one page of a master spread to a document page, click the icon of the master spread and then drag it onto the icon of the document page you want to format. When the target document page is highlighted (framed in a black rectangle as shown in Figure 29-5), release the mouse button. If both document pages are highlighted, both sides of the master spread are applied to the document spread.

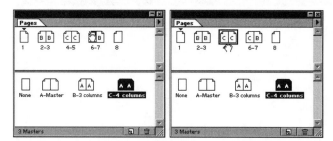

Figure 29-5: Left: Applying a single page of a master spread to a document page. Right: Applying both pages of a master spread to a document spread.

To apply both pages of a master spread to both pages of a document spread, drag the master spread's icon onto the document spread's icon. When both pages of the target document spread are highlighted, as shown in Figure 29-5, release the mouse button.

InDesign also lets you apply a master page to multiple document pages in a single operation. You can:

✦ Select the document pages to which you want to apply a master. You can click a page and then Shift+click another page to select a range of pages, or you can hold down the ⌘ or Ctrl keys and click pages to select nonconsecutive pages. After you've selected the document pages, press Option or Alt and click the master page you want to apply.

✦ Choose Apply Master to Pages from the Pages pane's palette menu. The Apply Master dialog box is displayed. Choose the master page you want to apply from the Apply Master pop-up menu and specify the pages to which you want to apply it in the To Pages field. Use commas to separate page numbers; use a hyphen to specify a range of pages. For example, you could enter 2, 4-6, 8, to apply the selected master to pages 2, 4, 5, 6, and 8.

You can also use the techniques explained previously to apply a different master page to a document page. If you want to dissociate a document page from its applied master page, you can apply the default None master page the same way you apply any other master page.

Modifying master items on document pages

As you work on a document page that's based on a master, you may find that you need to modify, move, or delete a master object. For example, you might apply a master to the first page of a newsletter and then decide that the page number you've placed on the master page isn't necessary for page 1. In this case, you'd select the master object on the document page and delete it. Any change you make to a master object on a local page is referred to as a *local override.*

If you remove a master object from a document page, you sever the object's relationship to the master page object for that document page only. If you subsequently move or modify the object on the master page, it won't affect the deleted object on the document page — it remains deleted on that particular document page.

However, you can modify a master object on a document page without completely breaking its relationship to the corresponding object on the master page. For example, if you change the size, position, or content of a master object on a document page, any subsequent size, position, or content change you make to the object on the master page does not affect the object you modified. But any changes you make to the stroke or fill of the object on the master page are applied to the overridden master object on the document page. Similarly, if you use any of the transformation tools or the corresponding controls in the Transform pane to modify a master object on a document page, any similar transformation applied to the corresponding object on the master page is not applied to the overridden object.

In other words, any type of attribute applied to the item on a particular document page prevents any changes to the same attribute on the master page from affecting that document page.

Tip The Display Master Items command (View ➪ Display Master Items, or ⌘+Y or Ctrl+Y) lets you show or hide master objects on document pages. When a check mark is displayed next to the name of the command, master objects are displayed.

To modify a master object on a document page, you must select it. However, master objects behave slightly differently from other objects on document pages. Specifically, to select a master object on a document page, you must hold down Shift+⌘ or Ctrl+Shift when you click the object with one of the selection tools. After you select a master object on a document page, you can modify it in the same manner as you modify nonmaster objects.

If you modify one or more master objects on a document page and then decide you want to revert to the original master objects, you can remove the local overrides. To do so, display the document page that contains the master objects you've modified, select the objects, and then choose Remove Selected Local Overrides from the Pages pane's palette menu. If no objects are selected, the command name changes to Remove All Local Overrides (if the selected spread doesn't have any modified master objects, the command is not available).

Using Templates

A template is a preconstructed InDesign document that you use as the starting point for creating multiple versions of the same design or publication. For example, if you were assigned the task of creating 10 testimonial ads that share the same layout but use different pictures and text, you would begin by creating a template that contains all the elements that are the same in every ad — placeholder frames for the pictures and text, guidelines, and so on. Along the same lines, if you produce periodicals such as a newsletter or a magazine, you should create a template for each one.

The process of creating a template is much the same as creating a document. You create the required character and paragraph styles, master pages, repeating elements (for example, the nameplate on the first page and mailing information on the back page), and so on. The only thing you don't add to a template is actual content.

It would be nice if designers had the luxury of creating a template for each new publication they produced. But in the real world, templates are often created by gutting an existing document. The first time you create a publication such as a newsletter, the main goal during production is getting a finished document to the printer — ideally on time. After you've finished the first issue of a publication (or a prototype), you can open the file, remove all objects and content that aren't repeated in every issue, and then save the gutted file as a template. This is probably how you'll wind up building many of your templates.

Tip If you're designing a template that will be used by others, you might want to add a layer of instructions. When it's time to print a document based on the template, simply hide the annotation layer. (See Chapter 30 for more information about working with layers.)

Steps: Saving a Document as a Template

1. Choose Save As from the File menu or press Shift+⌘+S or Ctrl+Shift+S to display the Save As dialog box, shown in Figure 29-6.

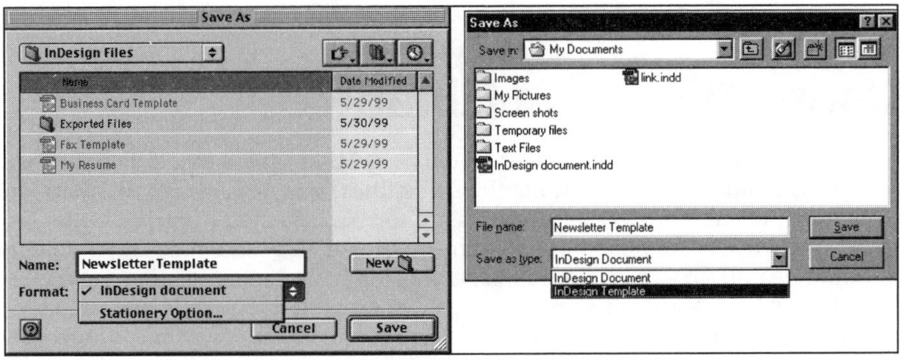

Figure 29-6: Saving templates is slightly different on a Mac (left) than on a PC (right).

2. Choose a storage folder and specify a name for the file. (It's not a bad idea to add "Template" to the file name, if possible. It enables whoever uses the file to know its purpose.)

3. On a Mac, choose Stationery Option from the Format pop-up menu, click Stationery in the Stationery Option dialog box, as shown in Figure 29-7, and then click OK. On a PC, choose InDesign Template from the Save as type pop-up menu.

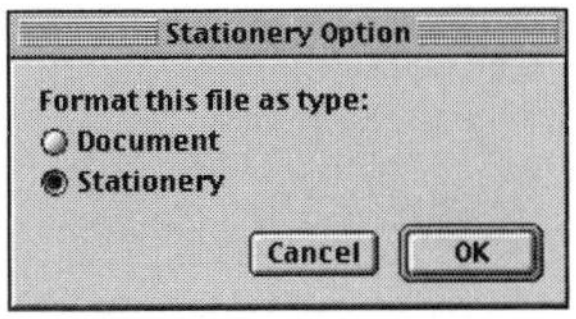

Figure 29-7: Macintosh users must choose the Stationery Option to save an InDesign document as a template.

4. Click OK to close the Save As dialog box.

A template is almost exactly the same as a standard InDesign document with one major exception: A template is slightly protected from being overridden. When you open a template, it's assigned a default name (Untitled-1, Untitled-2, and so on). The first time you choose File ⇨ Save, or press Shift+⌘+S or Ctrl+Shift+S, the Save As dialog box is displayed.

Note

As you use a template over time, you're likely to discover that you forgot to include something—perhaps a style, a repeating element on a particular master page, or an entire master page. To modify a template, you must open it, make your changes, and then use the Save or Save As command to save the file in the same place and with the same name as the original.

Storing Objects in Libraries

If you're a savvy InDesign user, you'll never build the same document twice. That's what templates are for. Along the same lines, you never have to create the same object twice. That's what libraries are for. An InDesign library is a file—similar in some ways to a document file—in which you can store individual objects, groups and nested objects, ruler guides, and grids (ruler guides and grids are covered in the next section). For example, if you've created a logo in InDesign and you want to use it in other documents, you could place it in a library. Once you've saved an object in a library, it's as though you have an endless supply of copies. Every time you need a copy, all you have to do is drag one out of the library.

Creating a library is easy: Use Window ⇨ Libraries ⇨ New, choose a location in which to save the library, give the library a name, and click OK. Figure 29-8 shows the dialog box.

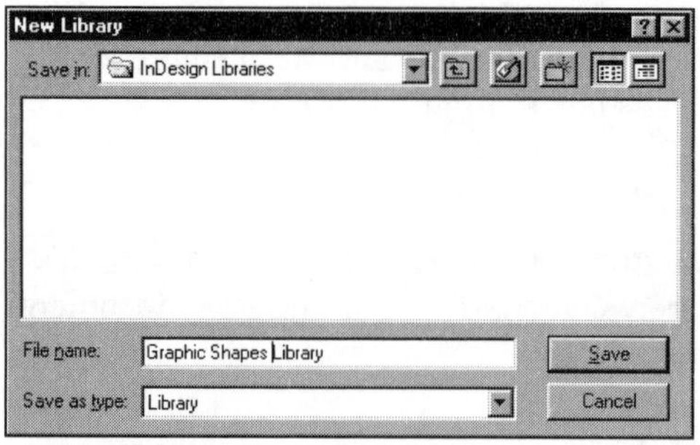

Figure 29-8: The dialog box in which you save a library.

You can create as many libraries as you want and store them wherever is most convenient, including a network server so other InDesign users can share them. When it comes to naming and organizing libraries, the choice is yours. If you work for an advertising agency, for example, you may decide to create a separate library for each client; each library could contain logos, images, boilerplate text (disclaimers, copyright information, legal blurbs, and so on). If you work for an in-house art department, you could create separate libraries for corporate logos (black-and-white, grayscale, and two-color or four-color variations), house ads, frequently used pictures, and standing art.

Tip InDesign libraries are cross-platform. That is, you can open libraries created on a Mac using a PC and vice versa. On the PC, libraries have the file-name extension .INDT, whereas on the Mac they have no file-name extension. In a cross-platform environment, add the PC file-name extensions even to Mac files so Windows can easily tell what type of file each file is.

After you create a new library, an empty library pane, as shown in Figure 29-9, is displayed. The name you assigned is displayed in its title bar. You can group the pane with other panes (by dragging its tab onto another pane) or close it by clicking its close box or choosing Close Library from its pop-up menu.

Objects currently displayed

Library Item Information

Show Library Subset

New Library Item

Delete Library Item

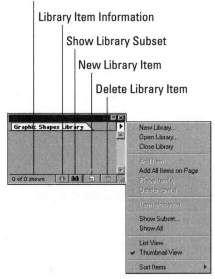

Figure 29-9: A new (empty) library and its accompanying pop-up menu.

At this point, you're ready to begin placing objects into the library, after which, you can begin copying the objects into other documents. Before we look at moving items into and out of libraries, here's a brief description of the controls in a library pane and the commands in the accompanying pop-up menu, which is shown in Figure 29-9:

✦ The numbers in the lower-left corner of the pane indicate the number of objects currently displayed in the pane (though not necessarily visible, depending on the size of the pane) and the number of objects in the library. Search capabilities let you display a subset of the entire library.

✦ Clicking the Library Item Information button displays the Item Information dialog box, shown in Figure 29-10. Here you can assign a name, type, and description to a library object. (You can search for library objects based on these attributes.)

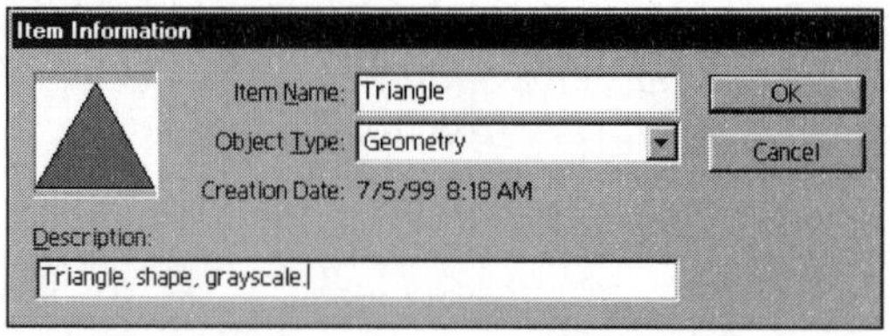

Figure 29-10: The Item Information dialog box.

✦ The Show Library Subset button displays a dialog box that enables you to locate and display objects that meet certain search criteria.

✦ The New Library Item enables you to add a selected object on a document page to a library.

✦ The Delete Library Item button enables you to delete highlighted objects in the library.

✦ New Library, Open Library, Close Library commands: The first two (New Library and Open Library) are duplicates of the same commands in the Windows menu. The Close Library command does the same thing as clicking a library pane's close box.

✦ The Add Items and Add All Items on Page commands enable you to add a selected item or all items on a document page to a library.

✦ Place Item(s) enables you to place copies of selected library objects into a document.

✦ Delete Item(s) enables you to remove selected library objects from the library.

✦ Item Information displays the Item Information dialog box, shown in Figure 29-10.

✦ Show Subset opens the same dialog box that's displayed if you click the Show Library Subset button. The dialog box enables you to locate and display objects that meet certain search criteria.

✦ Show All displays all library objects (rather than a subset identified by a search).

✦ When the List View option is checked, library objects are displayed in a list rather than as Thumbnails.

✦ When the Thumbnails View option is checked, each library object is displayed in its own thumbnail window.

To open an existing library, choose Window ➪ Libraries ➪ Open or press Option+Shift+⌘+L or Ctrl+Alt+Shift+L.

Note If a library pane is open, you can also choose Open Library from the pane's palette menu. If you've already opened the library in the current session (in this case, a session begins when you turn on your computer and ends when you shut down), you can choose its name from the submenu that's displayed when you choose Window ➪ Libraries. The same submenu enables you to toggle between show and hide for any open library. (This is a nice way to recover some screen real estate if you don't need immediate access to an open library.)

To delete a library, you must delete the file. Either drag the file icon to the Trash (Mac) or move the file icon to the Recycle Bin (Windows).

Adding objects to libraries

In addition to placing individual objects, such as text and graphics frames, into a library, you can also place multiple selected objects, groups, nested frames, ruler guides, guidelines, and all objects on a page.

You have several ways to add objects to a library. You can:

✦ Select one or more objects and then drag and drop them into an open library pane.

✦ Select one or more objects and then click the New Library Item button at the bottom of an open library pane.

✦ Select one or more objects and then choose Add Item from the pop-up menu of an open library pane.

✦ Choose Add All Items on Page from the pop-up menu of an open library pane to add all objects on the current page or spread.

Tip   If you hold down the Option or Alt key when adding an object to a library using any of the preceding methods, the Item Information dialog box is displayed. This dialog box enables you to add searchable attributes to the object.

To delete a library object, drag its icon to the Trash icon at the bottom of the pane or click the object once and then choose Delete Item(s) from the library pane's palette menu. You can select a range of objects by clicking the first one and then Shift+clicking the last one. You can select multiple, noncontinuous objects by holding down the ⌘ or Ctrl key and clicking their icons.

Figure 29-11 shows a library with several objects. The same library is displayed in thumbnails format and in list format.

Figure 29-11: On the left, the library is displayed in Thumbnails view; on the right in List view.

When you place an object into a library, all its attributes are saved. For example, if you import a picture into a document and then place a copy of the picture into a library, the path to the original picture file is saved, as are any transformations you've applied to the picture or its frame (scale, rotation, shear, and so on). If you save text in a library, all formats, including styles, are retained.

Cataloging library objects

If your libraries contain only a few objects, finding the one you're looking for won't be very hard. But a library can hold as many objects as you want, and as a library becomes bigger, locating a particular object gets increasingly difficult. To make library objects easier to find, InDesign lets you tag them with several searchable attributes.

To tag a library element, select it and then choose Item Information from the library pane's palette menu. You can also display the Item Information dialog box by double-clicking a library object or by clicking a library object once and then clicking the Library Item Information dialog box at the bottom of the library pane. (Figure 29-10 shows the Item Information dialog box.) Now specify a Name, Object Type, and/or Description. In the Description field, it's a good idea to enter one or more keywords that describe the object so that you can easily find it later. Click OK to close the dialog box and return to the document.

Library Caveats

Because the attributes of the original object are retained when you place a copy in a library, you have to watch out for some pitfalls:

✦ If you move, modify, or delete the original graphic files associated with a picture you've placed in a library and then copy the library object into a document, the Links pane will report that the graphics file is modified or missing (just as it would if you imported the picture and then moved, modified, or deleted the original). It's a good idea to store graphics files used in libraries in a common location, such as in a Standards folder on the network, so the graphics files aren't accidentally moved or deleted when you delete or archive a set of project files that happen to contain objects placed in libraries.

✦ If you copy a text frame from a library onto a document page, any character styles, paragraph styles, or colors in the library object that have the same name as character styles, paragraph styles, or colors in the target document are replaced by those in the target document. If the target document does not contain character styles, paragraph styles, or colors in the placed text, they're added to the document.

✦ If you copy a text frame from a library onto a document page, make sure that the fonts are available. (If they're not available, you'll have to choose alternative fonts.)

Performing searches on library objects

InDesign enables you to search for library objects based on the information specified in the Item Information dialog box. For example, if you've placed several different corporate logos into a library that includes many other objects, you could search for the term *logo* in the Name or the Description field. If you used the word *logo* in either of these fields for your logos, a search of these fields for the word *logo* would identify and display your logos. The ability to search for library objects based on name and description is a good reason to name your library objects carefully and consistently and to specify keywords in the Description field of the Item Information dialog box.

Steps: Searching for Library Objects

1. Choose Show Subset from a library pane's palette menu or click the Show Library Subset command at the bottom of the pane. The Subset dialog box, shown in Figure 29-12 displays.

2. To search the entire library, click Search Entire Library; to search only the objects currently displayed in the page, click Search Currently Shown Items.

3. From the left-most pop-up menu in the Parameters area, choose the Item Information category you want to search: Item Name, Creation Date, Object Type, or Description.

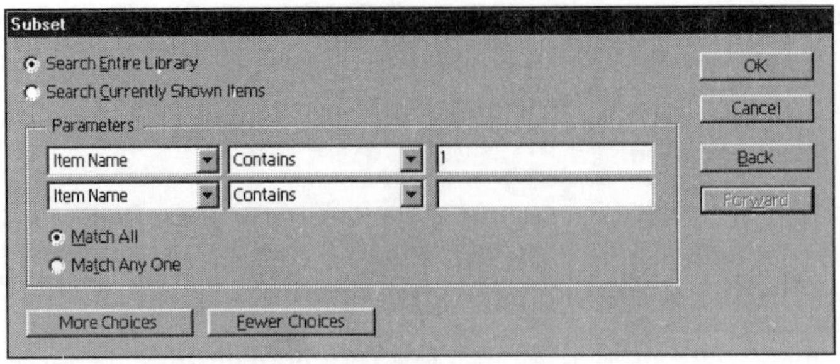

Figure 29-12: The Subset dialog box.

4. From the next pop-up menu, choose Contains if you intend to search for text contained in the chosen category; choose Doesn't Contain if you want to exclude objects that contain the text you specify.

5. In the right-most field, type the word or phrase you want to search for (if Contains is selected) or exclude (if Doesn't Contain is selected).

6. To add more search criteria, click More Choices; to reduce the number of search criteria, click Fewer Choices. You can add up to five levels of search criteria.

7. To display objects that match all search criteria, select Match All; to display objects that match any of the search criteria, select Match Any One. (These options are available only if two or more levels of search criteria are displayed.)

8. Click OK to conduct the search and close the dialog box.

All the objects that match the search criteria are displayed in the pane. The pane is empty if no objects matched the search criteria. If you want to display all objects after conducting a search, choose Show All from the library pane's palette menu.

Tip   The Sort Items command in a library pane's palette menu lets you sort objects by Name, Oldest, Newest, and Type. If you sort by Oldest or Newest, items are arranged based on the order in which they were placed into the library.

Copying library objects onto document pages

Once you've placed an object into a library and, optionally, specified item information for the object, you can place copies of the library object into any document or into another library. To place a copy of a library object onto the currently displayed document page, click the object's icon in the library pane and drag it onto the page. As you drag, the outline of the library object is displayed. Release the mouse button when the outline is positioned where you want to place the object. You can also place a library object onto a document by clicking its icon and then choosing Place Item(s).

Tip You can copy an object from one library to another by dragging its icon from the source library pane and dropping it onto the target library pane. If you hold down the Option or Alt key when dragging and dropping an object between libraries, the original object is removed from the source library (in effect moving it from one library to the other).

Using Ruler Guides and Grids

If you've every seen a carpenter use a chalked string to "snap" a temporary line to use as an aid for aligning objects, you understand the concept behind guidelines. They're not structurally necessary, and they don't show in the final product, yet they can still make your work easier. InDesign lets you create and display three types of nonprinting guidelines:

✦ *Ruler guides* are movable guidelines that you can create by hand or automatically. They're helpful for placing items precisely and aligning multiple items.

✦ A *baseline grid* is a series of horizontal lines that help in aligning lines of text and objects across a multicolumn page. When displayed, a baseline grid makes a page look like a sheet of lined paper.

✦ A *document grid* is a crisscross of horizontal and vertical lines that aid in object alignment and placement.

InDesign's grids and guides capabilities verge on overkill. Chances are you'll end up using a combination of ruler guides and the baseline, or ruler guides and the document grid, but using all three is more complicated than necessary.

Ruler guides

InDesign enables you to create individual ruler guides manually or a set of guides automatically with the Create Guides command (Layout ➪ Create Guides). (If the rulers are not displayed at the top and left of the document window, choose View ➪ Show Rulers or press ⌘+R or Ctrl+R.) Go to the page or spread onto which you want to place ruler guides. Now click the horizontal ruler or vertical ruler and drag the pointer onto a page or the pasteboard. Release the mouse button when the guideline is positioned where you want it. If you release the mouse when the pointer is over a page, the ruler guide extends from one edge of the page to the other (but not across a spread). If you release the mouse button when the pointer is over the pasteboard, the ruler guide extends across both pages of a spread and the pasteboard. If you want a guide to extend across a spread and the pasteboard, you can also hold down the ⌘ or Ctrl key as you drag and release the mouse when the pointer is over a page.

Tip   You can place both a horizontal and vertical guide at the same time by pressing ⌘ or Ctrl and dragging the ruler intersection point onto a page.

Ruler guides are cyan in color (unless you change the color using Layout ➪ Ruler Guides) and are associated with the layer onto which they're placed. You can show and hide ruler guides by showing and hiding the layers that contain them. You can even create layers that contain nothing but ruler guides and then show and hide them as you wish. (See Chapter 30 for more information about layers.)

Tip   You can also place a guide that extends across the page or spread and pasteboard by double-clicking the vertical or horizontal ruler.

Tip   If you want to create ruler guides for several document pages, create a master page, add the guides to the master page, and then apply the master to the appropriate document pages.

Steps: Creating a Set of Guides Automatically

1. If the document contains multiple layers, display the Layers pane (Window ➪ Layers or F7) and click the name of the layer to which you want to add guides. (See Chapter 30 for more information about layers.)

2. Choose Layout ➪ Create Guides. The Create Guides dialog box, shown in Figure 29-13, displays. Check Preview if you want to see the guides on the current document page as you create them.

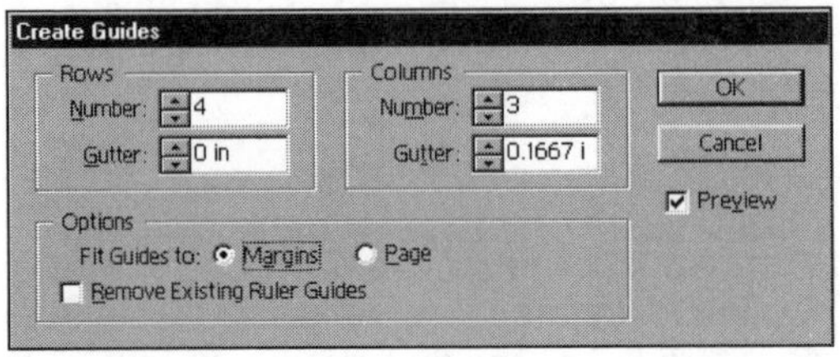

Figure 29-13: The Create Guides dialog box.

3. In the Rows and Columns areas, specify the number of guides you want to add in the Number fields and, optionally, specify a Gutter width between horizontal (Rows) and vertical (Columns) guides. Enter 0 in the Gutter fields if you don't want gutters between guides.

4. In the Options area, click Margins to fit the guides in the margin boundaries; click Page to fit the guides within the page boundary.

5. Check Remove Existing Guides to remove any previously placed ruler guides.

6. When you're done specifying the attributes of the ruler guides, click OK to close the dialog box. Figure 29-14 shows the guides created using the specifications shown in Figure 29-13.

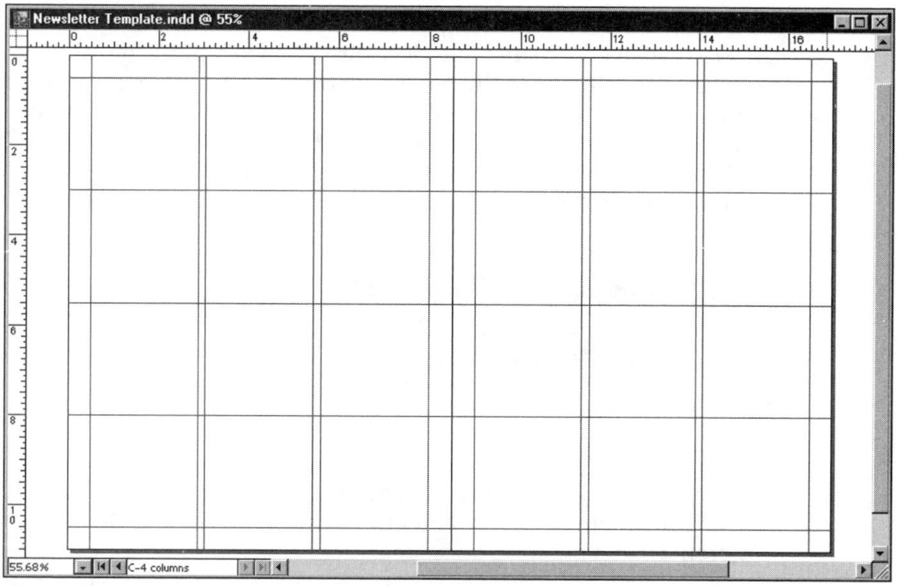

Figure 29-14: The spread to which we applied the guides specified in Figure 29-13.

Working with ruler guides

Once you've created ruler guides, you can show or hide them, lock or unlock them, and select and move, copy and paste them, or delete one or more guides at a time. Here are a few pointers for working with ruler guides:

✦ To display or hide ruler guides, choose View ➪ Show/Hide Guides or press ⌘+; or Ctrl+;.

✦ To lock or unlock all ruler guides, choose View ➪ Lock Guides. (If Lock Guides is checked, ruler guides are locked.)

✦ To select a ruler guide, click it with a selection tool. To select multiple guides, hold down the Shift key and click them. The color of a selected guide changes from blue to the color of its layer. To select all ruler guides on a page or spread, press Option+⌘+G or Ctrl+Alt+G.

✦ To move a guide, click and drag it as you would any object. To move multiple guides, select them and then drag them. To move guides to another page, select them, choose Edit ➪ Cut, or ⌘+X or Ctrl+X, or Edit ➪ Copy, or ⌘+C or

Ctrl+C, display the target page, and then choose Edit ⇨ Paste, or ⌘+V or Ctrl+V. If the target page is the same shape as the source page, the guides are placed in their original position.

✦ To delete ruler guides, select them and then press Delete or Backspace.

✦ To change the color of ruler guides and the view percentage above which they're displayed (the default view threshold is 5 percent), choose Layout ⇨ Ruler Guides. The Ruler Guides dialog box, shown in Figure 29-15, displays. Modify the View Threshold value and choose a different color from the Color pop-up menu, and then click OK. If you change the settings in the Ruler Guides dialog box when no documents are open, the new settings become defaults and are applied to all subsequently created documents.

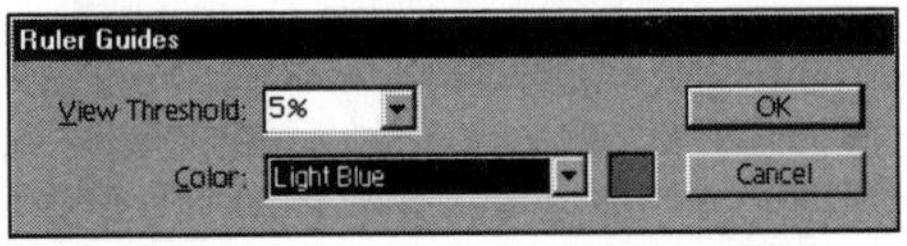

Figure 29-15: Ruler Guides dialog box.

✦ To display ruler guides behind objects instead of in front of them, choose File ⇨ Preferences ⇨ Guides and check Guides in Back in the Guides Preferences dialog box.

✦ If the Snap to Guides command (View ⇨ Snap to Guides, or Shift+⌘+; or Ctrl+Shift+;) is checked, objects edges will snap to ruler guides when you drag them in the snap zone. To specify the snap zone (the distance — in pixels — at which an object will snap to a guide), choose File ⇨ Preferences ⇨ Guides, or ⌘+K or Ctrl+K, and enter a value in the Snap to Zone field in the Guides Preferences dialog box.

Working with the baseline grid

Every new document you create includes a baseline grid. If the document you're working on uses a multicolumn page layout, a baseline grid can be helpful for aligning text baselines across columns and for ensuring that object edges align with text baselines. Baseline grids aren't much use for small documents — business cards, ads, and so on — and one-column designs.

Steps: Specifying a Custom Baseline Grid

1. Choose File ⇨ Preferences ⇨ Grids or press ⌘+K or Ctrl+K and choose the Grids pane from the pop-up menu. The Grids Preferences dialog box, shown in Figure 29-16 is displayed.

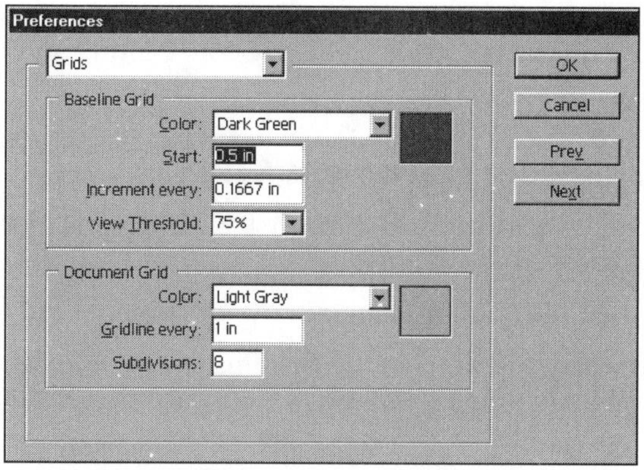

Figure 29-16: The Grids Preferences dialog box.

2. Choose a color from the Color pop-up menu in the Baseline Grid area..

3. In the Start field, enter the distance between the top of the page and the first grid line. If you enter 0, the Increment Every value determines the distance between the top of the page and the first grid line.

4. Enter the distance between grid lines in the Increment every field. Generally, the value you enter in this field will be the same as the leading value you use for the publication's body text.

5. Choose a View Threshold percentage from the pop-up menu or enter a value in the field. Generally, you don't want to display the baseline grid at reduced view percentages because grid lines become tightly spaced.

6. Click OK to close the dialog box and return to the document.

A baseline grid is document-wide (that is, you can't change it from page to page), and grid lines are displayed behind all objects, layers, and ruler guides. The default baseline grid begins a half-inch from the top of a document page, the grid lines are light blue lines and placed one pica apart; and grid lines are displayed at view percentages above 75 percent. If you change any of these settings when no documents are open, the changes are applied to all subsequently created documents; if a document is open, changes apply only to that document.

Tip   The Show/Hide Baseline Grid command (View ➪ Show/Hide Baseline Grid, or Option+⌘+" or Ctrl+Alt+") lets you display and hide a document's baseline grid.

Working with the document grid

Like the baseline grid, every document includes a default document grid, which is a set of horizontal and vertical lines. And like baseline grids, you may or may not find the document grid to be a useful aid for laying out pages. If you like working on graph paper in the real world, the document guide may be just your cup of tea. On the other hand, you may find document grids to be too constricting and opt not to use them.

Steps: Specifying a Custom Document Grid

1. Choose File ⇨ Preferences ⇨ Grids, or ⌘+K or Ctrl+K. The Grids Preferences dialog box, shown in Figure 29-16 displays.

2. Choose a color from the Color pop-up menu in the Document Grid area.

3. Enter the distance between grid lines in the Gridline every field. If your basic measurement unit is an inch, you'll probably want to use the default value of 1 inch.

4. Enter the number of divisions between grid lines in the Subdivisions field. If your basic measurement unit is an inch, you can specify a value of 6 to subdivide the grid into one-pica squares. Or, if you prefer, you can enter a value of 4, 8, 16, and so on to subdivide the grid into standard divisions of an inch.

5. Click OK to close the dialog box and return to the document.

Tip   The Show/Hide Document Grid command (View ⇨ Show/Hide Document Grid or ⌘+" or Ctrl+") lets you display and hide the document grid.

Summary

If you want to be a true InDesign expert, you must take advantage of three of its most powerful features: master pages, templates, and libraries. All of these features save time and ensure design consistency across documents. A master page is a preformatted page design that you can apply to document pages in a multipage publication; a template is a preconstructed document that serves as the starting point when you need to create multiple versions of the same publication; and a library is a storage file in which you can save any object you've created with InDesign for use in other publications.

To help you place and align objects, InDesign lets you create three types of guidelines: ruler guides, the baseline grid, and the document grid. You can show or hide guidelines, and you have the option to snap object edges to guidelines when you drag them in the specified snap zone.

✦   ✦   ✦

Working with Layers

Publishers seem to spend a lot of time doing the same things: creating several different versions of the same ad for different markets or flowing text in another language into a design. The goal of software is to automate the predictable so you have more time for creativity. Toward this goal, InDesign provides a method for preserving the time you put into creating and editing a layout that is used for more than one purpose: *layers*.

If you've ever seen a series of clear plastic overlays in presentations, it's easy to understand layers. In one of those old overhead presentations, the teacher might have started with one overlay containing a graphic, and then added another overlay with descriptive text, and then added a third overlay containing a chart. Each overlay contains distinct content, but you can see through each one to the others to get the entire message. InDesign's layers are somewhat like this, letting you isolate content on slices of a document. You can then show and hide layers, lock objects on layers, rearrange layers, and more.

Understanding Layers

Each document contains a default layer, Layer 1, which contains all of your objects until you create and select a new layer. Objects on the default layer — and any other layer for that matter — follow InDesign's standard stacking order. (The first object you create is the back-most, the last one you create is the front-most, and all the other objects fall somewhere in between. See Chapter 7 for complete information about stacking order.)

Like clear plastic overlays, the order of layers also affects the stacking order of the objects. Objects on the bottom layer are behind other objects, and objects on the top layer are in front of other objects. In Figure 30-1, the "Background Graphic" layer toward the bottom of the list contains the texture graphic and the main text of the menu. Two additional layers contain different prices, in separate text frames, for different markets.

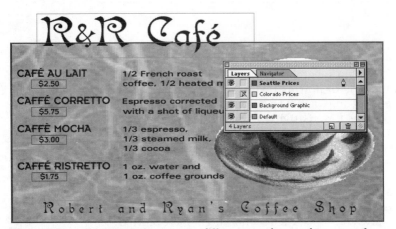

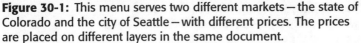

Figure 30-1: This menu serves two different markets — the state of Colorado and the city of Seattle — with different prices. The prices are placed on different layers in the same document.

Although layers are often compared to plastic overlays, you'll find one big difference: Layers are not specific to individual pages. Each layer encompasses the entire document, which doesn't make much difference when you're working on a one-page ad, but makes a significant difference when it comes to a 16-page newsletter. When you create layers and place objects on them, it's important that your strategy considers all the pages in the document.

The Layers pane (Window ➪ Layers or F7) is your gateway to creating and manipulating layers (see Figure 30-2). As with other panes, when Show ToolTips is checked in the General pane of the Preferences dialog box (Edit ➪ Preferences ➪ General, or ⌘+K or Ctrl+K), you can learn what controls do by pointing at them. If you know what the controls do, you can intuit a great deal about how to work with layers.

Eye icon indication a visible layer

Palette menus for manipulating layers

Pen icon indicating the active layer

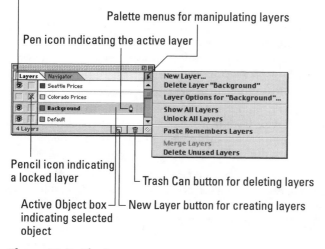

Pencil icon indicating
a locked layer

Trash Can button for deleting layers

Active Object box
indicating selected
object

New Layer button for creating layers

Figure 30-2: The Layers pane.

When, Where, and Why to Use Layers

The Layers feature is one that you can honestly ignore. If you never looked at the Layers pane, you could continue to do your work in InDesign. But you should take a look at the possibilities and see if they fit into your workflow. In the long run, you'll save time and prevent mistakes that can result when you need to track changes across multiple documents.

Say you've got an ad with the same text copy in it, but a different headline and image for each city it runs in. You can place the boilerplate information on one layer, and the information that changes on other layers. If any of the boilerplate information changes, you need to change it only once. To print different versions of the ad, you control which layers print. As already shown, the ad in Figure 30-1 contains two different versions of a menu, each with different prices.

You might use layers in the following situations:

✦ A project with a high-resolution background image, such as a texture, that takes a long time to redraw. You can hide the background image layer while designing other elements, and then show it occasionally to see how it works with the rest of the design.

Continued

(continued)

✦ A document that you need to produce in several versions — for example, a produce ad with different prices for different cities or a clothing catalog featuring different coats depending on the area's climate. You can place the content that changes on separate layers, and then print the layers you need.

✦ A project that includes objects you do not want to print. If you want to suppress printout of objects for any reason, the only way you can do this is to place them on a layer and hide it. You might have a layer that's used for nothing but adding editorial and design comments; you could then delete this layer when the document is final.

✦ A publication that is translated into several languages. Depending on the layout, you can place all the common objects on one layer, and then create a different layer for each language's text. Changes to the common objects need to happen only once — unlike if you created copies of the original document and flowed the translated text into the copies.

✦ You might use layers to experiment with different layouts of the same document. You can show and hide layers to present different options to your supervisor or client. This strategy enables you to use common elements, such as the logo and legal information, in several versions of the same design.

✦ A complex design that contains many overlapping objects, text wraps, and grouped objects. Say the background of a page consists of a checkerboard pattern made up of filled rectangular frames. You don't want to accidentally select the blocks while you're working with other objects. If you isolate complex objects on their own layer, you can show only that layer to work on it, hide that layer to concentrate on other layers, lock the layer so objects can't be selected, and otherwise manipulate the layer.

When determining whether objects should go on a layer, remember that layers are document-wide and not page-specific.

Creating Layers

Each document contains a default layer, Layer 1, that contains all the objects you place on master pages and document pages — until you create and activate new layers. You can create as many layers as you need; the number of layers in a document is limited only by the RAM available to InDesign. Once you create a new layer, it is activated automatically so you can begin working on it.

Creating a layer

The Layers pane (Window ⇨ Layers or F7) provides several methods for creating new layers. It doesn't matter which document page is displayed when you create a layer because the layer encompasses all the pages in the document. To create a layer, do one of the following:

✦ To create a new layer on top of all existing layers with the default name of "Layer #," click the New Layer button on the Layers pane, as shown in Figure 30-3.

Figure 30-3: Clicking the New Layer button on the Layers pane creates a new layer.

✦ To create a layer above the selected layer with the default name, ⌘+click or Ctrl+click the New Layer button.

✦ To create a new layer on top of all existing layers, but customize its name and identifying color, Option+click or Alt+click the New Layer button. Use the New Layer dialog box to specify options for the layer.

✦ To create a customized layer on top of all existing layers, choose New Layer from the Layers pane's palette menu. The New Layer dialog box lets you customize the layer.

Note

You can create a layer while a master page is displayed. Objects you create on a layer while a master page is displayed will be placed on all pages based on that master page. However, the layer is not specific to that master page. It is available for all document pages — even those based on other master pages — and you can place objects on it.

Customizing layers

A dialog box lets you customize the name, identifying color, guides, and lock status of objects on a new or existing layer. If you choose to customize the layer when you create it (by Option+clicking or Alt+clicking the New Layer button), the New Layer dialog box appears. If you choose to customize an existing layer, double-click it to display the Layer Options dialog box. (You can also choose Layer Options for [name of layer] from the Layers pane's palette menu.)

Whether you're using the New Layer dialog box shown in Figure 30-4 or the Layer Options dialog box, the options all work the same.

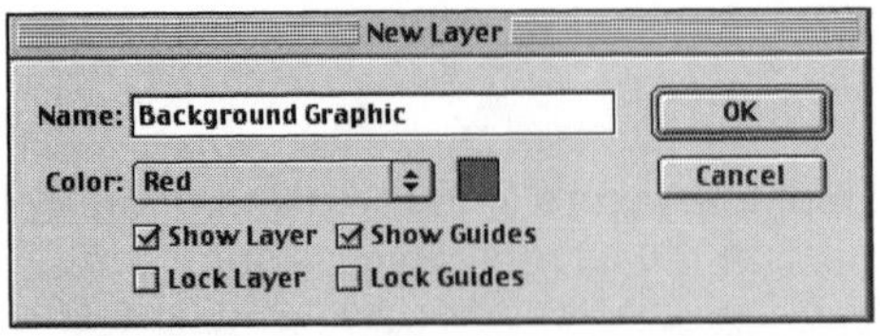

Figure 30-4: The New Layer dialog box, which works the same as the Layer Options dialog box.

Here are the New Layer dialog box options:

✦ **Name field:** Type a descriptive name of up to 32 characters for the layer. For example, if you're using layers for multilingual publishing, you might have a "U.S. English" layer, a "French" layer, and a "German" layer. If you're using layers so you can hide background objects while you're working, you might have a "Background Graphic" layer.

✦ **Color pop-up menu and button:** A layer's color helps you identify which layer an object is on. The color displays to the left of the layer name in the Layers pane, and displays on each object on that layer. The color is applied to frame edges, selection handles, bounding boxes, text ports, and text wraps. Note that the display of frame edges is controlled by the View ⇨ Show Frame Edges command. By default, InDesign applies a different color to each new layer, but you can customize it to something meaningful for your document and workflow. Choose a color from the list or double-click the color swatch to use from the operating system's color picker.

✦ **Show Layer checkbox:** Checked by default, this control lets you specify whether objects on a layer display and print. If you want to suppress printout of the objects on a layer (for example, to hide a different version of a document or to hide pictures while proofing), uncheck Show Layer. The Show Layer checkbox has the same effect as clicking the eye icon on the Layers pane.

✦ **Lock Layer checkbox:** Unchecked by default, this option lets you control whether objects on a layer can be edited. Check Lock Layer if you don't want to be able to select items and modify them. For example, in a document containing multiple versions of text on different layers, you might lock the layer containing background images and other objects that stay the same. The Lock Layer checkbox has the same effect as clicking the Pencil icon on the Layers pane.

✦ **Show Guides checkbox:** This option lets you control the display of guides that were created while the selected layer was active. When checked, as it is by default, you can create guides while any layer is active and view those guides on any layer. When unchecked, you cannot create guides. Any guides you created while that layer was active are not displayed, but you'll still be able to see guides created while other layers are active. Note that when guides are hidden entirely (View ➪ Hide Guides, or ⌘+; or Ctrl+;) this command has no apparent effect.

✦ **Lock Guides checkbox:** This option works similar to Show Guides in that it only effects guides that are created while the layer is active. When unchecked, as it is by default, you can move guides on any layer for which Lock Guides is unchecked. When checked, you cannot move guides created while that layer is active. You can, however, move guides on other layers for which Lock Guides is unchecked. Note that when all guides are locked (View ➪ Lock Guides, or Option+⌘+; or Ctrl+Alt+;) this command has no apparent effect.

Tip   You can multiple-select layers and customize them all at once. Because each layer must have a different name, the Name field is not available in the Layer Options dialog box when multiple layers are selected.

Working with Objects on Layers

Whether you're designing a magazine template from the ground up or modifying an existing ad, you can isolate specific types of objects on layers. You can create objects on a layer, move objects to a layer, or copy objects to a layer.

The active layer

The active layer is the one you are creating objects on — whether you're using tools, importing text or graphics, dragging objects in from a library, or pasting objects from other layers or other documents. A pen icon to the right of a layer's name means it's the active one (see Figure 30-5). And although more than one layer can be selected at a time, only one can be active. To switch the active layer to another layer, click to the right of the layer name to move the pen icon. To activate a layer, it must be visible.

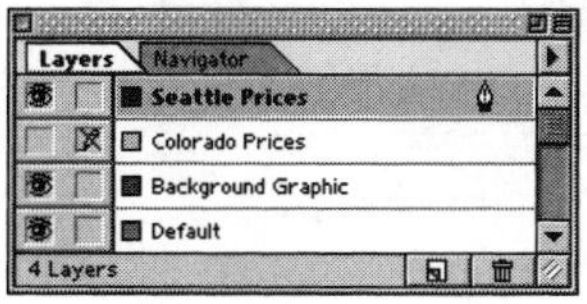

Figure 30-5: The pen icon indicates the active layer, which will contain any new objects you create.

Regardless of the active layer, you can select, move, and modify objects on any visible, unlocked layer. (The display and locking of layers is controlled by the eye and pencil icons on the Layers pane, respectively, and by the Show Layer and Lock Layer checkboxes in the Layer Options dialog box.)

Selecting objects on layers

Regardless of the active layer, you can select, move, and modify objects on any visible, unlocked layer. You can even select objects on different layers and manipulate them. The display and locking of layers is controlled by the eye and pencil icons on the Layers pane, respectively, and by the Show Layer and Lock Layer checkboxes in the Layer Options dialog box.

The Layers pane (Window ➪ Layers or F7) helps you work with selected objects in the following ways:

✦ To determine which layer an object belongs to, match the color on its bounding box, handles, and so on, to a color to the left of a layer name.

✦ To determine which layers contain active objects, look to the right of the layer names. A small box next to a layer name, as shown in Figure 30-6, indicates that it contains an active object.

✦ To select all the objects on a layer, Option+click or Alt+click the layer's name in the Layers pane.

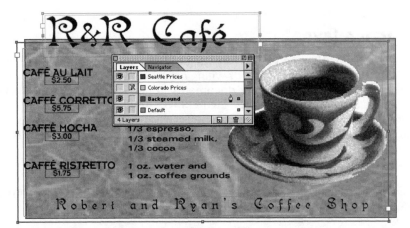

Figure 30-6: A small box next to the right of a layer's name indicates that an object on the layer is selected.

Tip Remember that, to select master page objects, you need to press Shift+⌘ or Ctrl+Shift.

Placing objects on layers

To place objects on a layer, the layer must be active, as indicated by the pen icon. To place objects on the layer, follow these steps:

Steps: Placing Objects on Layers

1. Use any tools to create paths and frames.

2. Use the Place command (File ➪ Place, or ⌘+D or Ctrl+D) to import graphics or text.

3. Use the Paste command (Edit ➪ Paste, or ⌘+V or Ctrl+V) to paste objects from the clipboard onto the layer.

4. Drag objects to the layer from a library or another document.

Note

When you create objects on master pages, they are placed on the default layer and are therefore behind other objects on document pages. To create objects on master pages that are in front of other objects, place the objects on a different layer while the master page is displayed.

Tip

You can cut and paste objects from one page to another, but have the objects remain on their original layer — without concern about the active layer. To do this, use the Paste Remembers Layers command in the Layers pane's palette menu rather than Edit ➪ Paste, or ⌘+V or Ctrl+V. You might do this if you're moving the continuation of an article from one page to another, but you want the text to remain on the same layer (for example, the French layer).

Moving objects to different layers

Once an object is on a layer, it's not stuck there. You can copy and paste objects to selected layers, or you can move them using the Layers pane. When you move an object to a layer, it is placed in front of all other objects on a layer. To select multiple objects, remember to Shift+click them, and then move them in one of the following ways:

✦ To paste objects on a different layer, first cut or copy objects to the clipboard. Activate the layer you want to put the objects on, and then use the Paste command (Edit ➪ Paste, or ⌘+V or Ctrl+V). This method works well for moving objects that are currently on different layers.

✦ To move objects to a different layer, drag the active object box (to the right of a layer's name) to another layer. (See Figure 30-7.) When you use this method, it does not matter which layer is active. However, you can't move objects from different layers to the same layer using this method. (If you select multiple objects that reside on different layers, dragging the box moves only objects that reside on the first layer on which you selected an object.)

Figure 30-7: Dragging an active object box moves the selection to a different layer.

✦ To move objects to a hidden or locked layer, press ⌘ or Ctrl while you drag the active object box.

✦ To copy rather than move objects to a different layer, press Option or Alt while you drag the active object box.

✦ To copy objects to a hidden or locked layer, press Option+⌘ or Ctrl+Alt while you drag the active object box.

Tip   After designing a new template, you might realize that working with it would be easier if you had isolated certain objects on layers. You can create new layers, and then move objects to them at this point. Just make sure the layers are in the same stacking order as the original objects.

Manipulating Layers

Using the Layers pane, you can select and manipulate entire layers. These changes affect all the objects on the layer — for example, if you hide a layer, all its objects are hidden; if you move a layer up, all its objects display in front of objects on lower layers. Functions that affect an entire layer include hiding, locking, rearranging, merging, and deleting.

Selecting layers

The active layer, containing the pen icon, is always selected. You can extend the selection to include other layers the same way you multiple-select objects: Shift+click for a continuous selection and ⌘+click or Ctrl+click for a noncontiguous selection. When layers are selected, you can move them within the stacking order of layers, modify attributes in the Layer Options dialog box, merge them, or delete them.

Hiding layers

When you hide a layer, none of the objects on that layer display or print. You might hide layers for a variety of reasons, including to speed screen redraw by hiding layers containing high-resolution graphics, to control which version of a publication prints, and to simply focus on one area of a design without the distraction of other areas. To show or hide layers using the Layers pane, do one of the following:

✦ Click the eye icon in the first column to the left of a layer's name. When the eye's column is blank, the layer is hidden. Click in the column again to show the layer, as shown in Figure 30-8. You can also double-click a layer and check or uncheck Show Layer in the Layer Options dialog box.

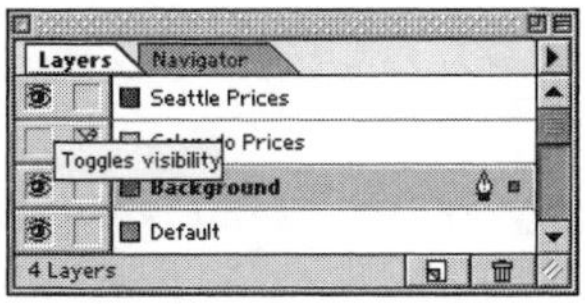

Figure 30-8: The eye icon indicates that objects on the layer are showing.

✦ If no layers are hidden, you can show only the active layer by choosing Hide Others from the palette menu.

✦ Regardless of the state of other layers, you can show only one layer by Option+clicking or Alt+clicking in the first column next to its name. All other layers will be hidden.

✦ If any layers are hidden, you can show all layers by choosing Show All Layers from the palette menu. You can also Option+click or Alt+click twice in the first column to show all layers.

> **Note**
>
> When you use the Package command (File ➪ Package, or Option+Shift+⌘+P or Ctrl+Alt+Shift+P) to prepare a document for a service bureau, InDesign includes only visible layers. This lets you hide the layers containing different versions of the document, and be sure that they are not accidentally printed.

Locking objects on layers

When you lock a layer, you cannot select or modify objects on it — even if the locked layer is active. Generally, you'll lock layers to prevent background elements or complex drawings from accidental changes — while still enabling you to view the objects in relation to the remainder of the layout. Because locking and unlocking is easy, you can lock layers while you're not working on them, and then unlock them to make changes. To lock or unlock layers using the Layers pane, do one of the following:

✦ Click the blank box in the second column to the left of a layer's name. When the pencil icon (with the slash through it) is displayed, as shown in Figure 30-9, the layer is locked. Click the pencil icon to unlock the layer. You can also double-click a layer and check or uncheck Lock Layer in the Layer Options dialog box.

Figure 30-9: The pencil icon indicates that objects on the layer are locked.

✦ If no layers are locked, you can lock all but the active layer by choosing Lock Others from the palette menu.

✦ If any layers are locked, you can unlock all layers by choosing Unlock All Layers from the palette menu.

✦ You can toggle between Lock Others and Unlock All Layers by Option+clicking or Alt+clicking the blank box or the pencil icon.

Note   When you lock an object to a page (Object ➪ Lock Object, or ⌘+L or Ctrl+L), the object stays locked regardless of its layer's lock status.

Rearranging layers

Each layer has its own front-to-back stacking order, with the first object you create on the layer being its back-most object. You can modify the stacking order of objects on a single layer using the Arrange commands in the Object menu. Objects are further stacked according to the order in which the layers are listed in the Layers pane. The layer at the top of the list contains the front-most objects, and the layer at the bottom of the list contains the back-most objects.

If you find that all the objects on one layer need to be in front of all the objects on another layer, you can move that layer up or down in the list. In fact, you can move multiple-selected layers up or down, even if the selection is noncontiguous. (When you move noncontiguous layers, they become continuous.) To move layers, click the selection and drag it up or down; a black bar indicates where the layers can be placed. (See Figure 30-10.) When you move layers, remember that layers are document-wide so you are actually changing the stacking order of objects on all the pages.

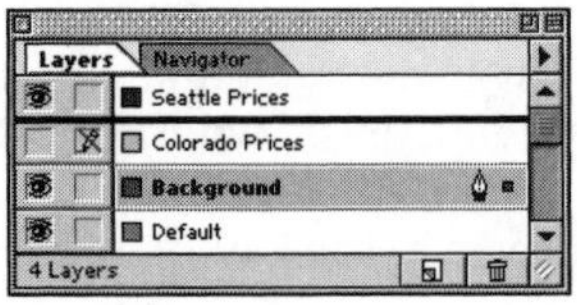

Figure 30-10: Dragging layers up and down in the Layers pane changes the stacking order of the layers.

Note   You might be accustomed to moving objects to the front of the stacking order to make them easily editable. Working this way, you might be tempted to bring a layer up to the top of the layer stacking order so you can edit it easily, and then move it back to its original location. Try to get out of that habit, though, and into the habit of simply showing the layer you need to work on and hiding the others.

Combining layers

If you decide that all the objects on one layer belong on a different layer — throughout the document — you can merge the layers. When you're learning about the power of layers, it's easy to create a document that is unnecessarily complex. For example, you might put each object on a different layer and realize that the document has become difficult to work with. You can also merge all the layers in a document to "flatten" it to a single layer.

Steps: Merging Layers

1. Select the target layer (where you want all the objects to end up) by clicking it.

2. Select the source layers (which contain the objects you want to move) in addition to the target layer. Shift+click, or ⌘+click or Ctrl+click, to add to the source layers to the selection.

3. Make sure the target layer contains the pen icon, and that the target and source layers are all selected.

4. Choose Merge Layers from the Layers pane's palette menu, as shown in Figure 30-11.

Figure 30-11: The Merge Layers command in the Layers pane's palette menu.

All objects on the source layers are moved to the target layer, and the source layers are deleted.

Note   When you merge layers, objects on higher layers are stacked on top of objects on lower layers. The stacking order is maintained and the design looks the same—with one notable exception. If you created objects on a layer while a master page was displayed, those objects go to the back of the stacking order with the regular master page objects.

Deleting layers

If you've carefully isolated portions of a document on different layers, and then find that you won't need that portion of the document, you can delete the layer. For example, if you have a U.S. English and an International English layer, and you decide that you can't afford to print the two different versions and one dialect's readers will simply have to suffer, you can delete the unneeded layer. You might also delete layers that you don't end up using to simplify a document.

When you delete layers, all the objects on the layer throughout the document are deleted. To ensure that you don't need any of the objects before deleting a layer, you can hide all other layers, and then look at the remaining objects on each page. If you will need any of them, you can drag them to the pasteboard or place them in a library.

Using the Layers pane, you can delete selected layers in the following ways:

✦ Dragging the selection to the trash can button (see Figure 30-12).

✦ Clicking the trash can button.

✦ Choosing Delete Layer from the Layers pane's palette menu.

Figure 30-12: The trash can button on the Layers pane lets you delete all selected layers.

If any of the layers contain objects, a warning reminds you that they will be deleted. And of course the ubiquitous Undo command (Edit ➪ Undo, or ⌘+Z or Ctrl+Z) lets you recover from accidental deletions.

Tip   To remove all layers that do not contain objects, choose Delete Unused Layers from the Layers palette.

Summary

If you take the time to integrate layers into your workflow, you can save time and effort in creating multilingual publications, producing multiple versions of a document, and benefiting from greater flexibility with objects. Until you create new layers, all the objects are placed on the default layers. Though each layer has its own stacking order, the order of layers also affects stacking order.

You can create objects on the active layer, and you can move objects to different layers. Even though objects are on layers, you can continue to select and modify them as you normally would — provided that the layers are visible and unlocked. Hiding layers suppresses the printout of objects, in addition to preventing their display. To streamline a document, you can merge and delete layers.

✦   ✦   ✦

Working with Pages

I t's a rare InDesign user who creates only one-page documents. Even if business cards, ads, and posters are your bread and butter, you'll probably produce at least a few multipage documents. If you'll be creating newsletters, newspapers, books, catalogs, or any other such multipage publications, you need to know how to add pages to your document, move pages around if you change your mind, and delete pages if necessary.

In addition to letting you create multipage documents — something that most illustration and image-editing programs don't — InDesign lets you divide multipage documents into independently numbered sections. As documents grow in size, your ability to navigate quickly to the page you want to work on becomes an important consideration. The longer you spend getting to the page you want, the less time you have to work on it. Fortunately, InDesign provides several navigation aids that make it easy to move around a page or a document.

InDesign does not include any long-document features, such as indexing or automatic table-of-contents generation, nor does it include any document-linking features. This means that if you produce a long publication, such as a book, and you decide to create a separate document for each chapter (which you should), you'll have to take care of the page numbering from chapter to chapter yourself.

Working with Multipage Documents

If you intend to create a multipage document, you should check the Facing Pages box in the New Document dialog box (File ➪ New, or ⌘+N or Ctrl+N) when you create the document.

You'll also want to display the Pages pane (Window ⇨ Pages or F12), shown in Figure 31-1, because it provides the controls that let you add pages (document and master), delete and move pages, apply master pages to document pages, and navigate through a document.

Figure 31-1: The Pages pane and its palette menu. This is how the pane looks when you open a new, one-page, facing-page document.

For more information about using the Pages pane to work on master pages, see Chapter 29.

The overwhelming majority of multipage documents are facing-page publications, such as books, catalogs, and magazines. Some exceptions are flip charts, Web pages, and three-hole-punched publications printed on only one side. In this chapter, the figures show examples of a facing-page document. If you're creating a single-sided multipage document, the techniques are the same as for facing-page documents, but the icons in the Pages pane will show only single-sided page icons (the icons aren't dog-eared).

Adding pages

An InDesign document can contain as many as 9,999 pages, though you'd never want to create a document nearly that long. In general, try to break up long publications into logical pieces. For example, if you're creating a book it's a good idea to create separate documents for the front matter, each chapter, the index, and any other parts (appendixes, and so on). Also, if you're producing a long document, you'll want to take advantages of master pages (covered in Chapter 29), which save you the work of building each page from scratch.

When you create a multipage document, you're free to add however many pages you want. But be careful. Even though InDesign lets you create a seven-page newsletter, in real life, facing-page publications always have an even number of pages — usually a multiple of 4 and often a multiple of 16 because of the way printers arrange multiple pages on a single large sheet of paper that is folded and trimmed after printing.

Steps: Adding Pages to a Document

1. If it's not displayed, open the Pages pane by choosing Window ➪ Pages or pressing F12.

2. From the Pages pane's palette menu, choose Insert Pages. The Insert Pages dialog box, shown in Figure 31-2, is displayed.

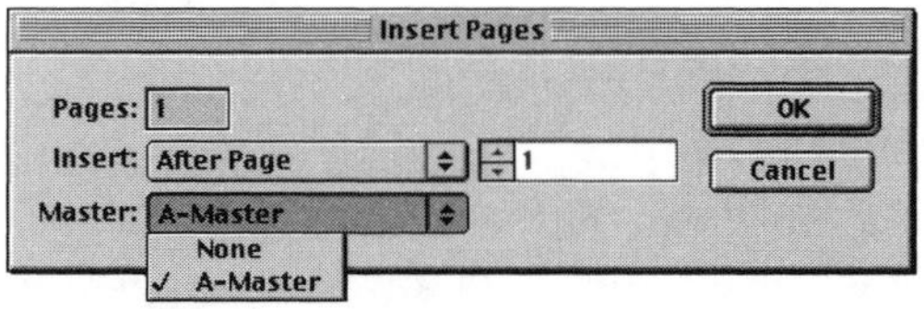

Figure 31-2: The Insert Pages dialog box.

3. In the Pages field, enter the number of pages you want to add.

4. Choose an option from the Insert pop-up menu: After Page, Before Page, At Start of Document, At End of Document. Be careful. If you've already started working on page 1, for example, make sure you add new pages after page 1. Otherwise, your first page won't be page 1 anymore and you'll have to move the objects you already created.

5. Enter a page number in the field next to Insert or use the arrows to increase or decrease the value in 1-page increments.

6. From the Master pop-up menu, choose the master page you want to apply to the new pages.

7. When you're finished, click OK to close the dialog box.

You can also add new pages one at a time at the end of a document by clicking the Create New Page icon at the bottom of the Pages pane. When you use this method, the master page applied to the last document page is applied to each new page.

To add a spread (two facing pages), you can click the name of the master spread (not the icons) at the bottom of the Pages pane, and then drag the hand icon between any pair of document page spreads or to the right of the last document spread. If a vertical bar is displayed when you release the mouse button, the spread is placed between the spreads on either side of the bar. If a vertical bar is not displayed between document page spreads when you release the mouse button, the new spread is placed at the end of the document.

 Caution If you add or remove an odd number of pages from a facing-page document, all pages after the new or deleted pages will change sides: Even pages get bumped to become odd pages, and odd pages get bumped to become even pages. This can wreak havoc with page designs. For example, a two-page opening spread for a magazine article could get split so that the original left-hand page is on the right and the original right-hand page gets bumped to the next (left-hand) page. Be careful when adding pages. It's a good idea to stick with even numbers to avoid the reshuffling that occurs with when you add or delete an odd number of pages.

Deleting pages

InDesign offers a couple of choices for deleting pages from a document. You can:

✦ Select one or more page icons in the Pages pane and either drag them to the pane's trash can or click the trash can button. Click a spread's page numbers to select both pages. You can click a page icon or spread number and then Shift+click another page icon or spread number to select a range of pages. Hold down the ⌘ or Ctrl key and click page icons or spread numbers to select multiple, noncontiguous pages.

✦ Select one or more page icons in the Pages pane and then choose Delete Page(s) or Delete Spread(s) from the pane's palette menu.

Moving pages

Although it's possible to move pages around in a document, this is something you should do with great care — if at all. Generally, if you want to move the objects on one page to another page, it's safer to cut or copy the objects (Edit ⇨ Cut, or ⌘+X or Ctrl+X; and Edit ⇨ Copy, or ⌘+C or Ctrl+C) than to move the page, which might cause subsequent pages to shuffle. If you absolutely need to move a single page, it's safer to move its spread. (Of course, if you're working on a single-sided facing-page document, shuffling is not an issue.)

To move a page, click its icon and then drag the hand pointer between two spreads or between the pages of a spread. A vertical bar indicates where the selected page will be placed. Release the mouse button when the vertical bar is where you want to move the page. To move a spread, click the page numbers beneath the icons (rather than on the page icons).

Numbering pages

You can add a page number manually to each page of a multipage document, but that can get old fast. As we mentioned earlier in this chapter, if you're working on a multipage document, you should be using master pages. And if you're using master pages, you should handle page numbers on document pages by placing page number characters on their master pages (further explained in Chapter 29).

If you want to add a page number to a page, you can choose Layout ⇨ Insert Page Number, or press Option+⌘+N or Ctrl+Alt+N, whenever the Type tool is active and the text cursor is flashing. If you move the page or the text frame, the page number character is automatically updated to reflect the new page number.

Creating island spreads

Have you ever seen a publication — a magazine, perhaps — that had a fold-out page? Often such pages are ads (publishers love advertisers who buy multipage ads) or special sections. Or maybe you've seen a two-sided, multifold brochure with several panels, each the same size. A multipage spread of this type is often called a gatefold or accordion page, or in InDesign terms, an *island spread*.

When you designate a spread as an island spread, the spread's pages don't move if you add or delete any document pages in front of it. (Normally, when you add or delete pages, all subsequent pages are bumped backward or shuffled forward.)

When you create a island spread of three pages in a facing-page publication, you should always create them in pairs because, in an actual printed publication, if you add a third page to a two-page spread, the back side of the page becomes the third page in another three-page spread. Along the same lines, if you create a four-panel, tri-fold brochure, both the front and the back have four panels.

One last word about island spreads. They require special care throughout the production process, and they'll cost you extra at the printer and bindery. If you're creating a modest, black-and-white newsletter for a local nonprofit organization, throwing in a three-panel gatefold probably isn't an option. On the other hand, if you can find an advertiser with deep pockets, InDesign lets you create island spreads with up to 10 pages.

To create an island spread, select it in the Pages pane, and then choose Island Spread from the pane's palette menu. (When you designate a spread as an island spread, the page numbers below the spread in the Pages pane are displayed in brackets.) To add pages to an island spread, drag a document page icon (a master page icon won't work) next to or between the pages of an island spread. A vertical bar indicates where the page will be placed. When the bar is where you want to place the page, release the mouse button. To clear an island spread, select it in the Pages pane and then choose Clear Island Spread from the pane's palette menu. Figure 31-3 shows a pair of three-page island spreads in a facing-page publication.

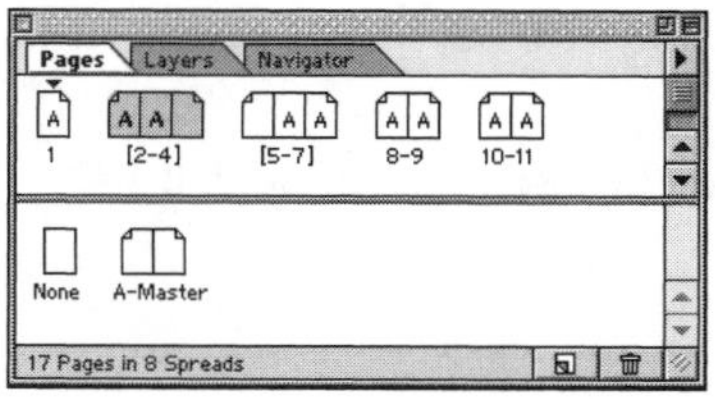

Figure 31-3: In this example, pages 2, 3, and 4 are an island spread, as are pages 5, 6, and 7. The extra page in each spread is based on the None master page.

Tip   You may want to create a section out of the extra pages in an island spread so that you can number them separately from the surrounding pages. Sections are covered later in this chapter.

Adjusting Page Layouts and Objects

If you've ever created and worked with a document all the way to the finishing touches, and then discovered that the page size was wrong from the beginning, you know the meaning of frustration. Manually adjusting the size and placement of all the objects in a document is an ugly chore, one you want to avoid at all costs. However, should the unthinkable happen — should you have to modify the size, orientation, or margins of a document that is partially or completely finished — InDesign can automatically resize and reposition objects when you change its basic layout.

For example, maybe you've created a magazine for an American audience that subsequently needs to be converted for publication in Europe. Most newsletters in the United States use letter-sized pages (8.5 by 11 inches), whereas in Europe the standard page size for such publications is A4 (210mm by 297mm), which is slightly narrower and slightly taller than U.S. letter size. Of course, you'll have to change "color" to "colour," "apartment" to "flat," and so on. But you'll also have to both squeeze (horizontally) and stretch (vertically) every item on every page to accommodate the A4 page's dimensions. The Layout Adjustment command (Layout ➪ Layout Adjustment) gives you the option of turning this chore over to InDesign, which automatically adjusts object shape and position according to the new page size, column guides, and margins.

Enabling and configuring layout adjustment

The Layout Adjustment dialog box lets you turn layout adjustment on or off and specify the rules used to adjust objects, when you change page size or orientation (via the Document Setup dialog box; File ➪ Document Setup, or Option+⌘+P or Ctrl+Alt+P) or margins or columns (via the Margin and Columns dialog box, accessed via Layout ➪ Margins and Columns).

Steps: Using Layout Adjustment

1. Choose Layout ➪ Layout Adjustment to display the Layout Adjustment dialog box, shown in Figure 31-4.

2. Check Enable Layout Adjustment to turn on the feature; uncheck it to turn it off.

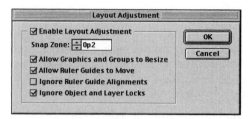

Figure 31-4: The Layout Adjustment dialog box.

3. In the Snap Zone field, enter the distance within which an object edge will automatically snap to a guideline when layout adjustment is performed.

4. Check Allow Graphics and Groups to Resize if you want InDesign to resize objects when layout adjustment is performed. If you don't check this box, InDesign moves objects but does not resize them (the preferred option).

5. Check Allow Ruler Guides to Move if you want InDesign to adjust the position of ruler guides proportionally according to a new page size. Generally, ruler guides are placed relative to the margins and page edges, so you'll probably want to check this box.

6. Select Ignore Ruler Guide Alignments if you want InDesign to ignore ruler guides when adjusting the position of objects during layout adjustment. If you think that objects may snap to ruler guides that you don't want them to snap to during layout adjustment, check this box. If it's checked, InDesign still snaps object edges to other margin and column guides.

7. When you're done, click OK to close the dialog box.

The Layout Adjustment feature works best when there's not much work for it to do. But if you radically change a document that you've already done considerable work on, the Layout Adjustment feature usually creates more work than it prevents. For example, the switch from a U.S. letter-sized page to an A4-sized page is a relatively minor change, and the layout adjustments will probably be barely noticeable. But if you decide to change a tabloid-sized poster into a business card in midstream, well, you're probably better off starting over.

Here are a few matters to keep in mind if you decide to use InDesign's Layout Adjustment feature:

✦ If you change page size, the margin widths (the distance between the left and right margins and the page edges) remain the same.

✦ If you change page size, column guides and ruler guides are repositioned proportionally to the new size.

✦ If you change the number of columns, column guides are added or removed accordingly.

✦ If an object edge is aligned with a guideline before layout adjustment, it remains aligned with the guideline after adjustment. If two or more edges of an object are aligned with guidelines, the object is resized so that the edges remain aligned with the guidelines after layout adjustment.

✦ If you change the page size, objects are moved so that they're in the same relative position on the new page.

✦ If you've used margin, column, and ruler guides to place objects on pages, layout adjustment will be more effective than if you've placed objects or ruler guides randomly on pages.

✦ Check for text reflow when you modify a document's page size, margins, or column guides. Decreasing a document's page size can cause text to overflow a text frame whose dimensions have been reduced.

✦ Check *everything* in your document after the adjustment is complete. You never know what InDesign has actually done until you see it with your own eyes.

Tip   If you decide to enable layout adjustment for a particular publication, you may want to begin by using the Save As command (File ⇨ Save As or Shift+⌘+S or Ctrl+Shift+S) to create a copy. This way, if you ever need to revert to the original version, you can simply open the original document.

Dividing a Document into Sections

Some long documents are divided into parts that are numbered separately from the other parts. For example, the page numbers of the front matter of books often use Roman numerals, whereas standard Arabic numerals are used for the body of the book. If the book has appendixes, a separate numbering scheme could be applied to these pages. In InDesign, such independently numbered parts are referred to as *sections*.

A multipage document can contain as many sections as you want (a section has to contain at least one page). If each section of a document uses a different page layout, you'll probably want to create a different master page for each section.

Steps: Starting a Section

1. If it's not displayed, open the Pages pane by choosing Window ⇨ Pages or pressing F12.

2. Click the icon of the page you want to start a section.

3. Choose Section Options from the pane's palette menu. The New Section dialog box, shown in Figure 31-5, is displayed. By default, the Start Section box is checked. Leave it checked.

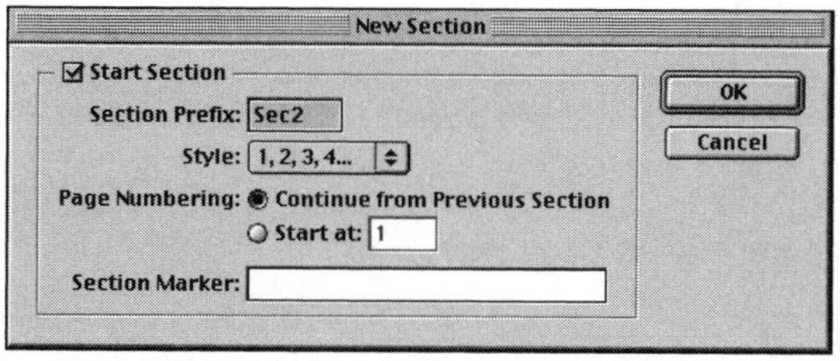

```
                    New Section
  ┌─ ☑ Start Section ──────────────────┐   ┌──────────┐
  │   Section Prefix: Sec2             │   │    OK    │
  │         Style: 1, 2, 3, 4...  ⬍   │   └──────────┘
  │   Page Numbering: ● Continue from Previous Section   │   ┌──────────┐
  │                   ○ Start at: 1   │   │  Cancel  │
  │   Section Marker:                 │   └──────────┘
  └────────────────────────────────────┘
```

Figure 31-5: The New Section dialog box.

4. In the Section Prefix field, enter up to five characters that will identify the section in the page number box at the lower-left corner of the document window. (For example, if you enter **Sec2**, the first page of the section will be displayed as "Sec2:1" in the page number box.)

5. From the Style menu, choose the Roman numeral, Arabic numeral, or alphabetic style you want to use for page numbers.

6. For Page Numbering, choose Continue from Previous Section if you want the first page of the section to be one number higher than the last page of the previous section. (The new section will use the specified style; the previous section may use this style or another style.) Choose Start At and enter a number in the accompanying field to specify a different starting number for the section. For example, if a book begins with a section of front matter, you could begin the body section of a book on page 1 by choosing Start At and entering 1 in the field. If you choose Continue from Previous Section, the first page of the body section would begin one number higher than the Roman numeral on the last page of the front matter.

7. In the Section Marker field, enter a text string that you can later automatically apply to pages in the section. You might want to enter something straightforward such as "Section 2" or, if the section is a chapter, the name of the chapter.

8. Click OK to close the dialog box.

When you create a section, it's indicated in the Pages pane by a small, black triangle over the icon of the first page in the section, as shown in Figure 31-6. (If you move the pointer over a black triangle, the name of the section is displayed.) The page-numbering scheme you've specified is reflected in the page numbers below the page icons. When you begin a section, it continues until the end of the document or until you begin a new section.

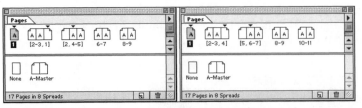

Figure 31-6: The three small triangles above the page icons represent section starts. The two extra pages in the pair of island spreads form a section; another section begins after the second island spread. On the left, section page numbers are displayed in the Pages pane; on the right, absolute page numbers are displayed.

Tip   By default, the Pages pane displays section numbers beneath the icons of document pages. If you want to display absolute page numbers—the first page is page 1 and all other pages are numbered sequentially—you can do so by choosing File ➪ Preferences ➪ General, or ⌘+K or Ctrl+K, and choose Absolute Numbering from the View pop-up menu. Figure 31-6 shows the difference between section numbering and absolute numbering.

Targeting versus Selecting Spreads

Depending on the task you're working on, you may want to use the Pages pane to *target* a spread or to *select* a spread. The choice you make determines the actions you can perform.

✦ A target spread is the spread to which copied objects will be placed when you choose Paste, or to which library objects will be placed when you choose Place Items from a library pane's palette menu. The target spread is the one that's in the center of the document window and is indicated by the page number displayed in the page number box at the lower-left corner of the document window. Only one spread can be the target spread at any one time. At reduced magnifications, it's possible to display several spreads in the document window. In this case, the number in the page number box indicates the target spread.

✦ When you select one or more spreads, you can then perform several page-level modifications, such as adjusting margin and column guides, applying a master page, or deleting the pages, in a single operation.

You have several ways to target a spread. You can:

✦ Modify an object on the spread or its pasteboard.

✦ Click a spread or its pasteboard.

✦ In the Pages pane, double-click the page numbers below the spread's page icons.

You also have several options for selecting a page or spread.

✦ Click once on a page icon to select one page of a spread; click the page numbers to select both pages. If you click twice, the page or spread is selected and targeted.

✦ Click a page icon or spread number and then Shift+click another page icon or spread number to select a range of pages.

✦ Hold down the ⌘ or Ctrl key and click page icons or spread numbers to select multiple, noncontiguous pages.

In the Pages pane, the page numbers of the target spread are displayed reversed, white numbers in a black rectangle, whereas the page icons of selected spreads are indicated by blackened page icons with white master page prefix letters (if any). The following figure shows the difference between how the target spread and selected spreads are displayed in the Pages pane. In this example, pages 4 and 5 are the target spread. Two spreads are selected: the "IV-V" spread and the "VI, 1" spread.

Removing a section

If you decide that you want to remove a section, navigate to the page that begins the section, choose Section Options from the Pages pane's palette menu, and then uncheck the Section Start box.

Adding a section marker to a document page

If you assign a Section Marker to a section (as explained previously), you can apply it to a document page in a single operation. All you have to do is select the Type tool and draw a text frame or click in an existing text frame. When the text cursor is flashing, Control+click or right-click to display the contextual menu. Choose Insert Special ⇨ Section Marker. The Section Marker text is placed at the text insertion point, and the formats applied at the insertion point are applied to the new text.

Navigating Documents and Pages

Moving from page to page in a long document and scrolling around a large or magnified page are among the most common tasks you'll perform in InDesign. The more time you spend displaying the page or page area you want to work on, the less time you have to do the work you need to do. As with most trips, the less time you spend between destinations, the better.

For navigating through the pages of a document, the Pages pane (Window ⇨ Pages or F12) offers the fastest ride. For navigating around in a page, you may want to switch to the Navigator pane (Window ⇨ Navigator).

Navigating with the Pages pane

When the Pages pane is displayed, you can use it to quickly move from page to page in a multipage document and to switch between displaying master pages and document pages. To display a particular document page, double-click its icon. The selected page is centered in the document window. To display a master spread, double-click its icon in the lower half of the pane.

Tip   The Fit Page in Window command (View ⇨ Fit Page in Window, or ⌘+0 or Ctrl+0) and Fit Spread in Window command (View ⇨ Fit Page in Window, or Option+⌘+0 or Ctrl+Alt+0) let you enlarge or reduce the display magnification to fit the selected page or spread in the document window. (Note that the shortcuts use the numeral 0, not the letter O.)

Using the Navigator pane

Although it's possible to use the Navigator pane (Window ⇨ Navigator) to move from page to page in a long document, the Pages pane is better for this task. The Navigator pane is more useful for scrolling within a page, particularly for doing detail work on a page that's displayed at a high magnification. If you're an Illustrator, PageMaker, or Photoshop user, you may already be familiar with the Navigator pane, which works the same in all three applications.

To display the Navigator pane, choose Window ⇨ Navigator. Figure 31-7 shows the Navigator pane and its palette menu.

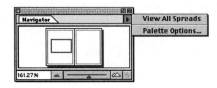
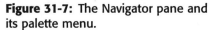

Figure 31-7: The Navigator pane and its palette menu.

Changing view magnification

You can use the Navigator pane to zoom in or zoom out on the current spread. You have several options for zooming in and out:

✦ Click the handle on the zoom slider and drag left to zoom out, or right to zoom in.

✦ Click the zoom-out icon to the left of the zoom slider to zoom out; click the zoom-in icon to the right of the zoom slider to zoom in.

✦ Enter a view percentage in the field at the bottom-left corner of the Navigator pane. Enter a smaller value to zoom out; enter a larger value to zoom in. Enter **100%** to display the page at actual size.

Tip   You can also use the Zoom tool or its keyboard shortcuts to zoom in or out (⌘+spacebar or Ctrl+spacebar to zoom in, or Option+⌘+spacebar or Ctrl+Option+spacebar to zoom out).

Scrolling with the Navigator pane

The rectangle displayed in the Navigator pane (on the actual screen it should show up red) indicates the area that's currently displayed in the document window. When you change the display magnification, the rectangle changes size (it gets larger as you zoom out and smaller as you zoom in). You can display a different area in the currently displayed spread by dragging the rectangle or by clicking outside it. If you click outside it, the point where you click is centered in the document window.

Other options in the Navigator pane

If red's not your favorite color, you can change the color of the rectangle displayed in the Navigator pane by choosing Palette Options from its palette menu and then choosing a different color from the Color pop-up menu in the Palette Options dialog box.

If you choose Show All Spreads from the Navigator pane's palette menu, all the document's spreads are displayed in the pane. The more spreads you have, the smaller they're displayed and the smaller the rectangle becomes that indicates the area that's displayed in the document window. By dragging the rectangle from page to page, you can navigate to a particular area on a page while remaining at the current display percentage. This can be a handy way of navigating, but if you're working on a document that has many pages, the page icons and rectangle can become too small to work with easily. Figure 31-8 shows the Navigator pane with the View All Spreads option selected.

Figure 31-8: The Navigator pane with View All Spreads selected.

Tip

You can also use the scroll bars at the right and bottom of the document window to move to different areas of a page or to a different page in a document or the keyboard shortcut (hold down the spacebar and then click and drag the hand pointer; the Type tool cannot be selected for this to work).

Platform Difference

The Pages and Navigator panes are resizable in the Windows version of InDesign, but they're not resizable in the Mac version.

Summary

If you're working on a multipage document, you'll want to display the Pages pane. It lets you add, move, and delete document pages and create multipage spreads called *island spreads*.

If you decide to change the layout of a publication after you've started work, you can use the Layout Adjustment feature to automatically adjust the size and position of objects and guidelines when you change the document's page size, margins, or columns.

If you're working on a long document with multiple parts, and you want to number each part separately, you can create sections to manage these multiple page-numbering schemes within the document.

As you work on a long document, you can use the Pages pane to target a specific page or spread in the document window, to select multiple pages or spreads so that you can move, modify, or delete them collectively, and to navigate from page to page in a multipage document. If you're doing detail work or working on a large page, you can use the Navigator pane to scroll around the page and to change the view magnification.

✦　　✦　　✦

Output Fundamentals

P A R T

✦ ✦ ✦ ✦

In This Part

Chapter 32
Preparing for Printing

Chapter 33
Printing Techniques

Chapter 34
Creating Output Files

✦ ✦ ✦ ✦

Few thrills are as exciting as seeing the results of countless hours of publication design. You labor over everything — from text creation to layout to graphics — until you wonder what you got yourself into. Then you send it off for printing, and later get your printed copies. You suddenly feel great — memories of long days and nights evaporate as you see all your work made real.

Ironically, the output step of publishing is often the last thing on people's minds when they begin a project, even though it's such a vital step. The chapters in Part IX show you what you need to be aware of and show you how to output your documents for printing or for use in the Adobe Portable Document Format often used for network- and CD-based documents, as well as for Web-based documents.

The first — and most tricky — step in document output is setting up your printer and the related driver files on your computer. This process varies considerably from platform to platform, and InDesign has expectations that vary from the other programs you use, so be sure to pay close attention to the setup details in **Chapter 32**.

With your document preflighted, you're ready to actually print. You have dozens of output decisions to make in printing, and **Chapter 33** walks you through each one.

In some cases, you won't actually print a document but instead will deliver a version in electronic form with all printing settings embedded. Here's where InDesign's several file-output options come in handy, as **Chapter 34** shows.

Preparing for Printing

After you've created your document and all elements are perfectly in place with the right colors, frame strokes, kerning, and so on, it's time to make tangible all that work you've done onscreen. You're ready to print the document.

Well, not quite. You may in fact be ready to just print your document. If, however, your document is at all complex or will be output at a service bureau, you should take a few minutes and dot your i's and cross your t's. You must also take extra care when outputting via your company's creative services group or print shop. Little things can go wrong as you or your team work on a document; a font might deactivate, a picture might move or be renamed, or a new output device might be acquired.

That's where InDesign's Preflight and Package tools come into play. The Preflight tool checks your document to make sure that all elements are available, whereas the Package tool copies all required elements — from fonts to graphics — to a folder so that you can give your service bureau all the pieces needed to accurately print your document.

Making Initial Preparations

Before you can do anything, you need to make sure that your system is set up with the right printer driver and printer description files. Without these, your output will likely not match your needs or expectations. It's important to set these up before you use the Preflight tool because the Preflight tool checks your document against the active printer settings (such as color separations), and you can't have selected printer settings until the printer is set up.

InDesign comes with its own PostScript printer drivers and may not work reliably with those that come with the Mac OS or with Windows. Typically, in a best-case scenario, you'll be able to print with another driver but will lose some output features provided by Adobe's driver — such as the ability to create color separations. In a worst-case scenario, you'll get unexpected results, which can be very expensive when outputting to film negatives or a color printer.

 Mac OS and Windows handle printing differently, so in this chapter we've divided all system-specific printing information, such as the coverage of drivers, into platform-specific sections.

Setting up your printer on the Macintosh

Make sure that you install the AdobePS 8.6 driver, which comes with InDesign. You can verify that the correct version is installed by going to the AdobePS file in the Extensions folder. Use File ➪ Get Info or ⌘+I to verify that you have version 8.6 installed.

Note   The LaserWriter driver version 8.6 installed with the Mac OS is *not* the same and should not be used in place of AdobePS.

You can use multiple printer drivers on your Mac, but you should choose the AdobePS driver when outputting from InDesign. (For example, you might use Apple's LaserWriter driver for other programs that have difficulty with Adobe's driver.) You may find that you have multiple versions of printer drivers because many programs install them or give you the option to do so (for example, Adobe Acrobat 4.0 comes with AdobePS 8.5.1, whereas InDesign comes with AdobePS 8.6). Always be sure to use the latest version. You may want to rename AdobePS to AdobePS 8.6 so you're sure another program won't overwrite it later with an earlier version of the driver.

Tip   If you get error messages saying that printer libraries are out of date or there is insufficient memory to use a printer driver, move all printer drivers — for PostScript, these are AdobePS and/or LaserWriter, Adobe Printing Library, and PrintingLib — out of the Extensions folder in your System Folder. Move them instead to the Extensions [Disabled] folder and reinstall the latest versions. You can move these drivers by dragging them from one folder to the other or by using an extension manager such as Apple's included Extensions Manager control panel or Casady & Greene's Conflict Catcher software.

You have several ways to switch printer drivers, as Figure 32-1 shows:

✦ Go to the Chooser (in the Apple menu), select the driver (AdobePS), and then the printer you want to print to (it must be turned on and connected to display).

✦ If you've installed the Mac OS's desktop printing feature (which lets you drag files on to a desktop printer icon for quick printing, as well as lets you double-click the icon to see the status of print jobs), you'll see icons for each printer installed. Click the icon of the printer you want to print to, and use ⌘+L or Printing ⇨ Set Default Printer to activate that printer. Note that the Printing menu displays only when you've selected a desktop printer icon.

✦ If you've installed the Desktop Printer Menu control panel as part of Mac OS's desktop printing software, you'll see a printer icon in the menu's right side. You can use that menu to switch active printers as well.

✦ If you installed the Control Strip extension and the Printer Selector control strip (in the System Folder's Control Strip Modules folder), you can switch printers via the printer icon in the Control Strip.

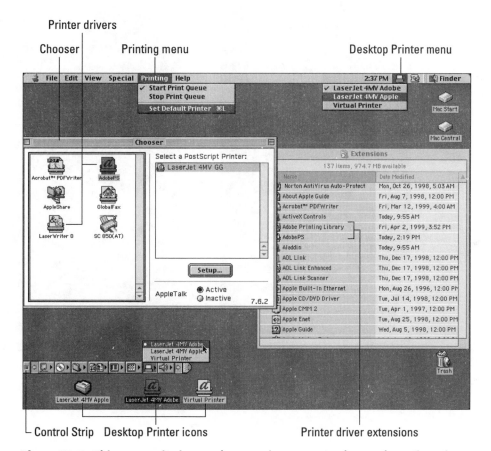

Figure 32-1: This composite image shows various ways to change the active printer on the Macintosh. Normally, only one at a time can be active.

Note

InDesign does not work with non-PostScript drivers, such as those for inkjet printers. Adobe PressReady lets you output to several such devices, including the Canon BubbleJet 8500, several models of the Epson Stylus Color line, and several models of the Hewlett-Packard line.

Tip

If you deal with a lot of printers, create a folder called Printers in your System Folder and then drag all printer icons to it. Make sure the Printers folder is open and then select View ➪ As Pop-up Window. This changes the folder to a pop-up folder with a tab at the top. Click that tab to reduce the folder at the bottom of the screen, as shown in the right half of Figure 32-2. Clicking the tab again will open the folder. Now you can get quick access to your printer icons without cluttering your desktop.

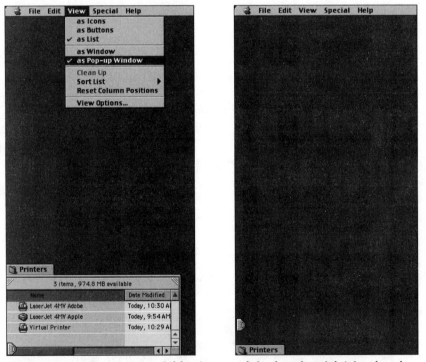

Figure 32-2: Using a pop-up folder (open at left, closed at right) is a handy way to store desktop printer icons, yet keep them easily accessible.

Setting Up a Mac Printer the First Time

If this the first time you've used this printer, you need to set it up. You must install the printer using the Chooser. Here's the correct sequence:

1. Make sure the printer is connected to the Mac and turned on.

2. Click the printer driver you'll be using and then the printer in the list of available printers at right.

3. Click the Create button to create a printer icon and set up the printer's configuration.

4. Select the Auto Setup option to let the Mac OS configure your printer.

Finally, double-check the settings. Make sure that the correct printer is listed under Current Printer Description File (PPD) Selected — you may need to add it to your system if the Mac OS can't find the right one (you can tell that's the case if something like Generic is used). These files tell InDesign and other programs what capabilities your printer has; they should go in the Printer Descriptions folder in your System Folder's Extensions folder. You can download many of these PPD files from Adobe's Web site, at `http://www.adobe.com/supportservice/custsupport/library/pdrvmac.htm`, as well as from your printer maker's Web site or on a disk that came with your printer. (You can also download the AdobePS driver from the Adobe site, in case yours is missing.)

Also, use the Configure button when you're done to make sure that the printer is properly configured (sometimes Auto Setup misses optional equipment such as extra paper trays).

In addition to printers connected to your Mac, you'll likely also need printer drivers set up for your final output device, such as an imagesetter. This is tricky because you likely don't have such devices connected to your Mac, even via a network. (If it is connected, you can set it up like any other printer.)

Steps: Adding a Remote Printer (or Other Output Device) Icon

1. For the printer you want to install, add the correct PPD file in the Printer Descriptions folder in your System Folder's Extensions folder (see the sidebar "Setting Up a Mac Printer the First Time").

2. Find the Desktop Printer Utility software installed with the Mac OS. The default location for it is in the Apple LaserWriter Software folder in the Apple Extras folder that the Mac OS installer will put on your startup drive.

3. Double-click the software's icon to run it.

4. Select Field ⇨ New, and make sure that you picked AdobePS from the list of drivers in the pop-up menu at the top. Also be sure to select the Printer (no printer connection) option. Figure 32-3 shows the New dialog box.

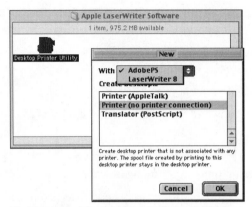

Figure 32-3: The Desktop Printer Utility lets you add desktop printer icons for output devices not connected to your Mac, such as imagesetters.

5. In the next dialog box, select the PPD file by clicking the Change button, scrolling down to the correct PPD file name in the window that appears, and clicking the Select button.

6. Use File ➪ Save, or ⌘+S, to save the desktop printer icon. You'll get a standard Mac Save dialog box that lets you put the icon anywhere. We recommend you save it in the same location as your other desktop printer icons.

7. Quit (File ➪ Quit, or ⌘+Q), or repeat steps 4 through 6 to add other desktop printer icons.

Setting up your printer in Windows 98

Make sure you install the AdobePS 4.3 driver, which comes with InDesign. You can verify that the correct version is installed by going to the Adobeps4.drv file in the System folder inside the folder that contains Windows (usually called Windows or Win98). Right-click the file name, choose the Properties option from the contextual menu, and click the Version pane to verify that you have version 4.3 installed.

Your PC will likely have the file Pscript.drv also installed; this is the Microsoft PostScript driver that comes with Windows. It's fine to keep that driver installed as long as you don't use it to print from InDesign. (You might use the Microsoft driver for other programs that have difficulty with Adobe's driver.)

Unlike the Mac version, InDesign for Windows can print to some non-PostScript inkjet printers for local color proofing. For these printers, you don't need to install any special software — just use the drivers that came with the printers.

The InDesign readme files list all supported printers; you'll need to use Adobe's PressReady software for several popular models, including the Canon BubbleJet 8500, several models of the Epson Stylus Color line, and several models of the Hewlett-Packard line. See the section "Making Proof Prints on an Inkjet Printer" in Chapter 33 for more on PressReady.

Before you use the AdobePS driver, you need to make sure that you have the right PostScript printer description (PPD) files installed — these contain the settings for your output device that tell InDesign how to configure the printer. You can download many of these from Adobe's Web site at http://www.adobe.com/supportservice/custsupport/library/pdrvwin.htm; your printer maker's Web site should also have current ones, and many printers come with a setup disk that contains them as well. (You can also download the AdobePS driver and utility from the Adobe site, in case yours is missing.)

Steps: Setting Up a Windows 98 Printer

1. Make sure you have the required PPD files on your PC. They can be anywhere, but we recommend that you create a folder named PPD Files in your Windows or Program Files directory so that later on you know where they are.

2. Run the AdobePS Utility program that came with InDesign or that you downloaded from the Adobe Web site. If you're sure you have the utility but are not sure where it is on your PC, search for the file name aps4eng.exe.

3. You'll have the option of installing a new printer — which you should do to add a printer, such as a remote printer that your documents will be output to at a service bureau — or updating your existing PostScript printer settings to the Adobe driver. Be sure to upgrade the existing drivers and then run the program again to install new printers.

4. When installing a new printer, you'll be asked whether it is connected directly to your computer or via a network. Choose whichever option is true. For a remote printer, choose the direct-connection (Local Printer) option. Then click the Next button.

5. In the next dialog box, Select Printer Model, you'll be asked for the printer description files. Click the Browse button to find the files on your hard disk or network, using the Browse for Printer dialog box. (Figure 32-4 shows this dialog box.) Click OK when you've found the correct driver, which returns you to the Select Printer Model dialog box, where you click the actual PPD file you want and then the Next button.

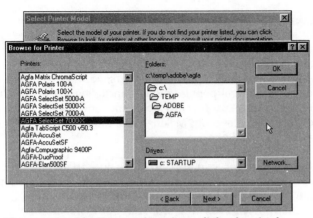

Figure 32-4: The Browse for Printer dialog box in the AdobePS utility lets you select the printer's PPD file.

6. You'll then be asked for a printer location. Choose FILE: and click Next>.

7. Finally, you'll be asked whether to make the printer the default printer (select No) and to print a test page (again, select No). Click Next.

8. In the next dialog box, click the Install button.

9. After a few seconds or minutes, you'll get a dialog box asking you whether to configure the printer. If you know the settings, go ahead and click Yes to go to the Properties dialog box. An example is shown in Figure 32-5. Otherwise, click No; you can always set the properties later by using Start ➪ Settings ➪ Printers to go to the Printers window, where you right-click the printer you want to update the settings for and choose Properties from the contextual menu.

10. Click Finish to complete the installation.

Now you're all set to print from InDesign. To make a printer the default printer for all applications, choose Start ➪ Settings ➪ Printers to go to the Printers window, where you right-click the printer you want to make the default printer and select Set as Default from the contextual menu, as Figure 32-6 shows. The default printer's icon will have a small black circle at upper left with a white checkmark in it.

Platform Difference

Unlike on the Mac, you don't need to select a printer before printing in Windows. Instead, you can select the printer from any program's Print dialog box and set it just for that job.

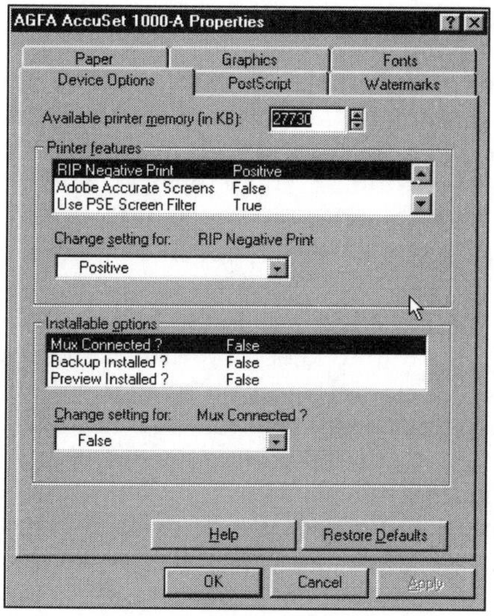

Figure 32-5: The Properties dialog box's Device Options tab lets you set printer-specific settings; the other panes handle basic printing issues such as font translation, PostScript error handling, and network settings.

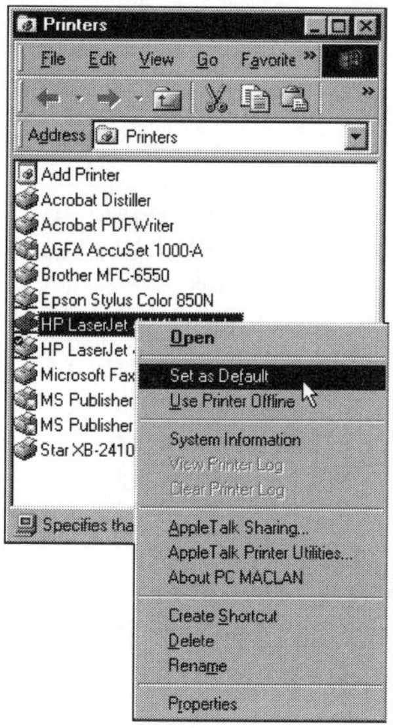

Figure 32-6: In the Printers window, you can set a printer as the default printer for all programs.

Setting up your printer in Windows NT 4.0

Make sure you install the AdobePS 5.1 driver, which comes with InDesign. You can verify that the correct version is installed by going to the Adobeps5.dll file in the w32x86 folder. (Follow this folder sequence to get there, starting from the folder that contains Windows, usually called Winnt4: system32, spool, drivers, and w32x86.) Right-click the file name, choose the Properties option from the contextual menu, and click the Version pane to verify that you have version 5.1 installed.

Your PC will likely have the file Pscript.dll also installed; this is the Microsoft PostScript driver that comes with Windows. It's fine to keep that driver installed, as long as you don't use it to print from InDesign. (You might use the Microsoft driver for other programs that have difficulty with Adobe's driver.)

Unlike the Mac version, InDesign for Windows can print to some non-PostScript inkjet printers for local color proofing. For these printers, you don't need to install any special software — just use the drivers that came with the printers. The InDesign readme files will list all supported printers; you'll need to use Adobe's PressReady software for several popular models, including the Canon BubbleJet 8500, several models of the Epson Stylus Color line, and several models of the Hewlett-Packard line.

See the section "Making Proof Prints on an Inkjet Printer" in Chapter 33 for more on PressReady.

Before you use the AdobePS driver, you need to make sure that you have the right PostScript printer description (PPD) files installed — these contain the settings for your output device that tell InDesign how to configure the printing. (They're kept in the same location as the Adobeps5.dll file.) You can download many of these from Adobe's Web site at http://www.adobe.com/supportservice/custsupport/library/pdrvwin.htm; your printer maker's Web site should also have current ones, and many printers come with a setup disk that contain them as well. (You can also download the AdobePS driver and utility from the Adobe site in case yours is missing.)

Note

You cannot update an existing printer to the AdobePS 5.1 driver. You must install it using the AdobePS Setup Utility. Any PostScript printers set up through the Windows NT Add Printer function will use the Microsoft driver.

Steps: Setting Up a New NT Printer

1. Make sure you have the required PPD files on your PC. They can be anywhere, but we recommend that you create a folder named PPD Files in your Windows or Program Files directory so you know where they are later on.

2. Run the AdobePS Utility program that came with InDesign or that you downloaded from the Adobe Web site. (If you're sure you have the utility but are not sure where it is on your PC, search for the file name aps5eng.exe.)

3. You'll be asked if you want to copy the utility to a local disk. Chances are it already has been, unless you're running it from a network disk. If you do have it copied, you'll be asked where to put it; we recommend that you keep it with your other utility programs or in an Adobe folder, such as that containing InDesign.

4. You'll be asked whether the printer is connected directly to your computer or via a network. Choose whichever option is true. For a remote printer, choose the direct-connection (Local Printer) option. Then click the Next button.

5. In the next dialog box, Select PPD, you'll be asked for the printer description files. Navigate the disk as you would with any standard Open dialog box to find the needed PPD file. Click the Network button if the PPD files reside on a network disk. Click Next when you've found the correct driver. Figure 32-7 shows this dialog box.

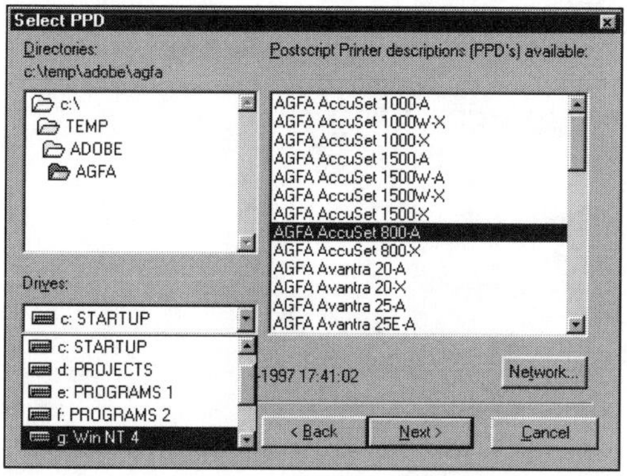

Figure 32-7: The Select PPD dialog box in the AdobePS utility lets you select the printer's PPD file.

6. You'll then be asked for a printer port. Choose FILE: and click Next.

7. Next, you'll be asked whether the printer should be set up as shared or not shared. Unless the printer is directly connected to your PC and you are acting as a printer server, select Not Shared and then click Next.

8. Finally, you'll be asked to name the printer, whether to make it the default printer (select No), and to print a test page (again, select No). Click Next.

9. After a few seconds or minutes, you'll get a Properties pane for the printer you selected; an example is shown in Figure 32-8. Click OK when done. Remember: You can always update the properties later by using Start ⇨ Settings ⇨ Printers to go to the Printers window, where you right-click the printer you want to update the settings for and choose Properties from the contextual menu. You set up basic settings, such as changing the PPD, setting security, or port location using the panes in the Properties dialog box, as shown in Figure 32-9.

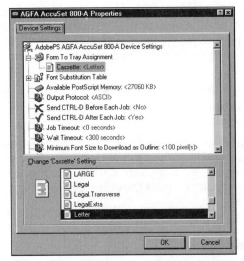

Figure 32-8: The Properties dialog box's Device
Options pane lets you set printer-specific settings.

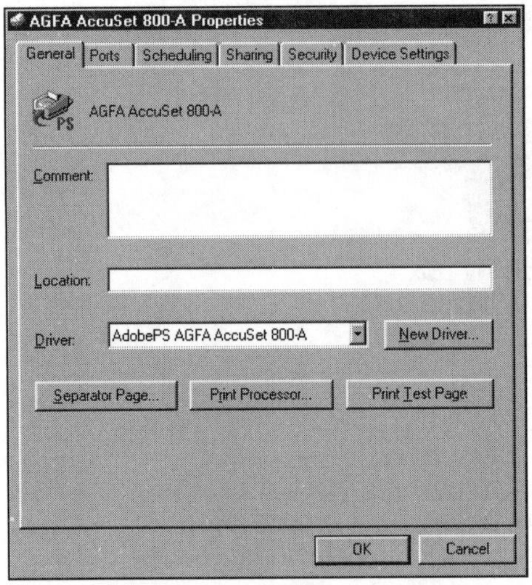

Figure 32-9: The Properties dialog box's other
panes let you set other printer defaults.

10. Click Exit to close the utility, or click Add Another to repeat Steps 4 through 9.
Note that you may be asked to restart Windows after exiting in some cases,
depending on whether the hard drive requires a system restart. You can defer
restart until later or do it immediately.

Now, you're all set to print from InDesign. To make a printer the default printer for all applications, choose Start ⇨ Settings ⇨ Printers to go to the Printers window, where you right-click the printer you want to make the default printer and select Set As Default from the contextual menu, as Figure 32-10 shows. Note that printers that are not directly connected (that is, set to print to FILE:) have a disk icon with their printer icon.

Figure 32-10: In the Printers window, you can set a printer as the default printer for all programs.

 Unlike on the Mac, you don't need to select a printer before printing in Windows. Instead, you can select the printer from any program's Print dialog box and set it just for that job.

Setting Printer Options

With your printer drivers installed and the correct PPD files in use, you should now set global printing settings — controls that affect all documents printed to each printer. You can always change these later for specific documents as needed.

Setting Mac-specific printer options

To get to printer options on the Mac, select File ⇨ Page Setup or use Shift+⌘+P; you'll get the dialog box shown in Figure 32-11.

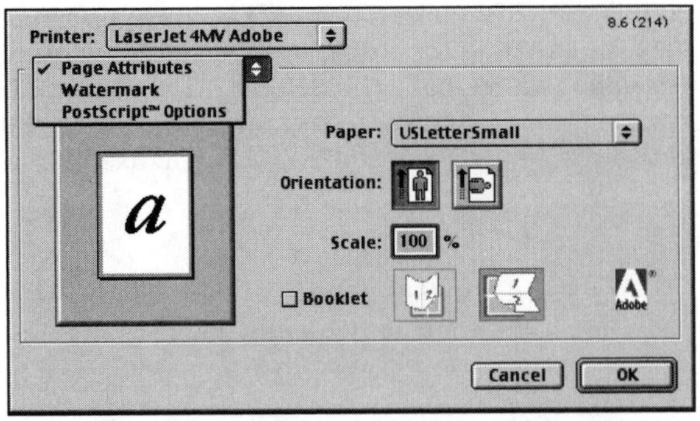

Figure 32-11: The Page Setup dialog box's Page Attributes pane lets you select paper, orientation, and scale.

A pop-up menu, as shown in the figure, lets you move within the dialog box's three panes. The controls will vary from printer to printer, but here are basic options:

✦ In the Page Attributes pane, set the paper size in the Paper pop-up menu, the orientation using one of the Orientation buttons, any magnification or reduction in the Scale field, and enable Booklet printing by checking the Booklet option and clicking the vertical or horizontal booklet icons. (*Booklet printing* essentially divides each page in half and prints the pages in the appropriate order so they can be arranged and folded in the proper sequence.)

✦ In the Watermarks pane, you can set the printer to include text or a graphic (PICT or EPS) that prints either on the background of all pages or just on the first page. You would use this, for example, to have the word *Confidential* printed in gray on the background of all pages. You'll almost never use this in publishing because you would include any such elements in your actual InDesign documents.

✦ The PostScript Options pane (shown in Figure 32-12) provides two sets of controls. The first, titled Visual Effects, will flip the page during printing (Flip Horizontal and Flip Vertical) and reverse the image so that white prints as black and vice versa, creating a negative image (Invert Image). The second set, titled Image & Text, controls how the printer adjusts text and graphics. In most cases, you should check only Unlimited Downloadable Fonts; the other options aren't really appropriate for professionally printed documents. (Substitute Fonts will replace the Mac's system fonts Monaco, Geneva, and New York with comparable PostScript fonts such as Courier, Helvetica, and Times — but you should use only PostScript fonts in the first place when using a PostScript printer. Smooth Text and Smooth Graphics adjust the objects so they look better on a coarse printer, such as an old inkjet or dot matrix, but InDesign doesn't support these, and the high resolution of PostScript printers makes these options unnecessary. Precision Bitmap Alignment forces pixels in a bitmap image to print at their original location — on a high-resolution printer, this can lead to moiré patterns and other visual oddities.)

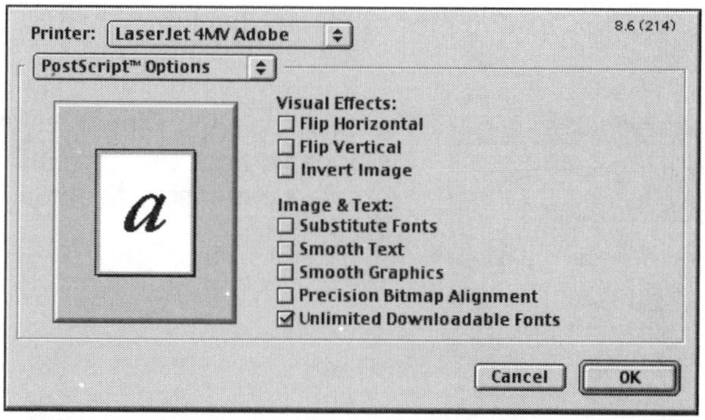

Figure 32-12: The Page Setup dialog box's PostScript Options pane lets you select special effects and tell the printer how to adjust text and graphics.

Setting Windows 98-specific printer options

Figure 32-13 shows some of the options specific to Windows 98. You get these options by selecting the Properties button in the InDesign Print dialog box. Note that these are a subset of the options you get if you go to the Printers window (Start ➪ Settings ➪ Printers), right-click the printer you want to adjust, and select Properties from the contextual menu. (Compare the Device Options pane in Figure 32-13 to that in Figure 32-8 to see the differences.)

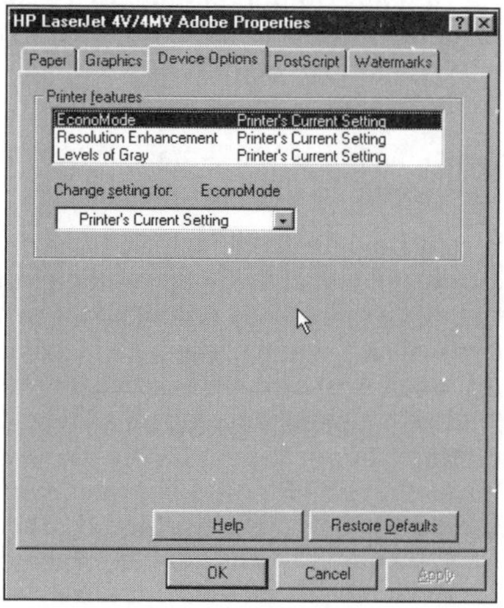

Figure 32-13: The Properties dialog box's Device Options pane, accessed from InDesign, gives you options specific to Windows 98.

The key options are as follows:

✦ In the Paper pane, shown in Figure 32-14, set the paper size, orientation (horizontal or vertical) and, if relevant, the paper source (for printers that have multiple trays or sources of paper or other imaging material).

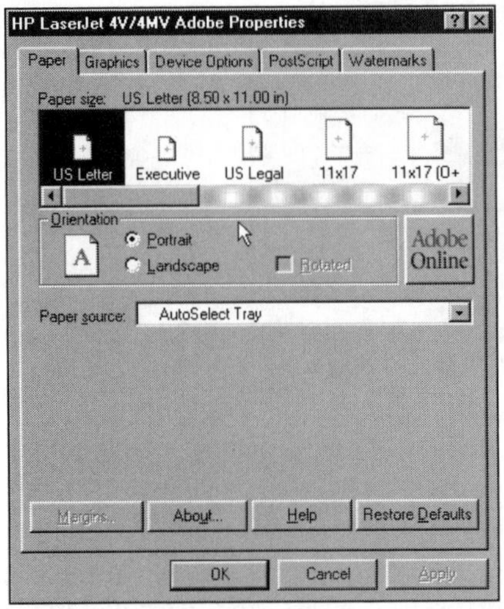

Figure 32-14: The Properties dialog box's Paper pane, accessed from InDesign, lets you select paper size, orientation, and source.

✦ In the Graphics pane, shown in Figure 32-15, make sure the resolution is set to be the highest your printer supports. Set the magnification or reduction in the Scaling field, and select one of the paper-handling options in the Layout pop-up menu (this divides the paper into sections for printing of small items such as business cards that you want to group — gang, in publishing lingo — onto one sheet). You can also set the printer to flip and/or reverse the image (make a photographic negative), but do so in InDesign instead, unless your service bureau or printing manager tells you to do so here.

✦ In the Device Options pane, already shown in Figure 32-12, make any necessary adjustments. The options are specific to each printer.

✦ In the PostScript Options pane, you can set how the PostScript file used for printing is created. In the Postscript output format pop-up menu, use Postscript (optimize for speed) when printing directly to a PostScript printer. Use PostScript (optimize for portability — ADSC) when creating a file that the service bureau may need to edit. Finally, use Encapsulated PostScript (EPS) when creating a file that will be imported into a page-layout program or illustration program (such as when creating a cover repeat for the table contents) or when sending a service bureau an EPS file that contains your document and all its components. Ask your service bureau which option it prefers.

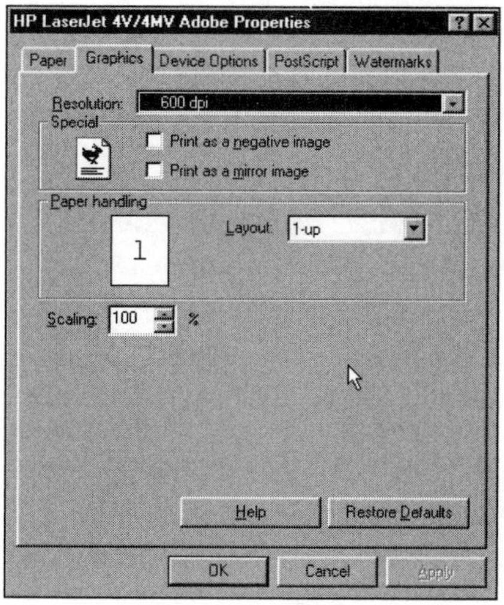

Figure 32-15: The Properties dialog box's Graphics pane, accessed from InDesign, lets you control scaling and adjust resolution to match your printer's capabilities.

✦ The optimization options in the PostScript pane (leave this untouched unless your service bureau asks for a change).

✦ In the Watermarks pane, you can set the printer to include text that prints either on the background of all pages or just on the first page, in full color, in gray, or as an outline. You would use this, for example, to have the word *Confidential* printed in gray on the background all pages. You'll almost never use this in publishing because you would include any such elements in your actual InDesign documents.

You should also set printer defaults through the Printers window (Start ➪ Settings ➪ Printers), right-click the printer you want to adjust, and select Properties from the contextual menu. Here are the key settings:

✦ The Fonts pane let you specify what happens to non-PostScript fonts when printing to a PostScript printer. The best setting is to have the printer translate TrueType fonts to PostScript (the Send as Type 42 option) and to substitute the standard PostScript fonts for the basic TrueType fonts, such as Arial and Times New Roman, as shown in Figure 32-16.

✦ The Device Options pane lets you configure items specific to the printer, such as RAM amount. Make sure this is set correctly, based on your printer's actual configuration. Figure 32-17 shows an example for an imagesetter.

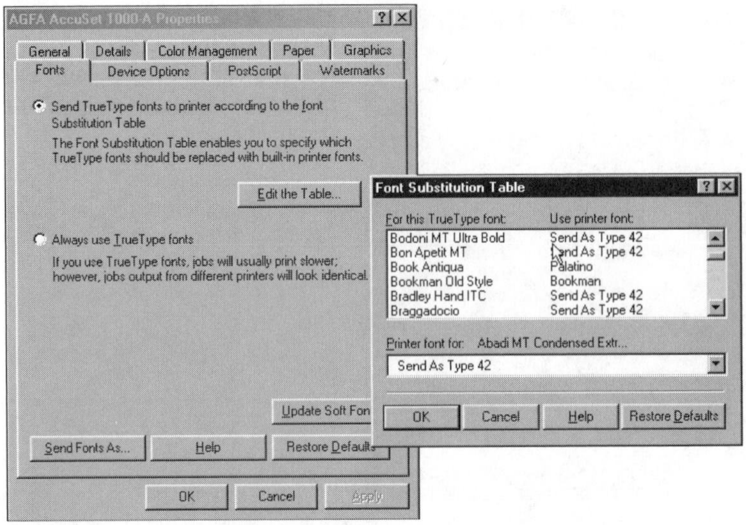

Figure 32-16: In the Properties dialog box's Fonts pane, accessed from the Printers window, you can specify what happens to non-PostScript fonts when you print to a PostScript printer.

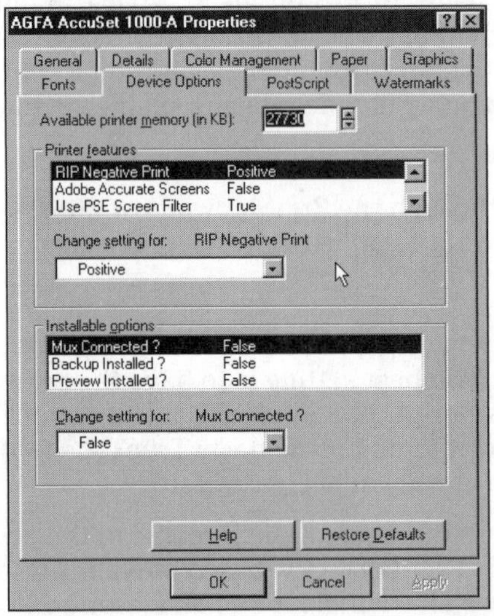

Figure 32-17: The Properties dialog box's Device Options pane for an imagesetter, accessed from the Printers window, lets you configure items specific to your printer.

Setting Windows NT 4-specific printer options

Figure 32-18 shows some of the options specific to Windows NT 4.0. You get these options by selecting the Properties button in the InDesign Print dialog box. Note that these are a subset of the options you get if you go to the Printers window (Start ➪ Settings ➪ Printers), right-click the printer you want to adjust, and select Properties from the contextual menu.

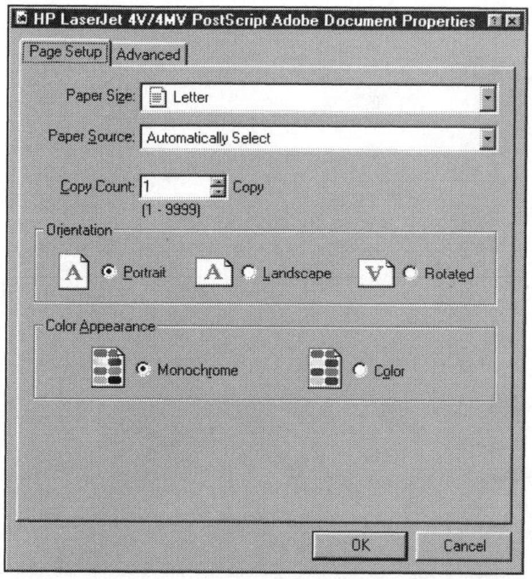

Figure 32-18: The Properties dialog box's Page Setup pane, accessed from InDesign, lets you select paper size, orientation, and source.

The key options are as follows:

✦ In the Page Setup pane, shown in Figure 32-18, you can set the paper size, orientation (horizontal or vertical), and if relevant the paper source (for printers that have multiple trays or sources of paper or other imaging material). If you're printing color documents to a black-and-white printer (such as a laser printer for proofing), select Monochrome; this will save you time in printing.

✦ In the Advanced pane, shown in Figure 32-19, you can set all other options, including resolution and how TrueType fonts are handled (converted to PostScript outlines, kept as TrueType, or converted to bitmaps). You can also set whether *n*-up printing is in effect (to gang several small elements such as business cards onto one page) and the PostScript output option. In the

PostScript output format area, use PostScript (optimize for speed) when printing directly to a PostScript printer and PostScript (optimize for portability — ADSC) when creating a file that the service bureau may need to edit. Finally, choose Encapsulated PostScript (EPS) when creating a file that will be imported into a page-layout or illustration program (such as when creating a cover repeat for the table contents) or when sending a service bureau an EPS file that contains your document and all its components. Ask your service bureau which option it prefers.

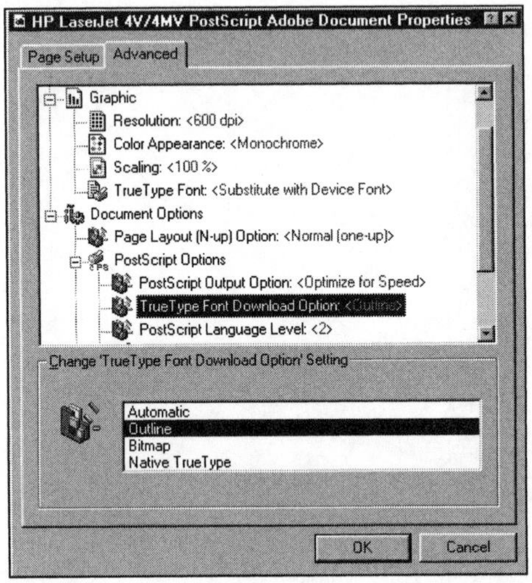

Figure 32-19: The Properties dialog box's Advanced pane, accessed from InDesign, lets you select additional refinements on basic printer options.

Note

The Advanced pane works differently from other panes. Click the + or − signs to expand or contract, respectively, a set of options (in Figure 32-19, Graphic, Document Options, and PostScript Options have all been expanded). To change an option, select it; a subset of additional options will appear at the bottom of the pane. Select the new option. Windows NT will display the changes in red and leave default settings in blue.

You should also set printer defaults through the Printers window (Start ➪ Settings ➪ Printers), right-click the printer you want to adjust, and select Properties from the contextual menu. Most of the panes concern network and printer connections; you'll be interested in the Device Settings pane, which is similar to the Advanced pane accessed via the InDesign Print dialog box. But there are some key settings in the Device Settings pane not available in the Advanced pane:

✦ You can edit the Font Substitution Table, which tells Windows NT which TrueType fonts to replace with equivalent PostScript fonts and which to send unmodified (the Don't Substitute setting), as Figure 32-20 shows. Note that how unmodified TrueType fonts are handled depends on how you set TrueType options in the Advanced panes, as shown in Figure 32-19.

✦ You can set any device-specific options by scrolling to the bottom of the dialog box's list of options. Make sure this is set correctly, based on your printer's actual configuration.

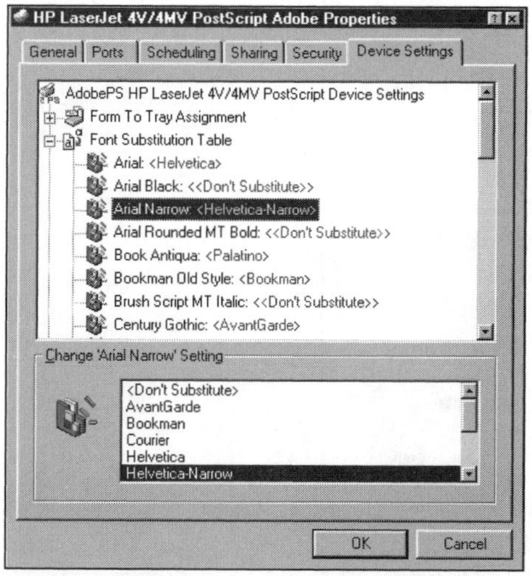

Figure 32-20: The Properties dialog box's Device Options pane, accessed from the Printers window, gives you some refinement options not available elsewhere.

Preflighting Your Document

Now that your printers are set up, you can use InDesign's printing and preprinting checkup tools. The Preflight tool that's part of InDesign will examine your document for any issues of concern and give you a report on what may need to be fixed.

You might wonder why you need a Preflight tool to check for things such as missing fonts and images when InDesign will list any missing fonts and graphics when you open a document. The answer is that sometimes fonts and graphics files could be moved after you've opened a file, in which case you wouldn't get the alerts from InDesign. This is more likely to happen if you're working with files and fonts on a network disk rather than with local fonts and graphics. Preflighting also checks for other problematic issues, such as the use of RGB files and TrueType fonts.

Before you run the Preflight tool, you may want to set up your printer output so the tool can accurately check your document's setup in anticipation of, for example, whether you plan to output color separations or spot colors. To do that, you need to go to the Print dialog box, set your output settings, and then use Save Settings then Cancel on the Mac and Apply then Cancel in Windows to put them into effect *without actually printing the document.* Figure 32-21 shows the dialog boxes for Mac and Windows.

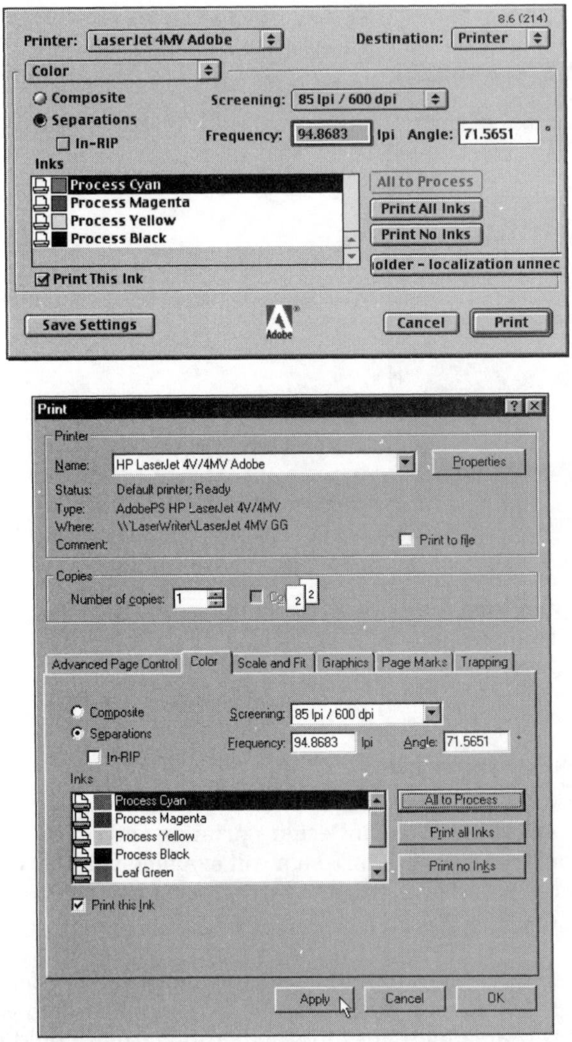

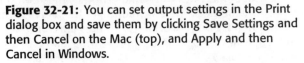

Figure 32-21: You can set output settings in the Print dialog box and save them by clicking Save Settings and then Cancel on the Mac (top), and Apply and then Cancel in Windows.

Selecting your output settings is covered in detail in Chapter 33.

InDesign's way of setting up printer settings without printing is unintuitive, and many users would likely not realize that they should take this step before preflighting.

Running the Preflight tool is easy. Choose File ➪ Preflight, or press Shift+Option+⌘+F or Ctrl+Alt+Shift+F. In a few seconds, you'll get a dialog box that shows the status of your document. Figures 32-22 through 32-26 show the five panes in the Preflight dialog box. Here's a walkthrough of what they do:

✦ The Summary pane (Figure 32-22) shows you a summary of alerts. If your document has layers, you can select or deselect the Show Data for Hidden Layers option. If selected, layers that won't print will be analyzed for font, image, and other issues. Check this option only if the person receiving your document plans on printing hidden layers. For example, in a French-and-English document, you may have hidden the French layer for proofing but still want it checked because the service bureau will be instructed to print the document twice — once with the English layer on and the French layer off, and once with the English layer off and the French layer on.

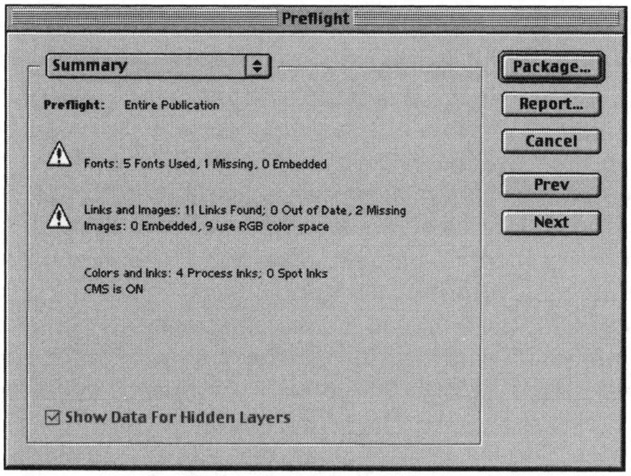

![Preflight dialog box Summary pane]

Figure 32-22: The Summary pane.

In a complex document with lots of graphics and fonts, you may want to select the Show Problems Only option in the Fonts and in the Links and Images panes. If selected, this option will display only elements flagged by the Preflight tool in that pane.

✦ The Fonts pane (Figure 32-23) shows the type (Type 1 PostScript or TrueType) of each font, so you can spot any TrueType fonts before they go to your service bureau. (TrueType fonts usually do not print easily on imagesetters, so use a program such as Macromedia Fontographer to translate them to PostScript instead.) It will also show if any fonts are missing from your system.

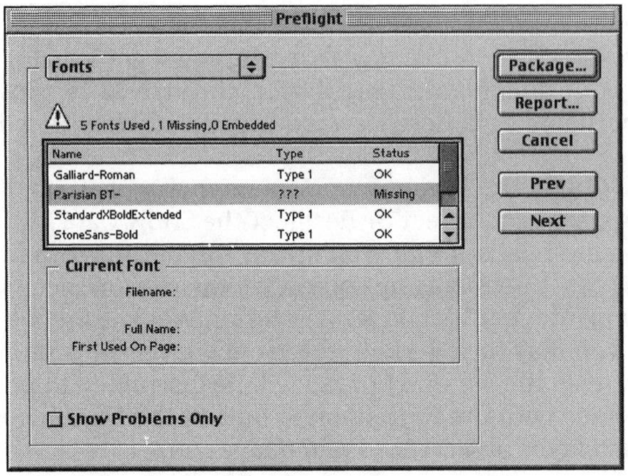

Figure 32-23: The Fonts pane.

✦ The Links and Images pane (Figure 32-24) shows whether any graphics files are missing or if the original image has been modified since you placed it in your layout. You can use the Relink button to correct any such bad links one at a time, or Repair All to have InDesign prompt you in turn for each missing or modified file. The pane will also show whether an ICC color profile is embedded in your graphics, in case files that should have them don't or in case a file that should not have an embedded profile does. It will also show an alert if you use RGB images; although such images will print or color-separate, InDesign provides the warning because it's usually better to convert such images to CMYK in an image editor or illustration program so you control the final appearance rather than rely on InDesign or the output device to do the translation.

The Colors and Inks pane (Figure 32-25) shows you what colors are being used in the document. But this pane's data should be taken with a grain of salt. For example, if you are printing color separations, it will show that you have 0 inks — unless you happened to define cyan, magenta, and yellow as color swatches in your document. Even without these swatches and the resulting alert in this pane, InDesign will color-separate your document to CMYK correctly. Likewise, the pane does not show what screen angle and dot resolution (lines per inch) the negatives will be set at, even if you have configured these settings in the Print dialog box.

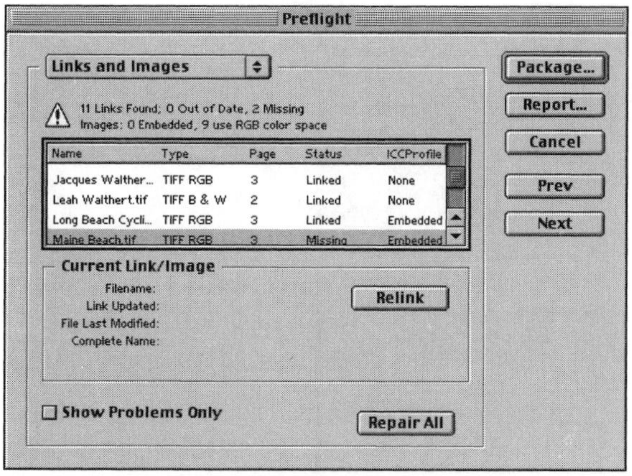

Figure 32-24: The Links and Images pane.

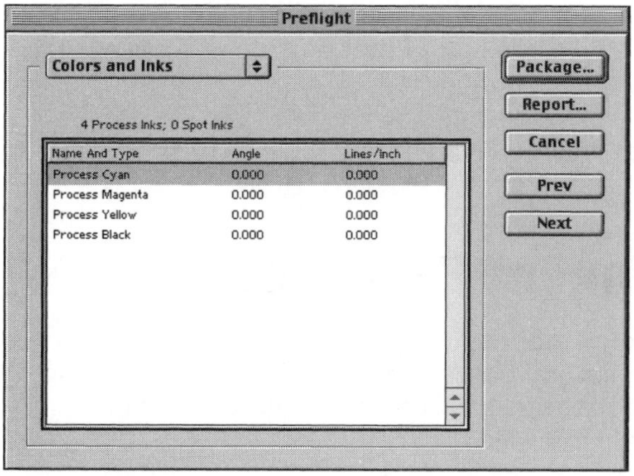

Figure 32-25: The Colors and Inks pane.

✦ The Print Settings dialog box (Figure 32-26) shows you how the document is configured to print in the Print dialog box. That's why it's key to configure the output settings, as described earlier, before preflighting your document.

You can create a report of the preflight information by clicking the Report button. It will generate a text file containing the information from the Preflight dialog box's panes, which you can give to your service bureau to check its settings and files against.

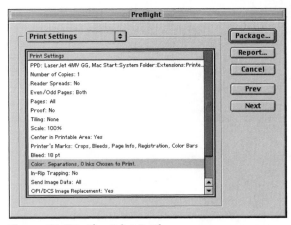

Figure 32-26: The Print Settings pane.

You can also click the Package button to gather all related fonts and files into one folder for delivery to a service bureau or other outside printing agency. The next section describes this option in more detail.

Click Cancel to exit the Preflight dialog box and go back to your document.

Creating a Document Package

If you've ever had the experience of giving a page-layout document to a service bureau, only to be called several hours later by the person outputting your document because some of the files necessary to output it are missing, you will love the Package feature in InDesign.

This command, which you access by choosing File ➪ Package, or Option+Shift+⌘+P or Ctrl+Alt+Shift+P, copies all the font, color-output, and picture files necessary to output your document into a folder. It also generates a report that contains all the information about your document that a service bureau is likely ever to need, including the document's fonts, dimensions, and trapping information. You can also create an instructions file that has your contact information and any particulars you want to say about the document.

When you run the Package command, InDesign will preflight your document automatically and give you the option of viewing any problems it encounters. If you elect to view that information, you'll be shown the Preflight dialog box shown in Figures 32-22 through 32-26. You can continue to package your document from that dialog box by clicking the Package button after you've assured yourself that none of the problems will affect the document's output.

Before you can actually package the document, you'll be asked to save the current document and then to fill in the Printing Instructions form shown in Figure 32-27. You can change the default file name from Instructions.txt to something more like the name of your job.

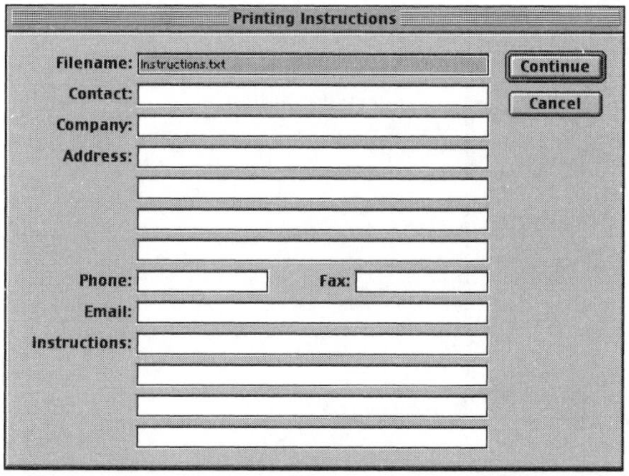

Printing Instructions

Filename: Instructions.txt	Continue
Contact:	Cancel
Company:	
Address:	
Phone: Fax:	
Email:	
Instructions:	

Figure 32-27: The Printing Instructions dialog box.

Caution

If you *don't* want to create an instructions form, don't click Cancel — that cancels the entire package operation. Just click Continue, leaving the form blank. Similarly, you must answer Save to the request to save the document; clicking Cancel stops the package operation as well.

The next step is to create the package folder.

Caution

Be careful here because the dialog box is a bit misleading. Although the dialog box on the Mac is labeled Create Package Folder, the name you enter in the Name field is the name for the InDesign document you are creating, not the name of the folder you intend to put it in. Use the New Folder icon to create the folder first, and then enter the name and select the other dialog box options.

Platform Difference

The Create Package Folder and Package Publication dialog boxes — different names for the same function — look substantively different between the Mac and Windows versions of InDesign, as Figure 32-28 shows. Both use their operating systems' standard Save dialog boxes for the top part, which is why the New Folder buttons, for example, are so different.

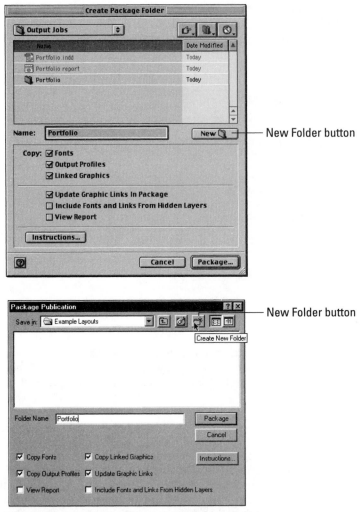

New Folder button

New Folder button

Figure 32-28: The Create Package Folder dialog boxes differ greatly between the Mac (top) and Windows. Even the dialog box's name is different in Windows.

In the dialog box, you can select what is copied: the fonts, color output profiles, and linked graphics (graphics pasted into an InDesign document rather than imported are automatically included). You can also have InDesign update the graphics links for those that were modified or moved; if this option is not selected, any missing or modified graphics files will not be copied with the document.

You can tell InDesign to include fonts and links from hidden layers (which you would do only if you want the service bureau to print those hidden layers or if you are giving the document's files to a colleague to do further work on).

The Package feature does not include any changes you made to the hyphenation and spelling dictionaries. This can cause real problems during output because if the service bureau opens the InDesign file, it will use their dictionaries, possibly causing incorrect hyphenation and even document reflow. So be sure to include these files, which are stored in the Proximity folder in the Dictionaries folder in the Plug-ins folder in the folder containing the InDesign program.

See Chapter 10 for more details on these dictionaries. Chapter 37 explains which files you should send to others using your documents.

Finally, you can view the report after the package is created. On the Mac, InDesign will launch SimpleText and display the report file, but on Windows it will launch the Notepad and display the report file.

Click the Package button when everything is ready to go. Your document will be placed in the folder you specified, as will the instructions file (the report). There will also be a folder called Fonts that includes the fonts, a folder called Links that has the graphics files, and a folder called Output Profiles that has the color output profiles.

We strongly recommend using the Package feature. It ensures that your service bureau has all the necessary files and information to output your document correctly.

Dealing with Service Bureaus

Service bureaus are great: They keep and maintain all the equipment, know the ins and outs of both your software and your printing press requirements, and turn jobs around quickly—at least most of the time. Working with a service bureau involves commitment and communication between both parties. They need your business; you need their expertise and equipment.

To ensure that you get what you want (fast, accurate service) and that the service bureau gets what it wants (no-hassle clients and printing jobs), make sure that you both understand your standards and needs. Keep in mind that the service bureau has many customers, all of whom do things differently. Service bureaus likewise must not impose unreasonable requirements just for the sake of consistency because customers can have good reasons for doing things differently.

Paying attention to a few basic issues can help you establish a productive relationship with your service bureau.

Sending documents versus output files

Because you have the Package feature, do you give the service bureau your actual InDesign documents or do you send an EPS, PostScript, or PDF output file?

 Cross-Reference   Chapter 34 shows you how to create the output files noted above.

The answer depends on several factors:

✦ A document file, even if the graphics files are copied with it, takes less space than an output file created from your document, which means fewer disks or cartridges to sort through and less time copying files from your media to theirs.

✦ A document file can be accidentally changed, resulting in incorrect output. For example, a color might be changed accidentally when the service bureau checks your color definitions to make sure that spot colors are translated to process colors. Or document preferences might be lost, resulting in text reflow.

✦ The service bureau cannot always edit an output file. So the service bureau may not be able to come to your rescue if you make a mistake such as forgetting to print registration marks when creating the output file or specifying landscape printing mode for a portrait document.

Basically, the question is whom do you trust more: yourself or the service bureau? Only you can answer that question. But in either case, there are two things that you can do to help prevent miscommunication: Provide the report file to the service bureau and also provide a proof copy of your document. The service bureau uses these tools to see if its output matches your expectations — regardless of whether you provided a document file or output file.

Determining output settings

A common area of miscommunication between designers and service bureaus is determining who sets controls over line screens, registration marks, and other output controls. Whoever has the expertise to make the right choices should handle these options. And it should be clear to both parties who is responsible for what aspect of output controls; you don't want to use conflicting settings or accidentally override the desired settings:

✦ Assuming you're sending InDesign documents to the service bureau, for output controls such as line screens and angles, the layout artist should determine these settings and specify them on the proof copy provided to the service bureau. That way the service bureau can use its own PPD files rather than take the chance you had incorrect or outdated ones.

✦ If the publication has established production standards for special effects or special printing needs or if the job is unusual, we recommend that the layout artist determine the settings for such general printing controls as the registration marks and the printer resolution.

Cross-Reference InDesign print-control setup is described in Chapter 33.

✦ But for issues related to the service bureau's internal needs and standards, such as how much gap between pages, we recommend that the service bureau determine their own settings. If you are sending the service bureau output files instead of InDesign documents, you will have to enter such settings in the Print dialog box pane before creating the file, so be sure to coordinate these issues with the service bureau in advance.

✦ Issues related to the printing press (such as which side of the negative the emulsion should be on), should be coordinated with the printer and service bureau. Again, let the service bureau enter this data unless you send output files.

In all cases, determine who is responsible for every aspect of output controls to ensure that someone does not specify a setting outside his or her area of responsibility without first checking with the other parties.

Note Smart service bureaus do know how to edit an output file to change some settings, such as dpi and line-screen, that are encoded in those files, but don't count on their doing that work for you except in emergencies. And then they should let you know what they did, and why. And remember: Not all output files can be edited (such as EPS and PostScript files created as binary files), or you can edit them only in a limited way (such as PDF files).

Ensuring correct bleeds

When you create an image that bleeds, it must actually print beyond the crop marks. There must be enough of the bleeding image that if the paper moves slightly in the press, the image still bleeds. (Most printers expect $1/8$ inch, or about a pica, of *trim* area for a bleed.) In most cases, the document page is smaller than both the page size (specified in InDesign through the File ➪ Document Setup option) and the paper size, so that the margin between pages is sufficient to allow for a bleed. If your document page is the same size as your paper size, the paper size limits how much of your bleed actually prints: Any part of the bleed that extends beyond the paper size specified is cut off. (This problem derives from the way PostScript controls printing; it has nothing to do with InDesign.)

Make sure that your service bureau knows that you are using bleeds and whether you specified a special paper or page size because that may be a factor in the way the operator outputs your job.

Sending oversized pages

If you use a paper size larger than U.S. letter size (8.5 by 11 inches), tell the service bureau in advance because the paper size might affect how the operator sends your job to the imagesetter. Many service bureaus use a utility program that automatically rotates pages to save film because pages rotated 90 degrees still fit along the width of typesetting paper and film rolls. But if you specify a larger paper size to make room for bleeds or because your document will be printed at tabloid size, this rotation might cause the tops and/or bottoms of your document pages to be cut off.

We've worked with service bureaus that forgot they loaded this page-rotation utility, so the operator didn't think to unload it for our oversized pages. It took a while to figure out what was going on because we were certain that we weren't doing the rotation (the service bureau assumed we had), and the service bureau had forgotten that it was using the rotation utility.

Summary

InDesign is a rarity among programs in that it requires you to use a specific printer driver rather than the one that came with your Mac or PC. Setting up this driver differs among the Macintosh, Windows 98, and Windows NT 4.0. With your printer driver installed, you should turn your attention to setting global printing defaults, the ones that affect all printing jobs, such as the use of paper trays and the handling of TrueType fonts.

Before you actually print, InDesign checks your document for possible output problems using its preflight tools. You also have the chance to create a print package—which collects all graphics, fonts, and a copy of the document file—to send to your service bureau or other output service.

✦   ✦   ✦

Printing Techniques

Your document is done. You've set up your printers, printer options, and Preflighted your document, as described in Chapter 32. You're ready to see all that effort become reality by printing a proof copy or an actual version on a high-resolution imagesetter or printer.

The good news is that your hard work is over. Printing from InDesign is straightforward once everything has been set up. Just use File ➪ Print, or ⌘+P or Ctrl+P, to go to the Print dialog box.

Note On the Mac, you normally have to remember to choose the printer before opening the Print dialog box, as explained in Chapter 32. But InDesign and the AdobePS driver let you choose the printer from the Print dialog box, similar to standard Windows behavior.

Selecting InDesign Printing Options

The Print dialog box has many panes — 13 on the Mac and six in Windows — as well as several options common to all the panes. Change any options and choose Print, and InDesign sends your document to the printer. Figure 33-1 shows the default Mac and Windows dialog boxes.

Figure 33-1: The default view for the Print dialog box
on the Mac (top) and in Windows.

Platform Difference

Most of the panes in Mac InDesign — but not in Windows InDesign — support Mac-specific options, such as choosing background printing, or are options that you set in the Windows printer properties, as described in Chapter 32. Also note that Windows InDesign displays tabs for all the available panes, whereas Mac InDesign uses a pop-up menu to move among panes. Other differences differentiate the two platforms' versions, as detailed throughout this chapter.

Choosing General options

The general options available in the dialog box no matter what pane is selected are as follows:

✦ The Printer pop-up menu and the Name pop-up menu in Windows let you select the printer to use. In Mac InDesign, only printers using the AdobePS driver are shown, whereas in Windows all printers (including Windows' built-in faxing function) are displayed. But Windows InDesign displays a note in red if you select a printer that does not use the AdobePS driver.

✦ The Destination pop-up menu on the Mac and the Print to File checkbox in Windows let you have the document printed to a printer or to a file that can then be output to a printer or other device later.

✦ The Save Settings button on the Mac and the Apply button in Windows save any settings you changed in the Print dialog box, making them the defaults for the next time you print using the same printer.

Oddity   QuarkXPress and PageMaker users will be disappointed that InDesign doesn't support printer styles, which let you save printer settings as named styles for reuse later, similar to how paragraph styles let you save text-formatting attributes. The Save Settings/Apply feature is as close as InDesign comes to this.

✦ Cancel closes the Print dialog box without printing. Use this option if you've clicked Save Settings or Apply but don't want to print, as well when you have any reason not to print.

✦ The Print button on the Mac and the OK button in Windows print the document based on the current settings.

Using the General pane

Macintosh InDesign has a General pane, whereas Windows InDesign does not. The General pane is a standard Mac pane, so Mac InDesign includes it for Mac compatibility. Windows InDesign places its Copies and Collate features in the common part of the dialog box, whereas the selection of pages to print is handled in the Advanced Page Control pane.

Using the Advanced Page Control pane

The Advanced Page Control pane, shown in Figure 33-2, is where you tell InDesign what pages to print.

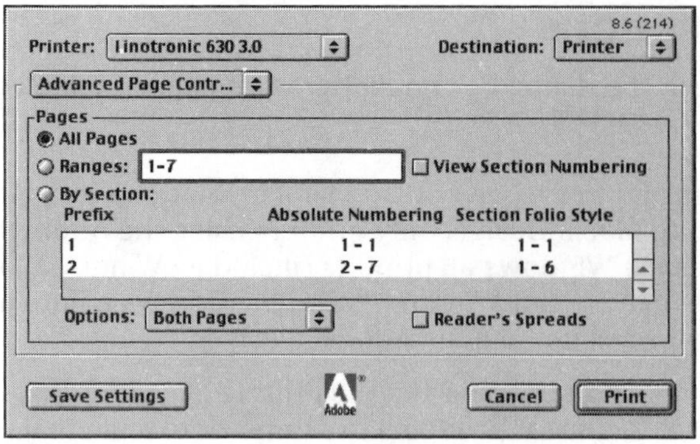

Figure 33-2: The Advanced Page Control pane.

You can select all pages, a range of pages, or — if your document uses sections — a specific section. If you want to see what pages in the document correspond to the section numbering, uncheck View Section Numbering. Remember, when specifying a range of pages, you can use nonconsecutive ranges, such as 1-4, 7, 10-13, 15, 18, 20.

Using the Options pop-up menu, you can also have InDesign print both pages on a sheet, just even pages, or just odd pages. For this option to be available, you must be using facing pages. A related option is Reader's Spreads, which prints facing pages on one sheet, just as they appear onscreen.

Tip You may not want to use the Readers Spreads option when outputting to an imagesetter if you have bleeds because no bleed will print between the spreads. If you use traditional perfect-binding (square spines) or saddle-stitching (stapled spines), which are printing methods where facing pages are not printed contiguously, do not use this option.

Using the Color pane

The Color pane, shown in Figure 33-3, is where you manage color output, particularly color separations.

If you're printing to a color printer, select Composite. On some printers, you may also have an option for the Screening pop-up menu, which lets you choose the resolution of the output.

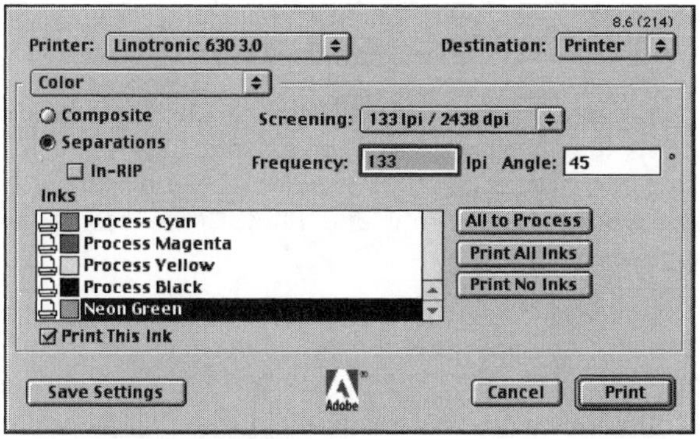

Figure 33-3: The Color pane.

If you're printing color separations, you have several options in this dialog box to work through:

✦ Select Separations to have InDesign output negatives for each color.

✦ If you're outputting to a PostScript Level 3 device with Adobe's In-RIP software, which does all the color-separation work, click the In-RIP box as well. Otherwise, InDesign does all the separation work as part of the output process.

✦ Choose the appropriate option from the Screening pop-up menu; you'll have a list of all resolution options supported by the target printer. The following sidebar "What *dpi* and *lpi* Mean" explains these terms.

✦ Now choose what inks you want to print. In the Inks section, all spot-color inks, plus the standard CMYK process colors (cyan, magenta, yellow, and black) will display. To convert all inks to process color, click the All to Process button. (The button then is renamed Revert to Spot so you can undo this action.) To select individual inks, click each one in turn and then uncheck or check the Print This Ink. Use Print All Inks to reactivate all inks, and Print No Inks to deactivate all inks. (This is handy if you want to print just one or a few inks: Click Print No Inks and then add back those you want to print, rather than deselecting all the ones you don't want.)

✦ For each selected ink, you can select an lpi setting in the Frequency field, as well as a screening angle. Unless you are doing a special effect, there's no reason that the lpi setting for an individual color should differ from that set in the Screening pop-up menu for all colors. For process colors, the screening angle should usually not be changed, but you may want to adjust it for spot colors. The section "Working with Spot Colors and Separations" later in this chapter explains the issues.

What *dpi* and *lpi* Mean

Lines per inch (lpi) and dots per inch (dpi) are not related because the spots in a line screen are variable-sized, whereas dots in a laser printer or imagesetter are often fixed-sized. (Because newer printers using techniques such as Hewlett-Packard's Resolution Enhancement Technology or Apple Computer's FinePrint and PhotoGrade use variable-sized dots, the distinction may disappear one day.)

Lines per inch specifies, in essence, the grid through which an image is filtered, not the size of the spots that make it up. Dots per inch specifies the number of ink dots per inch produced by the laser printer; these dots are typically the same size. A 100-lpi image with variable sized dots will therefore appear finer than a 100-dpi image. The following figure shows an example, with a fixed-dot arrow at left and a variable-size dot arrow at right.

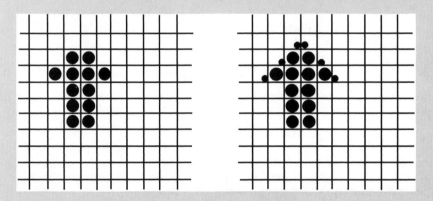

Depending upon the size of the line-screen spot, several of a printer's fixed-sized dots may be required to simulate one line-screen spot. For this reason, a printer's or imagesetter's lpi is far less than its dpi. For example, a 300-dpi laser printer can achieve about 60-lpi resolution; a 1,270-dpi imagesetter can achieve about 120-lpi resolution; a 2,540-dpi imagesetter about 200-lpi resolution. Resolutions of less than 100 lpi are considered coarse, and resolutions of more than 120 lpi are considered fine.

But there's more to choosing an lpi setting than knowing your output device's top resolution. An often overlooked issue is the type of paper the material is printed on. Smoother paper (such as *glossy-coated* or *super-calendared*) can handle finer halftone spots because the paper's coating (also called its *finish*) minimizes ink bleeding. Standard office paper, such as those used in photocopiers and laser printers, is rougher and has some bleed that is usually noticeable only if you write on it with markers. Newsprint is very rough and has a heavy bleed. Typically, newspaper images are printed at 85 to 90 lpi; newsletter images on standard office paper print at 100 to 110 lpi; magazine images are printed at 120 to 150 lpi; calendars and coffee-table art books are printed at 150 to 200 lpi.

Other factors affecting lpi include the type of printing press and the type of ink used. Your printer representative should advise you on preferred settings.

If you output your document from your computer directly to film negatives (rather than to photographic paper that is then shot to create negatives), inform your printer representative. Outputting to negatives produces a higher lpi than outputting to paper because negatives created photographically cannot accurately reproduce the fine resolution of negatives that are output directly on an imagesetter. (If, for example, you output to 120 lpi on paper and then create a photographic negative, even the slightest change in the camera's focus will make the fine dots blurry. Outputting straight to negatives avoids this problem.) Printer representatives often assume that you are outputting to paper and base their advised lpi settings on this assumption.

Using the Scale and Fit pane

The Scale and Fit pane, shown in Figure 33-4, lets you adjust the size of your document, as well as print documents that won't fit on an available paper size.

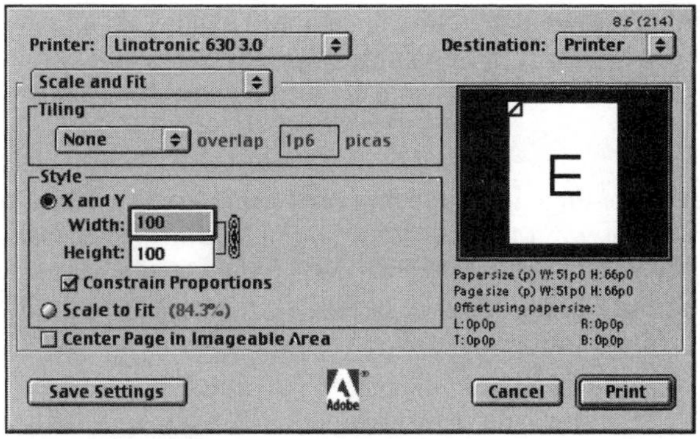

Figure 33-4: The Scale and Fit pane.

Use the Tiling options to print oversized documents. InDesign breaks the document into separate pages, called *tiles*, that you can assemble together later. Here's how:

✦ **None** is the default option in the Tiling pop-up menu. This prevents tiling, printing just what fits of the current page.

✦ **Auto** lets InDesign figure out where to divide the pages into tiles. You can change its default amount of overlap between tiles of 1p6 (0.25 inches) using the Overlap field. The overlap lets you easily align tiles by having enough overlap for you to see where each should be placed relative to the others.

✦ **Manual** lets you specify the tiles yourself. To specify a tile, you change the
origin point on the document ruler; this becomes the upper-left corner of the
current tile. To print multiple tiles this way, you need to adjust the origin
point, print, adjust the origin point to the next location, print, and so forth,
until done.

Cross-Reference   Chapter 2 covers the origin point in more detail.

In the Style section, you can magnify or reduce your document. Chances are that
you won't do so often because if you're outputting to negatives, you should print at
100 percent and select the right resolution. (In the old days, people often printed
small text larger so it could be photographically reduced when creating film
negatives. That was because the process of producing negatives could make small
text fill in. But that's not an issue when outputting directly to an imagesetter.)
Another reason to magnify or reduce a document is for proofing — to magnify small
pages to make them more legible when gathering comments, or to reduce large
pages so they fit on a local printer.

To adjust the output's scale, select the X and Y option and change the Width and
Height fields. If Constrain Proportions is unchecked, you can set them separately,
distorting the page. Or select the Scale to Fit option, which reduces the document's
size to fit within the target printer's page size. Note that Scale to Fit takes into
account bleeds and crop marks, so even if the document page size is the same as
the output device's paper size, Scale to Fit reduces it to make room for those
elements.

Caution   Be careful when using the Center Page in Imageable Area option when outputting
to an imagesetter. They may not want the pages centered because they may be
spacing them or rotating them to minimize wastage of paper or film negatives.
Remember: Imagesetters output to rolls of paper or film, so the service bureau has
some control over the page's size. Always check first. On a local laser printer or
other proofing device that outputs discrete pages, go ahead and use this option to
make room available on all sides where possible for crop marks and bleeds.

Using the Graphics pane

The Graphics pane, shown in Figure 33-5, controls how graphics are printed, as well
as how fonts are downloaded. The options here are meant for professional printing,
such as to imagesetters, in situations where you're working with a service bureau
or in-house printing department.

Your first option is the Send Image Data pop-up menu, which has three additional
options: All, Optimized Subsampling, and Low Resolution (72 dpi). Typically, use
All. The other two options are meant to increase speed of proof prints, with Low
Resolution (72 dpi) being the fastest. A related option is Proof Print — when
checked, all graphics are stripped out of the printing, replaced with an outline of
the graphics frame and an X through the frame to indicate a graphic. This is handy
for quick proofs meant to focus on the layout and the text.

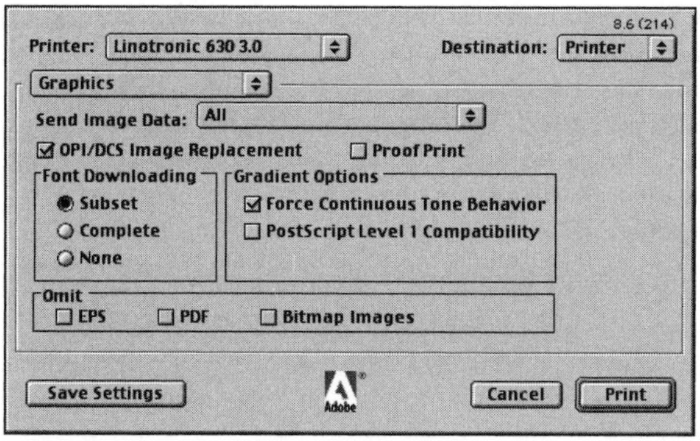

Figure 33-5: The Graphics pane.

If graphics files exist in high-resolution versions at your service bureau — typically, this occurs when the bureau scans in photographs at very high resolutions and sends you a lower-resolution version for layout placement — check OPI/DCS Image Replacement. This ensures that InDesign uses the high-resolution scans, as well as pre-color-separated versions of your EPS files. (OPI is the Open Prepress Interface, the standard for such image substitution. DCS is Document Color Separation, a variant of EPS that keeps each of the process colors in its own file, in effect preseparating the document.)

A related graphics-file-handling option is in the Omit section: You can have InDesign not include EPS, PDF, and bitmap images (such as TIFF files). You would omit these files either to speed printing of proof copies or when the service bureau has such files in higher-resolution or color-corrected versions and will substitute their graphics for yours. InDesign keeps any OPI links, so the graphics at the service bureau will relink to your document during output.

In the Gradient Options section of the dialog box, you have two options:

✦ **Force Continuous Tone Behavior** makes the output device treat gradients as a photo, which can improve appearance in some cases where the output device bands the colors, creating a step-like effect in color transitions.

✦ **PostScript Level 1 Compatibility** lets gradients print properly on PostScript Level 1 devices. Choose this option only if you're outputting to a Level 1 printer or creating PDF files that might be printed by readers who have Level 1 printers.

Finally, the Font Downloading options require that you understand how your output device is configured to handle fonts. Be sure to ask your service bureau what options it prefers:

✦ Normally, when printing to a local printer, keep the Font Downloading option set to Subset, which sends font data to the printer as fonts are used. This means that if you use just one character of a font on a page, only that character is sent for that page, and if more characters are used on later pages, they are sent at that time. This is an efficient way to send font data to printers that don't have lots of memory or hard drive space to store complete font information for many typefaces.

✦ If you're printing to a device that has a lot of font memory — or if your document has many pages and uses a font in bits and pieces throughout — use the Complete option. This sends the entire font to the printer's memory, where it resides for the entire print job; in cases such as those described, this option is more efficient than the standard Subset method.

✦ Use the None option if you're certain all the fonts you use reside in the printer's memory or in a hard disk attached to the printer. Many service bureaus will load all the fonts for a job into the printer memory and then print the job. They'll then clear out the printer memory for the next job, and load just the fonts that job needs. This is efficient when a service bureau has lots of clients who use all sorts of fonts. Alternatively, some service bureaus attach a hard drive loaded with fonts to their imagesetters, saving the font-loading time for them and for InDesign.

Using the Page Marks pane

The Page Marks pane, shown in Figure 33-6, lets you specify which printer marks are output with your pages.

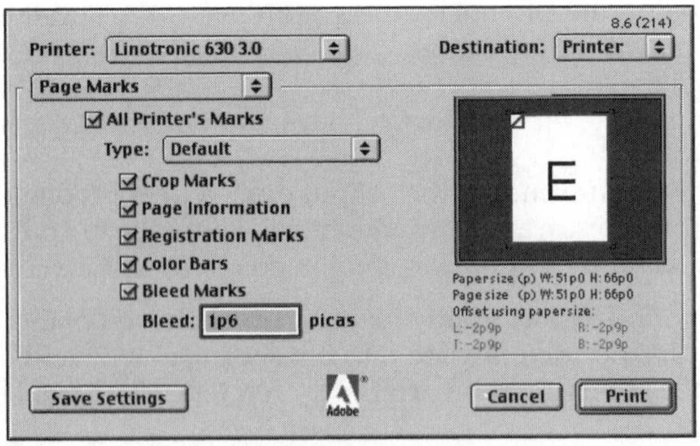

Figure 33-6: The Page Marks pane.

In most cases, you'd select All Printer's Marks and have all print on each sheet or negative. But you can select which ones you want to print. Here's what each option means:

✦ **Crop Marks** are lines at the corners of the page that tell a commercial printer where the page boundaries are, and thus where the paper will be trimmed to.

✦ **Page Information** lists the file name and page number.

✦ **Registration Marks** are cross-hair symbols that are used to ensure that the color negatives are properly aligned on top of each other when combined to create a color proof and when lined up on a printing press to make sure the final pages will not have the colors misregistered.

✦ **Color Bars** print the CMYK colors and tints so a commercial printer can quickly check during printing whether ink is under- or oversaturated—the shades could be too light or dark. The CMYK colors also help a commercial printer know which color a particular negative is for (after all, negatives are produced using transparent film with black images).

✦ **Bleed Marks** add a very thin box around your page that shows the bleed area—where you expect items to print into, even though they're past the page trim boundary. The default is 1p6 (0.25 inches), which is more than enough area for the bleed, but you can change that value in the Bleed field. (A *bleed* is an object that you want to be cut at the page boundary; you need to have the object overshoot that boundary in case during printing the page is not trimmed exactly where it should be. Normally, 0p9, or 0.125 inches, is a sufficient width for a bleed.)

Note

If a printer has options for printer's marks, they will display in the Type pop-up menu, but most will simply have one option: Default.

Tip

Using any printer's marks automatically increases the page size in PDF files exported from InDesign to add room for the printer's marks. This is handy because when you output EPS or other PostScript files, the page size selected determines the page boundary, and printer's marks often get eliminated because they fall outside that boundary. One solution is to use a larger page size than your final output will be, so there's naturally enough room for printer's marks. The preview window at right in the dialog box shows you if printer's marks fall outside the page's boundaries (as they do in Figure 33-6).

Using the Edit Trapping Inks dialog box

The next pane is the Trapping pane, which is covered in Chapter 28. But it does have one option, in the Edit Trapping Inks dialog box, that should be set when setting up print specifications. Figure 33-7 shows the dialog box; you access it by clicking the Inks button in the Trapping pane.

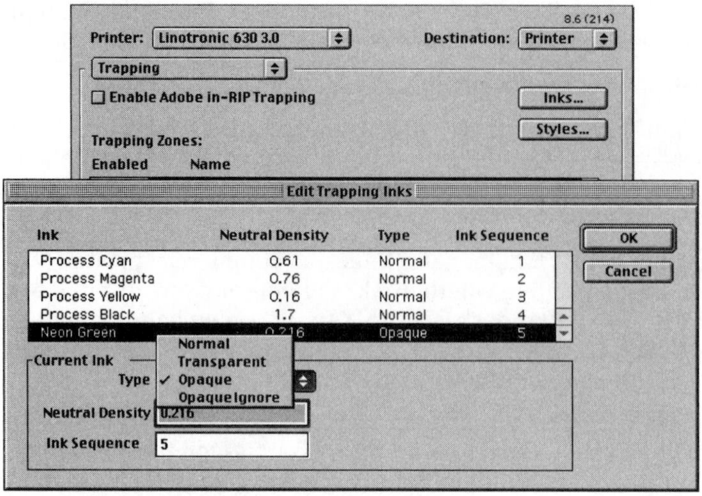

Figure 33-7: The Edit Trapping Inks dialog box.

Caution

These options should be specified in coordination with your service bureau and commercial printer – they can really wreak havoc with your printing if set incorrectly.

Here's what the options do:

✦ You can change the ink type in the Type pop-up menu. Most inks — including process inks — should be left at Normal. Use Transparent for varnishes and other finishes that let color through — you don't want InDesign to trap to such "colors"; if they did, no color would print under the varnish or finish. (A varnish is often used to highlight part of a page, such as making the text reflective in contrast to the rest of the page.) Use Opaque for metallics, pastels, and other thick colors; this setting lets adjacent colors trap to the edge of opaque objects but it prevents trapping of underlying colors (because they will be totally covered over). (In Figure 33-7, we set the Neon Green spot color to be treated as Opaque.) Finally, use OpaqueIgnore for inks that don't trap well with any other color — your service bureau or commercial printer will tell you when you need to do this.

✦ For each ink, you can change the neutral density, which tells InDesign how to handle the trapping of differently saturated inks. For example, a dark color (highly saturated) will need to be trapped more conservatively against a light color to prevent excess intrusion. In coordination with your commercial printer, you might want to override the default neutral density settings if you're finding that the defaults don't properly handle some trapping combinations. It's possible that your commercial printer is using a different brand of ink from what is assumed in the settings, for example, and this could require a density adjustment.

✦ Some commercial printers let you arrange the order in which color negatives print. This affects the trapping because InDesign presumes that the colors are printed in the standard order — cyan, then magenta, then yellow, then black, and then any spot colors — and factors that into its trapping adjustments. In some cases, changing the printing order can improve a publication's color balance because it happens to favor a range of tones that the standard order might not treat properly. For example, if there's a lot of black in the background, you might want to print black first, so other colors overprint it, giving it a warmer feel than if black were printed on top of the other colors as is normal. To change the order of output used by InDesign's trapping calculations, select a color and change its ink sequence number in the Ink Sequence field; all other colors' sequences will be automatically adjusted.

Using Macintosh-only panes

The other panes in InDesign's Print dialog box are available only on the Macintosh and exist for conformance to Macintosh standards. This section shows where Windows has equivalent functionality.

PostScript Settings

The PostScript Settings pane lets you control how a PostScript file is generated. You can set the format to PostScript Job (raw PostScript code, such as what goes to a printer) or to EPS (with options for no preview header, a Mac header, and a Windows header). You can also set the level of PostScript supported: Level 1, 2, and 3 (which will work on almost any PostScript device); Level 2, common among professional equipment; and Level 3, the newest version. Data format can be set to ASCII (which is editable but results in larger files) or Binary (uneditable but produces smaller files). Finally, you can decide which fonts are included in the file: None, All, All But Standard 13 (the fonts in the Courier, Times, Helvetica, and Symbol typefaces), and All But Fonts in PPD File (which lists those permanently in a printer's memory).

In Windows, you'll find these options in the PostScript pane in the Preferences dialog box for a printer (Start ➪ Settings ➪ Printers). Either way, you get these same options in InDesign's Export dialog box, which is where you should create such PostScript output files.

Cross-Reference   See Chapter 34 for more on InDesign's Export dialog box.

Error Handling

This pane lets you choose how PostScript error messages are handled: ignored, displayed onscreen, or printed on the printer. In Windows, you set this in the PostScript pane in the printer's Preferences dialog box.

Layout

This pane lets you add a border to pages and to set up *n*-up printing. In Windows, you do this in the Paper pane in the printer's Preference's dialog box (Start ⇨ Settings ⇨ Printers, and then right-click the appropriate printer icon, and select Properties from the contextual menu), if the printer driver supports these features.

Cover Page

This pane lets you print a cover page before or after the document proper, choosing an alternative paper source if available (such as for a report cover). Windows has no equivalent function.

Background Printing

This handy option lets you have printing occur in the background, so you can continue to work rather than wait for the job to finish. (Windows always prints in the background.) You can also set times for the job to print; in those cases, a *spool file* is created that contains the print job, and the Mac sends this file to the printer at the appointed time.

Printer-Specific Options

This pane contains any options for the current printer. In Windows, click the Properties button in the InDesign Print dialog box to get some of these options (in the Device Options pane in Windows 98, and in the Advanced pane in Windows NT 4.0). You can get to the complete set of options by using Start ⇨ Settings ⇨ Printers, right-clicking the appropriate printer icon, and selecting Properties from the contextual menu.

Cross-Reference See Chapter 32 for more on printer settings.

Working with Spot Colors and Separations

It's very easy to accidentally use spot colors such as red and Pantone 111 (say, for picture and text box frames) in a document that contains four-color TIFF and EPS files. The result is that InDesign outputs as many as six plates: one each for the four process colors, plus one for red and one for Pantone 111.

By default, each color defined in InDesign is set as a spot process color. And each spot color gets its own plate, unless you specifically tell InDesign to translate the color into process colors. You do so when defining a new color by selecting the Process option in the Color Type pop-up menu in the Swatch Options dialog box, described in Chapter 21, when you create or edit a color in the Swatches pane. No matter whether a color was defined as a process or spot color, you can also choose the All to Process option in the Print dialog box's Color pane when printing to convert all spot colors to process colors.

Tip The advantage to setting the colors to process in the Swatch Options dialog box is that the colors are permanently made into process colors; the All to Process option must be used each time you print. Note that you have no way to selectively have specific spot colors print as process colors from the Print dialog box's Color pane — you can have all or no spot colors print as processor colors from that pane.

If your work is primarily four-color work, edit the spot colors in the Swatches pane to make them process colors. If you make these changes with no document open, they become the defaults for all new documents.

If you do some spot-color work and some four-color work, duplicate the spot colors and translate the duplicates into process colors. Make sure that you use an understandable color-naming convention, such as Blue P for the process-color version of blue (which is created by using 100 percent each of magenta and cyan).

The same is true when you use Pantone colors (and Trumatch, Focoltone, Toyo, and DIC colors). If you do not select the Process option in the Swatch Options dialog box (double-click a color from the Swatches pane, which you can make visible via Window ⇨ Swatches, or F5), these colors are output as spot colors. Again, you can define a Pantone color twice, making one of the copies a process color and giving it a name to indicate what it is. Then all you have to do is make sure that you pick the right color for the kind of output you want.

Tip You still can mix process and spot colors if you want. For example, if you want a gold border on your pages, you have to use a Pantone ink because metallic colors cannot be produced using process colors. So use the appropriate Pantone color, and *don't* select the Process option when you define the color. When you make color separations, you get five negatives: one each for the four process colors and one for gold. That's fine because you specifically want the five negatives.

Working with screen angles

Normally, you'd probably never worry about the screening angles for your color plates. After all, the service bureau makes those decisions, right? Maybe.

If you have your own imagesetter, or even if you're just using a proofing device, you should know how to change screen angles for the best output. If you're working with spot colors that have shades applied to them, you'll want to know what the screen angles are so you can determine how to set the screening angles for those spot colors.

Screening angles determine how the dots comprising each of the four process colors — cyan, magenta, yellow, and black — or any spot colors are aligned so they don't overprint each other. The rule of thumb is that dark colors should be at least 30 degrees apart, whereas lighter colors (for example, yellow) should be at least 15 degrees apart from other colors. This rule of thumb translates into a 105-degree angle (also called –15 degrees; it's the same angle) for cyan, 75 degrees for magenta, 90 degrees for yellow, and 45 degrees for black.

But these defaults sometimes result in moiré patterns, which are distortions in the image's light and dark areas caused when the dots making up the colors don't arrange themselves evenly. With traditional color-separation technology, a service bureau would have to manually adjust the angles to avoid such moirés — an expensive and time-consuming process. With the advent of computer technology, modern output devices, such as imagesetters, can calculate angles based on the output's lpi settings to avoid most moiré patterns. (Each image's balance of colors can cause a different moiré, which is why there is no magic formula.) Every major imagesetter vendor uses its own proprietary algorithm to make these calculations.

InDesign automatically uses the printer's PPD values to calculate the recommended halftoning, lpi, and frequency settings shown in the Color pane of the Print dialog box. But for spot colors, it's basically a guess as to what screening angle a color should get. The default is to give it the same angle as yellow because if a spot color's dots overprint yellow dots, the effect is less noticeable than if it overprinted, say, black dots. But if you have multiple spot colors, this approach doesn't work. In such a case, choose a screening angle for the color whose hue is closest to the spot colors. And don't forget to consult your service bureau or printing manager.

Proofing on Non-PostScript Ink-jet Printers

With color ink-jet printers so inexpensive these days, they're becoming a part of the production process. Though no substitute for high-quality color proofs such as Matchprints, a color-ink-jet–printed page can serve as a good initial proofing device to show you roughly how the colors will look in your document. They're also handy for generating comps for clients or others in your staff to see. Given that they typically cost less than a dime per page to output — versus $30 or more for a Matchprint and $1 or more for a high-end color printer such as a thermal wax printer or color laser printer — and that such printers usually cost less than $500, color ink-jets are a fantastic addition to your production arsenal.

 Unfortunately, InDesign on the Mac won't let you print to non-PostScript printers, which includes every color ink-jet printer under $1,000. InDesign for Windows does support some ink-jet printers, but output quality for graphics is uneven — PostScript images in particular often output as low-resolution preview images.

That's why Adobe has released PressReady, a $99 package of printer drivers that let InDesign work with some color ink-jet printers. (PressReady also works with other PostScript-based programs — including PageMaker, QuarkXPress, CorelDraw, and Illustrator. Although these programs can output directly to color ink-jet printers, by using PressReady as the intermediary, you'll usually get better results because PressReady can work with the high-fidelity PostScript code directly rather than rely on the onscreen display to create the printed images, as most non-PostScript drivers do.)

At its most basic level, PressReady adds a virtual printer to your computer. It adds a PostScript Level 3 driver that InDesign thinks is a PostScript printer, which lets it output its pages properly. The PressReady software then translates this PostScript code generated by InDesign into the format native to your printer. (PressReady supports the Canon BubbleJet 8500; Epson Stylus Color 800, 850, 1520, and 3000; and the Hewlett-Packard DeskJet 895C, DeskJet 1120C, and 2000C. Other models may be added to future versions.) Figure 33-8 shows how the PressReady driver appears in the Mac's Chooser as just another printer, and Figure 33-9 shows how it appears in a Windows Print dialog box.

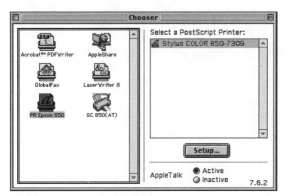

Figure 33-8: The PressReady printer icon (highlighted) in the Mac's Chooser; the native driver for this printer is to its right.

Using PressReady is as simple as choosing the PressReady driver, just as you would choose any printer on your computer.

Tip One way to circumvent InDesign's (and PressReady's) limited support for color ink-jet printers is to create a PDF version of your document and then print to your color ink-jet printer from Adobe Acrobat, which can print to most non-PostScript devices without special software.

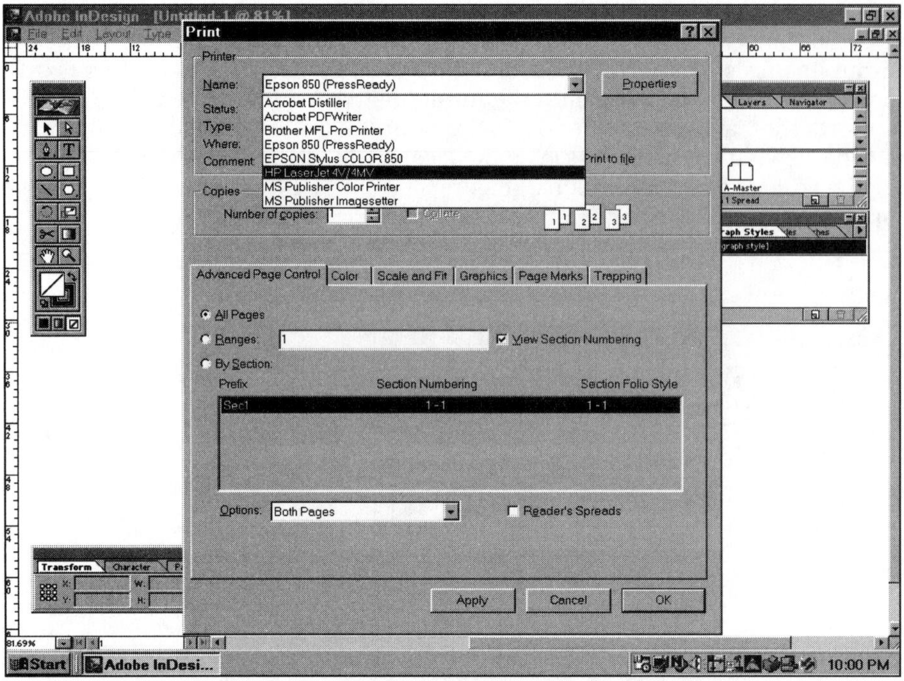

Figure 33-9: The PressReady printer option (highlighted) in Windows InDesign's Print dialog box; the native driver for this printer is listed immediately below.

Summary

When printing from InDesign, you have many options to choose from to control exactly how your document prints. The right options depend on the document's contents and the output device you're using.

Be sure to define your colors as process colors unless you want them to print on their own plates. Although InDesign lets you convert all colors to process colors when you print, at times you'll want some colors to print on their own plate (these are called spot colors) and others to be converted to process, and the only way to make this happen is to define colors as process or as spot in the first place.

If you want to make quick, inexpensive color proofs, you can use a color ink-jet printer. But on the Mac, you'll have to buy the Adobe PressReady product to do so, and it supports only a limited number of printers. In Windows, you'll be able to print to some color ink-jet printers without PressReady, although the output quality may be poor.

✦   ✦   ✦

Creating Output Files

In this electronic age, you have many reasons not to print a document, at least not directly. You may want to deliver the document to readers in electronic format, such as in HTML or Adobe Acrobat files. Or you may want to generate a file that your service bureau can output for you on an imagesetter — a file that you may send over a network, on a high-capacity disk, or even as an electronic-mail attachment to a device that could be down the hall or in another state.

Selecting the Best Output Option

InDesign has several options for creating output files: You can export to several variants of the PostScript printing language — Adobe Portable Document Format (PDF), Encapsulated PostScript (EPS), and a prepress-oriented version. You can print to file using all the settings described in Chapter 33 but save to a file — either in EPS or plain PostScript format — rather than output directly to a printer, creating a file tuned specifically to the printer driver chosen.

Tip If you're publishing on the Web, you can export to HTML format, as described in Part X, or to PDF, as described in this chapter. If using PDF files on the Web, you would have a link from an HTML-based Web page to the PDF file (using the same process in your Web-page-creation software for linking to any page or file on the Web).

The option you pick has several advantages and consequences; let's look at each choice separately.

Exporting to PDF

This option creates a file that can be linked to from a Web page, whether on the Internet or on a corporate intranet. It can also be accessed from a CD-ROM or other disk medium, as long as the recipient has the free Adobe Acrobat Reader program (included on this book's CD-ROM, as well as available for download from www.adobe.com/acrobat/).

This file can include some or all of the fonts, or expect the ultimate output device to have them. You also have control over the resolution of the graphics, letting you, for example, create a high-resolution file for output on an imagesetter or a low-resolution version for display on the Web.

The PDF file won't have information on the specific printer, so a service bureau or printing department could use it on any available output devices. But not all service bureaus and printing departments are geared to print from PDF files; while PDF is an increasingly popular option, it is by no means ubiquitous. To print a PDF file directly, the output device must be a PostScript 3 device; otherwise, the service bureau must print the PDF file from Adobe Acrobat or from Imation PressWise (go to http://ips.imation.com for more information on this product).

Exporting to EPS

This option creates a file that can be sent to many output devices or edited by PostScript-savvy graphics programs such as Illustrator, FreeHand, or CorelDraw. With InDesign, you can add a margin for bleeds — but you can't include printer's marks.

Most service bureaus can print directly from EPS files. But note that each page in your document is sent to a separate file, so a service bureau may prefer a prepress-oriented PostScript file or a PDF file that combines all pages into one file — which simplifies their output effort.

The lack of printer's marks might also bother your commercial printer, because they need them to properly combine film negatives. Using Imation PressReady, the service bureau can add printer's marks and integrate high-resolution and color-corrected images — so EPS could remain a solid output option depending on your service bureau's capabilities.

Tip   Exported PDF or EPS files can be imported back into InDesign (or other programs, including QuarkXPress, PageMaker, FreeHand, Illustrator, CorelDraw, Photoshop, and Photo-Paint) as a graphic. This is handy if, for example, you want to run a small version of the cover on your contents page to give the artist credit, or if you want to show a page from a previous issue in a letters section where readers are commenting on a story. If you're creating PDF files, be sure in these cases just to export the page or spread you want to use. Even though only the first page or spread will display when imported into a page-layout program, the file will contain the data for all other pages, possibly making its size unnecessarily unwieldy. (When exporting to EPS, a separate file is created for each page, so this is not an issue. But it also means you can't export a spread as one EPS file.)

Exporting to prepress PostScript

This option creates a file that contains all the fonts, graphics, printer's marks, and bleed margins needed to output a document to a device such as an imagesetter.

You can also export spreads as units, so the two pages comprising a spread can be output as if they were on one sheet. For professional output, this is not a good idea for several reasons. First, if you have a bleed across the gutter, you may end up with insufficient bleed because the two pages are joined during output. Second, printer's marks will be positioned as if the spread were one page, making it hard for the commercial printer if the spread is cut into two pieces when creating the final form — the series of pages that when arranged, printed, folded, and cut result in a section of your publication. (See the sidebar "Understanding Imposition" in this chapter.)

Printing to an EPS or PostScript file

This option has the same advantages as exporting, except all your printer settings are embedded, making the file print reliably only by the target printer.

Note Remember to work with your service bureau, commercial printer, or printing department — whoever will get the output file — to understand what their needs and expectations are. Although some output files are fully or partially editable, it's usually not easy to know what might be incorrect in a document until the expensive step of actually printing pages or negatives.

The easiest way to create a PDF, EPS, or PostScript prepress file from InDesign is to export it, using File ⇨ Export, or ⌘+E or Ctrl+E. You'll get the Export dialog box, which, like any standard Save dialog box, lets you name the file and determine what disk and folder the file is to be saved in. The key control in the Export dialog box is the Formats pop-up menu, where you choose the format: Adobe PDF, EPS, and Prepress File, respectively.

You can also create these formats by using the Print dialog box (see Chapter 33) and choosing File as the output location rather than Printer. The rest of the chapter shows both methods.

Understanding Imposition

Layout artists may work on single pages or spreads, but printing presses rarely do. Sure, for short-run jobs, your printer may actually work with one page at a time, but typically, they work with forms.

Forms are groups of pages aligned so that when they are folded, cut, and trimmed, they end up in proper numerical sequence. This arrangement of pages on a form is called *imposition*.

One popular printing method takes a huge sheet of anywhere from 4 to 64 pages, folds them, cuts them, and trims them. This results in a stack of pages in the right order—a process known as *perfect binding*—the technique used for square-backed publications such as books and many magazines and catalogs.

The other popular printing method also uses forms, but aligned in a different way. Here, the form is broken into two-page spreads that are cut and trimmed, and then stacked separately. A page from each stack is added to a pile, and the pile is then folded to create the right page sequence—this is called a booklet. These folded spreads are stapled in the center, in a process known as *saddle-stitching*. Many magazines and catalogs use this approach.

Both approaches usually use large sheets of paper, called a web, which is why such commercial printing is known as SWOP or standard web offset printing. (*Offset* refers to the way the ink is delivered to the page, with the ink offset to an intermediate roller between the color plate and the paper. This ensures that just the right amount of ink is placed on each sheet, sort of how an ink stamp works.)

Understanding how forms are configured shows why what InDesign calls a *reader's spread*—the two adjacent pages that a reader sees when reading (and that a layout artist sees when designing onscreen)—is usually not how you want to output pages for use at a commercial printer. Printing reader's spreads makes more sense if you are, for example, wanting to show a client a mockup of the document, so you print spreads together on large paper (such as printing two 8.5-by-11-inch pages on an 11-by-17-inch sheet of paper).

The following figure shows how a perfect-bound publication form is numbered, as well as a saddle-stitched form. Note that a form can have a number of pages other than 16, but must be in multiples of four pages.

To figure out the page sequence for a perfect-bound form, take a sheet of paper, and fold it as often as needed to create the number of pages on the form. You now have a booklet. Number the pages (front and back) with a pencil, and then unfold the paper to see how the form is put together. The front sides are one form, and the back sides another.

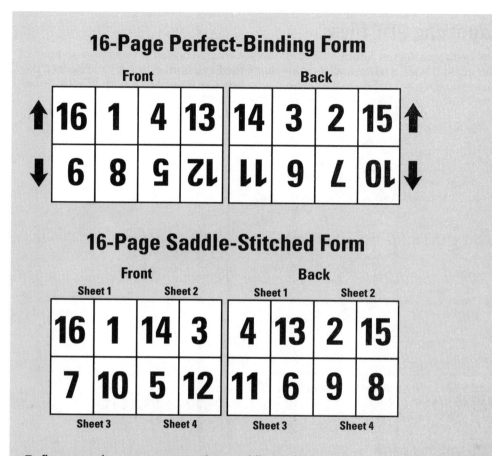

16-Page Perfect-Binding Form

16-Page Saddle-Stitched Form

To figure out the page sequence for a saddle-stitched form, you can take a sheet of paper for each spread, stack them, fold them once, and then number the pages (front and back) with a pencil, and then separate the sheets to see how the form is put together. The front sides are one form, and the back sides another. Another way to do it is to realize that the bottom sheet contains page 1 and the final page on the back, and page 2 and the next-to-final page on the front. The sheet on top would have pages 3 and FP–2 (where FP is the final page number) on the back and pages 4 and FP–3 on the back, and so on until the middle sheet.

Creating PDF Files

Typically, you'll want to directly export your InDesign files to PDF format rather than create a PostScript file and translate to PDF. This section shows how to export, and then explains how to print to PDF on those occasions when that's the better option.

Exporting PDF files

After you've selected Adobe PDF in the Export dialog box's Formats pop-up menu, and given the file a name and location, click the Save button to get the Export PDF dialog box, shown in Figure 34-1. The dialog box has four panes, with PDF Options being the one displayed when you open the dialog box.

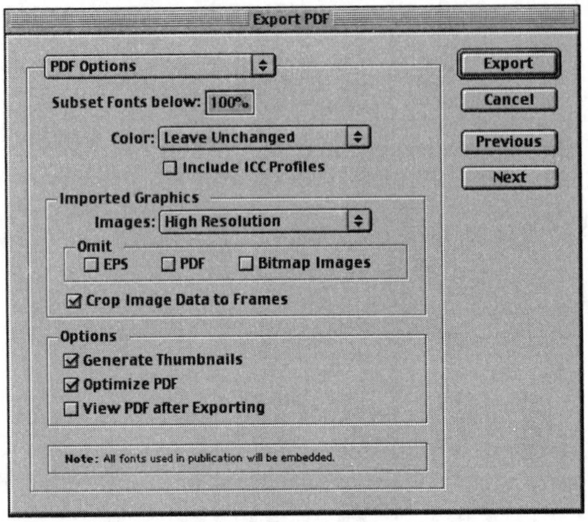

Figure 34-1: The Export PDF dialog box's PDF Options pane.

PDF Options pane

Here are what the options mean on the PDF Options pane:

✦ The Subset Fonts Below field tells InDesign how to embed fonts in the exported PDF file. The default value of 100 percent tells it to include the entire font for each typeface used. This is the best option because it ensures that if your service bureau needs to edit the file later, the file will include all font information. If you choose a lower value and the service bureau changes some text, there's a chance that some characters used in the editing won't be in the file. The value is a threshold, telling InDesign that if the file uses less than that percentage of the font's characters, to embed just the characters used; or, if the file uses more than that percentage, to embed them all. If your document uses many fonts but just a few characters in each, you might want to pick a value such as 35 percent, because chances are less that you have typos in such documents (they tend to be ads and posters that are heavily proofed beforehand).

✦ The Color pop-up menu lets you choose from Unchanged, which keeps the colors in whatever model they were defined in; RGB, which converts them all to RGB (use this for online documents); and CMYK, which converts them all to CMYK (use this if you are using no spot colors and are creating color negatives).

✦ Check Include ICC Profiles if your output device includes a color calibration feature that uses such profiles.

✦ In the Images pop-up menu, you can select from High Resolution and Low Resolution. Use High Resolution for all documents that will be printed, even if you're publishing the file electronically (on a CD-ROM or via the Web). Use Low Resolution only for documents that will be viewed onscreen and won't be printed (or where you don't care that the printouts will have low-quality graphics).

✦ Use the three options in the Omit section to strip out EPS, PDF, and/or bitmap images — you would use this only if you had high-resolution or color-corrected versions of these files at a service bureau and wanted them to substitute those files for the lower-resolution placeholder files you used during layout.

✦ Check Crop Image Data to Frames; this setting makes your files smaller by excluding any portion of an image that was imported but not visible because of cropping you applied to the frame. There's no reason not to select this option.

✦ In the Options section, select Generate Thumbnails if you are creating a PDF file to be viewed onscreen — these thumbnails will help people using the Acrobat Reader program navigate your document more easily. But if the PDF files are being sent to a service bureau or commercial printer for printing, there's no need to generate the thumbnails.

✦ Always select Optimize PDF — this setting minimizes the file size without compromising the output.

✦ If you want to see the results of the PDF export as soon as the export is complete, select View PDF after Exporting. Typically, you should not select this option, because you likely will have other tasks you want to do before launching Acrobat Reader (or the full Acrobat program, if you own it) to proof your files.

Compression pane

All the options in this pane, as shown in Figure 34-2, compress your document's graphics and fonts. For documents you're intending to print professionally, make sure that for all three image types, No Sampling Change is selected and that Compression is set to None. Also, make sure that Compress Text and Line Art is unchecked. You don't want to do anything that affects the resolution or quality of your images if you're outputting to a high-resolution device.

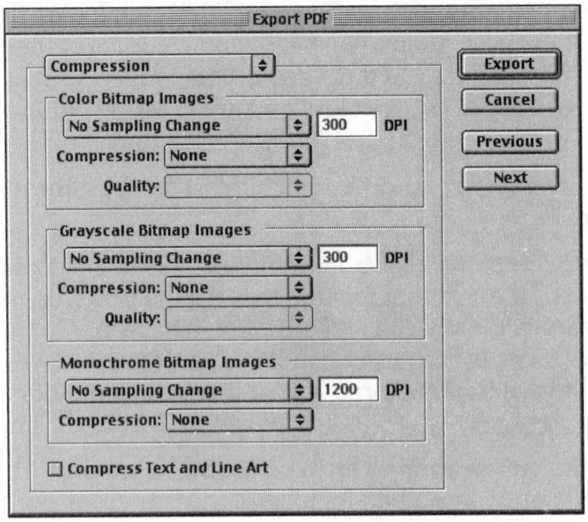

Figure 34-2: The Export PDF dialog box's Compression pane.

These compression settings are more appropriate for documents meant to be viewed online, as the sidebar "Settings for Onscreen Usage" explains later in this chapter.

Pages and Page Marks pane

Use this pane, shown in Figure 34-3, to specify which pages are output, as well as to set the page bleed and printer's marks.

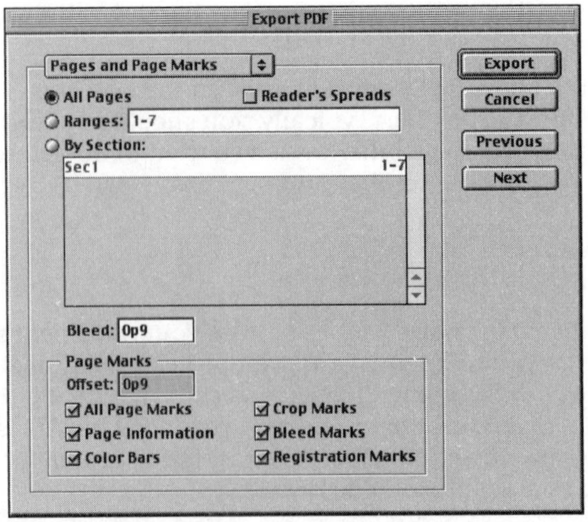

Figure 34-3: The Export PDF dialog box's Pages and Page Marks pane.

For selecting which pages are output, you can select All Pages, a range of pages (in the Ranges field; remember that you can specify nonconsecutive ranges such as 1-4, 7, 8-12, 15, 17), or a specific section (if your document uses sections).

Avoid selecting the Reader's Spreads options, which prints spreads as if they were on one sheet of paper. This usually is a bad idea when printing with a commercial printer, as the earlier sidebar "Understanding Imposition" explains.

For controlling bleed and printer's marks, use the options at the bottom of the pane:

✦ If you have elements bleeding off the page, you'll want a bleed setting of at least 0p9 (0.125 inches) that builds in enough forgiveness so that, when the pages are folded and trimmed, any elements that bleed off the page will, in fact, do so even if there's a slip in the page alignment.

✦ For printer's marks, choose which marks you want to print in the Page Marks section of the pane. Typically, you should select All Page Marks. (Chapter 33 covers each of these marks in detail.) Your Offset amount should be the same as or more than the bleed amount—if your Offset is less than the bleed, it's possible the marks could appear in your page's margins.

Security pane

The Security pane, shown in Figure 34-4, has no relevance to documents intended to be output at a service bureau or commercial printer, so make sure Use Security Features is unchecked.

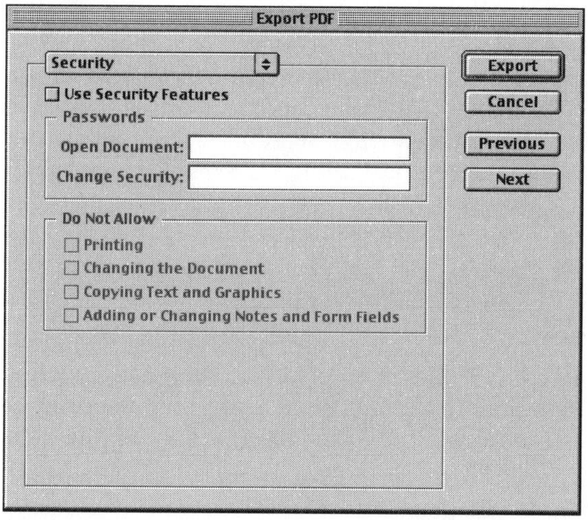

Figure 34-4: The Export PDF dialog box's Security pane.

These settings are useful if you are publishing the document electronically, because they control who can access the document and what they can do with the document once it's open.

Settings for Onscreen Usage

If your output is destined for use on a monitor—such as via CD-ROM, on the Web, or in a corporate intranet, the settings you choose will differ from the print-oriented ones described in the preceding "Exporting PDF files" section. Here's what you need to do:

✦ In the PDF Options pane, change the Color pop-up menu to RGB, change the Images pop-up menu to Low Resolution, and check Generate Thumbnails. This optimizes the color and file size for onscreen display.

✦ In the Compression pane, choose Downsample To or Subsample To in all three image types' sections. The DPI value should be either 72 (if you intend people just to view the images onscreen) or 300 or 600 (if you expect people to print the documents to a local ink-jet or laser printer—pick the dpi value that best matches most users' printers' capabilities). For the Compression pop-up menus, choose Automatic for the color and grayscale bitmaps, and CCITT Group 3 (the standard method for fax compression) for black-and-white bitmaps. Set Quality to Maximum for color and grayscale bitmaps. Finally, check Compress Text and Line Art.

✦ In the Pages and Page Marks pane, make sure no printer's marks are checked. Check Reader's Spreads if your facing pages are designed as one visual unit.

✦ In the Security pane, check User Security features and the options for which you want to add security. Use the Printing and Copying Text and Graphics options to prevent readers from copying and pasting your content, or to prevent printing—this is particularly aimed at Web-based readers or publicly distributed documents. The Changing the Document and Adding or Changing Notes and Form Fields options are meant for internally distributed documents, where you don't want a recipient who has the Acrobat program to modify the PDF file and then pass it on to someone else who might not realize it was altered. Similarly, you typically would use the passwords only for documents distributed internally, where you don't want all employees to have access to all documents. For Web-based documents, the presumption is that a page and its content are meant for public consumption unless the whole page has a password required, so these settings are usually irrelevant.

Printing to PDF format

Sometimes, you may want to create a PDF file when printing, such as to save printer-specific options such as trapping in the file. Note that you'll need the $249 Adobe Acrobat software (not the free Acrobat Reader) to create a PDF file using this method.

Set up your Print dialog box settings as described in Chapter 33. But don't click the Print button. Instead, follow these steps:

✦ On the Mac, go to the PostScript Settings pane, and choose PostScript Job in the Format pop-up menu. For PostScript Level, see the "EPS Options pane" section later in this chapter. (For documents to only be viewed onscreen, select Level 3 Only if you're using Acrobat 4, and Level 2 Only if you're using Acrobat 3.) Choose ASCII or Binary as the Data Format (as explained in the "EPS Options pane" section), and in the Font Inclusion pop-up menu, choose which fonts you want embedded in the file (this will depend on what fonts the output device has installed). Change the Destination pop-up menu to File. The Print button becomes Save; click it, specify a file name and location to save the file, and then click Save.

✦ In Windows, select Print to File and click OK. You'll get a Save dialog box that asks for a file name and location. (You can also choose Acrobat Distiller from the Name pop-up menu, instead of the printer you'll ultimately have the file output to, but then you won't be able to select any printer-specific output settings.) Leave the Save as Type pop-up menu at its default setting of PostScript.

✦ Now, whether you use a Macintosh or a Windows PC, open the Acrobat Distiller program (usually in the Distiller folder in the Adobe Acrobat 4.0 folder) and use File ➪ Open to open the PostScript file you generated for conversion to PDF format. Use Settings ➪ Job Options to set the output options. Although they're arranged differently, you have essentially the same options as in InDesign's Export PDF dialog box's panes. Differences include the ability to specify whether to save in Acrobat 3.0 or 4.0 PDF format and to embed specific fonts.

✦ Finally, open the resulting PDF file in Acrobat. Use File ➪ Document Info ➪ Prepress to turn trapping on (if you specified trapping in InDesign). Figure 34-5 shows the dialog box, as well as a converted InDesign file that shows printer's marks. If your output device supports the DeviceCMYK option for color calibration, also check the Print 4 color ICC profiles as DeviceCMYK option. Then save the document using File ➪ Save, or ⌘+S or Ctrl+S.

Note

You can also create PDF files by exporting to an EPS or PostScript file, and then using the Acrobat Distiller program to convert the file to PDF format. There's no need to do this if you have InDesign unless you happen to have EPS or PostScript files you've previously generated that you'd rather convert to PDF via Distiller than find the InDesign originals and export PDFs from InDesign. You can, of course, use Distiller to create PDFs from any PostScript or EPS file, no matter what program created it.

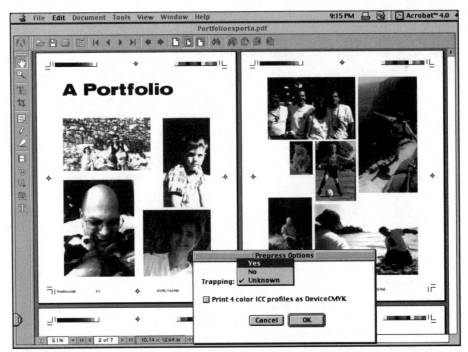

Figure 34-5: The Prepress Options dialog box in Acrobat, as well as an InDesign publication output as a PDF file that includes printer's marks.

Creating EPS Files

InDesign gives you two ways to create EPS files: exporting, and printing to file. Both methods have advantages and disadvantages: For example, exporting lets you create a file that any printer can handle, but each page is put into its own file (because InDesign assumes the reason for exporting is to reuse the EPS file in another program or in InDesign, treating the exported page as a graphic); while printing lets you embed printer settings, as well as all pages, in the EPS file so your service bureau has a ready-to-go file to send to the imagesetter or other output device.

Exporting EPS files

After you select EPS in the Export dialog box's Formats pop-up menu, and give the file a name and location, click the Save button to get the Export EPS dialog box, shown in Figure 34-6. The dialog box has two panes, with EPS Options being the one displayed when you open the dialog box.

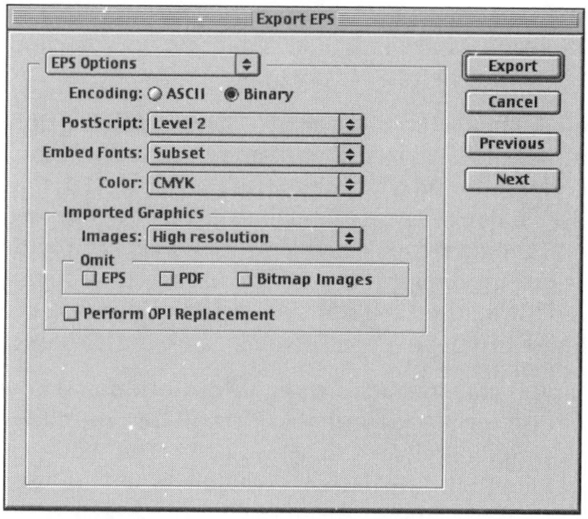

Figure 34-6: The Export EPS dialog box's EPS Options pane.

EPS Options pane

Most export options are in the EPS Options pane, shown in Figure 34-6:

✦ Select ASCII or Binary encoding at the top of the pane. ASCII creates a larger file but can be edited by someone who understands the PostScript language; Binary creates a smaller file that is not editable. The one you choose depends on whether you want or expect your service bureau or commercial printer to try to fix any problems in your file encountered during output. Be sure to talk to the service bureau or printer staff up front, so you and they agree on whether such efforts should be made.

✦ In the PostScript pop-up menu, choose the version of the PostScript language to use in creating the EPS file: Level 1, 2, and 3 Compatible files will print on any PostScript device or import into any program that supports EPS, but the file will be larger and gradients might appear banded; Level 2 will work on a PostScript Level 2 printer (the majority in professional environments); whereas Level 3 will work only on the newer PostScript 3 devices, which can include built-in color calibration, color separation, and trapping. Be sure to ask whoever is outputting your files which version to use.

✦ Use the Embed Fonts pop-up menu to determine whether all fonts, no fonts, or just the characters used will be embedded into the documents; the corresponding menu options are Complete, None, and Subset. Complete is the best option because it ensures that if your service bureau needs to edit the file later, the file will include all font information. If you choose Subset and the service bureau changes some text when editing the EPS file (such as to fix a typo), there's a chance that some characters used in the editing won't be in the file. Use None only if the service bureau has all the fonts you use and knows to load them into the printer before outputting this file.

✦ The Color pop-up menu determines what happens to colors; your options are CMYK (for commercial printing), RGB (for online display), gray (for black-and-white printing), or Device Independent (which lets the output device figure out what to do with the colors). For commercial printing, choose either CMYK or Device Independent, depending on your service bureau's recommendations and the capabilities of their output devices. If your file uses spot colors, you'll want to use Device Independent so they are not converted to process colors, but the service bureau will need to have a printer that can handle that format.

✦ In the Images pop-up menu, you can select from High Resolution and Low Resolution. Use High Resolution for all documents that will be printed, even if you're publishing the file electronically (on a CD-ROM or via the Web). Use Low Resolution only for documents that will be viewed onscreen and won't be printed (or where you don't care that the printouts will have low-quality graphics).

✦ Use the three options in the Omit section to strip out EPS, PDF, and/or bitmap images — you would use this only if you have high-resolution or color-corrected versions of these files at a service bureau and want them to substitute those files for the lower-resolution placeholder files you used during layout. By omitting these graphics files from the EPS file, you make the EPS file much smaller.

✦ The Perform OPI Replacement option flags the service bureau's output device to substitute high-resolution or color-corrected versions of your imported graphics. If you don't omit the files in the Omit section, the OPI function still substitutes the service bureau's graphics for the ones you imported.

Pages pane

Use the Pages pane, shown in Figure 34-7, to specify which pages are output, as well as to set the page bleed.

For selecting which pages are output, you can select All Pages, a range of pages (in the Ranges field; remember that you can specify nonconsecutive ranges such as 1-4, 7, 8-12, 15, 17), or a specific section (if your document uses sections).

If you have elements bleeding off the page, you'll want a bleed setting of at least 0p9 (0.125 inches) that builds in enough forgiveness so that, when the pages are folded and trimmed, any elements that bleed off the page will in fact do so, even if there's a slip in the page alignment.

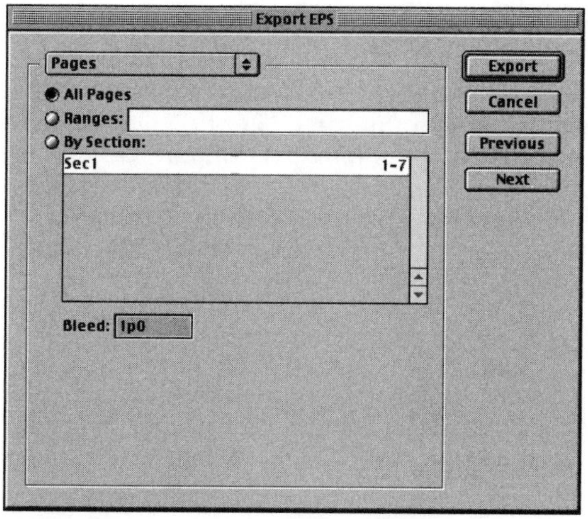

Figure 34-7: The Export EPS dialog box's Pages pane.

Printing to EPS format

You may at times want to create an EPS file when printing, possibly to save printer-specific options such as trapping in the file. Set up your Print dialog box settings as described in Chapter 33. But don't click the Print button. Instead, choose one of the following options:

✦ On the Mac, go to the PostScript Settings pane and choose one of the EPS options in the Format pop-up menu. Choose a Mac or Windows preview if the EPS file will be imported in a page-layout or illustration program, and the EPS No Preview option if the file will simply be sent to an output device. For PostScript Level, see the "EPS Options pane" section earlier in this chapter. Choose ASCII or Binary as the Data Format (as explained in the "EPS Options pane" section), and in the Font Inclusion pop-up menu, choose which fonts you want embedded in the file (this will depend on what fonts the output device has installed). Change the Destination pop-up menu to File. The Print button becomes Save; click it, specify a file name and location to save the file, and then click Save.

✦ In Windows, you cannot print to EPS format, just to regular PostScript. You'll have to use InDesign's export-to-EPS feature instead, as covered earlier in this chapter.

Creating PostScript Prepress Files

You'll use this option the least, because it generates a file that almost always gets sent directly to a printer. In most cases, generating an EPS or PDF file is a better option because it gives the service bureau or commercial printer a more structured document they can usually troubleshoot or print more easily. But sometimes, this option is what the service bureau will want, based on their equipment and expertise.

Exporting prepress files

After you select Prepress File in the Export dialog box's Formats pop-up menu, and give the file a name and location, click the Save button to get the Export Prepress File dialog box. The dialog box has two panes, with Prepress Options the one displayed when you open the dialog box.

Creating a PostScript prepress file is a cross between generating a PDF file and an EPS file: The Prepress Options dialog box is identical to the EPS Options dialog box shown in Figure 34-6, and the same options and considerations described in the "EPS Options pane" section earlier apply here as well. The second pane, Pages and Page Marks, is identical to the pane of the same name shown earlier in Figure 34-3, and the same options and considerations described in the "Pages and Page Marks pane" section earlier apply here as well.

Printing to PostScript prepress format

Sometimes, you may want to create a PostScript prepress file when printing, as when you wish to save printer-specific options such as trapping in the file. Set up your Print dialog box settings as described in Chapter 33. But don't click the Print button. Instead, choose one of the following options:

✦ On the Mac, go to the PostScript Settings pane, and choose the PostScript Job option in the Format pop-up menu. For PostScript Level, see the "EPS Options pane" section earlier in this chapter. Choose ASCII or Binary as the Data Format (as explained in the "EPS Options pane" section), and in the Font Inclusion pop-up menu, choose which fonts you want embedded in the file (this will depend on what fonts the output device has installed). Change the Destination pop-up menu to File. The Print button becomes Save; click it, specify a file name and location to save the file, and then click Save.

✦ In Windows, select Print to File and click OK. You'll get a Save dialog box that asks for a file name and location. Leave the Save as Type pop-up menu at its default setting of PostScript. You could choose the Printer Files option in the Save as Type pop-up menu, but there's really no reason to do so. This option generates a file that contains the raw data that the printer would get if directly connected. But because you're outputting to a PostScript device, you're going to get a PostScript file anyhow — this option is really for use when you're printing to non-PostScript printers and need to create a print file for one of them.

Summary

In many cases, you'll want to generate an output file that ensures that your service bureau prints your document exactly as you want it, with no chance to accidentally make a change to your InDesign document. The service bureau's equipment will dictate in most cases what format these output files are in: EPS, PostScript, or PDF. Each option has pros and cons, and varying levels of controls, so be sure to use the option that gives you the most control and works with your service bureau's equipment.

✦   ✦   ✦

Web
Fundamentals

Dozens of tools exist to help people create Web pages, so why bother using InDesign? After all, it's not meant to be a primary Web-page creation tool. Sure enough, but as Web publishing becomes a staple of creative communications, more print designers are also working on the Web, and Web-page designers of all backgrounds are considering whether and how they might reuse existing print documents.

InDesign can help you convert some print documents for use online as well as create basic Web pages. It's absolutely true that you'll still need a dedicated Web tool, but for those times where InDesign should be part of the process, the two chapters in this part will help you do things right.

First, you'll learn how Web-page creation differs from print-page creation. **Chapter 35** helps you set aside your print assumptions and prejudices so you can conceive your work from a Web perspective.

Then **Chapter 36** walks you through the conversion of actual pages to the Web's HTML format. You'll see where the conversion work is more than just creating the page from scratch in an HTML editor, as well as deciding where the work in InDesign requires a little follow-up in an HTML editor. You'll also learn some of the gotchas that anyone editing InDesign-generated Web pages should know.

◆ ◆ ◆ ◆

Web-Page Setup

More and more, Web page design is adopting the sophistication and variety of print, as well as adding scores of unique Web features. As both modems and computers get faster, more sophisticated techniques of Web page creation are becoming commonplace. For example, new technologies, such as cascading style sheets and embedded fonts, let you design pages that have pretty good typographic control, compared to the near lack of control Web publishers used to have in how the text appeared. And fancy Web-only technologies such as animated graphics are becoming commonplace.

So, it's no surprise that all major page-layout programs have some ability to create Web pages, either directly or through add-on software. The sophisticated skills of print publishing tools can more easily be exploited as Web page creation software (called *Hypertext Markup Language [HTML] editors*) to add print-like layout and typographic features.

InDesign is no exception to the Web bandwagon: It offers basic HTML export capabilities so you can produce Web pages with it. Make no mistake: InDesign is by no means capable of being your only Web-creation tool, or even your main one. You'll still need a professional HTML editor such as Microsoft FrontPage, SoftQuad HotMetal Pro, Barebones Software BBEdit, Macromedia Dreamweaver, or Adobe GoLive. But you can use InDesign to do the initial conversion of your print content to Web format.

Understanding Print/ Web Differences

Most InDesign users are aware of the fundamental differences between publications printed on paper and those that are displayed on a computer monitor. After all, InDesign users spend long hours staring at their monitor while creating pages that will ultimately be printed.

If you decide to become a Web publisher, you should be aware of the basic differences between print and Web publishing, and you should take advantage of the strengths of each medium. For print publishers, this means being open to some new concepts in communication. For example:

✦ **Making the information jump:** Most printed publications are designed to be read from beginning to end. But on the Web, stories can contain hyperlinks that let readers instantly jump to related information. The idea of reading stories from top to bottom, beginning to end, is a print-based concept. On the Web, hyperlinks provide publishers with a different paradigm for presenting information. An effective Web publication uses hyperlinks to make it easy for a viewer to access information and to present information in discrete chunks.

✦ **Losing control:** Most print designers are accustomed to having absolute control over the look of the publications they produce. They specify the fonts, design the pages, create and apply the colors, and print proofs to make sure that what they get is what they want. But the designers of Web pages don't have this level of control. That's because many display options are controlled by the Web page viewer — and more specifically, by the viewer's *browser.* (See the sidebar "Learning about HTML and the Web" to learn about Web browsers.) Although the trend in recent years has been toward WYSIWYG Web publishing, InDesign users should become comfortable with relinquishing some of the design control they've enjoyed while creating printed publications.

✦ **Creating without columns:** InDesign users are accustomed to pages that contain multiple columns, complex text runarounds, layered items, and so on. Not all of these page-layout options are available to designers of Web pages, and some of the design options that are available for both print and Web publishing behave differently. You have to be careful about using multicolumn formats for Web pages. For one thing, if a story is presented in two columns, one long one and one short one, the reader may have to do considerable scrolling to read everything. For another, if the columns are fixed-width, viewers with small monitors may have to deal with a truncated column.

✦ **Different kinds of color:** Print publishers use their eyes to tell them that the printed versions don't look exactly the same as the versions they saw onscreen during production. For example, InDesign users who have done spot-color publishing have probably held a Pantone swatchbook next to their monitor and mused, "Hmmm. They're close, but they're not the same." That's mostly because the colors that can be created on paper by mixing cyan, magenta, yellow, and black inks aren't the same as the colors that can be produced on a computer using red, green, and blue light. Ironically, when you create Web pages, you're creating the pages in the same medium in which they will be displayed. So the colors you see onscreen will be nearly identical to what your reader sees. Why not completely identical? Because no two monitors are quite the same — the ambient lighting, brightness and contrast settings, and internal electronics all can result in slight variations of the same color. Also, you may be used to working in a high-resolution color mode, such as 24-bit (true) color. But Web browsers typically display just 216 colors, so those subtle shades you see onscreen get translated to the nearest of those 216 supported colors.

✦ **Redefining the page:** The meaning of the term *page* is very different in an InDesign environment than on the Web. For InDesign users, a page is a finite area with a specified height, width, columns, and margins. The number of text boxes, picture boxes, and lines you place on an InDesign page is limited by the physical size of the page (and your tolerance for crowding). On the Web, a page is a single HTML file and all its embedded elements — pictures, sound, video, and so on. A Web page can contain very little information or a whole lot of information. Its size is determined by the amount of information it contains and its width by the size of the browser window in which it's displayed. This is a pretty foreign concept for print designers.

For many print designers accustomed to having absolute control over the appearance of the final, printed page, the idea of creating pages that will look different depending on the browser that's used to display them and the personal preferences of the person viewing them is a bit disconcerting. However, when designers understand the limitations of HTML, they can use its strengths to create effective Web pages. Freed from the burden of fine-tuning the look of the pages they create, Web page designers can focus on organizing the content of their publications so that viewers can access and digest it easily.

| **Tip** | If you're the curious type and would like to see what HTML codes look like, import an HTML text file into an InDesign text frame. You'll see lots of cryptic formatting codes that — mercifully — you don't have to understand. If you're the *really* curious type and want to learn more about HTML codes, tons of information is available on the Web. For starters, try NCSA's Beginner's Guide to HTML (`http://www.ncsa.uiuc.edu/general/internet/www/htmlprimer.html`). There are also several good books on Web publishing from the publisher of this book, IDG Books Worldwide, Inc.. |

Learning about HTML and the Web

The World Wide Web is a means of distributing information on the Internet, and it provides anybody with an Internet connection point-and-click access to documents that contain text, pictures, sound, video, and more. The Web was developed at the European Particle Physics Laboratory (known as CERN from its French name, Centre européen des récherches nucléaires) in the early 1990s as a way for physicists to exchange information in a more collaborative way than was possible with simple text documents.

Continued

(continued)

Web documents are text files that contain embedded HTML codes that add formatting to the text, as well as *hypertext links* (commonly called *hyperlinks* or simply *links*), which let a viewer access other Web pages or jump to another location within the same page with just a mouse click. How a computer monitor displays the various elements in an HTML document is determined in large part by the *browser*, a program that lets computer users view Web documents. Different browsers will render a single HTML document slightly differently. (See the sidebar, "A Brief Look at Browsers," for information about the most commonly used browsers.)

HTML is a semantic markup language that assigns meaning to the various parts of a Web page document. An HTML document might contain a headline, a number of paragraphs, an ordered list, a number of graphics, and so on. HTML documents are linear in structure, meaning that one element follows another in sequence. In general, the elements that make up a Web page are displayed from left to right and from top to bottom in a browser window, though the rigid structure that limited the appearance of early Web documents has evolved in recent years to give Web page designers more control over the way HTML documents look onscreen.

Despite the linear structure of HTML documents, viewers are free to access information in whatever order they want. That's because the hyperlinks embedded in Web pages let viewers choose their own path through the information. Think of it this way: Everybody enters a museum through the same door, but inside, viewers are free to meander from exhibit to exhibit in any sequence they want. Surfing the Web offers the same freedom. Once connected, you can linger as long as you want on a particular page or jump to other pages by clicking on a hyperlink.

HTML's greatest strength is its versatility. Web pages can be viewed on a wide range of computer platforms with any monitor using a variety of browsers. Granted, a particular document may look a bit different when viewed under difference circumstances, but that's considered a minor inconvenience in a publishing environment where content — not design — is king.

Getting Documents Ready for the Web

Before you jump into converting documents, you must first determine which publications you want to convert. For example, a book publisher probably wouldn't want to put its books online — reading long tracts of text on a computer monitor is no fun. If the company produces a catalog of its titles, however, converting the catalog into a Web page makes perfect sense. When you've determined which publications you want to convert into Web pages, you need to think about how the Web versions of these publications will relate to the rest of your Web site — assuming your company already has a Web site.

Page-layout artists are trained to think in terms of document construction, page design, color, typography, and picture manipulation as they create the electronic documents that will eventually become printed publications. Given that readers of this book are InDesign users, we approach Web page design from an InDesign user's perspective.

Instead of examining the nuts and bolts of HTML codes (not a pretty picture), we show how the decisions you made while creating an InDesign document affect the options you have when you export it as a Web page. We also explain some of the limitations of Web publishing that will ultimately determine the look of the pages you create.

Starting from scratch

If you're starting a Web site from scratch *and* you intend to convert InDesign documents into Web pages, you should decide on the overall structure of the site before you begin converting documents. If possible, get the corporate portion of the site up and running before you start adding publications. It's much easier to add a converted publication to an existing Web site — all you have to do is provide a link from an existing page — than to do everything at once.

Establishing a structure

Web sites offer even greater flexibility than printed publications. A viewer can bounce from place to place within a page, jump to another page that's part of the same Web site, or even across the world. Still, a good Web site, like a good printed publication, has a logical structure that provides a viewer easy access to the information.

Maintaining the original format

If you intend to convert, for example, a magazine into a Web site, not only will you want to convert the content, you'll probably want to maintain as much of the original structure as possible. This could be accomplished by creating a title page for the Web version that includes a scaled-down reproduction of the printed cover alongside a table of contents that contains hyperlinks to individual articles. Chances are, each of the articles is a separate InDesign document. Under these circumstances, you would create a separate Web page out of each InDesign document.

Making a map

You're probably already familiar with creating flowcharts for printed publications. You can do the same thing with your Web publications. Sit down with a printed version of the publication you're converting, determine which elements will be included in the Web version, and then create a map using page icons to represent Web pages and arrows to represent basic links. Figure 35-1 shows a simple structure for a generic Web publication that's part of a larger corporate Web site.

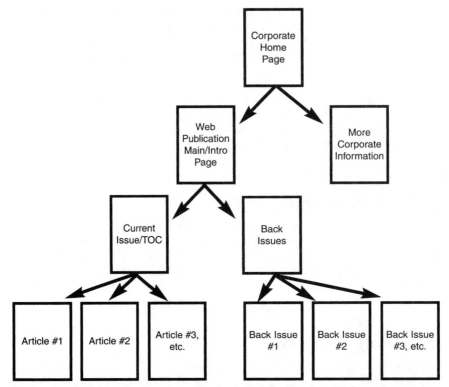

Figure 35-1: Before you begin converting a publication into Web pages, you should first determine how the publication will fit into the overall structure of your Web site. Start by creating a rough sketch like this one.

Determining the basics

After you've mapped out a plan for your Web publication, it's time to get down to the business of converting your InDesign documents. If this Web-publishing business is all new to you, start small before you get big. You may have grandiose plans to convert many of your InDesign-produced publications — back issues and all — into Web pages; to add sound and video; to provide search capabilities and database connectivity; to boldly create the greatest Web site of all time. That's fine. But start small.

Asking the content questions

Think for a moment about the many decisions that are made long before an InDesign user begins work on what will eventually become a printed publication. Let's begin with content:

✦ What content will the publication contain?

✦ Who will its audience be?

✦ How will the content be produced?

✦ How often?

Asking the production questions

After you've made the basic content decisions, consider the overall production issues:

✦ What tools and skills will be required to produce it?

✦ Will all work be done in house, or will parts be outsourced?

✦ What are the cost issues?

✦ Does the budget allow for full color, two colors, or one color?

✦ How will it be printed and by whom?

Asking the design questions

After all the preparatory groundwork has been done, you must make several design decisions before the InDesign work begins:

✦ What will the publication look like?

✦ How big will the pages be?

✦ What typefaces will be used?

✦ How will design elements be incorporated to give the publication a unified look?

✦ Will pages contain one column, multiple columns, or both?

Making a prototype

It's at this point that many layout artists pull out scissors, felt pens, ink, and spray mount and wrestle with thumbnail sketches of pages, galleys of dummy type, and fake headlines. The end result is a prototype that will serve as the blueprint for an InDesign document. (Granted, some designers — especially those who never had to learn traditional paste-up techniques — may do all the messy prototyping on their computer, but the process is much the same as using traditional tools.)

Getting to work

When it's finally time to begin work on the InDesign document, many of the details — the number of pages, the page size, the column formats, the typefaces that will be used, and so on — should have already been resolved. It's the InDesign user's job to implement all the decisions while creating an electronic document.

In many ways, creating a publication for the Web is similar to creating a printed publication, particularly for Web publishers who are starting from scratch: You first gather the content and then assemble it into Web pages.

Considering the conversion process

Converting existing documents into Web pages is easier than starting from scratch (see the sidebar on the evolution of HTML layout tools, later in this chapter). The content has already passed through the approval process, so you don't have to worry much about additional editorial and art reviews. Also, the typographic and page-layout options available for Web publishers are limited compared to those available to print publishers, which simplifies Web page design. Converting InDesign documents to HTML, however, has limitations and pitfalls of its own.

Keep it simple

In general, it's a good idea to keep the conversion process as simple you can. Yes, you can jazz up the HTML pages you export by opening them in an HTML editor and adding sound, video, and the like. Before you venture into multimedia Web publishing, however, ask yourself two questions:

✦ Do you have the resources to do it?

✦ Will adding sound and video significantly improve the quality of your Web publication?

Keep the look and feel

If your goal is simply to offer a Web version of a printed publication, why spend the time, energy, and money required to create something that bears little resemblance to the original printed version? The reason you'd start with an InDesign documents in creating your Web pages is that you want them to have a look and feel that's similar to the printed version. If after converting a publication — and solving all the unforeseen problems that occur during the initial conversion process — you have the resources and the desire to add bells and whistles to your pages, go for it.

Tip   Before you begin converting an InDesign document into HTML format, you should make sure that you're working with the final version of the document. You should also use the File ⇨ Save As command (or the keyboard shortcut Shift+⌘+S or Ctrl+Shift+S) to create a new version of the document. That way, if you then have to tweak any of the items in preparation for exporting an HTML file, the original document remains unchanged.

A Brief Look at Browsers

In 1993, the National Center for Supercomputing Applications at the University of Illinois released a program called Mosaic. This was the "killer app" that got the Web rolling. Mosaic is now gone, superseded by Netscape Navigator, which was developed by much of the same team that created Mosaic. Now, the most popular browsers are Netscape Navigator, Microsoft Internet Explorer, and America Online (which uses a version of Internet Explorer).

It's important to understand that a Web page will look different when displayed with each of these browsers. It will also look different when displayed on older versions of the browsers. To add to the confusion, pages displayed on Macintosh computers look different than pages displayed on Windows computers.

Not only are there differences between browsers, but each browser includes display-related preferences that can be customized by each user to control how Web pages look in the browser window. For example, most people are accustomed to seeing Web pages that use the Arial or Times fonts extensively. This is because Arial or Times is the default display font specified in most browsers. However, a Web surfer who doesn't like Arial or Times is free to choose any available font for text display. Similarly, most Web pages are displayed with gray backgrounds, but that's a browser preference that's easily changed.

The bottom line is that the fonts, font sizes, background color, and column formats may vary depending on the hardware and software being used to view a particular Web page. This means that no matter how careful you are when you export the contents of an InDesign document as a Web page and no matter how much subsequent tweaking you do, you have little control over the way that individual viewers see the pages. Although new technologies such as cascading style sheets and embedded fonts give you more control than in previous years, not all readers have browsers that support these features, so even if you use them, you still can't guarantee a common view of your documents. The only way to get such a common view is by using the Adobe Portable Document Format (PDF), as described in Chapter 34.

One decision that Web publisher must make is the minimum browser that will be supported. Typically, if you design your pages to work with Navigator, Internet Explorer, and America Online, you'll be fine.

Constructing Web-Ready Documents

When you create a new InDesign document, you must first specify the page size, margins, and the number of columns. If you're creating a template document, you'll probably add master pages with headers and/or footers, styles, and colors. If the publication will be the same length every time, you can insert pages with the appropriate master-page layout and add permanent items — for example, the banner or masthead on page 1, mailing information on the back page, and so forth. After you finish the framework, you're ready to begin creating a document that will ultimately be printed. This means adding text, pictures, and lines to pages and fine-tuning the look of the pages until the document is ready for final output.

For InDesign sites that have decided to convert their documents into Web pages, this is where the print production process ends and the Web-production process begins.

Rethinking your design decisions

The ability to create long documents with complex page layouts and sophisticated typography are trademarks of InDesign. You'll find, however, that you have to rethink many of the design decisions you made in InDesign when you convert a document into a Web page.

Among other things, you'll have to decide how much of the original document structure and page design you want to maintain on your Web pages, given the restrictions of Web publishing. You must then decide how much detail you want to maintain and what, if any, changes you want to make to the items you plan to export.

Working with pages

The fundamental unit in InDesign is a page, but pages in print differ greatly from pages on the Web.

Page size

Although InDesign gives you considerable leeway when you specify the page size of a document—pages can be as small as ⅙ inch by ⅙ inch or as large as 216 inches by 216 inches—every page in a print document must be the same size as every other page. By contrast, Web pages have no predetermined length or width. When displayed with a browser, a Web page is as wide as the browser window in which it's displayed, which is usually as wide as the monitor displaying it. And the page is as tall as it needs to be. It could all fit in the monitor's window, or it may require the reader to scroll down for more of the page, which could be infinitely long.

Note   Regardless of the default browser window size, a browser user is free to resize the window at any time. The bottom line is that the size of your InDesign pages becomes fairly meaningless when you export them as Web pages.

Keeping minimum monitors in mind

While surfing the Web, you may have landed on pages that were designed with a minimum monitor in mind. Such pages contain fixed-width items and often multicolumn layouts that look fine when displayed on monitors wide enough to hold the elements or columns but that get clipped when viewed on small monitors.

It's never a bad idea to let the viewer control the width of your Web pages and to make sure that design elements, image maps, and pictures aren't too wide to be displayed on most monitors. Figure 35-2 shows a two-column HTML layout for a fictional Web site. The header is narrow enough to be displayed on most monitors, and the single column of text surrounded by white space is easy to read.

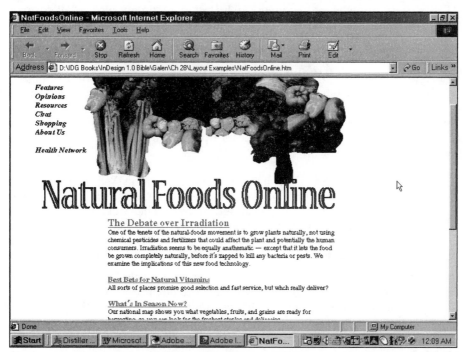

Figure 35-2: This page's two-column format — one with text and one that's blank and serves as a margin — works well for all browsers because everything is narrow enough to be viewed on even small monitors.

> **Tip** If you want to accommodate all viewers with 14-inch monitors and larger, restrict the width of your graphics and multicolumn layouts to about 6.5 inches or less.

Beware WYSIWYG thinking

Don't assume that the page you see on your screen is what the reader on the Web will see. It rarely is true.

But the assumption that what you see is what the reader will see *may* be appropriate if you are certain that all viewers will be accessing the pages under the same conditions — platform, browser, and monitor. For example, if all viewers will access your pages over a corporate intranet using the same hardware and software, you can design your pages so that they look good under these controlled circumstances.

Margins

In InDesign, margins are the strips along the edges of your pages (defined in the Margin area of the New Document dialog box, accessed via File ➪ New, or ⌘+N or Ctrl+N, or in the Margins and Columns dialog box, accessed via Layout ➪ Margins and Columns) that define the area within which you place text and pictures. Historically, Web pages haven't had margins, so usually they are tossed during HTML export. But when you convert an InDesign document into HTML format, you get the option of saving the margins or removing them.

Columns

When you create a new document with InDesign, you must specify the number of columns your pages will have. As you add pages to a document, you also have the option — through the use of master pages — to use different column formats for different pages. The column guides you specify in InDesign are used by automatic text frames and also serve as guidelines for placing items. Here are some column guidelines to follow:

✦ **Making multicolum pages:** If you're familiar with the Web, you've probably noticed that multicolumn pages are far less common than single-column pages — although that's been changing slowly. The latest generation of Web-layout applications has made it easier to create multicolumn page formats, and a growing number of sites are using such layouts. InDesign will keep your column settings during export — if you specify that option during export.

✦ **Losing column guides:** When you convert an InDesign document, the column guides established in the New Document dialog box and on master pages are disregarded. InDesign will do its best approximation — within the limits of HTML — to follow those guidelines.

Multiple pages

For InDesign users, designing pages in multipage publications usually begins by creating a master page or two. Pages are then added as needed to the publication, and finally text boxes, picture boxes, and lines are added and arranged on individual pages. When you export the pages of a multipage publication as Web pages, much of your document construction and page design work is disregarded.

When appearance doesn't matter

Remember that on the Web, content has always been king, not appearance. But this doesn't mean that your exported Web pages can't resemble the original printed pages. A Web site created from an InDesign document can maintain some of the appearance of the printed publication, but you'll want to create Web pages that work well for browsers — which means pages that are as lean as possible and designed to download and display quickly.

Freeing yourself of page-size concepts

In a multipage InDesign document prepared for printing, each page is the same size and for publications printed on offset presses, there are a specified number of pages (almost always a multiple of four to accommodate folding and binding). A Web page, however, can be as long as the information requires and as wide as the viewer's monitor. Consequently, you won't find page numbers on Web pages. Think of this as a bonus: Free from the size limitations imposed by printed pages, Web page designers can rest assured that all of their pages will be exactly the appropriate size for the information they contain.

But, having said that, you can still organize your documents by pages. For HTML export, InDesign lets you merge all pages into one long page (creating a single HTML document with a line separating the print version's pages) or choose which pages to export as separate documents (creating multiple HTML documents).

From page jumps to anchors and links

One challenge you don't have to worry about when exporting Web pages is jumping the text of a long article to a different page because there's too much text to fit on the printed page—a problem that often occurs in printed publications such as magazines and newspapers. If you create a Web page from a lengthy article, you can export all the text and graphics as a single Web page. If you export a multipage InDesign document as separate HTML pages, InDesign will add Next and Prev links so readers can move from page to page.

But InDesign doesn't let you create anchors (hyperlinks within documents) or hyperlinks to other documents or Web sites. This is odd, given how fundamental hyperlinks are to Web page organization and design. You'll need to use an HTML editor to add such links, so consider coloring intended links (perhaps blue because that is the standard color for a hyperlink on the Web) so you can find those pieces of text later in your HTML editor.

Headers, footers, and navigation bars

Another difference between print and Web publishing is the nature and appearance of headers and footers. In printed publications, headers and footers inconspicuously inform readers of their location within the publication. However, in Web pages, headers and footers play multiple roles. In addition to informing viewers of their current location, a Web page's header also must function as an attention grabber and often as a navigation tool. And on the Web, a "header" can actually run along the side as a menu bar—which makes a lot of sense because when people scroll, any header at the top will disappear from view.

Figure 35-3 shows a Web site based on a printed publication—*5280* magazine. The header at top contains the publication's logo, whereas the bar at the left side serves as an index with hyperlinks for jumping to other pages within the publication.

Figure 35-3: Using the same graphic and navigational elements at the top and bottom of all pages — or on the side, as in this site — gives a Web site a visual continuity that make it easy for a viewer to access the information.

In most cases, if you're exporting an entire publication as multiple Web pages, you'll want to create custom headers, footers, and navigation bars — in HTML format — that will be used on most if not all of the pages you generate. Because InDesign doesn't let you add hyperlinks, all you can do is create the text or images that you will later add the links to in an HTML editor.

One neat technique is to create a header or footer that includes a graphic with multiple clickable areas (called an *image map*) that link a page to several Web pages. You can do that in most modern HTML editors.

Dealing with multiple elements

InDesign lets you work with all sorts of elements — text, graphics, lines, and boxes. Although HTML has similar elements — text, images, lines, and frames — it doesn't have the ability to combine them. So InDesign converts grouped items into a single image for you, preserving your original look.

The ability to arrange items in layers lets InDesign users place text and lines in front of pictures, create intricate text runarounds, and build complex illustrations from multiple items. Although HTML doesn't support layers, InDesign combines layered items during export so they do display properly—text wraps, transparent cutouts, and all.

Using colors

Because nearly everybody who uses a computer these days has a color monitor, most Web page designers use color freely. But printing color on paper and displaying color on a computer monitor are different. Let's look at some of the differences between printed color and color displayed on a monitor and see how these differences affect the Web pages you export. Here are a couple of thoughts to bear in mind as you read the following sections:

✦ **The Web-safe palette:** Most graphics programs these days let you save files using the 216-color Web-safe palette—the one that most PC and Mac browsers support. Regardless of the colors you've applied to text and pictures in an InDesign document, the people who view the Web pages you create from these documents will see only the colors that their browser can display. The other factor is whether the graphic in your InDesign document was converted to GIF or JPEG format; this is covered in more depth later in this chapter. InDesign comes with a Web color swatch that contains only the Web-safe colors.

✦ **Check before you convert:** This is one of many reasons you should always preview the pages you export in a browser. This way, you can see how the color elements survived the trip. If the results are not what you want, you can always open the converted image—or the original image for that matter—in an illustration or image-editing program and make whatever modifications you want.

Formatting text

As much as any other feature, InDesign's claim to fame is its set of sophisticated typographic controls. In comparison, text-formatting options for Web page designers are quite limited. There's no tracking, kerning, or ligatures for controlling appearance of text on Web pages, and techniques such as specifying fonts and shifting text baselines are possible only using HTML editors and browsers that support HTML Version 4 and its cascading style sheets feature. As mentioned earlier, the look of text is determined as much—more in most cases—by the browser and the user of the browser than by the Web page designer. Here are the major issues:

✦ **The decision-making process:** The decisions that you make before converting InDesign text into HTML format are similar to the decisions you make when saving text in a word processing program for use in InDesign. If you're saving text for use in InDesign, you usually want to retain as much of the formatting as possible. The same is true when you convert InDesign text into HTML format.

✦ **Attribute and formatting issues:** Although you can't be certain of the typeface or point size that will ultimately be used to display the text you convert, the HTML export maintains several character attributes and paragraph formats during export, which helps maintain continuity between the text in a printed InDesign document and in its HTML counterpart.

Character attributes

Considering that the Web was designed on the UNIX computer platform nearly a decade ago, where all words looked the same and typography wasn't much of an issue, it's not surprising that content — not appearance — was the main concern of the first generation of Web page designers. But lately, a growing number of print designers have been making the transition to Web page design, and many have been shocked by the lack of typographic options for text on the Web. Still, a good part of the text formatting done in InDesign is retained when you export Web pages, as Table 35-1 shows.

Note

InDesign has two options for exporting text: Appearance and Editability. If you choose the former, your text effects will survive export to HTML — because InDesign creates a graphic of the page. That's not useful for most pages because it increases file size (and thus display time for your readers) and prevents readers from copying text. The Editability option applies HTML formatting to the text, so the text can be selected and, more important, displays quickly.

Table 35-1	
Text Formatting That Exports to HTML	
InDesign	**Exports to HTML**
All caps	Yes
Baseline shift	No
Boldface	Yes
Colors	Yes
Condensed/expanded	No
Fonts	Yes *
Gradients	No
Italics	Yes
Kerning	No
Outlines	No
Point sizes	Yes
Shading	Yes
Small caps	No

InDesign	Exports to HTML
Strikethrough	Yes
Subscript	Yes *
Superscript	Yes *
Underlines	Yes

* For some browsers

Font types

Most of the text you see on Web pages these days uses the same typefaces that have been used since the advent of the Web: Arial and Times. That's because most browsers support two typefaces — a proportional face and a fixed-width face — and either Arial or Times is the default proportional typeface used by most browsers; users can typically set different defaults for their own browsers if they choose to do so. (Courier is commonly used as the fixed-width face.) InDesign will export the font information, so browsers that support fonts will display the correct font if the user has it on his or her system.

InDesign does not support a new Web font technology called TrueDoc fonts. Bitstream's TrueDoc font technology, supported by Netscape Navigator 4.0 and later, embeds the fonts in the Web pages, similar to how Adobe's PDF technology does for PDF files.

Font sizes

Once again, the viewer has the final say about the display size of the text in your exported Web pages. Both Netscape Navigator and Microsoft Internet Explorer provide options for enlarging or reducing the size of the text displayed in the browser window. InDesign will approximate the original document's text size when it exports to HTML — the newer the browser you have, the more accurate the text size will be because newer browsers support more font sizes than older ones.

Paragraph formats

Other than paragraph alignment, you usually will get the paragraph formatting retained if your readers have current browser versions (at least Navigator 4 or Internet Explorer 5). HTML does support left-, right-, and center-aligned text, and these formats are retained when you export from InDesign to HTML. Depending on the browser, justified and forced-justified text either is retained as is or is converted to left-aligned text. Other paragraph attributes — indents, tabs, space before and after, and so on — are also either retained or ignored depending on the browser.

Tables

If you use tables in InDesign — created with tabs, as explained in Chapter 14 — don't expect them to export to HTML properly. Instead, the tabs will be removed, bunching all the text together. Any tab leaders (the series of characters — usually periods — used in some tables to connect data, such as in a table of contents) are removed as well.

Special characters

Print publishers have grown accustomed to using lots of fonts, as well as numerous special characters, such as bullets (•) and the degree symbol (°), in their publications. But when you export InDesign text to Web pages, special characters don't always survive the trip. Also, just because Macs and Windows PCs support many special characters doesn't mean that all Web browsers support them. They don't.

The good news is that, in general, all the characters you see on your keyboard, such as the percent sign (%) and the dollar sign ($), are exported intact. The bad news is that special characters created using a Ctrl, Alt, Option, or ⌘ key combination may not survive. To complicate matters further, different fonts offer different sets of special characters. Table 35-2 shows the special characters that can be used in an HTML document.

Tip   If you use numerous special characters and you want to convert as many as possible, the best way to begin is by exporting some test pages that contain the special characters. If your pages contain many accented characters used to display text in languages other than English, make sure to check your Web pages using the browsers that the majority of your readers will use.

Table 35-2 **Special Characters That Export to HTML**		
Character	*Windows*	*Macintosh*
Accented characters		
Ä À Á Á Ã Â ä à â á ã å Ä À Ç ç -Ë È Ê É ë è ê é Ï Ì Î Í ï ì î í Ñ ñ Ö Ò Ô Ó Õ Ø ö ò ô ó õ ø Š š Ü Ù Û Ú ü ù û ú Ý ý Ÿ ÿ	All but Š š Ý ý ÿ *	All but Š š Ý ý
Diphthongs		
Æ æ Œ œ	Æ æ Œ œ	Æ æ Œ œ
International Punctuation		
¿ ¡ « » £ ¥	¿ ¡ « » £ ¥	¿ ¡ « » £ ¥
Legal Symbols		
© ® ™	© ® ™	© ® ™

Character	Windows	Macintosh
Ligatures		
fi fl	None	none
Mathematical Symbols		
± × ÷ ≠ ≈ ∞ √ ¼ ½ ¾	± × ÷ ¼ ½ ¾	± × ÷
Miscellaneous Symbols		
¢ °	¢ °	¢ °
Text Symbols		
† ‡ § ¶	† ‡ § ¶	† ‡ §
Typographic Characters		
– — … ' ' " "	Quotes as keyboard " '	Quotes as keyboard " '

* Many fonts don't support Š and š.

Adding graphics

InDesign lets you import pictures in many different formats, and after you import a picture, you can modify its appearance in many ways. For example, you can scale, rotate, and skew any image, and you can modify the contrast, shade, and color of imported bitmaps. Additionally, you can apply frames to picture boxes and color to box backgrounds. The good news is that nearly all the modifications you make to imported pictures and the boxes that contain them are retained for the pictures you include in the Web pages you export. You can even export rounded corner, oval, straight-edged polygon, and Bézier-curved boxes.

Runarounds

As noted earlier, typographic options on the Web are limited and in the case of pictures, this means that text on Web pages will not wrap tightly around the edges of an irregular shape. Depending on the browser and whether you set InDesign to approximate the layout, you'll usually get a decent approximation of the original text wrap.

Picture file formats

The main decision you must make when you include pictures in your exported Web pages is the picture file format used for the converted picture files. Regardless of the original file type of any picture you export — be it TIFF, EPS, PICT, or whatever — when you create Web pages you must choose between two standard Web graphic formats: GIF and JPEG.

Although Adobe created the Portable Network Graphics (PNG) format as a more capable replacement for GIF. InDesign does not support PNG. That may be because PNG support in browsers is not universal, but it nonetheless is odd to not have the option.

GIF

The GIF (Graphics Interchange Format) format works best for relatively small images that don't have much detail. The biggest advantage of the GIF format is its relatively small file size. As the amount of material available on the Web proliferates and Internet traffic grows, users are growing increasingly impatient waiting for Web pages to download. Keeping image files small goes a long way in keeping viewers happy and interested. The GIF format works well for simple images, such as logos and vector graphics created with programs such as Adobe Illustrator, Macromedia FreeHand, and CorelDraw, and for graphics created in InDesign. The GIF format lets you use color palettes in a variety of ways, but will not let you use more than 256 colors in one image file.

If you choose to export images using the GIF format, InDesign provides the option to create interlaced GIF images. An interlaced GIF image looks exactly the same as a noninterlaced GIF image and is the same file size. However, when an interlaced GIF image is displayed in a browser window, a low-resolution version of the image is first displayed, and then as the rest of the file is downloaded, the resolution is steadily enhanced until the entire image is displayed with maximum possible clarity.

Noninterlaced GIF images are drawn at maximum resolution from top to bottom as the file is downloaded. Interlaced GIF images appear to draw faster than noninterlaced GIF images, although the total screen display time is the same for both. Interlacing GIF images, particularly those that are fairly large, softens the download experience for the viewer and also lets the viewer begin examining any surrounding text while the picture is drawn. It's usually a good idea to select this option for exported GIF images.

JPEG

Sometimes, using the GIF format for an exported picture produces an image file that's prohibitively large. Pictures such as large scanned images that contain a wide range of colors and considerable detail don't always work well when they're converted into GIF files. The alternative is to use the JPEG (Joint Photographic Experts Group) format. Unlike the GIF format, the JPEG format compresses a file by tossing out some of the detail. But the JPEG format retains true 24-bit color and generally produces a smaller file than the GIF format for complex images. Because it's a highly compressed format — more so than the GIF format — JPEG has become the format of choice on the Web for scanned photographs and other large images.

Deciding what's best

The learning process should begin with plenty of fiddling around. The best way to learn about the options for exporting pictures is to import a variety of pictures onto a test page, and then start exporting and experiment with the two image types for export.

It's easy to switch back and forth between your Web browser and InDesign as you try different combinations. While you're testing, save the same image in both the GIF and JPEG formats, and then check both the file size and the browser display of the resulting images.

Tip InDesign can make the choice for you — its Automatic option will choose for each image independently whether to use GIF or JPEG. Frankly, it's easy to rely on InDesign and not worry about choosing to use one over the other for all images. (InDesign doesn't let you make the choice on a per-image basis — it's all or nothing, or it's automatic.)

Backgrounds

If your InDesign document includes pictures with None-colored backgrounds, you can automatically create transparent GIF images during export. The JPEG format does not support transparent box backgrounds. Blended box backgrounds are maintained during export.

InDesign also lets you specify a GIF or JPEG file as the background for your page. The browser will repeat the image — like tiles on a floor — as often as needed to fill in the page's background.

Lines

All lines — like any other graphic created in InDesign — are converted into graphics, retaining any arrowheads, colors, stroke width, and dashes.

Adding Finishing Touches

No matter how careful you are when you export an InDesign document as a Web page, in many cases you're not going to be completely happy with the pages you produce. Your first option is to simply return to InDesign, modify the elements that were not exported as you wanted them or change the export settings, and then re-export another Web page. But also consider the following options:

✦ If you have enough RAM, you can run InDesign, a Web browser, an image-editing application, and, if necessary, an HTML editor, and switch among all of them as you build pages.

✦ Another option is to be content with exporting a "ballpark" version of a Web page — one that's acceptably close to what you want — and then performing a post-export checklist of tasks in an HTML editor to achieve the look you want. After all, you'll need to use an HTML editor anyhow to add the hyperlinks.

Despite its limitations, creating Web pages from InDesign documents can be a quick, easy, and painless process — particularly if you're satisfied with basic Web pages that contain text and graphics. Don't be surprised, however, if you become as enamored with the intricacies of Web page design as you've become with the intricacies of print design. If that happens, you can easily spend as much time tweaking the look of your Web pages as you do on your print pages.

Summary

InDesign supports just basic HTML export, so you'll likely use a dedicated HTML editor to continue working on any layouts you export from InDesign. The most glaring omission in InDesign's HTML export is support for hyperlinks, so be sure to use a color or other technique to identify hyperlinks in your InDesign document so whoever adds them to your exported HTML file knows where they should be. Another omission that will require work in an HTML editor is support for tables; your InDesign tables will lose all of their formatting when exported to HTML.

Despite being basic, InDesign's HTML export features will help some users create basic Web pages from their print publications, and help users who intend to do additional work in an HTML editor retain the basic elements of their print documents when trying to create Web versions.

✦　　✦　　✦

Converting from Print to Web

Understanding the differences between the Web and print described in Chapter 35 is one thing. Creating documents for export to the Web is quite another. The best way, of course, is to try it out. This chapter walks you through the conversion to HTML of a real magazine's content to a Web document, and shows the creation of a simpler Web page.

Remember, in all layout work you rarely have just one way to do things. The creative process is just that — creative — and different people will come up with different approaches in solving the same problem. Your own processes may differ, and that's fine as long as you end up in the same place.

Assessing Your Document

Figures 36-1 and 36-2 show the dining guide from *5280* magazine, which serves the Denver region. The goal is to publish this dining guide — updated listings and reviews — on the magazine's Web site, www.5280pub.com. Take a good look at both the closeup page in Figure 36-1 and the overview of the magazine pages in Figure 36-2.

In This Chapter

Converting a multipage document for the Web

Converting a single page for the Web

Understanding the HTML export options in InDesign

Converting a Print-Oriented Document

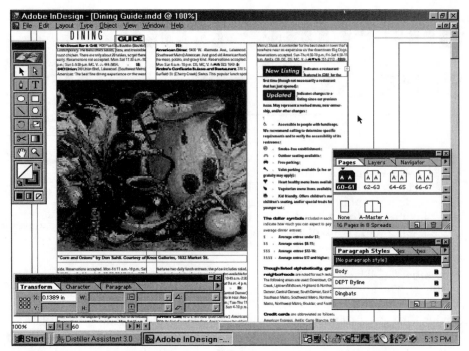

Figure 36-1: T The original dining guide layout, focusing on the first page.

It's quickly apparent that the Web-page designer needs to make several decisions in converting this publication to HTML format:

✦ **Noncontiguous layout:** The printed version jumps over several pages that contain ads. And ads could appear on the same page as the dining guide — there could easily be, for example, one column of text and a two-column ad next to it. Slavishly exporting this layout to HTML will include the ad pages (blank in the figures but with the actual images in the real file) — not something you will want. Also noncontiguous is the order of elements — the guide to the guide appears as the third column, so the restaurant listings begin on the first two columns and then jump past the guide to the next page. If you leave this order untouched when exporting to the Web, you'll have the guide in the middle of your listings, rather than as a separate page — which is what you'll likely want, so readers who need it can follow a hyperlink to it, and the rest need not worry about it.

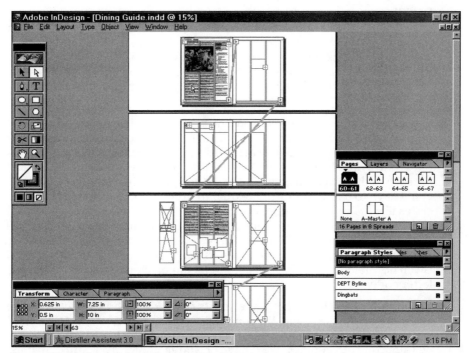

Figure 36-2: The original dining guide layout, showing several spreads (blank pages are ads).

✦ **Multicolumn layout:** As is typical in a magazine layout, the text is arranged in columns. But should the Web page be in columns or simply run through the list as one long series of items? In most cases, you *don't* want multiple columns of text on the Web, because scrolling up and down is much more work via mouse than it is for a person's eyes when scanning a printed page. (You might want multiple columns for items that you know will appear all in one Web screen, where no scrolling is needed, such as lists and other side-by-side elements.)

✦ **Lack of subheads:** The dining guide is arranged alphabetically, and no subheads appear for each letter to help a person quickly find listings under, say, the letter C. That was a decision that could have gone either way in the print version — and you'll have to make the same decision for the Web version. In a long list, we believe it's better to add such subheads, because they can serve as anchor points for quick access. (In that scenario, there would be a list of letters at the top of the page or on the side of the page that readers could simply click to jump to the first entry with that letter. Of course, you don't need to have a subhead to create such anchors — you could just put the anchor at the first restaurant that begins with a new letter, but then when restaurants come and go, your anchors could get lost.)

✦ **Dual listings:** A note at the bottom of the third column gives a cross-reference to the same set of restaurants that are organized by type of cuisine. The cross-reference is not easily visible on the page, but appears in the publication's index, and readers quickly learn where it is. On the Web, you'll have to decide whether such a cross-reference should be so subtle or should appear in an index along the side of each page. We usually opt for that side-index approach.

✦ **Special symbols:** To save room and help readers quickly spot certain aspects of restaurants they're considering visiting, the listings use many special symbols — for handicapped access, kid-friendly, vegetarian entrées, and so on. These symbols won't work on the Web, so you will need to create graphics for each and replace each symbol with the appropriate inline graphic, or you'll have to use some sort of textual treatment (such as using boldface codes like *KF* for *kid-friendly*) throughout. The latter is easier to execute, because you can do a search and replace, but you lose the visual punch. That visual punch, however, will require more effort for you, and a longer download time for your readers, because the graphics must load in their browsers. Given how many symbols *5280* uses in its dining guide, we'd opt for using letter codes.

✦ **Use of graphics:** The dining guide sports occasional photos, including the large one on the first page. Do you want to use graphics on the Web site? They could add visual interest as people scroll through the listings, but they also will slow download times. We'd have one large photo of a features restaurant at the top of the listings, and rotate that photo with others (perhaps weekly), so readers are reminded that the listings are updated.

Modifying your layout: the hard way

Now that you've assessed what you need to do to your print document to make it work for the Web, it's time to do the hard work. Based on the tasks to be done, the following set of steps is a logical approach to converting your document:

1. Most critical, save the print file under a new name, using File ➪ Save As, or Shift+⌘+S or Ctrl+Shift+S. In our example, the original file was called simply Dining Guide; we called the Web version Dining Guide Web. Now you can do your conversion work.

2. Convert the document from facing pages (spreads) to single pages. (This prepares you for Step 3.) To do this, use File ➪ Document Setup, or Option+⌘+P or Ctrl+Alt+P, and uncheck the Facing Pages option.

3. Delete all the ad pages and any ads and other elements (including empty frames and folios) on content pages *and* on master pages. To delete a page, go to the Pages pane, select the page(s) you want to delete, and then click the trash can icon at the bottom-right corner of the pane. Don't worry: Your text threads for the listings text will be maintained.

Why delete extraneous pages? Because InDesign puts a horizontal rule between pages, and if you have several blank pages in your layout and text that jumps over them as is the case in the example, you'll get some text, a series of horizontal rules, and then more text. Even if there were no blank pages, you'd still get the horizontal line in the middle of your text at the locations where the text threaded to a new page. Unfortunately, there's no way to tell InDesign to simply run all the text as one long string if that text threads across pages.

In the case of *5280*, the Dining Guide template has three-column text frames that are all linked on every page, so the text can be pored over easily. Ads are created as frames that are placed on top of the text frames, causing the text to reflow to the next open page. The designer keeps the listing's text frame underneath the ads' frames in case an ad is moved, added, or deleted — this causes the dining guide text to automatically fill the newly open space. This makes a lot of sense for this kind of flow-around-the-ads section.

4. Take any standalone elements — those you want on their own page — and move them to their own page. This example will have three pages total: one for the alphabetical listings, one for the by-cuisine listings, and one for the guide to the listings. There could also have been a fourth page for the index and links to the other elements, but we decided to incorporate that into the alphabetical-listings page, which doubles as the main page for this section of the Web site, as it does in the print magazine.

   For very long strings of text — such as the restaurant listings in the example — make a very large text frame on one page (go into the pasteboard if needed) and/or decrease the text size to hold all the text in one frame. Note that it's fine if the text frame extends down over subsequent pages, although for visual clarity you'll want those pages to be blank. You can also increase the page size if that helps you fit the frame (use File ⇨ Document Setup, or Option+⌘+P or Ctrl+Alt+P to do so).

   If necessary, add pages using the Pages pane (via the palette menu's Insert Pages menu). In this case, that means adding a page for the listings guide that contains all the codes.

Caution

Make sure that your text frame's upper-left corner starts on the actual page — any element that starts on the pasteboard or is only on the pasteboard is ignored during export.

Tip

One drawback to making the text fit on one frame by reducing its size is that InDesign exports the text to HTML in that small size. While you can edit the size in the HTML editor, that can be time-consuming. So you may end up using a series of threaded text frames across several pages rather than try to put all the text in one frame as previously recommended. If you use a series of threaded frames, you'll get line breaks between each page when you export to HTML, but removing those line breaks in an HTML editor is simple to do.

5. Change any multicolumn text frames to single-column frames. To do this, select the frame and use Object ➪ Text Frame Options, or ⌘+B or Ctrl+B, to open the Text Frame Options dialog box and change the Number setting to 1 in the Columns section of the dialog box. The only exceptions are those frames whose text you want to appear in multiple columns on the Web page.

6. You might add some missing elements. In this case, these include the alphabetical index to which we'll later apply hyperlinks so readers can quickly jump to a specific letter, as well as the side index that hyperlinks to the by-cuisine listing. Note that you can as easily add these in the HTML editor, which may make more sense in most cases because at that point you're dealing with the actual Web layout.

7. Save your work. Now you're ready to export to HTML.

Figure 36-3 shows how the document looks.

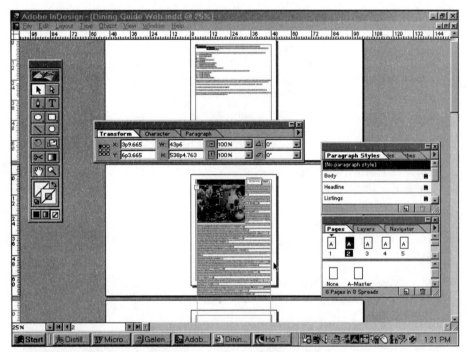

Figure 36-3: The dining guide layout reformatted for Web export.

Modifying your layout: the easy way

Although logical, the preceding steps require a lot of work to end up with three pages, one for the alphabetical listings, one for the by-cuisine listings, and one for the guide to the listings. Here's an easier way that may have more steps but takes less time:

1. Create a new InDesign document (File ➪ New, or ⌘+N or Ctrl+N), with three pages and no master text frame. Move to the second page.

2. Open the original dining guide layout and go to the first page.

3. Select the main standalone elements you want to keep: the Dining Guide logo frame and the photo's frame. (We'll deal with the text frames containing the listings and the guide to the listings later.) You can select all at once by holding the Shift key when clicking the second and subsequent items. Now use Edit ➪ Copy, or ⌘+C or Ctrl+C, to copy these items to the clipboard.

4. Paste the elements to the new document's second page by using Edit ➪ Paste, or ⌘+V or Ctrl+V.

5. Go back to the original document using the Window menu. Select the text frame containing the guide to the listings and copy it. Switch to the new document, and move to its first page. Paste the text frame on that page.

6. Go back to the original and, using the Type pointer, select the text frame containing the alphabetical listings. Use Edit ➪ Select All, or ⌘+A or Ctrl+A, to select all the text, including text on threaded text frames.

7. Return to the new document, and create a text frame. Paste the listings text into that frame.

8. Go back to the original document and find the page that has the by-cuisine listings, and then repeat Steps 3 through 7 for its elements. You'll place these on page 3 of the new document.

9. Save the new document with a name such as *Dining Guide Web*.

10. Adjust the text frames so all the text fits in by increasing the text frame size (go into the pasteboard if needed) and/or decreasing the text size. Note that it's fine if the text frame extends down over subsequent pages, but the text frame's upper-left corner must be on the page, not on the pasteboard.

11. Change any multicolumn text frames to single-column frames. To do this, select the frame and use Object ➪ Text Frame Options, or ⌘+B or Ctrl+B, to open the Text Frame Options dialog box and change Number setting to 1 in the Columns section of the dialog box. The only exceptions are those frames whose text you want to appear in multiple columns on the Web page.

12. Add any missing elements. In this case, these include the alphabetical index to which we'll later apply hyperlinks so readers can quickly jump to a specific letter, as well as the side index that hyperlinks to the by-cuisine listing.

13. Save your work. Now you're ready to export to HTML.

Figure 36-3, shown previously, shows how the document looks.

When Not to Start with an InDesign Document

As you can see from the first example of the dining guide, the work in converting to HTML a document not originally designed with the Web in mind can be tremendous. You might wonder why bother to go through all that hassle and instead just create a Web document in an HTML editor by using the same text files and graphics as used in the InDesign document.

In fact, the dining guide example shows why in most cases it's easier *not* to use InDesign to create your HTML documents. It would be much easier in this case to import the text file into an HTML editor, use a program such as Photoshop to convert graphics from such formats as TIFF and EPS to the Web's GIF and JPEG, import those images into your HTML editor, and add hyperlinks and so forth in that editor.

In some cases, you can use a more Web-savvy program such as Microsoft Word or Corel WordPerfect to create the HTML file — in cases such as a listing where there's not much layout work involved for components like the listings, a word processor can be a great tool to use — it already knows how to deal with text that can be of any length. Of course, word processors have their own HTML woes, so be sure to use an HTML editor to clean up HTML files created by other programs, and to build the bulk of your original Web pages.

So, should you use InDesign at all to create HTML files? Yes, for documents designed up front for use on the Web, such as in the next section.

Preparing a Web-Oriented Document

If you're creating a document for use on the Web, rather than converting a print-oriented document, you'll find the work to be much easier in InDesign. That's because you'll be setting up the document from a Web perspective in the first place.

Look at the InDesign document in Figure 36-4. The design for this home page eliminates most of the rework hassles we had in the listings document earlier.

Here's why this document is so much more Web-friendly:

✦ It's laid out on a 6.5-inch wide document, to ensure that it'll fit comfortably in most browser windows. (It's easy to forget that a browser window is smaller than a piece of paper, which is why we recommend you use a smaller document size when creating Web pages in InDesign.)

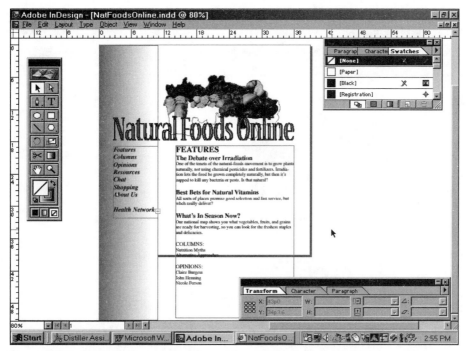

Figure 36-4: A simple home page layout for a Web site in InDesign.

✦ The layout is simple, putting the content in one main column, avoiding awkward alignment problems of a multicolumn document.

✦ It has no margins. That's key, because InDesign uses the margins to figure out the page boundaries when exporting to HTML. If you have no margins, the edge of the page becomes that boundary. Because few people actually place images and text right up to the page boundary, this in effects gives you a predictable margin.

✦ To the side is an index of site locations, to make it easy for readers to navigate.

✦ At the top, above the logo, is a space for a banner ad.

✦ The page has no special symbols or fonts to worry about.

This page can be exported as is, resulting in the clean Web page shown in Figure 36-5. We still need to use an HTML editor to add the hyperlinks and the ad, but that work will be straightforward in this clean design.

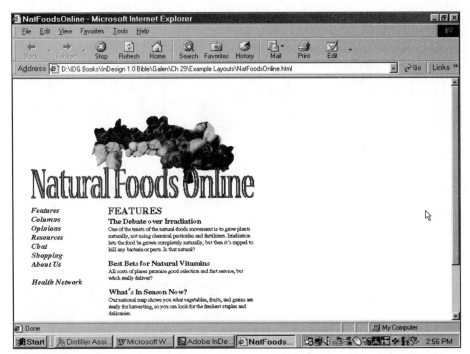

Figure 36-5: The HTML page after being exported from InDesign and displayed in Internet Explorer.

Understanding Export Options

Now that your document is set for HTML export — however you created it — it's time to actually do the export. In InDesign, the process is straightforward: Just use the Export dialog box (File ➪ Export, or ⌘+E or Ctrl+E).

First, choose HTML from the Save as Type pop-up menu in the dialog box. You can also change the file name and location — it works like any standard Mac or Windows Save dialog box.

Now you're ready to set the export settings. Understanding them is essential so you get the right HTML output. The Export dialog box has four panes — Documents, Formatting, Layout, and Graphics — that you can move among by using the Previous and Next buttons on the right-hand side of the dialog box or by using the pop-up menu at the top of the dialog box.

Document pane

The first pane in the Export dialog box is the Documents pane, shown in Figure 36-6, where you specify which pages of your document get exported and whether they are merged into one HTML page or exported as separate pages.

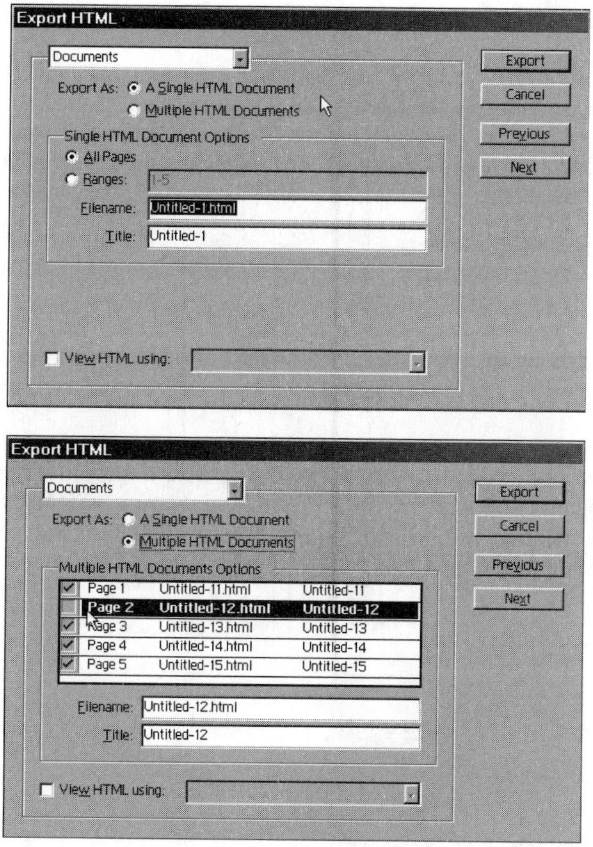

Figure 36-6: In the top Documents pane of the Export HTML dialog box are the options for single-HTML-page export, while in the bottom Documents pane are the options for multiple-HTML-page export.

If you decide to export to a single HTML page, the dialog box looks like the one at the top of Figure 36-6. You can export all pages or a range of pages to that HTML page. That's key, because in many cases (such as in the dining listings example earlier in this chapter), you'll want to export some pages separately (such as the listings) and others individually (such as the listings guide). By being able to select page ranges, you can do just that.

If you decide to export each document page to its own HTML page, the dialog box looks like the one at the bottom of Figure 36-6. In this version, you check the pages you want exported.

Either way, you can also change the HTML page's file name and internal name using the fields at the bottom of the dialog box. When exporting multiple pages, first click the page you want to rename from the list of pages; that's the page whose name will be affected by what you enter at the bottom of the dialog box.

> **Tip**   The View HTML Using option lets you link to a browser program that launches after you export the pages so you can see how it looks. If you leave it blank, as we recommend, you can export a series of pages before checking them out. It makes sense not to launch a browser to see the results of the HTML export, because you can see those same results in the HTML editor—which lets you do something about what you see.

Formatting pane

The second pane, Formatting, is where you specify how text and backgrounds are formatted during export.

> **Tip**   The key function in the Formatting pane, shown in Figure 36-7, is Maintain Non-Standard Text, in the Text section at the top of the dialog box. It should almost always be set to Editability. Otherwise, if you choose Appearance, you'll get a bitmap graphic in place of your text, which means the browser window can't change margins and other text settings to fit, and the file will usually take longer to display on readers' browsers.

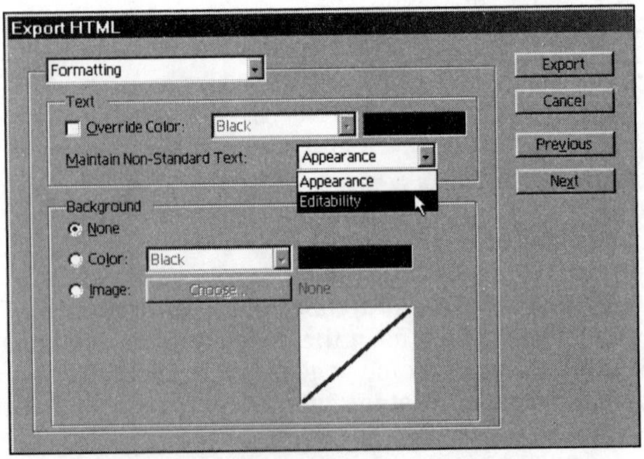

Figure 36-7: The Formatting pane of the Export HTLM dialog box is used to set text appearance and page background.

The other Text function is Override Color, which you use if you want all text in a document converted to one color (which you choose) during HTML export. A print document may use colors for formatting, or perhaps for annotation of changes by a copy editor, that you don't want to have to hunt down before exporting to the Web—that's a situation in which you'd use this option. But if you forget to use it, don't worry—you can add and remove color in an HTML editor as well.

The Background option is similar: Here, you set whether your pages have a background. That background can be a color or a GIF or JPEG image you select. Note that the image will be repeated in the background of your page as often as needed to fill it, like tiles on a floor.

Layout pane

The third pane, Layout, is key to getting the look you want for your HTML pages. Figure 36-8 shows the pane.

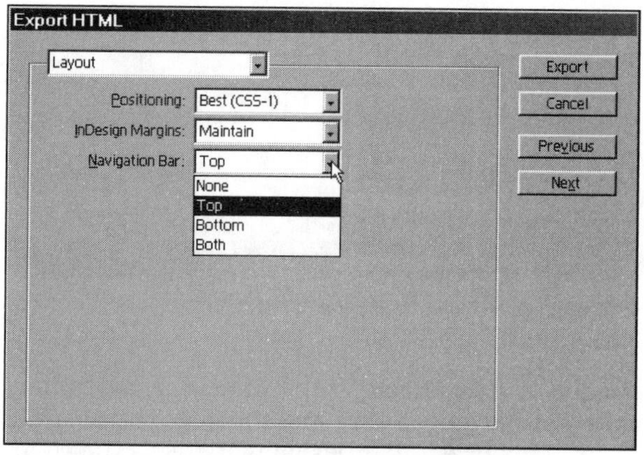

Figure 36-8: The Layout pane of the Export HTML dialog box is used to set layout fidelity.

The Positioning pop-up menu has two options: Best (CSS-1) and None. The first option uses cascading style sheets to place and size text for the most accurate replication of your print document's look. The second option lets the browser figure out the placement and size. You'd use the first option for a document such as the "Natural Foods Online" example, where you want a close approximation of the original layout. You'd use the second (None) for a document such as the restaurant listings in which the layout in InDesign is pretty much irrelevant to the final appearance on the Web. With None, all the objects are exported sequentially.

Figure 36-9 shows how the Natural Foods Online document looks with this option; compare it to the version in Figure 36-5, which used the Best (CSS-1) option.

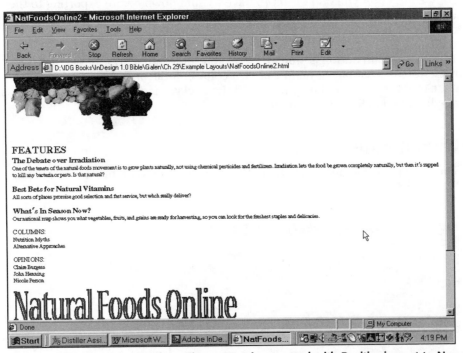

Figure 36-9: The Web page from Figure 36-5 is exported with Positioning set to None.

The InDesign Margins pop-up menu also has two options: Maintain and None. Maintain uses the space between the page boundary and the page margins as the margins around your HTML page. None uses the InDesign margins as the HTML page's boundary.

Finally, the Navigation Bar pop-up menu has four options: Top, Bottom, Both, and None. It places two buttons — Prev and Next — in the designated locations on your exported HTML pages.

Tip

The Navigation Bar is a silly option — you have no control over the formatting or placement, and the chances of them matching your other navigation buttons are slim. It's better to use text or graphics for buttons in InDesign, and then apply hyperlinks to them in your HTML editor, or to simply add them in the HTML editor.

Graphics pane

The final pane, Graphics, controls how graphics are exported. Remember, all graphics for use in HTML pages are converted to GIF or JPEG formats, and this pane lets you determine how that conversion works. Figure 36-10 shows the pane.

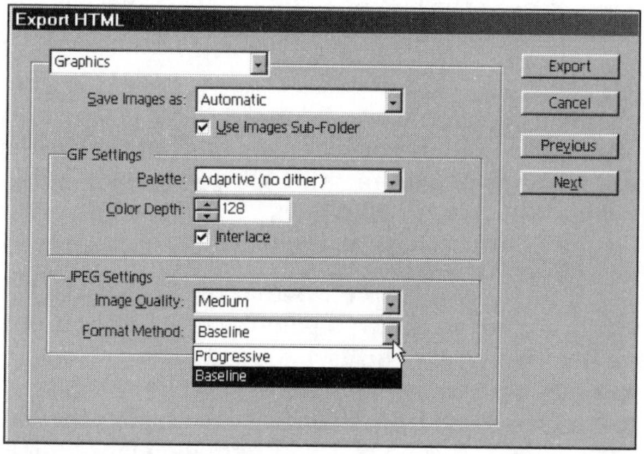

Figure 36-10: The Graphics pane of the Export HTML dialog box is used to set text appearance and page background.

The Save Images As pop-up menu gives you a choice of Automatic, GIF, and JPEG. Automatic has InDesign choose which format to use based on its characteristics (line drawings and simple bitmaps usually do better as GIF files, while photographic images usually do better as JPEG files). Unless you have a reason to choose to have all images be converted to GIF or JPEG, leave it at Automatic.

If checked, the Use Images Sub-Folder option places the converted images in a folder called Images inside the folder that holds the exported HTML file. Otherwise, the images are in the same folder as the HTML file. It doesn't really matter which option you pick.

The rest of the settings are broken into two groups: GIF and JPEG.

For GIF files, a key option is the palette used. The Palette pop-up menu gives you five choices:

✦ **Adaptive (no dither),** which lets the browser make the best representation possible given the kind of computer the reader has and the color settings for that computer. This is the best option to select. Fortunately, it's the default option.

✦ **Web**, which adjusts the colors so that only the 216 Web-safe colors — those available on all Windows PCs and Macs — are used. This is the safest choice, though it limits color fidelity for some images.

✦ **Exact**, which doesn't adjust the colors and leaves it to the browser and reader's computer settings to do the best display job they can. (The Adaptive setting helps the browser figure this out, while Exact basically tells the browser to just pass the pixels onto the screen unmodified.) Unless your readers are using systems whose display settings match yours and can be kept that way, avoid this setting.

✦ **System (Win)**, which uses the system colors in Windows. This is similar to Web, except that it includes a few colors that Windows has but the Macintosh does not (and thus are not in the Web palette either). If you know your readers are all using Windows, this is a good choice.

✦ **System (Mac)**, which uses the standard colors on the Macintosh. This is similar to Web, except that it includes a few colors that the Macintosh has but Windows does not (and thus are not in the Web palette either). If you know your readers are all using the Macintosh, this is a good choice.

The Color Depth option lets you pick a value from 2 to 256 — the higher the value, the richer and more accurate the colors. A value of 2 is essentially black-and-white. The default is 128 — a reasonable value that balances fidelity and download time.

The Interlace option controls how the GIF file displays in a browser. If checked, the reader sees the image build as the file is downloaded to their browser. If unchecked, the reader won't see the image until it has finished being downloaded. You should usually check this option.

Image Quality controls the quality and size of the JPEG images. You can choose from Low, Medium (the default), High, and Maximum. The lower the quality, the smaller the file and thus the faster the downloading to the reader's browser. You may want to experiment with various settings on your images — or simply leave it at Medium.

For JPEG files, the Format Method pop-up menu serves the same purpose as the Interlace option for GIF files. The Progressive option has the JPEG image build in the browser as it is downloaded, while the Baseline option means the entire image must be downloaded before displaying.

Fine-Tuning in an HTML Editor

As we've indicated several times, exporting to HTML from InDesign is almost never the final step in creating a Web page. At the least, you need to add hyperlinks to the pages. And you're likely to add other elements and even rearrange some of the elements exported from InDesign.

The next two figures show part of the restaurant listings HTML page being edited in Microsoft's FrontPage 98 HTML editor. Figure 36-11 shows the HTML code, with the added hyperlinks being added. The code `<A HREF="text">address</A>` defines a link around *text* to an address. A # as part of an address, such as #A, means a hyperlink within the same page, to a hyperlink anchor. The code `<A NAME="anchor">text</A>` defines that anchor. Here, we've made a hyperlink from the letter "A" in the index to the first restaurant whose name begins with "A," which here is "The Abstract Cafe."

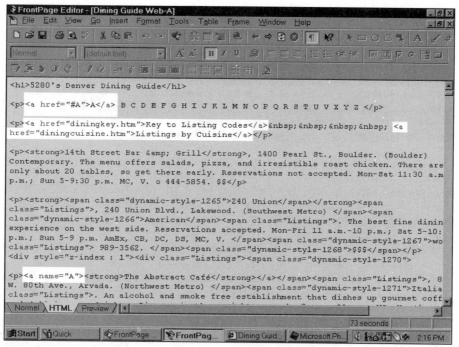

Figure 36-11: Adding hyperlinks via HTML code in FrontPage 98.

Figure 36-12 shows the results in a preview mode. You can see the underlined text that indicates hyperlinks at the top. The dotted underline under "The Abstract Cafe" is FrontPage 98's way of indicating an anchor; that indication won't display on a browser. (The dashed lines below indicate the use of a SPAN style definition, covered in a moment.)

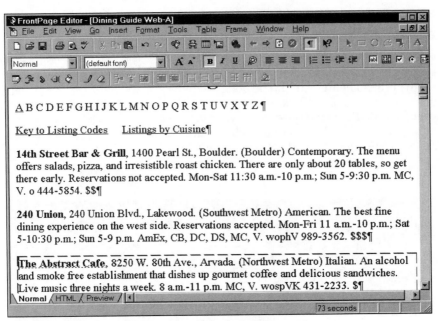

Figure 36-12: Previewing the hyperlinks in FrontPage 98.

Dozens of HTML editors are available—you can even use a simple text editor if you choose. Consequently, we can't describe all the possible steps and approaches. But we can give you pointers on what you'll likely have to do with an InDesign-generated HTML file:

✦ InDesign uses what are called SPAN commands, which not all HTML editors understand, for formatting text appearance and position. For simple documents, such as the restaurants listing, these codes are not needed and should be removed in the HTML editor. For Web pages such as the Natural Foods Online document, where they ensure the accurate placement of text and elements, leave them in. Figure 36-13 shows the use of these codes in an HTML editor (Microsoft's FrontPage Express) that does not understand them and thus flags them with question marks (?).

✦ InDesign also defines dynamic styles for text, even if you don't specify cascading style sheets—the Best (CSS-1) export option. This means that your text will be relatively at the same size as it was in your print document, whether or not that's appropriate for the Web. You'll need to delete those definitions (in the STYLE tag); Figure 36-14 shows this being done in SoftQuad's HotMetal Pro 5.0.

✦ InDesign places META tags, which are supposed to be used for comments at the beginning of an HTML file, within the body of the HTML page, which causes some HTML editors to generate error messages and may even disable some features. For example, HotMetal Pro 5.0 disables rule-checking—which verifies HTML coding syntax—because of how InDesign handles META tags.

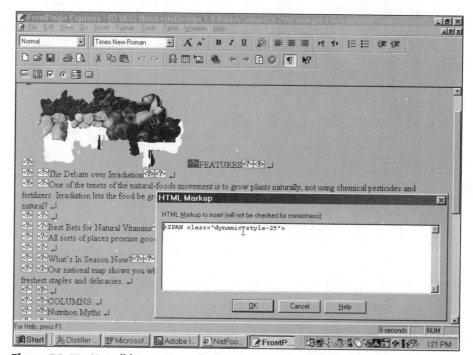

Figure 36-13: Not all browsers understand the SPAN codes used by InDesign to format and place text in HTML pages. The browser here is FrontPage Express.

There's a lot more to HTML editing, so consult an expert—and if you're that expert, check out the wealth of good books on HTML coding and Web page creation. No matter your level of knowledge, be sure to preview all your HTML changes in your HTML editor before saving them. For extra safety, work on a copy of the file that InDesign generated, in case anything goes wrong.

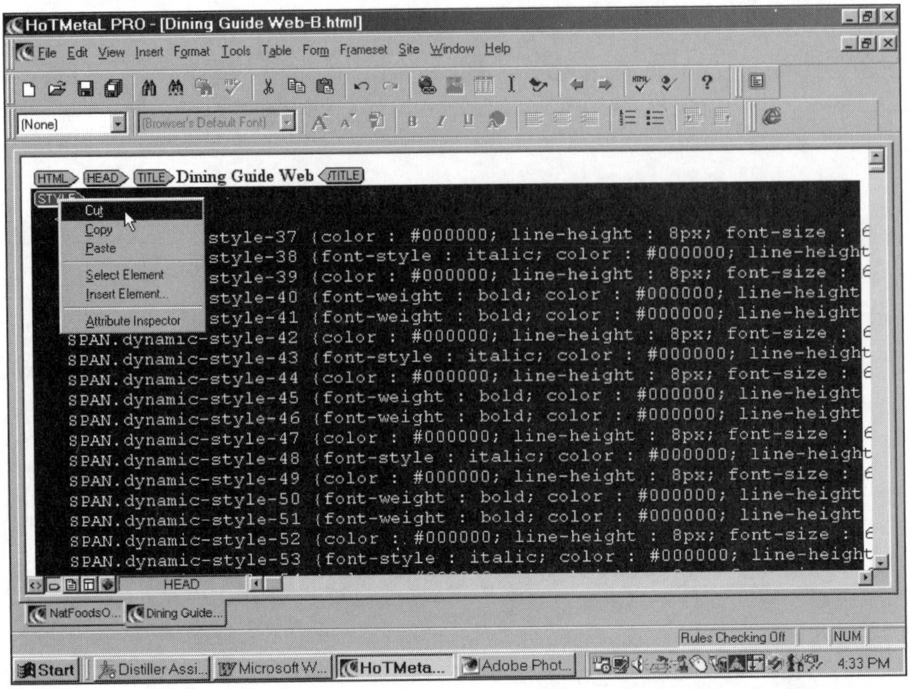

Figure 36-14: For documents that don't need SPAN commands or style definitions, you can simply delete them in your HTML editor. Here, we use HotMetal Pro 5.0 to delete a set of SPAN style definitions contained in a STYLE block.

Summary

Chapter 35 walked you through understanding the differences between the Web and print. This chapter walked you through the conversion to HTML of a real magazine's content to a Web document, as well as how to create a simpler Web page. The best way to learn, of course, is to try it out.

Web-page designers need to make several decisions in converting this publication to HTML format, such as following a noncontiguous or multicolumn layout, and whether or not to include subheads, dual listings, special symbols, or graphics.

Once your document is set for HTML export you must then do the actual export. In InDesign, you use the Export dialog box (File ➪ Export, or ⌘+E or Ctrl+E).

Finally, exporting to HTML from InDesign is almost never the final step in creating a Web page. At the least, you need to add hyperlinks to the pages. And you're likely to add other elements and even rearrange some of the elements exported from InDesign.

✦　　　✦　　　✦

Advanced Issues

Now that you're an expert at using InDesign, it's time to expand your horizons a little. Very few publishers work by themselves, and most have a whole raft of tools to work their miracles. The chapters in Part XI expose you to key insights in working beyond InDesign.

Working with others in a workgroup adds a whole level of complexity to using a program such as InDesign, and this complexity increases if you are working in a cross-platform environment. **Chapter 37** explains how to share preferences and other InDesign components with others in your workgroup, as well as how to integrate Macs and PCs.

As Adobe and other companies develop plug-ins for InDesign, you'll have the option to make InDesign do even more. This too adds to the complexity of using InDesign, but for a worthwhile reason. **Chapter 38** explains how to work with plug-ins.

Finally, InDesign rarely is the only application on your computer. **Chapter 39** explains how to choose the right computer, set up fonts, and work with other publishing tools. And if you're new to computers, you'll find the part at the end that explains the user interfaces of the Mac OS and Windows very handy.

Working with Others

Publishing is rarely a one-person enterprise. Chances are that the creators of your text and graphics are not the same people who do your layout. And in many environments, the chances are high that many people are involved in layout and production.

By its very nature, publishing is a group activity, so publishing programs must support workgroups. Yet a Mac or a PC is a *personal* computer, so it's easy to work on a Mac or PC without worrying about how your setup and work style might affect others. InDesign lets you create your own balance between the individual and the workgroup.

The key to working effectively in a workgroup environment is to establish standards and make sure they are easy to stick to. A basic way to accomplish this task is to place all common elements in one place so that people always know where to get the standard elements. This practice also makes it easy to maintain (to add, modify, and delete) these elements over time, which is essential because no environment is static. How you do this depends on your computing environment:

+ If you don't use a network, keep a master set of disks and copy elements from the master set in a folder with the same name on each person's computer. Update these folders every time a standard element changes on the master disk.

+ If you do use a network, keep a master set of disks (networks do go down, so you'll want your files accessible when that happens) and create a folder for your standard elements on a network drive accessible to all users. Update this folder whenever a standard element changes on the master disk.

Sharing with Other Users

Some standard elements can be accessed easily from a common folder because InDesign can import certain elements that are stored outside InDesign documents. These elements include graphics files, libraries, keyboard shortcut sets, and spelling dictionaries.

Other elements reside within documents and templates and cannot be saved in separate files. These elements include styles, swatch definitions, and master pages. But styles and swatches can be exported/imported from one document to another.

InDesign stores preference-related elements in different places on the Mac and in Windows. For both platforms, color swatches are stored in the Swatch Libraries folder in the InDesign application folder, whereas keyboard shortcut sets are stored in the Shortcut Sets folder in the InDesign application folder. On the Mac, however, spelling and hyphenation exception dictionaries are stored in the Proximity folder in the Dictionaries folder in the Plug-ins folder of the InDesign application folder. On Windows PCs, they are stored deep in the Windows directory: Profiles, then the user name (such as Joe Smith), then Local Settings, then Application Data, then Adobe, then InDesign, and finally in Version 1.0. The InDesign Defaults file on the Mac is stored in the InDesign application folder, while it is stored in the same place as the spelling and exception dictionaries in Windows.

Preference files

When no document is open and you change the preferences, add swatches and styles, modify tool settings (such as changing the number of sides on the polygon tool by double-clicking it), and modify some dialog box default settings (such as Text Wrap and Text Frame Options), these changes are saved in the InDesign Defaults file in the InDesign application's folder.

Tip

You can use the Mac's alias feature or Windows's shortcut feature to use an InDesign Defaults file stored in a folder other than the one in which InDesign resides. On a network, being able to use this technique means that everyone can share the same InDesign Defaults file. You can also set keyboard shortcuts sets, spelling and hyphenation dictionaries, libraries, and swatch libraries to be shared this way. Note that if you're sharing these across platforms, you'll need to create a Windows shortcut from Windows to these files as well as a Mac alias from the Mac.

The InDesign Defaults file cannot be shared across platforms, so if you want to have a master copy on a network server, you'll need to maintain two masters — one for Macintosh and one for Windows. Because the files have the same name on both platforms (no file name extension exists for this file in Windows), you'll need to store them in separate directories or add something to the name such as "Mac" and "Windows." If you do change the name, note that the alias and shortcut on each user's system must simply be named InDesign Defaults.

Color definitions

It's not unusual to want to keep color, tint, and gradient definitions consistent across documents. This consistency helps you ensure, for example, that corporate-identity colors, if you have them, are used instead of someone's approximations.

You can import swatches created in other documents (and templates) by having both documents open, and then dragging the swatch from the source document's Swatches pane (Window ⇨ Swatches) to anywhere in the other document's window. By creating a file that contains nothing but swatches, you can in effect create a color library for users.

You can't add swatches to a library, but any swatch used in a library element will be copied to a document along with that element. So you could use a library that has a series of rectangles each with a different swatch applied as another way of creating a color library.

InDesign also lets you share swatch libraries, even across platforms (just give the library the file extension .AI if you're transferring a swatch library from the Mac to Windows).

Cross-Reference

See Chapter 27 for more on creating swatches.

Note

In Windows, color profiles are stored in the Color folder inside the System folder inside the folder that contains Windows (usually called Windows or Win98). On the Mac, color profiles are stored in folders within the System Folder: ColorSync Profiles for ColorSync profiles, and CMSCP and KPCMS for Kodak and ICC profiles.

Styles

The Character Styles pane (Type ⇨ Character, or Shift+⌘+F or Ctrl+Shift+F) and the Paragraph Styles pane (Type ⇨ Paragraph) include an option in the palette menu to import styles from other InDesign documents and templates. Figure 37-1 shows this menu. Use Load Character Styles or Load Paragraph Styles to import just character or paragraph styles; use Load All Styles to load both from a document or template.

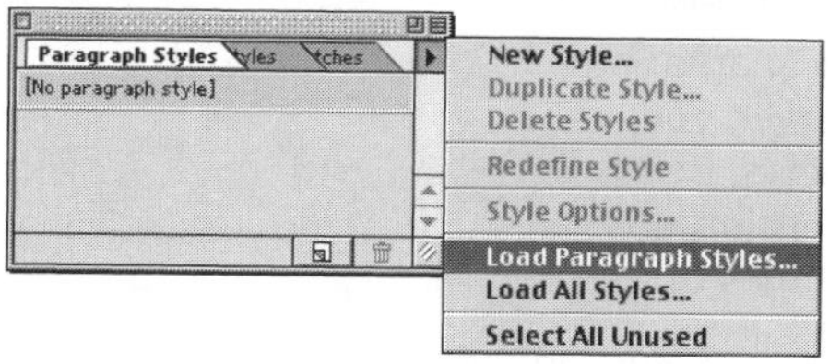

Figure 37-1: The palette menu used for importing styles.

Tip

By importing styles with no document open, you copy all new styles into your global defaults (those stored in the InDesign Defaults file covered earlier). This technique is a handy way of bringing new styles into your default settings without affecting existing styles.

Cross-Reference

See Chapter 15 for more on styles.

Spelling dictionaries

InDesign saves any spelling or hyphenation exceptions you add via Edit ➪ Dictionary or when spell-checking via Edit ➪ Check Spelling, or ⌘+I or Ctrl+I. These exception dictionaries can be copied from one computer to another (regardless of platform), or you can use an alias or shortcut from each computer to a central location on a server.

On both Mac and Windows, hyphenation exception files have the file name extension .NOT, while the spelling exception dictionaries have the extension .UDC. The files will have the same name as the language dictionaries (but different file name extensions) to which they are associated, such as FREN.NOT for French hyphenation exceptions and USA.UDC for U.S. English spelling exceptions.

Cross-Reference

See Chapter 10 for more on hyphenation and spelling dictionaries.

Graphics and text files

Perhaps the most obvious elements to standardize are the source elements — the text and graphics that you use in your documents — especially if you have common elements such as logos that are used in multiple documents.

The simplest method of ensuring that the latest versions of these common elements are used is to keep them all in a standard folder (either on each computer or on a network drive). This method works well when you first use a text or graphic element, but it does not ensure that these elements are updated in InDesign documents if the elements are changed after being imported.

For both text and graphics files, using InDesign's links feature — when you keep common elements in a common location — can ensure consistency across documents. You can also use libraries to store commonly used graphics and text blocks (including any formatting for the text and its frame).

Libraries

InDesign libraries are a great aid to keeping documents consistent. Because libraries are stored in their own files, common libraries can be put in common folders. You can even access them across the network. If you want, you can keep an alias to a library elsewhere on the network on your computer's local drive.

For many people, libraries offer more flexibility than just linking to graphics files because all attributes applied to graphics and their picture boxes are also stored in the library.

Libraries can be shared across platforms, and although Windows InDesign libraries have the file name extension .INDL, this extension is not required for Windows InDesign to open and use Mac libraries.

See Chapter 29 for more information on libraries.

Templates

In the course of creating documents, you are likely to evolve templates (also called *stationery* on the Mac) that you want to use over and over. InDesign can save a document as a template. The only difference between a template and a document is that a template forces you to use Save As rather than Save in the File menu so that you do not overwrite the template but instead create new documents based on it. (See Chapter 4 for more information on templates.)

Although the optimum approach is to design a template before creating actual documents, the truth is that no one can foresee all possibilities. Even if you create a template (and you should) with a style, swatches, and master pages intended for use in all new documents, you can expect to modify your template as working on real documents brings up the need for modifications and additions.

Whether or not you use templates, you still need to transfer basic layout elements such as styles and master pages from one document to another, as described earlier in this chapter.

Templates can be shared across platforms, and although Windows InDesign templates have the file name extension .INDT, this extension is not required for Windows InDesign to open and use Mac templates.

See Chapter 4 for more on templates.

Master pages

Moving master pages between documents is tricky because InDesign offers no feature that explicitly performs this task. But you can use InDesign libraries as way-stations for master pages that you want to move from one document to another. Here are the steps:

1. Open a library with Window ➪ Libraries ➪ Open, or Option+Shift+⌘+L or Ctrl+Alt+Shift+O, or create a library with Window ➪ Libraries ➪ New.

2. Open the document with the master page that you want to copy and display that master page (by double-clicking the master page in the Pages pane, which you open via Window ➪ Pages or F12). We recommend that you change the view to something small, such as 25 percent, so you can see the full page.

3. Select the Selection tool and then select all items (via Edit ➪ Select All, or ⌘+A or Ctrl+A).

4. Drag (or copy and paste) the items into an open library and release the mouse. All of the elements on the master page will appear in their own library box.

5. Open the document that you want to copy the master page into. You don't need to close the other document, but unless you intend to get other elements from it or work on it later, go ahead and close it to reduce clutter both on the screen and in the computer's memory. (Use the Window ➪ Cascade or Window ➪ Tile to manage how documents display if you have several open. Tile creates nonoverlapping windows — one at the top and one at the bottom if you have two documents open — while Cascade overlaps the windows. The names of all open documents also appear in the Window menu so you can switch among them. You can also resize windows manually by clicking and holding the mouse on the window's resize box on the Mac, or by clicking and holding any of its sides or corners in Windows.)

6. Insert a new blank master page in the second document, using the Pages pane.

7. Drag (or copy and paste) the library item containing the first document's master-page elements into the new master page.

8. Rename the new master page (using the Master Options option in the Pages pane's palette menu) so you can remember what it is. Now you're done.

See Chapter 29 for more on master pages.

Mixing Mac/Windows Environments

As a cross-platform application, InDesign appeals strongly to all sorts of users who find that they deal with "the other side." This includes corporate users whose various divisions have standardized on different platforms, service bureaus whose clients use different machines, and independent publishers or layout artists who deal with a range of clients.

InDesign differences

InDesign can read document files from either platform. However, the Windows version may not recognize a Mac-generated file as an InDesign file unless you do one of two things:

✦ Add the file extension .INDD for documents or .INDT for templates to the Mac-generated file's name.

✦ Select the All Files in the File of Type pop-up menu in the Open dialog box (File ⇨ Open, or Ctrl+O).

On the Mac, you'll typically not be able to double-click a PC-generated InDesign document (it'll have the PC icon rather than the InDesign icon; instead, you'll need to open it from the InDesign Open dialog box (File ⇨ Open, or ⌘+O).

Which elements transfer

The following elements may be transferred across platforms, with any limits noted:

✦ Color, tint, and gradient swatches are retained. They may also be imported across platforms. For swatch libraries copied from the Mac to Windows, be sure to add the file name extension .AI.

✦ Although color profile files cannot be exchanged across the two platforms, both the Mac and Windows InDesign versions retain color-profile information from the other platform's files. And if both platforms have color profiles for the same device (monitor, scanner, printer, and so forth), InDesign applies the correct color profiles. If a color profile is not available on the new platform, you can apply a new profile or ignore the issue. (If you ignore this issue, the correct profile will be in place when you bring the document back to the original platform.) If you print with a missing profile, InDesign substitutes the default profile based on the type of color model used (RGB or CMYK).

✦ Styles are retained. They may also be imported across platforms.

✦ Hyphenation and spelling exceptions are retained. These files use a file name extension on both the Mac and in Windows: .NOT for hyphenation additions, .UDC for spelling additions.

✦ Document preferences are retained, but the InDesign Defaults file cannot be shared across platforms.

✦ Plug-ins must be present on both platforms if you are moving documents that use specific plug-ins' features.

Which elements don't transfer

Adobe has removed most barriers between Mac and Windows in InDesign. Only the following elements cannot be moved across platforms:

✦ Shortcut sets

✦ Color profiles

✦ The InDesign Defaults preferences file

✦ Scripts

Platform differences

Windows and Macintosh systems have some general differences that add a few bumps along the road to cross-platform exchange.

File names

The most noticeable difference between Windows and the Macintosh is the file-naming convention. Macintosh files follow these rules:

✦ Names are limited to 31 characters.

✦ Any character may be used except for colons (:), which are used by the Macintosh system software internally to separate the folder name (which is not visible onscreen) from the file name.

✦ Case does not matter: "FILE," "file," and "File" are all considered to be the same name. If you have a file named "FILE" and create or copy a file named "file," "FILE" is overwritten.

Windows files follow these rules:

✦ Names are limited to 250 characters.

✦ Names must also have a file extension of up to 4 characters, which is almost always added automatically by programs to identify the file type. A period separates the file name from the extension: File Name.ext. Windows hides these file extensions from view, unless you use the View option in View ⇨ Options in a drive or folder window to make Windows display them.

✦ Names may use any characters except for most punctuation: pipes (|), colons (:), periods (.), asterisks (*), double quotes ("), less-than symbols (<), greater-than symbols (>), question marks (?), slashes (/), and backslashes (\), which are all used by Windows to separate parts of paths (file locations, such as drives and folders) or to structure commands. A period may be used as the separator between a file name and an extension.

✦ Case does not matter: "FILE," "file," and "File" are all considered to be the same name. If you have a file named "FILE" and create or copy a file named "file," "FILE" is overwritten.

When you bring Mac InDesign files and any associated graphics to Windows, you'll have to translate the Mac names into names that are legal on Windows. Similarly, you'll need to make Windows file names Mac-legal when going the other direction. This rule applies not only to InDesign documents but also to any associated files, such as graphics.

If you rename files, either before transferring or while transferring, you'll find that, within the InDesign document itself, the original names are still used. When InDesign tries to open these files, it looks for them by their original names.

The simplest way to assure that you won't have problems with transferred files looking for incompatible names is to use a naming convention that satisfies both Windows and Mac standards. That means you should:

✦ Keep file names to 26 characters.

✦ Always include the PC file extension (which adds 4 or 5 characters to the full name, hitting the Mac limit of 31). Use .INDD for documents, .INDT for templates, .INDL for libraries, .AI for swatch libraries, .NOT for hyphenation exceptions, and .UDC for spelling exceptions. Typical extensions for cross-platform graphics are .TIF for TIFF, .JPG for JPEG, .EPS for Encapsulated PostScript, .AI for Adobe Illustrator, .PCT for PICT, .PCX for PC Paintbrush, .BMP and .RLE for Microsoft bitmap, .MAC or .PNT for MacPaint, .GIF for Graphics Interchange Format, .WMF for Windows metafile, .SCT or .CT for Scitex, and .PSD for Adobe Photoshop.

✦ Don't use the pipe (|), colon (:), period (.), asterisk (*), double quote ("), less-than symbol (<), greater-than symbol (>), question mark (?), slash (/), or backslash (\) characters.

Font differences

Although the major typeface vendors such as Adobe Systems and Bitstream offer their typefaces for both Windows and Macintosh users, these typefaces are not always the same on both platforms. Cross-platform differences are especially common among typefaces created a few years ago, when multiplatform compatibility was not a goal for most users or vendors.

Differences occur in four areas:

✦ The internal font name—the one used by the printer and type scalers such as Adobe Type Manager—is not quite the same for the Mac and Windows version of a typeface. This discrepancy results in an alert box listing the fonts used in the document that are not on your computer. The solution is to use the Find/Replace dialog box (covered in Chapter 10) to replace all instances of the unrecognized font name with the correct one for the current platform.

✦ Even if typefaces use the same internal names, the font files' tracking, kerning, and other character width information may be different on the two platforms, possibly resulting in text reflow. The solution is to check the ends of all your columns, pages, and stories to make sure text did not get shorter or longer.

✦ Symbols do not always translate properly. Even when created by the same vendors, the character maps for each font file differ across platforms because Windows and the Macintosh use different character maps. This problem is complicated by the fact that some vendors didn't stick to the standard character maps for any platform or don't implement all symbols in all their typefaces. The solution is to proofread your documents, note the symbols that are incorrect, and then use the Find/Change dialog box to replace them with the correct symbol. (Highlight the incorrect symbol and use the copy and paste commands to put it in the Text field of the Find/Change dialog box rather than trying to figure out the right keypad code in Windows or the right keyboard shortcut on the Mac.)

✦ Ligatures are supported only on the Mac (Windows doesn't support ligatures at all). Windows InDesign uses just the regular fi, fl, ffi, and ffl letter combinations, and Mac InDesign can substitute the ligatures (fi , fl , ffi , and ffl) if you bring the file to the Mac.

Tip   To minimize font problems, use a program such as Macromedia's Fontographer or Pyrus FontLab (a demo version is included on the CD-ROM that accompanies this book) to translate your TrueType and PostScript files from Mac to Windows format or vice versa. (Fontographer and FontLab are available in both Mac and Windows versions.) This ensures that the internal font names, width information, and symbols are the same on both platforms.

Cross-Reference   See Chapter 16 for more information on fonts, and Chapter 18 for more information on special characters.

Transfer methods

Moving files between Macs and Windows PCs is easier now than ever before, thanks to a selection of products on both platforms that let each machine read the other's disks (floppies, removable disks such as Zip disks, and even hard drives). Here is a brief summary of the major products:

✦ **File Exchange.** This control panel included in the Mac OS lets you use Windows disks in a Mac floppy drive or removable drive and lets the Mac recognize files immediately and know which applications are compatible with each type of PC file. File Exchange also can automatically add the right Mac icon and file-type information to a Windows file transferred to the Mac based on the Windows file's extension.

✦ **MacLinkPlus, from DataViz** (203/268-0030, www.dataviz.com). This Mac utility includes file translation (DataViz's own translators). The version called MacLinkPlus/PC Connect includes a serial cable through which you can connect a Mac to a PC (making sort of a two-computer network). In Windows, DataViz's Conversions Plus gives PCs the ability to read and write Mac disks. The MacOpener program lets Macs read PC disks, although it includes none of the file-translation features of the other DataViz products. (A demo version of MacOpener is included on the CD-ROM that accompanies this book.)

✦ **MacDrive 98, from Media4 Productions** (800/528-7440, www.media4.com), is similar to DataViz's MacOpener in that it lets Windows 98 and NT 4.0 PCs open, read, write, and format Mac disks. (A demo version of MacDrive 98 is included on the CD-ROM that accompanies this book.)

Another method of transferring files is to use a cross-platform network — if you are using one:

✦ **Miramar Systems' PC MacLAN** (805/966-2432, www.miramarsys.com) lets a Windows PC be a server to Macs and other PCs via an Ethernet or TCP/IP network. It also lets a Windows PC be accessed on a Mac network. In both cases, it matches Windows file extensions with Mac icons, so files transferred between the two platforms have the expected icons. (Demo versions of PC MacLAN are included on the CD-ROM that accompanies this book.)

✦ **Thursby Software Systems' Dave** (817/478-5070, www.thursby.com) is software for the Mac that makes a Mac appear as a PC to a Windows server, using the TCP/IP network protocol.

✦ **Netopia's Timbuktu Pro** (510/814-5000, www.netopia.com) lets both Macs and PCs exchange files — as well as lets users chat electronically and even view and control each other's screens for collaborative work — via a TCP/IP- or AppleTalk-based Ethernet or Internet network. (A demo version of Timbuktu Pro is included on the CD-ROM that accompanies this book.)

✦ Windows NT Server includes a utility called **MacFile** that lets you designate specific directories on the server that Macs can access. (Note that this utility is not installed by default — you must select it as an option during installation of network services.) This is fine when you want the NT server to hold shared files, such as images, fonts, InDesign templates, shared InDesign projects, and so on. MacFile does not let the NT system access any Macs on the network.

✦ For larger networks, you'll likely want to use networks based on the TCP/IP protocol and on Ethernet wiring, using a server operating system such as Unix; you'll need a consultant or in-house network manager to set up such large networks.

The Macintosh assigns a hidden creator and file type attribute to each file; these hidden attributes tell it which icon to display for the file and which program to launch if you double-click the file. Windows files have no such hidden attributes, so they appear as either SimpleText or PC binary files when you move them to the Mac. To load these files into InDesign (or other Mac applications), you must first load your application and then use File ⇨ Open, or ⌘+O.

File Exchange, MacLinkPlus, Conversions Plus, MacOpener, MacDrive 98, Timbuktu Pro, Dave, and PC MacLAN all can be set to create these hidden attributes automatically based on the Windows file's extension, as well as to add the Windows file extension based on the Mac creator and file type. This means that you can double-click the transferred files to open them. Figure 37-2 shows a sample extension map in PC MacLAN and in the Mac OS's File Exchange.

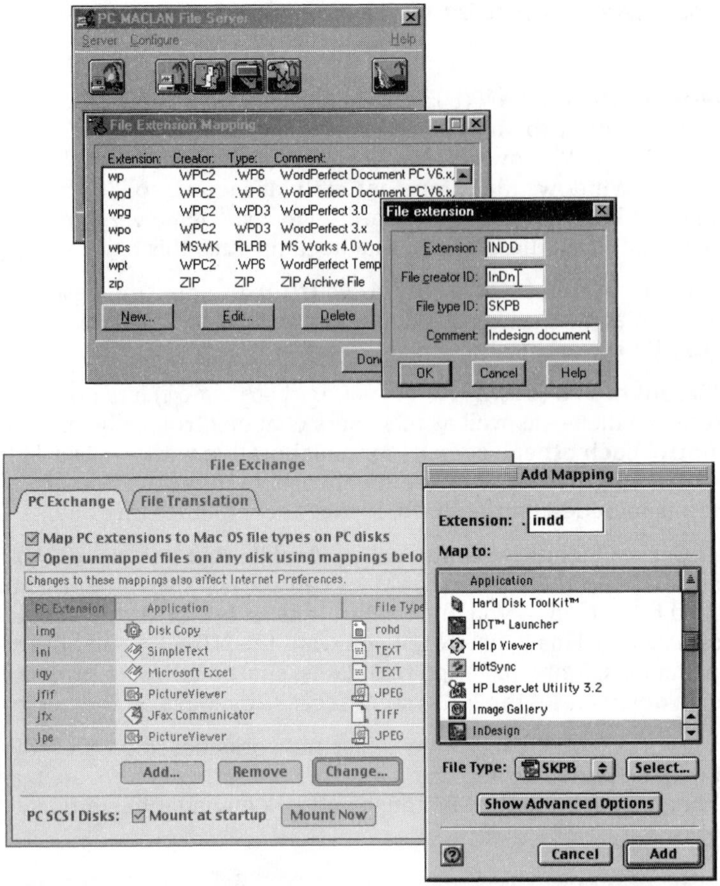

Figure 37-2: The file-extension mapping features in PC MacLAN
(top) and Apple File Exchange (bottom).

Most of these programs detect the file type and creator type when you add a file to
the extension map. But just in case, here are the file types for InDesign components:

+ **Documents:** InDn is the creator type, SKPB is the file type, and .INDD is
the extension.

+ **Templates:** InDn is the creator type, SKPB is the file type, and .INDT is
the extension.

+ **Libraries:** InDn is the creator type, InDl is the file type, and .INDL is
the extension.

✦ **Swatch libraries:** ART5 is the creator type, TEXT is the file type, and .AI is the extension.

✦ **Standard spelling and related dictionaries:** InDn is the creator type, .InDx is the file type, and .HYP, .LEX, .ENV, and .CLX are the extensions.

✦ **Spelling exceptions:** InDn is the creator type, .InDu is the file type, and .UDC is the extension.

✦ **Hyphenation exceptions:** InDn is the creator type, .InDu is the file type, and .NOT is the extension.

Caution　Proper capitalization is critical for file and creator types, but not for file name extensions.

Summary

When working with other users, you can share preferences by copying or making aliases to just one InDesign Defaults file, ensuring that all users have the same preferences. But the InDesign Defaults file is not compatible across platforms, so Windows users cannot use a Mac user's file or vice versa.

Except for shortcut sets, color profiles, the InDesign Defaults preferences file, plug-ins, and scripts, cross-platform users can share InDesign support documents. Otherwise, sharing file between PC and Mac users is very simple, thanks to a variety of disk- and network-based utilities now available for both platforms.

✦　　✦　　✦

Using Plug-Ins

The InDesign team engineered the software to be *extensible* — meaning you can extend its capabilities by adding more software. To do this, you use plug-ins, which are small software modules, often developed by third parties. If you're a Photoshop user, you might be familiar with plug-ins such as Kai's Power Tools; or if you're a QuarkXPress user, you're probably familiar with the concept of add-on software through XTensions. Even if you're new to publishing, you may have purchased add-on software for your operating system, such as a custom screen saver or virus-protection software.

Extensible programs solve the one-size-fits-all nature of most software, letting you customize your tools to your workflow. If InDesign doesn't meet a need of yours — say, indexing, table editing, or imposition — you can look for a plug-in that does. Although InDesign is in its infancy, many well-known QuarkXPress XTension developers and Photoshop plug-in developers were working on InDesign plug-ins before InDesign was even released. As InDesign grows up, more plug-ins are likely to become available.

Using the Default Plug-Ins

Many core features in InDesign are actually implemented through plug-ins. When you launch the application, you may notice the words "Caching plug-ins" on the InDesign startup screen — this is when the plug-ins load. Structuring the software this way lets Adobe update or modify a finite area of the software, and then distribute a new plug-in, rather than updating and distributing the entire application. It's a good idea to go to the Adobe Web site (www.adobe.com) periodically to look for both fixes and new plug-ins.

The default plug-ins are stored in a folder called Plug-ins inside your InDesign application folder. If you open the Plug-ins folder, as shown in Figure 38-1, you'll notice that the plug-ins have been consolidated into special-purpose folders such as Filters and Text. You should leave the default plug-ins alone, for the most part.

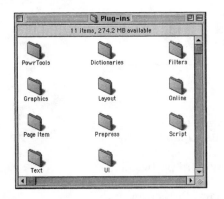

Figure 38-1: The InDesign Plug-ins folder stores the default plug-ins, as well as additional plug-ins you may install.

Caution   QuarkXPress users might be accustomed to removing XTensions to reduce launch time and consume less RAM. *Don't use this technique with InDesign.* Many core features of the application — such as the text handling — are implemented through plug-ins, and the program may not work at all if you remove required plug-ins.

Purchasing Special-Purpose Plug-Ins

With the backing of software and publishing giant Adobe, InDesign has enticed a variety a proven developers to create special-purpose plug-ins.

For example, A Lowly Apprentice Production, which made its name creating QuarkXPress XTensions and also develops Photoshop plug-ins, will release ShadowCaster and Imposer for InDesign. Because InDesign doesn't provide a feature for creating printer spreads or printer flats, this low-priced plug-in will be welcomed by many InDesign users, especially service bureaus and printers.

Another noticeable omission in InDesign, the lack of indexing, is solved by Virginia Systems' InDex plug-in. Other plug-ins focus on special types of publishing, such as Em Software's InData for database publishing.

Although the number of plug-ins for InDesign may be somewhat limited in the beginning, as the user base grows the number of plug-ins available is sure to grow as well. Once the user base figures out what small, daily problems InDesign can't handle, the plug-in developers should jump in with answers.

Most plug-in developers provide a free evaluation copy so you can try before you buy. This is important, so you can figure out if the plug-in really solves your problem, whether everyone in your workgroup will need it, and whether your service bureau will need it as well. One place to start looking for plug-ins is www.pluginsource.com, which sells Adobe plug-ins from many developers. Or check the individual Web sites of the current plug-in developers:

- ✦ A Lowly Apprentice Production: www.alap.com
- ✦ Cascade Systems: www.cascadenet.com
- ✦ Em Software: www.emsoftware.com
- ✦ Extensis: www.extensis.com
- ✦ Gannett: www.gannett.com
- ✦ HexMac Software Systems: www.hexmac.com
- ✦ LizardTech: www.lizardtech.com
- ✦ Managing Editor: www.maned.com
- ✦ Mapsoft Computer Services: www.mapsoft.com
- ✦ Pantone: www.pantone.com
- ✦ PowrTools Software: www.powrtools.com
- ✦ ShadeTree Marketing: www.borderguys.com
- ✦ Ultimate Technographics: www.ultimate-tech.com
- ✦ Virginia Systems: www.virginiasystems.com

Using Plug-ins

To use a new plug-in, the first task is install it. Many plug-ins include their own installers that search out your copy of InDesign and plant themselves in the Plug-ins folder. Figure 38-2 shows the installer for the PowrTable plug-in, which lets you create editable tables in documents. If a plug-in doesn't include an installer or installation instructions, you can probably try dragging it into the Plug-ins folder. Once a plug-in is in the correct location, you need to restart InDesign so the plug-in is recognized and its code is loaded. You cannot use a new plug-in if it's installed while InDesign is running — you should always quit the application before changing anything in the Plug-ins folder and then restarting.

Figure 38-2: The PowrTable installer places a PowrTools folder inside the Plug-ins folder.

If a plug-in cannot load with InDesign, an alert appears while the application is starting up. Usually, loading errors result from incompatible versions of InDesign and the plug-in. Check the plug-in's ReadMe file or contact the developer for assistance. To remove a plug-in, simply drag it out of the subfolder of the Plug-ins folder and store it someplace else. (You might create a folder called Disabled Plug-ins in which to store plug-ins that you're not using.)

When a plug-in is loaded with InDesign, new controls appear in the interface. You might see entire menus, menu commands, dialog boxes, panes, palettes, and tools added to the application by a plug-in. No matter the combination of interface elements, when you're using the features of a plug-in, it should look and feel as if you're using InDesign. Some plug-ins will meet this criterion, and others will not.

For example, the PowrTables plug-in adds a tool to the Toolbox, as shown in Figure 38-3. Although it leaves a gap in the Toolbox, the tool is consistent with other tools, even including a ToolTip and keyboard shortcut of B.

Figure 38-3: The PowrTable Tool in the InDesign Toolbox, along with its ToolTip and keyboard shortcut.

Once you click and drag to draw a table, the New Table dialog box shown in Figure 38-4 lets you specify the number of rows and columns, the gutter width, the width and color of borders, and the fill. Looks like InDesign — so far, so good.

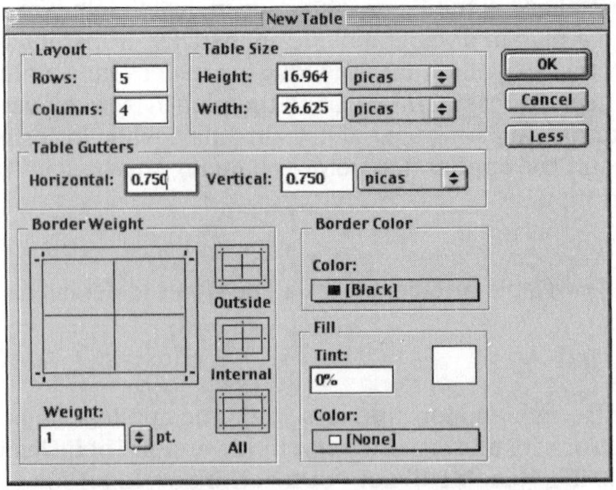

Figure 38-4: The PowrTable plug-in's New Table dialog box.

Here's where things get a little weird. Once you've created the table and you're ready to start working with it, you're no longer in InDesign. As shown in Figure 38-5, the menu bar has changed, no longer displaying InDesign options but instead displaying only PowrTable options. The plug-in works in two distinct modes, one that lets you edit tables and one that lets you edit the remainder of the document. While in table mode, you can use two powerful palettes to modify the tables. This is not the most seamless integration, but the developer may have had a good reason. (In this case, the tables actually display in the InDesign document as EPS files, indicating that the table cells are not of a type that InDesign can recognize and thus must be handled by an external program.)

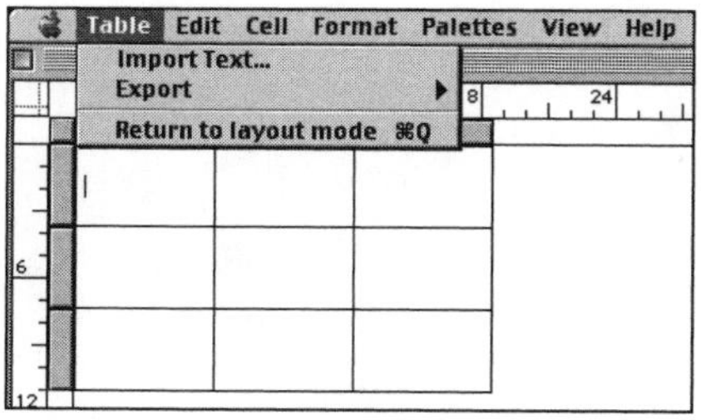

Figure 38-5: PowrTable's menu bar replaces the InDesign menu bar when you're in table mode.

In some cases, plug-ins may add objects or information to documents that can be recognized only when the plug-in is loaded. If the plug-in is missing, you may not be able to open the document, or the document may look different. If it turns out that a plug-in is required to open a document or preserve information, you'll need to ensure that each member of a workgroup and your service bureau owns the same plug-in.

Summary

Plug-ins are software modules that serve two purposes in InDesign: incorporating core features into the application and adding special functions. Plug-ins are stored in the Plug-ins folder within the application folder — and the default plug-ins should not be removed, especially while InDesign is running. Many established developers of QuarkXPress XTensions and Photoshop plug-ins have developed or are developing InDesign plug-ins to provide additional features such as table editing and imposition. Developers should design their plug-ins to integrate smoothly into the InDesign interface. When purchasing and using plug-ins, consider whether other users of your workgroup and your service bureau will need the plug-in as well.

✦   ✦   ✦

The Right Toolkit

InDesign by itself doesn't do anything — you need to work with it in the context of a computer, add-on hardware, other software, and of course the operating system of your Mac or PC. And once you have the equipment and platform that's right for you, you need to learn to make the most of it.

This chapter gives you the basic information you need to get the right equipment and to get started on your platform of choice. However, we do recommend that you pick up more detailed books on the Mac OS, Windows, PCs, and/or Macs; the publisher of this book, IDG Books Worldwide, has several good books for beginners (the *For Dummies* series) and for more experienced users (the *Bible* and *Secrets* series).

Note We assume most readers have used a computer, so the chapter starts with the more technical issues and concludes with a primer on using the Mac or Windows for new users. Moderately experienced users can use those sections to get new tips and as a refresher.

Recommended Equipment

Computer hardware and software seems to change by the minute, so keep in mind that our specific recommendations are based on what was available in summer 1999. But even with the pace of change, you can feel confident in our recommendations — and if there's a newer, faster version of something we recommend, and it's worth your money, go ahead and substitute it for our recommendations.

The computer

Computers have gotten so fast in recent years that they've outpaced users' needs. Pentium III-based PCs running at 500MHz, 600MHz, and faster are overkill for most professionals. Ditto for Power Macs using 450MHz, 500MHz, or faster PowerPC 750s (the G3 chip).

But, InDesign is a program that does require more horsepower than you might expect. We found it noticeably slower than other page-layout programs. The reason is its new architecture, which breaks the program into dozens of separate modules that must communicate with each other. This communication can cause delays of several seconds when opening dialog boxes or switching palettes or even selecting text. The beauty of this architecture is that with the right plug-in software you can add almost any capability to InDesign (see Chapter 38).

So, while you may not need the absolute fastest computer, do get the fastest one you can afford. For Mac users, we recommend a 300MHz or faster Power Mac G3 system (and a G4 wouldn't hurt); if you're using anything slower, consider an upgrade. For PC users, try to have a 400MHz or faster Pentium II system, or consider an upgrade. Of course, In Design will run on slower systems, but if you're doing a lot of complex work—such as for magazines and newspapers—you'll really want the faster speed.

> **Tip**   Many Macs and PCs are upgradable, so you don't have to always replace one to get a real speed boost. For example, some Macs accept accelerator cards that add a new processor. On the PC side, upgrades are more universal—practically any PC can accept a faster Pentium, which costs anywhere from $300 to $600, depending on speed, and if your PC isn't upgradable, a new motherboard adds less than $200 more to the upgrade cost.

Storage capacity

The best upgrades you can give yourself are usually more RAM (memory) and more storage capacity.

Memory

Adding RAM lets the computer work more efficiently, and you'll want 32 megabytes (MB) as a bare minimum (if you work with just one program at a time). Better for publishers is 64MB, and more than that is better if you are doing complex work on large files in Adobe Photoshop as well (128MB is typical for such users). Because RAM is so cheap, it's better to add more than to skimp.

> If you're using Windows NT, add 16MB to the recommended RAM amounts.

Hard drives

Programs and files eat through disk space, so these days, a 1-gigabyte (GB) drive (which holds about a billion characters) is considered small. Look for 4GB or more. Fortunately, most new Macs and PCs have at least 4GB, and often as much as 10GB. Disk storage is cheap, so load up. And remember that you can add hard drives to your Mac or PC—you don't have to replace your existing one in most cases.

Removable media

If you work with others or with service bureaus, you'll probably need to invest in an Iomega Zip drive, a $100–$150 device that uses 100MB cartridges that cost about $15 each. Most service bureaus have adopted these drives, replacing the SyQuest drives that had been standard. (Of course, most still support SyQuest cartridges, but the company that made them is out of business and those drives and their cartridges were also costlier.) Get an IDE (PC-only) or SCSI Zip drive — the parallel (PC-only) and USB versions are much slower.

Note You might consider a 250MB version of the Zip drive, because it reads and writes the 100MB format, but unless your service bureau or whomever you exchange data with intends to get one as well, you don't need to pay for its higher cost.

Also invest in a tape drive — prices range from $100 to $1,000 depending on the capacity, with the bulk under $400. These drives back up your system on inexpensive tapes, saving your work in case your hard drive gets damaged. If you're making a living from your computer, don't put that living at risk.

Tape backup is slow, so many people are looking at other removable media instead, such as the Iomega Jaz drives, which have 2GB cartridges, or recordable CD drives (CD-R and CD-RW), which use 650MB CDs. (They cost about $500.) Rewritable media such as Jaz and CD-RW are great for very large projects — particularly if you use them as surrogate hard drives and have everything you need on them, such as programs, fonts, and files. But these gizmos typically make sense only if you're working on very large projects with other people who aren't connected to you by a network. You'll also spend anywhere from about $40 for CD-RW media to $200 for a Jaz cartridge. CD-R is great because the media cost can be as low as $1, but they are not rewritable — they're better for archiving or for sending materials to coworkers or service bureaus to copy to their systems.

Connectivity

Publishing professionals don't work alone, so getting the right connectivity tools is key.

Networks

If you're in a workgroup, such as in a design department or service bureau or small consultancy, an essential component is a network.

At the very least, you want peer-to-peer networks, in which your Macs and PCs are connected to each other so they can share files. Both the Mac and Windows have this capability built in, and several programs let Macs and PCs connect to each other. Miramar Systems' PC MacLAN lets PCs join Mac-based networks, as does COPS's COPSTalk. They cost about $200 per person. Similarly, and at a comparable price, Thursby Software Systems' Dave lets Macs join Windows NT-based networks. (A demo version of PC MacLAN is included on the CD-ROM that accompanies this book.)

You'll likely want an Ethernet network. Ethernet is a kind of wiring, and it's pretty fast yet inexpensive. Most new Macs have Ethernet connectors built in, and so do a lot of PCs. For those that don't, the cost is $50 to $100 per computer for the needed card or adapter box. Macs also have a networking style called LocalTalk that is slower and cheaper (about $20 per computer for the required connector boxes). You can use both LocalTalk and Ethernet, although you need to tell the Mac to switch back and forth. We recommend you stick with Ethernet, using LocalTalk only if you have a printer that is not Ethernet-compatible (such as a color ink-jet printer).

Tip   Ethernet comes in two speeds — 10Mbps (called 10BaseT) and 100Mbps (called 100BaseT and also called Fast Ethernet). If you're sharing lots of 100MB-plus files, you'll want the faster Ethernet. Be sure, though, to get a dual-speed hub (the box that all the Ethernet cables plug into), so your older, 10Mbps devices (like most printers) can work on the same network as the faster devices.

Disk Exchange

For disk exchange, DataViz's MacOpener and Media4 Productions' MacDrive 98 read Mac disks (floppies, Zips, SyQuests, and so on); they cost about $75 per person. On the Macintosh, the built-in File Exchange control panel in Mac OS 8.5 and later lets Macs read PC disks.

Modem

You'll also want a modem, for sending and receiving files, connecting to the Internet to get program updates, and for use as a fax:

✦ Get 56 kilobits per second (Kbps) speed — the de facto standard. Prices range from $50 to $150, with Mac models usually costing at least $100. If it's available in your area, consider DSL (Digital Subscriber Line), a new technology that provides modem speeds of about 200Kbps to 1,000Kbps (the speed varies based on your telephone company's implementation). Access fees are as low as $50 a month. You'll need a special modem, which costs about $250.

✦ Another option is a cable modem, which works through your cable TV if your area has digital cable service. Prices are usually the same as for DSL. But note that cable modems have several drawbacks:

  • You rarely are wired for cable in your office or home office (and office buildings usually can't get cable service added).

- You usually have to use the cable company's Internet service provider, adding cost.

- Your computer may be exposed to others — cable modems put entire neighborhoods on the equivalent of one line, letting everyone get to the contents of everyone else's computer, unless you have enabled password protection on your PC or Mac. Make sure you know how to protect your system from outsiders if you use a cable modem.

Platform Difference

Mac users may find that their phone company won't install cable or DSL modems on a Macintosh. There's no compatibility problem, just that they're unfamiliar with Macs. A good resource is `www.macfixit.com`.

Output and input

Layouts may exist in electronic form on your computer or network, but the content in them likely comes from the outside, and to publish your work, you'll need to output your results.

Laser printer

Invest in a good printer. Whether you're in a home office or in a large business, you'll want a black-and-white laser printer that is capable of 600-dots-per-inch (dpi) output. Older printers support 300-dpi output, which is acceptable but not as sharp when it comes to printing text and images.

If you work in an office, you can buy one or two fast network printers (16 pages per minute [ppm] or faster) and share them. Such printers cost between $2,000 and $6,000 each, such as the Hewlett-Packard LaserJet 5si. They can hold lots of paper and often several sizes of paper.

If you work alone, not too many affordable laser printers are available; look for one that prints between 6 ppm (a minimum) and 10 ppm. Consider getting a refurbished printer, such as the workhorse LaserJet 4MV, especially if it has Ethernet built-in (Ethernet is an expensive option for personal laser printers).

Note

You want a PostScript Level 2-capable printer, because that's the language that all professional output devices, such as imagesetters, use. (InDesign requires Level 2 or later if you're using PostScript.)

Platform Difference

Printers aimed at Mac owners almost always have PostScript, while printers aimed at PC owners usually do not. Mac-oriented printers almost always work with PCs, so PC owners will find it easier to get PostScript by looking at Mac-oriented printers than looking at PC-oriented printers. In fact, most work with both at the same time — you can have Macs and PCs plugged into them or connected via a network, and use them simultaneously.

Ink-jet printer

Consider also getting an inexpensive color ink-jet printer, such as an Epson Color Stylus. They cost between $180 and $500, and provide glorious color output. They're too slow for most printing, but if you're doing color work and want to get cheap color proofs occasionally—or do low-volume color printing yourself— they're a great deal and very convenient. Note that most of these do not support PostScript, so you won't get as detailed output for many images. Also note that they may not work well on a network (even the networkable models), so you may need to get several and dedicate them to specific computers.

InDesign supports only a limited number of non-PostScript printers (most ink-jets don't use PostScript) in Windows and none on Macintosh. This limits most people's ability to generate color comps or proofs to expensive color laser printers, some pricey ink-jets that have PostScript, and some exotic color printing technologies such as thermal wax. If you want to proof on a non-PostScript ink-jet printer or on a high-end non-PostScript color proofer, you'll need Adobe's $149 PressReady software (see Chapter 33 for details).

Scanner

One device that has become very affordable is a color scanner. No matter what brand you buy, at their low prices and great quality, scanners are almost a requirement to own, even in a home office. They also can double as occasional-use copy machines or fax machines—you scan in a paper document and then print it to your printer or fax it from your modem. (You'll still want a dedicated fax machine for a busy home or small office.)

Tip

Umax Technologies' Astra line is inexpensive ($200 to $500) yet has color quality that approaches that of a professional scanner costing several thousand dollars. They have models for both Macs and PCs (a SCSI model works on both, if your PC has a SCSI card; a USB model can work on both if your Mac and PC are new enough to have USB ports).

Note

Service bureaus, creative-services departments, and other higher-end users will find scanners such as the Astra fine for basic work, but will want more expensive equipment if producing glossy magazines and catalogs.

Digital camera

Digital cameras are popular, but their image quality isn't up to snuff for print publishing (unless your laser printer is your final printing device) or unless you're using one of the new megapixel models. For Web publishing, however, even older digital cameras are fine, and using them is more convenient than having your 35mm film processed and scanned in, or processed and saved to CD-ROM format.

Odds and ends

There sometimes seems to be no limit in how you can accessorize a computer. We'll leave the toys and fashion accessories to you, but some add-ons are must-haves for any professional publisher.

CD-ROM or DVD-ROM

Every computer now comes with a CD-ROM drive, which is great, because it makes software installation a snap (no more floppy shuffle!). If your computer doesn't have a CD-ROM drive, invest $100 or so in one—you don't need anything faster than 4× speed, so don't pay more for a top-speed model. You can also use a DVD-ROM drive in place of a CD-ROM drive.

On the PC, look for the new multiread format when buying a CD-ROM drive, because it can read most CD formats, including CD-RW. The multiread option is not available on the Mac.

Mouse and pen

Consider getting a multibutton mouse. The extra buttons can save you strain on your hands and arms by being used for common operations such as dragging and double-clicking. For Mac OS users, a multibutton mouse lets you assign the awkward Control+click combination to a mouse button—use the right-hand mouse button to simulate the right-clicking in Windows. We advise both Mac and Windows users to get a three- or four-button mouse (or trackball, if that's your fancy); Kensington Microware and Logitech both offer good models for both platforms.

If you use the Web a lot, consider a mouse that has a scroll wheel, which lets you scroll through Web pages and other programs rather than click scroll icons.

Unfortunately, scroll-wheel mice are not yet available for Macs.

A pen-based tablet makes sense if you're also doing illustration work, but consider that a secondary input device, not a primary one.

Essential software

The hardware is half the battle. The other half is the software you use to do your creative work.

Plug-Ins

You'll probably want add-on programs, known as *plug-ins*, for InDesign that extend its capabilities. Chapter 38 covers these in more detail.

Art tools

Consider having an image editor (we recommend Adobe Photoshop on both Macintosh and Windows) and an illustration program (CorelDraw, Adobe Illustrator, and Macromedia FreeHand are all good and cross-platform, although each is different, so try them out first to see what feels best to you).

Font tools

You definitely want the $70 Adobe Type Manager (ATM), a utility that manages your fonts for you, even loading fonts that your document needs but are loaded when you start up your computer. On the Mac, the free companion Adobe Type Reunion (ATR) utility is also a must to streamline the list of fonts that appear on your menus (without it each version of a font, such as bold and italic, appears as a separate item).

Don't forget to get lots of fonts — you can never have enough, and so many interesting yet useful ones exist. More and more programs come with free fonts (all the image-editing and illustration programs mentioned earlier do, for example), so building a font collection is not nearly as expensive as it used to be. You can also get decent quality, special-purpose fonts on the Web at computer magazine Web sites, such as `www.publish.com`, as well as on the Desktop Publishing forum on CompuServe (the command is GO DTP).

Editing tool

You'll need a word-processing program. Use Microsoft Word or Corel WordPerfect, per your personal preference.

Web tools

If you're publishing to the Web, you'll need an HTML editor, such as Adobe's GoLive or SoftQuad's HotMetal Pro. You'll also need Adobe Acrobat to create PDF files. Finally, you'll want a Web browser — Microsoft's free Internet Explorer or America Online's free Netscape Navigator or Communicator — to both preview any Web pages you create and to get you to the Web for research and perhaps e-mail exchange.

Compression tools

Files are always too big, so compression utilities are a must. On the Mac, there's no substitute for StuffIt Deluxe, a $50 utility package that creates and decodes both Mac StuffIt files and PC .ZIP files, as well as several Internet compression formats. On Windows, the equivalent is the $30 shareware program WinZip, from Niko Mac Computing. The free Aladdin Expander for Windows is also useful for decompressing StuffIt and .ZIP files. Demo versions of StuffIt Deluxe and WinZip, as well as a full version of Aladdin Expander, are included on the CD-ROM that accompanies this book.

System utilities

Mac owners will want Connectix's Speed Doubler and RAM Doubler software (about $100 if sold together), which really do increase the amount of memory available and make your Mac work faster. Windows does much of this work itself, so no comparable utilities for the PC are worthwhile.

Printer drivers

InDesign is designed to use Adobe's PostScript language, and its newer PostScript drivers. You'll need AdobePS 8.6 or later on the Macintosh, Adobe PS 4.3 or later for Windows 98, and Adobe PS 5.1 or later for Windows NT 4. The InDesign CD-ROM comes with these drivers, so you don't have to buy anything extra. But be sure to install them. Also make sure that when you install other software, such as Adobe Acrobat or Illustrator, that you don't accidentally overwrite them with an older version of the driver — do a custom installation and uncheck the driver software if its version number is lower than that required by InDesign.

Caution

We found AdobePS 8.6 for Macintosh could crash during printing in a way that made it impossible to restart the Mac. (That's why you may want to use the standard Apple LaserWriter driver when printing from programs other than InDesign.) No matter what type of computer you use, one problem using the latest software is that not all other software and hardware you may have is compatible with it, at least not until they are revised. Be sure to check with your service bureau and test out such drivers before installing them across your company or client base. (If you encounter a crash that prevents your Mac from starting, you'll need to delete the AdobePS extension to be able to start the Mac. Do so by holding the Shift key during startup, and then go to the Extensions folder in the System Folder, move the AdobePS file to the trash can, and then restart. You'll need to reinstall the driver from the InDesign CD-ROM or other CD-ROM containing it.)

Favorite Shareware Utilities

Everyone has his or her favorite shareware utilities — programs sold for just a few dollars or given away — so we thought we'd share ours. On the book's bundled CD-ROM, we've included several free or demo versions of these shareware utilities. Please be sure to register and pay for the ones you use.

Macintosh

✦ The $20 NameCleaner from Sig Software translates PC files into Mac format, and vice versa.

✦ The $35 GraphicsConverter from Thorsten Lemke does just what its name says: translate graphics from one format to another. It supports a wide range of PC, Mac, and even Unix file formats.

Continued

(continued)

✦ PopChar Pro, a $39 program from Günther Blaschek that displays all available characters for the current font, so you can easily add special characters to your document. Its icon stays in the Mac's menu, so it's always accessible. We prefer it over the KeyCaps program that comes with the Mac.

✦ StuffIt Expander, a $50 utility from Aladdin Systems that decompresses all sorts of compressed files, including those widely used in Windows, on the Macintosh, and on the Web.

✦ ZipIt, a $15 utility from Tom Brown that lets Macs decompress the Zip compressed file format popular on PCs.

Windows

✦ PowerToys, a free but unsupported collection of Microsoft utilities from Microsoft's Web site (and on the Windows 98 CD-ROM) that enhance the interface — everything from letting audio CDs play automatically to letting you switch the monitor color depth and resolution with out restarting. The TweakUI control panel is very handy for customizing the Windows interface. Microsoft wouldn't let us include this on the CD-ROM that accompanies this book, but we thought it was worth mentioning anyhow.

✦ ShoveIt, a $15 program from Phil Hord, takes care of a flaw in Windows 98. We prefer having the Start button and menu at the top of the screen, not at the bottom. But while Windows 98 lets you move the Start button to the top, most programs don't notice that it's there, and so their menus are hidden beneath it. ShoveIt forces those other programs' menus to stay below the Start button's menu.

✦ WinZip, a $29 program from Niko Mac Computing that lets you compress and decompress files easily.

Working with Fonts

InDesign can do wonders with type in either the TrueType or PostScript Type 1 format, as well as the forthcoming OpenType format that merges TrueType and PostScript into one file. But for InDesign to see typefaces, you must install them properly. Even though Adobe Type Manager, Windows, and the Mac OS have simplified font installation, you should still know a few tricks and cautions.

For example, with PostScript fonts, the Macintosh and Windows both display fonts on the screen differently than it prints them. This means that, for your computer to print the font you see onscreen, it needs to have access to the corresponding printer font (also called an *outline font*).

Note Desktop publishing has changed the meaning of some fundamental typographic terms, which can lead to confusion. When you see the word *font* in the context of a computer, this means what a traditional typographer would call a *face* – one basic variant of a *typeface*. (In traditional typography, a *font* means a face at a particular point size, a context that digital typesetting has all but eliminated.) Thus, you'll see the word *font* used to mean, for example, Times Roman or Times Italic. A typographer would call these variants *faces*. Many people use the word *font* informally to mean *typeface*, which is the collection of related faces. Thus, your service bureau would understand the phrase "I'm using the News Gothic font in my brochure" to mean that you are using the News Gothic typeface, and that the bureau needs to ensure it downloads the whole family to the imagesetter when printing your job.

Macintosh font installation

Installing fonts on the Macintosh is a straightforward process: You install fonts by simply dragging them onto your Mac's System Folder. Keep in mind that any program that is open when you add fonts this way won't see them until you close the program and reopen it.

Note If you're using Adobe Type Manager, you don't need to drag the fonts to the System Folder – instead, you put them in any folder you like and activate them in ATM, as described later. The advantages of this approach are that you don't clutter your System Folder with fonts, and that you can more easily activate and deactivate fonts based on current project needs. Also, using ATM lets you have a large collection of fonts without having them all active at once, taking precious RAM.

 Note Either way, make sure you install both the screen fonts and the printer fonts for each PostScript font. You may have a font *suitcase* – a special font file – with several screen fonts for your PostScript font, or you may have separate files for each screen font, depending on which option the company decided to use. TrueType fonts don't come in several files – all variants are in one suitcase.

Figure 39-1 shows ATM 4.5 in action: You can simply click a font and the Activate button to activate it. For permanent activation (when you restart the Mac), drag the desired font into a font set (a group of fonts that can be activated or deactivated all at once) in the left pane and activate it there.

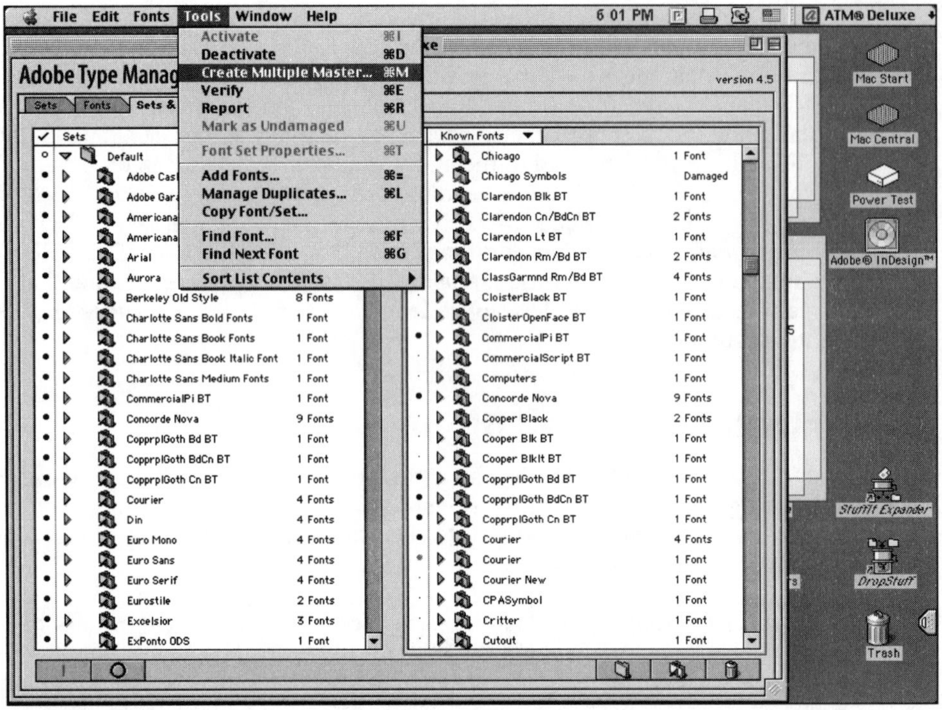

File   Edit   Fonts   **Tools**   Window   Help   6 01 PM 🖵 🖨 🖼 🖳 ☑ ATM® Deluxe ✦

Figure 39-1: Adobe Type Manager on the Mac lets you activate fonts at will and create sets of fonts to be activated at each startup.

Windows font installation

Windows does not support PostScript fonts on its own — you need Adobe Type Manager.

Separate versions of ATM are available for Windows 98 and for NT — unlike most Windows software, the same version does not work on both operating systems.

ATM finds all the fonts — TrueType and PostScript — residing on your PC and displays a list of them. To activate a font on the fly, go to the Font List pane and select the desired fonts and check the boxes to the left of their names or click the Activate button. To make fonts permanently available (after a restart), use the Sets pane to create font sets (groups of fonts that can be activated or deactivated all at once). You can add fonts from the font list to a set by using the Add Fonts pane, as shown in Figure 39-2, and dragging a font from the right pane into the sets pane at left, click the checkbox to the left of the name of the added font, or use the Activate button, and you're done.

Figure 39-2: Use Adobe Type Manager to install and manage PostScript fonts in Windows.

Steps: Adding TrueType Fonts to Windows

1. Use Start ➪ Settings to open the Control Panel, and then double-click the Fonts folder.

2. Use the menu command File ➪ Install New Font to get the Add Fonts dialog box shown in Figure 39-3.

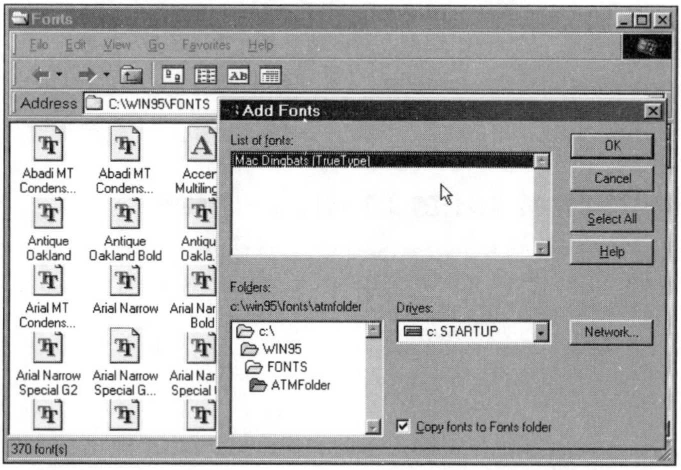

Figure 39-3: Windows has a built-in utility to install TrueType fonts.

3. Navigate the dialog box using the Folders and Drives scroll lists to get to the folder or disk that has the TrueType fonts you want to install. A list of fonts appears in the dialog box.

4. Select the fonts to install and click OK.

Use the Create Multiple Masters option that comes with Adobe Type Manager 4.0 or later, as shown in Figure 39-4. If you have installed Adobe Type Manager or Adobe's Acrobat portable-document software (which uses a version of ATM), you will have two multiple-master fonts automatically installed — Adobe Serif MM and Adobe Sans X MM. However, these fonts are designed for use only with ATM (they are what ATM uses to simulate fonts not installed on your system, so they will not show up in the editable multiple-master fonts.

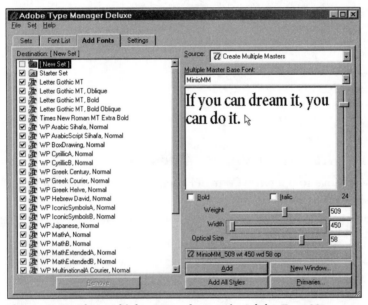

Figure 39-4: The multiple-master feature in Adobe Type Manager 4.0 for Windows.

Loading PostScript fonts to the printer

For faster printing, it's best to load PostScript fonts to printer memory. Otherwise, each time you print, your computer must load the fonts to the printer, which can be time-consuming. (TrueType fonts cannot be loaded to the printer.)

Should You Use TrueType or PostScript Fonts?

The most basic question about fonts usually is whether you should use TrueType or PostScript fonts. The answer depends on the work you do. If you produce newsletters, magazines, ads, or brochures that you output on a typesetter or imagesetter, use PostScript, because that is the standard format on these devices. If your final output is to a laser or inkjet printer, TrueType is probably the better bet because it prints faster in most cases, especially if you print to a non-PostScript printer. However, you do not have to use one font format exclusively:

✦ If you see a TrueType typeface that you want to use in your typeset document, use it — the Macintosh and Windows automatically convert TrueType fonts into PostScript format when printing to a PostScript device (or to a file designated for use by a PostScript device, such as an EPS file). This conversion process may make your files larger because the computer must download the converted TrueType font file into your document.

✦ Conversely, if you have PostScript typefaces, there's no reason to give them up if you switch to TrueType. On a PostScript printer, you can use both formats. On other printers, all you need is a program such as Adobe Type Manager to translate PostScript font files into a format the printer can use.

Don't base decisions about whether to use TrueType or PostScript fonts on assumptions about quality. Both technologies provide excellent results, so any quality differences are due to the font manufacturer's standards. If you purchase typefaces from recognized companies, you don't need to worry. (Many smaller companies produce high-quality fonts as well.)

Your Mac should have a font-loading utility (called the Apple Printer Utility; an older version is called the LaserWriter Font Utility) bundled with the system disks. Many printers come bundled with Adobe's font-loader utility (called Downloader; an old version is called SendPS). They all work basically the same way: you select the fonts you want to load and then tell the utility to do the work. Figure 39-5 shows the process in Apple Printer Utility.

 Platform Difference

Windows does not have an equivalent utility. Instead, it loads the fonts as they are used.

The one trick to loading fonts to printer memory is to not download too many. Each font takes up room in the printer memory that would otherwise go for processing your files. If you put too few fonts in printer memory, you'll waste a lot of time having your Macintosh send fonts repeatedly to the printer. But if you put too many fonts in printer memory, you'll waste a lot of time having the printer process the file under tight memory constraints, which slows it down.

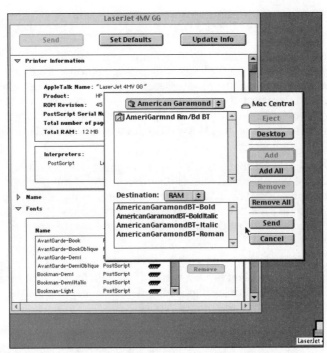

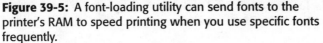

Figure 39-5: A font-loading utility can send fonts to the printer's RAM to speed printing when you use specific fonts frequently.

Tip

A good rule of thumb is to load no more than 10 fonts per megabyte of printer memory, after reserving 2MB for the printer's internal processing. For example, if your printer has 4MB of memory, download no more than 20 fonts to it. Keep in mind that *font* in this context means each distinct face, so loading the News Gothic family—News Gothic Medium, News Gothic Oblique, News Gothic Bold, and News Gothic Bold Oblique—counts as four fonts.

Another rule of thumb: Load fonts that appear on every page of your document, and let your Macintosh itself load fonts used just occasionally when it needs to (it will remove them when the print job is complete).

Note that fonts loaded to printer memory are removed from memory when you restart or shut down the printer. If you constantly use many fonts, get a printer with a built-in or external disk drive onto which you can load the fonts permanently.

The Macintosh Interface

It's been said that the Macintosh was *designed* for desktop publishing. Although that's not exactly true, one thing is certain: the Macintosh makes a near-perfect publishing platform. It handles high-end graphics with ease. It has the ability to run multiple programs simultaneously, to move elements between different documents or programs, and to work with a consistent set of tools, fonts, and device drivers.

If you are an experienced Macintosh user, you can skip the rest of this section. But if you are a relatively new Mac user who is now also using InDesign, read on for a brief review of some of the Macintosh basics you'll need to know. For a comprehensive look at Macintoshes, we recommend *Macs For Dummies* by David Pogue, *Macworld Mac Secrets, 5th Edition* by David Pogue and Joseph Schorr, *Macworld Complete Mac Handbook* by Jim Heid, and *Macworld Mac OS 8.5 Bible* by Lon Poole (all from IDG Books Worldwide).

The basic interface

When you turn on your Macintosh, the screen looks something like the screen in Figure 39-6. The Finder program, built into the Macintosh, creates this screen, which is also known as the *desktop*. In the upper-right corner is the *icon* for the computer's hard disk.

Icons

Most of the Macintosh interface is based on icons, which are small graphic illustrations that represent Mac programs, files, or functions. Icons represent applications, such as InDesign; file folders, which help you organize your hard disk by holding items such as documents and applications; disks (if you put a disk into the disk drive, a little picture of a disk appears on your desktop); and documents, including InDesign documents and those created by word-processing applications.

If an icon's label is in italics (slanted text), that means it is an alias to the original file or folder or drive; the original item exists somewhere else. The alias is a way of having items available in more than one location on your Macintosh without copying the actual item to several locations.

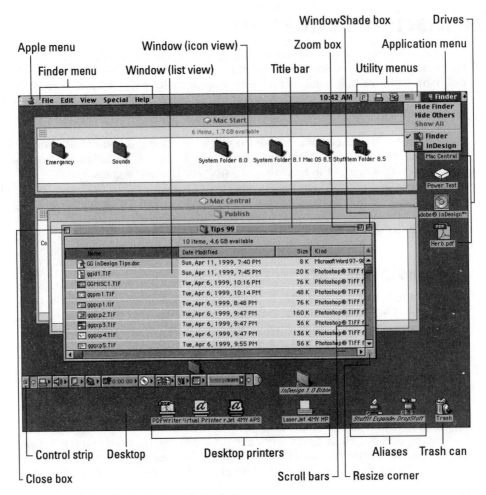

Figure 39-6: The basic Macintosh desktop.

Menus

Menus are another big part of the interface. The Mac always has a menu bar across the top of the screen, containing the commands available for the Finder or, if a program is running, for that program. As you switch among programs, the menu changes (you get a list of running programs by clicking and holding on the Application menu icon, which looks like the following symbol in Mac OS 8.x). The menu can also contain icons for programs that are always available—in Figure 39-6, you see these to the right of the menu, between the time and the application menu icon.

The Mac OS icon looks like this.

You can easily organize the contents of the Apple menu, which is a handy list of aliases to programs and other commonly used files. Just open the System Folder and then the Apple Menu Items folder. Now move, add, and remove folders and aliases (or even the original programs) as you prefer.

Across the top of the screen in Figure 39-7 is a menu bar. The menu bar includes the names of menu titles. To see a menu, you move the mouse so that the pointer appears on the menu title; then you hold the mouse button down and the menu appears.

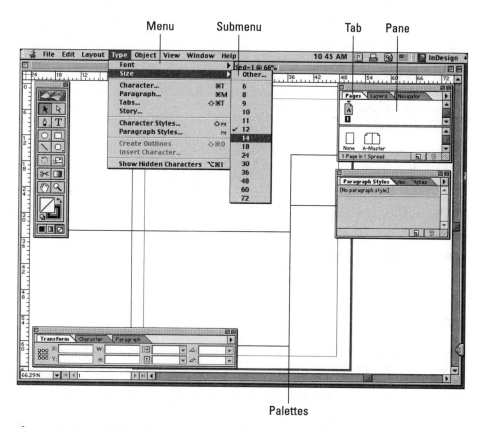

Figure 39-7: A Macintosh menu with a submenu and tabbed panes.

Note *Pointer* refers to the icon that moves on the Mac screen with the movement of the mouse. *Selecting* means using the mouse to get the pointer "on top of" something on the screen and then clicking the item (or clicking and holding the mouse button down if you are selecting a passage of text, for example). When something is selected, it reverses its appearance (white letters become black, black letters become white). You can also open something by *double-clicking* it, where you move the mouse to position it on top of the item, and click the mouse button twice with the second click immediately following the first. The difference is that double-clicking opens a document or launches a program. Single-clicking just selects it.

The names of active menu selections and menu titles are darker than inactive ones, which are lighter or "grayed out," as are some of the menu selections in Figure 39-7. An inactive menu selection is one that you can't make given the current circumstances on your Macintosh. For example, if you haven't already selected a section of text or a graphic and copied it to the Mac clipboard (by selecting Cut or Copy from the Edit menu, or using the keyboard shortcuts ⌘+X or ⌘+C, respectively), the Paste option in the edit menu is inactive because nothing exists on the clipboard to paste; if data does reside on the clipboard, the Paste command is active.

When you pull down a menu, some menu items have a keyboard shortcut listed to their right. You can use the shortcut keys to access these menu options directly, bypassing the need to select a series of menu options. An ellipsis (. . .) after a menu option means that, when you select the option, a dialog box appears offering more options. Dialog boxes have places where you can make selections by either typing in information, or by clicking buttons that appear in the boxes.

A right-pointing arrow to the right of a menu option means that when you select that option, a submenu appears next to the first menu. Figure 39-7 shows menu options with ellipses, right-pointing arrows, and keyboard equivalents.

Windows

You can resize an open Macintosh window by selecting the sizing box in the lower-right corner, holding the mouse button down, and dragging the window to the desired size. You can get the original size back by clicking the zoom box at the upper-right corner of the window. If the window is already at full size, clicking this box changes the size to the previous size you made the window.

Note *Drag* means to select an item with the mouse and keep the mouse button pressed while moving the selected item.

If you want to get rid of the window but keep it accessible, you can collapse it by clicking the WindowShade icon at the upper-right corner or double-clicking anywhere on the menu title. Clicking again opens the window back.

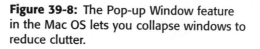 The WindowShade icon looks like this.

The Mac OS uses a second way to collapse windows, called pop-up windows, as shown in Figure 39-8. Select a window in the Finder and use View ⇨ As Pop-up Window to get it to be a pop-up. When you click the window's tab, it collapses the window and places the tab at the bottom of the desktop. Click a collapsed window's tab to get the window back. This technique does not work for program or document windows, just disk and folder windows.

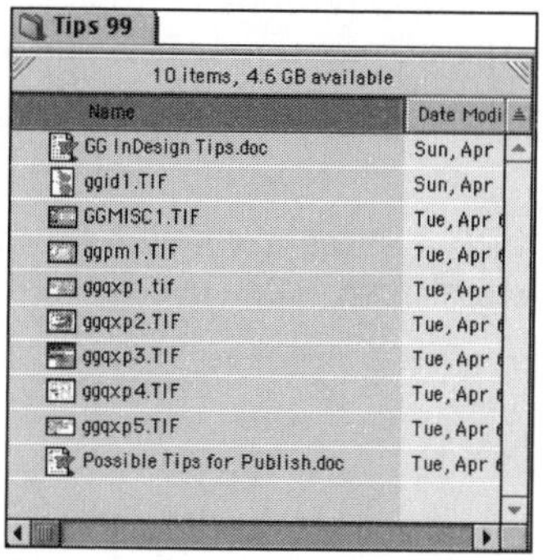

Figure 39-8: The Pop-up Window feature in the Mac OS lets you collapse windows to reduce clutter.

A scroll bar at the right and bottom of a window lets you move around within a window. You can click the scroll buttons (the arrows) or drag the scroll slider (the small open square) to access elements of a window that may be out of view. You can also click the scroll bar itself: Clicking above the scroll slider scrolls a window up one page; clicking below the scroll slider scrolls a window down one page.

If you want to move a window around on the screen, use the mouse to position the pointer in the window's title bar (the bar at the top of the window that displays its title), and hold down the mouse button as you move it to the desired location.

Working with files

The Macintosh interface, with its readily accessible icons of file folders and documents, makes working with files on the Macintosh a relatively easy and straightforward process. This part of the chapter reviews some of the basics of working with Macintosh files, with specific attention paid to how these basics work with InDesign.

Opening a file

Double-click the file folder or document to open it. If the folder you are opening contains an application, such as InDesign, you can launch the program by double-clicking its icon.

Tip If you double-click an InDesign document that is outside the folder containing the application, it may give you a message that the file could not be opened because the application that created it is missing. (This often happens when moving files from a PC to a Mac.) In this case, first open the InDesign application by double-clicking its icon. Then open the file by selecting Open from the File menu and locate the file by means of the controls in the Open dialog box or by dragging the document's icon to the InDesign icon.

Saving files

One of the best habits you can acquire is saving your work. With many Mac applications, you save your work by choosing Save from the File menu, or just use ⌘+S. (You would use Save As if the file has not previously been saved; Save would usually be grayed out in this case.)

Note InDesign has an automatic backup feature in which it saves a copy of your file every so often, so in case of a power outage or system crash, it can usually recover a recent version of your document.

Moving and deleting files

To move a file or document to another folder or disk, click its icon to select it. Then hold the mouse down as you drag it to its destination. If you move a file from one disk to another, the Macintosh copies the item. When you drag an element within a disk, it is simply moved from one location to another. To copy within a disk, hold the Option key down as you drag the element until you have moved the icon to its new location and then release the mouse button.

To delete a file or document, click its icon to select it and then drag it to the icon that looks like a trash can.

Tip You can also Control+click the item you want to delete and select Move to Trash from the pop-up menu (called a *context menu*). Figure 39-9 shows this context menu in action. Context menus are very handy to quickly get a list of relevant options for a specific file, program, or function.

Figure 39-9: The Mac OS lets you easily trash a file or folder by Control+clicking it.

Until you choose to empty the trash can by choosing Empty Trash from the Special menu, you can recover the file or document by double-clicking the trash can icon to open it and then dragging the item back from the trash can to the desktop or to a disk. (You open the trash can the same way you open a folder or disk: just double-click it.)

The Windows Interface

Windows for years was considered a poor stepchild by publishing and graphics pros — only a Mac would do for real work. But that was not so true once Windows 95 came out in August 1995. Borrowing heavily from the Mac, plus from OS/2 and Microsoft's own ideas, Windows became a professional-level operating system, and soon every major graphic and publishing program was available in a Windows 95 versions that worked almost exactly like its Mac original. InDesign is no exception to this trend. Windows NT 4.0, which debuted in late 1996, adopted the Windows 95 interface as well. And in 1998, Microsoft offered users the option of using a more Web-like interface in Windows 98.

While Windows is not quite as good for high-end publishing as the Mac (among other things, it doesn't support ligatures such as *fi*, has trouble handling fine typography and color output, and still has less-than-stable drivers for many important devices), it has everything that most publishers need: It creates and manipulates high-end graphics with ease. It has the ability to run multiple programs simultaneously, to move elements between different documents or programs, and to work with a consistent set of tools and fonts.

If you are an experienced Windows user, you can skip the rest of this section. But if you are a relatively new Windows user who is now also using InDesign, read on for a brief review of some of the Windows basics you'll need to know. For a comprehensive look at Windows PCs, we recommend *PCs For Dummies* and *Windows 98 For Dummies* by Dan Gookin, *Windows 98 Secrets* by Brian Livingston and Davis Straub, and *Alan Simpson's Windows 98 Bible*.

The basic interface

When you turn on your PC, the screen looks something like the screen in Figure 39-10. This screen is known as the *desktop*.

Window (icon view)

Icons for PC and network drive contents

Shortcuts to drives and programs

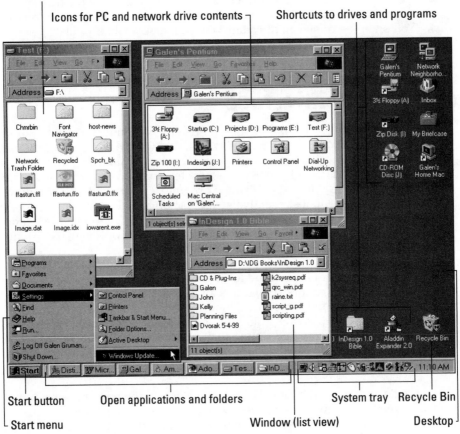

Start button

Start menu

Open applications and folders

System tray   Recycle Bin

Window (list view)

Desktop

Figure 39-10: The basic Windows 98/NT 4.0 desktop.

Windows 98 — but not NT 4 — has an option to make the operating system work more like a browser. Figure 39-11 shows the interface. Use Start ⇨ Settings ⇨ Folder Options to enable or disable this interface style.

Icons

In the upper-right corner of the desktop are icons for the computer (usually called My Computer, although the one shown in Figure 39-10 was renamed to Galen's Pentium) and the Network Neighborhood (which includes connected PCs, Macs, and printers). If you double-click these icons, you get a window that shows the available items (drives, computers, printers) — the Galen's Pentium window is open to the left of its icon and shows several hard drives available, as well as three folders to basic Windows control programs.

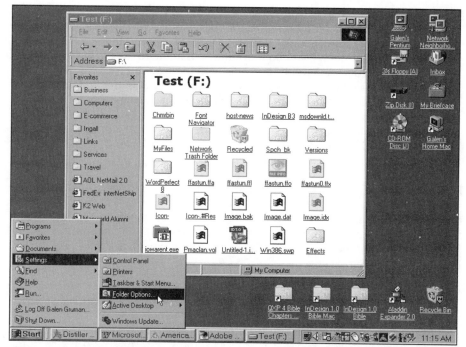

Figure 39-11: The Web-like interface option for Windows 98.

Also on the desktop are icons for drives that we use a lot (such as the floppy drive, CD-ROM drive, and Zip drive) as well as for programs we use a lot (such as the Explorer and File Manager). Those icons are shortcuts — aliases — to the real files. The curved arrow on those icons' lower-left corners shows that they are shortcuts. We placed these shortcuts on the desktop for easy access — your desktop could have different or no such shortcuts.

Most of the Windows interface is based on icons, which are small graphic illustrations that represent Windows programs, files, or functions. Icons represent applications, such as InDesign; file folders, which help you organize your hard disk by holding items such as documents and applications; disks; and documents, including InDesign documents and those created by word-processing applications.

Menus

Menus are another big part of the interface. The Windows interface has a permanent menu, called the Start menu. It lists all the windows that are open and programs that are running (the icons after the Start button), as well as showing all loaded special utilities in a space called the *system tray* (these utilities are always running, which is why they are in their own space).

Tip Although its location is typically at the bottom of the screen, we like to move the Start menu to the top (which is easier for us to use – perhaps a Mac convention we're imposing on Windows). All you have to do is drag it to the top (you can also drag it to either side). If you do move the Start menu to the top, be sure to get the shareware program ShoveIt, because some Windows programs will otherwise place their own menus so they're hidden behind the Start menu. (A demo version of ShoveIt is included on the CD-ROM that accompanies this book.)

Tip You can easily organize the contents of the Start menu. Just right-click the Start button and then choose Open to get it opened as a folder. Then move, add, and remove folders and icons, as you prefer.

Programs also have their own menu bars, which appear at the top of the screen. As you switch from program to program, the menu bar changes to the currently active one. Across the top of the screen in Figure 39-12 is the menu bar for InDesign. The menu bar includes the names of menu titles. To see a menu, you move the mouse so that the pointer appears on the menu title; then you click the mouse button once to have the menu appear.

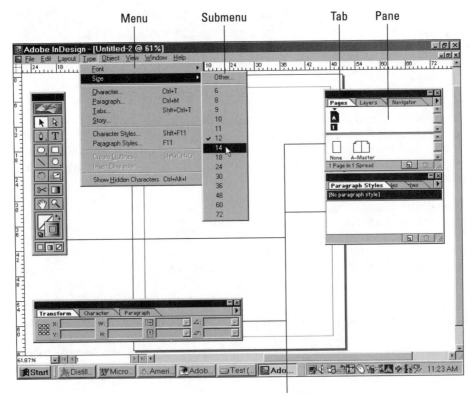

Figure 39-12: A Windows menu with a submenu and tabbed panes.

Note

Pointer refers to the icon that moves on the Windows screen with the movement of the mouse. *Selecting* means using the mouse to get the pointer "on top of" something on the screen and then clicking the item (or clicking and holding the mouse button down if you are selecting a passage of text, for example). When something is selected, it reverses its appearance (white letters become black, black letters become white). You can also open something by *double-clicking* it, where you move the mouse to position it on top of the item, and click the mouse button twice with the second click immediately following the first. The difference is that double-clicking opens a document or launches a program. Single-clicking just selects it.

The names of active menu selections and menu titles are darker than inactive ones, which are lighter or "grayed out," as are some of the menu selections in Figure 39-12. An inactive menu selection is one that you can't make given the current circumstances on your PC. For example, if you haven't already selected a section of text and copied it to the Windows clipboard (by selecting Cut or Copy from the Edit menu, or using the keyboard shortcuts ⌘+X or ⌘+C, respectively), the Paste option in the edit menu is inactive because nothing exists on the clipboard to paste; if data does reside on the clipboard, the Paste command is active.

When you pull down a menu, some menu items have a keyboard shortcut listed to their right. You can use the shortcut keys to access these menu options directly, bypassing the need to select a series of menu options. An ellipsis (. . .) after a menu option means that, when you select the option, a dialog box appears offering more options. Dialog boxes have places where you can make selections by either typing in information, or by clicking buttons that appear in the boxes.

A right-pointing arrow to the right of a menu option means that when you select that option, a submenu appears next to the first menu. Figure 39-12 shows menu options with ellipses, right-pointing arrows, and keyboard equivalents.

Windows

You can resize an open Windows window by clicking any side or corner, holding the mouse button down, and dragging the window to the desired size. If the window fills the screen (preventing you from selecting the sides or corners), click the Restore button at the upper-right corner of the window. That should reduce the window's size so you can select it for resizing.

The File Restore icon looks like this.

Note

Drag means to select an item with the mouse and keep the mouse button pressed while moving the selected item.

To make a window take the full screen, click the Maximize icon at the upper-right corner of the window. You can reduce a program window so that it only appears in the Start menu by clicking the Minimize icon. If you click the Minimize icon for a document window, you'll get a little tab with the window name at the bottom of the program window. To close a window, click the Close icon. Here's what the buttons look like:

 Maximize

 Minimize

☒ Close

A scroll bar at the right and bottom of a window lets you move around within a window. You can click the scroll buttons (the arrows) or drag the scroll slider (the small open square) to access elements of a window that may be out of view. You can also click the scroll bar itself: Clicking above the scroll slider scrolls a window up one page; clicking below the scroll slider scrolls a window down one page.

If you want to move a window around on the screen, use the mouse to position the pointer in the window's title bar (the bar at the top of the window that displays its title), and hold down the mouse button as you move it to the desired location.

Working with files

The Windows interface, with its readily accessible icons of file folders and documents, makes working with files on the PC a relatively easy and straightforward process. This part of the chapter reviews some of the basics of working with Windows files, with specific attention paid to how these basics work with InDesign.

Opening a file

Double-click the file folder or document to open it. If the folder you are opening contains an application, such as InDesign, you can launch the program by double-clicking its icon.

> **Tip**
> If you double-click an InDesign document that is outside the folder containing the application, it may give you a message that the file could not be opened because the application that created it is missing. (This often happens when moving files from a Mac to a PC.) In this case, first open the InDesign application by double-clicking its icon. Then open the file by selecting Open from the File menu and locate the file by means of the controls in the Open dialog box.

> **Tip**
> Many programs add a menu item for themselves in the Start button's Programs menu. Click the Start button to get the Start menu, and then click Programs to get a list of installed programs. Just because the program you're looking for is not there doesn't mean it's not on your system—but because most programs add themselves to the Programs menu, you'll probably find it.

Saving files

One of the best habits you can acquire is saving your work. With many Windows applications, you save your work by choosing Save from the File menu, or use Ctrl+S. (You would use Save As if the file has not previously been saved; Save would usually be grayed out in this case.)

Note   InDesign has an automatic backup feature in which it saves a copy of your file every so often, so in case of a power outage or system crash, it can usually recover a recent version of your document.

Moving and deleting files

To move a file or document to another folder or disk, click its icon to select it. Then hold the mouse down as you drag it to its destination. If you move a file from one disk to another, Windows copies the item. When you drag an element within a disk, it is simply moved from one location to another. To copy within a disk, hold the Ctrl key down as you drag the element until you have moved the icon to its new location and then release the mouse button.

To delete a file or document, click its icon to select it and then drag it to the icon that looks like an environmentalist's trash pail (the Recycle Bin).

Tip   Windows has an easier way to delete items: Right-click the item you want to delete and select Send To from the pop-up menu (called a *contextual menu*); then select Recycle Bin as the location to send it to. These contextual menus are all over Windows and its programs; use them to quickly get to relevant options for the selected file, folder, or program function. Figure 39-13 shows this contextual menu in action.

Figure 39-13: Windows lets you easily trash a file or folder by right-clicking it.

Until you choose to empty the Recycle Bin by right-clicking it and choosing Empty Recycle Bin from the context menu, you can recover the file or document by double-clicking the Recycle Bin icon to open it and then dragging the item back from the bin to the desktop or to a disk or folder. (You open the Recycle Bin the same way you open a folder or disk—just double-click it.)

Summary

Making the most out of InDesign means getting the right tools and environment for it. You'll want a speedy PC or Mac to run InDesign—don't try to use it on a three-year-old or older model, and be sure to have plenty of RAM installed. Other peripherals can make it easier to do tasks such as share data with others and bring images into your computer; prices have dropped considerably in recent years for most such items, making it easier to add tools to your publishing environment.

Make sure you have Adobe Type Manager on your Mac or PC to manage your fonts and assure top-quality output. And consider using some of the shareware we recommend and have demos of in the CD-ROM that accompanies this book—they'll help you work more easily.

✦   ✦   ✦

Installing Adobe InDesign

There's no trick to installing a version 1.0 product with a fine-tuned, automated installer application. The key is to make sure you have enough disk space, decide what you want to install, and then kick off the installer. Before you get started, close any open files and quit any applications. (It is not, however, necessary to disable virus protection software as some installers require or suggest.) Make sure you have your InDesign serial number, which is included in the product box.

Checking System Requirements

You probably haven't gone so far as to purchase InDesign without ensuring that it will run on your computer. However, you may have too much stuff on your hard drive to install it. Make sure you have 120MB of free hard disk space for a full installation and 75MB for a minimum installation. A quick summary of the other minimum system requirements follows. (Chapter 38 discusses the ideal operating environment for InDesign, including hardware, software, and other publishing utilities.)

Note   If you're installing InDesign on a computer without a CD-ROM drive, you can access the InDesign CD-ROM on a networked drive to install it.

Macintosh system requirements

At the time of this writing, InDesign 1.0 for Macintosh required the following:

◆ Power Macintosh PowerPC 603e processor or greater (a Mac with the G3 processor, also called the PowerPC 750, is recommended)

◆ Mac OS 8.5 or 8.6 (although Adobe had not at press time committed officially to support Mac OS X, product marketing staff have said such support is very likely; Mac OS X Server will *not* be supported)

◆ 48MB of RAM (64MB or more is recommended)

◆ 832×624-pixel or greater video resolution — the equivalent of a 17-inch monitor or larger (24-bit color is recommended)

Windows system requirements

At the time of this writing, InDesign 1.0 for Windows required the following:

◆ 300MHz Intel Pentium II or faster processor (although Adobe has not tested comparable processors such as the AMD K6-II, its technical staff have said any Windows-compatible processor should work fine with InDesign)

◆ Microsoft Windows 98, Windows NT 4.0 (Workstation or Server) with Service Pack 3 or later, or later Windows operating system (such as Windows 2000)

◆ 48MB of RAM (64MB or more is recommended)

◆ Video card that supports 256 colors (8-bit color) at 800×600-pixel or greater video resolution — the equivalent of a 17-inch monitor or larger (24-bit-color is recommended)

Installing InDesign for Mac OS

You'll need about 10 to 20 minutes to install InDesign. And while it's not necessary to quit other applications or break your Internet connection, it is a good idea to do so; if something goes wrong, you don't want to lose any unsaved work.

Steps: Installing on a Macintosh

1. Quit all applications and insert the InDesign CD-ROM into your CD-ROM drive.

2. If a window containing the InDesign installer does not automatically appear, double-click the Adobe InDesign CD-ROM icon on your desktop.

3. Double-click the Read Me First! file, which launches SimpleText. Skim through the file for late-breaking installation information (you can read its explanation of the CD-ROM contents later). If the text identifies any installation problems or conflicting software, resolve any issues before continuing with the installer.

4. Close the file and quit SimpleText.

5. Double-click the Install Adobe InDesign butterfly icon at the top of the CD-ROM's folder.

6. A large installer screen displays. While you might be tempted to click Continue and move on, take a second to confirm the language in the upper-right corner — a pop-up menu lets you choose U.S. English, Canadian English, or International English. The choice you make determines InDesign's default spelling and hyphenation dictionary, page size, and measurement system (although you can change these easily). After confirming the language, click Continue.

7. The next dialog box lets you specify your country so the installer can display the proper license agreement. If you can't find your country, choose All Other Countries. Click OK to continue.

8. Skim through to the End User License Agreement, and then click Accept if you agree. Clicking Decline cancels the installation.

9. Finally, you've reached the InDesign Installer dialog box. By default, it's set at Easy Install, which installs all the InDesign software and add-ons (although not the entire contents of the CD-ROM).

   • If you want to be sure you have everything you'll ever need with no further hassles, leave this Easy Install setting alone.

   • If you have limited hard drive space — or are simply opposed to cluttering your hard drive with unnecessary files — choose Custom Install. The installer makes a recommendation for you by leaving InDesign, Learning Adobe InDesign folder, and Adobe Online checked, while unchecking Kodak CMS Profiles and Dictionaries, as shown in Figure A-1. These are not necessarily the best choices, though. Consider whether you're really going to do the tutorial, use color management, or surf the Adobe Web site directly through InDesign rather than through a browser to decide whether to check or uncheck these options. You must check Adobe InDesign to get the software, and you should install some of the dictionaries. Click the arrow next to the Dictionaries check box, and then choose the ones you might use. For example, you might want to include English Legal, English Medical, and U.S. English if you're publishing primarily for a U.S. audience.

Tip   Click the little "I" to the right of an option for a basic reminder of what each option contains.

10. Now that you've decided what to install, focus your attention on the Install Location area in the lower-left corner of the dialog box to decide where to install InDesign. The default location is the root level of your hard drive. To change the location (for example, to your application folder, another drive, or even on another Mac), click Select Folder. Use the Select the Installation Folder dialog box to find (but not open) the folder or drive in which you want to install InDesign. Choose the destination folder or drive, and then click Select.

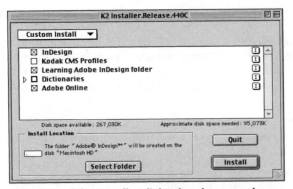

Figure A-1: The Installer dialog box lets you choose between Easy Install (everything) and Custom Install, which lets you choose what to install.

11. Click Install to continue the journey. (If there's not enough room in the selected location, the installer notifies you at this point. You'll need to install fewer options or delete contents from the destination, which you can do without quitting the installer.)

A dialog box asks you to enter your name, company, and serial number, as shown in Figure A-2. If you select A Business, you must complete every field in this dialog box—even making up your own salutation and company name, if necessary—to continue. (If you select An Individual, you can skip the company name.) When you finish, click Next. Review your information in the next dialog box, clicking Back to fix any errors and Install Now to continue. (Note that the serial number shown in Figure A-2 is not a valid one—sorry!)

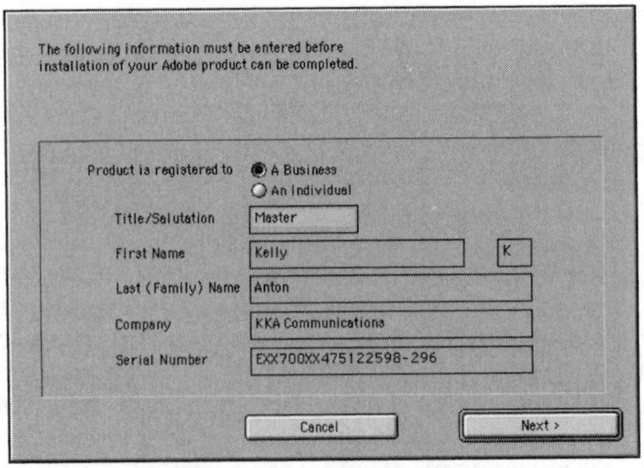

![Dialog box requesting registration information. "The following information must be entered before installation of your Adobe product can be completed." Product is registered to: A Business (selected), An Individual. Title/Salutation: Master. First Name: Kelly, K. Last (Family) Name: Anton. Company: KKA Communications. Serial Number: EXX700XX47512 2598-296. Cancel / Next > buttons.]

Figure A-2: Adobe uses the information you enter in this dialog box to address its communications to you.

12. While the Installing dialog box is running, you can take a few minutes to stretch or read the Adobe messages that appear. When the Installation was Successful alert appear, click Quit. (If you need to install additional copies of InDesign on other Macs on your network—Macs that maybe don't have CD-ROM drives—you can click Continue.)

13. Restart your computer. At this point, locate the InDesign folder on your computer and open it. Double-click the Read Me file for late-breaking product information. While the folder is open, create an alias to InDesign and place it in a convenient location (see Chapter 2 for more information about creating aliases).

Before you pack up the CD-ROM and start working, check the next section in this chapter, "Installing Additional Mac Components." If you have access to the CD-ROM, it doesn't really matter if you leave something off as it's easy to install stuff later. But if your IT department hoards the software, you might want to go ahead and install everything you might need.

Installing Additional Mac Components

After installing the InDesign program files—and before you put away the CD-ROM—make sure there's nothing else you need right away.

✦ You need the Adobe PostScript driver version 8.6 to print from InDesign. If you don't have it, install it from the CD-ROM as covered in Chapter 39.

✦ If you don't have Acrobat Reader 4.0, install it from the CD-ROM. You'll need it to read some of the InDesign documentation files.

✦ If you're planning to write scripts to automate processes in InDesign, copy the Scripting folder from the Adobe Technical Info folder.

✦ If you'll be working with Adobe's Tagged Text format (a method for saving formatting codes with ASCII text), copy the Tagged Text folder from the Adobe Technical Info folder.

✦ To run through Adobe's automated preview of the software, double-click the InDesign Tour icon. (There's no reason to copy this to your hard drive for future reference.)

After you begin working with InDesign, you may find that you need something from the CD-ROM—the tutorial, another language dictionary, or the CMS profiles, for example. You can drag-copy the Learning Adobe InDesign folder to your hard drive, but you'll need to run the installer again to access the Kodak CMS Profiles, the Dictionaries, or the Adobe Online software. Use the Custom Install option and select only the items you need—leaving the InDesign software itself unchecked as there's no need to reinstall it. Make sure to choose the same Install Location as your copy of InDesign so the files end up in the right spots.

Installing InDesign for Windows

You'll need about 10 to 20 minutes to install InDesign. The AutoPlay installer walks you through the installation, but it's not always intuitive.

Steps: Installing on Windows

1. Quit all applications and insert the InDesign CD-ROM into your CD-ROM drive.

2. The Adobe InDesign AutoPlay splash screen, shown in Figure A-3, should display automatically. If not, double-click your computer's icon (usually named My Computer) on the desktop to open it, and then double-click the Adobe InDesign CD-ROM icon.

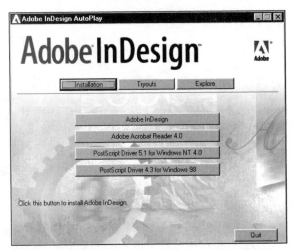

Figure A-3: The Adobe InDesign AutoPlay dialog box walks you through the installation process in Windows.

3. The AutoPlay dialog box contains three panes, which you access through the buttons across the top: Installation, Tryouts, and Explore. If the Installation pane isn't showing (as indicated by a red outline on the button), click its button.

4. Click the Adobe InDesign button to kick off the installer. The Adobe InDesign Setup dialog box reminds you to quit all applications. Click Next to continue.

5. The Language Selection pane appears, asking whether you want to install U.S. English, Canadian English, or International English. The choice you make determines InDesign's default spelling and hyphenation dictionary, page size, and measurement system (although you can change these easily). After confirming the language, click Next.

6. The Select License Agreement dialog box asks you to specify your country so the installer can display the proper license agreement. If you can't find your country, check All Other Countries. Click Next to continue.

7. Skim through the Software License Agreement, and then click Yes if you agree. Clicking No cancels the installation.

8. You've now reached the Adobe InDesign Setup dialog box shown in Figure A-4. By default, it's set at Typical, which installs all the InDesign software and add-ons.

   • If you want to be sure you have everything you'll ever need with no further hassles, leave this alone.

   • If you have limited hard drive space — or are simply opposed to cluttering your hard drive with unnecessary files — click Custom. Later, you will have the chance to decide what you want to install.

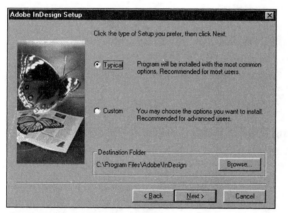

Figure A-4: A Typical installation provides just about everything you'll ever need, while a Custom installation lets you install only what you know you'll use. (This requires you to *know* what you'll use.)

9. The Destination Folder area at the bottom of the dialog box shows the default path. If this is where you usually store your software, leave it unchanged. To change the location (for example, to another drive or even another PC), click Browse. Use the Choose Folder dialog box to find (but not open) the folder or drive in which you want to install InDesign. Select the destination folder or drive, and then click OK. If you're doing a Typical installation, skip to Step 12.

10. If you selected a Custom installation, the Components area appears so you can choose what to install. The installer makes a recommendation for you by leaving InDesign, Learning Adobe InDesign folder, and Adobe Online checked, while unchecking Kodak CMS Profiles and Dictionaries. These are not necessarily the best choices, though. Consider whether you're really

going to do the tutorial, use color management, or surf the Adobe Web site directly through InDesign rather than through a browser to decide whether to check or uncheck these options. You must check Adobe InDesign to get the software, and you should install some of the dictionaries.

11. To install selected dictionaries, first check Dictionaries, as shown in Figure A-5. Then click the Change button in the Description area — this lets you check the dictionaries you might need (for example, you might want to include English Legal, English Medical, and U.S. English if you're publishing primarily for a U.S. audience). Click OK when you finish selecting dictionaries.

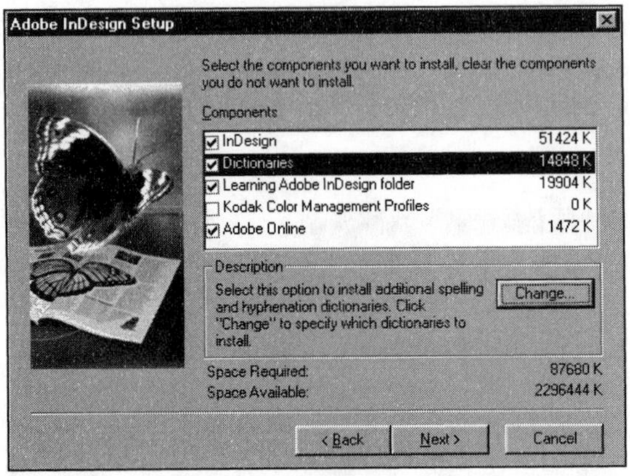

Figure A-5: The Change button in the Description area lets you choose which spelling and hyphenation dictionaries you want to install.

12. Click Next to continue the installation. (If there's not enough room in the selected location, the installer will notify you at this point. You'll need to install fewer options or delete contents from the destination.)

13. The User Information dialog box asks you to enter your name, company, and serial number. If you select A Business, you must complete every field in this dialog box — even making up your own salutation and company name, if necessary — to continue. (If you select An Individual, you can skip the company name.) When you finish, click Next. Review your information in the next dialog box, clicking No to fix any errors and Yes to continue.

14. Review the location you've selected and the items you want to install, and then click Next. To change anything at this point, click Back.

15. While the installer is running, you can take a few minutes to stretch or read the Adobe messages that appear. When the "Installation was successful" message appears, click OK. Click Quit if you're finished with the AutoPlay installer.

16. Restart your computer. At this point, locate the InDesign folder on your computer and open it. Double-click the Readme.doc file for late-breaking product information.

Tip

If you're planning to use InDesign on a daily basis, create a shortcut and put it somewhere convenient for you — such as on your desktop. See Chapter 2 for more information about creating shortcuts. The installer will also add an Adobe folder to your Start menu, which you can edit by using the instructions in Chapter 39.

Before you pack up the CD-ROM and start working, check the next section in this chapter, "Installing Additional Windows Components." If you have access to the CD-ROM, it doesn't really matter if you leave something off as it's easy to install stuff later. But if your IT department hoards the software, you might want to go ahead and install everything you might need.

Installing Additional Windows Components

After installing the InDesign program files — and before you put away the CD-ROM — make sure there's nothing else you need right away.

✦ You need the Adobe PostScript driver version 4.3 for Windows 98 or the Adobe PostScript driver version 5.1 for Windows NT 4.0 to print from InDesign. If you don't have the correct driver for your version of Windows, use the button in the Adobe InDesign AutoPlay dialog box to install it as covered in Chapter 39.

✦ If you don't have Acrobat Reader 4.0, use the button in the Adobe InDesign AutoPlay dialog box to install it. You'll need it to read some of the InDesign documentation files.

✦ If you're planning to write scripts to automate processes in InDesign, click the Explore button at the top of the Adobe InDesign AutoPlay dialog box. In the Explore pane, click the CD-ROM Contents button. Locate the Adobe Technical Info folder, and copy the Scripting folder to your PC.

✦ If you'll be working with Adobe's Tagged Text format (a method for saving formatting codes with ASCII text), copy the Tagged Text folder from the Adobe Technical Info folder.

✦ To run through Adobe's automated preview of the software, click the InDesign Tour button in the Explore pane of the Adobe InDesign AutoPlay dialog box. (There's no reason to copy this to your hard drive for future reference.)

After you begin working with InDesign, you may find that you need something from the CD-ROM — the tutorial, another language dictionary, or the CMS profiles, for example. You can access the Learning Adobe InDesign folder from the Explore pane, but you'll need to run the installer again to access the Kodak CMS Profiles, the Dictionaries, or the Adobe Online software. Use the Custom option and select only the items you need — leaving the InDesign software itself unchecked as there's no need to reinstall it. Make sure to choose the same Destination Folder as your copy of InDesign so the files end up in the right spots.

✦   ✦   ✦

Most Useful Shortcuts

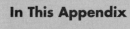

Shortcuts are essential to making the most of InDesign. Sure, you can access everything from a menu or pane, but shortcuts make the work much faster. This appendix covers InDesign's keyboard shortcuts and working with contextual menus, which lets you use the mouse to find out what options are available for specific objects.

Adobe InDesign Keyboard Shortcuts

Because there are so many keyboard shortcuts, we've broken them into functional areas to help you find them more easily in the following tables. NA indicates that a shortcut is not available.

Table B-1		
Keyboard Shortcuts for Opening, Closing, and Saving		
Action or Command	*Macintosh*	*Windows*
New document	⌘+N	Ctrl+N
New document based on previous	⌘Shift+N	Ctrl+Shift+N
Open document	⌘+O	Ctrl+O
Open library	Shift+Option +⌘+L	Ctrl+Alt+Shift+L
Close document	⌘+W	Ctrl+W *or* Ctrl+F4

Continued

Table B-1
(continued)

Action or Command	Macintosh	Windows
Quit program	⌘+Q	Ctrl+Q *or* Alt+F4
Save document	⌘+S	Ctrl+S
Save document as	Shift+⌘+S	Ctrl+Shift+S
Save copy of document	Option+⌘+S	Ctrl+Alt+D
Export document	⌘+E	Ctrl+E
Place text and graphics	⌘+D	Ctrl+D

Table B-2
Keyboard Shortcuts for Changing Views

Action or Command	Macintosh	Windows
Hide/show panes	Tab	Tab
Hide/show all panes but toolbox	Shift+Tab	Shift+Tab
Zoom in	⌘++ [plus sign]	Ctrl++ [plus sign]
Zoom out	⌘+- [hyphen]	Ctrl+- [hyphen]
Fit page/spread in window	⌘+0	Ctrl+Alt++ [plus sign]
Fit spread in window	Shift+⌘+0	Ctrl+Alt+0
Fit entire pasteboard in window	Option+Shift+⌘+0	Ctrl+Alt+Shift+0
Display actual size	⌘+1	Ctrl+1
Display at 50 percent	⌘+5	Ctrl+5
Display at 200 percent	⌘+2	Ctrl+2
Display at 400 percent	⌘+4	Ctrl+4
Switch between current and previous view	Option+⌘+2	Ctrl+Alt+2
Set magnification	Option+⌘+5	Ctrl+Alt+5
Set all pages to same view	⌘+*percent in view percent menu*	Ctrl+*percent in view percent menu*

Action or Command	Macintosh	Windows
Switch to previous document window	NA	Ctrl+Shift+F6
Switch to next document window	NA	Ctrl+F6
Show/hide master items	⌘+Y	Ctrl+Y
Show/hide text threads	Option+⌘+Y	Ctrl+Alt+Y
Show/hide frame edges	⌘+H	Ctrl+H
Show/hide rulers	⌘+R	Ctrl+R
Show hidden characters	Option+⌘+I	Ctrl+Alt+I
Redraw screen	NA	Shift+F5
Redraw high-resolution screen	NA	Ctrl+Shift+F5

Table B-3
Keyboard Shortcuts for Preferences and Setup

Action or Command	Macintosh	Windows
Show installed components	⌘+click *About InDesign in Apple menu*	Ctrl+click *Adobe Online tool*
Preferences dialog box	⌘+K	Ctrl+K
Edit shortcuts	Option+Shift+⌘+K	Ctrl+Alt+Shift+K
Document setup	Option+⌘+P	Ctrl+Alt+P
Page setup	Shift+⌘+P	NA

Table B-4
Keyboard Shortcuts for Accessing Tools

Action or Command	Macintosh	Windows
Selection tool	V	V
Direct Selection tool	A	A
Type tool	T	T

Continued

	Table B-4	
	(continued)	
Action or Command	**Macintosh**	**Windows**
Shift+T	Shift+T	Vertical Type tool
Pen tool	P	P
Add Anchor Point tool	+ [plus sign]	+ [plus sign]
Delete Anchor Point tool	- [hyphen]	- [hyphen]
Ellipse tool	L	L
Oval Frame tool	Shift+L	Shift+L
Rectangle tool	M	M
Rectangle Frame tool	Shift+M	Shift+M
Polygon tool	N	N
Polygon Frame tool	Shift+N	Shift+N
Rotate tool	R	R
Scale tool	S	S
Shear tool	Shift+S	Shift+S
Scissors tool	C	C
Hand tool	H	H
Temporary Hand tool	Shift+spacebar	Shift+spacebar
Zoom tool	Z	Z
Temporary zoom-in tool	⌘+spacebar	Ctrl+spacebar
Temporary zoom-out tool	Option+⌘+spacebar	Ctrl+Alt+spacebar
Gradient tool	G	G
Fill box	X	X
Stroke box	X	X
Swap Fill/Stroke box	Shift+X	Shift+X
Default Fill/Stroke box	D	D
Apply Color box	<	<
Apply Gradient box	>	>
Apply None box	/	/

Table B-5
Keyboard Shortcuts for Viewing Panes

Action or Command	Macintosh	Windows
Apply value in field	Option+Return	Shift+Enter
Show Links pane	Shift+⌘+D	Ctrl+Shift+D
Show Layers pane	F7	F7
Show Pages pane	F12	F12
Show Swatches pane	F5	F5
Show Color pane	F6	F6
Show Transform pane	F9	F9
Show Tabs pane	Shift+⌘+T	Ctrl+Shift+T
Show Character pane	⌘+T	Ctrl+T
Select Font Name field	NA	Ctrl+Alt+Shift+M
Show Paragraph pane	⌘+M	Ctrl+M
Show Character Styles pane	Shift+F11	Shift+F11
Show Paragraph Styles pane	F11	F11
Show Paragraph Rules pane	Option+⌘+J	Ctrl+Alt+J
Show Keep Options dialog box	Option+⌘+K	Ctrl+Alt+K
Show Text Wrap pane	Option+⌘+W	Ctrl+Alt+W
Show Text Frame Options pane	⌘+B	Ctrl+B
Show Align pane	F8	F8
Show Stroke pane	F10	F10

Table B-6
Keyboard Shortcuts for Navigation

Action or Command	Macintosh	Windows
Go to page	⌘+J	Ctrl+J
Go to previous spread	⌘+*left arrow button in navigation area*	Ctrl+*left arrow button in navigation area*
Go to next spread	⌘+*right arrow button in navigation area*	Ctrl+*right arrow button in navigation area*

Table B-7
Keyboard Shortcuts for Controlling Guides

Action or Command	Macintosh	Windows
Show/hide guides	⌘+; [semicolon]	Ctrl+; [semicolon]
Lock/unlock guides	Option+⌘+; [semicolon]	Ctrl+Alt+; [semicolon]
Snap to guides on/off	Shift+⌘+; [semicolon]	Ctrl+Shift+; [semicolon]
Show/hide baseline grid	Option+⌘+"	Ctrl+Alt+"
Show/hide document grid	⌘+"	Ctrl+"
Snap to document grid on/off	Shift+⌘+"	Ctrl+Shift+"
Select all guides	Option+⌘+G	Ctrl+Alt+G
Lock zero point	⌘+click *zero point when dragging guides*	Ctrl+click *zero point when dragging guides*

Table B-8
Keyboard Shortcuts for Object Selection

Action or Command	Macintosh	Windows
Select master page	Shift+⌘+click	Ctrl+Shift+click
Select topmost object	Option+Shift+⌘+]	Ctrl+Alt+Shift+]
Select object above current object	Option+⌘+]	Ctrl+Alt+]
Select bottommost object	Shift+Option+⌘+[	Ctrl+Alt+Shift+[
Select object below current object	Option+⌘+[	Ctrl+Alt+[
Go to last frame in thread	Shift+Option+⌘+ Page Down	Ctrl+Alt+Shift+Page Down
Go to next frame in thread	Option+⌘+Page Down	Ctrl+Alt+Page Down
Go to first frame in thread	Shift+Option+⌘+Page Up	Ctrl+Alt+Shift+Page Up
Go to previous frame in thread	Option+⌘+Page Up	Ctrl+Alt+Page Up

Table B-9
Keyboard Shortcuts for Moving Objects

Action or Command	Macintosh	Windows
Move selection*	Left, right, up, and down cursors	Left, right, up, and down cursors
Move selection increments*	Shift+left, right, up, and down cursors	Shift+left, right, up, 10 and down cursors
Bring object to front	Shift+⌘+]	Ctrl+Shift+]
Bring object forward	⌘+]	Ctrl+]
Send object to back	Shift+⌘+[	Ctrl+Shift+[
Send object backward	⌘+[	Ctrl+[

* Amount of movement is defined in Units & Increments pane in Preferences dialog box (File ⇨ Preferences, or ⌘+K or Ctrl+K).

Table B-10
Keyboard Shortcuts for Object Commands

Action or Command	Macintosh	Windows
Cut	⌘+X	Ctrl+X
Copy	⌘+V	Ctrl+V
Paste	⌘+P	Ctrl+P
Paste into	Option+⌘+P	Ctrl+Alt+P
Clear	Backspace	Backspace *or* Del
Duplicate object	Option+⌘+D	Ctrl+Alt+D
Step and repeat	Shift+⌘+V	Ctrl+Shift+V
Resize proportionately	Shift+drag	Shift+drag
Resize frame and content	⌘+drag	Ctrl+drag
Duplicate	Option+drag, or Option+left, right, up, and down cursors	Alt+drag, or Alt+left, right, up, and down cursors
Group	⌘+G	Ctrl+G
Ungroup	Shift+⌘+G	Ctrl+Shift+G
Lock	⌘+L	Ctrl+L
Unlock	Option+⌘+L	Ctrl+Alt+L
Corner effects	Option+⌘+R	Ctrl+Alt+R

Table B-11
Keyboard Shortcuts for Handling Graphics

Action or Command	Macintosh	Windows
Convert text to outlines	Shift+⌘+O	Ctrl+Alt+O
Image color settings	Option+Shift+⌘+D	Ctrl+Alt+Shift+D
Make compound path	⌘+8	Ctrl+8
Release compound path	Option+⌘+8	Ctrl+Alt+8

Table B-12
Keyboard Shortcuts for Selecting Text

Action or Command	Macintosh	Windows
Select all	⌘+A	Ctrl+A
Deselect all	Shift+⌘+A	Ctrl+Shift+A
Select word	double-click	double-click
Select one word to left	Shift+⌘+left cursor	Ctrl+Shift+left cursor
Select one word to right	Shift+⌘+right cursor	Ctrl+Shift+right cursor
Select range	Shift+left, right, up, and down cursors	Shift+left, right, up, and down cursors
Select paragraph	triple-click	triple-click
Select one paragraph before	Shift+⌘+up cursor	Ctrl+Shift+up cursor
Select one paragraph after	Shift+⌘+down cursor	Ctrl+Shift+down cursor
Select to start of story	Shift+⌘+Home	Ctrl+Shift+Home
Select to end of story	Shift+⌘+End	Ctrl+Shift+End

Table B-13
Keyboard Shortcuts for Moving Within Text

Action or Command	Macintosh	Windows
Move left one word	⌘+left cursor	Ctrl+left cursor
Move right one word	⌘+right cursor	Ctrl+right cursor
Move to start of line	Home	Home

Action or Command	Macintosh	Windows
Move to end of line	End	End
Move to previous paragraph	⌘+up cursor	Ctrl+up cursor
Move to next paragraph	⌘+down cursor	Ctrl+down cursor
Move to start of story	⌘+Home	Ctrl+Home
Move to end of story	⌘+End	Ctrl+End

Table B-14
Keyboard Shortcuts for Applying Text and Paragraph Formats

Action or Command	Macintosh	Windows
Bold	Shift+⌘+B	Ctrl+Shift+B
Italic	Shift+⌘+I	Ctrl+Shift+I
Normal	Shift+⌘+Y	Ctrl+Shift+Y
Underline	Shift+⌘+U	Ctrl+Shift+U
Strikethrough	Shift+⌘+/	Ctrl+Shift+/
All caps on/off	Shift+⌘+K	Ctrl+Shift+K
Small caps	Shift+⌘+H	Ctrl+Shift+H
Superscript	Shift+⌘++ [plus sign]	Ctrl+Shift++ [plus sign]
Subscript	Option+Shift+⌘++ [plus sign]	Ctrl+Alt+Shift++ [plus sign]
Align left	Shift+⌘+L	Ctrl+Shift+L
Align right	Shift+⌘+R	Ctrl+Shift+R
Align center	Shift+⌘+C	Ctrl+Shift+C
Justify full	Shift+⌘+F	Ctrl+Shift+F
Justify left	Shift+⌘+J	Ctrl+Shift+J
Justify right	Option+Shift+⌘+R	Ctrl+Alt+Shift+R
Justify center	Option+Shift+⌘+C	Ctrl+Alt+Shift+C
Increase point size*	Shift+⌘+>	Ctrl+Shift+>
Increase point size by 5 times*	Option+Shift+⌘+>	Ctrl+Alt+Shift+>
Decrease point size*	Shift+⌘+<	Ctrl+Shift+<

Continued

Table B-14 *(continued)*		
Action or Command	**Macintosh**	**Windows**
Decrease point size by 5 times*	Option+Shift+⌘+<	Ctrl+Alt+Shift+<
Increase leading*	Option+up cursor	Alt+up cursor
Decrease leading*	Option+down cursor	Alt+down cursor
Increase leading by 5 times*	Option+⌘+up cursor	Ctrl+Alt+up cursor
Decrease leading by 5 times*	Option+⌘+down cursor	Ctrl+Alt+down cursor
Use autoleading	Option+Shift+⌘+A	Ctrl+Alt+Shift+A
Increase kerning/tracking*	Option+right cursor	Alt+right cursor
Increase kerning/ tracking by 5 times*	Option+⌘+right cursor	Ctrl+Alt+right cursor
Decrease kerning/tracking*	Option+left cursor	Alt+left cursor
Decrease kerning/ tracking by 5 times*	Option+⌘+left cursor	Ctrl+Alt+left cursor
Clear all kerning/ tracking (set to 0)	Shift+⌘+Q	Ctrl+Shift+Q
Increase baseline shift*	Option+Shift+up arrow	Alt+Shift+up arrow
Increase baseline shift by 5 times*	Option+Shift+⌘+ up arrow	Ctrl+Alt+Shift+up arrow
Decrease baseline shift*	Option+Shift+down cursor	Alt+Shift+down arrow
Decrease baseline shift by 5 times*	Option+Shift+⌘+ down arrow	Ctrl+Alt+Shift+down arrow
Set horizontal scale to 100 percent	Shift+⌘+X	Ctrl+Shift+X
Set vertical scale to 100 percent	Option+Shift+⌘+X	Ctrl+Alt+Shift+X
Autohyphenation on/off	Option+Shift+⌘+H	Ctrl+Alt+Shift+H
Align to grid on/off	Option+Shift+⌘+G	Ctrl+Alt+Shift+G
Update character style based on selection	Option+Shift+⌘+C	Ctrl+Alt+Shift+C
Update paragraph style based on selection	Option+Shift+⌘+R	Ctrl+Alt+Shift+R

* Amount of change is defined in Units & Increments pane in Preferences dialog box (File ➪ Preferences, or ⌘+K or Ctrl+K).

Table B-15
Keyboard Shortcuts for Finding and Changing Text and Spelling

Action or Command	Macintosh	Windows
Find/change	⌘+F	Ctrl+F
Find next	Option+⌘+F	Ctrl+Alt+F
Search for selected text	Shift+F1	NA
Add selected text to Find What field	⌘+F1	Ctrl+F1
Add selected text to Change To field	⌘+F2	Ctrl+F2
Change current selection	⌘+F3	Ctrl+F3
Change current selection and search forward	Shift+⌘+F3	Ctrl+Shift+F3
Check spelling	⌘+I	Ctrl+I

Table B-16
Keyboard Shortcuts for Special Characters

Action or Command	Macintosh	Windows
Bullet (•)	Option+8	Alt+8
Ellipsis (...)	Option+; [semicolon]	Alt+; [semicolon]
Copyright (©)	Option+G	Alt+G
Registered trademark (®)	Option+R	Alt+R
Trademark (™)	Option+2	Alt+2
Paragraph (¶)	Option+7	Alt+7
Section (§)	Option+6	Alt+6
Switch between keyboard and typographic quotes	Option+Shift+⌘+"	Ctrl+Alt+Shift+"
Em dash (—)	Option+Shift+- [hyphen]	Alt+Shift+- [hyphen]
En dash (–)	Option+- [hyphen]	Alt+- [hyphen]
Nonbreaking hyphen	Option+⌘+- [hyphen]	Ctrl+Alt+- [hyphen]
Discretionary hyphen	Shift+⌘+- [hyphen]	Ctrl+Shift+- [hyphen]

Continued

Table B-16
(continued)

Action or Command	Macintosh	Windows
Em space	Shift+⌘+M	Ctrl+Shift+M
En space	Shift+⌘+N	Ctrl+Shift+N
Figure space	Option+Shift+⌘+8	Ctrl+Alt+Shift+8
Flush space	Option+Shift+⌘+J	Ctrl+Alt+Shift+J
Thin space	Option+Shift+⌘+M	Ctrl+Alt+Shift+M
Hair space	Option+Shift+⌘+I	Ctrl+Alt+Shift+I
Nonbreaking space	Option+spacebar *or* Option+⌘+X	Alt+spacebar *or* Ctrl+Alt+X
Soft return	Shift+Return	Shift+Enter
Insert section marker text	Option+Shift+⌘+N	Ctrl+Alt+Shift+N
Insert page number	Option+⌘+N	Ctrl+Alt+N

Table B-17
Keyboard Shortcuts for Printing and Output

Action or Command	Macintosh	Windows
Print document	⌘+P	Ctrl+P
Preflight document	Option+Shift+⌘+F	Ctrl+Alt+Shift+F
Package document	Option+Shift+⌘+P	Ctrl+Alt+Shift+P

Table B-18
Miscellaneous Keyboard Shortcuts

Action or Command	Macintosh	Windows
Help	Help	F1
Undo	⌘+Z	Ctrl+Z
Redo	Shift+⌘+Z	Ctrl+Shift+Z
Switch between single-line and multi-line composition	Option+Shift+⌘+T	Ctrl+Alt+Shift+T

Contextual Menus

Windows 98, Windows NT 4.0, and Mac OS 8.*x* all use a technique called contextual menus that give you quick access to functions for a selected object, saving you the hassle of hunting down the right menu or pane. In Windows, right-click the object for which you want the contextual menu. On the Mac, Control+click the object; note that you may first need to click it with the mouse button to make it the active selection.

Tip   We recommend that Mac users buy a multibutton mouse from a company such as Logitech or Kensington Microware and set the right-hand button to be Control+click, emulating Windows's right-click feature. Once you get the hang of it, you'll find it easier to access the contextual menus solely via the mouse rather than having to use a keyboard-and-mouse combination.

Figures B-1 through B-6 show which contextual menus display if you Control+click or right-click various elements. Unless noted, the Selection tool is used to select the object.

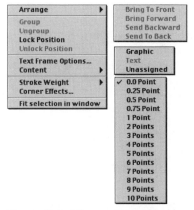

Figure B-1: The contextual menu that appears for a frame, path, or line, as well as its submenus.

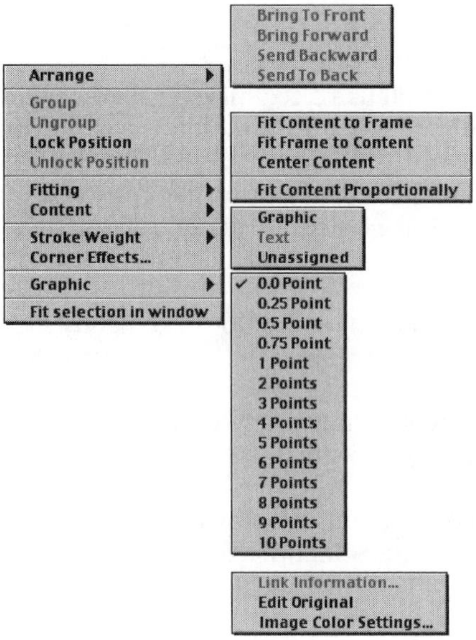

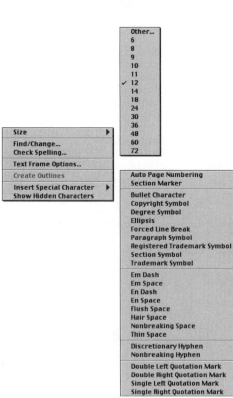

Figure B-2: The contextual menu that appears for a frame containing graphics, as well as its submenus.

Figure B-3: The contextual menu that appears
for text selected with the Type tool, as well as
its submenus.

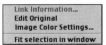

Figure B-4: The contextual menu that appears
when selecting a graphic with the Direct Selection tool.

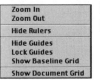

Figure B-5: The contextual menu that appears for the
pasteboard.

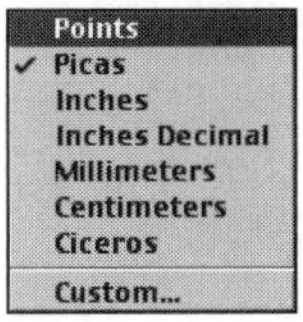

Figure B-6: The contextual menu that appears for rulers.

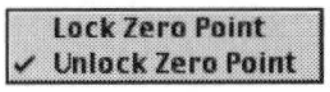

Figure B-7: The contextual menu that appears for the
ruler zero point.

✦   ✦   ✦

Top Tips for Using InDesign

The more you use a program, the more you learn to ease your work through shortcuts, techniques, and other methods. This appendix summarizes the best tips for using InDesign from the book, giving you an all-in-one-place compendium to help make your InDesign work that much easier.

Using Tools and General Functions

Working with tools and manipulating standard functions such as zoom and windows can get overwhelming. But using the following tips can save you time and make it easier to use these functions.

Tools and views

If you're working with text and have the Type tool selected, you can switch to the Selection tool by holding ⌘ or Ctrl rather than using the Toolbox palette.

You can configure the Polygon tool and the Polygon Frame tool to create either regular polygons or starburst shapes. Double-click either of the Polygon tools to display the Polygon Settings dialog box. The value in the Number of Sides field determines how many sides your polygons will have. If you want to create a starburst shape, specify a value in the Star Inset field. As you increase the percentage value, the spikes become longer and pointier. When you change the values in the Polygon Settings dialog box, the new values are used for both versions of the polygon tool.

You never have to actually select the Zoom tool. Instead, use its keyboard shortcuts: ⌘+spacebar or Ctrl+spacebar (for zooming in) and ⌘+Option+spacebar or Ctrl+Alt+spacebar (for zooming out).

Double-clicking the Zoom tool is the same as choosing View ⇨ Actual Size; it displays a document at 100 percent magnification.

To switch back and forth between the last two magnification percentages, press ⌘+Option-2 or Ctrl+Alt+2.

To temporarily access the Hand tool when the Type tool is not selected, press the spacebar. The hand pointer is displayed. Click and drag to move the page within the document window. (This is one of InDesign's most useful keyboard shortcuts!)

Windows and documents

To close all windows for the currently displayed document, press Shift+⌘+W or Ctrl+Shift+W. To close all windows for all open documents, press Option+Shift+⌘+W or Ctrl+Alt+Shift+W.

To create new documents bypassing the New dialog box (thus using the default settings), use Shift+⌘+N or Ctrl+Shift+N.

If you have more than one document open, you can save them all at once by pressing Option+Shift+⌘+S or Ctrl+Alt+Shift+S.

Undo

If you perform an action and then change your mind while InDesign is completing the action, pressing the Esc cancels the operation.

To undo any changes you've made after opening a dialog box, press Option or Alt, which changes the Cancel button into a Reset button, and then click Reset. (This feature is not available in all dialog boxes.)

Working with the Interface

The InDesign interface has many options and particulars. Although it can take a while to get used to using a new program's interface, with practice you'll soon be using the interface more easily.

File names

In the Open dialog box, use All Files in Windows InDesign to display Mac files with no extensions, and in Macintosh InDesign to display Windows files without the InDesign icons.

Defaults

You can use the Mac's alias feature or Windows's shortcut feature to use an InDesign Defaults file stored in a folder other than the one in which InDesign resides. On a network, being able to use this technique means that everyone can share the same InDesign Defaults file. (Windows users can all use a shortcut to the same InDesign Defaults file, while Mac users can all use an alias to the same InDesign Defaults file, but Windows users cannot use a shortcut to a Mac InDesign Defaults file or vice versa.) You can also set keyboard shortcuts sets, spelling and hyphenation dictionaries, libraries, and color swatch libraries to be shared this way. Note that if you're sharing these across platforms, you'll need to create a Windows shortcut from Windows to these files as well as a Mac alias from the Mac.

You might want to change the View Threshold to match or exceed the document's most common Fit in Window view. For example, a magazine page on a 15-inch monitor in a full window might display at around 65 percent when you choose View ➪ Fit in Window. Usually you use Fit in Window to get an overall look at the page, and the baseline grid would simply be in the way.

Measurement entry

When entering measurements in dialog boxes and panes, it doesn't matter whether you put a space between the value and the code: for example, *1inch* and *1 inch* are the same as far as InDesign is concerned.

Shortcuts

Consider adding a keyboard shortcut for Layout ➪ Create Guides, such as the unused Shift+G. Although you'll get a capital "G" while typing, when any other tool than Type is selected, you'll be able to create a guide. Another command sorely in need of a keyboard shortcut is Type ➪ Insert Character. Try the unused ⌘+U or Ctrl+U.

Palettes and panes

We suggest you make the following change to InDesign's default arrangement of panes: InDesign has combined the Transform, Character, and Paragraph panes into a single palette to mimic the QuarkXPress Measurements palette and PageMaker Control palette. We suggest you split these three panes into separate palettes. Use the Transform pane while performing layout tasks, and then keep both the Character and Paragraph panes open separately while formatting text so you can see all the attributes at once. (You might combine the Character pane with the Character Styles pane and the Paragraph pane with the Paragraph Styles pane. If you do this, use the menus on the Paragraph and Character panes to change their orientation to vertical to match the Styles panes.)

For color swatch libraries that you use a lot, drag them into the palette containing the Swatches pane. In fact, you might want to have a palette just for color-related panes: Swatches, any swatch libraries, Color, and Gradient.

Once you've clicked in a field in a pane with multiple fields, you can move around the pane by using the Tab and Shift+Tab shortcuts rather than selecting each one with the mouse. Tab goes to the right, whereas Shift+Tab moves to the left.

Guides

You can place both a horizontal and vertical guide at the same time by pressing ⌘ or Ctrl and dragging the ruler intersection point onto a page.

You can also place a guide that extends across the page or the spread and pasteboard by double-clicking the vertical or horizontal ruler.

Working with Objects

InDesign works with a great variety of objects, and it has several tools to do so. Having so many tools — especially given the subtle difference between the Selection and Direct Selection tools — can be confusing. But you can use the following techniques to more effectively work with objects, often without needing to follow complicated menu operations.

Import and creation

You can place an image or text on a page — and automatically create a new graphics frame or text frame — by dragging a supported file directly from the Mac Finder (desktop or folder) or Windows Explorer (desktop or folder) onto an InDesign page.

When you create a line, it takes on the characteristics specified in the Stroke pane (Window ➪ Stroke, or F10). When you first open a document, the default line width is 1 point. If you want to change the appearance of your lines, double-click the Line tool and adjust the Weight in the Stroke pane that appears. If you make this adjustment when no document is open, all new documents will use the new line settings.

Selection

You can't click in master text frames — text frames that are placed on the page by the master page in use — and simply start typing. To select a master text frame and add text to it, Shift+⌘+click or Ctrl+Shift+click it.

To select an object that's hidden behind one or more other objects without clicking, choose the Selection tool, and then move the pointer over the hidden object. Hold down ⌘+Option or Ctrl+Alt and press [. The first time you press [, the top object is selected. Each successive press selects the next lowest object. If the bottom object is selected, the next click selects the top object as the top-to-bottom selection cycle begins to repeat itself.

To use the mouse to select an object that's hidden behind one or more other objects, hold down the ⌘ or Ctrl key, and then click anywhere within the area of the hidden object. The first click selects the top-most object; each successive click selects the next lowest object in the stacking order. When the bottom object is selected, the next click selects the top object. If you don't know where a hidden object is, you can simply click the object or objects in front of it, and then send the object(s) to the back.

Groups

You cannot create a group if some of the selected objects are locked and some are not locked. All selected objects must have the same lock status before you can group them.

If you want to manipulate a group, choose the Selection tool, and then click any object in the group. The group's bounding box is displayed. Any transformation you perform is applied to all objects in the group. If you want to manipulate an object that's part of a group, select it using the Direct Selection tool.

To resize multiple objects simultaneously, you must first group them (Object ➪ Group, or ⌘+G or Ctrl+G). Otherwise, only the object whose handle is being dragged will resize. Ungroup via Object ➪ Ungroup, or Shift+⌘+G or Ctrl+Shift+G.

Positioning

You can use the arrow keys to nudge items when precise positioning is required. Each press of an arrow key moves the selected objects one point. If you hold down the Shift key when nudging, the increment is 10 points. You can set alternative nudge settings via the Cursor Key field after selecting File ➪ Preferences ➪ Units & Increments, or by pressing ⌘+K or Ctrl+K and then selecting the Units & Increments pane. Holding the Shift key when nudging moves the selected object(s) 10 increments of whatever Cursor Key is set to. If you need a tab flush with the right margin — for example, to position a dingbat at the end of the story — click the Right Tab Style button and position it on the right side of the tab ruler. Then, drag the right-aligned tab on top of the right indent arrow. (You can't actually click to place a tab on top of the arrow, but you can drag a tab on top of it.)

When you create a text frame with the Type tool, you can align the frame edge with a guideline by clicking within the number of pixels specified in the Snap to Zone in the Guides pane of the Preferences dialog box (File ➪ Preferences, or ⌘+K or Ctrl+K).

The Align buttons don't work with objects that have been locked with the Lock Position command (Object ⇨ Lock Position, or ⌘+L or Ctrl+L). If you need to align a locked object, you must first unlock it (Object ⇨ Unlock Position, or ⌘+Option+L or Ctrl+Alt+L).

Hold down the Shift key as you drag to restrict the angle of movement to multiples of 45 degrees.

If you drag immediately after clicking an object with the Rotation tool, the object is displayed in its original location and the object's bounding box moves as you drag. If you click and then pause until the stem of the arrow pointer disappears, the object is displayed as you drag.

Cloning

To create a clone of an object, use Option+Return or Alt+Enter after changing the X and/or Y value in the Transform pane. You can also create a clone by holding Option or Alt when dragging an object with the mouse or nudging an object via the arrow keys.

Frames

If you drag immediately after clicking a handle, only a frame's bounding box is displayed as you drag. If you click and then pause until the pointer changes, the contents within are displayed as you drag.

When you resize a picture frame by clicking and dragging a handle, the picture within isn't affected unless you hold down ⌘ or Ctrl as you drag. Holding down ⌘ or Ctrl and dragging changes the picture's scale as well as the size of the frame.

If you accidentally use the Type tool to create a frame that you want to use as a container for a graphic, you can change it to a graphics frame by choosing Object ⇨ Content ⇨ Graphic.

To delete an inline frame, you can select it, and then choose Edit ⇨ Clear or, if you wish to preserve it on the clipboard for pasting elsewhere, choose Edit ⇨ Cut, or ⌘+X or Ctrl+X, or you can position the cursor following it and then press the Delete or Backspace key.

You can flip the contents of a picture frame or text frame by dragging a bounding box handle across and beyond the opposite corner or edge.

Paths

As you create a path, you can move any anchor point, direction line handle, or the entire path by holding down the ⌘ or Ctrl keys, and then clicking and dragging whatever element you want to move.

If all you need to do is resize a path—particularly a simple rectangle—rather than change its shape, you should select it with the Selection tool rather than the Direct Selection tool, and then drag one of its bounding box handles.

When using the Convert Direction Point tool, you can temporarily switch to the most recently used selection tool by pressing the ⌘ or Ctrl key.

Working with Text

InDesign has some of the strongest text-manipulation features of any layout program. Following these tips will help you work with your text more easily and take fuller advantage of InDesign's capabilities.

Import

If you're importing a text-only file that contains paragraph returns at the end of each line, be sure to check the Show Import Options as it gives you the option to remove them.

Styles and formatting

If the Type tool is selected and no objects are active, the controls in the Character pane and Paragraph pane are still available. In this situation, any changes you make in these panes become the default settings for the document and are automatically used when you create new text frames.

If you hold down Option or Alt when clicking a name in the Paragraph Styles pane, any formatting that's been applied within selected paragraphs is removed. If you hold down Option+Shift or Alt+Shift when clicking a style name, all formatting within the selected paragraphs is retained.

If you click New Style after selecting a style from the Styles list, your new style inherits that selected style's options. This is a great way to create a variant of an existing style.

By importing styles with no document open, you copy all new styles into your global defaults (those stored in the InDesign Defaults file covered earlier). This technique is a handy way of bringing new styles into your default settings without affecting existing styles.

Tabs

Any tabs you set in the Tabs pane when no document is open are added to all future documents you create.

Rather than clicking a new Tab Style button for a selected tab, you can Option+click or Alt+click the tab on the ruler. This cycles through the four different styles; stop clicking when the alignment you need displays.

Hyphenation

You can prevent a word from being hyphenated by placing a discretionary hyphen (Shift+⌘+hyphen or Ctrl+Shift+hyphen) in front of the first letter.

Text effects

You can use the Offset feature in the Paragraph Rules pane of the New Paragraph Styles or Edit Paragraph Styles pane (Type ⇨ Paragraph Styles, or F11) and in the Paragraph Rules dialog box accessed by the palette menu of the Paragraph pane (Type ⇨ Paragraph, or ⌘+M or Ctrl+M) to create reversed type. To do this, you essentially move the rule into the text line associated with it. The key is to make the rule larger than the text. For example, if the text is 28 points, we'd set the rule to be 30 points, which provides a slight margin above and below the text. (Make your rule at least 2 points larger than the text to get an adequate margin.) We'd then offset the rule by –8 points to move it below the baseline (to cover any descenders in the text).

If you hold the Option or Alt keys when creating text outlines (via Type ⇨ Create Outlines, or Shift+⌘+O or Ctrl+Shift+O), the text in the resulting inline compound path will be editable.

Text wraps

If you want to wrap text around only a portion of a picture — perhaps you need to isolate a face in a crowd — the best solution is to open the graphics file in its original program, create a clipping path around that portion, and then resave the file and import it and its clipping path into an InDesign document.

To apply text-wrap settings to a master item on a document page, hold down Shift+⌘ or Ctrl+Shift to select the item, and then use the controls in the Text Wrap pane as described previously.

If you specify text-wrap settings when no objects are selected, the settings are automatically applied to all new objects. When you create outlines out of a range of highlighted characters, a compound path is created, and each of the characters becomes a subpath. You can use the Release (Compound Path) command (Object ⇨ Compound Path ⇨ Release, or Option+⌘+8 or Ctrl+Alt+8) to turn each of the subpaths into independent paths.

Working with Color

Using color can be tricky, but InDesign offers several features to simplify this work. Follow these tips to make working with color easy and to get the color you expect.

Swatches

Share color swatches by putting objects that use them in a library. When others use these objects, they'll get the swatch added to their document automatically.

InDesign offers a nice option to quickly find all unused colors in the Swatches pane: the palette menu's Select All Unused option. Then you can just delete them in one fell swoop. Note that you don't get the option to assign each deleted color separately to another color in the Delete Swatch dialog box—they are all replaced with the color you select or are made into unnamed colors. Because no object uses these colors, choosing Unnamed Swatch in essence is the same as replacing them with a color using the Defined Swatch option.

When you create a new gradient, InDesign uses the settings from the last one you created. If you want to create a gradient similar to an existing one, click that existing gradient before selecting New Gradient Swatch from the palette menu. InDesign copies the selected gradient's settings to the new one, which you can then edit. One reason to use this method is to create, say, a radial version of an existing linear gradient.

Trapping

You may want to overprint black strokes, because doing so ensures that no registration issues occur in four-color printing—no gap between the black stroke and the underlying color.

To change trapping styles for a document, create a trapping zone that is set for all pages for each trapping style. Then you can just click Enable for the particular trapping style you want to be used for the current document rather than open the Trapping Styles dialog box and choose one there.

Color calibration

Depending on what kinds of documents you produce, you'll likely want Perceptual (Images) or Saturation (Graphics) as your document-wide default, which you set in the Document Color Settings dialog box. Use the first for photographs and scanned images, the latter for drawn objects and charts.

To create a monitor profile if InDesign doesn't support your monitor, use the Adobe Gamma control panel that is installed with InDesign — it very nicely walks you through the necessary steps. One tip: When asked to make the center box fade into the background to adjust the image's gamma, focus your eyes between the monitor and you, to make the image fuzzy — this will help you better gauge when the colors become equivalent. You can also use commercial software tools such as Color Solutions' ColorBlind, as long as it creates an ICC profile. Remember to adjust the lighting in your work area so it's not too bright or dark; doing so affects how you perceive the monitor display and affects the profile you create. Windows users: You must use DOS-style names for your profile (eight characters maximum, followed by the file extension .icc); Adobe Gamma oddly doesn't support long file names for files it creates.

Working with Document-Wide Elements

A powerful approach used by InDesign is to have functions that affect the entire document. The following tips will help you use those functions more effectively.

Layers

If you're designing a template that will be used by others, you might want to add a layer of instructions. When it's time to print a document based on the template, simply hide the annotation layer.

You can multiple-select layers and customize them all at once. Because each layer must have a different name, the Name field is not available in the Layer Options dialog box when multiple layers are selected.

To remove all layers that do not contain objects, choose Delete Unused Layers from the Layers palette.

Master pages and spreads

To copy a master page or spread from one document to another, display the source document, click the master page's name in the Pages pane, drag it to the window of the target document, and then release the mouse button.

Libraries

InDesign libraries are cross-platform. That is, you can open libraries created on a Mac using a PC and vice versa. On the PC, libraries have the file-name extension .INDT, whereas on the Mac they have no file-name extension. In a cross-platform environment, add the PC file-name extensions even to Mac files so Windows users can easily tell what type of file each file is, and be sure to update any software on your PC that mounts Mac media or connects Macs to PCs over the network to include these extensions so InDesign files are recognized as such automatically (Chapter 37 explains how to do this).

If you hold down the Option or Alt key when adding an object to a library using any of the preceding methods, the Item Information dialog box is displayed. This dialog box lets you add searchable attributes to the object.

You can copy an object from one library to another by dragging its icon from the source library pane and dropping it onto the target library pane. If you hold down the Option or Alt key when dragging and dropping an object between libraries, the original object is removed from the source library (in effect moving it from one library to the other).

Working with Printers

On the Mac, if you deal with a lot of printers, create a folder called Printers in your System Folder, and then drag all printer icons to it. Make sure the Printers folder is open, and then select View ⇨ As Pop-up Window. This changes the folder to a pop-up folder, with a tab at top. Click this tab to reduce the folder at the bottom of the screen. Clicking the tab again will open the folder. Now you can get quick access to your printer icons without cluttering your desktop. (In Windows, all printers are available in the Printer pop-up menu in the Print dialog box.)

Using any printer's marks automatically increases the page size in PDF files exported from InDesign to add room for the printer's marks. This is handy because when you output EPS or other PostScript files, the page size selected determines the page boundary, and printer's marks often get eliminated because they fall outside that boundary. One solution is to use a larger page size than your final output will be, so there's naturally enough room for printer's marks. The preview window at right in the dialog box shows you if printer's marks fall outside the page's boundaries.

Working with Files

The easiest way to work smoothly with files on both platforms is to use the PC extension on all file names, even those created on the Mac. This way, you're assured that Windows users see the correct icon (at least for formats that exist on both Windows and the Mac — some formats have no PC equivalents and thus no PC extension). Macintosh users have to remember to look at files that have the PC icon.

If you can store all of your graphics files in a single location — not necessarily in a single folder, but perhaps within a folder hierarchy on your hard disk or a file server — you can minimize link problems. If you move or delete the original file after importing a graphic, you'll break the link, which causes printing problems. Keeping all graphics files in a single, safe place — a place that's backed up regularly — is a good idea.

✦   ✦   ✦

Switching from QuarkXPress or PageMaker

Learning to use new software, or even learning to use an upgrade of a familiar application, can be so intimidating that many users resist passionately. Even if an application is woefully out of date and lacking in functionality, you cling to it knowing you can accomplish your mission, even with workarounds, with less frustration than the untried, but powerful, new application. Users are particularly passionate about their choice of page-layout software — which is usually QuarkXPress or PageMaker — probably because they're involved with it for 8 to 12 hours a day. (A QuarkXPress user once said he spent more time with QuarkXPress than with his wife, so you can see where the dedication is coming from.)

But times, circumstances, and jobs change. Eventually, your old software won't run on your zippy new machine or you switch jobs or you simply prefer another vendor. No matter what circumstances lead you to choosing InDesign, this appendix is designed to help you let go and move forward, showing you the differences between your old layout application and InDesign, and pointing out a few benefits of InDesign as well. InDesign lets you open documents from both QuarkXPress and PageMaker so you can continue working with existing designs, and you can apply much of your page-layout knowledge to InDesign.

Opening QuarkXPress Documents

The Open command (File ➪ Open, or ⌘+O or Ctrl+O) lets you select and open documents and templates saved in QuarkXPress versions 3.3*x* through 4.04 on Macintosh or

Windows. (You can't open libraries, though.) All the text, graphics, items, master pages, styles, and more in the QuarkXPress document are converted to their InDesign equivalents. If the document contains items, content, or formatting that can't be converted, an alert notifies you of the issues. Once the document is converted, it displays as a new, untitled document.

Cross-Reference   See Chapter 4 for complete information about opening files.

Now that you know what InDesign is supposed to do, take a look at how well it actually does it. Yes, you can open QuarkXPress documents, save them as InDesign documents, and continue working with them. But the documents don't convert perfectly: You are likely to lose some formatting because InDesign doesn't have equivalent formatting or its options work differently. In general, you can expect to use a QuarkXPress document as a starting point for a design — usually with a little repair work — but you should not expect to simply open a QuarkXPress document and have it look and print exactly the same way.

Tip   After realizing which QuarkXPress features are not supported or not converted well, and considering how your own QuarkXPress documents are created, you can decide on a document-by-document basis whether conversion is worth the effort. In some cases, it might be easier to simply reconstruct a document, whereas in other cases, you might be able to start working almost immediately.

When you convert QuarkXPress documents to InDesign, you can expect the following:

✦ Master pages are converted, including all items, content, and guides.

✦ All line and frame styles are converted to dashed or plain strokes.

✦ Text boxes are converted to text frames; picture boxes are converted to graphics frames.

✦ Text paths, which are not supported in InDesign, are converted to rectangular text frames.

✦ All paragraph and character styles are converted to InDesign styles.

✦ Incremental autoleading (such as +4, which adds 4 points to the largest font size on the line) is converted to InDesign's standard autoleading.

✦ The Next Column (Enter on keypad) or Next Box (Shift+Enter) characters (which you use to bump text to the next column or next text rather than resizing the box) are not converted and the text is reflowed.

✦ The bold and italic type styles are converted to the appropriate typeface (if available), and Underline, Strikethru, Superscript, Subscript, All Caps, and Small Caps are converted. But Superior, Word Underline, Outline, and Shadow revert to plain text.

✦ Index tags are not maintained, and you may have difficulty opening chapters of a book.

✦ If a picture is missing or modified in QuarkXPress, it won't display in the InDesign document. If you want to retain the picture, you'll need to update the link in QuarkXPress (Utilities ➪ Usage ➪ Pictures) before converting it.

✦ Pasted (embedded) pictures, pictures imported using OLE or Publish and Subscribe, and pictures created with third-party XTensions will not convert.

✦ Clipping paths created in QuarkXPress are not converted, so the image's display will change.

✦ The Same as Clipping Runaround feature in QuarkXPress leaves a runaround shape based on the clipping path in InDesign — but if you've resized the image in QuarkXPress, the runaround path stays at 100 percent in InDesign.

✦ Items for which Suppress Printout is checked are placed on a separate layer called *Nonprinting layer*. To view these objects in InDesign, view the layer.

✦ If a group contains an item for which Suppress Printout is checked, all the items are ungrouped and the suppressed items are placed on the nonprinting layer.

✦ ICC-compliant color profiles (used in QuarkXPress 4.0 and greater) are retained; other profiles (the EfiColor profiles using in QuarkXPress 3.2 and 3.3x) are not retained.

✦ Colors in QuarkXPress 3.3x documents are converted to InDesign swatches according to their CMYK values (except for HSB colors, which are converted to RGB swatches).

✦ Colors in QuarkXPress 4.x documents are converted to InDesign swatches according to their RGB values (except for HSB and LAB colors, which are converted to RGB swatches). Hexachrome colors are not converted.

✦ Cool Blends are converted to linear or circular blends.

Opening PageMaker Documents

The Open command (File ➪ Open, or ⌘+O or Ctrl+O) lets you select and open documents and templates saved in PageMaker 6.5 on Macintosh or Windows. (You can't open libraries, though.) All the text, graphics, elements, layers, master pages, styles, and more in the PageMaker document are converted to their InDesign equivalents. If formatting can't be converted, an alert notifies you of the issues. Once the document is converted, it displays as a new, untitled document.

Cross-Reference   See Chapter 4 for complete information about opening files.

Because InDesign and PageMaker are similar, documents from PageMaker usually convert reliably. However, you still shouldn't count on PageMaker documents displaying and printing exactly the same way once they're converted in InDesign. You may need to do a little repair work, depending on the type of formatting you use.

When you convert PageMaker documents to InDesign, you can expect the following:

+ Master pages are converted, including all elements and content.

+ Guides on master pages are placed on a separate layer called *Guides*.

+ All line and stroke styles are converted to dashed or plain strokes.

+ All styles are converted to InDesign styles.

+ The Bold and Italic type styles are converted to the appropriate typeface (if available), Underline and Strikethru are converted, while Outline, Shadow, and Reverse revert to plain text.

+ Index tags are not maintained.

+ If an imported graphic's link is not intact, it won't display in the InDesign document. If you want to retain the graphic, you'll need to update the link in PageMaker (File ⇨ Links Manager) before converting it.

+ Pasted (embedded) graphics and graphics imported using OLE or Publish and Subscribe will not convert.

+ Items for which Suppress Printout is checked are placed on a separate layer called *Nonprinting layer*. To view these objects in InDesign, view the layer.

+ If a group contains an item for which Suppress Printout is checked, the items are ungrouped and suppressed items are placed on the nonprinting layer.

+ Color profiles are converted.

+ Colors are converted to InDesign swatches according to their CMYK values (except for HLS colors, which are converted to RGB swatches).

Switching from QuarkXPress

For the QuarkXPress veteran, the toughest thing about switching to InDesign is the set of tools. In your world, you've been using the Item tool (which you might call the pointer) and the Content tool (the little hand) for almost everything. Not only did you use them all the time, but the Item tool or Content tool was selected automatically for you most of the time (because object-creation tools snap back to the last-used selection tool). Over time, the two tools have evolved into almost one, so you might have been using the Content tool all the time, pressing ⌘ or Ctrl when you needed to manipulate an entire item.

You need to forget about this way of working entirely. In InDesign, you'll be switching tools constantly. When you create an object, its tool remains selected so you can't move or resize the objects immediately after creation. The Selection tool only lets you move and resize objects, whereas the Direct Selection tool lets you reshape objects and work with graphics. You must have the Type tool to work with text, but there's no moving or resizing of text frames while you're using it. This will seem restrictive to you at first, but the key is to embrace InDesign's single-letter shortcuts for selecting tools. (InDesign also provides QuarkXPress-like keyboard commands for temporarily activating tools, but it's easier to press a single letter to switch tools.)

As long as the Type tool isn't selected, you can activate any tool by pressing the letter displayed next to it in the tool's ToolTip. In particular, you'll want to memorize the following:

✦ Press V for the Selection tool.

✦ Press A for the Direct Selection tool.

✦ Press T for the Type tool.

✦ Press H for the Hand tool (you can also press the spacebar; when editing text, you can press Option or Alt).

✦ Press Z for the Zoom tool (you can also press ⌘+spacebar or Ctrl+spacebar to zoom in and Option+⌘+spacebar or Ctrl+Alt+spacebar to zoom out). Remember you can zoom to 1,600 percent in InDesign!

If you're also a Photoshop user, the single-letter shortcuts might be familiar to you, but it's an odd concept for a QuarkXPress-only user. But once you get the hang of it, you'll appreciate how fast and easy it is to switch tools.

Differing interfaces

A few overall interface differences between QuarkXPress and InDesign might hang you up initially. Keep in mind that many menu commands simply display a pane (which may already be open) rather than showing a dialog box. Get used to deciphering icons or using ToolTips on the panes because few dialog boxes contain named fields as you're used to in QuarkXPress's Character Attributes, Paragraph Attributes, and Modify dialog boxes. Contextual menus are implemented on a much broader scale than in QuarkXPress, so you can Control+click or right+click objects, rulers, and more to make changes quickly.

Most of the measurement system abbreviations are the same, with these exceptions:

✦ Type **0p** before an entry in points.

✦ Use **in** for inch rather than ".

✦ Use **m** for millimeter rather than "mm."

Tip

InDesign offers a set of keyboard commands similar to those in QuarkXPress (File ➪ Edit Keyboard Shortcuts, or Option+Shift+⌘+K or Ctrl+Alt+Shift+K). We recommend that you avoid this set and learn the commands in InDesign. This helps you in communicating about InDesign and working with other Adobe software. If you do choose to use the QuarkXPress set of keyboard commands, at least make the corrections to it recommended in Chapter 3.

Working with objects rather than items

In QuarkXPress, you're used to items such as text boxes, picture boxes, lines, and maybe text paths. In InDesign, you have paths and frames, with the only difference being that frames contain graphics or text. You can therefore make a one-to-one relationship between text boxes and text frames, and picture boxes and picture frames. Just keep in mind that, with InDesign, you're not restricted to using boxes for content — you can fill any path with text or graphics and have it become a frame. And if you don't make a box (or the right kind of box) up front, you can still import graphics and text in InDesign (unlike in QuarkXPress).

While selecting and manipulating objects with tools, remember the following:

♦ Use the Selection tool to move objects or resize frames.

♦ Use the Direct Selection tool to reshape objects, work with graphics, and change the endpoints of lines (it's kind of like QuarkXPress's Content tool).

♦ When reshaping objects, you can use the Pen tool, Anchor Point tool, and Remove Anchor Point tool in addition to the Direct Selection tool.

♦ You can't just click master page objects: Instead, use Shift+⌘+click or Ctrl+Shift+click to select them.

When modifying objects, remember the following:

♦ Use the Transform pane in InDesign instead of QuarkXPress's Measurements palette or Modify dialog box's Box or Line tab.

♦ To specify runaround, use the Object ⇨ Text Wrap command.

♦ To specify attributes of text frames, use the Object ⇨ Text Frame Options command, or ⌘+B or Ctrl+B.

♦ To suppress printout of objects, put them on a different layer and hide the layer.

Flowing text

Once you learn how to flow text in InDesign, you'll find it's easier and more flexible than QuarkXPress. It's easy to get stuck and to restrict yourself to QuarkXPress techniques. To prevent that, keep these differences in mind:

♦ To import a text file, use File ⇨ Place, or ⌘+D or Ctrl+D. You can also drag files and text from the desktop or any application that supports drag-and-drop.

♦ You do not need to create or select a text frame before you import text; you'll be able to create or select a text frame after choosing the file to import.

♦ InDesign does not have linking tools. To flow text from frame-to-frame, use a selection tool to click the out ports and in ports on text frames. (Make sure View ⇨ Show Text Threads is checked.)

✦ To flow text and add pages automatically, check Master Text Frame in the New Document dialog box (File ➪ New Document, or ⌘+N or Ctrl+N). Then, you'll need to Shift+⌘+click or Ctrl+Shift+click the master text frame on a document page. Finally, Option+click or Alt+click the loaded text icon. See Chapter 11 for complete information about flowing text.

Editing text

A few minor differences exist when it comes to editing and selecting text:

✦ InDesign doesn't support "smart space" the way QuarkXPress 4.0 does, so when you double-click to select, and then cut and paste a word, you won't get the trailing space.

✦ In QuarkXPress, clicking three times in text selects the line and clicking four times selects the entire paragraph. In InDesign, clicking three times selects the paragraph.

✦ To type special characters such as ñ, •, or ¶, you can use Type ➪ Insert Special Character rather than system utilities or key combinations.

✦ The control for showing invisible characters such as spaces, tabs, and paragraph returns is Type ➪ Show Hidden Characters.

Tip   Use the Edit Shortcuts feature (File ➪ Edit Shortcuts, or Option+Shift+⌘+K or Ctrl+Alt+Shift+K) to assign a keyboard command to the Insert Character command if you find yourself using it often.

Formatting text

In general, formatting text in InDesign will feel comfortable to QuarkXPress users. You'll miss those big Character and Paragraph Attributes dialog boxes (featuring real words, not icons!), but you have most of the same power. Review these differences, and keep them in mind while formatting text:

✦ Use the Character pane (Type ➪ Character, or ⌘+D or Ctrl+D) to format highlighted characters. You'll notice that no type style buttons appear — InDesign requires you to choose the appropriate version of a typeface rather than attributes such as bold and italic, whereas other type styles are listed in the Character pane's palette menu.

✦ Leading is a character-level format in InDesign, therefore the controls are in the Character pane rather than the Paragraph pane as you might have come to expect. Leading is always measured from baseline-to-baseline in InDesign.

✦ Unlike QuarkXPress, you can stroke and fill characters in InDesign.

✦ Use the Paragraph pane (Type ➪ Paragraph, or ⌘+M or Ctrl+M) to format selected paragraphs; the palette menu includes additional commands for adding rules and controlling hyphenation.

✦ InDesign does not have H&J sets, so set up your hyphenation using the Paragraph pane and save your settings in paragraph styles.

✦ Use the Tabs pane (Type ⇨ Tabs, or Shift+⌘+T or Ctrl+Shift+T) to set tabs for selected paragraphs.

✦ To create styles, use the new commands in the palette menus on the Character pane (Type ⇨ Character Styles, or Shift+F11) and the Paragraph pane (Type ⇨ Paragraph Styles, or F11). To share styles with other documents, use the load commands in the same menus.

✦ Applying styles to text with local formatting has the opposite effect as it has in QuarkXPress. Styles always wipe out local formatting when first applied. If you add local formatting later and want to revert the text to the style's formats, click the style twice. (Note that applying No Style and then the style does not work, as it does in QuarkXPress.)

Working with graphics

Importing and manipulating graphics in InDesign is very similar to QuarkXPress. As long as you remember to use the Direct Selection tool to select a graphic rather than its frame, you and the InDesign graphics features will get along fine. Differences between the programs include:

✦ To import a graphics file in InDesign, use File ⇨ Place, or ⌘+D or Ctrl+D. You can also drag files in from the desktop or other programs if InDesign supports their file formats.

✦ You do not need to create or select a graphics frame before you import a graphic; you'll be able to create or select a graphics frame after choosing the file to import.

✦ Use the Transform pane (Window ⇨ Transform or F9) to rotate, scale, and skew graphics. You can create clipping paths with the Object ⇨ Clipping Paths command.

✦ To automatically scale a graphic to fit within its frame — proportionally or not — use the Fitting commands in the Object menu or their keyboard commands. As a bonus, you get a Fit Frame to Picture command, a task you have to perform manually in QuarkXPress.

✦ To track the location of graphic files, use the Links pane (File ⇨ Links, or Shift+⌘+D or Ctrl+Shift+D).

Manipulating pages

You'll find the controls for working with document pages and master pages to be quite similar to QuarkXPress — if not slightly better. Once you realize the differences and start working, you can take advantage of InDesign's improvements. The differences mostly relate to guides and using the InDesign Pages pane rather than the QuarkXPress Document Layout palette:

✦ InDesign provides three methods for creating guides: Drag them off the ruler as you do in QuarkXPress, double-click the ruler where you want a guide, or choose Layout ⇨ Create Guides.

✦ To delete guides, you need to select them and click Delete. (To select all guides on a page, press Option+⌘+G or Ctrl+Alt+G.)

✦ Use the Pages pane (Window ⇨ Pages or F12) as you would the QuarkXPress Document Layout palette. To place more than two pages side-by-side, you'll need to use the Set as Island Spread command in the pane's palette menu.

✦ If you're missing the QuarkXPress Page menu, look for your favorite commands in the InDesign Layout menu and in the Pages pane's palette menu. There's a bonus in the Layout menu: an Insert Page Number command (Option+⌘+N or Ctrl+Alt+N) so you don't have to remember that odd ⌘+3 or Ctrl+3 command that QuarkXPress requires.

✦ You can base one master page on another, the same way you can base styles on each other.

✦ To share master pages among documents, you can drag a master page icon into another document window.

Working with color

Not to intimidate you, but color will confound you (although Photoshop users will have an easier transition). Basically, try to forget everything you know about creating and applying colors in QuarkXPress. Here's what you need to know to work with colors in InDesign:

✦ Most of your work with colors happens through the Swatches pane (Window ⇨ Swatches or F5), not through the Colors pane as QuarkXPress users might think.

✦ To create colors, use the New Swatches command in the Swatches pane's palette menu. You cannot create Hexachrome colors in InDesign.

✦ To apply colors, first click the Stroke or Fill button on the Toolbox to specify where the color goes on the selected object. Then, click a color in the Swatches pane.

✦ Use the Colors pane (Window ⇨ Colors or F6) to specify a shade (tint) of a color.

✦ InDesign's Paper color is equal to the QuarkXPress White color. Both programs use the color None for transparency, but InDesign provides None in both the Swatches pane and as a button on the Toolbox.

✦ To share colors among documents, drag a colored object into another document window.

Switching from PageMaker

As you might expect, because both come from the Adobe world, the transition from PageMaker to InDesign isn't that tough. The basic methods for working with frames, lines, and pages are the same in both programs. What you get with InDesign is more control, with improved tools for drawing, formatting text, and manipulating objects. With the exception of the indexing and book features, there's not much to miss about PageMaker, either.

Using tools and setting preferences

The basic selection, object creation, and navigation tools in InDesign are similar to those in PageMaker. You do have to remember that InDesign has two selection tools: the Selection tool for moving and resizing objects, and the Direct Selection tool for reshaping objects and working with graphics.

Because you'll be switching tools often, as you did in PageMaker, get in the habit of using the keyboard shortcuts. As long as the Type tool isn't selected, you can hop from tool to tool by simply pressing a letter on the keyboard. In particular, you'll want to memorize the following:

✦ Press V for the Selection tool.

✦ Press A for the Direct Selection tool.

✦ Press T for the Type tool.

✦ Press H for the Hand tool — you'll notice it's not included on the Toolbox as it is in PageMaker. (You can also press the spacebar; when editing text, you can press Option or Alt.)

✦ Press Z for the Zoom tool (you can also press ⌘+spacebar or Ctrl+spacebar to zoom in and Option+⌘+spacebar or Ctrl+Alt+spacebar to zoom out). Remember you can zoom to 1,600 percent in InDesign!

InDesign includes significantly more preferences than PageMaker. You'll definitely want to explore all the panes in the Preferences dialog box (File ➪ Preferences, or ⌘+K or Ctrl+K). You might find some power you've never had before (although you will be disappointed to see values for Superscript, Subscript, and Small Cap relegated to a document-wide preference rather than a character attribute as they were in PageMaker).

Working with objects rather than elements

As with other aspects of InDesign, when you work with objects, you gain more than you lose. The types of objects are similar: text frames, graphics frames, and lines. PageMaker is limited to creating closed frames and straight lines.

While selecting and manipulating objects with tools, remember the following:

✦ Use the Selection tool to move objects or resize frames.

✦ Use the Direct Selection tool to reshape objects, change the endpoints of lines, and work with objects in groups. The Direct Selection tool also works like PageMaker's Crop tool, enabling you to move graphics within a frame.

✦ You get Bézier curves in InDesign! Using the Pen tool, Anchor Point tool, and Remove Anchor Point tool, you can draw and manipulate curves to your heart's content.

✦ You can't just click master page objects: Use Shift+⌘+click or Ctrl+Shift+click to select them.

When modifying objects, remember the following:

✦ Look in the Object menu for familiar Elements menu commands, and use the InDesign Transform pane instead of the PageMaker Control palette.

✦ To specify runaround, use the Object ⇨ Text Wrap command.

✦ To specify attributes of text frames, use the Object ⇨ Text Frame Options command, or ⌘+B or Ctrl+B.

✦ To suppress printout of objects, put them on a different layer and hide the layer.

Working with text

When it comes to working with text, the big shock to the PageMaker user is that InDesign does not have an Edit Story mode. You work in layout mode all the time, viewing the text as it appears in the document. This gives you several advantages — for example, you can use Spell Check and Find/Change all the time. If you were a fan of story mode, you might consider spending more time on files up front in a word processor. If the display of graphics makes it difficult for you to edit text, choose Gray Out Images from the Display pop-up menu in the Preferences dialog box (File ⇨ Preferences ⇨ General, or ⌘+K or Ctrl+K and then selecting the General Pane).

Other differences between PageMaker and InDesign include:

✦ To type special characters such as ñ, •, or ¶, you can use Type ⇨ Insert Special Character rather than system utilities or key combinations.

Tip   Use the Edit Shortcuts feature (File ⇨ Edit Shortcuts, or Option+Shift+⌘+K or Ctrl+Alt+Shift+K) to assign a keyboard command to the Insert Character command if you find yourself using it often.

✦ In PageMaker's Edit Story mode, you can only see invisible characters such as spaces and tabs. But you can see them all the time in InDesign by choosing Type ➪ Show Hidden Characters.

✦ Use the Character pane (Type ➪ Character, or ⌘+D or Ctrl+D) to format highlighted characters. You'll notice no type style buttons appear — InDesign requires you to choose the appropriate version of a typeface rather than bold and italic, whereas other type styles are listed in the Character pane's palette menu.

✦ Unlike PageMaker, you can stroke and fill characters in InDesign.

✦ Use the Paragraph pane (Type ➪ Paragraph, or ⌘+M or Ctrl+M) to format selected paragraphs; the palette menu includes additional commands for adding rules and controlling hyphenation.

✦ Use the Tabs pane (Type ➪ Tabs, or Shift+⌘+T or Ctrl+Shift+T) to set tabs for selected paragraphs.

✦ To create styles, use the new commands in the palette menus on the Character pane (Type ➪ Character Styles, or Shift+F11) and the Paragraph pane (Type ➪ Paragraph Styles, or F11). To share styles with other documents, use the load commands in the same menus.

✦ When you apply styles in PageMaker, local formatting is retained. InDesign styles have the opposite effect — they wipe out all local formatting when applied.

Working with graphics

InDesign and PageMaker are very much alike when it comes to importing and manipulating graphics. There's no Crop tool in InDesign, but the Direct Selection tool functions pretty much the same way for graphics.

Other differences include:

✦ You can drag graphics files into a layout in addition to using the Place command (File ➪ Place, or ⌘+D or Ctrl+D).

✦ Use the Transform pane (Window ➪ Transform or F9) to rotate, scale, and skew graphics.

✦ You now get to create clipping paths — use the Object ➪ Clipping Paths command.

✦ InDesign can automatically scale pictures or frames for you. Use the Object ➪ Fitting commands: Fit Content to Frame, Fit Frame to Content, Center Content, and Fit Content Proportionally.

✦ To track the location of graphic files, use the Links pane (File ➪ Links, or Shift+⌘+D or Ctrl+Shift+D).

Manipulating pages

The one thing you'll miss about PageMaker is those neat little page icons in the lower-left corner of the document window. In shorter documents especially, the icons provided a quick, easy method for jumping to pages. Get used to using the Page Number box on the document window and the icons in the Pages pane instead.

Other differences between InDesign and PageMaker's page handling include:

✦ InDesign provides three methods for creating guides: Drag them off the ruler as you do in PageMaker, double-click the ruler where you want a guide, or choose Layout ⇨ Create Guides.

✦ To delete guides, you need to select them and click Delete. (To select all guides on a page, press Option+⌘+G or Ctrl+Alt+G.)

✦ Use the Pages pane (Window ⇨ Pages or F12) to create and apply master pages; to add, move, and delete document pages; and to display different pages.

✦ You can now place more than two pages side-by-side. Use the Set as Island Spread command in the Pages pane's palette menu.

✦ Some of your favorite commands from the Layout menu seem to be missing (such as Insert Pages), but you can access similar commands from the Pages pane's palette menu.

✦ You can base one master page on another, the same way you can base styles on each other.

✦ To share master pages among documents, you can drag a master page icon into another document window.

Working with color

Although creating colors is somewhat different in InDesign, applying colors is fairly similar. You can create colors in the same color models, and you can manage colors in a similar way. Differences between PageMaker and InDesign include:

✦ Most of your work with colors happens through the Swatches pane (Window ⇨ Swatches or F5), not through the Colors pane as PageMaker users might think.

✦ To create colors, use the New Swatches command in the Swatches pane's palette menu.

✦ To apply colors, first click the Stroke or Fill button on the Toolbox to specify where the color goes on the selected object. Then, click a color in the Swatches pane.

✦ Use the Colors pane (Window ➪ Colors or F6) to specify a shade (tint) of a color.

✦ Apply the color None to strokes and fills for transparency; you can also click the None button on the Toolbox.

✦ To share colors among documents, drag a colored object into another document window.

✦   ✦   ✦

What's on the CD-ROM

A wide variety of software — some free, some demo, and some shareware — can be found on the CD-ROM at the back of this book.

Exploring the Types of Software

The CD-ROM that accompanies this book has three types of software. Some won't cost you a dime, but others are meant to give you a chance to test it out before you decide to buy. Here's how it works:

✦ **Free software:** This is exactly that — free. You may use it at no charge. (You may not sell it to others, however. And you must get permission from the software's authors to redistribute it, even if you distribute at no charge.)

✦ **Demo software:** This is meant to be used on a trial basis, so you can see if you like it. If you do, you should buy the full version, usually available in stores and mail-order catalogs in a version that includes documentation and a CD-ROM or set of disks. Most demo software does one of the following three things to ensure that people don't use demo software instead of purchasing the retail product:

- Prevents you from being able to save documents while the software is loaded.

- Provides limited functionality until you purchase the full version.

- Expires after a certain number of days of usage.

✦ **Shareware:** This is also meant to be used on a trial basis, so you can see if you like it. If you do, you should buy the full version, usually available by sending in a registration fee and getting a code that converts the shareware into a fully functioning version or getting a fully functioning version on CD-ROM or disks mailed to you. Most shareware does one of the following three things to ensure that people don't use shareware instead of purchasing the full product:

- Prevents you from being able to save documents while the software is loaded.

- Provides limited functionality until you purchase the full version.

- Expires after a certain number of days of usage.

Note   Please pay for and register any demo software or shareware that you use regularly. It's fine to use these programs without paying while you're figuring out if they would really help you, but once you decide they are worthwhile, please support the companies and individuals who created the software so they can afford to create even better software in the future.

Touring the CD-ROM

The CD-ROM that accompanies this book contains both Macintosh and Windows software. Unless your system is equipped with software to read both Mac and Windows volumes on a CD-ROM, you'll see just the software that runs on your operating system: Mac OS or Windows.

Note   The programs on the book's CD-ROM were the most current available when this book went to press, but software developers frequently update their programs to work better. We recommend you check for updates at each developer's Web site if you decide to purchase the software. You'll find Web site or update information in their registration forms.

Macintosh

We've divided the CD-ROM contents into two broad sections: Publishing Utilities and System Utilities.

Publishing Utilities

This software helps you in your publishing work. The CD-ROM includes the following publishing utilities:

✦ **Acrobat Reader:** Free software from Adobe Systems that lets you read Portable Document Format (PDF) files created on Macs or PCs.

✦ **Adobe Euro Fonts:** Free fonts from Adobe that provide the euro currency symbol (only newer fonts have these symbols built in).

✦ **DiamondSoft FontReserve:** A shareware font-management utility.

✦ **FontBuddy:** A shareware utility that lets you view fonts to see what they look like, without having to use them in an actual document or install them in your system.

✦ **GraphicConverter:** A handy shareware program that translates among graphics formats.

✦ **GSF-FONDetective:** A troubleshooting shareware program that helps identify and fix problems in fonts.

✦ **Insider Software FontAgent:** A shareware utility that analyzes fonts to repair common problems.

✦ **Pyrus FontLab:** A demo version of a font-creation and editing utility.

✦ **Pyrus TransType:** A shareware utility that lets you convert Mac and Windows fonts from one platform to the other.

✦ **TextSpresso:** A shareware utility that cleans up formatting in text and HTML documents to make them import more easily into programs such as InDesign.

✦ **Ultimate Impostrip:** A demo version of software that lets you create page impositions from PostScript output files.

✦ **Ultimate IMPress:** A demo utility that help set up folded documents and other page-imposition arrangements.

✦ **Ultimate PrintDesk:** A demo program that manages print jobs in workgroups, letting a print server handle the heavy loads and letting users route their jobs to multiple printers.

✦ **Ultimate Trapeze:** A limited demonstration program that works with Adobe's trapping software to set trapping parameters for your output files.

System Utilities

This software helps you in your general work but has been selected because it is often used in publishing environments. The CD-ROM includes the following system utilities:

✦ **Aladdin DragStrip:** A handy shareware utility that makes it easier to access commonly used programs and files.

✦ **Aladdin ShrinkWrap:** A shareware utility that lets you create install-ation disks.

✦ **Aladdin StuffIt:** A demo utility that compresses and decompresses all sorts of compressed files, to make e-mail and disk exchange more efficient.

✦ **Gray Desktop Theme:** A color pattern to make your Mac's screen display neutral, to aid color fidelity of objects onscreen.

✦ **NameCleaner:** A shareware utility that helps convert PC-style file names to Mac standards.

✦ **Netopia HouseCall:** A demo program that lets you help remote users (over the phone or the Web).

✦ **Netopia Timbuktu Pro:** A demo program that lets you control remote PCs or Macs, share files, chat, and otherwise collaborate with and help remote users.

✦ **Sig Software Cross Platform:** A demo utility that tells you how Macintosh files can be used on Windows PCs.

Windows

We've divided the CD-ROM contents into two broad sections: Publishing Utilities and System Utilities.

Publishing Utilities

This software helps you in your publishing work. The CD-ROM includes the following publishing utilities:

✦ **Acute Systems CrossFont:** A shareware utility that lets you convert Windows fonts to Mac format and vice versa.

✦ **Acrobat Reader:** Free software from Adobe Systems that lets you read Portable Document Format (PDF) files created on Macs or PCs.

✦ **Adobe Euro Fonts:** Free fonts from Adobe that provide the euro currency symbol (only newer fonts have these symbols built in).

✦ **Electric Rain FontFX Express:** A demo utility that lets you create three-dimensional graphics based on your fonts.

✦ **Pyrus FontLab:** A shareware program that lets you edit and create fonts.

✦ **Pyrus ScanFont:** A shareware program that converts bitmap images, such as scanned signatures, letters, and shapes, into font characters.

✦ **Ultimate Impostrip:** A demo version of software that lets you create page impositions from PostScript output files.

System Utilities

This software helps you in your general work but has been selected because it is often used in publishing environments. The CD-ROM includes the following system utilities:

✦ **Aladdin Expander and DropStuff:** A set of demo utilities that compresses and decompresses all sorts of compressed files — including the StuffIt format popular on the Mac — to make e-mail and disk exchange more efficient.

✦ **DataViz MacOpener:** A demo version of software that lets your PC open, write, and format any removable Mac-formatted media — floppies, Zip disks, Jaz cartridges, SyQuest cartridges, and so forth — for which your PC has a compatible drive.

✦ **Media4 MacDrive 98:** A demo version of software that lets your PC open, write, and format any removable Mac-formatted media — floppies, Zip disks, Jaz cartridges, SyQuest cartridges, and so forth — for which your PC has a compatible drive.

✦ **Miramar PC MacLAN:** A demo version of networking software that adds AppleTalk networking to a PC, so it can easily share files with a Mac (and other AppleTalk-equipped PCs) without requiring a server system.

✦ **NicoMak WinZip:** The popular shareware utility that opens and creates compressed file formats to make e-mail and disk exchange more efficient.

✦ **ShoveIt:** A shareware program from Phil Hord that ensures that dialog boxes and other windows don't overlap the Start menu or other menus.

Installing the CD-ROM

To install the CD-ROM, insert the disc into your computer's CD-ROM drive. On a Mac, the CD-ROM automatically displays on your desktop like a floppy disk or hard disk. On a PC, you may have to open the CD-ROM from the Explorer or from the window that appears when you double-click your My Computer icon.

The programs on the CD-ROM come with their own installation programs, usually an .exe file, whose instructions you should follow, or with a readme file that describes the installation steps.

✦   ✦   ✦

Index

continued

continued

IDG Books Worldwide, Inc.
End-User License Agreement

5. Limited Warranty.

(a) IDGB warrants that the Software and Software Media are free from defects in materials and workmanship under normal use for a period of sixty (60) days from the date of purchase of this Book. If IDGB receives notification within the warranty period of defects in materials or workmanship, IDGB will replace the defective Software Media.

(b) IDGB AND THE AUTHORS OF THE BOOK DISCLAIM ALL OTHER WARRANTIES, EXPRESS OR IMPLIED, INCLUDING WITHOUT LIMITATION IMPLIED WARRANTIES OF MERCHANTABILITY AND FITNESS FOR A PARTICULAR PURPOSE, WITH RESPECT TO THE SOFTWARE, THE PROGRAMS, THE SOURCE CODE CONTAINED THEREIN, AND/OR THE TECHNIQUES DESCRIBED IN THIS BOOK. IDGB DOES NOT WARRANT THAT THE FUNCTIONS CONTAINED IN THE SOFTWARE WILL MEET YOUR REQUIREMENTS OR THAT THE OPERATION OF THE SOFTWARE WILL BE ERROR FREE.

(c) This limited warranty gives you specific legal rights, and you may have other rights that vary from jurisdiction to jurisdiction.

6. Remedies.

(a) IDGB's entire liability and your exclusive remedy for defects in materials and workmanship shall be limited to replacement of the Software Media, which may be returned to IDGB with a copy of your receipt at the following address: Software Media Fulfillment Department, Attn.: *Adobe InDesign Bible*, IDG Books Worldwide, Inc., 7260 Shadeland Station, Ste. 100, Indianapolis, IN 46256, or call 1-800-762-2974. Please allow three to four weeks for delivery. This Limited Warranty is void if failure of the Software Media has resulted from accident, abuse, or misapplication. Any replacement Software Media will be warranted for the remainder of the original warranty period or thirty (30) days, whichever is longer.

(b) In no event shall IDGB or the authors be liable for any damages whatsoever (including without limitation damages for loss of business profits, business interruption, loss of business information, or any other pecuniary loss) arising from the use of or inability to use the Book or the Software, even if IDGB has been advised of the possibility of such damages.

(c) Because some jurisdictions do not allow the exclusion or limitation of liability for consequential or incidental damages, the above limitation or exclusion may not apply to you.

7. U.S. Government Restricted Rights.
Use, duplication, or disclosure of the Software by the U.S. Government is subject to restrictions stated in paragraph (c)(1)(ii) of the Rights in Technical Data and Computer Software clause of DFARS 252.227-7013, and in subparagraphs (a) through (d) of the Commercial Computer — Restricted Rights clause at FAR 52.227-19, and in similar clauses in the NASA FAR supplement, when applicable.

8. General.
This Agreement constitutes the entire understanding of the parties and revokes and supersedes all prior agreements, oral or written, between them and may not be modified or amended except in a writing signed by both parties hereto that specifically refers to this Agreement. This Agreement shall take precedence over any other documents that may be in conflict herewith. If any one or more provisions contained in this Agreement are held by any court or tribunal to be invalid, illegal, or otherwise unenforceable, each and every other provision shall remain in full force and effect.